JEWISH TRAVEL GUIDE 2004

INTERNATIONAL EDITION

Published in association with
the *Jewish Chronicle*, London

VALLENTINE MITCHELL
LONDON • PORTLAND, OR

First published in 2004 in Great Britain by
VALLENTINE MITCHELL & CO. LTD
Crown House, 47 Chase Side, Southgate
London N14 5BP
Tel: 020 8447 8798
Email: jtg@vmbooks .com
Website: www.vmbooks.com

and in the United States of America by
VALLENTINE MITCHELL
c/o ISBS,
920 NE 58th Avenue, Suite 300
Portland, Oregon 97213-3786

ISBN 0 85303 500 8
ISSN 0075 3750

Printed in Great Britain by
Creative Print and Design (Wales), Ebbw Vale

Contents

Publisher's Note

WE NEED YOUR ASSISTANCE TO KEEP
THIS GUIDE UP TO DATE

The Editor and the Publishers have made every effort to ensure that this guide is as accurate and up to date as possible.

As in previous years, an update form is included at the back of this book for those who become aware of additions they would like to be considered for inclusion. In addition, of course, we wish to be notified of any errors that may have occurred in the preparation of this book.

Any information may be sent to:

The Editor
Jewish Travel Guide
Crown House
47 Chase Side
Southgate
London N14 5BP

Tel: +44(0)20 8447 8798
Fax: +44(0)20 8447 8548
Email: jtg@vmbooks.com
Website: www.vmbooks.com

Potential advertisers, or those who wish to stock and sell copies of the *Jewish Travel Guide*, may use any of the above means to contact us for details of advertising rates and trade terms.

Introduction

JAN SHURE
Travel Editor of the *Jewish Chronicle*

As the travel editor of the world's largest Jewish newspaper – unless of course you count the *New York Times*, which I prefer not to – and a long-standing champion of the manifold and manifest delights of vacationing in Israel, it gives me no pleasure to record how, in the last three-and-a-half years of renewed turmoil in the Middle East, Israel's tourism industry has continued to be wracked, while other places and types of holiday have hit new heights of popularity for Jewish visitors.

I will return, later to the many compelling reasons for visiting Israel, perhaps more than ever at the present time, but for now it is interesting to observe how Jewish people not only love to travel widely, but are frequently in the vanguard of those visiting destinations in the early stages of their ascendancy. Indeed, if one wants to catch the travel *zeitgeist*, one can do no better than to sit at a dinner party in Hampstead or St John's Wood or Altrincham, and listen to where the guests have recently been, or are planning to go.

Thus, 25 years ago, the newly popular silver-wedding trip for Jewish couples, was the Far East; ten years ago in it was a safari in Kenya; five years ago it was South Africa (unless you were an ex-pat South African, in which case you had been back often, though under duress during the apartheid period, to visit family), while Australia is the current hot ticket, with New Zealand coming up on the rails as the vacation spot for those looking for an excuse to return to the antipodes. Among other long-haul destinations, India, with its impossibly lavish hotels, draws a small but significant number of Jewish visitors among its European visitors (many of whom take in Cochin, with its synagogue and Jewish heritage, though sadly just a handful of elderly Jews), as do places like Bali, Thailand and the Indian Ocean islands. For those seeking a new Far East destination, Vietnam is definitely one of the hot new places to visit, while across the world, South America is attracting greater numbers of adventurous Jewish visitors who are going beyond the big cities of Buenos Aires and Rio de Janiero to take in Peru, Ecuador and Chile with their stunning lakes, glaciers and mountains.

When it comes to perennial long-haul favourites, one of those which has grown in popularity – perhaps especially since the 11 September terror outrages – is the USA. As well as New York, which is always high up on anyone's Top Ten weekending spots for its shopping, theatre, dining and sightseeing, other East Coast cities, such as Boston and Washington have edged into the limelight, while Florida, for lotus-eating or (for those with young families) Disney World, remains a real attraction. California, too, both for a nose around LA and San Francisco, and for taking in the sensational Pacific Coast, has become a popular 'Jewish' destination, while Vegas lures the curious for a couple of nights of over-the-top glitz and glitter. For those who want to avoid the bright lights, the Carolinas, including a trip to Charleston for the cathedral-like synagogue, or New England, make for superb driving holidays, with eating and accommodation of a standard that appeals to the Jewish traveller. The Caribbean (notably Barbados) has also become a popular, repeat long-haul winter-sun destination, while the smaller, more stylish islands like St Barthélemy and Nevis have become retreats of choice for their climate, luxurious hotels and generally friendly ambience.

Closer to Britain, certain European resorts maintain their popularity for Jewish holidaymakers. The South of France, which in Nice and Cannes and many of the smaller towns and resorts scattered like pretty jewels along the Côte d'Azure boast their own indigenous Jewish population, attract Jewish visitors in their droves. Some just visit for a couple of weeks in spring or summer, while thousands own a flat or villa to which they repair, *en famille*, for weeks at a time to enjoy the warm weather, the shopping, but perhaps most of all, the lifestyle and the food.

Marbella on Spain's Costa del Sol enjoys a similar loyalty from devotees, with probably the same split between those who visit for a week or two in spring, summer or autumn or even winter – Marbella enjoys warmer weather than France's south coast – and those who own properties which draw them for longer periods. Majorca, likewise, has its devotees, and both localities have synagogues and delis where one can buy kosher food and *challot*.

Italy and Portugal attract their fair share of Jewish visitors and, apart from its food and shopping, Italy has lots to offer in the way of Jewish history and heritage, with the stunning synagogues of Florence and Rome, the exquisite jewel-like shuls in Venice and the remnants of a vibrant Jewish community scattered across a dozen more Italian cities and towns.

Jewish visitors also flock to Eastern Europe to see their heritage and, in many cases, to see the homes which their families left just one or two generations earlier. Prague, which suffered terribly from flood-damage in October 2002, has cleaned and reopened the ancient Altneu Synagogue and the other beautifully restored shuls – some now converted into small museums. Indeed, the Jewish Quarter forms one of the key elements of the Prague tourist circuit and is a real jewel in this beautiful city.

Other countries and cities which have benefited from Jewish heritage tourism include Lithuania, Latvia and Budapest, which certainly has plenty to offer the visitor in addition to its places of Jewish interest. Most Jews who go to Poland do so to make the unbearably sad pilgrimage to Auschwitz, and to Cracow, where almost half of the pre-war population was Jewish. But it is worth spending a day or two in Warsaw, too. There is little left of the community and culture that flourished there for hundreds of years until the Nazis crushed it in 1945, but one synagogue does remain, as does the magnificent Jewish cemetery, along with one tiny section of the wall that once enclosed the infamous ghetto. There are also many moving memorials, as well as Yiddish theatre and a kosher restaurant.

Cruising, which has always been popular with a Jewish clientele, has probably seen the biggest explosion in popularity in the past five years or so, in both the general and the Jewish market. Both the quality and the variety of cruises has improved and, along with that, the cruise companies have marketed to a younger clientele. Thus, cruising is now a holiday of choice for honeymooners, young marrieds and the forty- and fifty-something empty-nesters – often accompanied by their grown-up children. The rise of the smaller, more luxurious lines, with restaurant-style dining (that is, being able to choose when you wish to eat, and with whom) and more exotic and recherché destinations, have also added to the popularity of cruising among discerning travellers.

For decades, cruise lines have accommodated the kashrut needs of Jewish passengers, usually by having limitless supplies of permitted fish, vegetarian dishes and mountains of smoked salmon, or, in some cases, bringing on board kosher meat and poultry, and storing and cooking it separately. But now there are full-on kosher cruises with their own chefs, rabbinic supervision and daily *shiurim* for the pious.

Several cruise lines also operate special Passover cruises that include *Sedarim* and festival services at sea. Indeed, a Passover cruise is just one of a range of options for Jewish families who wish to observe the Passover festival but do not wish to turn into drudges in order to do so. For about 20 years, the Passover destination of choice – for Europeans at least – was Israel. But as Israel been perceived as risky in the last three years, Passover package holidays have been organised in most of Europe's traditional vacation grounds (Spain, Portugal, France, Italy and Switzerland), as well as in Florida, the Caribbean, California and Mexico.

The other big growth area in travel among Jewish people has been the rise of the singles holiday. The increase in the rate of divorce in the Jewish community across the globe, combined with young people delaying marriage to their thirties or beyond, has led to an amazing increase in holidays, at all price levels and to all kinds of destinations, for the unattached. Certainly, no single man or woman with the cash to travel should ever have to forgo a holiday for want of a group of like-minded people to travel with. Of course, part of the growth in singles holidays has been facilitated by the huge increase in the Internet, where singles – who are perceived to be technologically advanced and desirable marketing targets – can find plenty of holidays and trips to weigh up.

Last, but by no means least, Israel remains the most definitively amazing holiday destination for the Jewish traveller. Throughout a country bursting with sights, scenes, history, heritage, colour and vibrancy, there is the entire gamut of amenities which visitors crave: hotels from the most opulent and beautiful to the modest and homely or the cool and quirky; restaurants, bars, cafés, fabulous shops, sensational spas, outdoor activities, water-sports and diving; and a climate which takes in the most benign sunshine spot on earth at the Dead Sea, or Eilat where it is often 80 degrees for most of the winter, or to the northern Galilee where you can ski in winter. It has astonishing cities, from buzzy, urban Tel Aviv, to historic, haunting Jerusalem; from Haifa with its endless beaches and stunning Bahai Terraces, to Herzliya with its trendy new marina; from Caesarea which blends California with ancient Rome, to a desert of stunning scenic beauty and secret oases.

London, November 2003.

ALBANIA

There have been Jews living on the territory now known as Albania since Roman times and there are remains in Dardania (in the north of the country) of an ancient synagogue. The community was re-established by Jews from Iberia escaping the Spanish Inquisition in the fifteenth and early sixteenth centuries.

The number of Jews in Albania never increased significantly, and, in 1930, there were only 204 Jews in the country. However, this number was soon augmented by refugees escaping the Nazis. The local population was not, on the whole, hostile to the Jews and helped most of them to hide during the war when Italy, and then Germany, occupied the country.

The strict communist regime which followed the war led to the isolation of the Jewish community until the fall of communism. In 1991, almost the entire community, about 300, was airlifted to Israel. The few Jews who remained in Albania live in the capital, Tirana.

The Albanian Israel Friendship Society will be happy to provide any further information.

GMT +1 hour
Country calling code: (+355)
Total population: 3,738,000
Jewish population: Under 100
Emergency telephone: (Police – 2445) (Fire – 23333) (Ambulance – 22235)
Electricity voltage: (Electricity voltage – 220)

TIRANA
CONTACT INFORMATION
Albanian-Israel Friendship Society
Rruga 'Barrikatave' 226
Telephone: (42) 22611

ALGERIA

Jews first settled in Algeria soon after the start of the Diaspora following the destruction of the Second Temple. A later influx occurred when Jews were escaping from Visigothic Spain.

In the twelfth and thirteenth centuries, Islamic conversion was forced on the Jews. Many Jews, however, crossed the Mediterranean from Spain during the time of the Inquisition, and these included some famous scholars. In 1830 the French occupied the country and, in due course, granted the Jews French citizenship.

Algerian Jews suffered anti-semitism from both the local Muslim population and the wartime Vichy government. After the Allied landings in 1942, the anti-Jewish laws were slowly lifted. In the late 1950s, 130,000 Jews lived in Algeria, but after the civil war, which led to independence from France in 1962, most of the community moved to France, with some to Israel, leaving very few behind. The present-day community, centred in Algiers, has a synagogue but no resident rabbi.

GMT +1 hour
Country calling code: (+213)
Total population: 29,050,000
Jewish population: Under 100
Emergency telephone: (Police – 24445) (Fire – 23333) (Ambulance – 2235)
Electricity voltage: (Electricity voltage – 117/220)

ALGIERS
COMMUNITY ORGANISATIONS
Association Consistoriale Israélite d'Alger
6 rue Hassena Ahmed
Telephone: (2) 62-85-72

SYNAGOGUES
6 rue Hassena Ahmed
Telephone: (2) 62-85-72

BLIDA
COMMUNITY ORGANISATIONS
Consistoire d'Algerie
29 rue des Martyrs
Telephone: (3) 49-26-57

ANDORRA

Andorra, which is governed by two co-princes - the Bishop of Urgel in Spain and the President of France, does not have a Jewish history. There are currently, however, around 15 Jewish families.

A synagogue was established inh 1997 in Escaldes and is the first in Andorra's 1,100-year history. While its liturgy leans towards Sephardism, it is also influenced by its Ashkenazi members. There is a community centre in Escaldes.

GMT +1 hour
Country calling code: **(+376)**
Total population: **66,000**
Jewish population: **Under 100**
Emergency telephone: **(Police – 825 225) (Fire – 118) (Ambulance – 118)**

CONTACT INFORMATION
Dr David ben-Chayil or Dr David Bezold
Francesco B.P. 244, Andorra la Vella
Telephone: 333 567
Email: bezold@andorra.ad
For visits to the synagogue contact Isaac Benisty
Telephone 860 758

ARGENTINA

The first Jewish arrivals (Conversos, or 'secret Jews') came in the sixteenth and seventeenth centuries from Portugal and Spain. They assimilated quickly. A more significant Jewish immigration occurred in the middle of the nineteenth century, from western Europe, and at the end of the nineteenth century many Jews arrived from eastern Europe, taking advantage of the 'open-door' policy towards immigrants. The new arrivals set up some Jewish agricultural settlements, under the auspices of the Alliance Israelita Universelle, and on the whole mixed with the local population.

The largest Jewish community is in Buenos Aires, with smaller communities in provincial centres. There are also some Jewish families remaining in the Jewish agricultural colonies, with Moiseville, Rivera and General Roca being the three most important.

There are Jewish newspapers, restaurants and other institutions. The Delegation of Argentine Jewish Associations (DAIA) represents all Jewish organisations

GMT -3 hours
Country calling code: **(+54)**
Total population: **35,672,000**
Jewish population: **200,000**
Emergency telephone: **(Police – 101) (Fire – 100) (Ambulance – 107)**
Electricity voltage: **(Electricity voltage – 226)**

BAHIA BLANCA
CONTACT INFORMATION
Beit Jabad
Chiclana 763 8000
Telephone: (291) 4453-6582
Fax: (291) 4456-5596
For details of Mikvah please phone.

BUENOS AIRES
The first recorded Jewish event in Buenos Aires was a wedding in 1860. Around 220,000 Jews live in Buenos Aires. There are fifty or so synagogues in the city and kosher food is widely available. The most interesting synagogues for visitors are in Once although fewer Jews live there now.

BAKERIES
Confitería Aielet
Aranguren 2911, Flores
Telephone: (11) 4637-5419

Confitería Ganz
Paso 752, Once
Telephone: (11) 4961-6918

Confitería Helueni
Tucumán 2620, Once
Telephone: (11) 4961-0541

Confitería Mari Jalabe
Bogota 3228, Flores
Telephone: (11) 4612-6991

Panadería Malena
Av. Pueyrredón 880, Once
Telephone: (11) 4962-6290

BOOKSELLERS
Kehot Lubavitch Sudamericana
San Luis 3281 1186
Telephone: (11) 4865-0625
Fax: (11) 4865-0625
Email: kehot@iname.com
Web site: www.kehot-lubavitch.com.ar
Librería Editorial Sigal
Av. Corrientes 2854 C1193AAN
Telephone: (11) 4861-9501; 4865-7208
Fax: (11) 4962-7931; 4865-7208
Email: libreriasigal@runbox.com
Web site: www.libreria-sigal.com

COMMUNITY ORGANISATIONS
AMIA (Central Ashkenazi community)
Pasteur 633
Telephone: (11) 4953-9777; 4953-2862
The community centre has now been reopened following the terror bomb attack in 1994.

Asociacion Israelita Sefaradi Argentina (AISA)
Paso 493
Telephone: (11) 4952-4707

DAIA (Political representative body of Argentine Jewry)
Pasteur 633, 7th Floor
Telephone: (11) 4378-3200
Fax: (11) 4378-3200
Email: daia@daia.org.ar

CONTACT INFORMATION
Asociacion Shuva Israel
Paso 557, Once
Telephone: (11) 4962-6255
Beit Jabad Belgrano
O'Higgins 2358, Belgrano 1428
Telephone: (11) 4781-3848
Fax: (11) 4783-4573
Email: shlomo@overnet.com.ar
Beit Jabad Villa Crespo
Serrano 69
Telephone: (11) 4855-9822
Chabad Lubavich Argentina
Agüero 1164, Flores 1425
Telephone: (11) 4963-1221
Congregacion Israelita de la Republica Argentina
Libertad 785, Centro
Telephone: (11) 4372-2474
Fax: (11) 4372-2474
The total number of synagogues in Buenos Aires where there is a minyan at least on Friday night and Shabbat morning exceeds fifty. Call any of the above numbers to locate the synagogue nearest you.

EMBASSY
Embassy of Israel
Avenida de Mayo 701-10° 1084
Telephone: (11) 4345-6207/08
Fax: (11) 4345-6207
Email: cidipal@israel-embassy.org.ar

GROCERIES
Almacén Behar
Campana 347, Flores
Telephone: (11) 4613-2033
Almacén Shalom
San Luis 2513, Once
Telephone: (11) 4962-3685
Autoservicio Ezra
Ecuador 619, Once
Telephone: (11) 4963-7062
Autoservicio Siman Tov
Helguera 474, Flores
Telephone: (11) 4611-4746
Azulay
Helguera 507, Flores
Battías
Paso 706, Once
Kahal Jaredim
Argerich 386, Flores
Telephone: (11) 4612-4590
Kaler
San Luis 2810, Once
Kol Bo Brandsen
Brandsen 1389, Barracas
Kol Bo I
Ecuador 855, Once
Telephone: (11) 4961-3838
Kol Bo II
Viamonte 2537, Once
Telephone: (11) 4961-2012
Kosher Delights
La Pampa 2547, Belgrano
Telephone: (11) 4788-3150
La Esquina Casher
Aranguren 2999, Flores
Telephone: (11) 4637-3706
La Quesería
Viamonte 2438, Once
Telephone: (11) 4961-3171
La Tzorja
Ecuador 673, Once
Telephone: (11) 4961-1096
Lidia's Macolet
Ecuador 586, Once
Telephone: (11) 4863-5595
Fax: (11) 4932-4443

Yehuda Kosher Foods
Moldes 2452, Belgrano
Telephone: (11) 4637-1465

KASHRUT INFORMATION
The Central Rabbinate of the Vaad Hakehillot
Ecuador 1110, Once
Telephone: (11) 4961-2944
The Orthodox Ashkenazi Chief Rabbi of Argentina is
Rabbi Shlomo Benhamu Anidjar.

LIBRARIES
Sociedad Hebraica Argentino
Sarmiento 2233
Telephone: (11) 4952-5570
Also has an art gallery.

YIVO Library
Pasteur 633, Third floor
Telephone: (11) 445-2474

MEDIA
Newspapers
Comunidades
Die Presse
Kesher Kehilari
Mundo Israelita

MIKVAOT
Helguera 270, Once
Telephone: (11) 4612-0410
Moldes 2431, Belgrano
Telephone: (11) 4786-8046
Email: ajdut@netcomputer.com.ar

MUSEUMS
Museo Judio de Buenos Aires
Libertad 769
Telephone: (11) 4123-0830
Email: kjba@netizen.com.ar
Hours: Tuesday and Thursday 4pm to 7pm.

RESTAURANTS
Confiterie Helueni
Tucuman 2620, Once
Telephone: (11) 4961-0541

Dairy
Soultani Café
San Luis 2601, Once
Telephone: (11) 4961-3913

Meat
Al Galope
Tucumán 2633, Once
Telephone: (11) 4963-6888

Mama Jacinta
Tucuman 2580 C-P 4052
Telephone: (11) 4962-9149

Fax: (11) 4962-7535
Email: mamajacintakosher@hotmail.com
Supervision: Gran Rasibo Josef Chehebar.

McDonald's
Shopping Abasto, (Corrientes and Anchorena),
Once
Supervision: Rav Oppenheimer - Ajdut Israel
There are two McDonalds. Only one is kosher.

Sucath David
Tucuman 2349
Telephone: (11) 4952-8878
Fax: (11) 4953-9656
Email: sucathdavid@sinectis.com.ar

SYNAGOGUES
Ashkenazi
Baron Hirsh
Billinghurst 664
Telephone: (11) 4862-2624
Beit Jabad Once "LITVISHE SHUL"
Jose Evaristo Uriburu 348
Telephone: (11) 4952-7968
Fax: (11) 4952-7968
Email: aharon@radar.com.ar
Bet Rajel
Ecuador 522
Telephone: (11) 4862-2701
Brit Abraham
Antezana 145
Telephone: (11) 4855-6567
Etz Jaim
Julian Alvarez 745
Telephone: (11) 4772-5324
Torah Vaaboda
Julian Alvarez 667
Telephone: (11) 4854-0462
Zijron le David
Azcuenaga 736
Telephone: (11) 4953-0200

Conservative
Beit Hilel
Araoz 2854, Palermo
Telephone: (11) 4804-2286
Colegio Wolfson, Comunidad Or-El
Amenabar 2972
Telephone: (11) 4544-5461
Comunidad Bet El
Sucre 3338
Telephone: (11) 4552-2365
Dor Jadash
Murillo 649, Villa Crespo
Telephone: (11) 4854-4467

Nueva Comunidad Israelita
Arcos 2319
Telephone: (11) 4781-0281

Or Jadash
Varela 850, Flores
Telephone: (11) 4612-1171

German Orthodox
Ajdut Yisroel
Moldes 2449
Telephone: (11) 4783-2831
Fax: (11) 4781-6725
Email: ajdut@netcomputer.com.ar

Progressive
Benei Tikva
Vidal 2049
Telephone: (11) 4795-0380

Reform
Templo Emanu-El
Tronador 1455
Telephone: (11) 4552-4343
Fax: (11) 4555-4004
Email: kol_emanuel@name.com

Sephardi
Centro Comunitario Chalom
Olleros 2876
Telephone: (11) 54-11-4552-2720
Fax: (11) 54-11-4552-6730
Email: secretaria@chalom.org.ar
Web site: www.chalom.org.ar

Sephardi Orthodox
Aderet Eliahu
Ruy Diaz de Guzman 647
Telephone: (11) 4303-1320
Fax: (11) 4303-1320

Agudat Dodim
Avellaneda 2874
Telephone: (11) 4611-0056

Asociacion Comunidad Israelita Sefaradi de Buenos Aires
Camargo 870
Telephone: (11) 54-11-4855-6945
Fax: (11) 54-11-4855-9377
Email: acisba@continuidad.com.ar

Bajurim Tiferet Israeil
Helguera 611
Telephone: (11) 4611-3376

Etz Jaim
Carlos Calvo 1164
Telephone: (11) 4302-6290

Jaike Grimberg
Campana 460
Telephone: (11) 4672-2347

Kehal Jaredim
Helguera 270, Once
Telephone: (11) 4612-0410

Od Yosef Jai
Tucuman 3326
Telephone: (11) 4963-2349

Or Misraj
Ciudad de la Paz 2555
Telephone: (11) 4784-5945

Shaare Sion
Helguera 453
Telephone: (11) 4637-5897
Fax: (11) 4637-1301
Email: editorial@shaaresion.org.ar
Web site: www.shaaresion.org.ar

Shaare Tefila
Paso 733
Telephone: (11) 4962-2865

Shuba Israel
Ecuador 627
Telephone: (11) 4862-0562

Sinagoga Rabino Zeev Grinberg
Felipe Vallese 3047, Ciudad Autonoma de Buenos Aires
Telephone: (11) 4611-3366

Sucath David
Tucuman 2750
Telephone: (11) 4962-1091
Fax: (11) 4962-1264
Email: perspect@satlink.com
Web site: www.judaicasite.com

Templo la Paz (Chalom)
Olleros 2876
Telephone: (11) 4552-6730

Yeshurun
Republica de la India 3035
Telephone: (11) 4802-9310

Yesod Hadat
Lavalle 2449
Telephone: (11) 4961-1615

CONCORDIA
CONTACT INFORMATION
Beit Jabad Concordia
Entre Rios 212 3200
Telephone: (45) 421-1934
Fax: (45) 421-7898

CORDOBA

CONTACT INFORMATION
Jabad Lubavitch Cordoba
Sucre 1380, Barrio Cofico 5000
Telephone: (351) 4471-0223
Fax: (351) 4411-9721
Email: jturk@elsitio.net

GROCERIES
Almacén
Sucre 1378, Barrio Cofico 5000
Telephone: (351) 471-0223

ROSARIO

CONTACT INFORMATION
Beit Jabad Rosario
S. Lorenzo 1882 P.A. 2000
Telephone: (341) 425-2899

GROCERIES
La Granja Kasher
Telephone: (341) 449-6210

TUCUMAN

CONTACT INFORMATION
Beit Jabad Tucuman
Lamadrid 752 4000
Telephone: (381) 424-8892
Fax: (381) 4248893
Email: jabadtucuman@amet.com.ar

GROCERIES
Almacén y Carnicería
9 de Julio 625
Telephone: (381) 431-0227

Beit Jabad Tucuman
Lamadrid 752 4000
Telephone: (381) 424-8892
Fax: (381) 4248893
Email: jabadtucuman@amet.com.ar

AUSTRALIA

The first Jews in Australia arrived with the first convict ships from the United Kingdom in 1788 and regular, organised worship started in the 1820s. The first free Jewish settler arrived with her husband, a deported convict, in 1816. The community grew in the nineteenth century, with the first synagogue being established in the mid-1840s. Events such as the gold rush and pogroms in eastern Europe were catalysts for more Jewish immigration.

The Jewish contribution to Australian life has been prominent, with the commander of the ANZAC forces in the First World War being a practising Jew, Sir John Monash. The twentieth century saw some 7,000 Jewish refugees from Nazi Europe settling in Australia, and the community contains the largest percentage of Holocaust survivors in the world. They are a major influence on the present community, which is expanding and comparatively religious. There have also been two Jewish Governors-General; one being Sir Issac Issacs, who was the first Australian - born to hold that position.

The community is led by the Executive Council of Australian Jewry. 75 per cent of primary and 55 per cent of secondary Jewish school children attend Jewish schools and there is a low level of inter-marriage. Melbourne has the largest community (42,000), with 35,000 in Sydney. There are Jewish newspapers, radio programmes of Jewish interest and museums on Jewish themes.

GMT +7 to +10 hours
Country calling code: **(+61)**
Total population: **19,105,000**
Jewish population: **100,000**
Emergency telephone: **(Police – 000) (Fire – 000) (Ambulance – 000)**
Electricity voltage: **(Electricity voltage – 240/250)**

Australian Capital Territory

CANBERRA

EMBASSY
Embassy of Israel
6 Turrana Street, Yarralumla 2600
Telephone: (262) 73-1309
Fax: (262) 73-4279
Email: israelembassy@israemb.org

SYNAGOGUES
The A.C.T. Jewish Community Synagogue
National Jewish Memorial Centre, cnr Canberra Ave & National Circuit, Forrest 2603
Telephone: (262) 951-052
Fax: (262) 958-608
Web site: www.actjewish.org.au
Postal address: POB 3105, Manuka 2603

New South Wales

NEWCASTLE
SYNAGOGUES
122 Tyrrell Street 2300
Telephone: (49) 26-2820
Contact: Dr L.E. Fredman, 123 Dawson St, Cooks Hill,
2300 N.S.W.

SYDNEY
The first Jewish convict settlers were generally
illiterate in both English and Hebrew, and there
was no Jewish organisation until a Chevrah
Kadishe was formed in 1817 and services were
held under the leadership of a former convict
Joseph Marcus.

Most of Sydney's Jews are now settled outside
the city in two suburban areas: the eastern
suburbs, including Bondi, and the North Shore.

BAKERIES
Carmel Cake Shop
14 O'Brien Street, Bondi
Supervision: NSW Kashrut Authority

BOOKSELLERS
Gold's World of Judaica
9 O'Brien Street, Bondi 2026
Telephone: (2) 9300-0495
Fax: (2) 9389-7345
Email: sydney@golds.com.au

BUTCHERS
Eilat
173 Bondi Road, Bondi
Telephone: (2) 9387-8881
Supervision: NSW Kashrut Authority

Hadassa
17 O'Brien Street, Bondi
Telephone: (2) 9365-4904
Fax: (2) 9130-4760
Supervision: NSW Kashrut Authority

COMMUNITY ORGANISATIONS
Executive Council of Australian Jewry
146 Darlinghurst Road, Second floor, Darlinghurst
2010
Telephone: (2) 9360-5415
Fax: (2) 9360-5416
Email: ecaj@tig.com.au

EMBASSY
Consul General of Israel
37 York Street, Level 6. 2000
Telephone: (2) 9264-7933
Fax: (2) 9290-2259
Email: sydney@israel.org

HOSPITAL
Wolper Jewish Hospital
8 Trelawney Street, Woollahra
Telephone: (2) 9328-6077

KASHRUT INFORMATION
Kosher Consumer Association
Telephone: (2) 9337-6657
Fax: (2) 9371-0348

NSW Kashrut Authority
4/58 Hall St, Bondi Beach 2026
Telephone: (2) 9365-2933
Fax: (2) 9365-0933
Email: rabbig@ka.org.au
Web site: www.ka.org.au

MEDIA
Newspaper
Australian Jewish News
146 Darlinghurst Road, Darlinghurst 2010
Telephone: (2) 9360-5100
Fax: (2) 9332-4207
Email: valhadeff@jewishnews.net.au
Web site: www.ajn.net.au

MIKVAOT
117 Glenayr Avenue, Bondi
Telephone: (2) 9130-2509

MUSEUMS
Sydney Jewish Museum
148 Darlinghurst Road, Darlinghurst 2010
Telephone: (2) 9360-7999
Fax: (2) 9331-4245
Email: sydjmus@tmx.mhs.oz.au
Has won many awards for its work documenting
Sydney's Jewish history and the Holocaust and has a
kosher (dairy) restaurant.

RELIGIOUS ORGANISATIONS
Sydney Beth Din
166 Castlereagh Street, Sydney, NSW 2000
Telephone: (2) 02-9267-2477
Fax: (2) 02-9264-8871
Email: rabbi@greatsynagogue.org.au

RESTAURANTS
Dairy
Red Tomato Café
50 Mitchell St, N Bondi 2026
Telephone: (2) 9300-0707
Fax: (2) 9130-4477

Toovya the Milkman
379 Old South Head Road, North Bondi 2026
Telephone: (2) 9130-4016
Supervision: NSW Kashrut Authority
Not Cholov Yisrael. Vegetarian and vegan food. Eat in or take away. Delivery to eastern suburbs, including to hotel room. Hours: Sunday to Thursday, 5 pm to 10 pm; Saturday, after Shabbat to midnight. Nearest metro: 387 bus from Bondi junction to the door.

Meat
Beaches Kosher Restaurant
11 O'Brien Street 2026
Telephone: (2) 9365-5544
Fax: (2) 9365-5577
Supervision: NSW Kashrut Authority
Lunch is only Pareve. Delivery to all Sydney addresses.

Café Maccabee
Corner Darlinghurst and Burton Street, Darlinghurst
Telephone: (2) 9360-7999
Fax: (2) 9331-4245
Email: ceo@sjm.com.au

Katzy's Food Factory
Shop 2, 113-115 Hall Street, Bondi Beach
Telephone: (2) 9130-6743
Fax: (2) 91306742
Supervision: NSW Kashrut Authority
Also take-away.

Lewis' Continental Kitchen
2 Curlewis Street, Bondi 2026
Telephone: (2) 9365-5421
Fax: (2) 9300-0037
Email: judith@lewiskosher.com
Web site: www.lewiskosher.com
Supervision: NSW Kashrut Authority
Glatt Kosher. Specialise in assisting tourists with their meals in Australia.

Tibby's Kosher Restaurant at Jaffa
61-67 Hall Street, Bondi Beach 2026
Telephone: (2) 9130-5051
Supervision: NSW Kashrut Authority
Open Saturday to Thursday for dinner. Continental, Chinese, Sephardi and Israeli food. Glatt kosher.

SYNAGOGUES
Adath Yisroel
243 Old South Head Road, Bondi
Telephone: (2) 9300-9447

Bondi Mizrachi Synagogue
101/60 Blair Street, North Bondi 2026
Telephone: (2) 02-9369-2345
Fax: (2) 02-9369-2345
Email: mizrachisydney@bigpond.com
Web site: mizrachi.org.au
Synagogue location is 339 Old South Head Road, Bondi 2026

Coogee Synagogue
121 Brook Street, Coogee
Telephone: (2) 9315-8291

Cremorne & District
12a Yeo Street, Neutral Bay
Telephone: (2) 9908-1853
Fax: (2) 9908-1852

Illawarra Synagogue
502 Railway Parade, Allawah
Telephone: (2) 9587-5643
Email: georgefoster1@compuserve.com

Kehillat Masada
9-15 Link Road, St Ives 2075
Telephone: (2) 9988-4417
Fax: (2) 9449-3897
Email: kmasada@dingoblue.net.au

Paramatta Synagogue
116 Victoria Road, Paramatta
Telephone: (2) 9683-5381

Sephardi Synagogue
40-44 Fletcher Street, Bondi Junction 2022
Telephone: (2) 02-9389-3982
Fax: (2) 02-9369-2143
Email: mail@sephardi.org.au

Shearit Yisrael
146 Darlinghurst Road, Darlinghurst 2010
Telephone: (2) 9365-8770

South Head & District Synagogue
666 Old South Head Road, Rose Bay 2029
Telephone: (2) 9371-7300
Fax: (2) 9371-7416
Email: admin@southhead.org
Web site: www.southhead.org

Strathfield & District Synagogue
19 Florence Street, Strathfield 2135
Telephone: (2) 9642-3550
Fax: (2) 9642-4803

Western Suburbs Synagogue
20 Georgina Street, Newtown

Conservative
Temple Emanuel
7 Ocean Street, Woollahra 2025
Telephone: (2) 9328-7833
Fax: (2) 9327-8715
Email: info@emanuel.org.au
Web site: www.emanuel.org.au
Look forward to welcoming visitors from abroad.

Orthodox

Great Synagogue
166 Castlereagh Street
Telephone: (2) 9267-2477
Fax: (2) 9264-8871
Email: admin@greatsynagogue.org.au
Web site: www.greatsynagogue.org.au
Houses the Rabbi L.A. Falk Memorial Library and the A.M. Rosenblum Jewish Museum. (Entrance for services: 187 Elizabeth Street.) There are synagogue tours on Tuesdays and Thursdays.

Maroubra Synagogue (K.M.H.C.)
635 Anzac Parade, Maroubra 2035
Telephone: (2) 9344-6095
Fax: (2) 9344-4298
Email: maroubrasyn@bigpond.com

North Shore Synagogue
15 Treatts Road, Lindfield
Telephone: (2) 9416-3710
Fax: (2) 9416-7659
Email: nss@bigpond.com

The Central Synagogue
15 Bon Accord Avenue, Bondi Junction
Telephone: (2) 9389-5622
Fax: (2) 9389-5418
Email: central@centralsynagogue.com.au
Web site: www.centralsynagogue.com.au

Yeshiva
36 Flood Street, Bondi 2026
Telephone: (2) 9387-3822
Fax: (2) 9389-7652
Email: info@yeshiva.org.au

Progressive

North Shore Temple Emanuel
28 Chatswood Avenue, Chatswood 2067
Telephone: (2) 02-9419-7011
Fax: (2) 02-9413-1474
Email: nste@nste.org.au
Web site: www.nste.org.au

Sefardim

Beth Yosef
Ground Floor, 243 Old South Head Road, Bondi

TOURS
Telephone: (2) 9328-7604
For information about tours of Jewish Sydney, contact the Great Synagogue at the number listed above or Karl Maehrischel at this number.

Queensland

BRISBANE

COMMUNITY ORGANISATIONS

Jewish Communal Centre
2 Moxom Road, Burbank 4156
Telephone: (7) 3349-9749

MIKVAOT

Queensland Mikvah
46 Bunya Street, Greenslopes 4120
Telephone: (7) 3848-5886

RELIGIOUS ORGANISATIONS

Chabad House of Queensland
43 Cedar Street, Greenslopes 4120
Telephone: (7) 3848-5886
Fax: (7) 3848-5886
Email: kthomas@onenet.au

SYNAGOGUES

Brisbane Hebrew Congregation
98 Margaret Street 4000
Telephone: (7) 3229-3412

Givat Zion
43 Bunya Street, Greenslopes 4000
Telephone: (7) 3397-9025
Fax: (7) 3397-9025

South Brisbane Hebrew Congregation
46 Burya Street, Greenslopes 4120
Telephone: (7) 3397-9025
Fax: (7) 3397-9025
Email: slatwall@ozemail.com.au

Progressive

Beit Knesset Shalom
13 Koolatah Street, Camp Hill 4152
Telephone: (7) 3398-8843/3391-2579
Fax: (7) 3391-2579
Email: bks@hotmail.com

GOLD COAST

BAKERIES

Goldstein's Bakery
509 Olsen Avenue, Ashmore City 4214
Telephone: (7) 5539-3133
Fax: (7) 5597-1064
Supervision: Rabbi Gurevitch, Gold Coast Hebrew Congregation
Under the umbrella of the NSW Kashrut Authority. Challah and kosher breads available at fourteen stores along the Gold Coast, including Surfers Paradise shop. (Tel) 5531-5808.

COMMUNITY ORGANISATIONS
Association of Jewish Organisations
31 Ranock Avenue, Benown Waters 4217
Telephone: (7) 5597-2222

SYNAGOGUES
Surfers Central Synagogue
4 River Terrace, Surfers Paradise 4217

Temple Shalom
25 Via Roma Drive, Isle of Capri 4217
Telephone: (7) 5570-1716

Orthodox
Gold Coast Hebrew Congregation
34 Hamilton Avenue, Surfers Paradise 4215
Telephone: (7) 5570-1851
Fax: (7) 5570-1851
Email: gchebrewcong@ausinfo.com.au

South Australia
ADELAIDE
BAKERIES
Bakers Delight
Frewville Shopping Centre, Glen Osmond Road

GROCERIES
Kosher Imports
c/o Hebrew Congregation, 13 Flemington Street, Glenside 5065
Telephone: (8) 8338-2922
Fax: (8) 8379-0142
Email: jewish@ozemail.com.au
Web site: www.adelaidejewish.com
Kosher and Judaica products available.

SYNAGOGUES
Orthodox
Adelaide Hebrew Congregation
13 Flemington Street, Glenside 5065
Telephone: (8) 8338-2922
Fax: (8) 8379-0142
Email: jewish@ozemail.com.au
Web site: www.adelaidejewish.com
Mikva on premises. Mailing address: PO Box 320, Glenside 5065.

Progressive
Beit Shalom
41 Hackney Road, Hackney 5000
Telephone: (8) 8362-8281
Fax: (8) 8362-4406
Email: bshalom@senet.com.au
Web site: www.beitshalomadelaide.com
Mailing address: PO Box 47, Stepney 5069.

Tasmania
Established as a penal colony in 1803. Jewish names first appeared in 1819. One being Ikey Solomons a famous Jewish convict who was said to be the model for Dicken's Fagin in Oliver Twist.

The community remained small. The Launcerlin synagogue was closed in 1871 and not reopened until 1939.

HOBART
CONTACT INFORMATION
Jewish Centre
Chabad House, 93 Lord Street, Sandy Bay 7005
Telephone: (3) 6223-7116
Fax: (3) 6223-7116
Email: jwc@southcom.com.au
Contact in advance for Shabbat meals and mikveh.

SYNAGOGUES
Progressive and Orthodox Services
GPO Box 128 7001
Telephone: (3) 03-6234-4720
Email: shule@hobart.org

Progressive
Hobart Hebrew Congregation
PO Box 128, Hobart 7001
Telephone: (3) 6234-4720
Email: shule@hobart.org
The oldest synagogue in Australia, having been consecrated in July 1845. Open 9.30 am Saturdays and one Friday per month 6.15 pm. Other days by arrangement.

LAUNCESTON
CONTACT INFORMATION
Chabad House of Tasmania
5 Brisbane Street, Launceston 7250
Telephone: (3) 61-03-6334-0705
Fax: (3) 61-03-6344-9960
Email: ghgoldsteen@netspace.net.au
For all enquiries please call or fax the Hon. Manager Mr Gershon Goldsteen at (3) 6344 9960 or email him as above.

SYNAGOGUES
St. John Street 7250
Telephone: (3) 6343-1143
The synagogue in St John Street is the second oldest in Australia, founded in 1846. It is shared by Reform and Orthodox congregation and still has the original "convict benches".

Victoria

BALLARAT

SYNAGOGUES
211 Drumond Street North 3350
Telephone: (353) 32-6330

MELBOURNE

With 42,000 Jews, Melbourne has the largest Jewish community in the country, and the largest Jewish school in the world (the Mount Scopus).

BAKERIES

Big K Kosher Bakery
316 Carlisle Street,, Balaclava 3183
Telephone: (3) 9527-4582
Supervision: Rabbi A.Z. Beck, Adass Israel

Glicks Cakes and Bagels
330a Carlisle Street, Balaclava 3183
Telephone: (3) 9527-2198
Supervision: Melbourne Kashrut

Greenfield Cakes
7 Willow Street, Elsternwick
Telephone: (3) 9528-4261
Supervision: Rabbi A.Z. Beck, Adass Israel
At same location is King David Kosher Meals on Wheels (Refuah), hospital meals, airline and TV dinners.

Haymishe Bakery
320 Carlisle Street, Shop 4 3183
Telephone: (3) 9527-7116
Supervision: Rabbi A.Z. Beck, Adass Israel

Kosher Delight Bakery
75 Glen Eira Road, Ripponlea
Telephone: (3) 9532-9994
Supervision: Rabbi A.Z. Beck, Adass Israel

Lowy's Cakes & Catering
59 Gordon Street, Elsternwick
Telephone: (3) 9530-0246
Supervision: Rabbi A.Z. Beck, Adass Israel

Meal-Mart
251 Inkerman Street, St Kilda 3182
Telephone: (3) 9525-5077
Fax: (3) 9525-4230
Supervision: Rabbi A.Z. Beck, Adass Israel
Pies, salads, pre-cooked and frozen foods.

BOOKSELLERS

Golds World of Judaica
3 - 13 William Street, Balaclava 3183
Telephone: (3) 9527-8775
Fax: (3) 9527-6434
Email: info@golds.com.au
Web site: www.golds.com.au

BUTCHERS

Continental Kosher Butchers
155 Glenferrie Road, Malvern 3144
Telephone: (3) 9509-9822
Fax: (3) 9509-9099
Email: ckb@bigpond.net.au
Supervision: Rabbi J.S. Cohen and Rabbi M. Gutnick, Melbourne Kashrut.

Melbourne Kosher Butchers
251 Inkerman Street, East St Kilda 3182
Telephone: (3) 9525-5077
Fax: (3) 9525-4230
Supervision: Rabbi A.Z. Beck, Adass Israel
Sell other kosher products as well. Hours: Monday, 10 am to 5:30 pm; Tuesday to Thursday, 7 am to 5:30 pm; Friday, 7 am to 3 pm. Winter 2 pm.

Solomon Kosher Butchers
140-144 Glen Eira Road, Elsternwick 3185
Telephone: (3) 9532-8855
Fax: (3) 9532-8896
Supervision: Rabbi Y.D. Groner, Agudas Chabad Kashrut Committee
Hours: Monday to Thursday, 7 am to 5:30 pm; Friday, 7 am to 3 pm.

Yumi's Kosher Seafoods
29 Glen Eira Road, Ripponlea 3183
Telephone: (3) 9523-6444
Fax: (3) 9532-8189
Email: yumis@bigpond.com
Supervision: Rabbi A.Z. Beck, Adass Israel
Also suppliers of kosher fresh fish.

CHOCOLATE SHOPS
Kosher

Alpha Kosher Chocolates
17 William Street, Balaclava
Telephone: (3) 9527-2453
Australia's only kosher chocolate factory. Handmade chocolates of export quality. Visitors welcome. Open Sunday mornings.

COMMUNITY ORGANISATIONS

Jewish Community Council of Victoria Inc.
306 Hawthorn Road, South Caulfield 3162
Telephone: (3) 9272-5566
Fax: (3) 9272-5560
Email: community@jccv.org.au
Web site: www.jccv.org.au
Head body of Melbourne Jewish community.

CONTACT INFORMATION

Mizrachi Hospitality Committee
81 Balaclava Road, Caulfield 3161
Telephone: (3) 9525-9833
Fax: (3) 9527-5665
Email: mizrachi@iprimus.com.au
Mailing address: P.O.Box 2247. Caulfield Junction. VIC 3161.

DELICATESSEN
E.S. Delicatessen
74 Kooyong Road, Caulfield 3161
Telephone: (3) 9576-0804
Supervision: Melbourne Kashrut

Eshel Take-Away Foods & Catering
59 Glen Eira Road, Ripponlea 3161
Telephone: (3) 9532-8309
Fax: (3) 9532-8089
Supervision: Rabbi A.Z. Beck, Adass Israel

GROCERIES
Dainty Foods (Kravsz)
62 Glen Eira Road, Ripponlea 3183
Telephone: (3) 9523-8463
Grocers/Importers.

Gefen Liquor Store
144 Chapel Street, Balaclava 3183
Telephone: (3) 9531-5032
Fax: (3) 9525-7388
Hours: Monday to Thursday, 9 am to 5 pm; Friday, 9 am
to 4 pm. Public transport access: #3 tram to corner of
Carlisle and Chapel Streets or Sandringham line train to
Balaclava Station.

Milecki's Balaclava Health Food
277 Carlisle Street, Balaclava 3183
Telephone: (3) 9527-3350
Open every day except Shabbat and all Jewish holidays.
Hours: 9 am to 9 pm. Close to rail station and on tram
line.

Rishon Foods Party Ltd.
23 Williams Street, Balaclava 3183
Telephone: (3) 9527-5142

Tempo Kosher Supermarket
5/320 Carlisle Street, St Kilda 3182
Telephone: (3) 9527-5021
Manufacturers of a range of kosher foods, including
cheese, butter and juice drinks.

HOTELS
Quest Kimberley Caulfield
441 Inkerman Street, Balaclava 3183
Telephone: (3) 9526-3888
Fax: (3) 9525-9691
Strictly Glatt kosher.

JUDAICA
The Antique Silver Co.
253 Carlisle Street, Balaclava 3183
Telephone: (3) 03-9525-8480
Fax: (3) 03-9525-8479
Large selection of Judaica and ritual objects.

KASHRUT INFORMATION
Melbourne Kashrut
81 Balaclava Road, Caulfield 3161

Telephone: (3) 9525-9895
Fax: (3) 9527-5665
Email: melbkash@iprimus.com.au
Mailing address: PO Box 2247 Caulfield Junction, Victoria
3161. Provides Kashrut information.

LIBRARIES
**Kadimah Jewish Cultural Centre & National
Library**
7 Selwyn Street, Elsternwick 3185
Telephone: (3) 9523-9817
Hours: 9.30 am-2.30 pm

Makor Jewish Community Library
306 Hawthorn Road, South Cantfield 3162
Telephone: (3) 9272-5611
Fax: (3) 9272-5629
Email: jlibrary@vicnet.net.au
Web site: www.vicnet.net.au/~jlibrary

MEDIA
Newspapers
Jewish News
PO Box 1000, South Cantfield
Publishes weekly newspaper.

MIKVAOT
Caulfield Mikva
9 Furneaux Grove, East St Kilda 3183
Telephone: (3) 9528-1116/9525-8585
Contact: Mrs C Sofer.

Lubavitch Mikva
38 Empress Road, East St Kilda 3183
Telephone: (3) 9527-7555
Fax: (3) 9525-8838
Email: ktrubin@wavenet.net.au

MUSEUMS
Jewish Holocaust Centre
15 Selwyn Street, Elsternwick 3185
Telephone: (3) 9528-1985
Fax: (3) 9528-3758
Email: hc@sprint.com.au
Hours: Monday and Wednesday 10.00 am to 4.00 pm,
Tuesday, Thursday and Friday 10.00 am to 2.00 pm,
Sunday 11.00 to 3.00pm.

Jewish Museum of Australia
26 Alma Road, St Kilda 3182
Telephone: (3) 9543-0083
Fax: (3) 9543-0844
Email: info@jewishmuseum.com.au
Web site: www.jewishmuseum.com.au

RELIGIOUS ORGANISATIONS
Council of Orthodox Synagogues of Victoria
C/- Level 10, 5 Queens Road 3004
Telephone: (3) 9864-4622
Fax: (3) 9864-4666
Email: yaron@jewishnews.net.au

Melbourne Beth Din
Synagogue Chambers, 572 Inkerman Road, North Caulfield 3161
Telephone: (3) 9527-8337
Fax: (3) 9527-8072

Rabbinical Council of Victoria
c/o Honorary Secretary, Rabbi Mordechai Gutnick, 7 Meadow St., East St Kilda 3183
Telephone: (3) 9525-9542
Fax: (3) 9525-9546

Progressive
Victorian Union for Progressive Judaism
78 Alma Road, St Kilda 3182
Telephone: (3) 9510-1488
Fax: (3) 9521-1229
Email: vupj@tbi.org.au

RESTAURANTS
Dairy
Sheli's Coffee Shop
306 Hawthorn Road, South Caulfield
Telephone: (3) 9272-5607

Meat
Delishes Restaurant
8-10 Glen Eira Ave., Ripponlea
Telephone: (3) 9523-1801

Klein's Kosher Gourmet
19 Glen Eira Road, Ripponlea
Telephone: (3) 9528-1200
Fax: (3) 9528-1300
Email: kleinsgourmetfoods@hotmail.com

Kosher Express
263-265 Carlisle St, Balaclava
Telephone: (3) 9527-9911
Fax: (3) 9527-9922

Lamzini's
219 Carlisle Street, St. Kilda
Telephone: (3) 9527-1283
Supervision: Melbourne Kashrut

SYNAGOGUES
Independent
Bet Hatikva Synagogue
233 Nepean Highway, Gardenvale 3185
Telephone: (3) 9576-9755

Liberal
Bentleigh Progressive Synagogue
549 Centre Road 3204
Telephone: (3) 9563-9208
Fax: (3) 9557-9880
Email: bpsadmin@bigpond.com.au
Web site: www.bps.org.au

Leo Baeck Centre
33-37 Harp Road, East Kew 3102
Telephone: (3) 9819-7160
Fax: (3) 9859-5417
Email: lbc@netspace.net.au
Web site: www.leobaeckcentre.org.au
PO Box 430 East Kew 3102

Temple Beth Israel
P O Box 128, St Kilda 3182
Telephone: (3) 9510-1488
Fax: (3) 9521-1229
Email: info@tbi.org.au
Web site: www.tbi.org.au

Orthodox
Brighton Hebrew Congregation
132-136 Marriage Road, East Brighton 3187
Telephone: (3) 9592-9179
Fax: (3) 9593-1682
Email: brightonshule@iprimus.com.au
Office hours: Monday to Friday 9 am-1 pm. PO Box 202 Bentleigh 3204. Visitors welcome.

Burwood Hebrew Congregation
38 Harrison Avenue 3125
Telephone: (3) 9808-3120

Caulfield Hebrew Congregation
572 Inkerman Road, Caulfield 3161
Telephone: (3) 9525-9492
Fax: (3) 9527-8463
Email: admin@caulfieldshule.com
Web site: www.caulfieldshule.com

East Melbourne City Synagogue
488 Albert St. East Melbourne 3002
Telephone: (3) 9662-1372
Fax: (3) 9662-1843
Email: office@melbournecitysynagogue.com
Web site: www.melbournecitysynagogue.com
The only synagogue in the inner city area. Within walking distance of all City hotels. A historically significant synagogue classified by the National Trust of Victoria.It celebrated its 125 year anniversary in 2002.

Elwood Talmud Torah Congregation
39 Dickens Street, Elwood 3184
Telephone: (3) 9531-1547

Kew Synagogue
53 Walpole Street, Kew 3101
Telephone: (3) 9853-9243
Fax: (3) 9853-1354
Email: kewshul@iprimus.com.au

Kollel Beth Hatalmud
362a Carlisle Street, East St Kilda 3183
Telephone: (3) 9527-6156
Fax: (3) 9527-8034
Email: kbt@blaze.net.au

Melbourne Hebrew Congregation
Cnr. Toorak & St Kilda Roads, S. Yarra 3141
Telephone: (3) 9866-2255
Fax: (3) 9866-2022
Email: mhc@bigpond.com

Mizrachi
81 Balaclava Road, Caulfield 3161
Telephone: (3) 9525-9833
Fax: (3) 9527-5665
Email: mizrachi@iprimus.com.au
Communication: P O Box 2247, Caulfield Junction, VIC 3161.

Moorabbin & District Synagogue
960 Nepean Highway, Moorabbin 3189
Telephone: (3) 9553-3845

North Eastern Malvern Chabad
Glenferrie Road, Malvern

South Caulfield Synagogue
47 Leopold Street, South Cantfield 3162
Telephone: (3) 9578-5922
Fax: (3) 9578-5299

St Kilda Hebrew Congregation Inc.
12 Charnwood Grove, St Kilda 3182
Telephone: (3) 9537-1433
Fax: (3) 9525-3759
Web site: www.stkildashule.org.au

The Sassoon Yehuda Sephardi Synagogue
79 Hotham Street, East St Kilda 3183
Telephone: (3) 9527-8863
Email: amar@netspace.net.au
Sephardi Kiddush follows Saturday service. Monday,
Thursday and Sunday services followed by breakfast.

Yeshiva Shule
92 Hotham Street, East St Kilda 3183
Telephone: (3) 9522-8222
Fax: (3) 9522-8266

TOURIST SITES
North Eastern Jewish War Memorial Centre Inc.
6 High Street, Doncaster 3108
Telephone: (3) 9816-3516
Fax: (3) 9857-4430
Email: nejc@one.au

Western Australia
PERTH
BUTCHERS
W.A. Kosher Butcher & Bakery
4 Bayley St., Dianella
Telephone: (8) 9276-2525

COMMUNITY ORGANISATIONS
Council of Western Australian Jewry
J.P. PO Box 763 6062

KOSHER FOOD
Aviv Catering
The Jewish Centre, 61 Woodrow Avenue, Yokinea 6060
Telephone: (8) 9276-6030
Fax: (8) 9276-6030
Supervision: Kashrut Authority of Western Australia
Open 10am-2pm

Kosher Food Centre
Freedman Road (cnr. Plantation St.), Menora
Telephone: (8) 9271-1133

SYNAGOGUES
Orthodox
Chabad House
396 Alexander Drive, Dianella 6062
Telephone: (8) 9275-4912

Dianella Shule
68 Woodrow Avenue, Yokine 6060
Telephone: (8) 9375-1276

Northern Suburbs Congregation
4 Vernon Street, Noranda 6062
Telephone: (8) 9275-5932

Perth Hebrew Congregation
Freedman Road, Menora 6050
Telephone: (8) 9271-0539
Email: phc@theperthshule.asn.au
Web site: www.theperthshule.asn.au
Also has a mikvah.

Reform
Temple David
34 Clifton Crescent, Mt Lawley 6050
Telephone: (8) 9271-1485
Fax: (8) 9272-2827
Email: temdavid@iinet.net.au
Web site: www.templedavid.org.au

AUSTRIA

The arrival of Jews in this area of Europe (probably with the Romans) was more than a 1,000 years ago. The community was expelled from Austria between 1420 and 1421, but Jews were allowed to return in 1451. The Jews were granted their own quarter of Vienna in 1624, but were expelled again in 1670. The economy declined after the expulsion, and so they were asked to return.

It was not until 1782 that the situation became more stable when Joseph II began lifting the anti-Jewish decrees that his mother, Maria Theresa, had imposed on her Jewish subjects. The Jews received equal rights in 1848 and, in 1867, legal and other prohibitions were lifted.

Anti-semitism did continue, however, and many influential anti-semitic publications were available in Vienna and were keenly read by many people, including the young Adolf Hitler. After the First World War, Austria lost its empire (which included Czech lands and Galicia, which had a very large Jewish community), and the Jewish population fell accordingly. At the time of the Nazi take-over in 1938, 200,000 Jews lived in the country. Some 70,000 were killed in the Holocaust, the rest having escaped or hidden.

Today there are several synagogues in Vienna. The city has an active Ultra-Orthodox community and kosher food is available. There are prayer rooms in some provincial cities.

Visitors to Vienna should not miss the new Jewish Museum opened in 2001. It combines Rachel Whiteread's memorial, the museum of medieval Jewish life and details of the excavation of a medieval synagogue built around the middle of the thirteenth century.

GMT +1 hour
Country calling code: **(+43)**
Total population: **8,086,000**
Jewish population: **10,000**
Emergency telephone: **(Police – 133) (Fire – 122) (Ambulance – 144)**
Electricity voltage: **(Electricity voltage – 220)**

BADEN
CEMETERIES
Jewish Cemetery
Halsriegelstrasse 4
Contains some 3,000 graves. (Keys to be obtained from the Jewish Community.)

SYNAGOGUES
Orthodox
Judische Gemeinde Baden
Grabengasse 14, POB 149 A-2500
Telephone: (2252) 210-6767
Fax: (2252) 217-0768
Email: synagogenverein@gmx.at
Web site: www.synagogenverein.at
Kosher meals are provided by the Jewish community on Shabbatot and Chagim.

EISENSTADT
CEMETERIES
Old Cemetery
The old cemetery, closed around 1875, contains the grave of Rav Meir Eisenstaat (Maharam Esh), who died in 1744. To this day it is the scene of pilgrimages, particularly on the anniversary of his death. Keys to the cemetery are with the porter of the local hospital, which adjoins the old cemetery.

MUSEUMS
Austrian Jewish Museum
Unterbergstrasse 6
Telephone: (2682) 65145
Fax: (2682) 65145; 65144
Email: info@oejudmus.or.at
The museum now also comprises the restored private synagogue of Samson Wertheimer, Habsburg court Jew and Chief Rabbi of Hungary (1658–1724). The museum is open daily except Monday from 10 am to 5 pm. The Eruv Arch, spanning Unterbergstrasse, is at the end near the Esterhazy Palace. The road chain was used in former times to prevent vehicular traffic on Shabbat and Yom Tov.

GRAZ
Graz is considered one of the oldest Jewish communities in Austria. There has been a self-contained Jewish quarter in Graz since 1142. In November 1938 (Kristallnacht) the synagogue was burnt and the Jews community was expelled.

The new synagogue, consecrated in November 2000, was partially rebuilt using bricks from the old synagogue.

Graz has been designated a European City of Culture for the year 2003.

SYNAGOGUES
Jewish Religious Community Synagogue
David-Herzog-Platz 1 A-8020
Telephone: (316) 712-468
Fax: (316) 720-433
Email: office@ikg-graz.at
Web site: www.ikg-graz.at

HINTERGLEMM

HOTELS
Hotel Knappenhof
Dorfstrasse 140 A574
Telephone: 6541-6497
Fax: 6541-64976
Email: info@kosher-hotel.at
Web site: www.kosher-hotel.at

INNSBRUCK

COMMUNITY ORGANISATIONS
Community Centre
Sillgassse 15
Telephone: (512) 586-892

KOBERSDORF

CEMETERIES
Jewish Cemetery
Waldgasse
The keys of the cemetery on the Lampelberg are with Mr Piniel, Waldgasse 25 (one of the two houses to the left of the cemetery) and Mr Grässing, Haydngasse 4.

LINZ

COMMUNITY ORGANISATIONS
Community Centre
Bethlehemstrasse 26
Telephone: (732) 779-805

SALZBURG
The Salzburg community dates back to 803 when Archbishop Arno summoned a Jewish doctor to set up a practice in the town.

COMMUNITY ORGANISATIONS
Lasserstrasse 8 A-5020
Telephone: (662) 872228
Fax: (662) 872228
Email: office@ikg-salzburg.at
Web site: www.ikg-salzburg.at
Community synagogue and mikva are to be found at the same address.

VIENNA
Vienna was in the past the most important centre for Central European Jews. From 180,000 Jews in the 1930s, there are about 1,000 Jews (mainly elderly) in Vienna today. Professor Freud's clinic is a popular attraction, and the Jewish Museum of Vienna gives much information on the history of the Jews.

BED AND BREAKFAST
Pension Lichtenstein
Grosse Schiffgasse 19 1020
Telephone: (1) 216-8498
Fax: (1) 214-7690
Web site: www.pension-lichtenstein.at

The pension consists of 'suites'. It is within walking distance of the old Jewish quarter of Vienna in one direction, and 5-20 minutes from some small synagogues and a kosher bakery in the other direction. Visits should be arranged in advance as there is no front desk reception; the key is kept in the owner's office around the block.

BOOKSELLERS
Chabad-Simcha-Center
Hollandstrasse 10 1020
Telephone: (1) 216-2924

Chai Vienna
Praterstrasse 40 1020
Telephone: (1) 216-4621
Fax: (1) 216-4621

BUTCHERS
B. Ainhorn
Stadtgutgasse 7 1020
Telephone: (1) 214-5621
Supervision: Rabbi David Grunfeld
Also supplies "Fast Food".

Rebenwurzel
Grose Mohrengasse 19 1010
Telephone: (1) 216-6640
Supervision: Rabbi Chaim Stern

CEMETERIES
Floridsdorfer Cemetery
Ruthnergasse 28 1210
Those wishing to visit must first obtain a permit from the community centre.

Rossauer Cemetery
Seegasse 9 1090
This is the oldest Jewish cemetery in Vienna, dating from the sixteenth century. It has now been restored after being devastated by the Nazis and is open daily from 8 am to 3 pm. Access is via the front entrance of the municipal home for the aged at Seegasse 9-11, but a permit must first be obtained from the community centre.

Vienna Central Cemetery
Simmeringer Haupstr.244 A-1110
Telephone: (1) 531 04 904, 767 6252
The Jewish section (the only one still in use) is at Gate 4 and there is an older Jewish part at Gate 1.

Währinger Cemetery
Semperstrasse 64a 1180
Those wishing to visit must first obtain a permit from the community centre.

CONTACT INFORMATION
Jewish Community Centre
Seitenstettengasse 4
Telephone: (1) 531 04104
Fax: (1) 531 04108
Email: office@ikg-wien.at

Jewish Welcome Service Vienna
Stephansplatz 10 1010
Telephone: (1) 43-1-533-2730
Fax: (1) 43-1-533-4098
Email: jewish.welcome@verkehrsbuero.at
Web site: www.jewish-welcome.at
Open: Monday to Friday 9.00 am to 5.30 pm.

DOCUMENTATION CENTRE
Documentation Centre of Austrian Resistance
Old City Hall, Wipplingerstrasse 8 1010
Telephone: (1) 534-36-90319
Fax: (1) 534-36-9990319
Email: office@doew.at
Web site: www.doew.at
Hours of opening: Monday to Thursday 9 am to 5 pm.

Documentation Centre of Union of Jewish Victims of the Nazis
Salztorgasse 6 A-1010
Telephone: (1) 533-9131
Fax: (1) 535-0397

EMBASSY
Embassy of Israel
Anton-Frankgasse 20 1180
Telephone: (1) 476-460

GROCERIES
Gross-Import-Wien
Nicklegasse 1 A-1020
Telephone: (1) 214-0607
Fax: (1) 214-7690

Koscherland
Kleine Sperlgasse 7
Telephone: (1) 212-8169

Kosher Supermarket & Shatnes Laboratory
Hollandstrasse 7 1020
Telephone: (1) 269-9675
Supervision: Rabbi Abraham Yonah Schwartz

Ohel Moshe
Hollandstrasse 10 A-1020
Telephone: (1) 216-9675
Supervision: Rabbi Abraham Yonah Schwartz

Rafael Malkov
Tempelgasse 6, Ferdinandstrasse 2 A-1020
Telephone: (1) 214-8394

HOTELS
Hotel Stefanie
Taborstrasse 12 1020
Telephone: (1) 211-500
Fax: (1) 211-50160
Email: stefanie@schick-hotels.com
Web site: www.schick-hotels.com
Four-star hotel with kosher breakfast on request.

MEDIA
Newspaper
Die Gemeinde
Telephone: (1) 531 04 271
Fax: (1) 531 04 279
Monthly.

MIKVAOT
Agudas Yisroel
Tempelgasse 3 1020
Telephone: (1) 214-9973

MONUMENT
Nameless Library
Judenplatz
Rachel Whiteread's monument, opened in 2001, depicts shelves of 9,000 books with their spines turned to the inside. The names of the concentration camps in which Austrian Jews were killed are engraved around the base. Underneath the memorial one can view the ruins of a synagogue razed in 1421.

MUSEUMS
Jewish Museum Vienna
Dorotheergasse 11 A-1010
Telephone: (1) 535-0431 ext. 112
Fax: (1) 535-0424
Email: susanna.koncar@jmw.at
Web site: www.jmw.at
Hours: Sunday to Friday, 10 am to 6 pm; Thursday, 10 am to 8 pm. Cafeteria and bookshop on site. The cafeteria is not supervised.

Museum Judenplatz
Judenplatz 8 A-1010
Telephone: (1) 535-0431
Fax: (1) 535-0424
Email: info@jmw.at
Web site: www.jmw.at
A memorial to the Austrian victims of the Holocaust. A place of rememberance was created that is unique in Europe. It combines Rachel Whiteread's memorial (Nameless Library, see above) and the excavations of a medieval synagogue with the Museum on Medieval Jewish Life to form a commemorative whole. Opening hours 10am to 6pm, Friday 10am to 2pm. Special guided tours for groups by prior arrangement only.

Sigmund Freud Museum
Berggasse 19 1090
Telephone: (1) 43-1-319-1596
Fax: (1) 43-1-317-0279
Email: office@freud-museum.at
Web site: www.freud-museum.at
Hours: March to June 9am to 5pm, July to September 9am - 6pm

RESTAURANTS
Dairy
Milk 'n' Honey
Kleine Sperlgasse 7
Telephone: (1) 219-6886

Meat
Restaurant Alef - Alef
Seitenstettengasse 2 A-1010
Telephone: (1) 535-2530
Fax: (1) 5352-53033
Web site: www.alef-alef.at

Snack Bar
Berl Ainhorn Koscher Fleisch und Imbiss
Gross Stadtgutgasse 7 1020
Telephone: (1) 214-5621

SITE
Mauthausen Memorial Site
Telephone: (1) 723-82269
Fax: (1) 723-83696
Those wishing to visit the site should contact the Jewish Welcome Service.

SYNAGOGUES
Orthodox
Agudas Yisroel
Grünangergasse 1 1010
Telephone: (1) 512-8331
Tempelgasse 3 1020
Telephone: (1) 214 9262

Machsike Haddas
Große Mohreng. 19 A-1020
Telephone: (1) 216 0679

Misrachi
Judenplatz 8 1010
Telephone: (1) 532-8301
Fax: (1) 214-8010
Email: daleno@utanet.at

Ohel Moshe
Lilienbrunngasse 19 1020
Telephone: (1) 216-8864

Rambam
Bauernfeldgasse 4 A-1190

Seitenstettengasse Synagogue
Seitenstettengasse 4 1010
Telephone: (1) 531-040
Fax: (1) 531-04108
Email: office@ikg-wien.at
Web site: www.ikg-wien.at
Built in 1824-26 and partly destroyed during the Nazi period, this beautiful synagogue was restored by the community in 1988. For information about guided tours, contact the Community Centre offices.

Sephardi Centre
Tempelgasse 7 1020
Telephone: (1) 214 3097

Shomre Haddas
Glasergasse 17 1090

Thora Etz Chayim
Grosse Schiffgasse 8 1020
Telephone: (1) 214-5206
Fax: (1) 216-2032
Email: Samikern@csi.com

Progressive
Or Chadasch
Rosentalgasse 5-7/4/3 1140
Telephone: (1) 967 1329
Fax: (1) 914 5245

AZERBAIJAN

Azerbaijan has a remarkable Jewish history, which can now be better explored now that the country is independent from the Soviet Union. The Tats (mountain Jews) believe that their ancestors arrived in Azerbaijan at the time of Nebuchadnezzar. The lived in several mountain villages, and adopted the customs of their non-Jewish neighbours. They spoke a north Iranian language, known as Judeo-Tat, to which they had added some Hebrew words. The Soviets clamped down on their way of life after 1928, changing the alphabet of their language from Hebrew to Latin, and then in 1938, to Cyrillic. Some of their synagogues were also closed down. Zionist feeling is high, with almost 30,000 emigrating to Israel since 1989.

The other strand in Azerbaijan's Jewish population are the Ashkenasis who arrived in the nineteenth century from Poland and other countries to the west.

The community has some 10–15 organisations in Baku, the capital, including Zionist and youth groups. The largest synagogue in Baku is the Tat synagogue, but there are also Ashkenazi and Georgian synagogues. Synagogues are found in other towns.

GMT +5 hours
Country calling code: (+994)
Total population: **7,625,000**
Jewish population: **10,000**
Emergency telephone:

BAKU
EMBASSY
Embassy of Israel
Stroiteley Prospect 1

SYNAGOGUES
Mountain Jews
Dmitrova Street 39 370014
Telephone: (12) 892-232-8867

Ashkenazi
Pervomoskaya Street 271
Telephone: (12) 892-294-1571

KUBA
SYNAGOGUES
Kolkhoznaya Street 46

BAHAMAS

Luis de Torres, the official interpreter for Columbus, was the first Jew in the Bahamas, as well as being one of the first Europeans there. He was a Converso, a 'secret Jew' who officially had converted to Catholicism, but who practised Judaism in private. The British arrived in 1620, and eventually gained control of the islands. Although there was a Jewish attorney-general and chief justice in the islands in the eighteenth century, few Jews settled there until the twentieth century, coming from eastern Europe and the UK after the First World War, and settling in Nassau, the capital.

There are approximately 100 Jewish residents in the Bahamas. However, it is estimated that about 350,000 Jews visit the Islands each year as tourists. There are congregations in Nassau and Freeport. Both cities have Jewish cemeteries, that in Nassau being more historic.

GMT -5 hours
Country calling code: **(+1242)**
Total population: **289,000**
Jewish population: **300**
Emergency telephone: **(Police – 919) (Fire – 919) (Ambulance – 919)**
Electricity voltage: **(Electricity voltage – 120)**

FREEPORT
SYNAGOGUES
Freeport Hebrew Congregation
Luis de Torres Synagogue, East Sunrise Highway, PO Box F-41761
Telephone: 373-9457

Fax: 871-5528
Email: hurst100@yahoo.com
Services every Friday evening at 8:30 pm from September through April, as well as Community Seder, Chanukah celebration and full-time certificated marriage officer.

NASSAU
SYNAGOGUES
Progressive
Bahamas Jewish Congregation
POB CB-11002
Telephone: 363-2305

BARBADOS

Jewish history in Barbados starts in 1628, a year after the British first settled there. Jewish settlers came from Brazil, Surinam, England and Germany, and were mainly Sephardi. The first synagogue was established in Bridgetown (the capital) in 1654. Early settlers were engaged in cultivating sugar and coffee.

The Jewish population was well treated, and in 1831 Barbados was the first British possession in which Jews were granted full political emancipation. Despite a largely favourable climate, the community suffered losses from hurricanes, which destroyed sugar plantations, and the Jewish population fell to 70 by 1848. In 1925, no Jews remained, but a new influx (30 families escaping Nazism) came shortly after.

The synagogue was restored in 1987, and postage stamps were produced which commemorated its restoration. The Jewish population remains small, but it was a group of Barbadian Jews who founded the Caribbean Jewish Congress. The Jewish cemetery, one of the oldest in the Americas, is now back in use.

GMT -4 hours
Country calling code: **(+1246)**
Total population: **262,000**
Jewish population: **Under 100**
Emergency telephone:
Electricity voltage: **(Electricity voltage – 110)**

BRIDGETOWN
COMMUNITY ORGANISATIONS
Barbados Jewish Community
PO Box 651, Bridgetown
Telephone: 427-0703
Fax: 436-8807

Caribbean Jewish Congress
PO Box 1331, Bridgetown
Telephone: 436-8163
Fax: 437-4992
Email: comphosting.sunbeach.net\cjc

Synagogue Restoration Project
PO Box 256, Bridgetown
Telephone: 432-0840
Fax: 432-2147
Email: altman@caribsurf.com
Local inquiries to Henry Altman, Little Mallows, Sandy Lane, St. James. Tel: 132-6462

SYNAGOGUES
Nidhe Israel
Synagogue Lane
Telephone: 427 7611
Services are held Friday evenings at 7 pm at 'True Blue', Rockley New Road, Christ Church, during the summer, and at the synagogue at 7.30 pm in winter.

BELARUS

For the adventurous traveller, who has a keen interest in Jewish history, Belarus (also known as White Russia) makes an interesting and unusual destination. Situated on the western side of the former Soviet Union, this largely flat country borders Poland and Lithuania to the west, Ukraine to the south and Russia to the east. Belarus finally achieved independence in 1991, and within its present borders are many towns and villages of Jewish interest, such as Minsk, Pinsk and Grodno. One of the most famous villages in Belarus is Lubavitch, a hamlet in the far east of the country, near the Russian border, where the world-wide Lubavitch movement had its origins.

The majority of this region's Jews died in the Holocaust and although emigration to Israel is high, the community is slowly rebuilding itself after decades of Soviet control. Americans and Israelis are contributing rabbis to help in this revival, and Jewish schools have been set up. Yiddish is used far more here than in other parts of the former USSR.

GMT +2 hours
Country calling code: (+375)
Total population: **10,179,000**
Jewish population: **30,000**
Emergency telephone: **(Police – 03) (Fire – 03) (Ambulance – 003)**
Electricity voltage: **(Electricity voltage – 220)**

BARANOVICHI
SYNAGOGUES
39 Svobodnaya St.

BOBRUISK
SYNAGOGUES
Engels St.

BORISOV
SYNAGOGUES
Trud St.

BREST
SYNAGOGUES
Narodnaya St.

GOMEL
CONTACT INFORMATION
Rosa Sorkina
Telephone: (23) 252-5808

SYNAGOGUES
13 Sennaya St.

GRODNO
CONTACT INFORMATION
Misha Kemerov
Telephone: (15) 2313-798

SYNAGOGUES
Menorah Jewish Community
Blk 43,Flat 37 230009
Telephone: (15) 2313 798
Email: sh10@grsu.grodno.by

MINSK
CONTACT INFORMATION
Rabbi Nelly Shulman
Telephone: (17) 2110-234
Email: nashulman@mail.ru

EMBASSY
Embassy of Israel
Partizanski Prospekt 6A 220002
Telephone: (17) 2304-444

MEMORIAL

This memorial devoted to 5,000 Jews killed by the Nazis on Purim 1942 was erected in 1946 and is the only one in what was the USSR devoted to the Holocaust which displays Yiddish writing.

SYNAGOGUES
22 Kropotkin Fstreet
Telephone: (17) 2558-270
13b Daumana Street
22 Kropotkin St.
Telephone: (17) 255-8270

Progressive
Association of Progressive Jewish Congregations in Belarus
Per K Chyornogo 4, apt 18, Simcha 220012
Telephone: (17) 2846-089
Fax: (17) 2662-928
Email: simcha@open.by

MOGHILEV
SYNAGOGUES
1 2nd Krutoy La.

ORSHA
SYNAGOGUES
Nogrin St.

RECHITSA
SYNAGOGUES
120 Lunacharsky St.

BELGIUM

Jewish settlement in the area now called Belgium dates back to the thirteenth century, and suffered a similar fate to other medieval European Jewish communities, taking the blame for the Black Death and suffering expulsions. The Sephardim were the first to resettle in Belgium, mainly in Antwerp. After independence in 1830, conditions for the Jews improved and more Jews began to settle there. The diamond centre of Antwerp later developed rapidly, attracting many Jews from eastern Europe.

By 1939, the Jewish population had grown to 100,000, a large proportion of whom were refugees hoping to escape to America. Some succeeded, but many became trapped after the German invasion. Some 25,000 Belgian Jews were deported and killed in the Holocaust. A national monument listing the names of the victims stands in Anderlecht in Brussels.

The present Jewish population includes a large Chassidic community in Antwerp, where there are some 30 synagogues. There are also more than ten synagogues in Brussels. There are Jewish schools in Antwerp and Brussels, and Jewish newspapers.

GMT +1 hour
Country calling code: (+32)
Total population: 10,188,000
Jewish population: 33,000
Emergency telephone: (Police – 101) (Fire – 101) (Ambulance – 101)
Electricity voltage: (Electricity voltage – 220)

ANTWERP
Seen by some as 'the last shtetl in Europe', Antwerp is a well-known Hassidic centre. Antwerp's Jewish population (15,000) has one of the highest numbers of Ultra-Orthodox in the Diaspora. Served by 30 synagogues (many of them small shtiebels), there are also kosher restaurants and food shops.

BAKERIES
Gottesfeld
Mercatorstraat 20
Telephone: (3) 230-0003
Kleinblatt
Provinciestraat 206
Telephone: (3) 233-7513; 226-0018
Fax: (3) 232-0920
Steinmetz
Lange Kievitstraat 64
Telephone: (3) 234-0947

BOOKSELLERS
I. Menczer
Simonstraat 40
Telephone: (3) 232-3026
N. Seletsky
Lange Kievitstraat 70
Telephone: (3) 232-6966
Fax: (3) 226-9446

BUTCHERS
Berkowitz
Isabellalei 9
Telephone: (3) 218-5111
Fruchter
Simonstraat 22
Telephone: (3) 233-1811; 1557
Fax: (3) 231-3903

Kosher King
Lange Kievitstraat 40
Telephone: (3) 233-6749
Isabellalei 7
Telephone: (3) 239-4189

Mandelovics
Isabellalei 96
Telephone: (3) 218-4779

Moszkowitz
Lange Kievitstraat 47
Telephone: (3) 232-6349
Fax: (3) 226-0471

CONTACT INFORMATION
Machsike Hadass (Israelitische Orthodoxe Gemeente)
Jacob Jacobsstraat 22
Telephone: (3) 233-5567

Shomre Hadass (Israelitische Gemeente)
Terliststraat 35 2018
Telephone: (3) 232-0187
Fax: (3) 226-3123
Email: shomre-hadas@net4all.be
Web site: www.members.net4all.be/shomre-hadas

DELICATESSEN
Weingarten
Lange Kievitstraat 124
Telephone: (3) 233-2828

GROCERIES
Col-Bo
Jacob Jacobsstraat 40
Telephone: (3) 234-1212

Grosz-Modern
Terliststraat 28
Telephone: (3) 232-4626

Stark
Mercatorstraat 24
Telephone: (3) 230-2520

Super Discount
Belgielei 104-108
Telephone: (3) 239-0666

Superette Lamoriniere
Lamboriniere Straat 199
Telephone: (3) 239-3110
Fax: (3) 281-3205

MEDIA
Newspaper
Belgisch Israelitisch Weekblad
Pelikaanstraat 106-108 2018
Telephone: (3) 233-7094
Fax: (3) 233-4810
Email: biw@wanadoo.be

MIKVAOT
Machsike Hadass
Steenbokstraat 22
Telephone: (3) 239-7588

MUSEUMS
Plantin-Moretus Museum
Vrijdagmarkt (nr Groenplaats)
Telephone: (3) 233-0688
Open daily (except Monday). Contains examples of early Jewish printing, such as the famous Polyglot Bible.

RESTAURANTS
Dairy
Garden of Eden
Plantin En Moretuslei 10 2018
Telephone: (3) 281-4281
Fax: (3) 700-4034
Open: 12 pm-2 pm and 6 pm-10 pm.

USA Pizza
118a Isabellalei
Telephone: (3) 281-2300
Supervision: Machzikey Hadas
Take away option.

Meat
Blue Lagoon
Lange Herentalsestraat 70
Telephone: (3) 226-0114
Supervision: Machsike Hadass
Also sells chocolates. Five minutes from Central station.

Hoffy's
Lange Kievitstraat 52
Telephone: (3) 234-3535
Fax: (3) 226-0282
Email: hoffys@pandora.be

Jacob
Lange Kievitstraat 49
Telephone: (3) 233-1124

Lamalo
Appelmanstraat 21
Telephone: (3) 213-2200

Vegetarian
Time Out
Lange Herentalse Straat 58 2018
Telephone: (3) 32-3-281-2300
Fax: (3) 32-3-281-2300
Email: time-out@pandora.be

SYNAGOGUES
Great Synagogue Romi Goldmuntz
Van Den Nestlei 1
Telephone: (3) 232-0187

Sephardic Synagogue
Hovenierstraat 31
Telephone: (3) 232-5339
Built in 1913. This synagogue is located in the middle of the Diamond district.

Orthodox
Machsike Hadass
Jacob Jacobsstraat 22
Telephone: (3) 232-0021
Fax: (3) 233-8797

Oosten Synagogue
Oostenstraat 43
Telephone: (3) 230-9246

TOURS
Toerisme Antwerpen
Grote Markt 15 2000
Telephone: (3) 232-0103
Fax: (3) 231-1937
Email: visit@antwerpen.be
Web site: www.visitantwerpen.be

ARLON
SYNAGOGUES
Synagogue
Rue St Jean
Telephone: (63) 217-985
Established 1863. The secretary, J.C. Jacob, can be reached at 11 rue des Martyrs, 6700. A monument has been erected in the new Jewish cemetery to the memory of the Jews of Arlon deported and massacred by the Nazis.

BRUSSELS
The capital of Belgium is less well endowed with kosher facilities than Antwerp, although there are 23,000 Jews living in the city. The headquarters of the European Union of Jewish Students is based there. The Anderlecht area has a monument to the Belgian Holocaust victims and a memorial to Jews who fought in the Belgian Resistance.

BAKERIES
Bornstein
62 rue de Suéde, St Gilles
Telephone: (2) 537-1679

BOOKSELLERS
Colbo
121 rue du Brabant
Telephone: (2) 217-2620

Menorah
12 Ave. J. Voldens 1060
Telephone: (2) 537-5073

BUTCHERS
Lanxner
121 rue de Brabant 1030
Telephone: (2) 217-2620
Supervision: Rabbinate of the Jewish Orthodox Community of Brussels
Grocery: Hours: Sun, Mon, Fri 8.30 am to 1.00 pm. Tues 8.30 am to 6.00 pm. Wed-Thurs 8.30 am to 7.30 pm.

COMMUNITY ORGANISATIONS
Centre Communautaire Laic Juif
Yitzhak Rabin Center, 52 rue Hotel des Monnaies
Telephone: (2) 543-0270
Fax: (2) 543-0271
Email: info@cclj.be
Web site: www.cclj.be

EMBASSY
Embassy of Israel
40 Avenue de l'Observatoire 1180
Telephone: (2) 373-5500

GROCERIES
Hod Taim
51 Boulevard Jamar
Telephone: (2) 527-1832

MEDIA
Newspapers
Centrale
91 Av. Henri Jaspar
Telephone: (2) 538-8036
Monthly

Fax de Jerusalem
68 Ave Ducpétiaux
Telephone: (2) 538-5673
Fax: (2) 534-0236
Email: alyabelgique@skynet.be
Weekly

Kehilatenou
2 rue Joseph Dupont B-1000
Telephone: (2) 512-4334
Fax: (2) 512-9237
Monthly

Regards
52 rue Hotel des Monnaies, 1060
Telephone: (2) 543-0281
Fax: (2) 537-5565
Email: Regards@cclj.be
Web site: www.cclj.be/Regards
Fortnightly

Radio
Radio Judaica (Jewish Radio) FM 90.2
Jewish interest programs 24-hours a day.

MIKVAOT
Machsike Hadass
67a rue de la Clinique
Telephone: (2) 537-1439

MUSEUMS
Jewish Museum
74 Ave de Stalingrad 1000
Telephone: (2) 512-1963
Fax: (2) 513-4859
Email: info@mjb-jmb.org
Web site: www.mjb-jmb.org
Hours: Mon-Thurs 12.00 - 5.00 pm. Sunday 10.00 am to 1.00 pm. Closed Friday, Saturday and Jewish holidays.

RELIGIOUS ORGANISATIONS
Communaute Israelite de Bruxelles
2 rue Joseph Dupont B-1000
Telephone: (2) 512-4334
Fax: (2) 512-9237

Machsike Hadass (Communauté Israélite Orthodoxe de Bruxelles)
67a rue de la Clinique
Telephone: (2) 524-1486; 521-1289

RESTAURANTS
Chez Gilles
Rue de la Clinique 21 1070
Telephone: (2) 522-1828
Open from 9 am - 5 pm.

El Assado
Roosendael 154
Telephone: (2) 346-3487

Restaurant Seven-Seventy
87 Avenue du Roi 1060
Telephone: (2) 537-1158

Meat
Athenee Maimonide
Boulevard Poincarte 67
Telephone: (2) 523-6336

SITE
National Monument to the Jewish Martyrs of Belgium
Corner rue Emile Carpentier and rue Goujons, Square of the Jewish Martyrs, Anderlecht.
This monument commemorates the Jews of Belgium who were deported to concentration camps and killed by the Nazis during the Second World War. The names of all 23,838 are engraved on the monument.

SYNAGOGUES
Brussels Airport
Situated in the transit lounge.

Liberal
Communaute Israelite Liberale de Belgique - Beth Hillel
Avenue de Kersbeek 96 1190
Telephone: (2) 332-2528
Fax: (2) 376-7219
Email: cilb.asbl@chello.be

Orthodox
Adath Israel
126 rue Rogier 1030
Telephone: (2) 241-1664
Near City Center

Ahavat Reim
73 rue de Thy
Telephone: (2) 648-3837

Beth Itshak
115 Ave du Roi 1060
Telephone: (2) 538-3374; 520-1359

Communaute Israelite d'Uccle-Forest
11 Avenue de Messidor 1180
Telephone: (2) 32-2-344-6094
Fax: (2) 32-2-344-6094
Email: info@maale.org
Web site: www.maale.org

The Great Synagogue
32 rue de la Regence 1000
Telephone: (2) 512-4334
Fax: (2) 512-9237
The synagogue built in 1878 survived the occupation.

Sephardi
Synagogue Simon and Lina Haim
47 rue du Pavilion 1030
Telephone: (2) 215-0525
Fax: (2) 215-0242
This is a memorial to the Jews deported from Rhodes, Greece

CHARLEROI
COMMUNITY ORGANISATIONS
Community Centre
56 rue Pige-au-Croly

GHENT
CONTACT INFORMATION
Jacques Bloch
Veldstraat 60
Telephone: (9) 225-7085
Email: blochjb@yahoo.com
The treasurer of the community will be happy to meet English-speaking visitors. As the community is a very small one, there is no permanent synagogue. Services are held on the High Holy Days.

KNOKKE
SYNAGOGUES
30 Van Bunnenlaan
Telephone: (50) 61-0372
Also has a mikva.

LIÈGE
COMMUNITY ORGANISATIONS
Community Centre
12 Quai Marcellis 4020

MUSEUMS
Musee Serge Kruglanski
19 rue L. Fredericq 4020
Telephone: (4) 438-043
Fax: (4) 226-0234

SYNAGOGUES
19 rue L. Frédéricq 4020
Telephone: (4) 436-106

MONS

CONTACT INFORMATION
SHAPE
Telephone: (65) 445-808; 444-809
Nearby, at Casteau, the International Chapel of NATO's Supreme Headquarters Allied Powers Europe, includes a small Jewish community, established 1951, that holds regular services. Call for further information.

OSTEND

SYNAGOGUES
Philip Van Maastrichtplein 4
Telephone: (59) 511-622
Services during July and August. Inquiries to Mrs Liliane Wulfowicz, Parklaan 21, B-8400, (59) 802-405.

WATERLOO

SYNAGOGUES
Traditionalist
Communaute Israelite de Waterloo et du Brabant Sud (CIWABS)
140 Avenue Belle-Vue, 1410 Waterloo
Telephone: (2) 354-6833
Fax: (2) 514-5977
Regular Services Shabbat and Festivals; English speaking visitors very welcome; tel:32-2-351-3631 (evenings).

BERMUDA

Jews have lived in Bermuda since the seventeenth century, but the first formal congregation was not established until the twentieth century.

The resident Jewish population is very small, but the transient population (of tourists largely from the USA, Britain and Canada) is much greater. There is a Jew's Bay but whether this is merely named to balance a nearby Christian Bay or has some other origin is not known.

GMT -4 hours
Country calling code: (+1 441)
Total population: 60,000
Jewish population: Under 100
Emergency telephone: (Police – 112) (Fire – 113) (Ambulance – 115)
Electricity voltage: (Electricity voltage – 110)

HAMILTON

COMMUNITY ORGANISATIONS
Jewish Community of Bermuda
PO Box HM 1793 HM05
Telephone: (441) 291-1785
Web site: www.jcb.bm

BOLIVIA

The history of the Jews of Bolivia dates back to the Spanish colonial period. Conversos (converts to Christianity who practised Judaism in secret) came with the Spaniards in the seventeenth century.

The main influx of Jews occurred in 1905, with immigrants from eastern Europe, but the number entering Bolivia was much smaller than that going to other South American countries. In 1933 there were only some 30 Jewish families. At the end of the decade, however, there was a small increase in Jewish immigration as German and Austrian Jews fled from Europe. Ironically, the Jewish community did not grow very much, even though the government granted every Jew an entry visa.

Many Jews started to leave Bolivia in the 1950s because of political instability and the apparent lack of educational opportunities. The present-day community has a central organisation known as the Circulo Israelita de Bolivia.

GMT -4 hours
Country calling code: (+591)
Total population: 8,140,000
Jewish population: 500
Emergency telephone:
Electricity voltage: (Electricity voltage – 110/220)

COCHABAMBA

COMMUNITY ORGANISATIONS
Asociacion Israelita de Cochabamba
PO Box 349, Calle Valdivieso

SYNAGOGUES
Calle Junin y Calle Colombia, Casilla 349

LA PAZ

SYNAGOGUES
Circulo Israelita de Bolivia
Casilla 1545, Calle Landaeta 346, PO Box 1545
Telephone: (2) 32-5925
Fax: (2) 34-2738
Representative body of Bolivian Jewry. All La Paz organisations are affiliated to it. Service Shabbat morning only.

Comunidad Israelita Synagogue
Calle Canada Stronguest 1846, PO Box 2198
Affiliated to the Circulo Israelita de Bolivia. Friday evening services are held here.

TOURS
Centro Shalom
Calle Canada Stronguest 1846

SANTA CRUZ
COMMUNITY ORGANISATIONS
Centro Cruceño
PO Box 469
WIZO
Castilla 3409

BOSNIA-HERCEGOVINA

Sephardi Jews were the first to arrive in the area, in the late sixteenth century. They established a Jewish quarter in Sarajevo, and this was home for poorer Jews until the Austrians conquered the land in 1878. It was the Turks, however, who emancipated the Jews in the nineteenth century when Bosnia-Hercegovina was under Ottoman rule.

When Bosnia-Hercegovina became part of the newly formed Yugoslavia, after the First World War, the community maintained its Sephardi heritage and joined the all-Yugoslav Federation of Jewish Religious Communities. The Jewish population numbered 14,000 in 1941. This number dropped sharply after the Germans conquered Yugoslavia.

After the war the survivors were joined by many who had decided to return. The Sephardi and Ashkenazi communities became unified. La Benevolencija, founded 100 years ago, is a humanitarian organisation which supported the plight of the community and became well known in the early 1990s at the time of the civil war. After the Yugoslav civil war, many made aliyah to Israel, reducing the community still further.

GMT +1 hour
Total population: **3,784,000**
Jewish population: **400**
Emergency telephone: **(Police – 664 211) (Fire – 93) (Ambulance – 94)**
(Emergency - 94)
Electricity voltage: **(Electricity voltage – 220)**

SARAJEVO
CEMETERIES
Kovacici
This historic Jewish cemetery is in town. Not far from the centre of town, on a hill called Vraca, there is a monument with the names of the 7,000 Jews from the area who fell victim to the Nazis.

COMMUNITY ORGANISATIONS
Sarajevo Jewish Community "La Benevolencija"
Hamdije Kresevljakovica 83 7100
Telephone: (71) 663-472
Fax: (71) 663-473

MUSEUMS
Jewish Museum
Mulamustafe Baseskije Street
This historic museum, placed in the oldest synagogue in Sarajevo, with priceless relics dating back to the expulsion from Spain, is temporarily closed to the public.

SYNAGOGUES
Synagogue and Community Centre
Hamdije Kresevljakovica 59
Telephone: (71) 663-472
Fax: (71) 663-473
Email: la_bene@soros.org.ba

TOURIST SITES
The National Museum of Bosnia and Herzegovina
Zmaja od Bosne 3
Telephone: (71) 387-33-668027; 387-33-668025
Fax: (71) 387-33-668-025; 387-33-262710
Email: z.muzej@zemaljskimuzej.ba
Web site: www.zemaljskimuzej.ba
The world famous Sarajevo Haggadah written around 1314 as a wedding gift to a young couple has now been fully repaired and restored. It is in a secure climate-controlled room.

BRAZIL

The first Jewish settlers in Brazil came with the Portuguese in 1500. They were mainly Conversos, escaping persecution in Portugal, and initially worked on the sugar plantations. In due course they played important roles as traders, artisans and plantation owners. The huge area which is called Brazil today was in the process of being conquered by the Dutch and the Portuguese. Two synagogues were opened in Recife during the 1640's and many Jews came from Holland. When the Dutch left

Brazil in 1654 one of the terms of surrender allowed the Jews who had been on their side to emigrate. Many fled and some went on to found the first Jewish community in New York, then known as New Amsterdam. A seventeenth-century Mikvah was discovered in 2000 in the basement of the Tsur Israel Synagogue in Recife.

With Brazilian independence in 1822, conditions became more favourable for Jews and many came from north Africa and Europe. The majority of Jews in Brazil today, however, originate from the immigration of east European Jews in the early twentieth century. From about 6,000 Jews in 1914, the community grew to 30,000 in 1930. After 1937 Brazil refused to allow Jewish immigrants into the country, but some limited immigration managed to continue despite the restrictions.

A central organisation was established in 1951 (the CONIB), and this includes 200 various Jewish organisations. Brazilian Jews live in an atmosphere of tolerance and prosperity, and assimilation is prominent.

There are synagogues in all the major cities.

GMT -3 to -5 hours
Country calling code: **(+55)**
Total population: **159,884,000**
Jewish population: **110,000**
Emergency telephone: **(Police – 147) (Fire – 193) (Ambulance – 192)**
Electricity voltage: **(Electricity voltage – 220/100)**

Amazonas
MANAUS
COMMUNITY ORGANISATIONS
Comite Israelita Amazonas
R. Leonardo Malcher, 630
Telephone: (92) 234-7647
Fax: (92) 233-6361

Bahia
SALVADOR
SYNAGOGUES
Rua Alvaro Tiberio 60
Telephone: (71) 321-4204
Fax: (71) 337-6412
Community centre and Zionist organisation are at the same address.

Goiás
BRASILIA
EMBASSY
Embassy of Israel
Av. das Nacoes Sul, Lote 38
Telephone: (61) 244-7675/244-7875
Fax: (61) 244-6129
SYNAGOGUES
ACIB
Entrequadras Norte 305-306, Lote A
Telephone: (61) 273-8255
Fax: (61) 366-3651
Email: goldner@tba.com.br
Community centre is at the same address.

Minas Gerais
BELO HORIZONTE
COMMUNITY ORGANISATIONS
Associacão Israelita Brasileira
Rua Rio Grande do Norte 477
Telephone: (31) 224-6673
Email: associacaoisraelita@bol.com.br
Uniao Israelita de Belo Horizonte
Rua Pernambuco 326
Telephone: (31) 224-6013
Email: ihim@pib.com.br
CONTACT INFORMATION
Lojinha do Beit Chabad
Av. Serzedelo Corrêa 276
Telephone: (31) 241-2250
MIKVAOT
Rua Rio Grande do Norte 477
Telephone: (31) 221-0690
SYNAGOGUES
Av. Leonardo Malchez 630, Centro

Reform
Congregacao Israelita Mineira
Rua Rio Grande do Norte 477
Telephone: (31) 3224-2129
Fax: (31) 3224-2129
Email: cim@pib.com.br

Para
BELÉM
COMMUNITY ORGANISATIONS
Community Centre
Travessa Dr. Moraes 37
Telephone: (91) 222-3184
Email: cip@zaz.com.br

SYNAGOGUES
Eshel Avraham
Travessa Campos Sales 733
Shaar Hashamaim
Rua Alcipreste Manoel Theodoro 842

Parana
CURITIBA
COMMUNITY CLUB AND JEWISH FEDERATION
Centro Israelita do Parana
Rua Mateus Leme 1431 80530
Telephone: (41) 338-7575
Fax: (41) 338-7922

SYNAGOGUES
Orthodox
Francisco Frischmann
Rua Cruz Machado 126
Telephone: (41) 224-5218
Fax: (41) 224-8172

Pernambuco
RECIFE
COMMUNITY ORGANISATIONS
Community Centre
Rua da Gloria 215

SYNAGOGUES
Rua Martins Junior 29

Rio de Janeiro
CAMPOS
COMMUNITY ORGANISATIONS
Community Centre
Rua 13 de Maio 52

GREATER RIO DE JANEIRO
The old Jewish area is situated around Rua
Alfandega. The country's first Ashkenazi
Synagogue (Grande Templo Israelite) is an
imposing building which was renovated in 1986.

BUTCHERS
Frigorifico
Rua Ronald Carvalho 265, Copacabana 22021-020
Telephone: (21) 295-7341
Supervision: Rav Stauber

COMMUNITY ORGANISATIONS
Confederacao Israelita de Brazil (Conib)
Avenida Nilo Pecanha 50
Telephone: (21) 240-0034
Fax: (21) 240-2717

Organizaco Israelita do Estado do Rio de Janeiro
Rua Tenente Possolo 8
Rabinado do Rio de Janeiro
Rua Pompeu Loureiro 40, Copacabana 22061
Telephone: (21) 2256-3587
Fax: (21) 2256-3587
Email: rabinatorio@aol.com

CULTURAL ORGANISATIONS
ASA - Associacao Scholem Aleichem
Rua Sao Clemente 155, Botafogo 22260
Telephone: (21) 2539-7740
Fax: (21) 2266-1980
Email: asa@asa.org.br
Web site: www.asa.org.br
The institution is dedicated to promote cultural events
(seminars, debates, video exhibitions, etc.).

EMBASSY
Consul General of Israel
Av. Copacabana 680
Telephone: (21) 255-5432

GROCERIES
Kosher House
Rua Anita Garibaldi 37 lj. A, Copacabana
Telephone: (21) 255-3891

MIKVAOT
Kehilat Yaakov
Rua Capelao Alvares da Silva 15, Copacabana 22041
Telephone: (21) 2236-3922

MUSEUMS
Museu Judaico do Rio de Janeiro
Rua Mexico 90, Andar 20031-141
Telephone: (21) 2524-6451
Fax: (21) 240-1598
Email: museujudaico@uol.com.br
Web site: www.museujudaico.org.br

RESTAURANTS
Rua Pompeu Loureiro 40, Copacabana
Telephone: (21) 236-0249
Hours: 10am to 5pm Sunday to Thursday.

Meat
Kosher House
Rua Anita Garibaldi 37A, Copacabana
Telephone: (21) 255-3891

SYNAGOGUES
Liberal
Associacão Religiosa Israelita
Rua General Severiano 170, Botafogo 22290
Telephone: (21) 2543-6320; 2542-5598
Fax: (21) 2542-6499
Email: ari.adm@arirj.com.br

Orthodox
Agudat Israel
Rua Nascimento Silva 109, Ipanema 22421
Telephone: (21) 267-5567

Beith Chabad of Rio de Janeiro
Rua Pompeu Loureiro No 40, Copacabana

Grande Templo Israelita
Rua Tenente Possolo 8, Centro 20230
Telephone: (21) 232-3656

Kehilat Yaakov
Rua Capelao Alvares da Silva, Copacabana 22041

TOURS
Michel Mekler
Av. Graca Aranha 81/608, Centro 20030
Telephone: (21) 220-8817
Web site: www.orbita.starmedia.com/via/~caritur

NITEROI
COMMUNITY ORGANISATIONS
Centro Israelita
Rua Visconde do Uruguai 25524030

Sociedade Hebraica
Rua Alvares de Azevedo 185, Icarai 24220

PETROPOLIS
RELIGIOUS ORGANISATIONS
Machane Israel Yeshiva
Rua Duarte de Silveira 1246 25600
Telephone: (242) 45-4952

SYNAGOGUES
Sinagoga Israelita Brasileira
Rua Aureliano Coutinho 48 25600

Rio Grande do Sul
ERECHIM
SYNAGOGUES
Av. Pedro Pinto de Souza 131

PASSO FUNDO
SYNAGOGUES
Rua General Osório 1049

PELOTAS
SYNAGOGUES
Rua Santos Dumont 303

PORTO ALEGRE
BUTCHERS
Kosher Butcher
Rua Fernandes Vieira 518
Telephone: (51) 250-441

CULTURAL ORGANISATIONS
**Instituto Cultural Judaico Marc Chagall -
Projeto Memoria**
Rua Dom Pedro II, 1220/sala 216
Telephone: (51) 343-5748

MIKVAOT
Rua Francisco Ferrer 170

MUSEUMS
Museu Judaico
Rua João Telles 329
Telephone: (51) 226-0379

RELIGIOUS ORGANISATIONS
City Rabbinate
Rua Henrique Dias 73
Telephone: (51) 219-649

SYNAGOGUES
Liberal
SIBRA
Mariante 772
Telephone: (51) 331-8133
Services on Shabbat only.

Orthodox
Beit Chabad
Rua Felipe Camarão 748
Telephone: (51) 330-7078
Daily services.

Centro Israelita Porto Alegrense
Rua Henrique Dias 73
Telephone: (51) 228-1935
Daily services.

Linath Ha-Tzedek
Rua Bento Figueredo 55
Telephone: (51) 332-1065
Daily services.

Poilisher Farband
Rua João Telles 329
Telephone: (51) 226-0379
Daily services.

União Israelita Porto Algrense
Rua Dr Barros Cassal 750
Telephone: (51) 311-6515
Fax: (51) 311-5886
Daily services.

Sephardi
Centro Hebraico Riograndense
Rua Cel. Machado 1008
Services on Shabbat only.

Sao Paulo

CAMPINAS

SYNAGOGUES
Beth Yacob Campinas
Rua Barreto Leme 1203
Telephone: (19) 231-4908

GUARUJA

SYNAGOGUES
Beit Yaacov
Av. Leomil 628
Telephone: (13) 387-2033

MOGI DAS CRUZES

COMMUNITY ORGANISATIONS
Jewish Society
Rua Dep. Deodato Wertheimer 421
Telephone: (11) 469-2505

SANTO ANDRE

SYNAGOGUES
Beit Chabad
Rua 11 de Junho 172
Telephone: (11) 449-1568

SANTOS

COMMUNITY ORGANISATIONS
Club
Rua Cons. Neblas 254
Telephone: (132) 32-9016

SYNAGOGUES
Beit Sion
Rua Borges 264

Sinagoga Beit Jacob
Rua Campos Sales 137

SAO CAETANO DO SUL

SYNAGOGUES
Sociedade Religiosa S. Caetano do Sul
Rua Para 67
Telephone: (11) 442-3514

SAO JOSE DOS CAMPOS

SYNAGOGUES
Beit Chabad
Rua Republica do Ira 91
Telephone: (11) 3064-6322

SAO PAULO

Many Conversos came to sao Paulo to escape the Inquisition, which was centred in northern Brazil. A number rose to positions of importance.

By 1972 the Jews of Sao Paulo build the Albert Einstein hospital as a contribution to the public health service.

BAKERIES
Buffet Mazal Tov
Rua Peixoto Gomide 1724
Telephone: (11) 883-7614
Fax: (11) 3064-5208

Matok Bakery
Al. Barros 921
Telephone: (11) 66-7514
Supervision: Rabbi I. Dichi
Rua P. João Manoel 709
Telephone: (11) 3064-6668
Supervision: Rabbi I. Dichi

BOOKSELLERS
Livraria Sêfer
Alameda Barros, 893 01232-001
Telephone: (11) 3826-1366
Fax: (11) 3826-4508
Email: sefer@sefer.com.br
Web site: www.sefer.com.br
Bookseller and Judaica.

BUTCHERS
Casa de Carnes Casher
Rua Fortunato 241
Telephone: (11) 221-2240
Under supervision of Rabbi Elyahu B. Valt.

Kosher Express
Rua Tupi No 506, Higienopolis 01233-000
Telephone: (11) 3367-0863
Fax: (11) 3825-4986
Email: kosherexpress@uol.com.br

Mehadrin
Rua S. Vicente de Paulo
Telephone: (11) 67-9090
Under supervision of Rabbi M.A. Iliovitz.
Rua Prates 689
Telephone: (11) 228-1771
Under supervision of Rabbi M.A. Iliovitz.

EMBASSY
Consul General of Israel
Rua Luis Coelho 308, 7th Floor
Telephone: (11) 257-2111; 257-2814

GROCERIES
All Kosher
Rua Albuquerque Lins 1170
Telephone: (11) 3825-1131

Casas Menora
Rua Guarani 114
Telephone: (11) 228-6105

Chazak
Rua Afonsa Pena 348a
Telephone: (11) 229-5607
Rua Haddock Lobo 1002
Telephone: (11) 3068-9093

Kosher Mart
Rua Tenente Pena 187, Bom Retiro
Telephone: (11) 221-7299
Web site: www.koshermart.com.br

Mazal Tov
Rua Peixoto Gomide 1724
Telephone: (11) 3083-7614
Fax: (11) 3064-5208

Sta. Luzia
Al. Lorena 1471
Telephone: (11) 883-5844
Look for kosher section.

Zilanna
Rua Itambé 506
Telephone: (11) 257-8671

MEDIA

Newspapers
O Hebreu
Rua Cunha Gago 158 05421-000
Telephone: (11) 3819-1616
Fax: (11) 3819-1616
Email: ohebreu@ohebreu.com.br
Web site: www.brasiljudaico.com.br
Monthly.

Tribuna Judaica
Rua Tanabi 299 05002-010
Telephone: (11) 3871-3234/3873-3020/3862-9074
Fax: (11) 3871-3234
Email: tjudaica@uol.com.br
Weekly.

Periodical
Morasha Magazine
Rua Dr Veiga Filho 547, Higienopolis 01229-000
Telephone: (11) 3825-9784
Fax: (11) 3030-5630
Email: morasha@uol.com.br
Web site: www.morasha.com

MIKVAOT
Rua Chabad 60 01417-030
Email: chabad@chabad.org.br

Beit Yaacov Synagogue
Rua Dr Veiga Filho 547, Higienopolis 01229-000
Telephone: (11) 3662-2154

Fax: (11) 3662-2154
Email: morasha@uol.com.br

Congregacao Mekor Haim
Rua Sao Vicente de Paulo 276 01229-010
Telephone: (11) 3662-6238; 3826-7699
Fax: (11) 3666-6960
Email: revista_nascente@hotmail.com
Orthodox

Congregacao Monte Sinai
Rua Piaui 624, Higienopolis 01241-000
Telephone: (11) 3824-9229
Fax: (11) 3824-9229
Email: cmsinai@sanet.com.br

Micre Taharat Menachem - Perdizes
Rua Dr. Manoel Maria Tourinho 261
Telephone: (11) 3865-0615
By appointment only.

RELIGIOUS ORGANISATIONS
Rabanut- Rabino Elyahu Baruch Valt
Rua Corre de melo 84 cj 308
Telephone: (11) 55-11-3331-5642
Fax: (11) 55-11-3064-9054
Email: ravvalt@hotmail.com
Office hours: 9 am to 1 pm weekdays.

RESTAURANTS
Kosher Center
Rua Corrèa de Melo 68 01123-020
Telephone: (11) 223-1175
Fax: (11) 223-3721
Supervision: Rabbi M.A. Iliovitch Shlita of Kehal Hachareidim
Restaurant and Bakery. Hours: Sun 9.00 am-4.00 pm. Mon-Thurs 8.00 am-6.00 pm. Fri 7.30 am-3.00 pm

Restaurante Kosher Delight
Rua Baronesa de Itu 436
Telephone: (11) 3661-3106

Meat
Bero
Rua peixoto Gomide 2020
Telephone: (11) 3086-2808
Fax: (11) 3086-2809
Email: berokosher@osite.com.br

Hebraica Kosher Restaurant
Rua Hungria 1000
Telephone: (11) 3815-6788/3818-8831
Fax: (11) 3815-6980
Email: kosher@hebraica.org.br
Supervision: Rabbi Elyahu B. Valt
Buffet Mosaico inside the Hebraica Sao Paulo club.
Closed Mondays, open Saturday night 90 minutes after Shabbat.

Milk
Cantina Do Bero
Rua Pe. Joao Manoel, 881
Telephone: (11) 3064-9022
Email: berokosher@osite.com.br
Open from Sunday to Thursday from 6.00 pm until 11.30 pm. Also delivers.

Milk and Parve
Jacky Gourmet Café
Rua Rosa e Silva 146, Higienopolis
Telephone: (11) 3823-3537
Fax: (11) 3664-7034
Email: jackycafe@webcable.com.br
Supervision: Kashrut supervision: Ha Rav Y.D. Horowitz Shlita

SYNAGOGUES
Hasidic
Uniao Ortodoxa Judaica
Rua Mamore 597
Telephone: (11) 3224-8639
Fax: (11) 3224-9029

Hungarian
Adas Yereim
Rua Talmud Tora 86
Telephone: (11) 282-1562; 852-9710

Liberal
Congregacao Israelita Paulista
Rua Antonio Carlos 653
Telephone: (11) 256-7811
Fax: (11) 257-1446
Email: scrtgeral@dialdata.com.br
Web site: www.cip.sp.com.br

Orthodox
Beit Chabad Augusta
Rua Augusta 259 01305-000
Telephone: (11) 258-7173

Beit Chabad Central
Rua Chabad 54-60 01417-010
Telephone: (11) 3060-9777
Fax: (11) 3060-9778
Email: chabad@chabad.org.br
Web site: www.chabad.org.br

Beit Chabad Perdizes
Rua Man. Maria Tourinho, 261
Telephone: (11) 3865-0615

Beit Yaacov
Rua Dr Veiga Filho 547, Higienopolis 01229-000
Telephone: (11) 3662-2154
Fax: (11) 3662-2154
Email: morasha@uol.com.br

Congregacao Mekor Haim
Rua Sao Vicente de Paulo 276 01229-010
Telephone: (11) 3826-7699
Fax: (11) 3666-6960
Email: revista_nascente@hotmail.com

Progressive
Comunidade Shalom
Rua Coronel Joaquim Ferreira Lobo 195 04544-150
Telephone: (11) 829-1477
Fax: (11) 828-9177

Sephardi
Templo Israelita Brasileiro Ohel Yaacov
Rua Abolicao 457
Telephone: (11) 606-9982
Fax: (11) 227-6793

TRAVEL AGENCIES
Carmel Tur
Rua Xavier de Toledo 121/10
Telephone: (11) 257-2244

Sharontur
Rua Sergipe 457, Cj. 607/608 01243-001
Telephone: (11) 11-3826-8388
Fax: (11) 11-3825-3828
Email: sharontur@sharontur.com.br
Web site: sharontur.com.br
Open: 8.00 am-6.00 pm. Closed Shabat (Saturday) & Sunday. International & domestic tickets. Car rental, exchange, hotel reservations. Languages spoken: English, Hebrew, Spanish. Contact person: Mr Dov Smaletz

Vertice
Rua Sao Bento 545/10
Telephone: (11) 3115-1970
Fax: (11) 3115-1970
Email: turismo@vertice.com.br

SOROCABA
SYNAGOGUES
Community Centre
Rua Dom Pedro II 56
Telephone: (11) 31-3168

BULGARIA

Dating back to the Byzantine conquest, the community in Bulgaria was established by Greek Jews in Serdica (Sofia, the capital). The Jewish community grew when the Bulgarian state was founded in 681. Czar Ivan Alexander (1331-71) had a Jewish wife (who converted to Christianity).

The community has included eminent rabbinic commentators, such as Rabbi Dosa Ajevani and Joseph Caro, the codifier of the Shulchan Aruch, who escaped to Bulgaria after the expulsion from Spain. The various Jewish groups joined to form a unified Sephardi community in the late seventeenth century.

About 50,000 Jews lived in Bulgaria in 1939. Bulgaria joined the war on the side of Germany but, despite much pressure from the Nazis, the government and general population refused to allow Bulgarian Jews to be deported. Only Jews from Macedonia and Thrace, then occupied by Bulgaria, were deported. Despite being saved, most of the community emigrated to Israel after the war. The 10 per cent who remained were then under the control of the communists and had little contact with the outside world.

Since the fall of communism, the community has been reconstituted and now has synagogues in Sofia and Plovdiv. The community is ageing, although 100 children attend a Sunday school run by the Shalom Organisation, the central Jewish organisation for Bulgaria.

GMT +2 hours
Country calling code: **(+359)**
Total population: **8,306,000**
Jewish population: **3,000**
Emergency telephone: **(Police – 166) (Fire – 160) (Ambulance – 150)**
Electricity voltage: **(Electricity voltage – 220)**

PLOVDIV
LIBRARIES
Library and House of Culture
Vladimir Zaimov St. 20
Telephone: (32) 761-376

SYNAGOGUES
Tsar Kalojan St. 15
In the courtyard of a large apartment complex.

ROUSSE
SYNAGOGUES
Community Centre
Ivan Vazov Sq. 4
Telephone: (82) 270-540

SOFIA
About half of Bulgarian Jewry lives in Sofia. The Great Synagogue of 1878 ranks among the largest of Sephardi synagogues.

CEMETERIES
Jewish Cemetery
Orlandovtzi suburb
Take a tram (Nos 2, 10 or 14) to the last stop for this large Jewish cemetery.

COMMUNITY ORGANISATIONS
Social & Cultural Organisation of Bulgarian Jews
Shalom, Alexander Stambolisky St. 50
Telephone: (2) 870-163
Publishes a periodical 'Evreiski Vesti' and a yearbook. It also maintains a museum devoted to "The Rescue of Bulgarian Jews, 1941–1944". At the same address are the offices of El Al, the Joint and the Jewish Agency.

EMBASSY
Embassy of Israel
1463 Sofia, 1 Bulgaria Sq, NDK-Admin. Building, 7th Floor
Telephone: (2) 359-2-951-50-29
Fax: (2) 359-2-952-11-01
Email: sofia@israel.org
Hours of opening: Consular Section - Mon-Fri - 9.30-12.30h

RELIGIOUS ORGANISATIONS
Central Jewish Religious Council
Ekzarh Josef St. 16
Telephone: (2) 983-1273
Fax: (2) 985-5085
Email: isaksaiu@mail.orbitel.bg

SYNAGOGUES
Sofia Central Synagogue
Ekzarh Josef St. 16
Telephone: (2) 983-1273
Fax: (2) 985-5085
Email: sofia_synagogue@mail.orbitel.bg
Web site: www.shalom.bg
Adjacent to the synagogue is a museum dedicated to the history of Bulgarian Jewry.

CANADA

The Jewish settlement of Canada began with the British expansion into Canada. In 1760, the Shearith Israel synagogue was founded in Montreal and in 1832 Jews received full civil rights. In the 1850s the community began to spread from Montreal to Toronto and Hamilton.

The community grew throughout the early twentieth century, from 16,000 in 1900 to 126,000 in 1921. After the Second World War, Jewish immigration increased and by 1961 the population was 260,000.

The headquarters of the Canadian Jewish Congress is in Montreal. This is the main national organisation for Canadian Jewry, and the community is provided with a full range of services, with Jewish schools, yeshivot, newspapers and the unique (in the Americas) Montreal Jewish Library. There are also several kosher restaurants.

GMT -3 to -8 hours
Country calling code: (+1)
Total population: 30.491,000
Jewish population: 365,000
Emergency telephone: (Police – 911) (Fire – 911) (Ambulance – 911)
In remote areas, calls have to be made via the operator.
Electricity voltage: (Electricity voltage – 110)

Alberta

CALGARY
BAKERIES
Tobey's Nosh Kosher Bakery
131, 2515 - 90th Avenue SW
Telephone: (403) 238-5300
Fax: (403) 238-3023
Supervision: Calgary Kosher
Hours of operation: Sunday 10 am to 2 pm, Tuesday to Thursday 9 am to 6 pm, Friday 8 am to 4 pm (winter 8 am to 2 pm). Closed Mondays and Shabbat.

COMMUNITY ORGANISATIONS
Calgary Jewish Community Council
1607 90th Av. S.W.
Telephone: (403) 253-8600
Fax: (403) 253-7915
Email: cjcc@cjcc.ca
Web site: www.cjcc.ca
The Council issues a booklet "Keeping Kosher in Calgary".

DELICATESSEN
Izzy's Kosher Meats and Deli
2515 90th Av. S.W. T2V 0L8
Telephone: (403) 251-2552
Fax: (403) 281-3322

RELIGIOUS ORGANISATIONS
Calgary Rabbinical Council
Telephone: (403) 253-8600
Fax: (403) 253-7915

RESTAURANTS
Karen's Cafe
Calgary Jewish Centre, 1607 90th Av. S.W.
Telephone: (403) 255-5311
Hours: Monday to Thursday, 10 am to 7 pm; Friday, 10 am to 1 pm. Closed on Sunday

SYNAGOGUES
Conservative
Beth Tzedec
1325 Glenmore Trail S.W. T2V 4Y8
Telephone: (403) 255-8688
Fax: (403) 252-8319
Email: bethtze@telus.net

Orthodox
Chabad Lubavitch of Alberta
28-S23 Woodpark blvd. T2W 4J3
Telephone: (403) 238-4880
Fax: (403) 281-0338
Email: mmatsusof@chabadalberta.org

Congregation House of Jacob-Mikveh Israel
1623 92nd Av., Jerusalem Rd. SW T2V 5C9
Telephone: (403) 259-3230
Fax: (403) 259-3240
Email: hojmi@telus.net
Web site: www.hojmi.org

Reform
Temple B'nai Tikvah
Calgary Jewish Centre, 1607 90th Av. S.W. T2V 4V7
Telephone: (403) 252-1654
Fax: (403) 252-1709
Email: temple@cadvision.com

EDMONTON
COMMUNITY ORGANISATIONS
Edmonton Jewish Federation
7200 156th St. T5R 1X3
Telephone: (780) 487-0585
Fax: (780) 481-1854
Email: edjfed@netcom.ca
Contact Gayle Tallman, Exec. Director, for additional information.

Shoshana Szlachter
B'nai Brith, Western Region Director, 7200 - 156
Street T5R 1X3
Telephone: (780) 780-483-6939
Fax: (780) 780-481-1854
Email: bnaibrith.westcan@shaw.ca

MEDIA

Newspapers
Edmonton Jewish Life
7200 156th Street T5R 1X3
Telephone: (780) 488-7276
Fax: (780) 484-4978
Email: ejlife@shaw.ca

Edmonton Jewish News
#330, 10036 Jasper Av. T5J 2W2
Telephone: (780) 421-7983
Fax: (780) 424-3951

SYNAGOGUES

Conservative
Beth Shalom
11916 Jasper Av. T5K 0N9
Telephone: (780) 780-488-6333
Fax: (780) 780-488-6259
Email: info@e-bethshalom.org
Web site: www.bethshalomedmonton.org

Orthodox
Beth Israel
131 Wolf Willow Road T5T 7T7
Telephone: (780) 482-2840
Fax: (780) 482-2470
Email: edbeth@telusplanet.net

Reform
Temple Beth Ora
7200 156th St. T5R 1X3
Telephone: (780) 780-487-4817
Fax: (780) 780-481-1854
Email: tboffice@shaw.ca
Services: the first Friday of the month

British Columbia

COQUITLAM
SYNAGOGUES
Sha'arei Mizrah
2860 Dewdney Trunk Road V3C 2H9
Telephone: 552-7221
Fax: 552-7201
Email: admin@burquest.org
Web site: www.burquest.org

KELOWNA
SYNAGOGUES
Traditional
Beth Shalom Sanctuary
OJCC, 102-1 North Glenmore Road V1V 2E2
Telephone: (250) 862-2305
Fax: (250) 862-2365
Email: shalom@ojcc.net
Web site: www.ojcc.net

RICHMOND
BAKERIES
Garden City Bakery
#360-9100 Blundell Road
Telephone: (604) 244-7888

SYNAGOGUES
Conservative
Beth Tikvah
9711 Geal Road V7E 1R4
Telephone: (604) 271-6262
Email: bethtikvah@btikvah.ca
Web site: www.btikvah.ca

Hasidic
Chabad of Richmond
200-4775 Blundell Road, Richmond
Telephone: (604) 277-6427
Fax: (604) 263-7934
Email: info@chabadrichmond.com
Web site: www.chabadrichmond.com

Orthodox
Eitz Chaim
8080 Frances Road V6Y 1A4
Telephone: (604) 275-0007
Fax: (604) 277-2225
Email: eitzchaim@telus.net

VANCOUVER
The most famous of early Jewish settlers were
the Oppenheimer brothers who settled there the
year the city was founded. David Oppenheimer
was the city's second mayor. The city's first
synagogue was built in 1912, although of course
services had been held much earlier.

BAKERIES
Sabra Bakery
3844 Oak Street
Telephone: (604) 733-4912

CONTACT INFORMATION
Shalom BC
950 West 41st Avenue V5Z 2N7
Telephone: (604) 257-5111
Fax: (604) 257-5119
Email: info@shalombc.org
Web site: www.shalombc.org

RESTAURANTS

Dairy

Chagall's
950 West 41st Avenue
Telephone: (604) 263-7507
Fax: (604) 263-7507

Green V Organics
2936 west Fourth Ave.
Telephone: (604) 730-1808
Supervision: British Columbia Kosher Council

Sabra Kosher Bakery, Restaurant and Grocery
3844 Oak Street V6H 2M5
Telephone: (604) 733-4912
Fax: (604) 733-4911

Meat

Omnitsky Kosher B.C.
5866 Cambie Street
Telephone: (604) 321-1818
Fax: (604) 321-1817
Email: kosher@telus.net

SYNAGOGUES

Conservative

Beth Israel
4350 Oak Street V6H 2N7
Telephone: (604) 731-4161
Fax: (604) 731-4989
Email: info@bethisrael.ca
Web site: www.bethisrael.ca

Congregation Har El
1305 Taylor Way, West Vancouver V7T 2Y7
Telephone: (604) 925-6488
Fax: (604) 922-8245
Email: office@harel.org
Web site: www.harel.org
Friday, 7 pm; Shabbat, 10 am (Seasonal). Visitors welcome.

Jewish Renewal

Or Shalom
710 East 10th Avenue V5T 2A7
Telephone: (604) 872-1614
Fax: (604) 872-4406
Web site: www.orshalom.bc.ca
Family Kabbalat Shabbat and potluck dinner monthly; Shabbat 10 am. Wheelchair access.

Orthodox

Louis Brier Home
1055 West 41st Avenue V6M 1W9
Telephone: (604) 261-9376
Fax: (604) 266-8172

Schara Tzedeck
3476 Oak Street V6H 2L8
Telephone: (604) 604-736-7607
Fax: (604) 604-730-1621
Email: gabriella@scharatzedeck.com
Web site: www.scharatzedeck.com
Monday and Thursday, 7 am; Tuesday, Wednesday and Friday, 7:15 am; weekdays, sunset; Friday, 7:30 pm; Shabbat, 9 am and half hour before sunset; Sunday, 8:30 am.

Torat Hayim Community
483 Eastcot Road
Telephone: (604) 984-4168
Fax: (604) 984-4168
Email: info@hayim.com
Web site: www.hayim.com/sponsor
Shabbat: 10.30 am followed by Kiddush

Reform

Temple Shalom
7190 Oak Street V6P 3Z9
Telephone: (604) 266-7190
Fax: (604) 266-7126
Email: templeshalom@telus.net
Web site: www.templeshalom.ca
Monday and Wednesday, 7:15 am; Friday, 8:15 pm; Shabbat, 10 am. Also has a gift shop.

Sephardi Orthodox

Beth Hamidrash
3231 Heather Street V5Z 3K4
Telephone: (604) 872-4222
Fax: (604) 872-4222

Traditional

Shaarey Tefilah
785 West 16th Avenue V5Z 158
Telephone: (604) 873-2700
Email: office@shaareytefilah.com
Web site: www.shaareytefilah.com
Friday evening, call for time; Shabbat and Sunday, 9 am. Wheelchair access.

VICTORIA

COMMUNITY ORGANISATIONS

Victoria Jewish Community Centre
3636 Shelbourne Street
Telephone: (250) 477-7184
Fax: (250) 477-6283

SYNAGOGUES

Conservative

Emanu-El
1461 Blanshard V8W 2J3
Telephone: (250) 382-0615
Fax: (250) 382-0615

Manitoba
WINNIPEG
BAKERIES
City Bread
238 Dufferin Avenue R2W 2X6
Telephone: (204) 586-8409

Goodies' Bake Shop
2 Donald Street R3L 0K5
Telephone: (204) 949-2480

Gunn's
247 Selkirk Avenue R2W 2L5
Telephone: (204) 582-2364

BUTCHERS
Omnitsky's Kosher Foods
1428 Main Street R2W 3V4
Telephone: (204) 204-586-8271
Fax: (204) 204-586-8270
Web site: www.omnitsky.com

COMMUNITY ORGANISATIONS
Asper Jewish Community Campus
C300 - 123 Doncaster Street R3N 1B2
Telephone: (204) 477-7400
Fax: (204) 477-7405
Email: info@jewishwinnipeg.org
Web site: www.jewishwinnipeg.org
Home to Winnipeg Jewish Theatre, Canadian Jewish
Congress and Jewish Heritage Centre.

Gwen Secter Creative
1588 Main
Telephone: (204) 339-1701

MIKVAOT
Herzlia-Adas Yeshurun
620 Brock R3N 0Z4
Telephone: (204) 489-6262
Fax: (204) 489-5899
Email: cbt@execulink.com

MUSEUMS
Jewish Heritage Centre of Western Canada
C116-123 Doncaster Street R3N 2B2
Telephone: (204) 477-7460
Fax: (204) 477-7465
Email: heritage@jhcwc.mb.ca
Web site: www.jhcwc.mb.ca

RESTAURANTS
Garden Café
146 Magnus Avenue R2W 2B4
Telephone: (204) 586-9781

Dairy
Mariner Neptune
472 Dufferin
Telephone: (204) 589-5341

Schmoozer's Café
located at the Asper Jewish Community Campus,
123 Doncaster Street R3N 2B2
Telephone: (204) 204-477-7418
WK Kosher - Dairy only.

SYNAGOGUES
Egalitarian Conservative
Beth Israel
1007 Sinclair Street R2V 3J5
Telephone: (204) 582-2353

Congregation Shaarey Zedek
561 Wellington Crescent R3M 0A6
Telephone: (204) 452-3711
Fax: (204) 474-1184
Email: administration@shaareyzedek.mb.ca
Web site: www.shaareyzedek.mb.ca

Orthodox
Chabad Lubavitch
2095 Sinclair Street R2V 3K2
Telephone: (204) 339-8737
Fax: (204) 586-0487
Email: aaltein@merlin.mb.ca

Chevra Mishnayes
700 Jefferson Avenue R2V OP6
Telephone: (204) 338-8503

New Brunswick
FREDERICTON
GROCERIES
Scoop & Save
934 Prospect
Telephone: (506) 459-7676

SYNAGOGUES
Orthodox
Sgoolai Israel
Westmorland Street E3B 3L7
Telephone: (506) 454-9698
Fax: (506) 452-8889
Email: sgoolai@nbnet.nb.ca
For information on availability of kosher food, call Rabbi
Yochanan Samuels: (506) 454-2717.

MONCTON
SYNAGOGUES
Orthodox
Tiferes Israel
56 Steadman Street E1C 8L9
Telephone: (506) 858-0258
Fax: (506) 859-7983
Email: tifisrl@nbnet.nb.ca
Mikva on premises.

SAINT JOHN

MUSEUMS

Saint John Jewish Historical Museum
29 Wellington Row E2L 3H4
Telephone: (506) 633-1833
Fax: (506) 642-9926
Email: sjjhm@nbnet.nb.ca
May-mid Octoberr 10am to 4pm Monday to Friday. Also,
during July and August, Sunday 1pm to 4pm or by
appointment. This is the only Jewish museum in the
Atlantic Provinces of Canada. There are eight display
areas as well as library and archives. Guided tours
available.

Newfoundland

ST. JOHN'S

SYNAGOGUES

Conservative
**Hebrew Congregation of Newfoundland &
Labrador (Beth El)**
Elizabeth Avenues A1B 1S3
Telephone: (709) 726-0480
Fax: (709) 777-6995
Email: mpaul@mun.ca

Nova Scotia

GLACE BAY

SYNAGOGUES

Orthodox
Sons of Israel
1 Prince Street B1A 3C8
Telephone: (902) 849-8605

HALIFAX

COMMUNITY ORGANISATIONS

Atlantic Jewish Council
5670 Spring Garden Road, Suite 508 B3J 1H6
Telephone: (902) 422-7491
Fax: (902) 425-3722
Email: atlanticjewishcouncil@theajc.ns.ca
Web site: www.theajc.ns.ca
Covers Jewish communities in Nova Scotia, New
Brunswick, Price Edward Island, Newfoundland and
Halifax. Also at this address: Canadian Jewish Congress,
Atlantic Region, Canadian Zionist Federation, United
Jewish Appeal, Canadian Young Judea, Hadassah, Jewish
National Fund, JSA (Jewish Student Association) for
Atlantic Canada.

GROCERIES

Barrington Meat Super Store
1145 Barrington
Telephone: (902) 492-3240

Sobeys
1120 Queen
Telephone: (902) 422-9884

SYNAGOGUES

Conservative
Shaar Shalom
1981 Oxford Street B3H 4A4
Telephone: (902) 423-5848
Fax: (902) 422-2580
Email: shaar.shalom@ns.sympatico.ca

Orthodox
Beth Israel
1480 Oxford Street B3H 3Y8
Telephone: (902) 422-1301
Fax: (902) 422-7251
Email: thebeth@eastlink.com
Web site: www.thebethisrael.com
Mikva on premises.

TOURIST SITES

Pier 21
1055 Marginal Road, Pier 21
Telephone: (902) 425-7770
Web site: pier21.ns.ca
Known as Canada's Ellis Island, Pier 21 was Canada's
"front door" to over one million immigrants. Visitors are
able to re-enact the immigrant experience through
various multimedia displays. In addition they can explore
their family trees.

SYDNEY

SYNAGOGUES

Conservative
Temple Sons of Israel
P.O. Box 311, Whitney Avenue B1P 6H2
Telephone: (902) 564-4650

YARMOUTH

CONTACT INFORMATION

R & V Indiq
13 Parade Street B5A 3A5
Will be happy to provide details of the local Jewish
community.

Ontario

BELLEVILLE

SYNAGOGUES

Conservative
Sons of Jacob
211 Victoria Avenue K8N 2C2
Telephone: (613) 962-1433
Email: jmarkus@intranet.ca
Web site: www.iks.net/~soj

CHATHAM
SYNAGOGUES
Conservative
Children of Jacob
29 Water Street N7M 3H4
Telephone: (519) 352-3544

HAMILTON
BUTCHERS
Hamilton Kosher Meats
889 King Street West L8S 1K5

COMMUNITY ORGANISATIONS
Hamilton Jewish Federation
1030 Lower Lions Club Road, Ancaster L9G 3N6
Telephone: (905) 905-648-0605
Fax: (905) 905-648-8350
Email: gfisheruja@on.aibn.com
Web site: www.jewishhamilton.org

DELICATESSEN
Westdale Deli
893 King Street West L8S 1K5
Telephone: (905) 529-2605
Fax: (905) 529-2605

MEDIA
Newspaper
Hamilton Jewish News
P.O. Box 7528, Ancaster L9G 3N6
Telephone: (905) 648-0605
Fax: (905) 648-8388

SYNAGOGUES
Conservative
Beth Jacob
375 Aberdeen Avenue L8P 2R7
Telephone: (905) 522-1351

Orthodox
Adas Israel
125 Cline Avenue S. L8S 1X2
Telephone: (905) 528-0039
Fax: (905) 528-7497

Reform
Anshe Sholom
215 Cline Avenue N. L8S 4A1
Telephone: (905) 528-0121
Fax: (905) 528-2994

KINGSTON
COMMUNITY ORGANISATIONS
B'nai B'rith Hillel Foundation
26 Barrie Street
Telephone: (613) 542-1120

SYNAGOGUES
Orthodox
Beth Israel
116 Centre Street K7L 4E6
Telephone: (613) 542-5012
Fax: (613) 542-9071
Email: bethisrael@kingston.net

Reform
Temple Iyr Hamelech
331 Union Street West K7L 2R3
Telephone: (613) 789-7022

KITCHENER
SYNAGOGUES
Orthodox
Beth Jacob
161 Stirling Avenue South N2G 3N8
Telephone: (519) 743-8422
Fax: (519) 743-9252
Email: bethjacob@on.albm.com

Reform
Temple Shalom
543 Beechwood N2T 2S8
Telephone: (519) 746-2234

LONDON
COMMUNITY ORGANISATIONS
London Jewish Federation
536 Huron Street N5Y 4J5
Telephone: (519) 673-3310
Email: admin@ljf.on.ca

SYNAGOGUES
Conservative
Or Shalom
534 Huron Street N5Y 4J5
Telephone: (519) 438-3081
Fax: (519) 439-2994
Email: or.shalom@sympatico.ca
Web site: www.uscj.org/canadian/london

Orthodox
Congregation Beth Tefilah
1210 Adelaide Street North N5Y 4T6
Telephone: (519) 433-7081
Fax: (519) 433-0616
Email: office@bethtefilah.org
Web site: www.bethtefilah.org
Mikva on premises.

Reform
Temple Israel
605 Windermere Road N5X 2P1
Telephone: (519) 858-4400
Fax: (519) 858-2070
Email: templeisrael@bellnet.ca
Web site: www.uahc.org/congs/cd/cdool

MISSISSAUGA

SYNAGOGUES

Reform
Solel Congregation
2399 Folkway Drive L5L 2M6
Telephone: (905) 820-5915
Fax: (905) 820-1956

NIAGARA FALLS

SYNAGOGUES

Reform
B'nai Tikvah
5328 Ferry Street L2G 1R7
Telephone: 354-3934

NORTH BAY

SYNAGOGUES

Conservative
Sons of Jacob
302 McIntyre Street West P1B 2Z1
Telephone: (705) 497-9288
Fax: (705) 497-9812
Email: martybig@hotmail.com
Friday evening services.

OAKVILLE

SYNAGOGUES

Reform
Shaarei-Beth El
186 Morrison Road L6J 4J4
Telephone: (905) 849-6000
Fax: (905) 849-1134
Email: sbeofc@idirect.com
Web site: www.sbe.ca

OSHAWA

SYNAGOGUES

Orthodox
Beth Zion
144 King Street East L1H 1B6
Telephone: (905) 723-2353

OTTAWA

Ottawa is the capital of Canada and its fourth
largest city. The first Jewish settler came in 1858
when Ottawa was still known as Bytown. Ottawa
has always been strongly traditional and has a
growing community presently numbering
around 13,000.

BAKERIES

Rideau Bakery
384 Rideau St K1N 5Y8
Telephone: (613) 789-1019

1666 Bank St
Telephone: (613) 737-3356

COMMUNITY ORGANISATIONS

Canadian Jewish Congress National Office
100 Sparks Street, Suite 650 K1P 5B7
Telephone: (613) 613-233-8703
Fax: (613) 613-233-8748
Email: canadianjewishcongress@cjc.ca
Web site: www.cjc.ca

Vaad Ha'ir (Jewish Community Council)
21 Nadolny Sachs Private K2A 1R9
Telephone: (613) 798-4696
Fax: (613) 798-4695
Web site: www.jewishottawa.org
Vaad Hakashruth located here for all kashrut
information.

EMBASSY

Embassy of Israel
Suite 1005, 50 O'Connor Street K1P 6L2
Telephone: (613) 567-6450
Fax: (613) 237-8865

MEDIA

Ottawa Jewish Bulletin
Telephone: (613) 798-4646
Fax: (613) 798-4730

RESTAURANTS

Dairy
Rideau Bakery
384 Rideau Street
Telephone: (613) 789-1019

Viva Pizza
Soloway JCC, 21 Nadolny Sachs Private
Telephone: (613) 798-9818

OWEN SOUND

SYNAGOGUES

Conservative
Beth Ezekiel
313 11th Street East N4K 1V1
Telephone: (519) 376-8774

PETERBOROUGH

SYNAGOGUES

Conservative
Beth Israel
Waller Street
Telephone: (705) 745-8398

RICHMOND HILL
SYNAGOGUES
Conservative
Beth Rayim
9711 Bayview Avenue L4C 9X7
Telephone: (905) 770-7639

ST CATHARINE'S
SYNAGOGUES
Traditional
B'nai Israel
190 Church Street L2R 3E9
Telephone: (416) 685-6767
Fax: (416) 685-3100

SUDBURY
SYNAGOGUES
Shaar Hashomayim
158 John Street P3E 1P4
Telephone: (705) 673-0831

THORNHILL
BOOKSELLERS
Israel's Judaica Centre
441 Clark Avenue West L47 6W7
Telephone: (905) 881-1010
Fax: (905) 881-1016
Email: contact@israelsjudaica.com
Web site: www.israel.judaica.com
Also sells gifts.

Matana Judaica Inc.
248 Steeles Avenue West, #6 L4J 1A1
Telephone: (905) 731-6543
Fax: (905) 882-6196

RESTAURANTS
Dairy
My Zaidy's Pizza
441 Clark Avenue West L4J 6W8
Telephone: (905) 731-3029

THUNDER BAY
SYNAGOGUES
Orthodox
Shaarey Shomayim
627 Grey Street P7E 2E4
Telephone: (807) 622-4867
Email: phlab@baynet.net

TORONTO
There have been one and a half centuries of organised Jewish life in Toronto since its start in 1849. The Jewish population increased significantly during the 1980s, and now Toronto is home to almost half of Canada's Jews. There is a good range of Jewish facilities in the city.

BAKERIES
Carmel Bakery
3856 Bathurst Street
Telephone: (416) 633-5315

Dairy Treats Bakery
3522 Bathurst Street
Telephone: (416) 787-0309
Fax: (416) 787-1935

Richman's Kosher Bakery
4119 Bathurst Street
Telephone: (416) 636-9710
Fax: (416) 636-9614

BOOKSELLERS
Israel's Judaica Centre
897 Eglinton Avenue West M6C 2C1
Telephone: (416) 256-2858
Email: contact@israelsjudaica.com
Web site: www.israel.judaica.com

Negev Importing Co Ltd
3509 Bathurst Street M6A 2C5
Telephone: (416) 905-9356 (Toll free: 1-888-618-9356)
Fax: (416) 905-0071
Email: negev_imp@hotmail.com
Web site: www.negevjudaica.com

COMMUNITY ORGANISATIONS
Bernard Betel (Senior Centre)
1003 Steeles Avenue West M2R 3T6
Telephone: (416) 225-2112
Fax: (416) 225-2097
Email: betelctr@idirect.com
Centre operates Conservative Synagogue - has two Sephardi congregations on site - Beth Yosef and Tehillat Yerushalayim.

Kashruth Council of Canada
4600 Bathurst Street, Ste 240 M2R 3V2
Telephone: (416) 635-9550
Fax: (416) 635-8760
All enquiries about kashrut here.

UJA Federation of Greater Toronto
4600 Bathurst Street, Toronto M2R 3V2
Telephone: (416) 635-2883
Fax: (416) 635-9565
Email: office@ujafed.org
Web site: www.jewishtoronto.net

CONTACT INFORMATION

Jewish Information Service - UJA Federation of Greater Toronto
4588 Bathurst Street, Suite 115 M2R 1W6
Telephone: (416) 416-635-5600
Fax: (416) 416-636-5813
Email: jinfo@ujafed.org
Web site: www.jewishtoronto.net
Information about the Jewish community in the Greater Toronto area, Canada including synagogues, kosher restaurants, sites of interest.

EMBASSY

Consul General of Israel
180 Bloor Street West, Suite 700 M5S 2V6
Telephone: (416) 640-8500
Fax: (416) 640-8555
Email: hasbara@idirect.com
Israel Government Tourist Office: 964-3784.

GIFT SHOP

Miriam's
3007 Bathurst Street
Telephone: (416) 781-8261
Fax: (416) 781-8261

MEDIA

Newspapers
Jewish Tribune
15 Hove Street, Downsview M3H 4Y8,
Telephone: (416) 633-6224
Fax: (416) 633-6224
Email: jewishtribune@jewishtribune.ca

MEMORIAL

Holocaust Education & Memorial Centre
4600 Bathurst Street, Willowdale M2R 3V2
Telephone: (416) 635-2883

MUSEUMS

Silverman Heritage Museum
Baycrest Centre for Geriatric Care, 3560 Bathurst Street M6A 2E1
Telephone: (416) 785-2500 Ext.2802
Fax: (416) 785-4228
Email: pdickinson@baycrest.org
One of the few Judaica museums in Canada. It has an active exhibit program.

RESTAURANTS

Dairy
Dairy Treats Cafe
3522 Bathurst Street M6A 2C6
Telephone: (416) 787-0309
Fax: (416) 787-1935

King David Pizza
3020 Bathurst Street M6B 3B6
Telephone: (416) 781-1326
3774 Bathurst Street M3H 3M6
Telephone: (416) 633-5678
221 Wilmington Avenue M3H 5K1
Telephone: (416) 636-3456

Milk'n Honey
3457 Bathurst Street, Downsview M6A 2C5
Telephone: (416) 789-7651
Fax: (416) 789-4788

Not just Yogurt
7117 Bathurst Street
Telephone: (416) 764-2525

Tov Li Pizza
5982 Bathurst Street, Willowdale M2R 1Z1,
Telephone: (416) 650-9800

Tov-Li Pizza & Falafel
5982 Bathurst Street
Telephone: (416) 650-9800

Yehudale's Falafel & Pizza
7241 Bathurst Street
Telephone: (416) 889-1400

Meat
Colonel Wong Restaurant
2825 Bathurst Street M6B 3A4
Telephone: (416) 784-9664

Hakerem Restaurant
3030 Bathurst Street M6B 3B6
Telephone: (416) 787-6504

Jerusalem One
3028 Bathurst Street M6B 3B6
Telephone: (416) 631-9602

King Solomon's Table
3705 Chesswood Drive, Downsview M3J 2P6
Telephone: (416) 630-0666
Fax: (416) 630-4585
Open Monday to Thursday 12.00 noon to 10.00pm. Sunday 4.00pm to 10.00pm. Closed Friday and Saturday. Kashrut: COR.

Marky's Deli & Restaurant
280 Wilson Avenue M3H 1S8
Telephone: (416) 638-1081

Miami Grill
441 Clark Avenue West
Telephone: (416) 709-0096

The Chicken Nest
3038 Bathurst Street M6B 4K2
Telephone: (416) 787-6378

SYNAGOGUES
Conservative
Adath Shalom
31 Nadolny Sachs Private K2A 1R9
Telephone: (416) 228-0570
Fax: (416) 228-0570
Email: ellencaplan@rogers.com
Web site: www.adath-shalom.ca/

Agudath Israel
1400 Coldrey Avenue K1Z 7P9
Telephone: (416) 728-3501
Fax: (416) 728-4468
Email: terry@agudathisrael.net
Web site: www.agudathisrael.net

Beth Tzedec Street
1700 Bathurst Street M5P 3K3
Telephone: (416) 781-3514
Fax: (416) 781-0150
Email: info@beth-tzedec.org
Web site: www.beth-tzedec.org

Orthodox
Anshei Minsk
10 St. Andrews Street M5T 1K6
Telephone: (416) 595-5723
Fax: (416) 595-9586
Email: minsk@bellnet.ca
Web site: www.theminsk.com

Beth Shalom
151 Chapel Street K1N 7Y2
Telephone: (416) 789-3501
Fax: (416) 789-4438
Email: gittel@magma.ca

Beth Shalom West
15 Chartwell Avenue K2G 4K3
Telephone: (416) 723-1800
Fax: (416) 723-6567
Email: bsw@bethshalomwest.org
Web site: www.bethshalomwest.org

Kiever Congregation
25 Bellevue Avenue M5T 2N5
Telephone: (416) 593-9956
Shabbat and holiday services.

Machzikei Hadas
2301 Virginia Drive K1H 6S2
Telephone: (416) 521-9700
Fax: (416) 521-0067
Email: cmh@cyberus.ca
Web site: www.cyberus.ca/~cmh/shul.htm

Ottawa Torah Center Chabad
79 Stradwick Avenue K2J 2Z2
Telephone: (416) 823-0866
Fax: (416) 823-7540
Email: OttawaTC@aol.com

Shaarei Shomayim
470 Glencairn Avenue M5N 1V8
Telephone: (416) 789-3213
Fax: (416) 789-1728
Email: info@shomayim.org
Web site: www.shomayim,org

The Village Shul - Aish Hatorah Learning Centre
1072 Eglinton Avenue West M6C 2E2
Telephone: (416) 416-785-1107
Fax: (416) 416-783-9870
Email: mbookbinder@aish.com
Web site: www.aishtoronto.com

Reform
Holy Blossom
1950 Bathurst Street M5P 3K9
Telephone: (416) 789-3291
Fax: (416) 789-9697
Email: templemail@holyblossom.org
Web site: www.holyblossom.org

Temple Israel
1301 Prince of Wales Drive K2C 1N2
Telephone: (416) 224-1802
Fax: (416) 224-0707
Email: temple@ca.inter.net
Web site: www.templeisraelottawa.ca

WINDSOR
COMMUNITY ORGANISATIONS
Jewish Community Council
1641 Ouellette Avenue N8X 1K9
Telephone: (519) 973-1772

MEDIA
Periodical
Windsor Jewish Community Bulletin
Fax: (519) 973-1774

SYNAGOGUES
Orthodox
Shaar Hashomayim
115 Giles Blvd East N9A 4C1
Telephone: (519) 256-3123
Fax: (519) 256-3124
Email: shaar@mnsi.net

Shaarey Zedek
610 Giles Blvd East N9A 4E2
Telephone: (519) 252-1594

Reform
Congregation Beth-El
2525 Mark Avenue N9E 2W2
Telephone: (519) 969-2422

Quebec

MONTREAL

1760 saw the arrival of the first Jews in Montreal as civilians attached to the British army. In the 1920s and 1930s the Boulevard St-Laurent was equivalent to London's East End or New York's Lower East Side. There are now just over 100,000 Jews in the city. Twenty percent of them are North African Sephardim.

BAKERIES

Andalos
266 Lebeau
Telephone: (514) 856-0983

Biscuit Adar
5458 Westminister
Telephone: (514) 484-1198

Boulangerie-Adir
6795 Darligton
Telephone: (514) 342-1991

Cheskie
359 Bernard West
Telephone: (514) 271-2253

Cite Cashere
4747 Van Horne
Telephone: (514) 733-2838

Delice Cashere
4655 Van Horne
Telephone: (514) 733-5010

Kosher Quality Bakery
5855 Victoria
Telephone: (514) 731-7883
Fax: (514) 731-0205
Hours: Sunday - Wednesday 6am to 9pm. Thursday 6am to 10pm. Friday 6am winter 2pm or summer 4pm.

Montreal Kosher
7005 Victoria
Telephone: (514) 739-3651
2765 Van Horne, Wilderton Shopping Centre
Telephone: (514) 737-0393
Fax: (514) 737-2427
Web site: www.montrealkosherbakery.com
Supervision: Vaad Ha'ir
2135 St. Louis, St. Laurent
Telephone: (514) 747-5116

New Homemade Kosher Bakery
6915 Querbes
Telephone: (514) 270-5567
Fax: (514) 270-5041
Supervision: Vaad Ha'ir
6685 Victoria
Telephone: (514) 733-4141
5638 Westminister
Telephone: (514) 486-2024

Patisserie Chez Ma Souer
5095 Queen Mary
Telephone: (514) 737-2272

Renfels Bakery
2800 Bates
Telephone: (514) 733-5538

BOOKSELLERS

Kotel Book & Gift Store
6414 Victoria Avenue H3W 2S6
Telephone: (514) 739-4142
Fax: (514) 739-7330

Rodal's Hebrew Book Store & Gift Shop
4689 Van Horne Avenue H3W 1H8
Telephone: (514) 733-1876
Fax: (514) 733-2373
Email: rodals@ican.net

Victoria Gift Shop
5875 Victoria Avenue H3W 2R6
Telephone: (514) 738-1414

COMMUNITY ORGANISATIONS

Federation CJA
5151 ch, de la Côte Ste-Catherine H3W 1M6
Telephone: (514) 735-3541
Operates the Jewish Information and Referral Service (JIRS), Tel: 737-2221.

Jewish Community Council of Montreal
6825 Decarie, Suite 100 H3W 3E4
Telephone: (514) 739-6363
Fax: (514) 739-7024
Email: semanuel@mk.ca
Web site: www.mk.ca
Visitors requiring additional information about kosher establishments should contact the Vaad Ha'ir at the above numbers. Also apply to them for a list of kosher butchers, bakeries, caterers and restaurants.

LIBRARIES

Jewish Public Library
1 carre Cummings Square H3W 1M6
Telephone: (514) 514-345-2627
Fax: (514) 514-345-6477
Email: info@jplmtl.org
Web site: www.jewishpubliclibrary.org

MEDIA

Newspaper
Canadian Jewish News
6900 Decarie Blvd, #341 H3X 2T8
Telephone: (514) 735-2612
Fax: (514) 735-9090
Email: montreal@cjnews.com

RESTAURANTS

Dairy

Bistrot Casa Linga
5095 Queen Mary H3W 1X4
Telephone: (514) 737-2272

Cummings Jewish Centre for Seniors Cafeteria
5700 av. Westbury Ave. H3W 3E8
Telephone: (514) 514-343-3529 local 7244
Fax: (514) 514-343-3524
Email: info@cummingscentre.org
Web site: www.cummingscentre.org

Foxy's
5987A Victoria Avenue
Telephone: (514) 739-8777
Supervision: Vaad Ha'ir

Pizza Pita
5710 Victoria Avenue
Telephone: (514) 731-7482
Supervision: Vaad Ha'ir
Open 9.30 am-11.30 pm daily, Saturday night until 2.30 am.

Tatty's Pizza
6540 Darlington
Telephone: (514) 734-8289
Supervision: Vaad Ha'ir

Meat

El Morocco II
3450 Drummond Street
Telephone: (514) 844-6888; 844-0203
Fax: (514) 844-1204
Email: elmorocco@spring.ca
Supervision: Vaad Ha'ir
Open for lunch and dinner until 10 pm. Located downtown near hotels and boutiques.

Ernie's & Ellie's Place
6900 Decarie Blvd H3X 2T8
Telephone: (514) 344-4444
Fax: (514) 344-0001
Supervision: Vaad Ha'ir

Exodus Restaurants
5395 Queen Mary
Telephone: (514) 483-6610
Fax: (514) 483-6810
Supervision: Vaad Ha'ir

SYNAGOGUES

Canadian Jewish Congress National Headquarters
Samuel Bronfman House, 1590 Docteur Penfield Avenue H3G 1C5
Telephone: (514) 931-7531
Fax: (514) 931-0548
Email: mikec@cjc.ca
Contact to find out which of the many synagogues in Montreal is nearest.

QUEBEC CITY

SYNAGOGUES

Orthodox

Beth Israel Ohev Shalom
1251 Place de Merici G1R 1Y2
Telephone: (418) 688-3277

TOURIST SITES

Beth Israel Ohev Sholom
Boulevard Rene Levesque, Sainte-Foy
Telephone: (418) 658-6677
This is an official monument and historic site - 5 miles from the old centre.

STE. AGATHE DES MONTS

A resort in the Laurentian Mountains known as the "Catskills" of Montreal where members of the Montreal community spend their summer months.

SYNAGOGUES

Orthodox

House of Israel Congregation
31 rue Albert J8C 3A3
Telephone: (819) 326-4320
Fax: (819) 326-8558
Web site: www.houseofisrael.org

Saskatchewan

REGINA

SYNAGOGUES

Orthodox

Beth Jacob
4715 McTavish Street S4S 6H2
Telephone: (306) 757-8643
Fax: (306) 352-3499

Reform

Temple Beth Tikvah
Box 33048, Cathedral Post Office S4T 7X2
Email: templebethtikvah@hotmail.com
Web site: www.uahc.org/cd/cd012

SASKATOON

SYNAGOGUES

Shir Chadash
610 Clarence South S7H 2E2
Telephone: (306) 242-3756

Conservative

Agudas Israel
715 McKinnon Avenue S7H 2G2
Telephone: (306) 343-7023
Fax: (306) 343-1244
Email: jewishcommunity@sk.sympatico.ca

CAYMAN ISLANDS

In addition to a very small permanent Jewish community there are a number of Jews who spend part of the year on the Islands.

GMT -5 hours
Country calling code: (+1 345)
Total population: 38,000
Jewish population: Under 100
Emergency telephone: (Police – 911) (Ambulance – 555)
Electricity voltage: (Electricity voltage – 110)

GRAND CAYMAN
CONTACT INFORMATION
Harvey DeSouza
PO Box 72 GT, Grand Cayman, B.W.I.
Telephone: (345) 949-7739

CHILE

The original Jewish settlers in Chile were Conversos. Rodrigo de Organos, a Converso, was the first European to enter the country in 1535. The Inquisition, however, curtailed the growth of the community.

The first legal Jewish immigration, albeit small, occurred only after Chile's independence in 1810. In 1914 the Jewish community numbered some 500, but this increased in the late 1930s with those refugees from Nazism who were able to avoid the strict immigration laws. Anti-semitism, however, also grew, and the Comite Representativo was formed to respond to it.

There is an umbrella organisation and a large Zionist body in Chile. Most of the community is not religious, but some keep kosher and there are several synagogues in Santiago (the capital) and a few kosher shops. There are two Jewish schools and several Jewish newspapers are published.

GMT -4 hours
Country calling code: (+56)
Total population: 14,622,000
Jewish population: 21,000
Emergency telephone: (Police – 133) (Fire – 132) (Ambulance – 131)
Electricity voltage: (Electricity voltage – 220)

ARICA
COMMUNITY ORGANISATIONS
Sociedad Israelita
Dr Herzl, Casilla 501

IQUIQUE
COMMUNITY ORGANISATIONS
Comunidad Israelita
Playa Ligade 3263, Playa Brava

LA SERENA
COMMUNITY ORGANISATIONS
Community Centre
Cordovez 652

RANCAGUA
COMMUNITY ORGANISATIONS
Comunidad Israelita
Casilla 890

SANTIAGO
The majority of Chilean Jews live in Santiago. The city has a couple of notable features in connection with its Jewish community. The Circulo Israelita Synagogue has an interesting stained glass design in its interior, and the "Bomba Israel" is a fire service, manned by volunteers who include a few rabbis. Two of their fire engines carry the Chilean and Israeli flags.

BUTCHERS
Kosher Deli
Av Las Condes 8400
Telephone: (2) 251-3145/848-6921
Fax: (2) 251-3149
Email: kd1301@123.cl
Supervision: Jabad

COMMUNITY ORGANISATIONS
Communal Headquarters (Comite Representativo de las Entidades Judias de Chile)
Miguel Claro 196
Telephone: (2) 235-8669

DELICATESSEN
Shemtov Kosher Delikatesen
47 La Niebla St
Telephone: (2) 56-2-325-4180
Fax: (2) 56-2-325-3595
Email: shemtovkosher@yahoo.com
Supervision: Rabbi Mensahe Perman
Delivery 24 hours a day

EMBASSY
Embassy of Israel
San Sebastian 2812, Casilla 1224
Telephone: (2) 246-1570

SYNAGOGUES
Ashkenazi
Comunidad Israelita de Santiago
Serrano 214-218

German
Sociedad Cultural Israelita B'nei Jisroel
Mar Jonico No 8860
Telephone: (2) 201-1623
Fax: (2) 201-1623
Email: bneisrael@entelchile.net

Hungarian
Maze
Pedro Bannen 0166
Telephone: (2) 274-2536

Orthodox
Bicur Joilim
Av. Matte 624

Jabad (Chabad) Lubavitch
Los Cactus 1575, La Dehesa
Telephone: (2) 56-2-228-2240
Email: mperman@vtr.net

Jafets Jayim
Miguel Claro 196

Sephardi
Maguen David
Av. R. Lyon 812

TEMUCO
COMMUNITY ORGANISATIONS
Comunidad Israelita
General Cruz 355

VALDIVIA
COMMUNITY ORGANISATIONS
Community Centre
Arauco 136 E.

VALPARAISO
COMMUNITY ORGANISATIONS
Comunidad Israelita
Alvarez 490, Vina del Mar
Telephone: (32) 680-373

CHINA

There is archaeological evidence of a Jewish presence in China in the eighth century but it is believed that their existance as a community only dates from the twelfth century. The largest established community of around 1,000 was in Kaifeng. The first Kaifeng synagogue was built in 1163.

The Treaty of Nanking in 1842 opened Shanghai to trade. In 1845 Elias Sassoon pioneered the Jewish settlement of Shanghai. Many Baghdadi Jews followed and were under the protection of the British government. In due course they were in the forefront of the development of the city. A second community was formed later, mainly by Russians and Poles fleeing religious persecution. The final influx was refugees from Nazi oppression in the period 1933-39. Almost all the community left Shanghai after the Second World War. In 1999 a community was again established.

Also included here is Hong Kong, previously listed as a separate entity but, since July 1997, again a region of China.

GMT +8 hours
Country calling code: **(+86)**
Total population: **1,284,100,000**
Jewish population: **2,100**
Emergency telephone: **(Police – 110) (Fire – 119)**
Electricity voltage: **(Electricity voltage – 220/240)**

BEIJING
EMBASSY
Embassy of Israel
1 Jianguo Menwai Da Jia 100004
Telephone: (10) 6505-2970/1/2
Fax: (10) 6505-0328

KOSHER FOOD
Mrs Shanen's Bagels
Telephone: (10) 6435-9561
Ask for kosher bagels

SYNAGOGUES
Chabad Lubavitch of Beijing China
Kings Garden Villa, 18 Xiao Yun Road, D-5A, Chao Yang District 16
Telephone: (10) 6468-1321
Fax: (10) 6468-1322
Email: chabadbeijing@hotmail.com
Shabbat services on Friday night and Shabbat as well as Friday night dinners and Shabbat lunches. All are welcome

HONG KONG

Although there were some Jewish merchants trading out of Hong Kong over the centuries, the first permanent community consisted of Jews who came from Baghdad in the early nineteenth century. The first synagogue was not established until 1901, the early settlers preferring to organise communal events from their homes. The majority of the community were Sephardi, but Nazi persecution led to more Ashkenazi settlers arriving in Hong Kong, via Shanghai. Since the Second World War many Chinese Jews have emigrated through Hong Kong to Australia and the USA, although some have remained in Hong Kong. Following the reversion to Chinese control in mid-1997, the Jewish community is still thriving, and the mood is optimistic.

The Jews have contributed greatly to the building of the infrastructure of Hong Kong and, since the 1960s, many Western Jews, attracted by the success of this major financial centre, have made their homes there. The first communal hall was founded in 1905, but a new, multi-purpose complex (the Jewish Community Centre) has recently been opened, which is one of the most luxurious in the world. This centre includes everything from a library and a strictly kosher restaurant to a swimming pool and sauna.

CEMETERIES
The Jewish Cemetery
Located in Happy Valley
Telephone: 2589-2621
Fax: 2548-4200

COMMUNITY ORGANISATIONS
Hong Kong Jewish Community Centre
One Robinson Place, 70 Robinson Road, Mid-Levels
Telephone: 2801-5440
Fax: 2877-0917
Email: csw@jcc.org.hk
Web site: www.jcc.org.hk
Two glatt kosher restaurants under the supervision of a full-time Mashgiach. Regular Shabbat and Festival Dinners. Kosher supermarket, full banquet facilities, library, swimming pool and leisure facilities and a full programme of activities and classes. Visitors are welcome.

CULTURAL ORGANISATIONS
The Jewish Historical Society of Hong Kong
Telephone: 2807-9400
Fax: 2887-5235
Publishes monographs on subjects of Sino-Judaic interest and maintains an archive. Information from Mrs Judith Green.

EMBASSY
Consul General of Israel
Room 701 Admiralty Centre, Tower 2, 18 Harcourt Street
Telephone: 2529-6091
Fax: 2865-0220
Email: isrcons@asiaonline.net

RESTAURANTS
Hong Kong Jewish Community Centre
One Robinson Place, 70 Robinson Road, Mid-Levels
Telephone: 2801-5440
Fax: 2877-0917
Email: info@jcc.org.hk
Web site: www.jcc.org.hk
Two glatt kosher restaurants under full-time Mashgiach supervision. Meals on Shabbat, take-away and delivery service available.

Shalom Grill
2/F Fortune House, 61 Connaught Road, Central
Telephone: 2851-6218; 2851-6300
Fax: 2851-7482
Email: darvick@darvick.com.hk
Glatt kosher restaurants under full-time Mashgiach supervision, Meals on Shabbat affer services, take-away and delivery service available. There is also a kosher supermarket, Sunday-Thursday Lunch 12.30 pm-2.30 pm. Dinner 6.30 pm-9.30 pm. Friday 12.30 pm-2.30pm.

SYNAGOGUES
Orthodox
Chabad of Hong Kong
Chabad House, Coda Plaza 3/F, 51 Garden Road
Telephone: 2523-9770
Fax: 2845-2772
Email: info@chabadhk.org
Web site: www.chabadasia.com
Shabbat Minyan & Meals in Central District.

Ohel Leah Synagogue
70 Robinson Road, Mid-Levels
Telephone: 2589-2621
Fax: 2548-4200
Email: mail@ohelleah.org
Web site: www.ohelleah.org
Built in 1902 and carefully restored in 1998, the Orthodox Ohel Leah Synagogue known by some as the "crown jewel" of Asian Jewry still remains the region's most vibrant centre of Jewish religious activity. Classes, daily services, a Beth Din, and a mikva operate on the premises. Gourmet catered shabbat meals - Friday eve is by reservation and shabbat community kiddush luncheon is complimentary following services. Book nearby hotels at discounted rates through the synagogue office.

Zion Congregation
21 Chatham Road, Kowloon
Telephone: 2366-6364
Corner of Mody Road (opposite to Kowloon Shangri-La Hotel).

Sephardi
Beit Midrash Shuva Israel and Community Centre
2/F Fortune House, 61 Connaught Road, Central
Telephone: 2851-6218; 2851-6300
Fax: 2851-7482
Email: darvick@darvick.com.hk
Daily Shacharil at 7.00 and Mincha-Ma'ariv fifteen minutes before sunset. Shabbat services are followed by Shabbat meals. Full day kollel.

KAIFENG
MUSEUMS
Kaifeng Museum
The Kaifeng Museum documents the ancient history of Kaifeng Jewry. The most significant artifact is a 15th-century etched stone with inscriptions describing Kaifeng's Jewish history and customs "from the times of Abraham".

SHANGHAI
Shanghai was opened to foreign trade in 1843. A flourishing Jewish community built up including Jews of many nationalities. There were three synagogues; one of which the Ohel Rachel built in 1917 was designated in 2001 as an endangered site. The current community is planning to raise money for its restoration.

RESTAURANTS
Meat
Kosher Café
Shangmira Garden, Villa #2, 1720 HongQiao Road 200336
Telephone: (21) 86-21-6278-0225
Fax: (21) 86-21-6278-0223
Email: rabbi@chinajewish.org
Web site: www.chinajewish.org
Supervision: Rabbi Shalom Greenberg
Daily 10-8.

SYNAGOGUES
Orthodox
Shanghai Jewish Center
Shanghai-Mira Garden, Villa #2, 1720 HongQiao Road 200336
Telephone: (21) 6278-0225
Fax: (21) 6278-0223
Email: rabbishalom@yahoo.com
Web site: www.chinajewish.org
Shabbat Meals are available. Kosher Restaurant.

COLOMBIA
The first Jews in Colombia were Conversos, as was common in South America. However, they were soon discovered by the Inquisition when it was established in Colombia.

The next influx of Jews came in the nineteenth century, followed by mass immigration from eastern Europe and the Middle East after 1918. Jews were banned from entering after 1939, but this restriction was eased after 1950.

The present community is a mix of Ashkenazi and Sephardi elements, each having their own communual organisations. There are also youth and Zionist organisations. There is a central organisation for Colombian Jewry in Bogota (the capital). There are also Jewish schools and synagogues, and Jewish publications and radio programmes.

GMT -5 hours
Country calling code: (+57)
Total population: 36,612,000
Jewish population: 5,000
Emergency telephone: (Police – 112) (Fire – 119) (Ambulance – 132)
Electricity voltage: (Electricity voltage – 110/120)

BARANQUILLA
COMMUNITY ORGANISATIONS
Centro Israelita Filantropico
Carrera 43, No 85-95, Apartado Aereo 2537
Telephone: (53) 342-310; 351-197

Comunidad Hebrea Sefaradita
Carrera 55, No 74-71, Apartado Aereo 51351
Telephone: (53) 340-054; 340-050

BOGOTA
EMBASSY
Embassy of Israel
Calle 35, No 7-25, Edificio Caxdax
Telephone: (1) 245-6603; 245-6712

MEDIA
Periodical
Menorah
Apartado Aereo 9081

RELIGIOUS ORGANISATIONS
Union Rabinica Colombiana
Tranversal 29, No 126-31
Telephone: (1) 625-4377
Fax: (1) 274-9069
Email: centrocib@tutopia.com

SYNAGOGUES
Congregacion Adath Israel
Carrera 7a, No 94-20
Telephone: (1) 257-1660; 257-1680
Fax: (1) 623-2237
Mikva on premises.

Ashkenazi
Centro Israelita de Bogota
Transversal 29, No 126-31
Telephone: (1) 625-4377
Fax: (1) 274-9069
Email: centrocib@tutopia.com
Kosher meals available by prior arrangement with Rabbi
Goldschmidt, 218-2500.

German
Asociacion Israelita Montefiore
Carrera 20, No 37-54
Telephone: (1) 245-5264

Orthodox
Comunidad Hebrea Sefaradi
Calle 79, No 9-66
Telephone: (1) 256-2629; 249-0372
Mikva on premises.

Jabad House
Calle 92, No 10, Apt. 405
Rabbi's Tel:(1)257-4920.

CALI
COMMUNITY ORGANISATIONS
Union Federal Hebrea
Apartado Aereo 8918
Telephone: (2) 443-1814
Fax: (2) 444-5544
An umbrella organisation co-ordinating all Jewish
activities in Cali.

SYNAGOGUES
Ashkenazi
Sociedad Hebrea de Socoros
Av. 9a Norte # 10-15, Apartado Aereo 011652
Telephone: (2) 668-8518
Fax: (2) 668-8521

German
Union Cultural Israelita
Apartado Aereo 5552
Telephone: (2) 668-9830
Fax: (2) 661-6857

Sephardi
Centro Israelita de Beneficiencia
Calle 44a, Av. 5a Norte Esquina, Apartado Aereo 77
Telephone: (2) 664-1379
Fax: (2) 665-5419

MEDELLIN
COMMUNITY ORGANISATIONS
Union Israelita de Beneficia
Carrera 43B, No 15-150, Apartado Aereo 4702

COSTA RICA

The first Jews arrived in Costa Rica in the nineteenth century, from nearby islands in the Caribbean, such as Jamaica. The next wave of immigrants came from eastern Europe in the 1920s. Thereafter Costa Rica did not welcome new Jewish immigrants, and passed laws against foreign merchants and foreign land ownership. However, the Jewish community in Costa Rica established a communual organisation in 1930. There is a monthly newsletter, and a synagogue in San Jose. Most Jewish children attend the Haim Weizmann School, which has both primary and secondary classes.

It is interesting to note that the Costa Rican embassy in Israel is in Jerusalem and not Tel Aviv, where most other embassies are situated.

GMT -6 hours
Country calling code: **(+506)**
Total population: **3,464,000**
Jewish population: **2,500**
Emergency telephone: **(Police – 911) (Fire – 911)**
(Ambulance – 911)
Electricity voltage: **(Electricity voltage – 110/220)**

SAN JOSE
CONTACT INFORMATION
Centro Israelita Sionista de Costa Rica
PO Box 1473-1000
Telephone: 233-9222
Fax: 233-9321
Email: cisdcr@racsa.co.cr
Web site: www.centroisraelita.com

EMBASSY
Embassy of Israel
Edificio Centro Colon, Piso 11, PO Box 5147-1000
Telephone: 221-60-11/221-64-44
Fax: 257-0867
Email: embofisr@sol.racsa.co.cr

GROCERIES
Little Israel Pita Rica
Frente a Shell Pavas Rd. 1055-1200
Telephone: 290-2083
Fax: 262-5425
Email: pitarica@hotmail.com
Web site: www.kosherfoodcostarica.com
The only kosher bakery and mini-market in Costa Rica.
Delivers to hotels.

HOTELS
Barcelo San Jose Palacio
Apdo 458-1150
Telephone: 220-2034; 220-2035
Fax: 220-2036
Email: Palacio@sol.racsa.co.cr
Hotel has separated kosher kitchen, with the key in the
mashgiach's (Rabbi Levkovitz) hands. The hotel is about a
half hour walk to the synagogue.

Camino Real
Prospero Fernandezy, Camino Real Boulevard
Telephone: 289-7000
Fax: 289-8930
Email: caminoreal@ticonet.co.cr
Hotel has separated kosher kitchen, with the key in the
Mashgiach's (Rabbi Levkovitz) hands.

Melia Confort Corobici
PO Box 2443-1000
Telephone: 232-8122
Fax: 231-5834
Email: melia.confort.corobici@solmelia.com
There is no separate kosher kitchen, but it is fairly close
to the Orthodox synagogue. The hotel has two separate
storage rooms for kosher cookware.

SYNAGOGUES
Shaarei Zion

CROATIA

Jews were in the land now known as Croatia
before the Croats themselves. The Croats
arrived in the seventh century, the Jews
some centuries before with the Romans:
there are remains of a third-century Jewish
cemetery in Solin (near Split).

The first Jewish communites were involved
in trade with Italy across the Adriatic Sea,
and also in trade along the River Danube.
Their success was brief, however, and they
were expelled in 1456, only returning more
than 300 years later. The area became part
of the newly formed Yugoslavia after the
First World War, and the Jewish community
became part of the Federation of Jewish
Communities in Yugoslavia.

The Croatian Jews suffered greatly under
the German occupation in the Second
World War when the local Ustashe
(Croatian Fascists) assisted the Germans.
Despite their efforts, some Jews survived
and even decided to rebuild their community when peace returned.

Today, after the civil war, there are synagogues in towns across the country. There
are some Hebrew classes and newsletters
are published. There are also many places
of historical interest, such as Ulicia
Zudioska (Jewish Street) in Dubrovnik.

GMT -1 hours
Country calling code: (+385)
Total population: **4,498,000**
Jewish population: **2,000**
Emergency telephone: (**Police – 92**) (**Fire – 93**)
(**Other emergency - 94**)
Electricity voltage: (**Electricity voltage – 220**)

DUBROVNIK
MUSEUMS
Jewish Museum
Zudioska Street 3
The first Jewish museum in Croatia opened in May 2003.
It is located in the Dubrovnik Synagogue and has Torah
scrolls dating back to the 13th century.

SYNAGOGUES
Zudioska Street 3
Zudioska means "Street of the Jews". This is the second
oldest synagogue in Europe and is located in a very
narrow street off the main street – the Stradun or Placa.
The Jewish community office is in the same building.
Zudioska Street is the third turning on the right from the
town clock tower. There are about thirty Jews in the city.
Tourists help to make up a minyan in the synagogue on
Friday night and High Holy Days.

OSIJEK
COMMUNITY ORGANISATIONS
Brace Radica Street 13
Telephone: (31) 211-407
Fax: (31) 211-407
The community building contains objects from the
synagogue that was destroyed during the Second World
War. The community numbers about 150 members and
has two cemeteries. No regular services are held. A
former building of the pre-war synagogue in Cvjetkova
Street is a Pentecostal church today. There is a plaque at
the site of the destroyed synagogue in Zupanijska Street.

RIJEKA
SYNAGOGUES
Filipovieva ul. 9, PO Box 65 51000
Telephone: (51) 425-156/336-032
The community numbers about sixty. Services are held in the well maintained synagogue on Jewish holidays.

SPLIT
COMMUNITY ORGANISATIONS
Zidovski Prolaz 1
Telephone: (21) 45-672
The synagogue at Split is one of the few in Yugoslavia to have survived the wartime occupation. The Jewish community numbers about 200. There is a Jewish cemetery, established in 1578. More information from the community offices at the above number.

ZAGREB
BOOKSELLERS
Voice of the Jewish Communities of Croatia
Email: jcz@oleh.srce.hr

COMMUNITY ORGANISATIONS
Jewish Community of Zagreb
Palmoticeva Street 16, PO Box 986
Telephone: (1) 434-619
Fax: (1) 434-638
Email: jcz@public.stce.hr
Before the War Zagreb had 11,000 Jews. There are now only about 1,500, but they remain very active in Jewish communal life. Services are held in the community building on Friday evenings and holidays.

MONUMENT
Central Synagogue
Praska Street 7
There is a plaque on the spot of this pre-war synagogue.

Mirogoj Cemetery
There is an impressive monument in this cemetery to the Jewish victims of the Second World War.

TOURIST SITES
National Museum
The Sarajevo Haggadah, created in the 14th century in Spain, and considered one of the most precious Jewish illuminated manuscripts in the world is currently being restored. It is expected to again be placed on display in the National Museum during 2003.

CUBA

The first Jew to set foot in Cuba (1492) was Luis de Torres. Although hundreds arrived following the Spanish Inquisition, they were prohibited from practising their religion. This changed in 1898 following Cuba's liberation from Spain. With the end of Spanish colonial rule in that year, Jews from nearby areas, such as Jamaica and Florida, and Jewish veterans of the Spanish American War began to settle in Cuba. A congregation was established in 1904. Later, Turkish Sephardim formed their own synagogue. The community was then augmented by immigrants from eastern Europe who had decided to stay in Cuba, which was being used as a transit camp for those seeking to enter America. A central committee was established for all Jewish groups in the 1930s. Cuba imposed severe restrictions on immigration at that time, and the story of the German ship *St Louis* (full of Jewish refugees), which was refused entry into Cuba, is well known.

About 12,000 Jews lived on the island in 1952. Havana had by far the largest community, and 75 per cent of the Cuban community was Ashkenazi. Although the Cuban revolution did not target Jews, religious affiliations were initially discouraged and many Jews emigrated (as did many non-Jews). The remaining community has synagogues, and a Sunday school. Kosher food and Judaica are imported, mainly from Canada and Panama. Cuba broke off diplomatic relations with Israel in 1973, although in 1998/99 a number of Jews were allowed to emigrate to Israel.

GMT -5 hours
Country calling code: (+53)
Total population: 11,509,000
Jewish population: 600
Emergency telephone: (Police – 82 0116) (Fire – 81 115) (Ambulance – 404 551)
Electricity voltage: (Electricity voltage – 110/220)

HAVANA
SYNAGOGUES
Conservative
Patronado de la Casa de la Comunidad Hebrea de Cuba
Calle 13 e I, Vedado
Telephone: (8) 32-8953
This is also the location of a modern community centre.

Orthodox
Hadath Israel
Calle Picota 52, Habana Vieja
Telephone: (8) 61-3495

CYPRUS

During the Roman Empire, Jewish merchants made their home on Cyprus. However, after a revolt that destroyed the town of Salamis, they were expelled. In medieval times, small Jewish communities were established in Nicosia, Limassol and other towns, but the community was never large.

It is interesting to note that Cyprus was seen as a possible 'Jewish Homeland' by the early Zionists. Agricultural settlements were established at the end of the nineteenth century, but they were not successful. Herzl himself tried to persuade the British government to allow Jewish rule over Cyprus in 1902, but met with failure.

Some German Jews managed to escape to Cyprus in the early 1930s. After the war, many Holocaust survivors who had tried to enter Palestine illegally were deported to special camps on the island. Some 50,000 European Jews were held there. Since the establishment of the state of Israel, the Jewish community on the island has become small; the Israeli embassy serves as a centre for community activities.

GMT +2 hours
Country calling code: **(+357)**
Total population: **766,000**
Jewish population: **Under 100**
Emergency telephone: **(Police – 112) (Fire – 112) (Ambulance – 112)**
Electricity voltage: **(Electricity voltage – 240)**

NICOSIA
COMMUNITY ORGANISATIONS
Committee of the Jewish Community of Cyprus
PO Box 24784 1303
Telephone: (22) 694758
Fax: (22) 662077
Email: amiyes@spidernet.com.cy
Contact Mrs Z. Yeshurun for information.

EMBASSY
Embassy of Israel
4 Grypari Street
Telephone: (22) 664195
Fax: (22) 666338
Email: press@nicosia.mfa.gov.il

CZECH REPUBLIC

Prague, the capital of this small central European country, has become a major tourist attraction. It is one of the few cities actively to promote its Jewish heritage, which dates from early medieval times. The oldest (still functioning) synagogue in Europe is there (the Altneuschul), as well as other interesting Jewish sites.

After the arrival of the first Jews in the country, in the tenth century, they suffered similar tragedies to those of other medieval Jewish communities forced baptism by the Crusaders and expulsions, together with some tolerance. Full emancipation was reached in 1867 under the Hapsburgs. The celebrated Jewish writer, Franz Kafka, lived in Prague and did not neglect his Judaism, unlike many other Czech Jews who assimilated and intermarried.

The German occupation led to 85 per cent of the community (80,000 people) perishing in the Holocaust. Further difficulties were faced in the communist period after the war, but since the 1989 'Velvet Revolution', Judaism is being rediscovered. The community (mostly elderly) has several synagogues around the country, a kindergarten and a journal, and there are kosher restaurants in the old Jewish quarter in Prague.

GMT +1 hour
Country calling code: **(+420)**
Total population: **10,304,000**
Jewish population: **5,000**
Emergency telephone: **(Police – 158) (Fire – 150) (Ambulance – 155)**
Electricity voltage: **(Electricity voltage – 220)**

BOSKOVICE

MUSEUMS
Medieval Ghetto
Telephone: (501) 454601; 452077
Fax: (501) 452077
Email: museum@mas.cz
Seventeenth-century Jewish town, synagogue and cemetery.

BRNO

COMMUNITY ORGANISATIONS
Community Centre
tr. Kpt. Jarose 3 60200
Telephone: (5) 4524-4710
Fax: (5) 4521-3803
Email: zob@zob.cz
Web site: www.zob.cz
The community president can be reached on 77-3233.

SYNAGOGUES
Skorepka 13

HOLESOV

MUSEUMS
Schach Synagogue
Dating from 1650, this synagogue is now a museum. Open in the mornings. At other times the curator will show visitors around, if contacted. The old cemetery is close by.

KARLOVY VARY

Carslbad (as it was then called) was popular among Jews as a spa and resort. The beautiful synagogue, destroyed on Kristallnacht, is recorded by a plaque on the wall of the Bristol Hotel.

RESTAURANTS
Meat
Shalom
Mariauskolazenska 21
Telephone: (17) 322-4921
Fax: (17) 322-3206

LIBEREC

SYNAGOGUES
Community Centre
Matousova 21, Reichenberg 46001
Telephone: (48) 510-3340
Each weekday 9 am-11 am.

MIKULOV

SITE
Only one synagogue, still being restored, remains of the many which flourished here when the town was the spiritual capital of Moravian Jewry and the seat of the Chief Rabbis of Moravia. The cemetery contains the graves of famous rabbis.

OLOMOUC

SYNAGOGUES
Community Centre
Komenskeho 7
Telephone: (68) 522-3119

PILSEN

SYNAGOGUES
Smetanovy Sady 5, Pilsen
Telephone: (19) 723-5749
Services Friday evenings. The Great Synagogue is now closed.

POLNA

MUSEUMS
A museum was opened in 2000 in a reconstructed seventeenth century synagogue. It charts the spread of anti-Semitism in Central Europe.

PRAGUE

Most of the Jews in the Czech Republic live in Prague, which has had a thousand-year history of Jewish settlement. The impact of the Jews in Prague has been great, the Golem has entered Prague folklore, and the Altneushul is the oldest functioning synagogue in Europe. The Jewish Quarter in the old town contains many historical sites.

Terezin is some forty miles from Prague and is easily visited. On the way is the town of Lidice, destroyed in June 1942 by the Nazis in retaliation for the assassination of Reinhard Heydrich.

CEMETERIES
Old Jewish Cemetery
U Stare Skoly 1,3 11001
Telephone: (2) 2171-1511
Fax: (2) 2481-9458
Email: office@jewishmuseum.cz
The oldest Jewish cemetery in Europe, containing the graves of such famous rabbis & scholars as Avigdor Karo (died 1439), Yehuda Low ben Bezalel (1609), David Gans (1613) & David Oppenheim (1736).

CONTACT INFORMATION
Jewish Town Hall
Maislova 18
Houses the Federation of Jewish Communities in the Czech Republic . It has the world famous Hebrew clock.

EMBASSY
Embassy of Israel
Badeniho 2, Praha 7 17076
Telephone: (2) 00420-2-33 09 75 00
Fax: (2) 0420-2-33 09 75 29
Email: israemba@bohem-net.cz
Web site: www.prague.mfa.gov.il

HOTELS
President Hotel
Namesti Curieovych 100 116-88
Telephone: (2) 231-4812
Fax: (2) 231-8247
A few minutes walk from the old Jewish quarter.

JUDAICA
Precious Legacy
Maiselova 16, Prague 1, Josefov
Telephone: (2) 232-1951
Fax: (2) 232-0398, 472-1068
Email: legacy_tours@oasanet.cz

MUSEUMS
Jewish Museum in Prague
Ul Stare Skoly 1,3
Telephone: (2) 2481-9456
Fax: (2) 2481-9458
Email: office@jewishmuseum.cz
Web site: www.jewishmuseum.cz
In 2001 a new set of facilities were opened. The complex includes art restoration workshops, a library, and an exhibition hall. Reservation centre: Tel: (2)231-7191. Fax: (2)231-7181.

RESTAURANTS
Dairy
Jerusalem
Brehova 5 1
Telephone: (2) 232-4729
Fax: (2) 232-4729
Supervision: Chabad Lubavitch Prague
Sells a few groceries. Boxed lunches and Shabbat meals can be ordered.

Meat
Aarons Burger
Brehova 8
Telephone: (2) 481-8752
Fax: (2) 786-4664

Carmel
Brehova 6
Telephone: (2) 232-1749

Casablanca
Na Prikope 10 1
Telephone: (2) 24-21-05-19
Fax: (2) 24-23-15-02

King Solomon
Siroka 8, Prague 1 110 00
Telephone: (2) 420-2-24818752
Fax: (2) 420-2-74864664
Email: solomon@kosher.cz
Web site: www.kosher.cz

SYNAGOGUES
Orthodox
Altneuschul
Cervena ul.7 1
Telephone: (2) 231-0909
Dates back to 1275. The synagogue has recently reopened after the devastating floods of 2002.

Chabad Center Prague
3 Parizska Street, Prague 1 11000
Telephone: (2) 232-0896
Fax: (2) 232-0200
Email: chabadprague@mbox.vol.cz
Web site: chabadprague.cz

Jubilee Synagogue
Jerusalemska 7

TOURS
Heritage Tours
Telephone: (2) 472-1068

Precious Legacy Tours
Maiselova 16, Prague 1, Josefov
Telephone: (2) 232-0398
Fax: (2) 472-1068
Email: legacy_tours@oasanet.cz
Web site: legacytours

Wittmann Tours
Manesova 8, 120 00 Praha 2
Telephone: (2) 2225-2472
Fax: (2) 2225-2472
Email: sylvie@wittmann-tours.com
Web site: www.wittmann.tours.com

TEPLICE
SYNAGOGUES
Community Centre
Lipova 25, Teplitz-Schönau
Telephone: (417) 26-580

TEREZIN
MUSEUMS
, Theresienstadt
There is a new museum in the town dedicated to the Jews who were deported from Theresienstadt to Auschwitz.

DENMARK

Jews were allowed to settle in Denmark in 1622, earlier than in any other Scandinavian country. Thereafter, the community grew, with immigration largely from Germany. The Danish king allowed the foundation of the unified Jewish community of Copenhagen in 1684, and the Jews were granted full citizenship in 1849.

In the early part of the twentieth century many refugees arrived from eastern Europe, and Denmark welcomed refugees from Nazi Germany. When the Germans conquered Denmark and ordered the Jews to be handed over, the Danish resistance managed to save 7,200 (90 per cent of the community) by arranging boats to take them to neutral Sweden. Some Jews did, however, stay behind and were taken to the transit ghetto of Theresienstadt (Terezin), and many died.

After the war, most of the Jews returned, and there is now a central Jewish organisation based in Copenhagen. There are also homes for the elderly, synagogues and a mikvahh. Kosher food is available.

GMT +1 hour
Country calling code: (+45)
Total population: 5,284,000
Jewish population: 8,000
Emergency telephone: (Police – 112) (Fire – 112) (Ambulance – 112)
Electricity voltage: (Electricity voltage – 220)

COPENHAGEN

With a Jewish population of almost 9,000, the vast majority of Danish Jews live in the capital. The Community Centre contains most of the offices of the Jewish community, and three old-age homes are jointly run with the Copenhagen Municipality. The Great Synagogue and the cemetery dating from 1693 are interesting sites.

BAKERIES
Mrs Heimann
Telephone: 3332-9443

BUTCHERS
Kosher Delikatesse
87 Lyngbyvej 2100
Telephone: 3918-5777
Fax: 3918-5390

COMMUNITY ORGANISATIONS
Jewish Community Centre
Ny Kongensgade 6 1472
Telephone: 3312-8868
Fax: 3312-3357
Email: mt@mosaiske.dk

EMBASSY
Embassy of Israel
Lundevangsvej 4, Hellerup 2900
Telephone: 3962-6288
Fax: 3962-1938
Email: israel@pip.dknet.dk

GROCERIES
I. A. Samson
Roerholmsgade 3 1352
Telephone: 3313-0077
Fax: 3314-8277
Kosher grocery, provisions and delicatessen. Catering for groups, twenty persons plus.

MIKVAOT
12 Krystalgade 1172
Telephone: 3393-7662; 3332-9443

Jewish Community Centre
Ny Kongensgade 6 1472
Telephone: 3312-8868
Fax: 3312-3357

SYNAGOGUES
Orthodox
Great Synagogue of Copenhagen
12 Krystalgade 1172
Telephone: 3929-9520
Fax: 3929-2517
Email: bent_lexner@hotmail.com
Web site: www.mosaiske.dk
Daily and Shabbat services.

Machsike Hadass
Ole suhrsgade 12 1354
Telephone: 3315-3117
Fax: 4396-9729
Email: machsike-hadas@subnet.dk
Web site: www.machsike-hadas.subnet.dk
Daily and Shabbat services.

TOURIST SITES
Copenhagen Walking Tours
Telephone: 4081-1217
Email: info@copenhagen-walkingtours
Web site: www.copenhagen-walkingtours.dn
Walking tours of sites of Jewish interest in the old city.

STRAND BEACH HOTEL
HORNBAEK, DENMARK

Situated 40 minutes from Copenhagen. Suites/balcony/family/
garden rooms. Danish-Jewish cuisine. Mikveh and synagogue on
premises. Special playground for children.
Pesach package: 4-14 April. Shavuot: 21-28 May.
Kosher Mehadrin Machsike Hadas.

Tel: 00 45 60 94 71 32 (also from 1 April) 00 45 49 70 00 88
Fax: 00 45 43 96 91 37
Email: ek@bongout.dk

HORNBAEK

A resort and seaside town where many members
of the Copenhagen community spend the
summer months, or weekends. It is the area of
the coast from which the Jewish community
escaped in 1943.

HOTELS
Kosher
Hotel Villa Strand
Kystvej 12 3100
Telephone: 2176-8680
Fax: 4596-9137

SYNAGOGUES
Granavenget 8
Telephone: 4220-0731
Open from Shavuot to Succot.

DOMINICAN REPUBLIC

Jewish settlement in the Dominican
Republic is comparatively late the oldest
Jewish grave dates back to 1826. Descended
from central European Jews, the community was not religious and many married
Christians. President Francisco Henriquez
y Carvajal (1916) traced his ancestry back to
the early Jewish settlers.

In 1938 the republic decided to accept
refugees from Nazism (one of the very few
countries of the world that did so freely),
and even provided areas where they could
settle. As a result, there were 1,000 Jews
living there in 1943. This number declined
as, once again, the Jewish community
assimilated and married the local non-
Jewish population. Despite this, many non-
Jewish husbands, wives and children take
part in Jewish events.

Two synagogues and a rabbi who divides
his time between them are features of
Jewish life. There is also a Sunday school in
Santo Domingo and a bi-monthly magazine
is produced. There is a small Jewish
museum in Sosua.

GMT -4 hours
Country calling code: (+1 809)
Total population: 8,097,000
Jewish population: 150
Emergency telephone: (Police – 999) (Fire – 999)
(Ambulance – 999)
Electricity voltage: (Electricity voltage – 220/240)

GMT -5 hours
Country calling code: (+593)
Total population: 11,937,000
Jewish population: 1,000
Emergency telephone: (Police – 101) (Fire – 102)
(Ambulance – 131)
Electricity voltage: (Electricity voltage – 110/220)

SANTO DOMINGO

COMMUNITY ORGANISATIONS
Consejo Dominicano de Mujeres Hebreas
PO Box 2189
Telephone: (809) 535-6042
Fax: (809) 688-2058

EMBASSY
Embassy of Israel
Av. Pedro Henriquez Urena 80 1404
Telephone: (809) 542-1635; 542-1548

SYNAGOGUES
Conservative
Centro Israelita de la Republica Dominicana
Av. Sarasota 21, Belle Vista
Telephone: (809) 535-6042
Fax: (809) 533-0168
Email: lalo@codetel.net.do

SOSUA

SYNAGOGUES
Liberal
Calle Alejo Martinez, El Batey, Next door to Hotel
Casa Marina Reef
Telephone: (809) 533-0168
Fax: (809) 533-0168
Services; Monthly, last Friday and Saturday.

ECUADOR

As in most Latin American countries, Conversos comprised the earliest Jewish settlers in Ecuador. It was not until 1904 that East European Jews began to arrive, and numbers increased further following the Nazi take-over in Germany, as Ecuador granted refuge to more Jews than other neighbouring countries. About 3,000 Jews entered Ecuador in the 1930s. The Jewish population peaked in 1950 at 4,000, but this number declined owing to emigration. In recent years, some Jews have moved to Ecuador from elsewhere in South America.

There are no Jewish schools, but children do have access to Jewish education.

QUITO

COMMUNITY ORGANISATIONS
Comunidad Judia del Ecuador
Calle Roberto Andrade, OE3 580 y Jaime, Roldos
Urbanizacion Einstein (Carcelen)
Telephone: (2) 5932-2483-800/927
Fax: (2) 5932-2486-755
Email: aiq@uio.satnet.net

EMBASSY
Embassy of Israel
Av. Eloy Alfaro 969, Casilla 2463
Telephone: (2) 547-322 & 548-431

EGYPT

For more than 2,000 years there has been a virtually continuous Jewish presence in the vicinity of Cairo and an even more ancient Jewish presence in Egypt is recounted in the Bible. After the exodus, Jews returned to Egypt during the time of Alexander the Great and at that time the Ben Ezra synagogue was built. The Bible was translated into Greek during that period. In the first century CE, the Jewish presence declined but a renaissance occurred with Moses Maimonides's arrival in Egypt in the twelfth century. Most of his books were written in Cairo and his yeshiva still exists in the Jewish quarter. From then on, the Jewish community expanded and flourished, especially with the arrival of refugees from pogroms and during the First and Second World Wars.

Before 1948 there were about 70,000 Jews in Egypt. The 1956 Suez War and the 1967 Six Day War encouraged Jewish emigration. At present, the community is small but the Jewish heritage, mostly synagogues classified as antiquities, represents an inestimable treasure worth visiting, as, for example, the recently restored Ben Ezra synagogue, home of the world-famous

Genizah of some 400,000 documents (the majority of which are now in Cambridge, England).

GMT +2 hours
Country calling code: **(+20)**
Total population: **67,974,000**
Jewish population: **Under 100**
Emergency telephone:
Electricity voltage: **(Electricity voltage – 220)**

ALEXANDRIA
SYNAGOGUES
Eliahu Hanavi
69 Nebi Daniel Street, Ramla Station
Telephone: (3) 492-3974; 597-4438

CAIRO
Cairo, has had a long and important Jewish history. The community has however declined in line with the rest of Egyptian Jewry. However, there are a number of interesting sites, such as the recently restored Ben Ezra Synagogue, where the Cairo Genizah used to be located.

COMMUNITY ORGANISATIONS
13 Rue Sabyl El Khazindar, Abbassieh
Telephone: (2) 824-613 & 824-885
Web site: www.geocities.com

EMBASSY
Embassy of Israel
6 Ibn Malek St., Gizeh
Telephone: (2) 3610528
Fax: (2) 3610414
Email: isremcai@mail.rite.com

SYNAGOGUES
Ben-Ezra
6 Harett il-Sitt Barbara, Mari Girges, Old Cairo
Telephone: (2) 847-695
The synagogue was built in 1892 and is the oldest in Egypt. According to legend under the building is the site where Pharaoh's daughter found Moses.
Meir Enaim
55 No.13 Street, Maadi
Under the supervision of the Jewish Community of Cairo and can be visited on request.
Shaarei Hashamayim
17 Adli Pasha Street, Downtown Cairo
Telephone: (2) 392-9025
Fax: (2) 736-9639
Services are held on holidays. There is an interesting library across from the synagogue, which is only accessible with a key. Ask the guards.

EL SALVADOR
The Jewish connection to El Salvador is not a strong one. It is believed that some Portuguese Conversos crossed the country a few hundred years ago. After that, some Sephardis from France moved to Chaluchuapa. Other Jews came from Europe, but in smaller numbers than those settling in other Latin American countries. There were only 370 Jews in 1976, a number reduced during the civil war, when many emigrated. Some returned, however, when the war was over.

An official community was set up in 1944 and a synagogue was opened in 1950.

El Salvador is one of the few countries to have an embassy in Jerusalem, rather than Tel Aviv.

GMT -6 hours
Country calling code: **(+503)**
Total population: **5,928,000**
Jewish population: **120**
Emergency telephone: **(Police – 123) (Fire – 123) (Ambulance – 123)**
Electricity voltage: **(Electricity voltage – 110)**

SAN SALVADOR
EMBASSY
Embassy of Israel
Alameda Roosevelt y63 Avenida Sur, Centro Financiero Gigante Torre B, 11o piso
Telephone: 503-211-3434
Fax: 503-211-3443
Email: elsalvador@israel.org
Web site: www.sansalvador

SYNAGOGUES
Conservative
Comunidad Israelita de El Salvador
Boulevard del Hipodromo 626 # 1, Colonia San Benito, PO Box 06-182
Telephone: 263-8074
Fax: 264-5499
Email: cisraelita@yahoo.com
Services Friday, Shabbat morning and Holy Days.

Synagogue
23 Blvd. del Hipodromo 626, Colonia San Benito
Telephone: 237-366
Friday evening services only.

ESTONIA

Despite being the only country officially declared 'Judenrein' (free of Jews) at the Wannsee conference in 1942, there is a Jewish community here today. The community has always been small, and is believed to have begun in the fourteenth century. However, most Jews arrived in the nineteenth century, when Czar Alexander II allowed certain groups of Jews into the area.

The first community was established in Tallinn in 1830. By 1939, the community had grown to 4,500 and was free from restraints. After the Soviet and Nazi occupations in the Second World War the Jews returned, mainly from the Soviet Union. Now that Estonia is independent, the Jewish community is able to practise its religion freely.

GMT +2 hours
Country calling code: **(+372)**
Total population: **1,454,000**
Jewish population: **2,500**
Emergency telephone: **(Police – 002 in Tallinn, 02 elsewhere) (Fire – 001 in Tallinn, 01 elsewhere) (Ambulance – 003 in Tallinn, 03 elsewhere)**
Electricity voltage: **(Electricity voltage – 220)**

TALLINN
COMMUNITY ORGANISATIONS
Jewish Community of Estonia
Karu Street 16, PO Box 3576 10507
Telephone: (6) 6623-034
Fax: (6) 6623-034
Email: community@jewish.ee
Publishes a monthly, called 'Hashaher', in Estonian and operates a radio programme on Radio 4 (Thursday 10:15pm-11:00pm). Information on vegetarian restaurants available.

SYNAGOGUES
Orthodox
16A Karu Street, PO Box 3576 10120
Telephone: (6) 623-050
Fax: (6) 623-001
Email: rabbi@jewishestonia.com

ETHIOPIA

The Falashas (Ge'ez for 'stranger', applied to the Ethiopian Jews) of Ethiopia became known world-wide in the early 1980s, when many were airlifted to Israel. The origins of the Beta Israel, as they call themselves, are unclear and little is known for certain. Historians have concluded that they may have become Jewish as early as the second or third century.

As the area became known to the West through nineteenth-century explorers, some Western Jews set up schools in the country. The Jewish population was believed to have been about 50,000 in 1934. After the establishment of Israel, more interest was taken in the Ethiopian community and the Ethiopian civil war was the catalyst for Operation Moses, when 10,000 people were airlifted to Israel in 1984–85. A further 15,000 left for Israel in 1991.

GMT +2 hours
Country calling code: **(+251)**
Total population: **63,495,000**
Jewish population: **500**
Emergency telephone:
Electricity voltage: **(Electricity voltage – 220)**

ADDIS ABABA
COMMUNITY ORGANISATIONS
PO Box 50
Telephone: (1) 111-725 & 446-471

FIJI

When Henry Marks, at the age of 20, moved to Fiji from Australia in 1881, he was the first recorded Jew on the island. Over the years, he developed a successful business across the region, and was later knighted.

Indian and other Jews later moved to Fiji but did not organise any official community. In recent years the Fiji Jewish Association has been created. The Israeli embassy organises an annual Seder.

GMT +12 hours
Country calling code: **(+679)**
Total population: **772,000**
Jewish population: **Under 100**
Emergency telephone: **(Police – 000) (Fire – 000) (Ambulance – 000)**
Electricity voltage: **(Electricity voltage – 240)**

SUVA
COMMUNITY ORGANISATIONS
Fiji Jewish Association
PO Box 882, Suva
Telephone: 387-980
Fax: 387-946
Email: contex@is.com.fj

FINLAND

When Finland was occupied by Russia in the nineteenth century, many Jewish conscripts in the Russian army settled in Finland after their discharge. They were still subject to several restrictions, but these ended after Finland's independence in 1917. In addition to these 'Cantonists', as they were known, immigrants came to Finland from eastern Europe. Finland proved a safe haven, as the government refused to hand over Finnish Jews to the Nazis, despite being allied to Germany in its war with Soviet Russia.

The community is keen to preserve a sense of Jewish identity among the young generation, who are encouraged to experience Jewish life in Israel. The community is also keen to help other Jews in the newly independent Baltic states across the sea to the south of the country. There is a central body for Jewish communities, and kosher food is available. There are also a school and synagogues.

GMT +2 hours
Country calling code: (**+358**)
Total population: **5,140,000**
Jewish population: **1,200**
Emergency telephone: (**Police – 10022**) (**Fire – 112**)
(**Ambulance – 112**)
Electricity voltage: (**Electricity voltage – 220**)

HELSINKI
Some 1,200 Jews (the majority of the Jewish population in Finland) live in Helsinki. The community centre is next to the synagogue. There is also a Jewish cemetery containing an area dedicated to the Jews who fought in the Finnish army in various wars, including the Russo-Finnish war.

DELICATESSEN
Community Centre
Malminkatu 26
Telephone: (9) 586-0310
Fax: (9) 694-8916
Email: srk@jchelsinki.fi
Web site: www.jchelsinki.fi

EMBASSY
Embassy of Israel
Vironkatu 5A 170
Telephone: (9) 681-2020
Fax: (9) 135-6959
Email: israemb@pp.htu.fi

MONUMENT
A monument was unveiled in 2000 in a park opposite the harbour where Jewish refugees were deported in 1942 to Germany

RESTAURANTS
Butcher/Deli
Kosher Deli
Malminkatu 24
Telephone: (9) 685-4584
Fax: (9) 694-8916
Email: srk@jchelsinki.fi
Hours: Wednesday 1.00pm to 5.00pm, Thursday 9.00am to 5.00pm and Friday 9.00am to 2.00pm.

SYNAGOGUES
Orthodox
Jewish Community Synagogue
Malminkatu 26 100
Telephone: (9) 586-0310
Fax: (9) 694-8916
Email: srk@jchelsinki.fi
Built in 1906. Preserved in the synagogue is a wreath presented in 1944 by the then President of Finland in memory of Jews who died in the Russo-Finnish War. Services Monday and Thursday morning, 7:45 am, other weekdays 8 am; Friday evening, 7 pm (summer), 5 pm (winter); Shabbat and Sunday mornings, 9 am.

TURKU
SYNAGOGUES
Brahenkatu 17
Telephone: (2) 231-2557
Fax: (2) 233-4689
The secretary is always pleased to meet visitors.

FRANCE

France now boasts the largest Jewish community in Europe. The Jewish connection with France is a long one: it dates back over 1,000 years as there is evidence of Jewish settlement in several towns in the first few centuries of the Jewish Diaspora. The community grew in early medieval times, and contributed to the economy of the region. Two great Jewish commentators, Rashi and Rabenu Tam, both lived in France. However, French Jewry suffered both from the Crusaders and from other anti-semitic outbursts in the medieval period.

Napoleon's reign heralded the emancipation of French Jewry and, as his armies conquered Europe, the emancipation of other communities began. Despite this, incidents such as the Dreyfus Affair highlighted the fact that anti-semitism was not yet dead. The worst case of anti-semitism in France occurred under the German occupation, when some 70,000 Jews were deported from the community of 300,000. After the war, France became a centre for Jewish immigration, beginning with 80,000 from eastern Europe, and then many thousands from North Africa, which eventually swelled the Jewish population to nearly 700,000.

The community is well served with organisations. Paris alone has 380,000 Jews, more than in the whole of the UK. There are many kosher restaurants, synagogues in many towns throughout the country, newspapers, radio programmes and schools in several cities. In Carpentras and Cavaillon there are synagogues which are considered to be national monuments.

GMT +1 hour
Country calling code: (+33)
Total population: 58,607,000
Jewish population: 600,000
Emergency telephone: (Police – 17) (Fire – 18)
(Ambulance – 15)
Electricity voltage: (Electricity voltage – 220)

North East

AMIENS
SYNAGOGUES
38 rue du Port d'Amont 8000

BAR-LE-DUC
SYNAGOGUES
7 Quai Carnot

BEAUVAIS
SYNAGOGUES
Rue Jules Isaac 60000
Telephone: 03.44.05.46.90

BELFORT
COMMUNITY ORGANISATIONS
27 rue Strolz 90000
Telephone: 03.84.28.55.41
Fax: 03.84.28.55.41
Publishes 'Notre Communaute' (quarterly).

SYNAGOGUES
6 rue de l'As-de-Carreau 90000
Telephone: 03.84.28.55.41
Fax: 03.84.28.55.41

BENFELD
SYNAGOGUES
7a rue de la Dime 67230
Telephone: 03.88.74.47.11

BESANCON
BUTCHERS
M. Croppet
18 rue des Granges 25000
Telephone: 03.81.83.35.93
Thursdays only.

COMMUNITY ORGANISATIONS
10 rue Grosjean 25000
Telephone: 03.81.80.82.82

SYNAGOGUES
23c Quai de Strasbourg 25000

BITCHE
SYNAGOGUES
28 rue de Sarreguemines 57230
Services, Rosh Hashana & Yom Kippur.

BOULAY
SYNAGOGUES
Rue du Pressoir 57220
Telephone: 03.87.79.28.34

BOULOGNE-SUR-MER
SYNAGOGUES
63 rue Charles Butor 62200

BOUZONVILLE
SYNAGOGUES
3 rue des Benedictins 57320

CHALON-SUR-SAONE
SYNAGOGUES
10 rue Germiny 71100

CHALONS-SUR-MARNE
SYNAGOGUES
21 rue Lochet 51000

CHAMBERY
SYNAGOGUES
44 rue St-Real 73000
Services, Friday, 7pm and festivals.

COLMAR
COMMUNITY ORGANISATIONS
3 rue de la Cigogne 68000
Telephone: 03.89.41.38.29
Fax: 03.89.41.12.96
Kosher food can be purchased in the community centre on Wednesdays and Thursdays. Kosher restaurant; Wednesday noon during the school period.

SYNAGOGUES
3 rue de la Cigogne 68000
Telephone: 03.89.41.38.29
Fax: 03.89.41.12.96

COMPIEGNE
SYNAGOGUES
4 rue du Dr.-Charles-Nicolle 60200

DIEUZE
SYNAGOGUES
Av. Foch 57260

DIJON
BUTCHERS
Albert Levy
25 rue de la Manutention 21000
Telephone: 03.80.30.14.42

SYNAGOGUES
5 rue de la Synagogue 21000
Telephone: 03.80.66.46.47
Mikva on premises.

TOURIST SITES
Archaelogical Museum
Has an important collection of old Jewish tombstones.

DUNKIRK
SYNAGOGUES
19 rue Jean-Bart 59140

EPERNAY
SYNAGOGUES
2 rue Placet 51200
Telephone: 03.26.55.24.44
Services, Yom Kippur only.

EPINAL
SYNAGOGUES
9 rue Charlet 88000
Telephone: 03.29.82.25.23

FAULQUEMONT-CREHANGE
SYNAGOGUES
Place de l'Hotel de Ville 57380
Services, festivals & High Holydays only.

FORBACH
SYNAGOGUES
98 Av. St.-Remy 57600
Telephone: 03.87.85.25.57

GROSBLIEDERSTROFF
SYNAGOGUES
6 rue des Fermes 57520

HAGONDANGE
SYNAGOGUES
Rue Henri-Hoffmann 57300

HAGUENAU
SYNAGOGUES
3 rue du Grand-Rabbin-Joseph-Bloch 67500
Telephone: 03.88.73.38.30

INGWILLER
SYNAGOGUES
Cours du Chateau 67340

INSMING
SYNAGOGUES
Rue de la Synagogue 57670

LILLE
GROCERIES
Monoprix
Shopping Centre Euralille, rue du Molinel 59000
Telephone: 03.20.06.81.25

SYNAGOGUES
5 rue Auguste-Angellier 59012
Telephone: 03.20.51.12.52
Fax: 03.20.31.35.46
Mikva on premises. Phone 03.20.85.27.37.

LUNEVILLE
SYNAGOGUES
Orthodox
5 rue Castara 54300
Telephone: 03.83.74.08.07
The synagogue built in 1785 has been listed as an historic monument.

MERLEBACH
SYNAGOGUES
19 rue St-Nicolas 57800

METZ
BUTCHERS
Claude Sebbag
22 rue Mangin, Moselle 57000
Telephone: 03.87.63.33.50
Supervision: Chief Rabbi of Moselle

GROCERIES
Galaries Lafayette
4 rue Winston Churchill, Moselle 57000
Telephone: 03.87.38.60.60

Atac
23 rue de 20e Corps Américain, Moselle 57000

MIKVAOT
30 rue Kellerman
Mme Rivkah Elalouf, Tel: 03.87.32.38.04

SYNAGOGUES
Main Synagogue and Community Centre
39 rue du Rabbin Elie-Bloch, Moselle 57000
Telephone: 03.87.75.04.44

Adass Yechouroun
41 rue de Rabbin Elie-Bloch, Moselle 57000

MONTBELIARD
SYNAGOGUES
Rue de la Synagogue 25200

MULHOUSE
SYNAGOGUES
2 rue des Rabbins 68100
Telephone: 03.89.66.21.22
Fax: 03.89.56.63.49
Mikva on premises. The old cemetery is also worth a visit.

NANCY
COMMUNITY ORGANISATIONS
Communal Centre
19 blvd Joffre 54000
Telephone: 03.83.32.10.67

MIKVAOT
53 rue Hoche
Telephone: 03.83.41.34.48
Mme Myriam Dahan

MUSEUMS
The Musee Historique Lorrain
64 Grand rue 54000
Whilst Jewish buildings were plundered in 1944 an important Jewish collection in the museum survived.

RESTAURANTS
Restaurante Universitaire
19 blvd Joffre 54000
Telephone: 03.83.32.10.67
Open weekdays at noon.

SYNAGOGUES
17 blvd Joffre 54000
Telephone: 03.83.32.10.67

OBERNAI
SYNAGOGUES
Rue de Selestat 67210

TOURIST SITES
41, rue du General-Gouraud
There are the remains of an old synagogue.

PHALSBOURG
SYNAGOGUES
16 rue Alexandre-Weill 57370

REIMS
SYNAGOGUES
49 rue Clovis 51100
Telephone: 03.26.47.68.47

SAINT-AVOLD
CEMETERIES
The American Military Cemetery
Contains many graves of the USA servicemen who fell in the Second World War.

SYNAGOGUES
Pl. Saint-Nabor 57500
Telephone: 03.87.91.16.16

SAINT-DIE
SYNAGOGUES
Rue de l'Eveche 88100
Services, festivals and Holy-days only.

SAINT-LOUIS
CEMETERIES
The Hegenheim Cemetary
This cemetery dates from 1673.

COMMUNITY ORGANISATIONS
19 rue du Temple 68300
Telephone: 03.89.70.00.48
Kosher products available.

SYNAGOGUES
Rue de la Synagogue 68300

Orthodox
3 rue de General Cassagnou 68300
Telephone: 03.89.69.07.05
Fax: 03.89.70.15.15
Kosher shop Tel: 03.89.70.00.48

SAINT-QUENTIN
SYNAGOGUES
11 ter blvd Henri-Martin
Telephone: 03.23.08.30.72

SARREBOURG
SYNAGOGUES
12 rue du Sauvage

SARREGUEMINES
SYNAGOGUES
Rue Georges-V 57200
Telephone: 03.87.98.81.40
Mikva on premises.

SEDAN-CHARLEVILLE
SYNAGOGUES
6 av. de Verdun 8200

SELESTAT
SYNAGOGUES
4 rue Ste.-Barbe 67600

SENS
SYNAGOGUES
14 rue de la Grande-Juiverie 89100
Telephone: 03.86.95.16.65
Fax: 03.86.65.02.11

STRASBOURG
With a Jewish population of 16,000, this city, contested by France and Germany throughout history, currently has an important Jewish community, with several kosher restaurants, butchers and even a kosher vineyard. The earliest evidence of jewish life dates from 1188. A 13th century Mikvahhh was recently discovered.

BAKERIES
Crousty Cash
4 rue Sellénick, Bas-Rhin 67000
Telephone: 03.88.35.68.21

BOOKSELLERS
Fraenckel
19 rue du Marechal-Foch 67000
Telephone: 03.88.36.38.39
Fax: 03.88.37.96.60

Schne-or
15 rue de Bitche 67000
Telephone: 03.88.37.32.37

Fax: 03.88.35.63.11
Email: nfraenckel@aol.com
Also Judaica antiquities.

BUTCHERS
Buchinger
63 rue du Faubourg de Pierre 67000
Telephone: 03.88.32.85.03
13 rue Wimpheling 67000
Telephone: 03.88.61.06.98
David
20 rue Sellenick 67000
Telephone: 03.88.36.75.01
FB Espace Casher
2-4 Av. Foret Noire 67000
Telephone: 03.90.41.18.68
Fax: 03.90.41.19.69

COFFEE SHOP
Coffee Shop
4 rue Strauss-Durkheim 67000

GROCERIES
Cash Center
22 rue Finkmatt 67000
Telephone: 03.88.35.12.38
Yarden
13 Blvd. de la Marne 67000
Telephone: 03.88.60.10.10/Office 03.88.60.51.96
Fax: 03.88.61.71.11

MEDIA
Newspaper
Echos-Unir
1a rue du Grand-Rabbin-Rene-Hirschler 67000
Telephone: 03.88.14.46.50
Fax: 03.88.24.26.69
Monthly publication.

MIKVAOT
1a rue du Grand-Rabbin-Rene-Hirschler 67000
Telephone: 03.88.14.46.68

MUSEUMS
Musee Alsacien
23, quai Saint-Nicolas 67000
Telephone: 03.88.52.50.01
Fax: 03.88.43.64.18
Web site: www.musees-strasbourg.org
Has a section on Jewish Art.

Musee Judeo-Alsacien
62a, Grand Rue, Bouxwiller 67330
Telephone: 03.88.70.97.17
Fax: 03.88.70.97.17
Web site: www.sdv.fr/judaisme
Visiting hours: from Easter to mid September: Tuesday to Friday from 10.00 am to 12 noon and 2.00 pm to 5.00 pm. Sundays from 2.00 pm to 6.00 pm. The museum, which is housed in an old synagogue, traces the history of the Jews of Alsace.

RELIGIOUS ORGANISATIONS
Consistoire Israelite du Bas-Rhin
23 rue Sellenick 67000
Telephone: 03.88.25.05.75
Fax: 03.88.25.12.75
Email: cibr1@libertysurf.fr

Regional Chief Rabbi, Rene Gutman
5 rue du General-de-Castelnau 67000
Telephone: 03.88.25.05.75
Fax: 03.88.25.12.65
Email: cibri1@libertysurf.fr

RESTAURANTS
Restaurant Universitaire
ORT-Laure Weil, 11 rue Sellenick 67000
Telephone: 03.88.76.74.76
Fax: 03.88.76.74.74
Email: ort.strasbourg@ort.asso.fr

Dairy
Autre Part
60, blvd Clemenceau
Telephone: 03.88.37.10.02

Meat
Le King
28 rue Sellenick 67000
Telephone: 03.88.52.17.71

SYNAGOGUES
There are in all more than fifteen synagogues in
Strasbourg; the following are among the largest and
oldest.

Esplanade
17, rue de Nicosie 67000

Ets Hayim
7, rue Turenne 67000
Telephone: 03.88.24.38.36
Fax: 03.88.24.38.36
Email: etzhaim@free.fr

Synagogue de la Paix
1a rue du Grand-Rabbin-Rene-Hirschler 67000
Telephone: 03.88.14.46.50
Fax: 03.88.24.26.69
Email: cis@media-net.fr
Web site: www.cisonline.org

THIONVILLE
SYNAGOGUES
31 av. Clemenceau 57100
Telephone: 03.82.54.47.89
Fax: 03.82.53.03.76

TOUL
SYNAGOGUES
Rue de la Halle 54200

TROYES
MEMORIAL
A statue of Rashi stands in place Jean Moulin.

MIKVAOT
15 rue Brunneval
Telephone: 03.25.73.34.44

SYNAGOGUES
5 rue Brunneval
The only half-timbered shul in France.

VALENCIENNES
SYNAGOGUES
36 rue de l'Intendance 59300
Telephone: 03.27.29.11.07

VERDUN
SYNAGOGUES
Synagogues
Impasse des Jacobins 55100
Telephone: 03.83.41.34.48

VITTEL
SYNAGOGUES
211 rue Croix-Perrot 88800
Telephone: 03.29.08.10.87
Open in July and August only.

WASSELONNE
SYNAGOGUES
Rue des Bains 67310

North West

ANGERS
SYNAGOGUES
12 rue Valdemaine 49100

BISCHEIM-SCHILTIGHEIM
SYNAGOGUES
9 Place de la Synagogue 67800
Telephone: 02.38.33.02.87

BREST
SYNAGOGUES
40 rue de la Republic 29200
Services, Friday, 7:30pm.

CAEN
BUTCHERS
Boucherie Marcel
26 Rue de l'Engannerie 14000
Telephone: 02.31.86.16.25

SYNAGOGUES
46 Av. de la Liberation 14000
Telephone: 02.31.43.60.54

CHATEAUROUX
CONTACT INFORMATION
Michel Touati
3 Allee Emile Zola, Montierchaume, Deols 36130
Telephone: 02.54.26.05.47

DEAUVILLE
SYNAGOGUES
14 rue Castor 14800
Telephone: 02.31.81.27.06

ELBEUF
SYNAGOGUES
29 rue Gremont 76500
Telephone: 02.35.77.09.11

LE HAVRE
GROCERIES
Super U Porte Oceane
Bd Francois 1 er
Telephone: 02.35.21.31.35

SYNAGOGUES
38 rue Victor-Hugo 76600
Telephone: 02.35.21.14.59

LE MANS
SYNAGOGUES
4-6 Blvd. Paixhans 72000
Telephone: 02.43.86.00.96

LORIENT
SYNAGOGUES
18 rue de la Patrie 56100
Services, Friday nights, festivals & Holy Days only.

NANTES
SYNAGOGUES
5 Impasse Copernic 44000
Telephone: 02.41.87.48.10
Fax: 02.41.37.11.79
Mikva on premises.

ORLEANS
SYNAGOGUES
14 rue Robert-de-Courtenay, (to the left of the cathedral) 45000
Information on services to be had from Marcus Sellem 02.62.89.18.

RENNES
COMMUNITY ORGANISATIONS
Centre Edmond Safra
Rue de la Heronniere, 5, Allee du Mont dol 35000
Telephone: 02.99.63.57.18
Services held. Telephone for times.

ROUEN
SYNAGOGUES
55 rue des Bons-Enfants 76100
Telephone: 02.35.71.01.44
The Jewish Youth Club can provide board residence for student travellers and holiday-makers.

TOURIST SITES
Old Jewish Quarter
Excavations in the 1970s uncovered the ruins of what is the only known medieval Jewish structure whose walls have survived. Now called "The house of the Jews" it is considered to most likely have been a yeshiva but it may in fact have been a synagogue.

TOURS
SYNAGOGUES
37 rue Parmentier 37000
Telephone: 02.47.05.56.95

Paris

PARIS
The city of Paris is divided into districts (*arrondissements*) designated by the last two digits of the postcode. In the categories below, establishments are listed in numerical order according to the postcode (that is, -01, -02, -03 and so on).

The historic centre of Paris Jewish life is found in the Marais area (4th *arrondissement*), although a synagogue stood on Ile de la Cité before Notre Dame was built, Jews having lived in the city since Roman times. Another more central area is that around rue Richer (9th *arrondissement*) which, although not historic as such, has many kosher restaurants of varying styles and prices. A most important new site to be visited is the Musee d'art and d'histoire du Judaisme which opened in December 1998.

BAKERIES
Charles Tr. Patissier
10 rue Corentin Cariou 75019
Telephone: 01.47.97.51.83
Supervision: Beth Din of Paris

Douieb
11 bis rue Geoffroy Marie 75009
Telephone: 01.47.70.86.09
Supervision: Beth Din of Paris

Golan
10 rue Geoffroy Marie 75009
Telephone: 01.48.00.94.71
Supervision: Beth Din of Paris

Kadoche
2 av. Corentin Cariou 75019
Telephone: 01.40.37.00.14
Supervision: Beth Din of Paris

Korcarz
29 rue des Rosiers 75004
Telephone: 01.42.77.39.47
Fax: 01.48.58.28.44
Supervision: Beth Din of Paris/Chief Rabbi Mordechai Rottenberg

Korcarz
25 rue Trévise 75009
Telephone: 01.42.46.83.33
Supervision: Beth Din of Paris/Chief Rabbi Mordechai Rottenberg

Le Relais Sucre
135 rue Manin 75019
Telephone: 01.42.41.20.98
Supervision: Beth Din of Paris

Les Ailes
34 rue Richer 75009
Telephone: 01.47.70.62.53
Supervision: Beth Din of Paris

Lilo
20 rue Desnoyer 75020
Telephone: 01.47.97.63.20
Supervision: Beth Din of Paris

Mat'amim
17 rue de Crimée 75019
Telephone: 01.42.40.89.11
Supervision: Beth Din of Paris

Medayo
71 rue de Meaux 75019
Telephone: 01.40.03.04.20
Supervision: Beth Din of Paris

Mendez
3 ter rue de la Présentation 75011
Telephone: 01.43.57.02.03
Supervision: Beth Din of Paris

Mezel
1 rue Ferdinand Duval 75004
Telephone: 01.42.78.25.01
Supervision: Beth Din of Paris

Nani
104 blvd de Belleville 75020
Telephone: 01.47.97.38.05
Supervision: Beth Din of Paris

Nathan de Belleville
67 blvd de Belleville 75011
Telephone: 01.43.57.24.60
Supervision: Beth Din of Paris

Zazou
20 rue du Faubourg Montmartre 75009
Telephone: 01.47.70.81.32
Supervision: Beth Din of Paris

BUTCHERS

Adolphe
14 rue Richer 75009
Telephone: 01.48.24.86.33

Andre Manin
135 rue Manin 75019
Telephone: 01.42.38.00.43

Aux Viandes Cacheres
6 av. Corentin Cariou 75019
Telephone: 01.40.36.02.41

Berbeche
15/17 rue Henri Ribiere 75019
Telephone: 01.42.08.06.06

Berbeche
39 rue Jouffroy 75017
Telephone: 01.44.40.07.59

Berbeche
46 rue Richer 75009
Telephone: 01.47.70.50.58

Berbeche
5 rue Vandrezanne 75013
Telephone: 01.45.88.86.50
6 rue du Moulinet 75013
Telephone: 01.45.80.89.10

Boucherie Guy
266 rue de Charenton 75012
Telephone: 01.43.44.60.90

Boucherie Claude
174 rue Lecourbe 75015
Telephone: 01.48.28.02.00

Boucherie Smadja
90 blvd de Belleville 75020
Telephone: 01.46.36.25.36

Charlot
33 rue Richer 75009
Telephone: 01.45.23.10.34

Chez Andre
69 blvd de Belleville 75011
Telephone: 01.43.57.80.38

Chez Jacques
19 rue Bouchardon 75010
Telephone: 01.42.06.76.13

Chez Jojo
20 rue Louis Bonnet 75011
Telephone: 01.43.55.10.29

Charly Halak B. Y.
51 rue Richard Lenoir 75011
Telephone: 01.43.48.62.26

Emsalem
17 quai de la Gironde 75019
Telephone: 01.40.36.56.64
18 rue Corentin Cariou 75019
Telephone: 01.40.36.56.64

Espaces Courses Elles
177 rue de Courcelles 75017
Telephone: 01.47.63.36.26

Gm Levy
83 rue de Lonchamp 75016
Telephone: 01.45.53.04.24

Henrino
122 blvd de Belleville 75020
Telephone: 01.47.97.24.52

J V (Temim)
2 rue de Dr Goujon 75012
Telephone: 01.43.45.78.77

Kassab
88 blvd Murat 75016
Telephone: 01.40.71.07.34

Krief
104 rue Legendre 75017
Telephone: 01.46.27.15.57

La Rose Blanche
43 rue Richer 75009
Telephone: 01.48.24.84.65

Maurice Zirah
91 rue de la Roquette 75011
Telephone: 01.43.79.62.53

Saada
17 rue des Rosiers 75004
Telephone: 01.42.77.76.22

Ste Delicatess
209 av. de Versailles 75016
Telephone: 01.44.40.07.59

EMBASSY
Embassy of Israel
3 rue Rabelais 75008
Telephone: 01.40.76.55.00
Fax: 01.40.76.55.55
Email: info@amb-israel.fr

GROCERIES
Chekel
14 av. de Villiers 75017
Telephone: 01.48.88.94.97
Supervision: Beth Din of Paris
Also sells delicatessen and sandwiches. Hours: 9 am to 8 pm. Nearest Metro: Villiers. Near Champs-Elysées/Opéra.

Chochana
54 av. Secretan 75019

Compt Pdts Alimentaires
111 av. de Villiers 75017
Telephone: 01.42.27.16.91

Doueib
11 bis rue Geoffroy Marie 75009
Telephone: 01.47.70.86.09

Keter David
5, rue Benjamin Franklin 75016
Telephone: 01.42.24.04.42
Fax: 01.42.24.04.41

Le Haim
6 rue Paulin Enfert 75013
Telephone: 01.44.24.53.34

HOTELS
Hôtel Aida Opéra
17 rue du Conservatoire 75009
Telephone: 01.45.23.11.11
Fax: 01.47.70.38.73
Email: reservation@aida-opera.com
Supervision: Beth Din of Paris.
Kosher breakfast.

Hotel Geoffroy-Marie Opera
12 rue Geoffroy-Marie 75009
Telephone: 01.47.70.11.85
Fax: 01.42.46.09.36
Email: hotelgmopera@wanadoo.fr
Supervision: Beth Din of Paris
Breakfast / Brunch is open to non residents.

Hotel Touring
21 rue Buffault 75009
Telephone: 01.48.78.09.16
Fax: 01.48.78.27.74
Email: infos@hotel-touring.fr
Web site: www.hotel-touring.fr

L'Hotel de Mericourt
50 rue de la Folie Mericourt 75011
Telephone: 01.43.38.73.63
Fax: 01.43.38.66.13
Email: hoteldemericourt@wanadoo.fr
Situated in an area with many kosher facilities.

Pavillon De Paris
7 rue de Parme 75009
Telephone: 01.55.31.60.00
Fax: 01.55.31.60.01
Email: mail@pavillondeparis.com
Web site: www.pavillondeparis.com

LIBRARIES

Library Judaica of the Seminaire Israelite de France
9 rue Vauquelin 75005
Telephone: 01.47.07.22.94
Visit only by appointment.

MIKVAOT
176 rue du Temple 75003
Telephone: 01.42.71.89.28
The mikvah is located in the centre of Paris, near Place de la République, at the rear of the building. The staff is English-speaking.
19-21 rue Galvani 75017
Telephone: 01.45.74.52.80

Mayan Hai Source de Vie Haya Mouchka
2-4 rue Tristan Tzara 75018
Telephone: 01.40.38.18.29; 01.46.36.11.09
1 rue des Annelets 75019
Telephone: 01.42.45.57.87
For men and women. Telephone is an answer-machine, for women only.

Mikve Haya Mouchka
25 rue Riquet 75019
Telephone: 01.40.36.40.92
Fax: 01.40.36.88.90
75 rue Julien Lacroix 75020
Telephone: 01.46.36.39.20; 01.46.36.30.10
For men and women.

MONUMENT
Memorial To The Unknown Jewish Martyr
rue Geoffroy-l'Asnier 17 75004
The memorial is a tribute to the Jews who perished in the Holocaust. Erected in 1956 it contains the Archives of the Centre Documentation Juive Contemporaine. At the centre is an "eternal flame".

MUSEUMS
Musée d'art et d'histoire du Judaisme
Hotel de Saint-Aignan, 71 rue du Temple 75003
Telephone: 01.53.01.86.53
Fax: 01.42.72.97.47
Email: info@mahj.org
Web site: www.mahj.org
Open Monday to Friday from 11 am to 6 pm and Sunday from 10 am to 6 pm.

Musee Nissim de Camondo
63, rue de Monceau 75008
Telephone: 01.53.89.06.40
Fax: 01.53.89.06.42
Web site: www.ucad.fr
Reconstruction of an eighteenth century aristocratic home. This home and its collections were bequeathed to France in 1935 by Comte Moise de Camondo in memory of his son Nissim, who died in combat in 1917.

RELIGIOUS ORGANISATIONS
Communauté Israélite Orthodoxe de Paris
10 rue Pavée 75004
Telephone: 01.42.77.81.51
Fax: 01.48.87.26.29

RESTAURANTS

Dairy

Bistrot Blanc
52 rue Blanche 75009
Telephone: 01.42.85.05.30
Supervision: Beth Din of Paris

Casa Rina
18 Faubourg Monmartre 75009
Telephone: 01.45.23.02.22
Supervision: Beth Din of Paris

Cine Citta Café
7 rue d'Aguesseau 75008
Telephone: 01.42.68.05.03
Supervision: Beth Din of Paris

Cocktail Café
82 av. Parmentier 75011
Telephone: 01.43.57.19.94
Supervision: Beth Din of Paris

Contini
42 rue des Rosiers 75004
Telephone: 01.48.04.78.32
Supervision: Beth Din of Paris

Dizengoff Café
27 rue Richer 75009
Telephone: 01.47.70.81.97
Email: dizengoff@caramail.com
Supervision: Beth Din of Paris
Open from 12:00 am to 10:30 pm

Gin Fizz
157 blvd Serrurier 75019
Telephone: 01.42.00.51.28
Supervision: Beth Din of Paris

Hamman Café
4 rue des Rosiers 75004
Telephone: 01.42.78.04.46
Supervision: Beth Din of Paris

King Salomon
46 rue Richer 75009
Telephone: 01.42.46.31.22
Supervision: Beth Din of Paris

Le New's
56 av. de la République 75011
Telephone: 01.43.38.63.18
Supervision: Beth Din of Paris

Maestro Pizza
19 rue d'Anjou 75008
Telephone: 01.47.42.15.60
Supervision: Beth Din of Paris

Meat

Adolphe
14 rue Richer 75009
Telephone: 01.47.70.91.25
Supervision: Beth Din of Paris

Berbeche Burger
47 rue Richer 75009
Telephone: 01.47.70.81.22
Supervision: Beth Din of Paris

Brasserie du Belvedere
109 av. de Villiers 75017
Telephone: 01.47.64.96.55
Supervision: Beth Din of Paris

Cash Food
63 rue des Vinaigriers 75010
Telephone: 01.42.03.95.75
Supervision: Beth Din of Paris

Centre Edmond Fleg
8 bis, rue de l'Eperon 75006
Telephone: 01.46.33.43.31
Supervision: Beth Din of Paris

Chez David
11 rue Montyon 75009
Telephone: 01.44.83.01.24
Supervision: Beth Din of Paris

Chez François
5 rue Ramponeau 75020
Telephone: 01.47.97.40.06
Supervision: Beth Din of Paris

Chez Rene et Gabin
92 blvd de Belleville 75020
Telephone: 01.43.58.78.14
Supervision: Beth Din of Paris

Darjeeling
1 bis, rue des Colonels Renard 75017
Telephone: 01.45.72.09.32
Fax: 01.45.72.03.27
Web site: www.darjeeling-ontable.com
Supervision: Chief Rabbi Mordechai Rottenberg

Dolly's Food
9 rue cité Riverain 75010
Telephone: 01.48.03.08.40
Supervision: Beth Din of Paris

Douieb
11 bis rue Geoffroy Marie 75009
Telephone: 01.47.70.86.09
Supervision: Beth Din of Paris

Elygel
116 blvd de Belleville 75020
Telephone: 01.47.97.09.73
Supervision: Beth Din of Paris

Fradji
42 rue Poncelet 75017
Telephone: 01.47.54.91.40
Supervision: Beth Din of Paris

Georges de Tunis
42 rue Richer 75009
Telephone: 01.47.70.24.64
Supervision: Beth Din of Paris

Juliette
14 rue Duphot 75001
Telephone: 01.42.60.18.05
Fax: 01.42.60.18.98
Supervision: Beth Din of Paris

La Petite Famille
32 rue des Rosiers 75003
Telephone: 01.42.77.00.50
Supervision: Beth Din of Paris

Le Cabourg
102 blvd Voltaire 75011
Telephone: 01.47.00.71.43
Supervision: Beth Din of Paris
Hours: 12 pm to 2:30 pm and 7 pm to 11 pm.

Le Chateaubriand
125 rue de Tocqueville 75017
Telephone: 01.47.63.96.90
Fax: 01.47.63.42.55
Supervision: Beth Din of Paris

Le Gros Ventre
7/9 rue Montyon 75009
Telephone: 01.48.24.25.34
Supervision: Beth Din of Paris

Le Lotus de Nissan
39 rue Amelot 75011
Telephone: 01.43.55.80.42
Supervision: Beth Din of Paris

Le Manahattan
231 blvd Voltaire 75011
Telephone: 01.43.56.03.30
Supervision: Beth Din of Paris

Les Ailes
34 rue Richer 75009
Telephone: 01.47.70.62.53
Supervision: Beth Din of Paris

Les Cantiques
16 rue Beaurepaire 75010
Telephone: 01.42.40.64.21
Supervision: Beth Din of Paris
Deliver.

Lumieres de Belleville
102 blvd de Belleville 75020
Telephone: 01.47.97.51.83
Supervision: Beth Din of Paris

Mille Delices
52 avenue Secrétan 75019
Telephone: 01.40.18.32.32
Supervision: Beth Din of Paris

Nini
24 rue Saussier Leroy 75017
Telephone: 01.46.22.28.93
Supervision: Beth Din of Paris

Synagogue Beth El
4 rue Saulnier 75009
Telephone: 01.45.23.34.89
Supervision: Beth Din of Paris
Shabbat meals by arrangement.

Yun-Pana
115 Boulevard Voltaire 75011
Telephone: 01.43.79.20.48
Supervision: Beth Din of Paris

Zazou Burger
19 rue du Faubourg Montmartre 75009
Telephone: 01.40.22.08.33
Supervision: Beth Din of Paris

SYNAGOGUES
Liberal
Union Liberale Israelite de France
24 rue Copernic 75116
Telephone: 01.47.04.37.27
Fax: 01.47.27.81.02
Email: communication@ulif.com
Web site: www.ulif.com

Masorti
Communaute Juive Massorti de Paris
8 rue George Bernard Shaw (off rue Dupleix) 75015
Telephone: 01.45.67.97.96
Fax: 01.45.56.89.79
Email: RuzieDr@aol.com
Web site: www.jtsa.edu/synagogues/adathsfr/
The Paris Jewish Masorti (Conservative) Community.
Services Friday night 6:30pm. Shabbat morning 10 am
festivals and Rosh Chodesh.

Orthodox
15 rue Notre-Dame de Nazareth 75003
Telephone: 01.42.78.00.30
Fax: 01.42.78.05.18

Adass Yereim
10 rue Cadet 75009
Telephone: 01.42.46.36.47; 01.48.74.51.78
Fax: 01.48.74.35.35
Nussach Ashkenez

Adath Israël
36 rue Basfroi 75011
Telephone: 01.43.67.89.20

Adath Yechouroun
25 rue des Rosiers 75004
Telephone: 01.44.59.82.36

Agoudas Hakehilos
10 rue Pavée 75004
Telephone: 01.48.87.21.54
Fax: 01.48.87.26.29
A striking Art Nouveau synagogue designed by Hector Guimard, the creator of the world famous Metro entrances, in 1913.

Avoth Ouvanim
59 av. d'Ivry 75013
Telephone: 01.45.82.80.73
Fax: 01.45.85.94.39
223 rue Vercingétorix 75014
Telephone: 01.45.45.50.51
6 bis villa d'Alésia 75014
Telephone: 01.45.40.82.35
Fax: 01.45.40.72.89

Beth Chalom
11-13 rue Curial 75019
Telephone: 01.40.37.65.16; 01.40.37.12.54

Beith Chalom
25 villa d'Alésia 75014
Telephone: 01.45.45.38.71
Fax: 01.43.37.58.49

Beth-El
3 bis rue Saulnier 75009
Telephone: 01.47.70.09.23
Fax: 01.45.23.15.75
Email: bethel@eboom.com

Beth Hamidrach Lamed
67 rue Bayen 75017
Telephone: 01.45.74.52.80

Beth-Israël
4 rue Saulnier 75009
Telephone: 01.45.23.34.89

Beth Loubavitch
53 rue Compans 75019
Telephone: 01.42.02.20.35

Beth Loubavitch
93 rue des Orteaux 75020
Telephone: 01.40.24.10.60

Beth Loubavitch
25 rue Riquet 75019
Telephone: 01.40.36.93.90
Fax: 01.40.36.60.15

Chaare Tora
1 rue Henri-Turot 75019
Telephone: 01.42.06.41.12
Fax: 01.42.06.95.47

Centre Edmond Fleg
8 bis rue de l'Epéron 75006
Telephone: 01.46.33.43.31
Houses the Union des Centres Communautaires (UCC), which can be contacted via the same telephone number. Their fax number is 01.43.25.86.19. Tikvaténou, the Jewish youth movement of the Consistoire, is also located here, Tel: 01.46.33.43.24; Fax: 01.43.25.20.59.

Centre Rachi
30 blvd du Port-Royal 75005
Telephone: 01.43.31.98.20

Centre Rambam
19-21 rue Galvani 75017
Telephone: 01.45.74.52.80

Chivtei Israel
12-14 Cité Moynet 75012
Telephone: 01.43.43.50.12
Fax: 01.43.47.36.78
Email: ravatlan@club-internet.fr

Consistorial Synagogue
14 place des Vosges 75004
Telephone: 01.48.87.79.45
Fax: 01.48.87.57.58
Email: templedesvosges@noos.fr
Web site: www.synadesvosges.com
Possibilities of "Shabbat meals".

E.E.I.F.
27 av. de Ségur 75007
Telephone: 01.47.83.60.33

Ets Haim
18 rue Basfroi 75011
Telephone: 01.43.48.82.42

Fondation Roger Fleishmann
18 rue des Ecouffes 75004
Telephone: 01.48.87.97.86

Grande Synagogue de Paris
44 rue de la Victoire 75009
Telephone: 01.40.82.26.26 ext. 2773 or 01.45.26.95.36
Fax: 01.45.26.95.36
Email: infos@lavictoire.org
Web site: www.lavictoire.org

Groupe Rabbi Yehiel de Paris
25 rue Michel-Leconte 75003
Telephone: 01.42.78.89.17

Hékhal Moché
218-220 rue du Faubourg St-Honoré 75008
Telephone: 01.45.61.20.25
Located behind the Golden Tulip Hotel.

Kollel Ysmah Moché
36 rue des Annelets 75019
Telephone: 01.43.63.73.94

Maor Athora
16 rue Ramponeau 75020
Telephone: 01.47.97.69.42

Merkaz Beth Myriam
19 rue Domrémy 75013
Telephone: 01.45.86.83.99
Fax: 01.45.86.83.99

Névé Chalom
29 rue Sibué 75012
Telephone: 01.43.42.07.70
Fax: 01.43.48.44.50

Ohaley Yaacov
11 rue Henri-Murger 75019
Telephone: 01.42.49.25.00

Ohel Avraham
31 rue Montevideo 75016
Telephone: 01.45.05.66.73
Fax: 01.40.72.83.76
23 bis rue Dufrénoy 75016
Telephone: 01.45.04.94.00; 01.45.04.66.73

Ohel Mordekhai
13 rue Fondary 75015
Telephone: 01.40.59.96.56

Ohr Chimchon Raphaël
5 passage Dagorno 75020
Telephone: 01.46.59.39.02
Fax: 01.46.59.14.99

Ohr Tora - AJJ
15 rue Riquet 75019
Telephone: 01.40.38.23.36
Fax: 01.40.36.42.23
Email: ajj@free.fr

Ohr Yossef
48 quai de la Marne 75019
Telephone: 01.42.45.74.20
Fax: 01.40.18.10.74

Oratoire de la Fondation Rothschild (Maison de Retraite)
76 rue de Picpus 75012
Telephone: 01.43.44.72.98
Fax: 01.43.44.71.39

Oratoire Mahziké Adath Mouvement Loubavitch
17 rue des Rosiers 75004

Ora Vesimha
37 rue des Trois-Bornes 75011
Telephone: 01.43.57.49.84

Pah'ad David
11 rue du Plateau 75019
Telephone: 01.42.46.47.03
Fax: 01.42.46.47.56

Rachi Chull
6 rue Ambroise-Thomas 75009
Telephone: 01.48.24.86.95

Rav Pealim (Braslav)
49 blvd de la Villette 75010
Telephone: 01.42.41.55.44

Séminaire Israélite de France
9 rue Vauquelin 75005
Telephone: 01.47.07.21.22
Fax: 01.43.37.75.92

Siège du Beth Loubavitch
8 rue Lamartine 75009
Telephone: 01.45.26.87.60
Fax: 01.45.26.24.37

Synagogue ACIP
42 rue des Saules 75018
Telephone: 01.46.06.71.39
Fax: 01.46.06.71.39

Synagogue Achkenaze & Sephardi
49 rue Pali Kao 75020
Telephone: 01.46.36.30.10

Synagogue Berit Chalom
18 rue Saint-Lazare 75009
Telephone: 01.48.78.45.32; 01.48.78.38.80

Synagogue Bet Yaacov Yossef
5 square des Cardeurs, 43 rue Saint-Blaise 75020
Telephone: 01.43.56.03.11

Synagogue de Montmartre
13 rue Sainte-Isaure 75018
Telephone: 01.42.64.48.34

Synagogue des Tournelles
21 bis rue des Tournelles 75004
Telephone: 01.42.74.32.65; 01.42.74.32.80
Fax: 01.40.29.90.27
Email: david-halim@septodont.fr

Synagogue Don Isaac Abravanel
84-86 rue de la Roquette 75011
Telephone: 01.47.00.75.95

Synagogue Michkan-Yaacov
118 boulevard de Belleville 75020
Telephone: 01.43.49.39.59

Synagogue Michkenot Israel
6 rue Jean-Nohain 75019
Telephone: 01.48.03.25.59
Fax: 01.42.00.26.87

Synagogue Tephilat Israël Frank-Forter
24 rue du Bourg-Tibourg 75004
Telephone: 01.46.24.48.94

Synagogue Torath-Hayim
130 rue du Faubourg Saint-Martin 75010
Telephone: 01.40.05.98.34

Tiferet Yaacob
71 rue de Dunkerque 75009
Telephone: 01.42.81.32.17; 01.42.49.65.12
4 rue Martel 75010
9 rue Guy-Patin 75010
Telephone: 01.42.85.12.74

Paris Region

ALFORTVILLE

BUTCHERS
Tiness
12 Etienne Dollet, Val-de-Marne 94140
Telephone: 01.49.77.95.79

SYNAGOGUES
Orthodox
1 rue Blanche, Val-de-Marne 94140
Telephone: 01.43.78.86.43

ANTONY

SYNAGOGUES
Orthodox
Community Centre and Synagogue
1 rue Sdérot, angle 1, rue Barthélémy, Hauts-de-Seine 92160
Telephone: 01.46.66.19.17

ASNIERES

MIKVAOT
82 rue du R.P. Christian-Gilbert, Hauts-de-Seine 92600
Telephone: 01.47.99.26.59

SYNAGOGUES
Orthodox
73 bis rue des Bas, Hauts-de-Seine 92600
Telephone: 01.47.99.32.55

ATHIS-MONS

SYNAGOGUES
Orthodox
55 rue des Coquelicots, Essonne 91200
Telephone: 01.69.38.14.29

AULNAY-SOUS-BOIS

SYNAGOGUES
Orthodox
80 rue Maximilien Robespierre, Seine-Saint-Denis 93600
Telephone: 01.48.69.66.93

BAGNEUX

BAKERIES
Princiane
1 rue de l'Egalité, Parc de Garlande, Hauts-de-Seine 92220
Telephone: 01.47.35.90.77
Fax: 01.47.35.93.67
Email: princiane@princiane.com
Supervision: Beth Din of Paris. Orthodox Union.

BUTCHERS
Isaac
188 av Aristide Briand, Hauts-de-Seine 92220
Telephone: 01.45.47.00.21

BAGNOLET

BAKERIES
Sonesta
27 rue Adélaide Lahaye, Seine-Saint-Denis 93170
Telephone: 01.43.64.92.93
Fax: 01.43.60.51.26
Supervision: Beth Din of Paris

SYNAGOGUES
Orthodox
15-17 rue D. Vienot, Seine-Saint-Denis 93170
Telephone: 01.43.60.39.93

BOBIGNY

RESTAURANTS
Dairy
Chez Daryl
22-24 rue Henri Barbusse, Seine-Saint-Denis 93000
Telephone: 01.48.43.79.00
Supervision: Beth Din of Paris

BONDY

SYNAGOGUES
Orthodox
Maison Communautaire
28 av. de la Villageoise, Seine-Saint-Denis 93140
Telephone: 01.48.47.50.79

BOULOGNE SUR SEINE

BAKERIES
Ariel
143 avenue J.B. Clément, Hauts-de-Seine 92100
Telephone: 01.46.04.24.42
Supervision: Beth Din of Paris

GROCERIES

Ednale
28 rue Georges Sorel, Hauts-de-Seine 92100
Telephone: 01.46.03.83.37

SYNAGOGUES

Orthodox
43 rue des Abondances, Hauts-de-Seine 92100
Telephone: 01.46.03.90.63
Fax: 01.46.03.90.63

CHAMPIGNY
SYNAGOGUES
Orthodox
Synagogue Beth-David
25 av. du Général-de Gaulle, Val-de-Marne 94500
Telephone: 01.48.85.72.29

CHELLES
SYNAGOGUES
Orthodox
14 rue des Anémones, Seine-et-Marne 77500
Telephone: 01.60.20.92.93

CHOISY-LE-ROI
MIKVAOT
28 av. de Newbum, Val-de-Marne 94600
Telephone: 01.48.53.43.70; 01.48.92.68.68

SYNAGOGUES
Orthodox
28 av. de Newburn, Val-de-Marne 94600
Telephone: 01.48.53.48.27

CLICHY-SUR-SEINE
SYNAGOGUES
Orthodox
26 rue de Mozart (Espace Clichy), Hauts-de-Seine 92210
Telephone: 01.47.39.02.43

CRÉTEIL
BAKERIES

Caprices et Delices
5 rue Edouard Manet, Val-de-Marne 94000
Telephone: 01.43.39.20.20
Supervision: Beth Din of Paris

La Nougatine
20 Esplanade des Abîmes, Val-de-Marne 94000
Telephone: 01.49.56.98.56
Supervision: Beth Din of Paris

Les Jasmins de Tunis
C.C. Kennedy, Val-de-Marne 94000
Telephone: 01.43.77.50.66
Supervision: Beth Din of Paris

Quick Chaud
26 allée Parmentier, Val-de-Marne 94000
Telephone: 01.48.99.08.30
Supervision: Beth Din of Paris

Tov 'Mie
25 rue du Dr Paul Casalis, Val-de-Marne 94000
Telephone: 01.48.99.00.39
Supervision: Beth Din of Paris

BUTCHERS

Boucherie Patrick
2 rue Edouard Manet, Val-de-Marne 94000
Telephone: 01.43.39.29.64

La Charolaise Julien
Cte Commercial Kennedy, Loge 13 rue Gabriel Peri, Val-de-Marne 94000
Telephone: 01.43.39.20.43

MIKVAOT
Rue du 8 Mai 1945, Val-de-Marne 94000
Telephone: 01.43.77.01.70; 01.43.77.19.68

SYNAGOGUES
Orthodox
Consistorial Synagogue
rue du 8 Mai 1945, Val-de-Marne 94051
Telephone: 01.43.77.01.70; 01.43.39.05.20
Fax: 01.43.99.03.60
Email: templedesvosges@noos.fr
Web site: www.synadesvosges.com
Possibilities of "Shabbos meals".

ENGHIEN
MIKVAOT
47 rue de Malleville, Val-d'Oise 95880
Telephone: 01.34.17.37.11

SYNAGOGUES
Orthodox
47 rue de Malleville, Val-d'Oise 95880
Telephone: 01.34.12.42.34

FONTAINEBLEAU
SYNAGOGUES
Orthodox
38 rue Paul Seramy, Seine-et-Marne 77300
Telephone: 01.64.22.68.48

FONTENAY AUX ROSES
SYNAGOGUES
Orthodox
Centre Moise Meniane
17 av. Paul-Langevin, Hauts-de-Seine 92660
Telephone: 01.46.60.75.94

FONTENAY SOUS BOIS

MIKVAOT
Haya Mossia
177 rue des Moulins, Val-de-Marne 94120
Telephone: 01.48.77.53.90; 01.48.76.83.84

SYNAGOGUES
Orthodox
79 blvd de Verdun, Val-de-Marne 94120
Telephone: 01.48.77.38.67

GARGES-LES-GONESSE

BUTCHERS
Boucherie Berbeche
C C Pal de la Dame Blanche, Val-d'Oise 95140
Telephone: 01.39.86.42.06

Chez Harry
1 rue J B Corot, Val-d'Oise 95140
Telephone: 01.39.86.53.81

MIKVAOT
15 rue Corot, Val-d'Oise 95140
Telephone: 01.39.86.75.64

SYNAGOGUES
Orthodox
Maison Communautaire Chaare Ra'hamim
14 rue Corot, Val-d'Oise 95140
Telephone: 01.39.86.75.64

ISSY-LES-MOULINEAUX

SYNAGOGUES
Orthodox
72 blvd Gallieni, Hauts-de-Seine 92130
Telephone: 01.46.48.34.49

LA COURNEUVE

SYNAGOGUES
Orthodox
13 rue Saint-Just, Seine-Saint-Denis 93120
Telephone: 01.48.36.75.59

LA GARENNE-COLOMBES

SYNAGOGUES
Orthodox
Synagogue and Community Centre of
Courbevoie / La Garenne-Colombes
13 rue L.M. Nordmann, Hauts-de-Seine 92250
Telephone: 01.47.69.92.17

LA VARENNE ST-HILAIRE

SYNAGOGUES
Orthodox
10 bis avenue du chateau, Val-de-Marne 94210
Telephone: 01.42.83.28.75

LE BLANC MESNIL

SYNAGOGUES
Orthodox
65 rue Maxime-Gorki, Seine-Saint-Denis 93150
Telephone: 01.48.65.58.98

LE CHESNAY

MIKVAOT
39 rue de Versailles, Yvelines 78150
Telephone: 01.39.54.05.65; 01.39.07.19.19

LE KREMLIN-BICETRE

SYNAGOGUES
Orthodox
41-45 rue J.F. Kennedy, Val-de-Marne 94270
Telephone: 01.46.72.73.64

LE PERREUX NOGENT

SYNAGOGUES
Orthodox
Synagogue-Nogent/Le Perreux/Bry-Sur-Marne
165 bis av. du Gal-de-Gaulle, Val-de-Marne 94170
Telephone: 01.48.72.88.65

LE RAINCY

MIKVAOT
67 blvd du Midi, Seine-Saint-Denis 93340
Telephone: 01.43.81.06.61

SYNAGOGUES
Orthodox
Maison Communautaire
19 allée Chatrian, Seine-Saint-Denis 93340
Telephone: 01.43.02.06.11

LE VESINET

MIKVAOT
29 rue Henri Cloppet, Yvelines 78110
Telephone: 01.30.53.10.45; 01.30.71.12.26

SYNAGOGUES
Orthodox
Maison Communautaire
29 rue Henri-Cloppet, Yvelines 78110
Telephone: 01.30.53.10.45

LES LILAS

BUTCHERS
Boucherie Des Lilas
6 rue de la Republique, Seine-Saint-Denis 93260
Telephone: 01.43.63.89.15

LEVALLOIS PERRET
RESTAURANTS
Meat
Delicates Eden
102 rue Rivay, Hauts-de-Seine 92300
Telephone: 01.42.70.97.06
Supervision: Beth Din of Paris

SYNAGOGUES
Orthodox
Jewish School
63, rue Louis Rouquier 92300
Telephone: 01 47 57 11 15
Fax: 01 47 57 39 12
Email: accil@accil.org
Web site: www.accil.org
Opening hours: 7am to 8pm daily.

MAISONS ALFORT
MIKVAOT
92-94 rue Victor-Hugo, Val-de-Marne 94700
Telephone: 01.43.78.95.69

SYNAGOGUES
Orthodox
Synagogue
68 rue Victor Hugo 94700
Telephone: 01 43 78 95 69

MASSY
MIKVAOT
Allée Marcel-Cerdan 91300
Telephone: 01.42.37.48.24

SYNAGOGUES
Orthodox
2 allee Marcel Cerdan 91300
Telephone: 01.69.20.94.21

MEAUX
SYNAGOGUES
Orthodox
11 rue P. Barennes, Seine-et-Marne 77100
Telephone: 01.64.34.76.58

MELUN
SYNAGOGUES
Cnr. rues Branly & Michelet 77003
Telephone: 01.64.52.00.05

MEUDON-LA-FORET
MIKVAOT
Rue de la Synagogue, Hauts-de-Seine 92360
Telephone: 01.46.32.64.82; 01.46.01.01.32

SYNAGOGUES
Orthodox
Maison Communautaire
Rue de la Synagogue, Hauts-de-Seine 92360
Telephone: 01.48.53.48.27

MONTREUIL
BAKERIES
Korcarz
134 bis rue de Stalingrad, Seine-Saint-Denis 93100
Telephone: 01.48.58.33.45
Supervision: Beth Din of Paris/Chief Rabbi Mordechai Rottenberg
Le Relais Sucre
62 rue des Roches, Seine-Saint-Denis 93100
Telephone: 01.48.70.22.60
Supervision: Beth Din of Paris
Nat Cacher
21 rue Gabriel Péri, Seine-Saint-Denis 93100
Telephone: 01.48.58.05.25
Supervision: Beth Din of Paris

BUTCHERS
Andre Volailles
62 rue des Roches, Seine-Saint-Denis 93100
Telephone: 01.41.58.58.58
Boucherie Andre
64 rue des Roches, Seine-Saint-Denis 93100
Telephone: 01.41.58.58.58

MONTROUGE
MIKVAOT
Ismah-Israel
90 rue Gabriel-Péri, Hauts-de-Seine 92120
Telephone: 01.42.53.08.54

SYNAGOGUES
Orthodox
Centre Communautaire Regional Malakoff-Montrouge
90 rue Gabriel-Péri, Hauts-de-Seine 92120
Telephone: 01.46.32.64.82
Fax: 01.46.56.20.49

NEUILLY
BUTCHERS
Neuilly Cacher
2/6 rue de Chartres, Hauts-de-Seine 92200
Telephone: 01.47.45.06.06

GROCERIES
King David
14 rue Paul-Chatrousse, Hauts-de-Seine 92200
Telephone: 01.47.45.18.19

RESTAURANTS
Meat
14 rue Paul-Chatrousse, Hauts-de-Seine 92200
Telephone: 01.47.45.18.19
Supervision: Beth Din of Paris
Deliver. Hours: 8 am to 10 pm.

SYNAGOGUES
Orthodox
12 rue Ancelle, Hauts-de-Seine 92200
Telephone: 01.47.47.78.76
Fax: 01.47.47.54.79
Web site: www.synaneuilly.com

NOISY LE SEC
SYNAGOGUES
Orthodox
Beth Gabriel
2 rue de la Pierre Feuillère, Seine-Saint-Denis 93130
Telephone: 01.48.46.71.79

PANTIN
BUTCHERS
Levy Baroukh
5/7 rue Anatole France, Seine-Saint-Denis 93500
Telephone: 01.48.91.02.14

RESTAURANTS
Dairy
Chez Jacquy
24 rue du Pré-Saint-Gervais, Seine-Saint-Denis 93500
Telephone: 01.48.10.94.24
Supervision: Beth Din of Paris

SYNAGOGUES
Orthodox
8 rue Gambetta, Seine-Saint-Denis 93500

RIS-ORANGIS
SYNAGOGUES
Orthodox
1 rue Jean-Moulin, Essone 91130
Telephone: 01.69.43.07.83

ROISSY-EN-BRIE
MIKVAOT
rue Paul-Cézanne, Centre Commercial Bois
Montmartre, Seine-et-Marne 77680
Telephone: 01.60.28.34.65; 01.60.29.09.44

SYNAGOGUES
Orthodox
Maison Communautaire
1 rue Paul Cézanne, Centre Commercial Bois
Montmartre, Seine-et-Marne 77680
Telephone: 01.60.28.36.38

ROSNY-SOUS-BOIS
SYNAGOGUES
Orthodox
62-64 rue Lavoisier, Seine-Saint-Denis 93110
Telephone: 01.48.54.04.11
Fax: 01.69.43.07.83

SAINT GERMAIN
SYNAGOGUES
Liberal
Kehilat Gesher (Franco-American)
10 rue de Pologne 78100
Telephone: 01.39.21.97.19
Email: rabbenutom@compuserve.com

Orthodox
Synagogue
6 impasse Saint Leger 78103
Telephone: 01 34 51 26 60

SAINT-LEU-LA-FORET
MIKVAOT
2 rue Jules Vernes, Val-d'Oise 95320
Telephone: 01.39.95.96.90; 01.34.14.24.15

SYNAGOGUES
Orthodox
2 rue Jules Verne, Val-d'Oise 95320
Telephone: 01.39.95.96.90
Fax: 01.39.95.72.13

SAINT-OUEN-L'AUMÔNE
SYNAGOGUES
Orthodox
Maison Communautaire
9 rue de Chennevières, Val-d'Oise 95310
Telephone: 01.30.37.71.41

SARCELLES
BAKERIES
Louis D'or
90 av. Paul Valéry, Val-d'Oise 95200
Telephone: 01.39.90.25.45
Supervision: Beth Din of Paris

Natania
34 blvd Albert Camus, Val-d'Oise 95200
Telephone: 01.39.90.11.78
Supervision: Beth Din of Paris

Oh Delices
71 av. Paul Valéry, Val-d'Oise 95200
Telephone: 01.39.92.41.12
Supervision: Beth Din of Paris

Zazou
C.C. les Flanades, Val-d'Oise 95200
Telephone: 01.34.19.08.11
Supervision: Beth Din of Paris

BUTCHERS
Boucherie Du Coin
60 blvd Albert Camus, Val-d'Oise 95200
Telephone: 01.39.90.53.02
Hazout
5 av. Paul Valery, Val-d'Oise 95200
Telephone: 01.39.90.72.95

MIKVAOT
Mayanot Rachel
14 av. Ch.-Péguy, Val-d'Oise 95200
Telephone: 01.39.90.40.17
Postal address: c/o 1 A C 15 av. de l'Escouvrier 95200

RESTAURANTS
Dairy
Marina
103 av. Paul-Valéry, Val-d'Oise 95200
Telephone: 01.34.19.23.51
Supervision: Beth Din of Paris

Meat
Berbeche Burger
13 av. Edouard-Branly, Val-d'Oise 95200
Telephone: 01.34.19.12.02
Supervision: Beth Din of Paris

SYNAGOGUES
Orthodox
Maison Communautaire
74 av. Paul-Valéry, Val-d'Oise 95200
Telephone: 01.39.90.59.59
Mikva on premises.

SARTROUVILLE
SYNAGOGUES
Orthodox
Synagogue Rabbi Shimon bar Yohai et Rabbi Meir Baal Hannes
1 rue de Stalingrad, Yvelines 78500
Telephone: 01.39.15.22.57

SAVIGNY SUR ORGE
MIKVAOT
1 av. de l'Armée-Leclerc, Essonne 91600
Telephone: 01.69.24.48.25; 01.69.96.30.90

SYNAGOGUES
Orthodox
1 av. de l'Armee Leclerc, Essonne 91600
Telephone: 01.69.96.30.90

SEVRAN
MIKVAOT
25 bis du Dr Roux, Seine-Saint-Denis 93270
Telephone: 01.43.84.25.40
Mikva Kelim.

SYNAGOGUES
Orthodox
Synagogue Mayan-Thora
25 bis rue du Dr Roux, BP. 111, Seine-Saint-Denis 93270
Telephone: 01.43.84.25.40

STAINS
SYNAGOGUES
Orthodox
8 rue Lamartine (face n°2), Clos St-Lazare, Seine-Saint-Denis 93240
Telephone: 01.48.21.04.12
Provisional address: 8 av. Louis Bordes (Ancien Conservatoire Municipal).

THIAIS
COMMUNITY ORGANISATIONS
Community Centre Choisy-Orly-Thiais
Voie du Four, 128 av. du Marechal de Lattre de Tassigny, Val-de-Marne 94320
Telephone: 01.48.92.68.68
Fax: 01.48.92.72.82

TRAPPES
SYNAGOGUES
Orthodox
7 rue du Port-Royal, Yvelines 78190
Telephone: 01.30.62.40.43

VERSAILLES
SYNAGOGUES
10 rue Albert-Joly, Yvelines 78000
Telephone: 01.39.07.19.19
Fax: 01.39.50.96.34
Mikva on premises.

VILLEJUIF
SYNAGOGUES
Orthodox
106 av. de Gournay, Val-de-Marne 94800
Telephone: 01.46.78.76.53

VILLENEUVE-LA-GARENNE
MIKVAOT
42-44 rue du Fond-de-la Noue, Hauts-de-Seine 92390
Telephone: 01.47.94.89.98

SYNAGOGUES
Orthodox
Maison Communautaire
44 rue du Fond-de-la-Noue, Hauts-de-Seine 92390
Telephone: 01.47.94.89.98

VILLIERS SUR MARNE
SYNAGOGUES
Orthodox
30 rue Léon-Douer, B.P. 15, Val-de-Marne 94350
Telephone: 01.49.30.01.47
Fax: 01.49.30.85.40

VILLIERS-LE-BEL-GONESSE
MIKVAOT
1 rue Léon Blum, Val-d'Oise 95400
Telephone: 01.39.94.45.51; 01.34.19.64.48

SYNAGOGUES
Orthodox
1 rue Léon-Blum, Val-d'Oise 95400
Telephone: 01.39.94.30.49; 01.39.94.94.89

VINCENNES
BUTCHERS
Boucherie Des Levy
32 rue Raymond du Temple, Val-de-Marne 94300
Telephone: 01.43.74.94.18
Boucherie Hayache
146 av. de Paris, Val-de-Marne 94300
Telephone: 01.43.28.16.04

SYNAGOGUES
Orthodox
Synagogue Achkenaze
30 rue Céline-Robert, Vincennes 94300
Telephone: 01.43.28.82.83
Synagogue Sepharade
30 rue Céline-Robert, Val-de-Marne 94300
Telephone: 01.47.55.65.07

VITRY-SUR-SEINE
SYNAGOGUES
Orthodox
133-135 av. Rouget-de-l'Isle, Val-de-Marne 94400
Telephone: 01.46.80.76.54; 01.45.73.06.58
Fax: 01.45.73.94.01

YERRES
MIKVAOT
Beth Rivkah
43/49 rue R. Poincare, Essone 91330
Telephone: 01.69.49.62.74; 01.69.49.62.62
Fax: 01.69.79.27.70
Email: beth-rivkah@wanados.fr

South East
AIX-EN-PROVENCE
BUTCHERS
Zouaghi
7 rue de Sevigne, Bouches du Rhône 13100
Telephone: 04.42.59.93.94
Supervision: Grand Rabbinate of Marseille

SYNAGOGUES
5 rue de Jerusalem 13100
Telephone: 04.42.26.69.39

AIX-LES-BAINS
BUTCHERS
Berdah
29 Av. de Tresserve 73100
Telephone: 04.79.61.44.11

HOTELS
Kosher
Auberge de La Baye
Chemin du Tir-Aux-Pigeons, Savoie 73100
Telephone: 04.79.35.69.42
Strictly kosher.

MIKVAOT
Pavillon Salvador
rue du President Roosevelt 73100
Telephone: 04.79.35.38.08

SYNAGOGUES
Synagogues
Rue Paul Bonna 73100
Telephone: 04.79.35.28.08
Mikva on premises

ANNECY
SYNAGOGUES
18 rue de Narvik 74000
Telephone: 04.50.67.69.37

ANNEMASSE
BUTCHERS
Yarden
59 av. de la Liberation, Gaillard 74100
Telephone: 04.50.92.64.05

SYNAGOGUES
Orthodox
8 rue du Docteur Coquart 74100

ANTIBES-JUAN-LES-PINS
BUTCHERS
Berreche
12 av. Courbet 6160
Telephone: 04.93.67.16.77

Le Kineret
25 av. D l'Esterel 6160
Telephone: 04.92.93.16.01
Fax: 04.93.88.14.76

RESTAURANTS
Maxime
6 Blvd de la Pinede 6160
Telephone: 04.92.93.99.40

SYNAGOGUES
Villa La Monada, 30 Chemin des Sables 6160
Telephone: 04.93.61.59.34

AVIGNON
The first archaeological evidence of a Jewish presence dates from the fourth century. For years the Avignon Jewish population flourished and there were many Jewish scholars and writers who were born and lived there. The first printing venture in Hebrew was attempted in Avignon in 1446 before Gutenberg's success in 1450.

BUTCHERS
Cachere Royale
15 rue Chapeau Rouge 84000
Telephone: 04.90.82.47.50
Supervision: Grand Rabbinate of Marseille

MIKVAOT
Vaucluse
Telephone: 04.90.86.30.30
Mme Cohen Zardi

SYNAGOGUES
Orthodox
2 Place de Jerusalem 84000
Telephone: 04.90.85.21.24
Fax: 04.90.85.21.24
This circular synagogue was built in 1847 on the site of a 13th-century synagogue.

BEZIERS
MIKVAOT
19 place Pierre-Semard
Mme Smolinski Tel: 04.67.28.44.24

SYNAGOGUES
19 Place Pierre-Semard 34500
Telephone: 04.67.28.75.98
Operates a Kosher Food Store.

TOURIST SITES
Ghetto
To visit the old Ghetto (Beziers was known as "the Little Jerusalem"); contact Mr Benyacar (04 67 31 14 23).

CALUIRE- ET- CUIRE
SYNAGOGUES
107 Av. Fleming 69300
Telephone: 04.78.23.12.37

CANNES
BUTCHERS
Cannes Casher
9 rue Marceau 6400
Telephone: 04.93.39.85.08
Chez Sylvie
15 rue Mal. Joffre 6400
Telephone: 04.93.39.57.92

COMMUNITY ORGANISATIONS
20 Boulevard d'Alsace 6400
Telephone: 04.93.38.16.54
Fax: 04.93.68.92.81

GROCERIES
La Emounah
32 rue de Mimont 6400
Near the main synagogue.

Monoprix
Rue Marechal Fox
Has a comprehensive kosher section.

MIKVAOT
20 boulevard d'Alsace
Telephone: 04.93.99.79.03
Contact: Mme Annie Rebibo

RESTAURANTS
Dairy
Le Dany's
18 Rue Marechal Joffre
Telephone: 04.92.59.35.50
Pizza Dick
7 bis, rue de Mimont 6400
Telephone: 04.92.59.10.82

Meat
Le Tovel
3 rue du Dr Gerard Monod 6400
Telephone: 04.93.39.36.25

SYNAGOGUES
Chabad Lubavitch
22 Rue Commandant Vidal 6400
Telephone: 04.92.98.67.51
Fax: 04.92.98.81.29
Email: canorhabad@aol.com
Web site: www.jewish-cannes.com
Sephardi
20 Boulevard d'Alsace 6400
Telephone: 04.93.38.16.54
Fax: 04.93.68.92.81

CARPENTRAS

Jews first settled in Carpentras in the 12th century. In 1343 permission was granted for the erection of a synagogue in which one of the women were situated in the basement. A "rabbi of the women" was employed to guide them through the service; the only direct contact being a small window.

SYNAGOGUES
Place de la Mairie
Telephone: 04.90.63.39.97
The synagogue originally built in 1367and the oldest in France was reconstructed in 1741-43 and again in 1959. The French government has declared it a historic site.

TOURIST SITES
Cathedral St Siffrein
The 15th-century door on the south side is where Jews had to go on their way to conversion and is known as "Porte des Juifs".

CAVAILLON

The Jews originally lived in Rue Hebraique. The present synagogue, classified as a historical monument, was built in 1772 and incorporates parts of the 16th-century former building.

MUSEUMS
Musee Judeo-Comatdin
Telephone: 04.90.76.00.34
The museum, a part of the synagogue, contains items dating back to the 14th century.

SYNAGOGUES
Telephone: 04.90.76.00.34
Fax: 04.90.71.47.06

CLERMONT-FERRAND

SYNAGOGUES
6 rue Blatin 63000
Telephone: 04.73.93.36.59

EVIAN

SYNAGOGUES
Adjacent to 1 av. des Grottes, 74502
Telephone: 04.50.75.15.63

EZE-VILLAGE

HOTELS
Hotel les Terrases d'Eze
Route de la Turbie 6360
Telephone: 04.92.41.55.55
Fax: 04.92.41.55.10
Supervision: Nice Beth Din.

FREJUS

SYNAGOGUES
Orthodox
Rue de Progres, Frejus-Plage 83600
Telephone: 04.94.52.06.87

GRENOBLE

BUTCHERS
C. Cohen
19 rue de Turenne 38000
Telephone: 04.76.46.48.14

GROCERIES
Aux Delices du Soleil
49 rue Thiers 38000
Telephone: 04.76.46.19.60
Ghnassia
15 place Gustave Rivet 38000
Telephone: 04.76.87.80.90

MEDIA
Radio
Radio Kol Hachalom 100 FM
BP 342 - 38013, Isère 38000
Telephone: 04.76.87.21.22
Fax: 04.76.47.58.31
Email: rkh@rkhfm.com
Web site: www.rkhfm.com
24 hours a day broadcasting.

SYNAGOGUES
Rachi
11 rue Maginot, Isère 38000
Telephone: 04.76.87.02.80
Fax: 04.76.87.27.14
Email: rabbin38@aol.com
Mikva at same address.

Synagogue and Community Centre
4 rue des Bains, Isère 38000
Telephone: 04.76.46.15.14

HYERES

SYNAGOGUES
Chemin de la Ritorte 83400
Telephone: 04.94.65.31.97

IZIEU

MUSEUMS
The Izieu Children's Home
Bouches du Rhône 1300
Telephone: recording 04.79.87.20.00; booking 04.79.87.20.08
Fax: 04.79.87.25.01
Email: izieu@alma.fr
Web site: www.izieu.alma.fr
The Izieu Children's Memorial Museum is dedicated to the memory of forty-four children and their guardians, taken away on 6 April 1944 by the Gestapo under the command of Klaus Barbie. The Museum's mission is to defend dignity, justice and to contribute to the fight against all forms of intolerance. Two buildings may be visited: the House takes the visitors back to the everyday life of the children's home, the Barn presents the historical background through permanent and temporary exhibitions. Meetings, conferences and discussions are organized throughout the year.

LA CIOTAT
SYNAGOGUES
1 Square de Verdun 13600
Telephone: 04.42.71.92.56
Services, Friday 7pm (Winter), 7.30pm (Summer).
Saturday 9am.

LA SEYNE-SUR-MER
BUTCHERS
Elie Benamou
17 rue Batistin-Paul 83500
Telephone: 04.94.94.38.60

SYNAGOGUES
5 rue Chevalier-de-la-Barre 83501
Telephone: 04.94.94.40.28

LYONS
BAKERIES
Jo Delice
44, rue Rachais
Telephone: 04.78.69.22.98

Nassy Gourmand
41, rue A Boutin, Villeurbanne 69100
Telephone: 04.78.85.72.88

BUTCHERS
William (Mr Dahan)
50, rue Tete d'Or 69006
Telephone: 04.78.24.10.10

Ittah David
267, av. Berthelot 69008
Telephone: 04.78.00.82,35

COMMUNITY ORGANISATIONS
Consistoire Israelite de Lyon
13 Quai Tilsitt 69002
Telephone: 04.78.37.13.43
Fax: 04.78.38.26.57
Email: acil@free.fr

Consistoire Israelite Sepharade de Lyon
Yaacov Molho Community Centre, 317 Rue
Duguesclin 69007
Telephone: 04.78.58.18.74
Fax: 04.78.58.17.49

MEDIA
CIV News
4 rue Malherbe, Villeurbanne 69100
Telephone: 04.78.84.04.32

Hachaar
18 rue St. Mathieu 69008
Telephone: 04.78.00.72.50

La Voix Sepharade
317 rue Duguesclin 69007
Telephone: 04.78.58.18.74

MIKVAOT
Chaare Tsedek (N. African)
18 rue St.-Mathieu 69008
Telephone: 04.78.00.72.50

Rav Hida (N. African)
La Sauvegarde, La Duchere 69009
Telephone: 04.78.35.14.44

Orah Haim
17 rue Albert-Thomas, St-Fons 69190
Telephone: 04.78.67.39.78

RELIGIOUS ORGANISATIONS
Beth Din
34 rue d'Armenie, 3e
Telephone: 04.78.62.97.63
Fax: 04.78.95.09.47

RESTAURANTS
Dairy
Le Pinocchio
5 Rue A. Boutin, Villeurbanne 69100
Telephone: 04.78.68.62.95

Lippo
9 Rue Michel Servet, Villeurbanne 69100
Telephone: 04.78.84.15.00

Pizza Cach
13 Rue d'Inkerman, Villeurbanne 69100
Telephone: 04.72.74.44.98

Prestopizza
61 Rue Greuze, Villeurbanne 69100
Telephone: 04.78.68.08.41

Meat
Croq Sandwiches
32 Crs Emile-Zola, Villeurbanne 69100
Telephone: 04.78.84.16.07

La Palmeraie
27 Rue des charmettes, Villeurbanne 69100
Telephone: 04.78.24.37.03

La Petite Maison
35, rue P. Corneille 69006
Telephone: 04.78.24.99.43

Le Belvedere
14, rue Jean-Jaures, Villeurbanne 69100
Telephone: 04.78.54.72.31

Lippmann Henry
4 rue Tony Tollet, Villeurbanne 69002
Telephone: 04.78.42.49.82
Supervision: Lyon Beth Din

Mac David
28 rue Michel Servet, Villeurbanne 69100
Telephone: 04.78.03.31.62

SYNAGOGUES
Orthodox
Chaare Tsedek
18 rue Saint Mathieu (8e) (T.T.)
Telephone: 04 78 00 72 50
Fax: 04 78 75 89 74

Grande Synagogue
13 qui Tilsitt
Telephone: 04.78.37.13.43
Fax: 04.78.38.26.57
Email: acil@free.fr

Rav Hida
501 Sauvegarde La Duchere (9e) (T.T.)
Telephone: 04 78 35 14 44
Fax: 04 78 64 95 90

Sephardi
Neveh Chalom
13 rue Duguesclin 69007
Telephone: 04.78.58.18.74
Fax: 04.78.58.17.49

MACON
SYNAGOGUES
32 rue des Minimes 71000

MARIGNANE
SYNAGOGUES
9 rue Pilote-Larbonne 13700

MARSEILLES
BAKERIES
Atteia et Fils
19 Place Guillardet, Bouches du Rhône 13013
Telephone: 04.91.66.33.28
Supervision: Grand Rabbinate of Marseille

Avyel Cash
28 rue St Suffren, Bouches du Rhône 13006
Telephone: 04.91.87.95.25
Supervision: Grand Rabbinate of Marseille

Cacher Food
31 blvd Barry, Bouches du Rhône 13013
Telephone: 04.91.70.13.43
Supervision: Grand Rabbinate of Marseille

Erets
205 rue de Rome, Bouches du Rhône 13006
Telephone: 04.91.92.88.73
Supervision: Grand Rabbinate of Marseille

Le Parve
72 av. Alphonse Daudet, Bouches du Rhône 13013
Telephone: 04.91.66.95.16
Supervision: Grand Rabbinate of Marseille

BUTCHERS
Chez David
9 blvd G. Ganay, Bouches du Rhône 13009
Telephone: 04.91.75.04.56
Supervision: Grand Rabbinate of Marseille

Jamap
13 place Mignard, Bouches du Rhône 13009
Telephone: 04.91.71.11.70
Supervision: Grand Rabbinate of Marseille

Sebane
59 rue Alphonse Daudet, Bouches du Rhône 13013
Telephone: 04.91.66.98.76
Supervision: Grand Rabbinate of Marseille

Zennou Raphael
20 marché Capucin, Bouches du Rhône 13001
Telephone: 04.91.54.02.54
Supervision: Grand Rabbinate of Marseille

EMBASSY
Consul General of Israel
146 rue Paradis, Bouches du Rhône 13006
Telephone: 04.91.53.39.87
Fax: 04.91.53.39.94

GROCERIES
Av bon gout
28 rue St Suffren, Bouches du Rhône 13006
Telephone: 04.91.37.95.25

Delicash
94 blvd Barry, Bouches du Rhône 13013
Telephone: 04.91.06.39.04

Emmanuel
93 avenue Clot Bey, Bouches du Rhône 13008
Telephone: 04.91.77.46.08

King Kasher
25 rue François Mauriac, Bouches du Rhône 13010
Telephone: 04.91.80.00.01

Raphael Cash
299 avenue de Mazargues, Bouches du Rhône 13009
Telephone: 04.91.76.44.13

MEDIA
Radio
Radio JM
4, impasse Dragon 13006
Telephone: 04.91.37.78.78

MEMORIAL
Memorial of the Death Camps
Quai de la Tourette 13002
Telephone: 04.91.90.73.15

MIKVAOT
Mikve Esther
47 rue St Suffren 13006
Telephone: 04.91.81.45.15
There are some eight mikvaot in Marseilles. This one is close to the main synagogue. The Consistoire will provide details of others.

RELIGIOUS ORGANISATIONS
Consistoire de Marseille
117 rue de Breteuil, Bouches du Rhône 13006
Telephone: 04.91.37.49.64; 04.91.81.13.57
Fax: 04.91.37.83.90
Email: consistoire.israelile@wanadoo.fr

RESTAURANTS
Dairy
Pizzeria Gan Eden
225, Paul Claudel 13010
Telephone: 04.91.75.12.72

Meat
Erets
205, rue de Rome, Bouches du Rhône 13006
Telephone: 04.91.92.88.73
Supervision: Grand Rabbinate of Marseille

Nathania
17 rue du Village, Bouches du Rhône 13006
Telephone: 04.91.42.05.31
Supervision: Grand Rabbinate of Marseille

SYNAGOGUES
Merlan
La Cerisaie, Batiment G1 13014
Telephone: 04.91.98.53.92

Ohel Yaakov
20 Chemin Ste-Marthe 13014
Telephone: 04.91.62.70.42

Ashkenazi
8 Impasse Dragon 13006

Reform
337 Rue Paradis Marseille 13008
Telephone: 04.91.37.54.31
Fax: 04.91.37.54.31
Email: rabbi.liebermann@voila.fr

Sephardi
Bar Yohai
171 rue Abbe-de-l'Epee 13005
Telephone: 04.91.42.38.19

Beth Simha
31 av. Des Olives 13013
Telephone: 04.91.70.05.45

Main Synagogue
117 rue Breteuil 13006
Telephone: 04.91.37.49.64
Fax: 04.91.37.83.89

Merkaz Netivot Chalom
27 blvd Bonifay 13004
Telephone: 04.91.89.40.62
There are over forty more synagogues in Marseilles. The Consistoire de Marseilles will supply details if required.

MENTON
SYNAGOGUES
Centre Altyner, 106 Cours du Centenaire 6500
Telephone: 04.93.35.28.29

MONTPELLIER
BUTCHERS
Eretz
41 rue de Lunaret 34000
Telephone: (4) 04.67.72.67.94

COMMUNITY ORGANISATIONS
Centre Communautaire et Cultural Juif
500 blvd d'Antigone 34000
Telephone: (4) 04.67.15.08.76

GROCERIES
A.C.P.C.
45 rue Proudhon
Telephone: (4) 04.67.02.10.99

SYNAGOGUES
Ben-Zakai
7 rue General-Laffon 34000
Telephone: (4) 04.67.92.92.07

Mazal Tov
18 rue Ferdinand-Fabre 34000
Telephone: (4) 04.67.79.09.82

NICE
The first reference to Jews in Nice was in 1342. The first cemetery was established in 1408 and the synagogue in 1492.

The main synagogue, built in 1886 is worth a visit. Nice is home to the Chagall Museum which contains a permanent collection of his work including a number of stained glass mosaics.

BOOKSELLERS
Librairie Tanya
25 rue Pertinax 6000
Telephone: 04.93.80.21.74
Fax: 04.93.13.87.90
Email: librairie.tanya@wanadoo.fr

BUTCHERS
K'Gel
18, rue Dante 6000
Telephone: 04.93.86.33.01

GROCERIES
Mickael
37 Rue Dabray 6000
Telephone: 04.93.88.81.23

Riviera Cacher
11 Avenue Villermont 6000
Telephone: 04.93.92.92.00

KASHRUT INFORMATION
Telephone: 04.93.85.82.06
A list of kosher butchers and bakers can be obtained from the Chief Rabbi.

KOSHER FOOD
Galleries Lafayette
Has a kosher food section.

MIKVAOT
22 rue Michelet 6100
Telephone: 04.93.51.89.80

MUSEUMS
Chagall Museum
Avenue Docteur Menard 6000
Telephone: 04.93.53.87.20
Fax: 04.93.53.87.39
The Museum presents to the public a permanent exhibition of the largest collection existing of the works of Marc Chagall

RELIGIOUS ORGANISATIONS
Centre Consistorial
22 rue Michelet 6100
Telephone: 04.93.51.89.80
Publishes an annual calendar and guide to Nice and district.

Regional Chief Rabbinate of Nice, Cote d'Azur and Corsica
1 rue Voltaire 6000
Telephone: 04.93.85.82.06

RESTAURANTS
Dairy
Le Leviathan
1 ave Georges Clemenceau
Telephone: 04.93.87.22.64

Meat
Le Dauphin Bleu
22, av. Malaussena 6000
Telephone: 04.93.82.98.74

L'Alliance
13, rue Andrioli 6000
Telephone: 04.93.44.11.94

SYNAGOGUES
Main Synagogue
7, rue Gustave-Deloye 6000
Telephone: 04.93.92.11.38

Ashkenazi
Synagogue Achkenaze
1, rue Blacas
Telephone: 04 93 62 38 68

NIMES
COMMUNITY ORGANISATIONS
5 rue d'Angouleme 30000
Telephone: 04.66.26.19.51

SYNAGOGUES
40 rue Roussy 30000
Telephone: 04.66.29.51.81
Mikva on premises.

PERPIGNAN
BUTCHERS
Gilbert Sabbah
3 rue P.-Rameil 66000
Telephone: 04.68.35.41.23
Fax: 04.68.51.09.83

SYNAGOGUES
54 rue Francois Arago 66000
Telephone: 04.68.34.75.81
Fax: 04.68.51.13.31

ROANNE
SYNAGOGUES
9 rue Beaulieu 42300
Telephone: 04.77.71.51.56

SAINT-ETIENNE
SYNAGOGUES
34 rue d'Arcole 42000
Telephone: 04.77.33.56.31

SAINT-FONS
SYNAGOGUES
17 av. Albert-Thomas 69190
Telephone: 04.78.67.39.78

SAINT-LAURENT-DU-VAR
SYNAGOGUES
Villa 'Le Petit Clos', 35 Av. des Oliviers 6700

TOULON
BUTCHERS
Abecassis
8 rue Vincent Courdouan, Var 83000
Telephone: 04.94.97.39.86
Supervision: Grand Rabbinate of Marseille

Fennech
15 av. Colbert, Var 83000
Telephone: 04.94.92.70.39
Supervision: Grand Rabbinate of Marseille

SYNAGOGUES
184 av. Lazare Carnot 83050
Telephone: 04.94.92.61.05
Mikva on premises.

VALENCE
SYNAGOGUES
1 place du Colombier 26000
Telephone: 04.75.43.34.43

VENISSIEUX
SYNAGOGUES
Synagogue
10 av. de la Division-Leclerc 69200
Telephone: 04.78.70.69.85

VICHY
SYNAGOGUES
2 bis rue du Marechal Foch 3200
Telephone: 04.70.59.82.83

South West
AGEN
SYNAGOGUES
52 rue Montesquieu 47000
Telephone: 05.53.66.24.20

TOURIST SITES
rue des Juifs 47000
Site of the old ghetto of the 15th century.

Museum of the Deportation
rue Montesquieu 47000

ARCACHON
SYNAGOGUES
Orthodox
36 av Gambetta
Telephone: 05.56.83.63.40
Fax: 05.56.83.63.40

BAYONNE
SYNAGOGUES
35 rue Maubec 64100
Telephone: (5) 05.59.55.03.95

BORDEAUX
BAKERIES
Boucherie Peres
64 rue Bouquiere
Telephone: 05 56 52 88 18

COMMUNITY ORGANISATIONS
Centre Yavneh
11 rue Poquelin Moliere 330
Telephone: 05.56.52.62.69
Fax: 05.56.51.71.95
Meals are available on Shabbat and other occasions.

MIKVAOT
213 rue Ste. Catherine 33000
Telephone: 05.56.91.79.39

RESTAURANTS
Mazal Tov
137 cours Victor Hugo 33000
Telephone: 05.56.52.37.03

SYNAGOGUES
8 rue du Grand-Rabbin-Joseph-Cohen 33000
Telephone: 05.56.91.79.39
Fax: 05.56.94.05.12

LA ROCHELLE
CONTACT INFORMATION
Pierre Guedj
20 rue Chef de Ville 17000
Telephone: 05.46.67.38.91
Fax: 05.46.41.24.68

SYNAGOGUES
Orthodox
Centre Communautaire
M.C.I. 40 cours des Dames 17000
Telephone: 05 46 41 17 66

LIBOURNE
SYNAGOGUES
33 rue Lamothe 33500

LIMOGES
SYNAGOGUES
25-27 rue Pierre-Leroux 87000
Telephone: 05.55.77.47.26

MONTAUBAN
SYNAGOGUES
12 rue St-Claire 82000
Telephone: 05.63.03.01.37

PAU
SYNAGOGUES
8 rue des Trois-Freres-Bernadac 64000
Telephone: 05.59.62.37.85

PÉRIGVEUX
SYNAGOGUES
13 rue Paul-Louis-Courrier 24000
Telephone: 05.53.53.22.52

POITIERS
SYNAGOGUES
Synagogue
1 rue Guynemer 86000

TOULOUSE

BUTCHERS
Cacherout Diffusion
37 blvd Carnot 31000
Telephone: 05.61.23.07.59

Lasry
8 rue Matabiau 31000
Telephone: 05.61.62.65.28

Maalem
7 rue des Chalets 31000
Telephone: 05.61.63.77.39

COMMUNITY ORGANISATIONS
Community Centre
2 place Riquet 31000
Telephone: 05.61.23.36.54

GROCERIES
Novogel
14 rue Edmund Guyaux 31200
Telephone: 05.61.57.03.19

MIKVAOT
13 rue Francisque Sarcey 31000
Telephone: 05.61.48.89.84

RELIGIOUS ORGANISATIONS
Grand Rabbinat du Toulouse et des Pays de la Garonne - A.C.I.T.
2 place Riquet 31000
Telephone: 05.62.73.46.46
Fax: 05.62.73.46.47

RESTAURANTS
Community Centre
2 place Riquet 31000
Telephone: 05.62.73.56.56

SYNAGOGUES
Chaare Emeth
35 rue Rembrandt 31000
Telephone: 05.61.40.03.88

Ashkenazi
Adat Yechouroun
3 rue Jules-Chalande 31000
Telephone: 05.61.62.30.19
Fax: 05.61.62.86.79

Orthodox
Hekhal David
2, place Riquet 31000
Telephone: 05 62 76 46 46

Sephardi
Palaprat
2 rue Palaprat 31000
Telephone: 05.61.21.69.56

Overseas Region

CORSICA

CONTACT INFORMATION
Jo Michel Reis
La Grande Corniche, Routes des Sanguinaires, Ajaccio
Telephone: 9521-5752.
There are between ten and fifteen families in the town.

SYNAGOGUES
3 rue du Castagno Bastia, Bastia 20200
Services Shabbat morning and festivals.

Overseas Territories

GUADELOUPE

SYNAGOGUES
Bas du Fort, Gosier, Lot 1
Telephone: 90.99.09
The synagogue, community centre and restaurant/kosher store are all located here.

MARTINIQUE

SYNAGOGUES
Kenafe Haarets
12 Anse Gouraud, Schoeler, Fort-de-France 97233
Telephone: 61.71.36
Fax: 61.66.71
A community centre is also located here, which supplies kosher food, plus a kosher meat restaurant.

RÉUNION

CONTACT INFORMATION
Leon Benhamou
Telephone: 29.05.45

SYNAGOGUES
Communauté Juive de la Réunion
8 rue de l'Est, St-Denis 97400
Telephone: 23.78.33
High Holy Day services and communal seder held here.

TAHITI

The first known Jew in Tahiti was Alexander Salmon, the son of a Rabbi from Hastings (England), who arrived in 1841 and later married the Queen's sister. No community developed however until the 1960s when refugees came from Algeria.

SYNAGOGUES
Synagogue
Rue Morenhouy, Quartier Fariipti, Papette
Telephone: 41.03.92
Fax: 41.03.92
Email: Acispo@mail.pf

GEORGIA

Georgia has had a very long history of Jewish settlement, dating back to two centuries before the destruction of the Second Temple, if the archaeological findings are correct. These earliest Jewish communities may have descended from the Babylonian exiles. Like the Jews in the other Caucasus regions (Armenia and Azerbaijan) they are known as 'mountain Jews'.

Synagogues are found in major towns, there is a school in Tbilisi (the capital) and there are some newsletters. It is worth noting that the non-Jewish population has traditionally been far less anti-semitic than the populations of some other ex-Soviet republics.

GMT +4 hours
Country calling code: (+995)
Total population: 5,434,000
Jewish population: 9,000
Emergency telephone: (Police – 02) (Fire – 01)
(Ambulance – 03)
Electricity voltage: (Electricity voltage – 220)

AKHALTSIKHE
SYNAGOGUES
109 Guramishvili Street

BATUMI
SYNAGOGUES
6 9th March Street

GORI
SYNAGOGUES
Chelyuskin Street

KUTAISI
SYNAGOGUES
12 Gapanove Street
Near the main square.

ONNI
SYNAGOGUES
Baazova Street

POTI
SYNAGOGUES
23 Ninoshivili
Tskhakaya Street

SUKHUMI
SYNAGOGUES
56 Karl Marx Street

SURAMI
SYNAGOGUES
Internatsionalaya Street

TBILISI
COMMUNITY ORGANISATIONS
Jews of Georgia Assoc.
Tsarity Tamari Street 8 380012
Telephone: (32) 234-1057

SYNAGOGUES
Ashkenazi
65 Kozhevenny Lane

Sephardi
45-47 Leselidze Street

TSHKINVALI
SYNAGOGUES
Isapov Street

TSKHAKAYA
SYNAGOGUES
Mir Street

VANI
SYNAGOGUES
4 Kaikavadze Street

GERMANY

It may be a surprise to many that Germany comes immediately after France and the UK in the population table of Western European Jews. German Jews have contributed much to the culture of European Jews in general since their arrival in what is now Germany in the fourth century. The massive Jewish presence in Poland and other east European states stemmed from German Jews escaping persecution in the late Middle Ages. They took the early Medieval German language with them, which formed Yiddish, the old lingua franca of European Jews.

The Jews who stayed behind in Germany contributed much towards Jewish and German culture, with the Reform movement starting in nineteenth-century Germany, and Heine and Mendelssohn contributing to German poetry and music respectively. The Enlightenment and modern Orthodoxy also began in Germany.

The rise of Nazism destroyed the belief that the German Jews were more German than Jewish. Many managed to escape before 1939, but 180,000 were killed in the Holocaust (of the 503,000 who lived in Germany when Hitler came to power). Following the events of 1933-45, it seems incredible that any Jew should want to live in Germany again. However, the community began to re-form, mainly with immigrants from eastern Europe, especially Russia. Now there are again Jewish shops in Berlin, and kosher food is once more available. There are many old synagogues which have been restored, and several concentration camps have been kept as monuments to history. There is also a great interest in Jewish matters among some of the non-Jewish younger generation.

Visitors to Berlin should try to visit the new Jewish Museum (officially opened in September 2001). It covers the history of German Jewry through the Middle Ages and up to the present. It revives the tradition of an earlier museum opened in 1933 before the Nazis came to power.

GMT +1 hour
Country calling code: (+49)
Total population: 82,071,000
Jewish population: 100,000
Emergency telephone: (Police – 110) (Fire – 112) (Ambulance – 112)
Electricity voltage: (Electricity voltage – 220)

AACHEN
COMMUNITY ORGANISATIONS
Bundesverband Jüdischer Studenten in Deutschland
Oppenhoffallee 50 52066
Telephone: (241) 75998

ALSENZ
SITE
Synagogue
Kirchberg 1 67821
Telephone: (636) 23149
Fax: (636) 23149
Restored eighteenth-century synagogue.

ANDERNACH
TOURIST SITES
Rhine Valley
This Rhine Valley town contains an early fourteenth-century mikva. Key obtainable from the Town Hall.

ANNWEILER
TOURIST SITES
Telephone: (623) 53333
The oldest cemetery in the Palatinate dating from the 16th century.

BAD NAUHEIM
RESTAURANTS
Judische Gemeinde
Karlstr. 34 61231
Telephone: (6032) 5605 or 0171-9509084
Fax: (6032) 938956
In the Jewish Community Centre. Entry for the restaurant is from Friedenstrasse.

SYNAGOGUES
Karlstr. 34 61231
Telephone: (6032) 5605; 0171-9509084
Fax: (6032) 5605
Synagogue is in the Jewish Community Centre.

BADEN-BADEN
SYNAGOGUES
Conservative
Werderstr. 2 76530
Telephone: (722) 21 39 10 21
Fax: (722) 21 39 10 24
Email: info@ikg-bad-bad.de

BAMBERG
COMMUNITY ORGANISATIONS
Community Centre
Willy-Lessing-Str. 7 96047
Telephone: (951) 23267

BAYREUTH
COMMUNITY ORGANISATIONS
Munzgasse 2 95444
Telephone: (921) 65407

BERLIN
Jewish life is beginning to grow again in Berlin, formerly an important centre for German Jewry. There are many sites which testify to the tragedy that befell the community before and during the war, such as the ruined Oranienburgerstrasse Synagogue, which has been turned into a Jewish centre. The site of the Wannsee Conference, to the south west of the city, (where the Holocaust was officially planned), has been turned into a museum.

BAKERIES
Backerei Kadtler
Danzigerstrasse 135 10407
Telephone: (30) 030-423-3233
Supervision: Rabbi Ehrenberg
Kastanien Allee 88 10349
Telephone: (30) 030-449-3214
Supervision: Rabbi Ehrenberg

BED AND BREAKFAST
Guestrooms
Tucholskystrasse 40, Mitte 10117
Telephone: (30) 281-3135
Fax: (30) 281-3122
Web site: www.adassjisroel.de
A synagogue and a kosher restaurant is in the house.

BOOKSELLERS
Literaturhandlung
Joachimstaler-Str. 13 10719
Telephone: (30) 882-4250
Fax: (30) 885-4713

BUTCHERS
Kosher Butcher
Goethestr. 61 10625
The butcher sells certain groceries. Opening hours: 10 am to 5 pm (Friday until 2 pm only).

CEMETERIES
Adass Jisroel
Wittlicherstrasse 2, Weissensee 13088
Telephone: (30) 925-1724
Established in 1880, this historic cemetery is still in use. Rabbi Esriel Hildesheimer, Rabbi Prof. David Zvi Hoffmann, Rabbi Eliahu Kaplan and many other wise and pious Jews are buried here.

COMMUNITY ORGANISATIONS
Community Centre
Fasanenstr. 79-80, off the Kurfurstendamm 10623
Telephone: (30) 88028-250
Fax: (30) 88028-250
This has been built on the site of a famous synagogue, destroyed by the Nazis.

Ignatz Bubis-Gemeindezentrum
Tucholskystrasse 40, Mitte 10117
Telephone: (30) 281-3135
Fax: (30) 281-3122
Open daily, except Shabbat, from 11 am to 10 pm. Closes Friday two hours before Shabbat.

Judische Gemeinde zu Berlin
Joachimstaler Str 13 10719
Telephone: (30) 88020-0
Fax: (30) 88028-150

Judischer Kulturverein (Jewish Cultural Association)
Oranienburgerstr. 26, Berlin-Mitte 10117
Telephone: (30) 282-6669; 285-98052
Fax: (30) 285-98053
Email: jkv.berlin@t-online.de
Hours: Monday-Thursday 11am to 5pm, Friday 11am to 2pm and 1 hour before evening and Sunday events. Friday for Kiddush 6-9 pm. (Summer 7 pm). (Entrance around the corner.)

Zentralrat der Juden in Deutschland
Tucholskystr. 9 10117
Telephone: (30) 284-4560
Fax: (30) 284-45613
Email: info@zentralratdjuden.de

EMBASSY
Embassy of Israel
Auguste-Viktoria Strasse 74-78 14193
Telephone: (30) 89045-500
Fax: (30) 89045-555
Email: botschaft@israel.de
Web site: www.israel.de

GROCERIES
Kolbo
Auguststrasse 77-78, Mitte 10117
Telephone: (30) 281-3135
In addition to kosher food and wines, sifrei kodesh as well as general literature about Jewish subjects can be obtained here.

Platzl
Passauer Str.4 10789
Telephone: (30) 217-7506

Schalom
Wielandstr. 43 10625
Telephone: (30) 312-1131
Fax: (30) 318-09905
Opening hours: 11.00 am to 5.00 pm (Fridays until 3.30 pm).

LIBRARIES
Jewish Community
Fassenstrasse 79 10623

Jewish Library
Oranienburger Str. 28 10117
Telephone: (30) 880-28-427/429

MEDIA
Newspapers
Allgemeine Judische Wochenzeitung
Postfach 04 03 69, Tucholskystrasse 9 10117
Telephone: (30) 2844 5650
Fax: (30) 2844 5699
Email: ajw@Juedische-Presse.de
Fortnightly.

Hadshot Adass Jisroel
Tucholsky str. 40 10117
Telephone: (30) 281-3135
Published by Adass Jisroel.

Periodicals
Judischer Kulturverein Berlin e.V.
Oranienburgerstr. 26, Berlin-Mitte 10117
Telephone: (30) 282-6669; 285-98052
Fax: (30) 285-98053
Email: jkv.berlin@t-online.de
Monthly.

Judisches Berlin
Oranienburger Str. 31 10117
Telephone: (30) 88028-260;88028-269
Fax: (30) 88028-266
Email: jued.berlin@jg-berlin.org
Monthly

MUSEUMS
Jewish Museum
Lindenstrasse 9-14 10969
Telephone: (30) 30878-5681
Fax: (30) 25993-409
Email: info@jmberlin.de
Web site: www.jmberlin.de
The building is now open and well worth visiting.The
permanent exhibition is a journey through German-
Jewish history and culture. In addition there are relevant
changing exhibitions. There is a restaurant on the
premises. Opening hours: Monday from 10.00 am to
10.00 pm Tuesday-Sunday from 10.00 am to 8.00 pm

RESTAURANTS
Meat
Restaurant Arche Noah
Fasanenstr. 79-80 10623
Telephone: (30) 882 6138
Shabbat reservations and payment have to be arranged
before beginning of Shabbat. The restaurant is located in
the first floor of the community building. Opening hours:
Daily 12 noon to 3.30 pm and 6.30 pm to 10.30pm.

SYNAGOGUES
Liberal
Synagogue
Pestalozzistr. 14, 1000 10625
Telephone: (30) 313-8411

Orthodox
Joachimstaler Strasse 13, Mitte 16719
Daily minyan

Adass Jisroel
Tucholskystrasse 40, Mitte 10117
Telephone: (30) 281-3135
Fax: (30) 281-3122
Web site: www.adassjisroel.de

Established 1869. Rabbinate, kashrut supervision and
mohel can all be reached at this number. Near its
community centre, there is a guest house, a kosher
restaurant and a shop which sells kosher products.

TOURIST SITES
Jewish Culture Edition
Leo-Baeck-House, Tucholsky Street 9 10117
Telephone: (30) 28445659
Fax: (30) 28445661
Email: Verlang@Judaicum.de

BONN
SYNAGOGUES
Templestr. 2-4, cnr. Adenauer Allee 53113
Telephone: 213560
Fax: 2618366

BRAUNSCHWEIG
COMMUNITY ORGANISATIONS
Community Centre
Steinstr. 4 38100
Telephone: (531) 45536

MUSEUMS
Braunschweigisches Landesmuseum
Abt. Judisches Museum, Burgplatz 1 D-38100
Telephone: (531) 1215-0
Fax: (531) 1215-2607
Email: derda@landesmuseum-bs.de
Web site: www.landesmuseum-bs.de
Founded in 1746, this museum was formerly the oldest
Jewish museum in the world. It was re-opened in 1987
under the auspices of the Braunschweigisches
Landesmuseum. Hours Tuesday-Sunday: 10am to 5pm.

BREMEN
SYNAGOGUES
Schwachauser Heerstr. 117 28211
Telephone: (421) 498-5104
Fax: (421) 498-4944

CELLE
MUSEUMS
Im Kreise 24 29221
Formerly a beautiful synagogue, it now houses travelling
exhibits on various themes of Jewish history and of
Jewish life in Celle where a community started between
1671 and 1691. There are now enough Jews in the town
to form a minyan. Opening hours: Tuesday to Thursday
3.00pm to 5.00pm, Friday 9.00am to 11.00am and
Sunday 11.00am to 1.00pm. Conducted tours of the
synagogue and tours on the history of the Jews of Celle
are also available by arrangement. Inquire at the tourist
Office, Celle, telephone +49.5141.1212.

COBLENZ (KOBLENZ)
COMMUNITY ORGANISATIONS
Community Centre
Schlachthof Str. 5
Telephone: (261) 42223

COLOGNE
BAKERIES
Koscher Backerei Lipowitz, Roonstr. 61, Koln 50674
Telephone: (221) 801-7895

HOTELS
Leonet
Rubensstr. 33
Telephone: (221) 272-300
Fax: (221) 210-893
Email: leonetkoeln@netcologne.de

RESTAURANTS
Meat
Community Centre
Roonstr 50, 50674
Telephone: (221) 240-4440
Fax: (221) 240-4440
Phone in advance. Glatt kosher.

SYNAGOGUES
Liberal
Judische Liberale Gemeinde
Stammheimer Str 22, Koeln-Riehl 50735
Telephone: (221) 287-0424
Fax: (221) 719-5024
Email: jlg.koeln@gmx.de

Orthodox
Roonstr. 50, Köln 50674
Telephone: (221) 921-5600
Fax: (221) 921-5609
Email: synagoge-koeln@netcologne.de
Web site: www.sgk.de
Daily services. There is a Youth centre, mikva, glatt-kosher restaurant (meat), Jewish museum and library at the same address. A kosher bakery is located nearby.

DORTMUND
COMMUNITY ORGANISATIONS
Landesverband der Judischen Gemeinden von Westfalen
Prinz-Friedrich-Karl-Str. 12 44135
Telephone: (231) 528495
Fax: (231) 5860372
Email: lvjuedwest@aol.com

SYNAGOGUES
Prinz-Friedrich-Karl-Str. 9 44135
Telephone: (231) 528497

DRESDEN
In November 2001 the first new synagogue, in what was East Germany, was consecrated. It is on the site of the Semper synagogue originally built in 1838 and destroyed one hundred years later on Kristallnacht.

A three-foot high Star of David, one of the two that was on the top of the synagogue, was all that remained. It will stand above the new synagogue's gate.

Up to date information may be found on www.Synagogue-dresden.de

COMMUNITY ORGANISATIONS
Landesverband Sachsen der Judischen Gemeinden K.d.o.R.
Bautzner Str 20 1099
Telephone: (351) 804-5491;802-2739
Fax: (351) 804-1445
A memorial to the six million Jews killed in the Holocaust stands on the site of the Dresden Synagogue, burnt down by the Nazis in November 1938.

SYNAGOGUES
Fiedlerstr. 3 1307
Telephone: (351) 693317

DUSSELDORF
SYNAGOGUES
Zietenstr. 50 40476
Telephone: (211) 469120
Fax: (211) 485156

EMMENDINGEN
COMMUNITY ORGANISATIONS
Community Centre
Kirchstr. 11 D-79312

SYNAGOGUES
Orthodox
Juedische Gemeinde Emmendingen
Landvogtei 11, D-79312
Telephone: (764) 571-989
Fax: (764) 571-980
Email: juedgemam@aol.com
Web site: www.juedgemen.de

ERFURT
COMMUNITY ORGANISATIONS
Community Centre
Juri-Gagarin-Ring 16 99084
Telephone: (361) 24964

ESSEN
COMMUNITY ORGANISATIONS
Sedanstr. 46 45138
Telephone: (201) 273413
Fax: (201) 287112

ESSINGEN

TOURIST SITES

Largest cemetery in the Palatinate dating from the sixteenth century where Anne Frank's ancestors are buried. Key at the Mayor's Office.

FRANKFURT

BUTCHERS

Aviv Butchery & Deli
Hanauer Landstrasse 50 60314
Telephone: (69) 433013
Fax: (69) 448064
Email: avivgmbh.kosherfood@rhein-main.net
Under the supervision of the Frankfurt Rabbinate.

COMMUNITY ORGANISATIONS

Community Centre (Jgnatz-Bubis-Gemeindezentrum)
Westendstr. 43 60325
Telephone: (69) 768-0360
Fax: (69) 746874
Email: jg.ffm@t-online.de
This community produces a magazine, "Judische Gemeinde-Zeitung Frankfurt".

Zentralwohlfahrtsstelle der Juden in Deutschland
Hebelstrasse 6 60318
Telephone: (69) 94 43 71-15
Fax: (69) 49 48 17
Email: zentrale@zwst.org

GROCERIES

Koschermarket
36 Bornheimer Landwehr 60385
Telephone: (69) 9441-1238
Fax: (69) 9441-2174

MIKVAOT

Judische Gemeinde
Westendstr 43 D-60325
Telephone: (69) 7680360
Fax: (69) 746874

MUSEUMS

Jewish Museum
Untermainkai 14-15, 60311
Telephone: (69) 212-35000
Fax: (69) 212-30705
Email: info@juedischesmuseum.de
Web site: www.juedischesmuseum.de
Sunday, Tuesday to Saturday 10.00 am-5.00 pm.
Wednesday 10.00am-8.00pm. Closed Monday.

RESTAURANTS

Sohar's
Savignystrasse 66 60325
Telephone: (69) 75 23 41
Fax: (69) 741 0116
Supervision: Rabbi Menachem Halevi Klein, Frankfurt Rabbinate.
Hours: Tuesday to Thursday and Sunday, 12 pm to 8 pm; Friday, 12 pm to Shabbat; Shabbat, 1:30 pm to 4 pm; Monday, closed. Special arrangements can be made by phone. Friday and Shabbat meals must be ordered in advance. Provides party service, airline catering and delivery to hotels. Fifteen-minute walk from synagogue, fair centre and main train station.

SYNAGOGUES

Synagogues
Baumweg 5-7 60316
Telephone: (69) 439381

Westend Synagogue
Freiherr-vom-Stein-Str. 30 60323
Telephone: (69) 726263
Email: verwaltung@jg-ffm.de
This is the city's main synagogue.

FREIBURG

COMMUNITY ORGANISATIONS

Community Centre
Engels Strasse
Telephone: (761) 383096
Fax: (761) 382332
Services: Erev Shabbat in Summer 7.30pm in Winter 6.30pm. Shabbat morning 9.30 am. Kosher Kiddush after services.

FRIEDBERG

TOURIST SITES
Judengasse 20 61169
A Gothic style mikva, built in 1260, is located here. The town council has issued a special explanatory leaflet about it. It has been restored and it is now scheduled as a historical monument of medieval architecture.

FURTH

COMMUNITY ORGANISATIONS

Community Centre
Blumenstr. 31 90762
Telephone: (91) 177-0879

TOURIST SITES
Julienstr. 2
There is a beautifully restored synagogue as well as a historic mikva.

GELSENKIRCHEN

COMMUNITY ORGANISATIONS

Community Centre
Von-der-Recke-Str. 9 45879
Telephone: (20) 923143 & 206628

HAGEN

COMMUNITY ORGANISATIONS
Potthofstr. 16 58095
Telephone: (2331) 711-3289

HALLE

COMMUNITY ORGANISATIONS
Grosse Markerstr. 13 6108
Telephone: (345) 233-110
Fax: (345) 233-1122
Email: jghalle@gmx.net

HAMBURG

COMMUNITY ORGANISATIONS
Schaferkampsallee 27 20357
Telephone: (40) 440-9440
Fax: (40) 410-8430
Mikvah on premises.

SYNAGOGUES

Orthodox
Hohe Weide 34 20253
Telephone: (40) 4409-4429
Email: kieseler@gmx.de

HANOVER

COMMUNITY ORGANISATIONS

Community Centre
Haeckelstr. 10 30173
Telephone: (311) 810-472

SYNAGOGUES
Haeckelstr. 10 30173
Telephone: (311) 810-472

HEIDELBERG

RESTAURANTS

College Restaurant
Theaterstr.9 69117
Telephone: (6221) 168-767
Kosher meals are available (by arrangement - it is not open all year round) Monday-Friday at the college restaurant, 100 yards from the College of Jewish Studies, situated at Friederichstrasse 9.

HERFORD

COMMUNITY ORGANISATIONS

Community Centre
Keplerweg 11 32049
Telephone: (52) 212039

HILDESHEIM

SYNAGOGUES

Jewish Community in Hildesheim
Postfach 10 07 07, Lower Saxony D31135
Telephone: (512) 1704962
Fax: (512) 1704964
Rabbi Dr Walter Homolka is responsible for all Lower Saxony.

HOF

COMMUNITY ORGANISATIONS

Community Centre
Am Wiesengrund 20 95032
Telephone: (92) 815-3249

ICHENHAUSEN

MUSEUMS

Museum of Jewish History
Located in the fine baroque synagogue, not far from Ulm.

INGENHEIM

TOURIST SITES
Klingenerstr. 20 76831
Sixteenth century cemetery can be visited. Key obtained from Klingenerstr. 20.

KAISERSLAUTERN

COMMUNITY ORGANISATIONS

Community Centre
Basteigasse 4 67655
Telephone: (63) 169720

KARLSRUHE

COMMUNITY ORGANISATIONS
Knielinger Allee 11 76133
Telephone: (72) 172035

KIEL

SYNAGOGUES

Orthodox
Wikingerstrasse 6 24143
Telephone: (431) 739-9096
Fax: (431) 739-9095

KIPPENHEIM

An extensive restoration of the synagogue, built in 1850-1852, and destroyed on Kristallnacht was started in 1987. The exterior renovation is complete and work is now taking place on the interior. It is classified by the state of Burden-Wurrrtenberg as a 'cultural monument of significance'.

There are no other specific locations of interest to travellers.

KONSTANZ

COMMUNITY ORGANISATIONS
Community Centre
Sigismundstr. 19 78462
Telephone: (75) 312-3077

KREFELD

COMMUNITY ORGANISATIONS
Wiedstr. 17b 47799
Telephone: (21) 512-0648

LANDAU

SYNAGOGUES
Frank-Loebsches Haus, Kaufhausgasse 9 D-76829
Telephone: (6341) 86472
Fax: (6341) 13294
Email: sabine.haas.landau.de

LUBECK

SYNAGOGUES

Orthodox
Synagogue & Community Centre
St.-Annen-Str 13 23552
Telephone: (451) 798-2182
Fax: (451) 7074-9207
Email: jgh_hl@gmx.de

MAGDEBURG

COMMUNITY ORGANISATIONS
Community Centre
Groperstr. 1a 39106
Telephone: (391) 52665

MAINZ

COMMUNITY ORGANISATIONS
Forsterstr. 2 55118
Telephone: (6131) 613990
Fax: (6131) 611767

TOURIST SITES
Untere Zahlbacherstr. 11
The key to the twelfth-century Jewish cemetery can be obtained at the 'new' Jewish cemetery.

MARBURG AN DER LAHN

COMMUNITY ORGANISATIONS
Community Centre
Unterer Eichweg 17 35041
Telephone: (642) 132881

MICHELSTADT

TOURIST SITES
Michelstadt
The town has an old synagogue which is now a museum of both Judaism and Jewish history. It is open every day in the summer except Saturday.

MINDEN

COMMUNITY ORGANISATIONS
Community Centre
Kampstr. 6 32423
Telephone: (57) 123437

MONCHENGLADBACH

SYNAGOGUES
Albertusstr. 54 41363
Telephone: (216) 23879
Fax: (216) 14639
Email: juedischegemeindemg@t-online.de

MULHEIM

COMMUNITY ORGANISATIONS
Kampstr. 7 45468
Telephone: 835191

MUNICH

BOOKSELLERS
Literaturhandlung Literatur Zum Judentum
Fürstenstr. 17 80333
Telephone: (89) 89-2800135
Fax: (89) 89-281601
Email: literaturhandlung@t-online.de

COMMUNITY ORGANISATIONS
Community Centre
Reichenbachstr. 27 80469
Telephone: (89) 202-4000
Fax: (89) 201-4604
Email: info@ikg-m.de

GROCERIES
Danel Feinkost
Pilgersheimerstrabe 44 81543
Telephone: (89) 669-888
Fax: (89) 669-820
Email: danel@t-online.de
Web site: www.koscher.net/danel/
Will deliver to hotels or other addresses, throughout Germany.
Viktualien-Markt, Westenriederstrabe 9 80331
Telephone: (89) 2280-0258

MUSEUMS
Judisches Museum Munchen
Maximilian Str. 36 80539
Telephone: (89) 2000-9693
Fax: (89) 2024-4838
A very small museum.

RESTAURANTS
Community Centre
Telephone: (89) 202 38252
Run by the community centre at Reichenbachstrasse.
Hours: 12pm - 2.30pm; 6pm - 9pm. Shabbat meals must
be ordered by Friday noon. Closed Sunday; August.

SYNAGOGUES
Possartstr. 15 81679
Telephone: (89) 474-440
Mikva on premises.
Reichenbachstr. 27 80469
Telephone: (89) 202-4000
Fax: (89) 201-4604
Mikva on premises.

Schwabing Synagogue (Schaarei Zion)
Georgenstr. 71 80798
Telephone: (89) 2602-3337
Fax: (89) 2602-3338
Friday evenings and Sabbath mornings only.

Liberal
Beth Shalom
Telephone: (89) 8980-9373
Fax: (89) 8980-9374
Email: obeth.shalom@hagalil.com
Please ask for address and timetable.

NEUSTADT
COMMUNITY ORGANISATIONS
Community Centre
Ludwigstr. 20 67433
Telephone: 212652

ODENBACH
TOURIST SITES
Kirchhofstrasse 9
Telephone: (67) 532745
There is a unusually shaped historic synagogue built in
1752 with baroque paintings in this small village.
Arrangements to visit need to be made in advance.

OFFENBACH
COMMUNITY ORGANISATIONS
Community Centre
Kaiserstr. 109 63065
Telephone: (69) 820036
Fax: (69) 820026

OSNABRUCK
COMMUNITY ORGANISATIONS
In der Barlage, 41 49078
Telephone: (541) 148420
Fax: (541) 143-4701
Kashrut information or visitors who wish to eat kosher on
Shabbat, please contact Rabbi Marc Sterm at Tel: 49 541-
48553.

SYNAGOGUES
Orthodox
Jewish Congregation Synagogue
In der Barlage, 41 49078
Telephone: (541) 48420
Fax: (541) 434701
Email: Rabbistern@t-online.de
Web site: www.jiddischkeit.org

TOURIST SITES
The Felix-Nussbaum House
Lotter Str 2 49078
Telephone: (541) 323-2207
Fax: (541) 323-2739
Email: jaehner@osnabrueck.de
About 20 minutes walk from the synagogue.

PADERBORN
COMMUNITY ORGANISATIONS
Community Centre
Pipinstr. 32 33098
Telephone: (52) 512-2596

REGENSBURG
COMMUNITY ORGANISATIONS
Am Brixener Hof 2 93047
Telephone: (94) 157093; 21819

SAARBRUCKEN
SYNAGOGUES
Synagogengemeinde Saar
Lortzingstr 8 66111
Telephone: (681) 910-380
Fax: (681) 910-38-13
Email: info@synagogengemeindesaar.de
Web site: www.synagogengemeinde.de

SCHWERIN
COMMUNITY ORGANISATIONS
Judische Gemeinde Schwerin
Schlachtermarkt 7 19055
Telephone: (38) 5550-7345
Fax: (38) 5593-60989
Email: jgemeinde@gmx.net

SPEYER
TOURIST SITES
Telephone: (62) 353332
This town contains the oldest (eleventh-century) mikva in
Germany, Judenbadgasse. To visit it, obtain the key by
contacting the Tourist Office (Maximilianstrasse 11).
Guided tours are available.

STRAUBING

COMMUNITY ORGANISATIONS
Community Centre
Wittelsbacherstr. 2 94315
Telephone: (94) 211387

STUTTGART

RELIGIOUS ORGANISATIONS
Israelitische Religionsgemeinschaft
Hospitalstr. 36 70174
Telephone: (711) 228360
Fax: (711) 2283618

RESTAURANTS
Meat
Schalom Kosher Restaurant
Hospitalstrasse 36 70174
Telephone: (711) 294752
Supervision: Orthodox Rav of the Stuttgart community.
Open during morning hours through to about 7.00pm
except Mondays (when its closed). Located on the
premises of the Stuttgart Jewish community centre.

TRIER

COMMUNITY ORGANISATIONS
Community Centre
Kaiserstr. 25 54290
Telephone: (65) 140530; 33295

VEITSHOCHHEIM
Located a few miles from Wurzburg is the town
of Veitshoechheim, which reconsecrated a pre-
First World WarI Synagogue and opened as a
Jewish Museum in March 1994. Originally built
in 1730, the synagogue was the community
centre for local Jews, who had lived in the area
for nearly three hundred years, from 1644 to
1942, when the last Jews were deported from
Veitshoechheim to the Nazi concentration
camps.

In 1986 the stone fragments of the original
interior, including the Bima and the Ahron
Hakodesch, were discovered beneath the floor,
where they had been buried in 1940. This find
prompted local officials to transform the
Synagogue back to its original function and
splendour, using photographs from the 1920s as
a guide.

MUSEUMS
Judisches Kulturmuseum Veitshoechheim
Thuengersheimer Strasse 17 97209
Telephone: (931) 9802-764
Fax: (931) 9802-766
Email: museum@veitschoechheim.de
Web site: www.veitshoechheim.de
Recently restored. Museum hours: Thursday 3pm to 6pm,
Sunday 2pm to 5pm.

WIESBADEN

RESTAURANTS
Judische Gemeinde Wiesbaden
Friedrichstr. 31-33 65185
Telephone: (611) 933-030
Fax: (611) 933-0319
Email: JG.WI@T-online.de

SYNAGOGUES
Community Centre
Friedrichstr. 31-33 65185
Telephone: (611) 933-030
Fax: (611) 933-0319
Email: JG.WI@T-online.de

WORMS
The original Rashi Synagogue, built in the 11th
century and the oldest Jewish place of worship
in Europe, was destroyed by the Nazis in 1938.
After the Second World War, it was
reconsecrated and was reconsecrated in 1961.
The building also contains a 12th century
mikvahh and a Jewish museum. There is also an
ancient Jewish cemetery, (the oldest in Europe).

**There are no other specific locations of
interest to travellers.**

WUPPERTAL

COMMUNITY ORGANISATIONS
Community Centre
Friedrich-Ebert-Str. 73 42103
Telephone: (202) 300233

WURZBURG
There are old Jewish cemeteries in Wurzburg,
Heidingsfeld and Hochberg.

COMMUNITY ORGANISATIONS
Valentin-Becker-Str. 11 97072
Telephone: (931) 151190
Fax: (931) 118184
Also guest rooms for tourists; kosher meals available.

MIKVAOT
Valentin-Becker-Str. 11 97072
Telephone: (931) 151190
Fax: (931) 118184
Appointments to be made.

SYNAGOGUES
Valentin-Becker-Str. 11 97072
Telephone: (931) 151190
Fax: (931) 118184
Email: mail@juedischegemeindewuerzburg.de
Web site: www.juedischegemeindhewuerzburg.de

TOURIST SITES
There are old Jewish cemeteries in Wurzburg,
Heidingsfeld and Hochberg.

GIBRALTAR

The first Jewish people in Gibraltar were Sephardi, who had crossed over the border from Spain before the Inquisition began in the fourteenth century. Many more followed in the ensuing centuries. When Britain took possession, Jews were banned, but later they were allowed in as traders and finally, in 1749, they were granted full permission to live there. The community began to flourish and the Jewish population, which now also included many North African Jews rose to 2,000.

At the end of the Second World War, some of the community returned after being evacuated to Britain. There are now fairly good Jewish facilities, namely four synagogues, and newsletters. There are no kosher hotels in Gibraltar.

Gibraltar has an Eruv. Gibraltar has had a Jewish prime minister and a Jewish mayor, both Gibraltar's highest offices.

GMT +1 hour
Country calling code: **(+350)**
Total population: **28,000**
Jewish population: **650**
Emergency telephone: **(Police – 999) (Fire – 999) (Ambulance – 999)**
Electricity voltage: **(Electricity voltage – 220/240)**

BAKERIES
J. Amar
47 Line Wall Road
Telephone: 73516

BUTCHERS
A. Edery
26 Public Market
Telephone: 75168
Fax: 42529
Email: edery@gibnet.gi
Web site: www.ederykosher.com

COMMUNITY ORGANISATIONS
Managing Board of Jewish Community
10 Bomb House Lane
Telephone: 72606
Fax: 40487

CONTACT INFORMATION
Solomon Levy M.B.E. J.P
3 Convent Place, PO Box 190
Telephone: 77789; 42818, 78047 (home)
Fax: 42527
Email: slevy@gibnet.gi
The vice-president of the Jewish community is happy to provide information for Jewish travellers.

CULTURAL ORGANISATIONS
Jewish Social & Cultural Club
7 Bomb House Lane
Telephone: 79636
Email: asuissa@gibnet.gi
Mailing address: Avner Suissa, 20 Lime Tree Lodge, Montagu Gardens, Gibraltar.

DELICATESSEN
Uncle Sam's Deli
62 Irish Town
Telephone: 51236; 51226
Fax: 42516
Email: dabamick@gibnet.gi.com
Provides kosher groceries and wine. Catering and takeaway service. Full glatt kosher service. Fully licensed.

EMBASSY
Consul General of Israel
Marina View, Glacis Road, PO Box 141
Telephone: 77244

GROCERIES
I&D Abudarham
32 Cornwall's Lane, PO Box 216
Telephone: 78506
Fax: 73249
Email: djabudar@gibnet.gi
Kosher wines, meats & poultry.

HOTELS
The Rock Hotel
Telephone: 73000
Fax: 73513
The hotel has kosher facilities (meat and dairy) and can cater for pre-booked groups of 10 or more. Kosher takeaway food can also be delivered to a room.

JUDAICA
A.Cohen
3 Convent Place, PO Box 190
Telephone: 52734
Email: sofergib@prontomail.com
Supplier of Mezuzot ,Tephilim and Shaatnez.

MIKVAOT
12 Bomb House Lane
Telephone: 77658 & 73090
Fax: 72359

RESTAURANTS
Jewish Club
Open daily from 10 am to 11 pm, except Shabbat, but arrangements can be made with this restaurant owner for Shabbat meals.

SYNAGOGUES
Abudarham
20 Parliament Lane 78506
Telephone: 78047
Fax: 42527

Nefusot Yehuda
65 Line Wall Road 73037

Shaar Hashamayim
19 Engineer Lane 78069
Telephone: 74030
Fax: 74029
Enquiries: Joseph de M. Benyunes PO Box 1474.

Orthodox
Etz Hayim
Irish Town 75955
Telephone: 75563
Fax: 42939

GREECE

After the Hellenistic occupation of Israel (the Jewish revolt during this occupation is commemorated in the festival of Hanukah), some Jews were led into slavery in Greece, beginning the first recorded Jewish presence in the country. The next significant Jewish immigration occurred after the Inquisition, when many Spanish Jews moved to Salonika, which was a flourishing Jewish centre until the German occupation in the Second World War. In 1832 Jews were granted equal civil rights to all other Greek citizens.

By the early 1940s, the Jewish population had grown to over 70,000, with 45,000 living in Salonika. The country was occupied in July 1941 and split among the Axis (German, Italian and Bulgarian) forces. During the occupation a relatively large number of Jews joined the partisans. Many local Christians did protect their Jewish neighbours in Athens. After the war, many of the survivors emigrated to Israel.

Today, there are Sephardi synagogues in Greece and, in Athens, a community centre and a Jewish museum. There are Jewish publications and a library in the community centre. In Aegina, Corfu and other Greek islands, ancient synagogues may be visited.

GMT +2 hours
Country calling code: **(+30)**
Total population: **10,552,000**
Jewish population: **4,500**
Emergency telephone: **(Police – 100) (Fire – 199) (Ambulance – 166)**
Electricity voltage: **(Electricity voltage – 220)**

ATHENS
Almost 3,000 Jews live in Athens. The community has access to a centre, containing a library, and the opportunity to have a kosher meal. The Jewish museum in the centre of the city details the rise and tragic fall of Greek Jewry. Kosher meals are served at the Athens Jewish Cultural Centre upon request (contact Mrs Rachel Sasson, Tel. (1) 213 3371. ñ Delivery to hotels in Athens can also be arranged).

COMMUNITY ORGANISATIONS
Central Board of the Jewish Communities of Greece
36 Voulis Street 10557
Telephone: (210) 324-4315-18
Fax: (210) 331-3852
Email: hhkis@hellasnet.gr
Web site: www.ris.gr

EMBASSY
Embassy of Israel
Marathonodromou Street 1, Paleo Psychico, POB 65140
Telephone: (210) 671-9530

MUSEUMS
Jewish Museum of Greece
39 Nikis Str 105 57
Telephone: (210) 322-5582
Fax: (210) 3223-1577
Email: jmg@otenet.gr
Web site: www.jewishmuseum.gr
Open: Monday to Friday 9.00am to 2.30pm, Sunday 10.00am to 2.00pm, Saturday closed.

RESTAURANTS
Meat
5 Averof St 10433
Telephone: (210) 520-2880
Fax: (210) 520-2881
Email: chabad@otenet.gr
Telephone for orders.

Vegetarian
Eden
Odos Flessa 3, Plaka

SYNAGOGUES
Sephardi
Beth Shalom
5 Melidoni Street 10553
Telephone: (210) 325-2773; 2823; 2875
Fax: (210) 322-0761

TOURIST INFORMATION
Community Office
8 Melidoni Street 10553
Telephone: (210) 210-325-2875
Fax: (210) 210-322-0761
Email: isrkath@hellasnet.gr

CHALKIS
COMMUNITY ORGANISATIONS
Community Centre
35 Kotsou Street 34100
Telephone: (2221) 80690

KASHRUT INFORMATION
Community Centre
Telephone: (2221) 27297

SYNAGOGUES
36 Kotsou Street
This synagogue has been rebuilt and renewed many times on its original foundations. Tombstone inscriptions in the cemetery go back more than fifteen centuries. Only open on High Holy Days.

CORFU
COMMUNITY ORGANISATIONS
Community Centre
5 Riz. Voulephton St. 49100
Telephone: (2661) 45650
Fax: (2661) 43791

TOURIST SITES
Velissariou St.
Telephone: (2661) 38802
There was an ancient synagogue and cemetery here, destroyed by the Nazis.

IOANNINA
COMMUNITY ORGANISATIONS
18 Josef Eliyia St. 45221
Telephone: (2651) 25195
Contact: John Kalef-Ezra on 32390.

LARISSA
SYNAGOGUES
Community Centre
29 Kentavron St. 41222
Telephone: (241) 532 965

RHODES
SYNAGOGUES
Khal Shalom Kadosh
1 Simmiou St., Dodecanese Islands
Telephone: (2241) 22364
Fax: (2241) 73039
The synagogue belongs to the Jewish Community of Rhodes which has 38 members. It was built around 1577 in the old Jewish Quarter. A photographic museum is functioning next to the synagogue. The synagogue is on the World Monuments Fund list of 100 most endangered sites. Tourists wishing to visit these sites should contact: Jewish Community of Rhodes, No. 5 Polydorou St. Old City. Tel: (0030) 241-22364 or Fax (0030) 241-73039.

THESSALONIKI
For many years around the turn of the 20th century, Jews formed the majority of Salonika's inhabitants. It was known as the "Jerusalem of the Balkans". The official day off was Saturday.

CULTURAL ORGANISATIONS
The Israelite Fraternity House
24 Vassileos Irakliou St.
Telephone: (231) 221030

Yad le Zikaron
24 Vassileos Irakliou St.
Telephone: (231) 275701

MUSEUMS
Jewish Museum of Thessaloniki
13, Agiou Mina str. 54624
Telephone: (231) 302310-250406-7
Fax: (231) 302310-250-406-7
Email: jctmuseo@compulink.gr
Web site: www.jmth.gr
Tuesday, Friday & Sunday: 11.00am - 2.00pm.
Wednesday & Thursday: 11.00am - 2.00pm and 5.00pm - 8.00pm. Guided tours for groups, educational programs for youngsters.

SYNAGOGUES
Monastirioton
35 Sygrou Str. 54630
Telephone: (231) 524968

TRIKKALA
SYNAGOGUES
Synagogue
15 Athanassiou Diakou St

Yad Lezicaron
24 Vassileos Irakliou Str.
Telephone: (231) 223231

VOLOS

COMMUNITY ORGANISATIONS
Xenophontos & Moisseos Streets 38333
Telephone: (2421) 25302
Fax: (2421) 25302

KASHRUT INFORMATION
20 Parodos Kondulaki

SYNAGOGUES
Xenophontos & Moisseos Streets
Open primarily on High Holy Days.

TOURIST SITES
Holocaust Monument
Riga Ferreou Square.

GUATEMALA

Conversos were the first recorded Jews in the country, but, a few centuries later, the next Jewish immigration occurred with the arrival of German Jews in 1848. Later, some east European Jews arrived, but Guatemala was not keen to accept refugees from Nazism and, as a result, passed some laws which, although not mentioning Jews directly, were aimed against Jewish refugees.

Even though these laws were in place, in 1939 there were 800 Jews in Guatemala. An Ashkenazi community centre was built in 1965, but, despite accepting some Jewish Cuban refugees, the community is shrinking owing to assimilation and intermarriage.

Most Jews live in Guatemala City, and others in Quetzaltenango and San Marcos. There is a Jewish school and kindergarten.

GMT -6 hours
Country calling code: (+502)
Total population: 10,517,000
Jewish population: 1,000
Emergency telephone: (Police – 110) (Fire – 110) (Ambulance – 125)
Electricity voltage: (Electricity voltage – 110)

GUATEMALA CITY

COMMUNITY ORGANISATIONS
Comunidad Judia Guatemalteca
Apartado Postal 502
Telephone: (2) 360-1509
Fax: (2) 360-1589
Email: comjugua@guaweb.net
Web site: www.comunidadjudia.com
Has a kosher grocery.

EMBASSY
Embassy of Israel
13 Av. 14-07, Zona 10
Telephone: (2) 371305

SYNAGOGUES
Ashkenazi
Centro Hebreo, 7a Av. 13-51, Zona 9
Telephone: (2) 367643

Sephardi
Maguen David
7a Av. 3-80, Zona 2
Telephone: (2) 232-0932

HAITI

Christopher Columbus brought the first Jew to Haiti – his interpreter, Luis de Torres, a Converso who had been baptised before the voyage. Thereafter more Jews settled but the community was destroyed in an anti-European revolt by Toussaint L'Ouverture in 1804. A hundred or so years later, Jews from the Middle East and some refugees from the Nazis settled in Haiti, but many subsequently emigrated to Israel.

The remaining community has benefited from the help of the Israeli embassy, and services are held in the embassy or in private homes. There is no central Jewish organisation, and the community is too small to support other Jewish facilities.

GMT -5 hours
Country calling code: (+509)
Total population: 7,492,000
Jewish population: Under 100
Emergency telephone: (Police – 114) (Ambulance – 118)
Electricity voltage: (Electricity voltage – 110)

PORT AU PRINCE

CONTACT INFORMATION
Religious services are held at the home of the Honorary Israeli Consul, Mr Gilbert Bigio.

HONDURAS

During the Spanish colonial period, some Conversos did live in Honduras, but it was only in the nineteenth century that any significant Jewish immigration occurred. In the early twentieth century, refugees from Nazism followed a handful of immigrants from eastern Europe. Honduras was one of the small number of countries to aid refugees from Nazism, and many Jews owe their lives to the help of Honduran consulates which issued visas in wartime Europe.

Tegucigalpa (the capital) contains the largest Jewish population, but the only synagogue in the country is in San Pedro Sula (services are held in private homes in Tegucigalpa). There is also a Sunday school and WIZO branch.

GMT -6 hours
Country calling code: (+504)
Total population: 6,338,000
Jewish population: Under 100
Emergency telephone: (Police – 119) (Fire – 198) (Ambulance – 37 8654)
Electricity voltage: (Electricity voltage – 110/220)

BALATONFURED
GUEST HOUSE
Holiday center Udulo, Liszt Ferenc utca 6
Telephone: 8734-3404
Open May to September. It is also a restaurant and there is a synagogue on the premises.

SAN PEDRO SULA
CONTACT INFORMATION
Telephone: 530157
Services Friday and Shabbat at synagogue and community centre.

TEGUCIGALPA
CONTACT INFORMATION
Telephone: 315908
Services usually held in private homes. Contact secretary at above number.

EMBASSY
Embassy of Israel
Palmira Building, 5th Floor
Telephone: 324232; 325176

HUNGARY

There were Jews living in Hungary in Roman times, even before the arrival of the Magyars (ancestors of the present-day Hungarians). The Jews suffered during the Middle Ages, when there was some anti-semitism, but conditions improved under Austro-Hungarian rule, and Judaism was recognised as being on a legal par with Christianity in 1896.

Hungary lost a considerable amount of territory after the First World War, and as a result many of its original Jewish communities (such as Szatmar) found themselves within other countries. Anti-semitism reached a peak in March 1944, when, during the German occupation, most Jewish communities began to be transported to Auschwitz. A number of those who were deported survived when Auschwitz was liberated by the Red Army in January 1945.

After the war, Hungary had the largest Jewish community in central Europe. Inevitably, the community dwindled through emigration (especially after the 1956 uprising) and assimilation. Communism in Hungary was far more lenient than in other Warsaw Pact countries, and synagogues were allowed to operate. Since 1989, religious interest has increased, and the government has recently renovated the Dohany Synagogue, the second biggest synagogue in the world and the largest in Europe. The Jewish population is still the largest in the region, although most are not religious. The Hungarian national tourist office had published 'Shalom', an excellent guide to Jewish Hungary.

GMT +1 hour
Country calling code: (+36)
Total population: 10,153,000
Jewish population: 60,000
Emergency telephone: (Police – 107) (Fire – 105) (Ambulance – 104)
Electricity voltage: (Electricity voltage – 220)

BUDAPEST

Once known in the nineteenth century as 'Judapest', this city contains the majority of Hungarian Jews. At its prewar peak its Jewish population was around 200,000. There are several functioning synagogues, from Orthodox to 'neolog' (Hungarian reform). The recently restored Doh·ny synagogue was built to accommodate 3,000 in prayer.

BAKERIES
Kosher Bakers
Kazinczy u. 28, 1074 Budapest
Telephone: (1) 342-0231

BOOKSELLERS
Biblical World Judaica Gallery
Wesselenyi utca. 13 H-1077
Telephone: (1) 267-8502
Fax: (1) 354-1561
Email: gallery@judaica.hu
Web site: www.judaica.hu

COMMUNITY ORGANISATIONS
Central Board of the Federation of Jewish Communities in Hungary
VII, Sip utca 12
Telephone: (1) 342-1355
Fax: (1) 342-1790
Email: bzsh@mail.matav.hu

CULTURAL ORGANISATIONS
Tourism and Cultural Center of the Budapest Jewish Community
H-1075 Budapest, Sip u. 12
Telephone: (1) 00-36-0-343-0420
Fax: (1) 00-36-1-462-0478
Email: zsikk@axelero.hu
Web site: www.jewishfestival.hu

EMBASSY
Embassy of Israel
Fullank utca 8 1026
Telephone: (1) 2000-781

GROCERIES
Koser Bolt
Dob utca 12, 1072 Budapest
Telephone: (1) 267-5691
Kosher products, bread, etc.

The Orthodox Central Synagogue
VII, Kazinczy utca 27
Kosher milk and cheese are available here three mornings a week.

HOTELS
Kosher
King's Hotel
Nagydiofa u. 27-29, 1075 Budapest 1074
Telephone: (1) 352-7617
Fax: (1) 352-7675
Strictly kosher hotel with a restaurant.

MEDIA
Newspaper
Uj Elet (New Life)
Central Board Hotel

MIKVAOT
VII Kazinczy utca 16 1074

MUSEUMS
Hungarian Jewish Museum and Archives
Dohany u.2 1077
Telephone: (1) 343-6756
Fax: (1) 343-6756
Email: bpjewmus@mail.c3.hu
Web site: www.c3.hu/~bpjewmus

RELIGIOUS ORGANISATIONS
The Central Rabbinical Council
VII, Sip utca 12
Telephone: (1) 142-1180
Rabbi Schweitzer is Chief Rabbi of Hungary and Director of the Rabbinical Seminary.

RESTAURANTS
Meat
King's Hotel
Nagydiofa Utca 25-27
Telephone: (1) 352-7675
Supervision: Orthodox Community

Restaurant King David
H-1075 Budapest Dohany u. 10
Telephone: (1) 5129773
Fax: (1) 36-1-4137304
Email: kinordavid@hotmail.com
Web site: www.zsido.com/kinor
Supervision: Chug Hatam Szofer Bne-Brak
Opening hours: 11am to 9.30pm

SYNAGOGUES
Dohany Street Synagogue
VII Dohany Utca 4-6
Telephone: (1) 342-2353
Built in 1859, it is the largest in Europe and the second largest in the world. In its grounds lie buried Hungarian Jewish victims of the Nazis. There is also a commemorative plaque to Hanna Senesh, the Jewish parachutist who was captured and tortured before being shot by the Nazis. A plaque commemorating Theodor Herzl, the founder of Zionism is in the Jewish Museum.

Heroes Synagogue
VII Wesselenyi utca 5
Telephone: (1) 342-2353

Orthodox
The Orthodox Central Synagogue
Kazinczy 27
Telephone: (1) 351-0526
Fax: (1) 322-7200

TOURIST INFORMATION
Jewish Information Service
Telephone: (1) 166-5165
Fax: (1) 166-5165

TOURS
Chosen Tours
Telephone: (1) 185-9499
Fax: (1) 166-5165
Tours of Jewish sites are provided by telephone arrangement.

Jewish Heritage in Budapest
Dohany utca 2
Telephone: (1) 317-2754
Email: hukonc@enternet.hu
Web site: www.ticket.info.hu
A walking tour of Jewish Budapest, arranged by the Municipality

TRAVEL AGENTS
AVIV Travel-Trade 2000 Kft.
H-0175 Budapest, Sip u. 12
Telephone: (1) 00-36-1-344-5409
Fax: (1) 00-36-0-462-0478
Email: aviv@aviv.hu
Web site: www.aviv.hu

SOPRON

MUSEUMS
The Old Synagogue Museum
utca 22-24 H-9400
Telephone: (99) 311327
Fax: (99) 311347
Email: smuzeum@mail.c3.hu
A department of the Sopron Museum. A medieval synagogue, originally a private one, situated on the ground floor of a baroque house, restored as a museum in 1976. Open from 1 May to 1 October, daily between 9am and 5pm. Closed Tuesdays.

SYNAGOGUES
Orthodox
Jewish Orthodox
Kiss Janos u. 3. H-9400
Telephone: (99) 313-508

TOURIST SITES
utca 11
A second medieval synagogue which formerly housed the museum is undergoing restoration.

The Neologue Cemetery
Dating from the nineteenth-century. There is a memorial wall dedicated to the 1,600 local victims of the Holocaust.

INDIA

The Jewish population of India can be divided into three components: the Cochin Jews, the Bene Israel and the Baghdadi Jews. The Cochin Jews are based in the south of India in Kerala. This community can be further divided into Black (believing themselves to be the original settlers) and White (of European or Middle Eastern origin), the Paradesi. Most of the community has emigrated, but there is still a synagogue in Cochin that is a major tourist attraction.

The Bene Israel believe they are descended from Jewish survivors of a ship wrecked on its voyage from ancient Israel during the period of King Solomon. No reliable documentary evidence, however, exists to support this claim. More reliable evidence dates settlement to around the tenth century. The Bene Israel follow only certain Jewish practices, such as kosher food and Shabbat, and also adhere to certain Muslim and Hindu beliefs; for example, they abstain from eating beef. In the eighteenth century, they settled in Bombay and now form the largest group of Indian Jews.

Baghdadi Jews, immigrants from Iraq and the other Middle Eastern countries, arrived in India in the late eighteenth century, and followed British Colonial rather than local custom. Many emigrated to Israel in the 1950s and 1960s.

During the Indo-Pakistan war of 1972, the leading Indian military figure was General Samuels. In 1999 Lt-Gen J.F.R. Jacob was appointed Governor of Punjab State.

There is a central Council of Indian Jewry, based in Mumbai, where most of the Indian Jews live. Kosher food is available, and there are three Jewish schools in the city. Relations with Israel have recently improved and it is now a major trade partner.

GMT +5 1/2 hours
Country calling code: **(+91)**
Total population: **1,013,662,000**
Jewish population: **5,000**
Emergency telephone:
Electricity voltage: **(Electricity voltage – 220)**

ALIBAG
SYNAGOGUES
Magen Aboth Synagogue
Alibag
Established in 1848 the synagogue is in what is known as "Israel" alley to the south-east of the town.

COCHIN
COMMUNITY ORGANISATIONS
Association or Kerala Jews
Thekkumbhagom Synagogue, Jews Street
Telephone: 366-247; 362-454
Fax: 363-747

CONTACT INFORMATION
Inquiries
Princess Street, Fort
Telephone: 24228; 24988

SYNAGOGUES
Chennamangalam
Jew Street, Chennamangalam
Built in 1614 and restored in 1916, this synagogue has been declared a historical monument by the Government of India. A few yards away is a small concrete pillar into which is inset the tombstone of Sara Bat-Israel, dated 5336 (1576).

Paradesi
Jew Town, Mattancherry 2
The only Cochin synagogue that is still functioning. Built in 1568.

ERNAKULAM
TOURIST SITES
Kadavumbagom Synagogue
Built in 1200 and rebuilt in 1690.

Thekkumbagon Synagogue
Telephone: (484) 390-187
Email: anithamsamson@yahoo.co.in
Built in 1580 and rebuilt in 1939.

KHAMASA
SYNAGOGUES
Magen Abraham
Bukhara Mohalla, opp. Parsi Agiari 380001
Telephone: (79) 535-5224

KOLKATA
COMMUNITY ORGANISATIONS
Jewish Association of Kolkata
1&2 Old Court House Corner
Telephone: (33) 224861
General inquiries to this telephone number.

SYNAGOGUES
Bethel Synagogue
26/1 Pollack Street

Magen David Synagogue
109a Peplabi Rash, Bihari Bose Road, 1, (formerly Canning Street)

Neveh Shalome Synagogue
9 Jackson Lane, 1

MUMBAI
EMBASSY
Consul General of Israel
50 Kailash, G. Deshmukh Marg, 26
Telephone: (22) 386-2793

GROCERIES
ORT India
68 Worli Hill Estate, PO Box 6571 400018
Telephone: (22) 496-2350; 8423; 8457
Fax: (22) 496-2350; 491-3203
Email: ortbbay@bom5.vsnl.net.in
Web site: www.ortindia.com
The Jewish Education Resource Centre provides kosher food from its bakery and kitchen to all travellers. ORT India also arranges conducted tours to places of Jewish interest in Mumbai and to ancient synagogues in the Konkan region of Maharashtra State.

SYNAGOGUES
Beth El Synagogue
Mirchi Galli, Mahatma Gandhi Road, Panvel 410206

Etz Haeem Prayer Hall
2nd Lane, Umerkhadi 400009
Telephone: (22) 377-0193

Gate of Mercy (Shaar Harahamim)
254 Samuel Street, Nr Masjid Railway Station 400003
Telephone: (22) 345-2991
This is the oldest Bene Israel synagogue in use in India, established in 1796 and known as the Samaji Hasaji Synagogue or Juni Masjid until 1896 when its name was changed to Shaar Harahamim.

Knesseth Eliahu Synagogue
V.B. Ghandi Road (Forbes Street), Fort 400001
Telephone: (22) 283-1502
The synagogue was constructed in 1884. Freddie Sofer welcomes visitors to join him for lunch after Shabbat service.

Magen David Synagogue
J.J.Nagpada, Byculla 400008
Telephone: (22) 300-6675
The synagogue built in 1861 with the assistance of the Sasoon family has a gothic character.

Magen Hassidim Synagogue
8 Mohammaed Shahid Marg, (formerly Moreland Road), Agripada 400011
Telephone: (22) 309-2493
Most marriages and bar mitzvahs are held here; it can seat 1000. Only Bene Israel carpenters were used, and they gave their services free.

Rodef Shalom Synagogue
Sussex Road, Byculla 400027

Shaar HaRahamim Synagogue
Tembi Naka, opp. Civil Hospital, Thane 400601
Telephone: (22) 853-4817
Established in 1796, it is the oldest Bene Israel synagogue in India.

Shaare Rason Synagogue
90 Tantanpura Street, 3rd Road, Don Tad, Israel Mohalla, Khadak 400009

Tifereth Israel Synagogue
92 K. K. Marg, Jacob Circle 400011
Telephone: (22) 305-3713

Orthodox
Kurla Bene Israel Prayer Hall
275 S. G. Barve Road (C.S.T. Road), Kurla, West Bombay 400070
Telephone: (22) 511-8795

TOURS
ORT India
68 Worli Hill Estate, PO Box 6571 400018
Telephone: (22) 496-2350; 8423
Fax: (22) 364-7308
Email: jhirad@giasbm01.vsnl.net.in
The Travel and Tourism Department arranges tours in Bombay & Raighad District.

TOV Jewish India Tours
96 Penso Villa, 1st Floor, Mbraut Rd, Shivaji Park 400028
Telephone: (22) 022-24450134
Fax: (22) 022-24449391
Email: indoisr@hotmail.com
Tours of Jewish India.

NEW DELHI
SYNAGOGUES
Judah Hyam Synagogue
2 Humayun Road 110003
Telephone: (11) 463-5500
A/7 Nirman Vihar, Patparganj 110092
Telephone: (11) 224-3136
The Judah Hyam Annexe houses a library and centre for Jewish and inter-faith studies.

PARAVUR
SYNAGOGUES
Parur Synagogue
Built in 1165, the synagogue was rebuilt in 1616 by the local Jewish community with the help of David Kastiel, who was not a Paradesi Jew, but a man of local origin. Paradesi Jews were associated with Mattancherry and their synagogue was built in 1568.

PUNE
SYNAGOGUES
Succath Shelomo
93 Rasta Peth 411011
Inquiries to Hon. Sec. 247/1 Rasta Peth, Trupti Apt., Pune 411011 or Dr S. B. David 9, Bund Garden Road, Pune 411001

Orthodox
Ohel David Synagogue
9 Dr Ambedkar Road 411001
Telephone: (20) 91-20-613-2048
Email: oheldavid@ip.eth.net
The synagogue was built by David Sasoon in 1867. His grave is in the synagogue grounds.

TOURS
Tov Jewish India Tours
118 Citadel Palace Orchard, rdindhari, Green Forest Hills 411028
Telephone: (20) 693-1488
Fax: (20) greenforesthills

THANE
KASHRUT INFORMATION
Pearl Farm, A/1 Dhobi Alley, Sulabha, Maharashtra 400601
Telephone: (22) 536-0539
Kosher goat meat and fish.

IRAN

Iran, formerly known as Persia, has an ancient connection with Jews. The first Jewish communities in Persia date from the time of the First Temple. King Cyrus, the Persian king who conquered Babylon, allowed the Jews to return to Israel from their exile. Not all returned, however, and some settled in Persia. The Persian community grew over time, suffering oppression after the Islamic conversion in 642. Certain segments of the Jewish community also grew in wealth in early medieval times.

In the twentieth century, there was a brief period of hope for the Jews in Iran when the country became more western-oriented after 1925. However, the 1979 revolution quashed the hope for a more tolerant Iran, and many thousands of Jews decided to emigrate. Association with Zionism became a capital offence and a number of Jews have been executed since 1979. The Jews are seen as 'dhimmi', (subordinates), to Islam, and as such are allowed some religious practices, but are so closely watched that maintaining a Jewish life is difficult. The tombs of Esther and Mordechai (from the Purim story) are in Hamadan, south-west of the capital Tehran. Iran currently has the largest Jewish community in the Middle East outside Israel.

Kosher food has become expensive and is difficult to obtain.

GMT +3 1/2 hours
Country calling code: (+98)
Total population: 60,694,000
Jewish population: 18,000
Emergency telephone:
Electricity voltage: (Electricity voltage – 220)

ISFAHAN
SYNAGOGUES
Synagogue
Shah Abass Street

TEHRAN
SYNAGOGUES
Haim
Gavamossaltaneh Street

TOURIST SITES
Jewish Quarter of Tehran, Mahalleh, off Sirus Avenue

IRISH REPUBLIC

The first report of Jews in Ireland records that in 1079 'five Jews came over the sea'. The small community was expelled in 1290, along with the Jews from the rest of the British Isles. The community slowly grew again after Jews were allowed to return and a few conversos settled in Dublin. There was never a strong community, however, and only in 1822 did a significant influx of Jews occur when immigrants came from England and eastern Europe.

Immigration continued and large numbers arrived from the Russian Empire after 1881. Some settled in Ireland intentionally but others believed that they had landed in America, deceived by the ships captains. In 1901, the community was 3,800 strong. The highest figure for the Jewish population of Ireland has been estimated at 8,000.

Robert Briscoe (1894-1969) who played an important role in the struggle for Irish independence was twice Lord Mayor of Dublin.

Currently, most Jews live in Dublin although the community is now shrinking.

GMT +0 hours
Total population: 3,626,000
Jewish population: 1,200
Emergency telephone: (Police – 999) (Fire – 999) (Ambulance – 999)
Electricity voltage: (Electricity voltage – 220)

CORK
SYNAGOGUES
Orthodox
10 South Terrace
Telephone: (21) 487-0413
Fax: (21) 487-6537
Email: rosehill@iol.ie
Services: For information contact Fred Rosehill (21) 487-0413.

DUBLIN

The centre of Irish Jewry, Dublin's position on the east coast meant that many Jews settled there in the flight from Eastern Europe in the nineteenth century. The Jewish Museum in Dublin, opened by the then President of Israel, Irish-born Chaim Herzog, in 1985 during a state visit to Ireland, gives much information on the town's Jewish history.

Dublin was also the home of possibly the world's most famous fictional Jew, Leopold Bloom of James Joyce's 'Ulysses'.

BAKERIES
Hemmingway's Deli
Ballsbridge Terrace 4

Rowan's Deli
Main Street, Rathfarnham 14

CONTACT INFORMATION
Vegetarian Society of Ireland
PO Box 3010, Ballsbridge 4
Email: vegsoc@ireland.com
Web site: www.vegetarian.ie
The society will provide details of establishments which cater for vegetarians.

DELICATESSEN
The Big Cheese
St Andrew's Lane 2
Telephone: (1) 671-1399
Fax: (1) 490-9917
Has a Kosher section and is open on Sunday Morning

EMBASSY
Embassy of Israel
Carrisbrook House, 122 Pembroke Road, Ballsbridge 4
Telephone: (1) 668-0303
Fax: (1) 668-0418
Email: info@embisrael.iol.ie

MIKVAOT
Terenure Hebrew Congregation, Rathfarnham Road
Telephone: (1) 490-5555

MUSEUMS
Irish Jewish Museum
3-4 Walworth Road 8
Telephone: (1) 453-1797
Fax: (1) 490-1857
Open Tuesday, Thursday and Sunday. May to September 11 am to 3.30 pm; October to April 10.30 am to 2.30 pm. Group visits by arrangement. (1) 490-1857.

RELIGIOUS ORGANISATIONS
Board of Shechita
1 Zion Road, Dublin 6
Telephone: (1) 492-3751
Email: irishcom@iol.ie
Web site: www.irishjewishcommunity.com

The Chief Rabbinate of Ireland
Herzog House, 1 Zion Road 6
Telephone: (1) 492-3751
Fax: (1) 492-4680
Email: irishcom@iol.ie

RESTAURANTS
Vegetarian
Blazing Salads
25c Powerscourt Town House 2
Telephone: (1) 671-9552

Café Paradiso
16 Lancaster Quay, Cork City
Telephone: (1) 277-939

Cornucopia
19 Wicklow St. 2
Telephone: (1) 677-7583

Juice
South Great Georges St. 2
Telephone: (1) 475-7856

SYNAGOGUES
Orthodox
Machzikei Hadass
Rathmore Villas, Rear of 77 Terenure Road North 6W
Telephone: (1) 493-8991
Email: machadass@jerusalemail.com
Web site:
www.jpostmail.com/jpost/users/machadass

Terenure Hebrew Congregation
Rathfarnham Road, Terenure 6
Telephone: (1) 490-8307

The Jewish Home of Ireland
Denmark Hill, Leinster Road West, Rathmines, Dublin 6
Telephone: (1) 497-6258
Fax: (1) 497-2018
Email: thejewishhomeofirl@tinet.ie
Services are held Friday evening at start of Sabbath and Sabbath morning. Kosher meals may be had in the home's dining room. Forty-eight hours notice is required..

Progressive
7 Leicester Avenue, Rathgar, Po Box 3059 6
Telephone: (1) 490-7605
Email: djpc@ulps.org
Friday evening at 8.15pm, first Sabbath in the month and Festivals at 10.30am.

ISRAEL

General Information

Israel, the Promised Land of the Bible, is today a modern, thriving, bustling and vibrant country. For centuries, the sites of many of the most stirring events in the history of mankind lay dormant beneath shifting sands and crumbling terraces, until the land was reclaimed by the People of Israel returning from exile. In today's Israel, cities, towns and villages, fertile farms and green forests, sophisticated industries and well-developed commercial enterprises have replaced barren hillsides, swamps and desert wilderness.

Climate

Israel enjoys long, warm, dry summers (April–October) and generally mild winters (November–March), with somewhat drier, cooler weather in hilly regions, such as Jerusalem and Safed. Rainfall is relatively heavy in the north and centre of the country with much less in the northern Negev and almost negligible amounts in the southern areas. Regional conditions vary considerably, with humid summers and mild winters on the coast; dry summers and moderately cold winters in the hill regions; hot, dry summers and pleasant winters in the Jordan Valley; and year-round semi-desert conditions in the Negev.

Languages

Hebrew, the language of the Bible, and Arabic, are the official languages of Israel. Hebrew, Arabic and English are compulsory subjects at school. French, Spanish, German, Yiddish, Russian, Polish and Hungarian are widely spoken. Local and international newspapers and periodicals in a number of languages are readily available. All street and most commercial signs are in Hebrew and English and often in Arabic.

Passports and Visas

Every visitor to Israel must hold a valid passport; valid for a minimum of six months beyond the intended date of arrival, stateless persons require a valid travel document with a return visa to the country of issue. Visitors may remain in Israel for up to three months from the date of arrival, subject to the terms of the visa issued. Visitors who intend to work in Israel must apply to the Ministry of the Interior for a special visa (B/1).

Electrical Appliances

The electric current in Israel is 220 volts AC, single phase, 50 Hertz. Most Israeli sockets are of the three-pronged variety but many can accept some European two-pronged plugs as well. Electric shavers, travelling irons and other small appliances may require adapters and/or transformers which can be purchased in Israel.

Health Regulations

There are no vaccination requirements for visitors entering Israel.

Pets

Dogs or cats accompanying visitors must be over four months old, inoculated against rabies and bear a valid official veterinary health certificate from the country of origin.

Accommodation

Kashrut

In Israel, kosher means under official rabbinical supervision. Most hotels (but not all) do adhere. Kosher restaurants, hotels and youth hostels are by law required to display a kashrut certificate.

Hotels

Israel has over 300 hotels, offering a wide choice of accommodation to suit all tastes, purposes and budgets, ranging from small, simple facilities to five-star luxury establishments, with prices varying according to grade and season. Hotel rates are generally quoted in US dollars and do not include the 15 per cent service charge.

Kibbutz Hotels

The kibbutz (collective settlement) is an Israeli social experience, in which all property is collectively owned and members receive no salaries but are provided with housing, education for their children, medical services, social amenities and all other necessities. Most of the 280 kibbutzim throughout Israel are essentially agricultural settlements but many are moving to a more industrially orientated economy.

Several kibbutzim, mostly in northern and central Israel, have established hotels on their premises, providing visitors with a close view of this world-renowned lifestyle. They offer guests the opportunity of a relaxed, informal holiday in delightful rural surroundings. Some present special evening programmes about the kibbutz experience.

For further information and a special tour of Israel's kibbutzim and kibbutz hotels, contact any Israel Government Tourist Office (IGTO), or the tourist information offices (TlO) in Israel, or Kibbutz Hotels, 1 Smolinskin St., Tel Aviv. Tel.: 03-527 8085. Fax: 03-523 0527.

Youth Hostels
The Israel Youth Hostels Association (IYHA), affiliated with the International Youth Hostels Association, operates some 32 youth hostels throughout the country for guests of all ages. All offer dormitory, usually single sex, accommodation and most also provide meals and self-service kitchen facilities. Some hostels also provide family accommodation for parents accompanied by at least one child. Individual reservations should be booked directly at specific hostels and group reservations with the IYHA.

The IYHA also arranges individual 14-, 21- or 28-day package tours, called 'Israel on the Youth Hostel Trail'. These include nights in any of 25 hostels with breakfast and dinner, unlimited bus travel, a half-day guided tour, free admission to National Parks, a map and other informative material.

For further information, contact the Israel Youth Hostels Association, 1 Sazar Street, 91060 Jerusalem, Tel: 02-655 8400, Fax: 02-655 8401.

Currency and Bank Information
The currency of Israel is the New Israeli Sheqel (NIS) (plural sheqalim). Each sheqel is divided into 100 agorot (singular agora).

Bank notes circulate in denominations of NIS 200, 100, 50 and 20 sheqels and coins in denominations of 5 sheqels, 10 sheqels, 1 sheqel and 50 and 10 agorot. One may bring an unlimited amount of local and foreign currency into Israel in cash, travellers' cheques, letters of credit, or State of Israel Bonds. Foreign currency may be exchanged at any bank and at many hotels.

Most banks are open from Sunday to Thursday from 08:30 am to 12:00 midday, and from 4:00 pm to 6:00 pm on Sunday, Tuesday and Thursday. On the eve of major Jewish holidays, banks are open from 08:30 am to 12.00 midday. Bank branches in major hotels usually offer convenient additional banking hours.

Shopping
Colourful oriental markets and bazaars may be found in the old city of Jerusalem and in several other towns and villages, bargaining is often expected. The unique variety of goods available includes handmade items of olive wood, mother-of-pearl, leather and straw, as well as hand-blown glass and exotic clothing. In all cities and towns there are shopping malls which are open from 08:00 pm to 10:00 pm. There are duty-free shops at Ben Gurion, Eilat and Ovda International Airports.

Opening Hours:
Most shops are open daily, Sunday to Thursday, from 9:00 am to 7:00 pm, although some close for a mid-day break between 1:00 pm and 4:00 pm. On Fridays and the eve of major Jewish holidays, shops close early in the afternoon. Some Muslim-owned establishments are closed on Fridays and some Christian shops on Sundays

Radio and Television
Radio programmes are broadcast daily in English, Arabic, French, Yiddish, Russian and other languages. There are three daily news programmes in English and French. Many programmes shown on Israeli TV are in English with Hebrew, Arabic and Russian subtitles.

The Israel Broadcasting Authority news in English is screened nightly on Channel 1 at 6.00 pm

Facilities for the Handicapped

Many hotels and public institutions in Israel (including Ben Gurion International Airport) provide ramps, specially equipped lavatories, telephones and other conveniences for the handicapped.

Milbat, the Advisory Centre for the Disabled at Sheba Medical Center in Tel Aviv (Tel: 03-5303 739), will be pleased to answer visitors' questions.

The Yad Sarah Organisation with branches located throughout Israel provides wheelchairs, crutches and other medical equipment on loan, free of charge (a small deposit is requested). For more specific information, contact the organisation's main office in Jerusalem, Tel: 02-624 4242.

Travellers to Israel, especially those with specific medical/paramedical needs, can turn to Traveller Hotline operated by Ezer Mizion, the Israel Health Support Fund. This volunteer organisation provides all paramedical information and needs free of charge to the traveller, via the International Office (02-537 8070) and Travellers Hotline (02-500 211). Transport and other arrangements can be organised prior to arrival and special inquiries/needs can be seen to while in Israel.

Organised Tours

Numerous organised tours, mostly in air-conditioned buses or minibuses, are conducted by licensed tour operators. Itineraries and prices are determined in accordance with the Ministry of Tourism guidelines to ensure a full sightseeing programme in maximum comfort. Half-day, full-day and longer tours are available, some combining air with road travel. Tours depart regularly from major cities as well as from popular resort areas during the peak season. All organised tours are accompanied by experienced, licensed multilingual guides identified by an official emblem bearing the words Licensed Tourist Guide.

Smaller groups may hire a licensed driver-guide and a special touring limousine or minibus, identified by the red Ministry of Tourism emblem.

Full details of itineraries, prices and schedules are available at travel agencies, tour companies, IGTOs and TIOs.

Major public institutions and organisations such as WIZO, Hadassah, universities and the Knesset (Parliament) conduct guided tours of their facilities. Walking tours of the larger cities are arranged by the municipalities.

Visitors should be aware that certain tourist sites such as the Tomb of the Patriachs and Jericho are now within the boundaries of the Palestinian Authority. They should consult the local tourist offices in Israel concerning travel to those areas.

When visiting religious sites always take care to be modestly dressed; if not you may be refused entry.

Buses

Buses are the most popular means of urban and inter-city transport throughout Israel. The Egged Bus Cooperative operates nearly all inter-city bus lines and also provides urban services in most cities and towns. (The greater Tel Aviv area is serviced by the Dan Cooperative and independent bus companies operate in Beer Sheva and Nazareth.) Fares are reasonably priced and service is regular. Most bus lines do not operate on the Sabbath (Friday evening to Saturday evening) and on Jewish holidays. Students are eligible for discount fares on inter-urban bus routes on presentation of an International Student Card. Special monthly tickets are available for Dan and Egged urban bus lines. Overseas visitors can purchase Israbus passes valid on all Egged bus lines for periods of 7,14, 21 and 30 days. Tickets can be obtained at any Egged bus station.

Taxis

These are both shared taxis (sheruts) and normal taxis. Taxis are required to operate a meter.

Traffic Regulations

A valid International Driving Licence is recognised and preferred, although a valid national driving licence is also accepted, provided it has been issued by a country maintaining diplomatic relations with Israel and recognising an Israeli driving licence.

An excellent system of roads connects all towns. Traffic travels on the right and overtakes on the left. It is compulsory for the driver and all passengers to wear seat belts. Drivers coming from the right have priority, unless indicated otherwise on the road signs, which are international. Distances on road signs are always given in kilometres (1 km is equal to 0.621 miles).

The speed limit is 50 km (approx. 31 miles) per hour in built-up areas; 80-90 km (approx. 50-56 miles) per hour on open roads.

Special Programmes For Tourists
Plant a Tree With Your Own Hands

Tree-planting centres have been established by the Jewish National Fund at several locations throughout Israel. For a nominal contribution, visitors may plant trees and receive a certificate and pin to mark the event. For further information, contact the Jewish National Fund, PO Box 283, 91002 Jerusalem, Tel: 02-670 7402, or 96 Hayarkon Street, 63432 Tel Aviv, Tel: 03-523 4367, Fax: 03-5246084.

GMT +2 hours
Country calling code: **(+972)**
Total population: **6,100,000**
Jewish population: **5,000,000**
Emergency telephone: **(Police – 100) (Fire – 102) (Ambulance – 101)**

AFULA
RESTAURANTS
La Cabania
Ha'atzmaut Square
Telephone: (4) 659-1638

San Remo
4 Ha'atzmaut Square
Telephone: (4) 652-2458

AKKO
HOTELS
Palm Beach
P.O. Box 2192 24101
Telephone: (4) 981-5815
Fax: (4) 991-0434
Hotel, Restaurant and Convention Centre.

Palm Beach Sport E Spa Hotel
Sea Shore 24101
Telephone: (4) 972-4-987-7777
Fax: (4) 972-4-991-0434
Email: palmbech@netvision.net.il
Web site: www.palmbeach.co.il

MUSEUMS
Akko Municipal Museum
Old City
Telephone: (4) 991-8251
Fax: (4) 981-6686

RESTAURANTS
Vegetarian
Amirei Hagalil
Akko-Safed Road, nr. Moshav Amirim 20115
Telephone: (4) 698-9815/6

YOUTH HOSTELS
Acre Youth Hostel
Telephone: (4) 991-1982
Fax: (4) 991-1982

ARAD
HOTELS
Arad
6 Hapalmach Street
Telephone: (8) 995-7040
Fax: (8) 995-7272

Margoa
Mo'av Street, POB 20 89100
Telephone: (8) 995-1222
Fax: (8) 995-7778
Email: margoa@mail.inter.net.il

Nof Arad
Moav Street
Telephone: (8) 995-7056
Fax: (8) 995-4053

YOUTH HOSTELS
Blau-Weis
Telephone: (8) 995-7150
This organisation is located in the centre of town.

AVIHAIL

MUSEUMS
Beit Hagedudim (History of Jewish Brigade W.W.I)
Telephone: (9) 882-2212
Fax: (9) 862-1619

B'NEI BERAK

HOTELS
Wiznitz
16 Damesek Elizier Street
Telephone: (3) 777-1413

RESTAURANTS
Dairy
Dairy Capit
34 Rabbi Akiv St
Telephone: (3) 579-6927

BEERSHEBA

HOTELS
Desert Inn
Tuviyahu Av.
Telephone: (8) 642-4922
Fax: (8) 641-2722

MUSEUMS
Man in the Desert Museum
Situated five miles north-east of the city.

TOURS
Bedouin Market
The market is held every Thursday but it has been affected negatively by tourism and modernization. Permanent Bedouin encampments can be seen south of town.

CAESAREA

HOTELS
Dan Caesarea Golf Hotel
PO Box 1120 30600
Telephone: (4) 626-9111
Fax: (4) 626-9122
Email: caesarea@danhotels.com
Web site: www.danhotels.com

RESTAURANTS
Caesarean Self Service
Paz Petrol Station
Telephone: (4) 633-4609

DAN

MUSEUMS
Natural History and Archaeology
Beit Ussishkin Nature Reserve 12245
Telephone: (4) 694-1704
Fax: (4) 695-1480
Email: ussishkin@kdan.co.il

DEAD SEA

HOTELS
Caesar Premier
Telephone: (8) 668-9666
Fax: (8) 652-0303
Contact the Caesar Group sales office in Tel Aviv for information, Tel: (03) 696-8383; Fax: (03) 696-9896.

Crown Plaza
Telephone: (8) 659-1919

Grand Nirvana
Telephone: (8) 668-9444
Fax: (8) 668-9400
Email: info@nirvana.co.il

Hod
Telephone: (8) 658-4644

Hyatt Regency
Telephone: (8) 659-1234

Moriah Gardens
Telephone: (8) 659-1591
Fax: (8) 658-4238

Radisson Moriah Plaza
Telephone: (8) 659-1591

DEGANIA ALEF

MUSEUMS
Beit Gordon
Telephone: (4) 675-0040
Fax: (4) 670-9514

EILAT

HOTELS
Ambassador
Coral Beach, PO Box 390 88103
Telephone: (8) 638-2222
Fax: (8) 638-2200
Email: info@ambassador.co.il
Web site: www.ambassador.co.il

Americana Eilat
PO Box 27, North Beach 88000
Telephone: (8) 633-3777
Fax: (8) 633-4174
Email: info@americanahotel.co.il
Web site: www.americanahotel.co.il

Caesar
North Beach
Telephone: (8) 630-5555
Fax: (8) 633-3497

Club-In Villa Resort
Rte. 90 (Eilat-Taba Road), Box 1505 Coral Beach 88000
Telephone: (8) 633-4555
Fax: (8) 633-4519

Dalia
North Beach
Telephone: (8) 633-4004
Fax: (8) 633-4072

Dan Eilat
Promenade, North Beach
Telephone: (8) 636-2222
Fax: (8) 636-2333

Edomit
New Tourist Center
Telephone: (8) 637-9511
Fax: (8) 637-9738

King Solomon's Palace
Promenade, North Beach
Telephone: (8) 633-3444
Fax: (8) 633-4189
Email: cro@isrotel.co.il
Web site: www.isrotel.co.il

Marina Club
North Beach
Telephone: (8) 633-4191
Fax: (8) 633-4206

Orchid
Rte. 90 (Eilat-Taba Road), Box 994 88000
Telephone: (8) 636-0360
Fax: (8) 637-5323

Princess
Rte. 90 (Eilat-Taba Road), Box 2323 88000
Telephone: (8) 636-5555
Fax: (8) 637-6333

Radisson Moriah Plaza
Promenade, North Beach
Telephone: (8) 636-1111
Fax: (8) 633-4158

Red Rock
North Beach
Telephone: (8) 637-3171
Fax: (8) 637-1705

Royal Beach
North Beach
Telephone: (8) 636-8888
Fax: (8) 636-8811
Email: cro@isrotel.co.il
Web site: www.isrotel.co.il

The Neptune Hotel
North Beach
Telephone: (8) 636-9369
Fax: (8) 633-4389

RESTAURANTS
Café Royal
King Solomon's Palace Hotel, North Beach
Telephone: (8) 667-6111

Chinese Restaurant
Shulamit Gardens Hotel, North Beach
Telephone: (8) 667-7515

Dolphin Baguette
Tourist Centre

Egged
Central Bus Station
Telephone: (8) 667-5161

El Morocco
Tourist Centre

Golden Lagoon
New Lagoona Hotel, North Beach
Telephone: (8) 667-2176

Halleluyah
Building 9, Tourist Centre
Telephone: (8) 667-5752

Dairy
La Trattoria
Radisson Moriah Plaza Hotel, North Beach
Telephone: (8) 636-1111

Meat
El Gaucho
Arrava Road. (Rte. 90)
Telephone: (8) 633-1549

Shipudei Habustan
The Dan Eilat Promenade
Telephone: (8) 636-2294

GALILEE
HOTELS
Ayelet Hashahar
Upper Galilee, Katzrin 12200
Telephone: (4) 693-2611
Fax: (4) 693-4777

Hacienda
Ma'a lot
Telephone: (4) 957-9000
Fax: (4) 997-4404

Rakefet
Mishgav, Western Galilee
Telephone: (4) 980-0403
Fax: (4) 980-0317

MUSEUMS
Bar-David Museum of Jewish Art
Kibbutz Bar'am, off Route 899
Telephone: (4) 698-8295
Fax: (4) 698-7505
Web site: www.galil-elion.org.il

Sculpture Gallery for Peace and Co-existence
Kawkab Abu Elhija, Gush Segev, Lower Galilee
Telephone: (4) 852-5251
Fax: (4) 852-9166
Email: bhagefen@netvision.il
Web site: www.haifa.gov.il/beit-hagefen/index

Tel Hai Sculpture Garden
Tel Hai, Upper Galilee Region
Telephone: (4) 694-3731
Fax: (4) 695-0697

The Museum of Photography
Tel Hai Industrial Park
Telephone: (4) 695-0769
Fax: (4) 695-0771
Web site: www.iscar.com

The Open Museum
Tefen Industrial Park, Migdal Tefen
Telephone: (4) 987-2977
Fax: (4) 987-2861
Web site: www.iscar.com

RESTAURANTS
Lev Hagolan
30 Dror. Street, Katzrin
Telephone: (4) 961-6643

Orcha
Commercial Centre, Katzrin
Telephone: (4) 696-1440

YOUTH HOSTELS
Karei Deshe (Tabgha)
Yoram
Telephone: (4) 672-0601
Fax: (4) 672-4818
Eleven miles north of Tiberias.

GOLAN HEIGHTS
LEISURE
Hamat Gader
The Golan Heights rise steeply fron the Sea of Galilee to the Mount Avital plateau. The Hamat Gader were thought to be the nicest spa baths in the whole Roman world, according to the Byzantine empress Eudocia. There are impressive ruins including the extensive Roman and Byzantine spa, which served as a grand bathing resort for six centuries, and an ancient synagogue. Four mineral springs and a freshwater spring emerge at Hamat Gader and so it is used today as a modern bathhouse. There is also an alligator farm where dozens of alligators and crocodiles can be seen lazing around.

MUSEUMS
The Golan Archeological Museum
Katzrin
Telephone: (4) 696-9636
Fax: (4) 696-9637

NATURE RESERVE
Gamla Nature Reserve
Telephone: (4) 682-2282
Fax: (4) 682-2285
Fifteen kilometres southeast of Katzrin.

RESTAURANTS
Hamat Gader Restaurant
Telephone: (4) 675-1039

GUSH ETZION
RESTAURANTS
Pizzeria Efrat
Te'ena Shopping Center, Efrat
Telephone: (2) 993-1630

Meat
The Oak Tree Restaurant
Judaica Center, Gush Etzion Junction
Telephone: (2) 993-4370
Fax: (2) 993-4949
Email: judaica1@netvision.net.il
Available for groups and events.

TOURS
Gush Etzion Judaica Center
Gush Etzion Junction
Telephone: (2) 993-4040; Tourism Dept. 993-8388
Fax: (2) 993-4949
Email: judaica1@netvision.net.ill
Web site: www.judaica.org.il
Display and sales hall that features the items of over 200 items of Israeli Judaica. Can be combined with a visit to Kibbutz Kfar Etzion to see an audio visual show that movingly describes the history of Gush Etzion.

HADERA
MUSEUMS
The Khan Museum
74 Hagiborim Street, POB 3232 38131
Telephone: (4) 632-2330; 632-4562
Fax: (4) 632-2072
Web site: www.khan-hadera.org.il
Hours: Sunday to Thursday, 8 am to 1 pm; Friday, 9 am to 12 pm; Sunday and Tuesday, 4 pm to 6 pm.

HAIFA
HOTELS
Dan Carmel
85 Hanassi Avenue
Telephone: (4) 830-3030
Fax: (4) 830-3040
Email: dancarmel@danhotels.com
Web site: www.danhotels.com

Dan Panorama
107 Hanassi Avenue
Telephone: (4) 835-2222
Fax: (4) 835-2235
Email: panorama-haifa@danhotels.com

Dvir
124 Yafe Nof Street
Telephone: (4) 838-9131
Fax: (4) 838-1068

Nof Haifa
101 Hanasi Avenue
Telephone: (4) 835-4311
Fax: (4) 838-8810
Email: s1@actcom.co.il
Web site: nof-hotels.co.il

Shulamit
15 Kiryat Sefer Street 34676
Telephone: (4) 834-2811
Fax: (4) 825-5206

MUSEUMS

Beit Pinchas Biological Insititute
124 Hatishbi Street
Telephone: (4) 837-2390
Fax: (4) 837-7019
Email: biolinst@netvision.net.il
Includes nature museum, zoo and botanical garden. Entrance via Gan Ha'em. Hours: Sunday to Thursday, Winter, 8 am to 4 pm, July to August, 8 am to 7 pm; Friday and holiday eves, 8 am to 2 pm; Saturday, 9 am to 5 pm; Winter, 9 am to 4 pm.

Israel Edible Oil Industry Museum
Shemen Factory, 2 Tovim Street, POB 136 31000
Telephone: (4) 865-4237
Fax: (4) 862-9237

Israel Railways Museum
Haifa East Railway Station
Telephone: (4) 856-4293
Fax: (4) 856-4310
Email: paulc@rail.org.il

Mane Katz Museum
89 Yafe-Nof Street 34641
Telephone: (4) 838-3482
Fax: (4) 836-2985

Museum of Clandestine Immigration & Navy Museum
204 Allenby Street 35472
Telephone: (4) 853-6249
Fax: (4) 851-2958
Open: Sunday-Thursday 08.30 am - 16.00 pm.

Museum of Haifa
26 Shabbtai Levy Street 33043
Telephone: (4) 852-3255
Fax: (4) 855-2714
Email: haifa4@netvision.net.il
Web site: www.haifa.gov.il
Includes Museums of Ancient Art, Modern Art and Music & Ethnology. Hours: Sunday, Monday, Wednesday, Thursday, 10 am to 4 pm; Tuesday, 4 pm to 7 pm; Friday and holidays, 10 am to 1 pm; Saturday, 10 am to 2 pm.

Museum of Pre-History
124 Hatishbi Street, Entrance from Gan Ha'em
Telephone: (4) 837-1833
Fax: (4) 855-2714

Reuben & Edith Hecht Museum
Haifa University 31905
Telephone: (4) 825-7773
Fax: (4) 824-0724
Email: mushecht@research.haifa.ac.il
Web site: www.mushecht.haifa.ac.il
Hours: Sunday, Monday, Wednesday, Thursday, 10 am to 4 pm; Tuesday, 10 am to 7 pm; Friday, 10 am to 1 pm; Saturday, 10 am to 2 pm. Admission free. All resturantes at the University are Kosher.

The Israel National Museum of Science, Planning and Technology.
The Historic Technion Building, Balfour Street, Hadar Ha carmel
Telephone: (4) 862-8111
Fax: (4) 867-9103
Email: museum@mustsee.org.il
Web site: www.mustsee.org.il

The National Maritime Museum
198 Allenby Road
Telephone: (4) 853-6622
Fax: (4) 853-9286
Hours: Sunday, Monday, Wednesday, Thursday, 10 am to 4 pm; Tuesday, 4 pm to 7 pm; Friday and holidays, 10 am to 1 pm; Saturday, 10 am to 2 pm.

Tikotin Museum of Japanese Art
89 Hanassi Avenue, Mount Carmel 34642
Telephone: (4) 838-3554
Fax: (4) 837-9824
Email: japanmus@netvision.net.il
Web site: www.haifamuseums.org.il
Hours: Monday, Wednesday, Thursday, 10 am to 5 pm; Tuesday, 10 am to 2 pm and 5 pm to 8 pm; Friday and holiday eves, 10 am to 1 pm; Saturday, 10 am to 2 pm.

University of Haifa Art Collection
University of Haifa, Mount Carmel
Telephone: (4) 824-0660
Fax: (4) 824-0309

RESTAURANTS

Egged
Central Bus Station
Telephone: (4) 851-5221
Self-service.

Hamber Burger
61 Herzl Street
Telephone: (4) 866-6739

Rondo
Dan Carmel Hotel, 87 Hanassi Blvd
Telephone: (4) 838-6211

Technion
Neve Shaanan
Telephone: (4) 823-3011
Self service. Lunch only.

The Chinese Restaurant of Nof
Nof Hotel, 101 Hanassi Blvd
Telephone: (4) 838-8731

Dairy
Milky Pinky (Milk Bar)
29 Haneviim Street
Telephone: (4) 866-4166

Meat
Mac David
131 Hanassi Blvd
Telephone: (4) 838-3684

TOURIST INFORMATION
48 Ben-Gurion Street
Telephone: (4) 853-5606
Fax: (4) 853-5610
What's on in Haifa
Telephone: (4) 864-0840

TOURS
Telephone: (4) 867-4342
Bahai shrine and gardens, Druse villages, Muchraka, the Moslem village of Kabair, the Carmelite monastery and Elijah's cave, Wednesday, 9:30am.
Mt Carmel, Druse villages, Kibbutz Ben Oren and Ein Hod artists' colony: Sundays, Mondays, Tuedays, Thurdays, Saturdays, 9:30am.

HANITA
MUSEUMS
Tower & Stockade Museum
Route 8990
Telephone: (4) 985-9677
Fax: (4) 985-9677

HAON
HOLIDAY VILLAGE
Kibbutz Haon
Jordan Valley
Telephone: (4) 675-7555/6

HAZOREA
MUSEUMS
Wilfrid Israel House of Oriental Art
Telephone: (4) 989-9566
Fax: (4) 989-0942

HERZLIA
HOTELS
Dan Accadia
Herzlia on Sea
Telephone: (9) 959-7070
Fax: (9) 959-7092
Email: danhtls@danhotels.co.il

Tadmor
38 Basel Street
Telephone: (9) 952-5000
Fax: (9) 957-5124
Email: hotel@tadmor.co.il
The Sharon
4 Ramot Yam Street, Herzlia on Sea 46748
Telephone: (9) 972-9-952-5777
Fax: (9) 972 9-927-3448
Email: sharon@sharon.co.il
Web site: www.sharon.co.il

MUSEUMS
Herzliya Museum of Contemporary Art
4 Habanim Street 46379
Telephone: (9) 950-2301
Fax: (9) 950-0043
Email: info@herzliyamuseum.co.il
Web site: www.herzliyamuseum.co.il

RESTAURANTS
Tadmor Hotel School
38 Basel Street 46660
Telephone: (9) 952-5050
Fax: (9) 957-5124
Email: hotel@tadmor.co.il

Meat
Steak.com
27 Rehov Maskit, Herzliya Pituah
Telephone: (9) 956-1145

TOURIST INFORMATION
English-Speaking Residents Association
PO Box 3132 46104
Telephone: (9) 950-8371
Fax: (9) 954-3781
Email: esra@trendline.co.il

JAFFA
MUSEUMS
The Antiquities Museum of Tel Aviv-Yafo (Jaffa Museum)
10 Mifratz Shlomo Street, Old Jaffa 68038
Telephone: (3) 682-5375
Fax: (3) 681-3624
Part of Eretz Israel Museum Tel Aviv. Opening hours: Sunday-Thursday 9 am to 1 pm.

JERUSALEM
ACCOMMODATION INFORMATION
Good Morning Jerusalem
9 Coresh Street 94146
Telephone: (2) 623-3459
Fax: (2) 625-9330
Email: gmjer@netvision.net.il
Web site: www.accommodation.co.il
Lists rooms and apartments available for tourists.

BED AND BREAKFAST
Le Sixteen
16 Midbar Sinai Street, Givat Hamivtar 97805
Telephone: (2) 532-8008
Fax: (2) 581-9159
Email: le16@le16-bnb.co.il
Web site: www.le16-bnb.co.il
Member of the Jerusalem Home Accommodation
Association. Can provide guest studios with kosher dairy
kitchenettes.

CONTACT INFORMATION
Jeff Seidel's Jewish Student Information Centre
5 Bet-El, Jewish Quarter, Old City
Telephone: (2) 628-2634
Fax: (2) 628-8338
Email: jseidel@jeffseidel.com
Web site: www.jeffseidel.com

Jeff Seidel's Student Centre for Hebrew University Students
14 Lechi
Telephone: (2) 581-2240
Fax: (2) 02-628-8338
Email: jseidel@jeffseidel.com
Web site: www.jeffseidel.com

GUEST HOUSE
Bet Shmuel
6 Shamma Street 94101
Telephone: (2) 620-3473; 620-3465
Fax: (2) 620-3467
Single and family guest rooms with a capacity of 240
beds; conference facilities and banquet services;
restaurant and coffee shop; international culture and
education centre with a central location.

HOTELS
Ariel Hotel Jerusalem
31 Hebron Road
Telephone: (2) 568-9999
Fax: (2) 673-4066
Email: info@arieljrm.co.il
Walking distance from Old City.

Caesar
208 Jaffa Road
Telephone: (2) 500-5656
Fax: (2) 538-2802
Email: caesarjm@netvision.net.il

Central
6 Pines Street
Telephone: (2) 538-4111
Fax: (2) 5381-480

Four Points
4 Vilnai Street 96110
Telephone: (2) 655-8888
Fax: (2) 651-2266
The hotel is located in the hotel area at the entrance to
the city and is within walking distance of the Israel
Museum and the Knesset.

Hyatt Regency Jerusalem
32 Lehi Street
Telephone: (2) 533-1234
Fax: (2) 581-5947
Email: hyattjrs@trendline.co.il
Web site: www.hyattjer.co.il

Inbal
Liberty Bell Park, 3 Jabotinsky Street 92145
Telephone: (2) 675-6666
Fax: (2) 675-6777
Email: rsv@inbal-hotel.co.il
Web site: www.inbal-hotel.co.il

Jerusalem Hilton
7 King David Street 94101
Telephone: (2) 621-1111
Fax: (2) 621-1000

Jerusalem Tower
23 Hillel Street 94581
Telephone: (2) 620-9209
Fax: (2) 625-2167
Email: towerhotels@012.net.il
Web site: www.towerhotels.com

King David
23 King David Street 94101
Telephone: (2) 620-8888
Fax: (2) 620-8882
Email: kingdavid@danhotels.com

King Solomon
32 King David Street
Telephone: (2) 569-5555
Fax: (2) 624-1174
Email: solhotel@netvision.net.il

Lev Yerushalayim
18 King George Street
Telephone: (2) 530-0333
Fax: (2) 623-2432

Menorah
44 Jaffa Road
Telephone: (2) 622-3122
Fax: (2) 625-0707

Mount Zion
17 Hebron Road
Telephone: (2) 568-9555
Fax: (2) 673-1425
Email: hotel@mountzion.co.il

Palatin
4 Agripas Street
Telephone: (2) 623-1141
Fax: (2) 625-9323
Email: info@hotel-palatin.co.il
Web site: www.hotel-palatin.co.il

Radisson Moriah Plaza Jerusalem
39 Keren Hayessod Street 94188
Telephone: (2) 569-5695
Fax: (2) 623-2411

Reich
1 Hagai Street, Bet Hakerem
Telephone: (2) 652-3121
Fax: (2) 652-3120

Renaissance Jerusalem Hotel
Ruppin Bridge, at Herz Blvd 91033
Telephone: (2) 659-9999
Fax: (2) 651-1824
Email: renjhot@netvision.net.il
Contact: Eli Velter.

Sheraton Jerusalem Plaza
47 King George Street
Telephone: (2) 629-8666
Fax: (2) 623-1667

Windmill
3 Mendele Street
Telephone: (2) 566-3111
Fax: (2) 561-0964

MUSEUMS
Ammunition Hill Memorial & Museum, Ramat Eshkol
Levy Eshkol Boulevard 91181
Telephone: (2) 582-8442
Fax: (2) 582-9132

Bible Lands Museum Jerusalem
25 Granot Street, POB 4670 91046
Telephone: (2) 561-1066
Fax: (2) 563-8228
Email: contact@blmj.org
Web site: www.blmj.org
The home of one of the most important collections of ancient artifacts displaying rare works of art from the dawn of civilisation to the Byzantine period. Gift shop, special exhibitions,weekly lectures and concerts. Daily guided tours in English and an audio guide are available. Groups by advance reservation. Open daily except Shabbat and Holidays. Call or email the museum for hours and program details. "Kosher restaurant". Daily English guided tours.

Herzl Museum
Herzl Blvd, Mount Herzl
Telephone: (2) 651-1108

L.A. Mayer Museum for Islamic Art
2 Hapalmach Street 92542
Telephone: (2) 566-1291/2
Fax: (2) 561-9802

Museum of Italian Jewish Art
27 Hillel Street 94581
Telephone: (2) 624-1610
Fax: (2) 625-3480
Web site: www.itcham.org.il/museum/

Museum of Natural History
6 Mohilever Street
Telephone: (2) 563-1116
Fax: (2) 566-0666

Nahon Museum of Italian Jewish Art
27 Hillel Street 94581
Telephone: (2) 624-1610
Fax: (2) 625-3840
Email: jija@netvision.net.il
Web site: www.jija.org
This special museum collects and preserves objects pertaining to the life of the Jews in Italy from the Middle Ages to the present day. The main attraction is the ancient synagogue of Conegliano Veneto, a township some 60 km from Venice relocated entirely to Israel. Hours: Sunday, Tuesday, Wednesday, 9.00am to 5.00pm, Monday, 9.00am to 2.00pm, Thursday, Friday, 9.00am to 1.00pm. For guided tours contact the numbers above.

Old Yishuv Court Museum
6 Or Hayim Street 91016
Telephone: (2) 628-4636
Fax: (2) 628-4636
The museum is located in the heart of the Jewish Quarter in the Old City of Jerusalem in a sixteenth-century building. It displays the story of the Jewish community from the periods under Ottoman rule, through the final days of the British Mandate. Hours Sunday to Thursday, 9 am to 2 pm.

S.Y. Agnon's House
16 Joseph Klausner Street, Talpiot 93388
Telephone: (2) 671-6498
Fax: (2) 673-8285
Email: agnon-h@zahav.net.il
Hours: Sunday to Thursday, 9 am to 1 pm.

Siebenberg House of Archaeological Museum
7 Hagittit Street, Jewish Quarter
Telephone: (2) 628-2341

The Chagall Windows at the Hadassah University Hospital
Ein Kerem
Telephone: (2) 972-2-6776271
Fax: (2) 972-2-6430934
Email: tourism@hadassah.org.il

The Israel Museum, Jerusalem
Ruppin Blvd
Telephone: (2) 02-670-8811
Fax: (2) 02-677-1332
Web site: www.imj.org.il
Includes Bezalel National Museum, Samuel Bronfman Biblical & Archaeological Museum, Shrine of the Book & the Rockefeller Museum in East Jerusalem.

The Sir Isaac & Lady Edith Wolfson Museum, Hechal Shlomo
4th Floor, 58 King George Street
Telephone: (2) 624-7908
Fax: (2) 623-1810
Email: hechalshlomo@bezeqint.net
Opening hours Sunday to Monday 10.00 - 14.00

Tourjeman Post Museum
4 Hail Hahandasa Street
Telephone: (2) 628-1278
Fax: (2) 627-7061

Tower of David Museum of the History of Jerusalem
Jaffa Gate
Telephone: (2) 626-5333
Fax: (2) 628-3418
Email: shivuk@tower.org.il
24-hour information line: 972-2-6265310

Yad Vashem, The Holocaust Martyrs' and Heroes' Remembrance Authority
Har Hazikaron, PO Box 3477 91034
Telephone: (2) 972-2-644-3400
Fax: (2) 972-2-644-3443
Email: general.information@yadvashem.org.il
Web site: www.yadvashem.org
Open 9 am-5 pm Sunday-Thursday, 9 am-2 pm Friday and eves of holidays, closed on Saturday and all Jewish holidays.

ORGANISATIONS
Ezer Mizion "Help from Zion"
25 Yirmiyahu St. 94467
Telephone: (2) 537-8070
Fax: (2) 538-3315
Email: ezerm@netvision.net.il
Web site: www.ezer-mizion.org.il
Opening hours are 8.00 am - 8.00 pm. Mailing address (midweek) - POB 41130 Jerusalem 91410.

Friends of Yad Sarah International Public Relations
Yad Sarah House, 124 Herzl Blvd. 96187
Telephone: (2) 972-2-6444425
Fax: (2) 972-2-6444423
Email: pata@yadsarah.org.il
Web site: www.yadsarah.org.il

Yad Sarah home care organization lends, free against a returnable deposit, regular and high-tech medical rehab. equipment. Visitors in wheelchairs can use the Yad Sarah special transportation vans, at a low fee. By pre-arrangement you can have the van and driver waiting at Ben Gurion airport. Minimum two weeks notice please for this service. Yad Sarah has 85 branches in Israel.

Travelers Aid of Israel
PO Box 2828
Telephone: (2) 582-0126
Fax: (2) 623-2742
Email: wolfilaw@netvision.net.il
Legal counselling, social and human services, accident victims legal assistance, immigrant assistance, interest free-loans, stranded travellers, medical assistance, crime-victim assistance, homelessness, emergency assistance.

RELIGIOUS ORGANISATIONS
Israel Council of Young Israel
Heichal Shlomo Building, 58 King George Street 91072
Telephone: (2) 623-1631
Fax: (2) 623-1363
Email: young-il@internet-zahav.net
Mailing address: POB 7306, 91072 Jerusalem, Israel. Office hours: Sunday through Thursday 9.00 am to 3.00 pm.

RESTAURANTS
Clafouti
2 Hasoreg Street
Telephone: (2) 624-4491

Pampa
3 Rehov Yosef Rivlin
Telephone: (2) 623-1455

Ye Olde English Tea Room
68 Jaffa Road
Telephone: (2) 537-6595

Dairy
Besograyim
45 Ussishkin Street
Telephone: (2) 624-5353

Café Rimon
4 Luntz Street (off Midrehov)
Telephone: (2) 624-3712

Chamomille
6 Yoel Solomon Street
Telephone: (2) 625-2750

Dagim Beni
1 Mesilat Yesharim Street
Telephone: (2) 622-2403

Daglicatesse
1 Rachel Imenu
Telephone: (2) 563-2657

Little Italy
38 Keren Hayesod Street
Telephone: (2) 561-7638

Mamma Mia
38 King George Street 94262
Telephone: (2) 624-8080
Fax: (2) 623-3336
Located in the centre of town in an old (1899) restored building. Air-conditioned. Hours: Sunday to Thursday, 12 pm to midnight, Friday 12 pm to 4 pm; Saturday, from the end of Shabbat.

Michael Andrew
12 Emil Bota
Telephone: (2) 624-0090

Of Course!
Zion Confederation House, Emile Botta Street
Telephone: (2) 624-5206

Off The Square
8 Ramban Street

Poire et Pomme
The Khan Theatre, 2 Remez Square
Telephone: (2) 671-9602

Rienzi
10 King David Street
Telephone: (2) 622-2312

Rimon
4 Lunz Street
Telephone: (2) 622-2772

Theatre Lounge
Jerusalem Theatre, 20 Marcus Street
Telephone: (2) 566-9351

Zeze
11 Bezalel Street
Telephone: (2) 623-1761

Meat
El Marrakesh
4 King David Street
Telephone: (2) 622-7577

Hanevi'im
54 Hanevi'im Street, Jerusalem
Telephone: (2) 624-7433

Marvad Haksamim
16 King George Street

Marziano & Toledano
15 Rehov Yad Harutzim
Telephone: (2) 672-8672

Norman's Steak 'n Burger
27 Emek Refaim Street
Telephone: (2) 566-6603
Fax: (2) 673-1768
Email: burger@normans.co.il
Web site: www.normans.co.il

American steakhouse. Reservations recommended. Easy walking distance from main hotels. Hours: Sunday to Thursday, 12 pm to 11 pm; Friday, closed; Saturday, from after Shabbat.

Rungsit
2 Jabotinsky Street
Telephone: (2) 561-1757

Shaul's Shwarma Centre
14 Ben-Yehuda Street
Telephone: (2) 622-5027

Shemesh
21 Ben-Yehuda Street
Telephone: (2) 622-2418

Shipodei Hagefen
74 Agrippas Street
Telephone: (2) 622-2367

Vanqueiro
54 Hanevi'im Street
Telephone: (2) 624-7432
Email: vanqueiro@softhome.net

Yemenite Step
12 Yoel Salamon Street
Telephone: (2) 624-0477

Pizzerias
Pizzeria Rimini
15 King George Street
Telephone: (2) 622-6505
7 Paran Street, Ramat Eshkol

Pizzeria Trevi
8 Leib Yaffe Street
Telephone: (2) 672-4136

Vegetarian
Belinda
20 King George Street
Telephone: (2) 624-5717
Fax: (2) 561-1176
Email: belindacatering@hotmail.com

Chamomile
6 Yoel Solomon St.
Telephone: (2) 625-2750

Village Green
33 Jaffa Street
Telephone: (2) 625-3065
Fax: (2) 625 3062
Catering takeaway function hall.

SYNAGOGUES
Great Synagogue
60 King George Street

Yeshurun
44 King George Street
Telephone: (2) 624-3942
Fax: (2) 622-4528
Email: netypjer@netvision.net.il

TOURIST INFORMATION
Ministry of Tourism
24 King George Street
Telephone: (2) 675-4811

Tourism Coordinator with the Palestinian Authority
Israel Ministry of Tourism, PO Box 1018, Jerusalem 91009
Telephone: (2) 675-4903
Fax: (2) 624-0571
Email: zvin@tourism.gov.il

TOURS
American P'eylim Student Union
10 Shoarim Street
Telephone: (2) 653-2131
Free tours of Jewish Quarter and free accommodation, in the hostel quarters.

Knesset (Parliament)
Telephone: (2) 675-3416
Fax: (2) 561-1201
Sunday & Thursday 8.30am and 2.30pm

Society for the Protection of Nature in Israel: Israeli Nature Trails
13 Helen Hamalka Street 95101
Telephone: (2) 624-4605
Fax: (2) 625-4953
Email: spnijeru@inter.net.il

YOUTH HOSTELS
Bet Bernstein
1 Keren Hayesod Street
Telephone: (2) 625-8286
80 rooms.

Davidka
67 HaNevi'im Street, PO Box 37110
Telephone: (2) 538-4555
Fax: (2) 538-8790
Seventy-five rooms; 4-6 bedded.

Ein Karem
Telephone: (2) 641-6282
Ninety-seven rooms. Ten minutes from the Louise Waterman-Wise Hotel in Bayit Vegan

Israel Youth Hostels Association
Youth Travel Bureau, Jerusalem International Convention Center, POB 6001, Jerusalem 91060
Telephone: (2) 655-8442
Fax: (2) 655-8431
Email: iyha@iyha.org.il
Web site: www.iyha.org.il
There are thirty-one youth hostels in Israel for students, youth groups and adults, which are supervised by the Israel Youth Hostels Association (a member of the International Youth Hostels Federation). All hostels offer the standard facilities of dormitories, kosher dining rooms, etc. Most hostels also have a guest house section, with double and family rooms and private facilities. Most are air-conditioned.

KFAR GILADI
MUSEUMS
Beit Hashomer
Telephone: (4) 694-1565
Fax: (4) 695-1505

KIBBUTZ HARDUF
RESTAURANTS
Vegetarian
Jutka's Restaurant
Telephone: (4) 905-9229
Fax: (4) 986-1106

KIBBUTZ YOTVATA
LEISURE
Biblical Wildlife Reserve Hai Bar Arava
The reserve is situated thirty-seven miles north of Eilat. Biologists have settled every breed of animal that is mentioned in the Bible. Animals include herd of Somalian wild asses, oryx antelope, ibex, ostriches, desert foxes, lynx, hyenas and the last desert leopard in the Negev, living out her days on the reserve. Guided tours start at 9 am and 10.30 am, noon and 1.30 pm.

RESTAURANTS
Dairy
Dairy Restaurant
Telephone: (8) 635-7449

KORAZIM
HOLIDAY VILLAGE
Amnon Bay Recreation Centre
Telephone: (4) 693-4431

Vered Hagalil Guest Farm
Telephone: (4) 693-5785
Fax: (4) 693-4964
Email: vered@veredhagalil.co.il

LOD
MUSEUMS
Museum of Jewish Ethnic Heritage
20 David Ha'melech Boulevard, Lod
Telephone: (8) 924-1160
Fax: (8) 924-9466
Email: zmalachi@post.tau.ac.il
P.O.B 383 Lod, 71101.

TOURIST INFORMATION
Ministry of Tourism
Ben Gurion International Airport
Telephone: (8) 971-1485

LOHAMEI HAGETAOT

MUSEUMS
Ghetto Fighters' House, Holocaust & Resistance Museum
M.P. (Mobile Post) 25220
Telephone: (4) 995-8080
Fax: (4) 995-8007
Email: simstein@gfh.org.il
Web site: www.gfh.org.il
Hours: Sunday-Thursday 9.00am to 4.00pm. Friday: Main museum closed. Yad Layeled open: 9.00am-1.00pm, Saturdays and holidays: Main museum closed. Yad Layeled open: 10.00am-5.00pm.

MAAGAN

HOLIDAY VILLAGE
Maagan Holiday Village
Sea of Galilee 15160
Telephone: (4) 665-4400
Fax: (4) 665-4455
Email: maaganhv@netvision.net.il

MAAYAN HAROD

YOUTH HOSTELS
Hankin
Telephone: (4) 658-1660
Seven miles east of Afula.

MAHANAYIM

TOURIST INFORMATION
Zomet Mahanayim
Telephone: (4) 693-5016

MOSHAV SHORESH

HOTELS
Shoresh Hotel
Harey Yehuda
Telephone: (2) 533-8338
Fax: (2) 534-0262
Email: info@shoresh.co.il
Web site: www.shoresh.co.il

NAHARIYA

HOTELS
Carlton
23 Ha'agaaton Blvd
Telephone: (4) 900-5555
Fax: (4) 982-3771
Email: carlton2@netvision.net.il
Web site: www.carlton-hotel.co.il

Rosenblatt
59 Weizmann Street
Telephone: (4) 992-0069
Fax: (4) 992-8121

LEISURE
Rosh Hanikra
Rosh Hanikra is situated four miles north of Nahariya, on the Lebanese border, and has an extensive system of caves which the sea has washed out of the soft chalk. There is also a lookout point with an adjacent restaurant which reveals a gorgeous panorama of the coast.

MUSEUMS
Nahariya Municipal Museum
19 Hagaaton Blvd
Telephone: (4) 987-9863
Fax: (4) 992-2303

NAZARETH

RESTAURANTS
Iberia
Rassco Centre, Nazareth Elite
Telephone: (4) 655-6314

NEGEV

RESTAURANTS
Bulgarian
112 Keren Kayemet Street, Beersheba
Telephone: (8) 623-8504

YOUTH HOSTELS
Bet Noam
Mitzpeh Ramon
Telephone: (8) 658-8433
Fax: (8) 658-8074

Bet Sara
Ein Gedi
Telephone: (8) 658-4165
1.5 miles north of Kibbutz Ein Gedi on Dead Sea.

Hevel Katif: Hadarom
Telephone: (8) 684-7597
Fax: (8) 684-7680
For more detailed information, apply either to the Israel Youth Hostels Assoc. or to the nearest Israel Government Tourist Office.

NETANYA

FOOD DELIVERY
Kosher Services Worldwide
Hashaked 16 42214
Telephone: (9) 98-626-422
Fax: (9) 98-847-673
Email: kosherisrael@013.net.il

HOLIDAY VILLAGE
Green Beach Holiday Village
Telephone: (9) 865-6166
Fax: (9) 835-0075

HOTELS
Arches
4 Remez Street 42271
Telephone: (9) 860-9860
Fax: (9) 860-9866
Email: arches-hotel@correy.com
Galei Hasharon
42 Ussishkin Street 42273
Telephone: (9) 834-1946
Fax: (9) 833-8128
Galil
26 Nice Blvd
Telephone: (9) 862-4455
Fax: (9) 862-4456
Ginot Yam
9 David Hamelech Street
Telephone: (9) 834-1007
Fax: (9) 861-5722
Goldar
1 Ussishkin Street
Telephone: (9) 833-8188
Fax: (9) 862-0680
Email: order@goldar.co.il
Grand Yahalom
15 Gad Machnes Street
Telephone: (9) 862-4888
Fax: (9) 862-4890
Green Beach
PO Box 230
Telephone: (9) 865-6166
Fax: (9) 835-0075
Jeremy
11 Gad Machnes Street
Telephone: (9) 862-2651
Fax: (9) 862-2651
King Koresh
6 Harav Kook Street
Telephone: (9) 861-3555
Fax: (9) 861-3444
King Solomon
18 Hamaapilim Street
Telephone: (9) 833-8444
Fax: (9) 861-1397
Margoa
9 Gad Machnes Street
Telephone: (9) 862-4434
Maxim
8 King David Street
Telephone: (9) 862-1062
Fax: (9) 862-0190

Metropol Grand
17 Gad Machnes Street
Telephone: (9) 862-4777
Fax: (9) 861-1556
Orly
20 Hamaapilim Street
Telephone: (9) 833-3091
Fax: (9) 862-5453
Palace
33 Gad Machnes Street
Telephone: (9) 862-0222
Fax: (9) 862-0224
Email: palacent@012.co.il
Park
7 David Hamelech Street
Telephone: (9) 862-3344
Fax: (9) 862-4029
Residence
18 Gad Machnes Street
Telephone: (9) 862-3777
Fax: (9) 862-3711
The Seasons
1 Nice Blvd
Telephone: (9) 860-1555
Fax: (9) 862-3022
Email: seasons@netmedia.net.il

SYNAGOGUES
Netanya Cultural Center
4 Raziel Street
Telephone: (9) 861-1687
Fax: (9) 861-7555
Email: Rina@netanya-cultural.co.il

Orthodox
New Synagogue of Netanya
7 MacDonald Street
Telephone: (9) 861-4591
Email: macshul@netvision.net.il
Young Israel Congregation of North Netanya
39 Shlomo Hamelech Street
Telephone: (9) 862-6472

TOURIST INFORMATION
Ha-Atzma'ut Square
Telephone: (9) 882-7286

PETACH TIKVA
MUSEUMS
Beit Yad Labanim
30 Arlozorov Street
Telephone: (3) 922-3450
Fax: (3) 922-3450

QATZRIN
MUSEUMS
Golan Archaeological Museum
Telephone: (4) 696-9636
Fax: (4) 696-2412
Email: museum@golan.org.il

RA'ANANA
RESTAURANTS
Lady D
158 Achuza
Telephone: (9) 791-6517
Limosa
5 Eliazar Jaffe
Telephone: (9) 790-3407
Pica Aduma
87 Achuza
Telephone: (9) 791-0508

RAMAT GAN
MUSEUMS
Museum of Israeli Art
146 Abba Hillel Street 52572
Telephone: (3) 752-1876
Fax: (3) 752-7377
Email: meirmusun@mail.inter.net.il
Pierre Gildesgame Maccabi Sports Museum
Kfar Hamaccabiah
Telephone: (3) 671-5729
Fax: (3) 574-6565
Email: lod@netvision.net.il
Yechiel Nahari Museum of Far Eastern Art
18 Hibat Zion Street
Telephone: (3) 578-1216
Fax: (3) 619-5837

RAMAT HANEGEV
TOURIST INFORMATION
Zomet Mashabay Sadeh
Telephone: (8) 655-7314

RAMAT YOHANAN
YOUTH HOSTELS
Yehuda Hatzair
Telephone: (4) 844-2976
Fax: (4) 844-2976
Eleven miles north-east of Haifa.

REHOVOT
MUSEUMS
Havayeda - Science Through Fun Science Park
5 Yechezkai Habibi Street 76000
Telephone: (8) 945-2949
Fax: (8) 945-2949
Web site: www.weizmann.ac.il

Weizmann Institute of Science
Yad Haim Weizmann, Marcus Sieff Blvd 76100
Telephone: (8) 934-4499
Fax: (8) 934-4960
Web site: www.weizmann.ac.il

ROSH HANIKRA
YOUTH HOSTELS
Rosh Hanikra
Telephone: (4) 998-2516
Near the grottos.

ROSH PINA
YOUTH HOSTELS
Hovevei Hateva
Telephone: (4) 693-7086
Sixteen miles north of Tiberias

SAFED
HOTELS
David
Mount Canaan
Telephone: (4) 692-0062
Nof Hagalil
Mount Canaan
Telephone: (4) 692-1595
Rimon Inn
Artists' Colony
Telephone: (4) 692-0665/6
Ron
Hativat Yiftah Street
Telephone: (4) 697-2590

MUSEUMS
Beit Hameiri Institute(History & Heritage of Safed)
Keren Hayesod Street 13110
Telephone: (4) 697-1307
Fax: (4) 692-1902
Israel Bible Museum
Citadel Hill
Telephone: (4) 699-9972
Fax: (4) 699-9972
Near Ron Hotel
Museum of Printing History
Artists' Colony
Telephone: (4) 692-3022

TOURIST INFORMATION
50 Jerusalem Street
Telephone: (4) 692-0961/633

YOUTH HOSTELS
Bet Benyamin
Telephone: (4) 692-1086
Fax: (4) 697-3514
In southern part of town.

TEL AVIV

CONTACT INFORMATION

Jewish Student Information Centre
Tel Aviv University Off-Campus Center, 82/10
Levanon Street, Ramat Aviv
Email: jseidel@netmedia.net.il

HOTELS

Adiv
5 Mendele Street
Telephone: (3) 522-9141

Ambassador
56 Herbert Samuel Street
Telephone: (3) 510-3993
Fax: (3) 517-6308

Armon Hayarkon
268 Hayarkon Street
Telephone: (3) 605-5271
Fax: (3) 605-8485

Avia
Ben Gurion Intl Airport Area
Telephone: (3) 539-3333
Fax: (3) 539-3319

Basel
156 Hayarkon Street
Telephone: (3) 520-7711
Fax: (3) 527-0005

Bell
12 Allenby Street
Telephone: (3) 517-7011
Fax: (3) 517-4352

Carlton Tel Aviv
10 Eliezer Peri Street
Telephone: (3) 520-1818
Fax: (3) 527-1043
Email: request@carlton.co.il

City
9 Mapu Street
Telephone: (3) 524-6253
Fax: (3) 524-6250

Dan Panorama
Charles Clore Park
Telephone: (3) 519-0190

Dan Tel Aviv
99 Hayarkon Street
Telephone: (3) 520-2525
Fax: (3) 524-9755
Email: dantelaviv@danhotels.com

Grand Beach
250 Hayarkon Street
Telephone: (3) 543-3333
Fax: (3) 546-6589
Email: reservation@grandbeach.co.il
Web site: www.grandbeach.co.il
Synagogue on premises.

Howard Johnson - Shalom
216 Hayarkon Street
Telephone: (3) 524-3277
Fax: (3) 523-5895
Email: h_shlom@netvision.net.il

Maxim
86 Hayarkon Street, P.O.B. 3442 63903
Telephone: (3) 517-3721/5
Fax: (3) 517-3726

Metropolitan
11-15 Trumpeldor Street 63803
Telephone: (3) 519-2727
Fax: (3) 517-2626
Email: reserve@metrotlv.co.il
Web site: www.hotelmetropolitan.co.il

Ramat Aviv
151 Namir Road
Telephone: (3) 699-0777
Fax: (3) 699-0997

Renaissance Tel Aviv
121 Hayarkon Street 63453
Telephone: (3) 521-5555
Fax: (3) 521-5588
Email: reserv@renaissance-tlv.co.il

Sheraton Moriah
155 Hayarkon Street
Telephone: (3) 521-6666
Fax: (3) 527-1065
Email: shermor@inter.net.il

Sheraton Tel Aviv Hotel & Towers
115 Hayarkon Street
Telephone: (3) 521-1111
Fax: (3) 523-3322
Email: shtelviv@netvision.net.il

Tal
287 Hayarkon Street
Telephone: (3) 542-5500
Fax: (3) 542-5501

Tel Aviv Hilton
Independence Park 63405
Telephone: (3) 520-2222
Fax: (3) 527-2711
Email: fom_tel-aviv@hilton.com

Yamit Park Plaza
79 Hayarkon Street
Telephone: (3) 517-7111
Fax: (3) 517-4719
Email: yamit@netvision.net.il

MUSEUMS

Beit Bialik
22 Bialik Street
Telephone: (3) 525-3403
Fax: (3) 525-4530

Ben Gurion House
17 Ben Gurion Boulevard
Telephone: (3) 522-1010
Fax: (3) 524-7293

Eretz Israel Museum
2 Haim Levanon Street 69975
Telephone: (3) 641-5244
Fax: (3) 641-2408

Hagana Museum
23 Rothschild Blvd. 65122
Telephone: (3) 560-8624
Fax: (3) 566-1208

Helena Rubenstein Pavilion for Contemporary Art
6 Tarsat Street
Telephone: (3) 528-7196

Jabotinsky Museum
38 King George Street 62398
Telephone: (3) 528-7320
Fax: (3) 528-5587
Email: jabo@actcom.co.il
Web site: www.jabotinsky.org
Hours: Sunday to Thursday, 8 am to 4 pm.

Lehi Museum
8 Stern Street 66085
Telephone: (3) 682-0288
Fax: (3) 681-9264

Museum of the Jewish Diaspora (Beth Hatefutsoth)
Klausner Street, Ramat Aviv
Telephone: (3) 646-2020
Fax: (3) 646-2134
Email: bhmuseum@post.tav.ac.il
Web site: www.bh.org.il

Tel Aviv Museum of Art
27 Shaul Hamelech Boulevard 61332
Telephone: (3) 972-3-695-7361
Fax: (3) 972-3-695-8099
Web site: www.tamuseum.com
Hours: Monday and Wednesday 10 am - 4 pm, Tuesday and Thursday 10 am to 10 pm , Friday 10am to 2 pm and Saturday, 10 am to 4 pm Public transport: buses 9, 11 18, 28, 70, 82, 90, 91, 111. Parking facilities.

RESTAURANTS
Dairy
Apropo
Alexander Hotel, 3 Havakuk Street
Telephone: (3) 544-4442

Felafelim Shop
86 Rehov Ibn-Gvirol
Telephone: (3) 524-6781

Hungarian Blintzes
35 Yirmiyahu Street

Telephone: (3) 605-0674

Meat
China Lee
102 Hayarkon Street
Telephone: (3) 524-6119

Olive Leaf
Sheraton Tel Aviv Hotel and Towers, 115 Hayarkon Street
Telephone: (3) 521-9300
Fax: (3) 521-9301
Web site: www.sheraton-telaviv.com
Innovative cuisine with Mediterranean flavours.

Shaul's Inn
11 Elyashiv Street, Kerem Hatemanim
Telephone: (3) 517-3303
Fax: (3) 517-7619
Oriental and Yemenite food. Popular and exclusive sections. Hours: 12 pm to 12 am.

SYNAGOGUES
Bilu
122 Rothschild Blvd.

Ihud Shivat Zion
86 Ben-Yehuda Street
Central European rite.

Ashkenazi
Main Synagogue
110 Allenby Road

TOURIST INFORMATION
ISSTA
109 Ben Yehuda Street

The Ministry of Tourism
6 Wilson Street
Telephone: (3) 556-2339
The Ministry of Tourism publishes a guide called 'The Best of Israel', detailing shops participating in the VAT refund scheme and recommended restaurants.

TIBERIAS
HOTELS
Ariston
19 Herzl Blvd
Telephone: (4) 679-0244
Fax: (4) 672-2002

Astoria
13 Ohel Ya'akov Street
Telephone: (4) 672-2351
Fax: (4) 672-5108

Caesar
103 The Promenade
Telephone: (4) 672-7272
Fax: (4) 679-1013

Carmel Jordan River
Habanim Street
Telephone: (4) 671-4444
Fax: (4) 672 2111

Gai Beach
Derech Hamerchatzaot
Telephone: (4) 670-0700
Fax: (4) 679-2766

Galei Kinnereth
1 Kaplan Street
Telephone: (4) 672-8888
Fax: (4) 679-0260

Golan
14 Achad Ha'am Street
Telephone: (4) 679-1901
Fax: (4) 672-1905

Kinar
N.E. Sea of Galilee
Telephone: (4) 673-8888
Fax: (4) 673-8811
Email: kinarmamag@kinar.co.il

Lavi Kibbutz Hotel
Lower Galilee 15267
Telephone: (4) 679-9450
Fax: (4) 679-9399
Email: hotel@lavi.co.il
Web site: www.lavi.co.il

Pagoda
Lido Beach, PO Box 253 14102
Telephone: (4) 672-5513
Fax: (4) 672-5518
Email: liz@kinneret.co.il
Open Sunday to Thursday 12.30-11.30pm. Saturday - opens for dinner only.

Quiet Beach
Gedud Barak Street
Telephone: (4) 679-0125
Fax: (4) 679-0261

TOURIST INFORMATION
Tourist Office
Ha-banim Street, In the Archaeological Park
Telephone: (4) 672-5666

ZICHRON YA'ACHOV
MUSEUMS
Nili Museum & Aaronson House
40 Hameyasdim Street 30950
Telephone: (4) 639-0120
Fax: (4) 639-0119

RESTAURANTS
Dairy
Habayit Bayekev
Carmel Mizrachi Winery, Rehov Hayayin
Telephone: (4) 629-0977
Fax: (4) 629-0957

TOURS
Old City Guesthouse and Youth Centre
9 Shoney Halachot Street, Old City of Jerusalem 97501
Telephone: (4) 972-2-628-9313
Fax: (4) 02-628-9314
Email: Olyshapira@yahoo.com
Free accommodation.

ITALY

Italy has an ancient connection with the Jews, and was home to one of the earliest Diaspora communities. Before the Roman invasion of ancient Israel, Judah Maccabee had a representative in Rome, and one of the reasons for the invasion was the Romans' desire to access the salt supply from the Dead Sea. There were Jewish communities in Italy after the destruction of the Second Temple, as Italy was the trading hub of the Roman empire. After Christianity became the official religion in 313CE, restrictions began to be placed on the Jewish population, forcing the community to migrate from town to town across the country.

In the medieval period, there was a brief flourishing of learning, but the Spanish conquered southern Italy in the fifteenth century, expelling the Jews from Sicily, Sardinia and, eventually, Naples. The first ever ghetto was established in Venice in 1516. Later in the century descendants of those expelled from Spain and Portugal arrived. Conquest by Napoleon led to the emancipation of Italian Jewry, and full equal rights were granted in 1870.

Ironically, the Italian Fascist party contained some Jewish members, as Mussolini was not anti-semitic and, even under pressure from Hitler, did not instigate any major anti-semitic policy. The situation changed after Germany's occupation of the north in

1943. Eventually, almost 8,000 Italian Jews were killed in Auschwitz, although the local population hid many of those who survived.

Today there is a central organisation which provides services for Italian Jews. There are kosher restaurants in Rome, Milan and other towns. There are also Jewish schools.

GMT +1 hour
Country calling code: (+39)
Total population: 57,523,000
Jewish population: 30,000
Emergency telephone: (Police – 112) (Fire – 115) (Ambulance – 116)
Electricity voltage: (Electricity voltage – 220)

ANCONA
COMMUNITY ORGANISATIONS
Community Offices
Via Fanti 2 bis
Telephone: (71) 202638

MIKVAOT
Via Astagno

ASTI
MUSEUMS
Via Ottolenghi 8, Torino
Telephone: (141) 539281

SYNAGOGUES
Synagogue
Via Ottolenghi 8, Torino

BOLOGNA
CAFETERIA
Comunita Ebraica Bologna
Via Gombruti 9 40123
Telephone: (51) 232-066
Fax: (51) 229-474
Email: comebrbol@libero.it
Supervision: Rabbi Alberto Sermoneta
Lunch Sunday to Friday; dinner Friday; closed mid-July and August.

COMMUNITY ORGANISATIONS
Via Gombruti 9 40123
Telephone: (51) 232-066 & 227-931 (office of Rabbi)
Fax: (51) 229-474
Email: comebrbol@libero.it
Web site: www.menorah.it/ceb/indice.htm

MIKVAOT
Mikveh Chaya Mushkah
Via Oreste Regnoli 17/1
Telephone: (51) 623-0316

MUSEUMS
Museo Ebraico
Palazzo Pannolini, via Valdonica, 1/5 40126
Telephone: (51) 2911280
Fax: (51) 235430
Email: info@museoebraicobo.it
Web site: www.museoebraicobo.it
The Jewish Museum of Bologna is located in Via Valdonica, in the area of the former ghetto. It was established as a means of conserving the Jewish cultural heritage that for centuries has been deeply rooted in Bologna and in the Emila Romagna region. It has a bookshop specialising on Jewish matters. Jewish itineraries.

SYNAGOGUES
Via Mario Finzi

CASALE MONFERRATO
SYNAGOGUES
Community Offices
Vicolo Salomone Olper 44
Telephone: (142) 71807
Fax: (142) 76444
Email: qqcasale@mail.dex-net.com
Web site: www.menorah.it/qqcasale/indice.htm
The synagogue, built in 1595 is one of the most interesting in North Italy. It also contains a Jewish museum. Casale-Monferrato is on the Turin-Milan road, and can be reached by turning off it about thirteen miles beyond Chivasso. Casale may also be reached via tollway A26 (exit Casale north or south, whichever comes first). It is advisable to make advance appointments for visiting either the synagogue or Museum. Closed in the months of January, February and August.

CUNEO
TOURIST SITES
Via Mondovi
Telephone: (171) 692-007
A beautiful synagogue; parts dating from the fifteenth century. Services are now only held on Yom Kippur. In 1799 a special Purim was established after the synagogue was saved from destruction by a shell.

FERRARA
COMMUNITY ORGANISATIONS
Community of Ferrara
Via Mazzini 95 44100
Telephone: (532) 24 70 04
Fax: (532) 24 70 04

MIKVAOT
Via Mazzini 95
Telephone: (532) 24 70 04

MUSEUMS
Jewish Museum of Ferrara
Via Mazzini 95 44100
Telephone: (532) 21 02 28
Fax: (532) 21 02 28
Email: museoebraico@comune.fe.it
Web site: www.comune.fe.it/museoebraico
Guided tours in English on Sunday to Thursday 10.00 am, 11.00 am, 12.00 pm. Closed on Fridays and Saturdays.

SYNAGOGUES
Via Mazzini 95
Telephone: (532) 24 70 33

FLORENCE
Although there is a belief that Jewish merchants lived in the city during Roman times there is no real evidence to substantiate this.

The known community was established in 1437 when Jewish financiers were invited to the city. The Medici family protected the community. Following their leaving in 1494 the Jews were expelled. In due course they returned and a ghetto was established in 1571. Emancipation was only achieved with the entry of Napoleon in 1799.

BAKERIES
Forno dei Ciompi
Piazza dei Ciompi
Telephone: (55) 241-256

BUTCHERS
Bruno Falsettini
Mercato Coperto di S., Ambrogio
Telephone: (55) 248-0740
8 am to 10 am. Order in advance specifying kosher.

Gionvannino
Via dei Macci 106
Telephone: (55) 248-0734
7.30 am to 1.00 pm. Order in advance specifying kosher.

COMMUNITY ORGANISATIONS
Community Offices
Via L.C. Farini 4, Firenze 50121
Telephone: (55) 245252
Fax: (55) 241811
Email: comebrfi@fol.it
Web site: www.fol.it/sinagoga
Open from Sunday to Friday from 9.30 am to 12.30 pm (Sunday closed in July and August).

HOTELS
Regency
Massimo D'Azeglio 3
Telephone: (55) 245247
Fax: (55) 2346735
Email: info@regency-hotel.com
Web site: www.regency-hotel.com
Located in the square, near the synagogue.

MIKVAOT
Via L.C. Farini 4, Firenze 50121
Telephone: (55) 245252
Fax: (55) 241811
Email: comebrfi@fol.it
Web site: www.fol.it/sinagoga

MUSEUMS
Jewish Museum
Via L.C. Farini 4, Firenze 50121
Telephone: (55) 245252
Fax: (55) 241811
Email: comebrfi@fol.it
Web site: www.fol.it/sinagoga
There is also a religious and artistic souvenir shop. Open Sunday - Thursday. Groups are kindly requested to book in advance. For further information and booking, please contact the Administation Office. (055) 2346054.

RESTAURANTS
Vegetarian Kosher
Ruth's
Via Farini 2/A
Telephone: (55) 248-0888
Bookings required for Shabbat meals and groups. Take-away.

SYNAGOGUES
Orthodox
Via L.C. Farini 4, Firenze 50121
Telephone: (55) 245252
Fax: (55) 241811
Email: comebrfi@fol.it
Web site: www.fol.it/sinagoga
Services on Shabbat and holidays, not daily. After service there is a public Kiddush. The synagogue is open for tourists from Sunday to Thursday (hours vary). Groups should book in advance.

Via De Banchi
Telephone: (55) 212-474
After the service there is a public Kiddush. For the timetable of services ask in the Community Office.

GENOA
SYNAGOGUES
Synagogue and Community Offices
Via Bertora 6 16122
Telephone: (101) 839-1513
Fax: (101) 846-1006
Email: comgenova@tin.it
Every Friday evening and Shabbat morning.

GORIZIA
SYNAGOGUES
Via Ascoli 19, Gradicia
Telephone: (3831) 532115

LEGHORN

BUTCHERS
Corucci
Banco 25, Mercato Centrale, Livorno
Telephone: (586) 884596

MIKVAOT
Community Offices
Piazza Benamozegh 1, Livorno
Telephone: (586) 896290

MUSEUMS
Jewish Museum
via Micali 21, Livorno
Telephone: (586) 893361
Visits only by appointment.

SYNAGOGUES
Community Offices
Piazza Benamozegh 1, Livorno
Telephone: (586) 896290
Fax: (586) 896290

MANTUA

SYNAGOGUES
Via G. Govi 11, Mantova
Telephone: (379) 321490

MERANO

MUSEUMS
Jewish Museum
Via Schiller 14
Telephone: (473) 236127
Fax: (473) 206210
Email: meranoebraica@hotmail.com
Hours: Tuesday and Wednesday 3 pm-6 pm. Thursday 9 am-12 am. Friday 3 pm-5 pm.

SYNAGOGUES
Community Offices
Via Schiller 14
Telephone: (473) 236127
Fax: (473) 206210
Email: meranoebraica@hotmail.com

MILAN

Home for the second largest community in Italy, (10,000). The Ambrosiana Museum (Piazza Pio xi) contains a number of Hebrew books, manuscripts and other Judaica.

COMMUNITY ORGANISATIONS
Sally Mayer 2
Telephone: (2) 483-02806
Fax: (2) 483-04660

DOCUMENTATION CENTRE
Contemporary Jewish Documentation Centre
Via Eupili 8
Telephone: (2) 316338
Fax: (2) 336-02728

GROCERIES
Eretz
Largo Scalabrini 5
Telephone: (2) 423-6891
Fax: (2) 423-4753
Hours: 9 am to 7:30 pm. Buses, 50, 95, 13, 61, subway 1 (red), stop, Bande-Nere.

MIKVAOT
Central Synagogue
Via Guastalla 19
Telephone: (2) 551-2101
Fax: (2) 5519-2699

Chaya Mushka
35 Carlo Poerio

Persian
Angelo Donati Beth Hamidrash
Via Sally Mayer 4-6

RESTAURANTS
Eshel Isroel
Via Benvenuto Cellini 2
Telephone: (2) 545-5076
Supervision: Rav G. H. Garelik
Open weekdays.

Mifgash Jewish Center
via Montecuccoli 35 20146
Telephone: (2) 4156199
Fax: (2) 41291105
Email: sissirattan@libero.it

Dairy
Carmel
viale San Gimignano 10 20146
Telephone: (2) 2-416368
Fax: (2) 2-416368
Email: info@carmelbylolita.com
Web site: www.carmelbylolita.com
Supervision: Kasrut supervision: Rav M Malri
Hours 12.00 noon to 2.30pm and 6.00pm to 11.30pm.

Meat
Glat Kosher Beit Yosef
via Montecuccoli 35 20146
Telephone: (2) 4156199
Fax: (2) 41291105
Email: sissirattan@libero.it

Re Salomone
Via Washington, 9
Telephone: (2) 469-4643
Fax: (2) 43318049
Email: resalomone@tiscalinet.it
International Meat restaurant with mediterranean, Italian and oriental food and take-away.

SYNAGOGUES
Beth Shlomo
Galleria Vittorio Emanuele, (Via Ugo Foscolo 3.)
20121
Telephone: (2) 8646-6118
Fax: (2) 8646-6118
Email: fweb.shlomo@bethshlomo.it
Web site: www.bethshlomo.it
Services are held on Friday evening, Shabbat, Sunday morning and Holy Days.

Central Synagogue
Via Guastalla 19
Telephone: (2) 551-2101
Fax: (2) 5519-2699

Merkos L'Inyonei Chinuch
Via Carlo Poerio 35 20129
Telephone: (2) 295-31213

New Home for Aged
Via Leone XIII
Telephone: (2) 498-2604
Services on Sabbaths and festivals. Kosher food available upon reservation.

New Synagogue
Via Eupili 8
Service on Sabbaths and festivals.

Orthodox
Ohel Yacob
Via Benvenuto Cellini 2
Telephone: (2) 545-5076

Orthodox Sephardi
Via Guastalla 19
Telephone: (2) 551-2029
Fax: (2) 551-92699
Rabbi Dr Laras is the Chief Rabbi.

MODENA
BUTCHERS
Macelleria Duomo
Mercato Coperto (Covered Market), Stand 25
Telephone: (59) 217269

SYNAGOGUES
Community Offices
Piazza Mazzini 26
Telephone: (59) 223978

NAPLES
SYNAGOGUES
Via Cappella Vecchia 31, Napoli
Telephone: (81) 764-3480
Email: c.l.na@virgilio.it

PADUA
MIKVAOT
Via S. Martino e Solferino 9, Padova
Telephone: (49) 871-9501

SYNAGOGUES
Community Offices
Via S. Martino e Solferino 9, Padova
Telephone: (49) 875-1106

PARMA
SYNAGOGUES
Vicolo Cervi 4

TOURIST SITES
Biblioteca Palatina
Palazzo della Pioltta 1-43100
Telephone: (521) 282-217
Fax: (521) 235-662
The collection of 1700 Hebrew manuscripts, derived from the collection of Giovanni Bernardo Rossi (1742-1831) the first bibliographer of Hebrew incunabula is said to be the greatest collector of Judaica put together by a Christian scholar.

PERUGIA
SYNAGOGUES
P. della Republica 77
Telephone: (75) 21250

PISA
SYNAGOGUES
Community Offices
Via Palestro 24
Telephone: (50) 542580
Services are held on festivals and Holy Days. During the week the resident beadle will be glad to show visitors round the synagogue, which is famed for its beauty. It is very near the Teatro Verdi.

RICCIONE
HOTELS
Vienna Touring Hotel
Telephone: (54) 160-1245
In the summer, kosher food is obtainable. Provides vegetarian food and particularly welcomes Jewish guests.

ROME

About half of Italian Jewry (some 15,000) live in Rome. As there has been such a long period of Jewish settlement, a Nusach Italki (Italian prayer ritual) has developed, which is practised in some synagogues in the town. Kosher restuarants and kosher food are available. Titus' Arch, depicting the destruction of Jerusalem by the Romans, is in the city, and Jews were forbidden to walk under it. The ghetto of Rome is behind the Great Synagogue. A visit worth considering is to the ancient Jewish burial sites along the Appian Way. Check about tour arrangements with the Jewish Community offices, Tel: 580-3667.

BAKERIES
Limentani Settimio
Via Portico d'Ottavia 1 186
Telephone: (6) 687-8637

Pasticceria Bernasconi
Piazza Benedetto Cairoli 16 00186
Telephone: (6) 6880-6264

BED AND BREAKFAST
Italian Kosher Bed & Breakfast
Via Nazionale 00184
Telephone: (6) 627-6995
Fax: (6) 4893-0253
Email: kosherbedbreakfast@tiscali.it
Situated in the heart of the historic center.

Locanda Carmel
via Goffredo Mameli 11 153
Telephone: (6) 580-9921
Fax: (6) 581-8853
Email: reservation@hotelcarmel.it
Web site: www.hotelcarmel.it
Pension situated in the old district of Trastevere, ten minutes from the main synagogue. Kosher breakfast only

Simcha Labi
Via Imperia 2, CAP 00161
Telephone: (6) 4423—0332
Supervision: Chabad Rabbi

Soggiorno il Boschetto
Via del Boschetto 13 00184
Telephone: (6) 0039-349-182-0287
Fax: (6) 0039-06-48907215
Email: info@soggiornoilgirasole.com
Web site: www.soggiornoilgirasole.com
Kosher pension situated in the old town center. Kosher breakfast. Accommodation for Shabbat dinner and lunch.

BOOKSELLERS
Menorah
Via del Tempio 2 00186
Telephone: (6) 687-9297
Email: menorah@menorah.it
Web site: www.menorah.it

BUTCHERS
Babani Ben David
Via Lorenzo il Magnifico 70 00161
Telephone: (6) 4424-3959
Supervision: Chief Rabbinate of Rome

Di Porto
Via Damaso Cerquetti 2 00152
Telephone: (6) 534-6992
Supervision: Chief Rabbinate of Rome

Di Veroli
Via Galla e Sidama 51 00199
Telephone: (6) 8620-7971
Supervision: Chief Rabbinate of Rome

Gepe-Gean
Via Stamira 2/B 00162
Telephone: (6) 4424-4055
Supervision: Chief Rabbinate of Rome

Ouazana
Via S. Gherardi 16-18 00146
Telephone: (6) 556-5231
Supervision: Chief Rabbinate of Rome
Via Giacomo Boni 18 00162
Telephone: (6) 4420-2626

Pascarella
Via Cesare Pascarella 36 00153
Telephone: (6) 588-1698
Supervision: Chief Rabbinate of Rome

Spizzichino
Via del Forte Bravetta 148 00164
Telephone: (6) 6615-7796
Supervision: Chief Rabbinate of Rome

Terracina
Via S. Maria del Pianto 62 00186
Telephone: (6) 6880-1364
Supervision: Chief Rabbinate of Rome

COMMUNITY ORGANISATIONS
Unione delle Comunita Ebraiche Italiane (Union of Italian Jewish Communities)
Lungotevere R. Sanzio 9
Telephone: (6) 580-3667
Fax: (6) 589-9569
Email: info@ucei.it
Web site: www.ucei.it
Information on Italian Jewry, its monuments and history may be obtained from here.

DELICATESSEN
Kosher Bistrot
Terracina Angelo, via Santa Maria del Pianto 68-69
Telephone: (6) 686-4398
Supervision: Chief Rabbinate of Rome

Kosher Point Minimarket
Via Orso Maria Corbino 17 00146
Telephone: (6) 556-5760

Sciunnah

Via A. lo Surdo 27/a 00146
Telephone: (6) 556-5760
Supervision: Chief Rabbinate of Rome
Hand made kosher pasta and ravioli.

EMBASSY

Embassy of Israel

Via Michele Mercati 14 197
Telephone: (6) 322-1541
Via Michele Mercati 14 00197
Fax: (6) 3619-8555
Email: info-coor@roma.mfa.gov.il
Web site: www.israel-amb.it

Embassy of Israel c/o The Holy See

Via Michele Mercati 12 00197
Telephone: (6) 3619-8690
Fax: (6) 3619-8626
Email: ambsec-vat@holysee.mfa.gov.il

Embassy of Israel to The Holy See

Via Michele Mercati 12 197
Telephone: (6) 3619-8690
Fax: (6) 3619-8626

MEDIA

Newspaper

Shalom

Lungotevere Cenci 1
Telephone: (6) 687-6816
Fax: (6) 686-8324
Email: shalom.mensile@flashnet.it
Web site: www.shalom.it
Monthly.

MIKVAOT

Lungotevere Cenci (Tempio) 9
Telephone: (6) 6840-0651
Ask for Mrs Elena Di Capua
Via Balbo 33
Telephone: (6) 7214210
Ask for Mrs. Gabriella Del Monte.

MUSEUMS

Museum of the Italian Resistance

Via Tasso 145
Telephone: (6) 700-3866
The museum was extended in 2001 with new displays dedicated to the fate of Roman Jews between 1938 and 1944.

The Jewish Museum

Lungotevere Cenci
Telephone: (6) 6840-0661
Fax: (6) 6840-0684
Email: museo.ebraico@romacer.org

The main synagogue building contains a permanent exhibition covering the 2000 year history of the Italian Jewish community. Another link with this long history is the Rome Ghetto almost adjoining. It is a maze of narrow alleys dating from Imperial Roman times, within which, until 1870, all Roman Jews were confined under curfew. A striking monument has been erected to the memory of 335 Jewish and Christian citizens of Rome who were massacred in 1944 by the Nazis in the Fosse Ardeatine: It lies just outside the Porta San Paolo.

RELIGIOUS ORGANISATIONS

The Italian Rabbinical Council

Headquarters, Lungotevere Sanzio 9
Telephone: (6) 580-3667; 580-3670

RESTAURANTS

Dairy

Ristorante Yotvate

Piazza Cenci 70 186
Telephone: (6) 6813-4481
Supervision: Chief Rabbinate of Rome
Open at noon.

Meat

Kasher Pizza

Via Luigi Magrini 12 146
Telephone: (6) 559-0790

Kosher Bistrot

Via S. Maria del Pianto, 68-69 186
Telephone: (6) 686-4398
Fax: (6) 6880-1364

La Taverna Del Ghetto

Via Portico D'Ottavia 8
Telephone: (6) 6821-2309

Oriental Foods Kosher

Via Livorno, 8-10
Telephone: (6) 440-4840
Fax: (6) 440-4840

SYNAGOGUES

Orthodox - Ashkenazi

Agudat Ashkenazim

Via Cesare Balbo 33 00184
Daily services in the basement.

Beth Habad Synagogue

Via Ruggero Fauro 94 00197
Telephone: (6) 8069-2277

Orthodox Nussah Italk

Oratorio Di Castro

Via Ceszie Balbo 33
Daily services.

The Great Synagogue

Lungotevere Cenci (Tempio)
Telephone: (6) 6840-0061
Fax: (6) 6840-0655
Email: info@romacer.org
Daily services.

Orthodox - Sephardi
Tempio Beth-El
Via Padova 92 00161
Telephone: (6) 4424-2857

Tempio Spagnolo
Via Catalana, (behind the great synagogue)
Daily services.

TOURS
G. Palombo
Via Maggia 7
Telephone: (6) 810-3716; 993-2074
Guides can be contacted also through the Jewish
Museum, Tel 0668400661.

Ruben E. Popper
12 Via dei Levii
Telephone: (6) 761-0901
Fax: (6) 761-0901
Telephone number is afternoons only.

SARDINIA

There is no Sardinian Jewish community today,
but the island is of more than passing Jewish
interest. In 19 CE, the Emperor Tiberius exiled
Jews to Sardinia. There was a synagogue at
Cagliari, the island's capital, at least as early as
599, for in that year a convert led a riot against it.
Sardinia eventually came under Aragonese rule,
and when the edict of expulsion of the Jews
from Spain was issued in 1492, the Jews of the
island had to leave. Since then there has been no
community.

**There are no other specific locations of
interest to travellers.**

SENIGALLIA
SYNAGOGUES
Via dei Commercianti

SICILY

Although there are very few Jews in Sicily today,
there is a long and varied history of Jewish
settlement on the island stretching back to at
least the sixth century and possibly according to
some scholars to the first or second centuries.

By the late Middle Ages, the community
numbered 40,000. In 1282, Sicily came under
Spanish rule. A century or so later, there was a
wave of massacres of Jews, and another in 1474.
These culminated in the introduction of the
Inquisition in 1479, and the expulsion of the
Jews in 1492.

**There are no other specific locations of
interest to travellers.**

SIENA
SYNAGOGUES
Vicolo delle Scotte 14
Telephone: (577) 284647
The committee has issued a brochure in English, giving
the history of the community which dates back to
medieval times. The synagogue dates from 1750.
Services are held on the Sabbath and High Holy-days.
Further information from Burroni Bernardi, Via del
Porrione. M. Savini, via Salicotta 23. Tel: 283140 (close to
the synagogue).

SPEZIA
SYNAGOGUES
Synagogue
Via 20 Settembre 165

TRIESTE
COMMUNITY ORGANISATIONS
Community Offices
Via San Francesco d'Assisi 19 34133
Telephone: (40) 371466
Fax: (40) 371226
Chief Rabbi: Rav Dr. Avraham Umberto Piperno. Tel:
3722681.

SYNAGOGUES
Synagogue
Via Donizetti 2
Telephone: (40) 631898

TOURS
Smile Service
via Martiri della Liberta' 17 34134
Telephone: (40) 375-5638
Fax: (40) 375-5638
Email: smile@com.area.trieste.it
This service agency organises tours around the Jewish
sites of Friuli Venezia-Giulia.

TURIN
BOOKSELLERS
Biblioteca "E. Artom"
P.tta Primo Levi 12, Torino 10125
Telephone: (11) 669-9097

Libreria Claudiana
Via Principe Tommaso 1, Torino 10125
Telephone: (11) 011-669-2458
Fax: (11) 011-669-2458

COMMUNITY ORGANISATIONS
Community Centre
P.tta Primo Levi 12, Torino 10125
Telephone: (11) 658-585
Fax: (11) 669-1173
Email: comebrato@libero.it

GROCERIES
Panetteria Bertino
Via B. Galliari 14, Torino 10125
Telephone: (11) 669-9527

MIKVAOT
P.tta Primo Levi 12, Torino 10125
Telephone: (11) 658-585
Fax: (11) 669-1173
Email: comebrato@libero.it

RESTAURANTS
Salomon e Augusto Segre - Jewish rest home
Via B. Galliari 13, Torino 10125
Telephone: (11) 658-585
Only by reservation

SYNAGOGUES
P.tta Primo Levi 12 10125
Telephone: (11) 658-585
Fax: (11) 669-1173
Email: comebrato@libero.it
Daily 6.50 am and sunset; Shabbat 9 am and half an hour
before sunset (winter) or 6.30 pm (summer); on Shabbat
(in winter) between Minchah and Maariv a Seudat
Shelishit is held.

TOURIST SITES
Mole Atonellianta
Now the National Cinema Museum, it was originally
built in the nineteenth century and was meant to be the
grandest synagogue in Europe but was never completed.

URBINO
SYNAGOGUES
Via Stretta

VENICE
Jews settled in Venice early in the tenth century
and became an important factor in the economic
life of the city. In 1516 however the authorities
banished the Jews to the Ghetto Nuovo (new
foundry), district so establishing the first ghetto.
The high walls surrounding the area still exist.
The 14th-century Jewish cemetery (the second
oldest in Europe after the one in Worms) has
recently been restored and was reopened in 1999
for guided tours (for details call the Jewish
Museum).

COMMUNITY ORGANISATIONS
Community Offices
2899 Cannaregio , Ghetto Nuovo 30121
Telephone: (41) 715-012
Fax: (41) 524-1862
Email: com.ehza.ve@lihero.it

GIFT SHOP
David's
Campo del Ghetto Nuovo 2880
Telephone: (41) 716278
Email: dcuriel@iol.it
Jewish articles & religious appurtenances are available.

Mordehai Fusetti
Ghetto Nuovo 1219
Telephone: (41) 714024
Jewish articles & religious appurtenances are available.

GUEST HOUSE
Jewish Rest Home
2874 Cannaregio, Ghetto Nuovo 30121
Telephone: (41) 716002
Fax: (41) 714394
Kosher meals and accommodation available. Early
booking is advised.

HOTELS
Buon Pesce
50 S. Nicolo , Lido island
Telephone: (41) 526-8599
Fax: (41) 526-0533
Email: info@hotelbuonpesce.com
Open February to November.

Kosher
Locanda del Ghetto
Campo del Ghetto Novo, Cannaregio 2892 30121
Telephone: (41) 3904-1275-9292
Fax: (41) 3904-1275-7987
Email: ghetto@veneziahotels.com
Web site: www.veneziahotels.com

LIBRARIES
Jewish Library and Archives "Renato Maestro"
2899 Cannaregio , Ghetto Nuovo 30121
Telephone: (41) 718833
Fax: (41) 5241862
Email: renatomaestro@libero.it

MIKVAOT
Jewish Rest Home
2874 Cannaregio , Ghetto Nuovo
Telephone: (41) 715-118
Fax: (41) 718-474
Email: chiefrabbivenice@virgilio.it
Booking 24 hours in advance.

MUSEUMS
Jewish Museum
Cannaregio, Ghetto Nuovo 2902/B
Telephone: (41) 715-359
Fax: (41) 723-007
Jewish Museum (Open Sunday through Friday from
10.00am to 4.30pm from October to May and from
10.00am to 7.00pm from June to September). Closed on
Saturdays and Jewish holidays. Guided visits to the
synagogues in English start every hour from the Jewish
Museum. Sandwiches and drinks are available.

RESTAURANTS
Meat
Gam-Gam
1122 Cannaregio , Sottoportico di Ghetto Vecchio
Telephone: (41) 715284
Fax: (41) 715284
Email: jewishvenice.org
Shabbat arrangements available. Open lunch and dinner.
Glatt kosher.

Jewish Rest Home
2874 Cannaregio, Ghetto Nuovo
Telephone: (41) 716-002
It is necessary to book in the morning.

SYNAGOGUES
Orthodox
Chabad of Venice
Cannaregio, Ghetto Nuovo 2915
Telephone: (41) 715284
Fax: (41) 715284
Email: guide@jewishvenice.org
Web site: www.jewishvenice.org
Shabbat and Holiday hospitality available.

Schola Levantina
1228 Cannaregio , Ghetto Vecchio
Telephone: (41) 715-012
Fax: (41) 5241-862
Shabbath services are held during winter. Friday about
one hour before sunset and Saturday at 9.00am; on
Saturday at 4.00pm (later in spring and summer). Tefillah
Mincha and Seuda Shelishit.

Schola Spagnola
1149 Cannaregio , Ghetto Vecchio
Telephone: (41) 715-012
Fax: (41) 524-1862
Shabbath services are held here during summer. Friday
about one hour before sunset and Saturday at 9.00am;
on Saturday at 4.00pm (later in spring and summer).
Tefillah Mincha and Seuda Shelishit.

VERCELLI
COMMUNITY ORGANISATIONS
Community Offices
Via Oldoni 20

SYNAGOGUES
Via Foa 70

VERONA
COMMUNITY ORGANISATIONS
Community Centre
Via Portici 3
Telephone: (45) 800-7112
Fax: (45) 596627
Email: comebraica@libero.it
SYNAGOGUES
Via Portici 3

VIAREGGIO
CONTACT INFORMATION
Mr Sananes
via Pacinotti 172/B
Telephone: (584) 961-025
Private office: Tirreno Tour, 26 Viale Carducci, Tel: 30777,
during daytime.

JAMAICA

During the time of Spanish colonisation,
Jamaica witnessed many Conversos arriving from Portugal. After the British took
over in 1655, many of these could again
practise Judaism openly. Soon, other Jews,
mainly Sephardim, followed from Brazil
and other nearby countries. The community received full equality in 1831 (before a
similar step was taken in England).

The Jews played an important role in
Jamaican life, and in 1849 the House of
Asembly did not meet on Yom Kippur!
However, assimilation and intermarriage
took their toll and in 1921 the Ashkenazi
and Sephardi synagogues combined. There
is now only one synagogue on the island,
but there are remains of old synagogues in
Kingston, Port Royal and other towns.

Community life includes WIZO, B'nai B'rith
and a school (the Hillel Academy). The
community lost members after the Cuban
revolution, because many feared a similar
revolution in Jamaica. However, this was
not the case.

GMT -5 hours
Country calling code: **(+1 809)**
Total population: **2,590,000**
Jewish population: **300**
Emergency telephone: **(Police – 119) (Fire – 110)
(Ambulance – 110)**
Electricity voltage: **(Electricity voltage – 110)**

KINGSTON
SYNAGOGUES
Shaare Shalom
Duke Street & Charles Street
Telephone: (876) 927-7948
Fax: (876) 978-6240
Services, Friday, 5:30 pm (all year), Shabbat, 10 am;
festivals, 9 am all year round.

JAPAN

After Japan became open to Western ideas and Westerners in the mid-nineteenth century, a trickle of Jewish immigrants from the Russian Empire, the UK and the USA began to make their homes there. The first Jewish communtiy at Yokohama was founded in 1860. Many were escaping anti-semitism and by 1918 there were several thousand in the country.

Individual Japanese, despite being allied to Nazi Germany, did not adopt the anti-Semitic attitude of the Nazis, and the Japanese consul in Kovno Lithuania even helped the Mir Yeshivah escape from occupied Europe in 1940.

The post-war American occupation of the country brought many Jewish servicemen, and the community was also augmented by Jews escaping unrest in China. In recent years, there have been some Jewish 'gaijin', or (foreign workers).

In Tokyo there is a synagogue, which provides meals on Shabbat, a Sunday school, and offices for the Executive Board of the Jewish Community of Japan, which is the central body.

GMT +9 hours
Country calling code: (+81)
Total population: **125,638,000**
Jewish population: **1,500**
Emergency telephone: (**Police** – 110) (**Fire** – 119) (**Ambulance** – 119)
Electricity voltage: (**Electricity voltage** – 110)

HIROSHIMA
TOURIST SITES
Holocaust Education Centre
866 Nakatsuhara, Miyuki, Fukuyama 720
Telephone: (849) 558001
Fax: (849) 558001
Email: hecjpn@urban.ne.jp
Web site: www.urban.ne.jp/home/hecjpn/
Open Tuesday, Wednesday, Friday and Saturday, 10:30 am to 4:30 pm.

KOBE
SYNAGOGUES
Orthodox Sephardi
Ohel Shelomoh (Jewish Community of Kansai)
4-12-12 Kitano-cho, Chuo-ku 650-0002
Telephone: (78) 81-078-221-7236
Fax: (78) 81-078-242-7254
Email: jiyohay@nava21.ne.jp
Web site: chabonline.com/kobe
Kabalat Shabbat sunset Fri., Shacharit 10.00 Sat., each followed by kiddush, meal (groups please enquire in advance); Mincha 14.30. Mikveh by prior appt.

NAGASAKI
Nagasaki
Now there are no known Jews living in Nagasaki. As a centre of foreign trade in the mid-19th century it had a community. The old Jewish cemetery is located at Sakamoto Gaijin Bochi. The site of the first synagogue in Japan is Umegasaki Machi.

There are no other specific locations of interest to travellers.

TOKYO
COMMUNITY ORGANISATIONS
8-8 Hiroo, 3-chome, Shibuya-ku 150
Telephone: (3) 3400-2559
Fax: (3) 3400-1827
Email: jccmanager@gol.com
Web site: www.jccjapan.co.jp

EMBASSY
Embassy of Israel
3 Niban-cho, Chiyodaku
Telephone: (3) 3264-0911

RESTAURANTS
Japan Jewish Community Center
8-8 Hiroo, 3-chome, Shibuya-ku 150
Telephone: (3) 3400-2559
Fax: (3) 3400-1827
Email: jcc@crisscross.com
They sell prepared foods and kosher wine, as well as serve meals on Friday evening and Shabbat. Reservation strongly recommended.

SYNAGOGUES

Beth David Synagogue
8-8 Hiroo, 3-chome, Shibuya-ku 150
Telephone: (3) 3400-2559
Fax: (3) 3400-1827
Services are held Friday evening at 6:30 pm (7 pm during summer); Shabbat morning, 9:30 am; and on Holy-days and festivals. Advance notification requested. Mikvah on premises.

KAZAKHSTAN

Essentially this community began when the Soviets rescued several thousand Jews at the time of the Nazi invasion of the Soviet Union in 1941. Others joined after the war. The community is mainly based in Almaty, the former capital, and also in Chimkent. Some 2,000 Bukharan and Tat Jews also live in the country.

The central organisation is the Mitzvah Association, which heads various Jewish groups. It even has a chair on the All-Peoples Assembly of Kazakhstan. There is a high rate of emigration to Israel.

GMT +6 hours
Country calling code: **(+7)**
Total population: **16,223,000**
Jewish population: **10,000**
Emergency telephone: **(Police – 03) (Fire – 03) (Ambulance – 03)**
Electricity voltage: **(Electricity voltage – 220)**

ALMATY

COMMUNITY ORGANISATIONS
206 e Raimbek St.
Telephone: (3272) 439-358
Fax: (3272) 507-770
Email: info@chabad.kz
Also has a store, kosher butcher, library and mikvah.

SYNAGOGUES
Orthodox
206 e Raimbek St.
Telephone: (3272) 439-358
Fax: (3272) 507-770
Email: synagogues@chabad.kz

ASTANA

SYNAGOGUES
Jewish Center of Astana
11 Respublki Street, #3 473000
Telephone: (3172) 216-913
Email: astana@chabad.kz

CHIMKENT

SYNAGOGUES
Sephardi
Svobody Street, 47th Lane

KENYA

Kenya could have been the site of the first Jewish state for two thousand years as this offer was made to the Zionists in 1903. It was, however, rejected in 1905. There were some Jews living in Kenya at that time, and a synagogue was built in 1912. Many more Jews came here after the Second World War as Holocaust survivors, and recently some Israelis have worked on a short-term basis in the country.

Kenya was an ally to Israel in its rescue of the Jews from Entebbe in Uganda. Jews have contributed much to the hotel industry and professional life of the country.

Regular services are held every Saturday in the Nairobi Hebrew Congregation, and there is a Community Centre next to the synagogue. The centre, the Vermont Memorial Hall, offers educational and social events.

GMT +3 hours
Country calling code: **(+254)**
Total population: **33,144,000**
Jewish population: **400**
Emergency telephone: **(Police – 999) (Fire – 999) (Ambulance – 999)**
Electricity voltage: **(Electricity voltage – 220/240)**

NAIROBI

COMMUNITY ORGANISATIONS
Community Centre
Vermont Memorial Hall
Open Monday, Tuesday, Friday 9 am to 1 pm; Wednesday 2.30 pm to 5.30 pm; Services Friday evening at 6.30 pm; Saturday morning at 8 am. All festivals. Kosher chickens available.

SYNAGOGUES
Nairobi Hebrew Congregation
cnr. University Way & Uhuru Highway, P.O.Box 25233
Telephone: (2) 577871
Fax: (2) 573345
Email: azfactor@africaonline.co.ke

KYRGYZSTAN

This central Asian ex-Soviet republic has only a short history of Jewish settlement. The community originated from migrants after the Russian Revolution and evacuees from the German advance into the Soviet Union in the Second World War. As a result, community members are almost all Russian speakers and are assimilated into the Russian minority of the country.

Before the collapse of the Soviet Union, there was no organised community. Following 1991, there is a synagogue in Bishkek (the capital), where there is also a Jewish library and an Aish HaTorah centre. The main umbrella group is the Menorah Society of Jewish Culture.

GMT +5 hours
Country calling code: (**+996**)
Total population: **4,856,000**
Jewish population: **2,500**
Emergency telephone: (**Police – 03**) (**Fire – 03**)
(**Ambulance – 03**)
Electricity voltage: (**Electricity voltage – 220**)

BISHKEK
SYNAGOGUES
193 Suymbaeva (Karpinsky) Street
Telephone: (3312) 681966
Fax: (3312) 681966
Email: chabad@netmail.kg

LATVIA

The Jews in the medieval principalities of Courland and Livonia represent the earliest Jewish settlement in Latvia. Tombstones from the fourteenth century have been found. After the Russian take-over, Jews were only allowed to live in the area if they were considered 'useful', or had lived there before the Russians took control, because the area was outside the 'Pale of Settlement' that the Russian Empire had designated for the Jews.

The Jews contributed much to Latvia's development, but this was never recognised by the government, which tried to restrict their influence in business matters.

Religious Jewish life, however, was strong. When the Nazis invaded Latvia, 90 per cent of the 85,000 Jews were systematically murdered by them and their Latvian collaborators.

The bulk of today's community originates from immigration into Latvia after the war, although 3,000 Holocaust survivors did return to Latvia. Before the collapse of communism, there was much Jewish dissident activity. There is a Jewish school and a Jewish hospital. There are some Holocaust memorial sites, in Riga (the capital), and also in the Bierkernieki Forest, where 46,000 Holocaust victims were shot.

GMT +2 hours
Country calling code: (**+371**)
Total population: **2,474,000**
Jewish population: **10,000**
Emergency telephone: (**Police – 02**) (**Fire – 01**)
(**Ambulance – 03**)
Electricity voltage: (**Electricity voltage – 220**)

DAUGAVPILS
COMMUNITY ORGANISATIONS
Jewish Community
Saules Street 47
Fax: (54) 8254-24658

SYNAGOGUES
Gogol Street
Suvorov Street

LIEPAJA
COMMUNITY ORGANISATIONS
Jewish Community
Kungu Street 21
Telephone: (34) 25336

REZHITSA
SYNAGOGUES
Kaleyu St.

RIGA
CULTURAL ORGANISATIONS
Latvian Society for Jewish Culture
Skolas 6 LV1322
Telephone: (2) 289-580
Fax: (2) 821-494

EMBASSY
Embassy of Israel
Elizabetes Street 2a LV1340
Telephone: (2) 732-0980
Fax: (2) 783-0170
Email: press@rig.mfa.gov.il

MUSEUMS
The Jewish Museum of Riga
6 Skolas Street LV-1322
The museum is small but has many moving exhibits and photos. A short video is shown depicting the tragedy of the Holocaust in Latvia.

SYNAGOGUES
Orthodox
Chabad Lubavitch Latvia
141 Lacplesa St., LV-1003
Telephone: (2) 720 4022
Fax: (2) 783 0444
Email: chabad@mailbox.riga.lv
Web site: www.jewish.lv/www.chabad.lv
Visitors welcomed for Shabbat and holiday meals. Take-out by order.

Riga Central Synagogue
6/8 Peitavas Street, L.V. 1050
Telephone: (2) 721-4507
Fax: (2) 721-4507
Email: rerd@inbox.lv
Web site: www.jrcr.com
Hot kosher meals may be ordered in advance. Also has a mikva.

LITHUANIA

The history of Lithuania Jewry is as old as the state of Lithuania itself. There were Jews in the country in the fourteenth century, when Grand Duke Gedeyminus founded the state. The community eventually grew, and produced many famous yeshivas and great commentators, such as the Vilna Gaon. The community began to emigrate (particularly to South Africa) at the beginning of the nineteenth century; even so in 1941 there were still 160,000 Jews in the country. Ninety-five per cent of these were murdered in the Holocaust, by the local population as well as the Nazis.

The remaining post-war community included some who had hidden or had managed to survive by other means and some Jews from other parts of the Soviet Union. Interestingly, the Lithuanian Soviet Socialist Republic was more tolerant of Jewish activity than some of the neighbouring republics, such as Latvia. Now that Lithuania is independent, Jewish life is free once again.

The Lubavitch movement is present, and there are synagogues in Vilnius (known to many as Vilna), the capital, and Kaunas. There is also a school and it is possible to study Yiddish. There are tours available to show the old Jewish life in Lithuania. The grave of the Vilna Gaon can be visited, as well as Paneriai, otherwise known as Ponary, where thousands of Jews were shot during the Holocaust.

GMT +2 hours
Country calling code: **(+370)**
Total population: **3,701,000**
Jewish population: **5,000**
Emergency telephone: **(Police – 02) (Fire – 01) (Ambulance – 03)**
Electricity voltage: **(Electricity voltage – 220)**

DRUSKININKAI
COMMUNITY ORGANISATIONS
Jewish Community
9/15 Sporto Street
Telephone: 54590

KAUNAS
COMMUNITY ORGANISATIONS
26 B Gedimino Street
Telephone: (7) 203717
Fax: (7) 7201135
Hours of opening: Sunday to Thursday 3 pm-6 pm.

SYNAGOGUES
11 Ozheshkienes Street

KLAIPEDA
COMMUNITY ORGANISATIONS
Jewish Community
3 Ziedu Skersqatvis
Telephone: (6) 93758

PANEVEZYS
COMMUNITY ORGANISATIONS
6/22 Sodu Street 5300
Telephone: (54) 68848

SHIAULIAI
COMMUNITY ORGANISATIONS
24 Vyshinskio
Telephone: (1) 26795

VILNIUS
Otherwise known as Vilna, this town used to be known as the 'Jerusalem of the North'. Jews started to live in Vilnius during the middle of the sixteenth century. In due course it became a pre-eminent centre for rabbinical studies. The town still has the largest community of Lithuanian Jews, and there are many sites of historical interest, including the Vilna Gaon's grave and the State Jewish Museum.

BAKERIES
Matzah Bakery
39 Pylimo Street
Telephone: (2) 61-2523

COMMUNITY ORGANISATIONS
Jewish Community of Lithuania
Pylimo St. 4 2001
Telephone: (2) 61-3003
Fax: (2) 5212-7915
Email: jewishcom@post.5ci.lt
Web site: www.litjews.org
Opening hours: Monday to Thursday 10.00am to 6.00pm, Friday 10.00am to 4.00pm.

CULTURAL ORGANISATIONS
The Israel Centre of Cultures and Art in Lithuania
4 Pylimo, 2nd Floor 2001
Telephone: (2) 61-1736 or 652139

MUSEUMS
The Vilna Gaon Jewish State Museum
4 Pylimo, LT 2001
Telephone: (2) 62-0730
Fax: (2) 22-7083
Email: jmuseum@puni.osf.lt
The Tarbut School, Exhibitions and seat of Jewish Community. Opening hours Monday to Thursday 9am to 5pm and Friday 9am to 4pm.

SYNAGOGUES
Central Synagogue of Vilnius Chabad
12 Saltiniu g. St. 2006
Telephone: (2) 250-387

Main Synagogue (Choral Synagogue)
39 Pylimo Street
Telephone: (2) 61-2523

LUXEMBOURG

The small community in Luxembourg faced massacres and expulsions during medieval times and Jews only began to resettle here several hundred years later. Napoleon heralded the rebirth of the community when he annexed Luxembourg, and by 1823 a synagogue had been built, but the community remained small, although in 1899 another synagogue was built.

Later many refugees from the Nazis arrived in the country, bringing the number of Jews to nearly 4,000. After the Nazi take-over, 750 Luxembourg Jews were killed, but many others were saved by the local population.

The present community is generally prosperous and assimilated. The Consistoire Israelite, established by Napoleon, is recognised by the government as the representative of the community, and is also financed by the government. The Orthodox synagogue is situated fairly centrally in Luxembourg City.

GMT +1 hour
Country calling code: (+352)
Total population: 417,000
Jewish population: 600
Emergency telephone: (**Police – 133**) (**Fire – 112**) (**Ambulance – 112**)
Electricity voltage: (**Electricity voltage – 220**)

ESCH-SUR-ALZETTE
SYNAGOGUES
Synagogue
52 rue de Canal
Services held on Friday evenings.

LUXEMBOURG CITY
COMMUNITY ORGANISATIONS
Consistoire Israelite de Luxembourg
45 av. Monterey 2018
Telephone: 452914
Fax: 473772

GROCERIES
Calon
rue de Reins 3

KASHRUT INFORMATION
34 rue Alphonse munchen 2172
Telephone: 452366

SYNAGOGUES
45 av. Monterey
Telephone: 452914
Fax: 250430

MACEDONIA

At the southern end of the former Yugoslavia, this new country has an ancient Jewish heritage dating back to Roman times. The Jews took advantage of the area's favourable commercial position, lying between Turkey and Western Europe, and the remains of a synagogue at Stobei dating back to the second and third centuries is evidence of a once thriving Jewish community.

Iberian Jews escaping the Inquisition settled in the area, and brought with them Sephardi customs and the Ladino language (based on Spanish). The fate of the 8,000 Macedonian Jews under Bulgarian occupation during the Second World War is in stark contrast to the fate of the Bulgarian Jews the Macedonian Jews were deported to their deaths, yet the Bulgarian Jews were saved by the defiance of the king and the people. Only ten per cent of the Macedonian community survived, of whom many have emigrated to Israel.

Today's community is mainly based in the capital Skopje, but there are no synagogues and there is little access to Jewish life. However, the community does have contact with Jews in Serbia and Greece.

GMT +1 hour
Country calling code: (+389)
Total population: 2,190,000
Jewish population: Under 100
Emergency telephone: (Police – 92) (Fire – 93) (Ambulance – 94)
Electricity voltage: (Electricity voltage – 220)

SKOPJE
COMMUNITY ORGANISATIONS
Community Offices
Borka Talevski Street 24
Telephone: (91) 237-543

MALAYSIA

Malaysia is a Muslim state, and the Jewish population is tiny, barely into double figures. There is, however, a Jewish cemetery on the island of Penang, in Georgetown in Jalan Yahudi (Jewish Street). The cemetery is looked after by Selvaraj Sundram, a Hindu. Decades ago the then vibrant Jewish community hired his great-grandfather to look after the site. His family has done so ever since, funds now being provided by an anonymous German. The Jews who today live on Penang originate from refugees from Russia. There was a synagogue, but it is now closed.

GMT +8 hours
Country calling code: (+60)
Total population: 21,667,000
Jewish population: Under 100
Emergency telephone: (Police – 999) (Fire – 999) (Ambulance – 999)
Electricity voltage: (Electricity voltage – 220)

There are no other specific locations of interest to travellers.

MALTA

There is evidence of an ancient Jewish community on Malta, as archaeologists have discovered remains from 2,000 years ago. Malta fell into Arab hands in the early Middle Ages, when there were still a few Jews on the island. The island then changed to Sicilian hands and, in 1492, the Jews were expelled.

Between the sixteenth and eighteenth centuries, the island was used as a prison for Jewish captives of the Knights of St John. They were held for ransom, but managed to find time to build a synagogue. A synagogue in Spur Street Valetta, opened in 1912, was demolished in 1995 as part of a redevelopment scheme.

GMT +1 hour
Country calling code: (+356)
Total population: 378,000
Jewish population: 100
Emergency telephone: (Police – 191) (Fire – 199) (Ambulance – 196)
Electricity voltage: (Electricity voltage – 240)

BIRKIRKARA
COMMUNITY ORGANISATIONS
P O Box 4
Telephone: 445924

TA-XBIEX
SYNAGOGUES
Orthodox
Jewish Community of Malta
Flat 1, Florida Mansions, Enrico Mizzi St., MSD 02
Telephone: 21237309 & 21386266. Spokesperson:
21 386266
Fax: 356/21249410
Email: jewsofmalta@digigate.net
Web site: www.maltesejewishcommunity.org
Synagogue services on the 1st & 3rd Sabbath of the
month, and on all high holidays.

MEXICO

Conversos were the first Jews in the country, and some achieved high positions in early Spanish colonial Mexico. As the Inquisition was still functioning here some 200 years after the sixteenth century, the number of Jewish immigrants was small. When Mexico became independent of Spain, Jews gradually began to enter the country, coming from German and other European communities.

It was during the twentieth century that most Jewish immigrants entered Mexico. There were both Ashkenazis and Sephardis, and they settled throughout the country. The communities grew on a parallel level, rather than together, with two languages, Yiddish and Ladino.

The current community is largely middle class and all the various factions come under the Comite Central Israelita. There are numerous synagogues and there are also kosher restaurants. The community is well equipped with Jewish schools and yeshivas.

GMT -6 to 8 hours
Country calling code: **(+52)**
Total population: **96,400,000**
Jewish population: **41,000**
Emergency telephone: **(Police – 080) (Fire – 080)
(Ambulance – 080)**
Electricity voltage: **(Electricity voltage – 110)**

ACAPULCO
HOTELS
The Hyatt Regency
Costera Miguel Aleman 1 39869
Telephone: (744) 69-1234
Fax: (744) 84-3087
Email: hyatta@netmex.com
The hotel has a synagogue and a mikva.

RESTAURANTS
Costera Miguel Aleman 1 39869
Telephone: (744) 69-1234
Fax: (744) 84-3087
Email: hyatta@netmex.com
Open only during the high season (generally Nov/Dec to March/April).

CUERNAVACA
SYNAGOGUES
Madero 404
Telephone: (777) 186-846
At the old age home.

GUADALAJARA
COMMUNITY ORGANISATIONS
Comunidad Israelita de Guadalajara
Juan Palomar y Arias 651
Telephone: (33) 416-463
Fax: (33) 427-168
Includes kosher restaurant, mikva and two synagogues.
Phone in advance.

MEXICO CITY
Despite the fact that the first auto-da-fe at which Conversos were burnt at the stake took place in Mexico City it has been said that in 1550 there were more crypto-Jews in Mexico City than Roman Catholics. There are now many Jews, the vast majority of Mexican Jewry. With twenty-three synagogues, kosher restuarants and Jewish schools, the city is well equipped with Jewish facilities. Polanco is a Jewish area in the city with some synagogues. The first synagogue, dating from 1912, is in the downtown area.

BUTCHERS
Fuente de Templanza 17, Tecamachalco
Mehadrin.

Carniceria Sary
Tecamachalco
Mehadrin.

Pollos Mugrabi
Platon 133, Polanco
Mehadrin.

COMMUNITY ORGANISATIONS
Comunidad Monte Sinai
Tennyson 134, Polanco
Telephone: (55) 280-6369
Fax: (55) 281-3969

EMBASSY
Embassy of Israel
Sierra Madre 215 11000
Telephone: (55) 201-1500
Fax: (55) 201-1555
Email: israel@prodigy.net.mx

GROCERIES
Casa Amiga
Horacio 1719, Col. Polanco
Telephone: (55) 540-1455

Kurson Kosher
Acuezunco 15, San Miguel
Telephone: (55) 905-589-9823, 9860 or 3225
Emilio Castelar , Polanco 204-G 11560
Telephone: (55) 280-3500
Fax: (55) 280-3361
Email: kkurson@aol.com
Web site: www.kursonkosher.com
Will also deliver and ship to any resort in Mexico.

MEDIA
Newspapers
CDI
Centro Deportivo, Plaza de toros of Cuatro Caminos
Telephone: (55) 557-3000
Spanish weekly.

Foro de Vida Judia en el Mundo
Aviacion Commercial 16, Col. Polanco 15700
Telephone: (55) 571-1114
Spanish monthly.

Kesher
Leibnitz 13-10, Colonia Anzures CP 11590
Telephone: (55) 203-0446
Fax: (55) 203-9084
Email: info@kesher.org.mx
Spanish bi-weekly.

La Voz de la Kehila
Acapulco 70, 2nd Floor
Telephone: (55) 211-0501
Spanish monthly.

MIKVAOT
Platon 413
Telephone: (55) 520-9569
Av. de los Bosques 53, Tecamachalco
Telephone: (55) 589-5530
Bernard Shaw 110, Polanco
Telephone: (55) 203-9964

Tevila Cuernavaca
Priv. de Antinea 4, Col. Delicias
Telephone: (55) 15 08 41; 18 16 55

MUSEUMS
The Holocaust Museum
Acapulco 70, Col Condesa
Telephone: (55) 211-051

RELIGIOUS ORGANISATIONS
Comite Central
Telephone: (55) 520-9393; 540-7376

Comunidad Maguen David
Email: mdavid@ort.org.mx
Contact for any religious questions.

Jerusalem de Mexico
Anatore France 359, Local C, Polanco
Telephone: (55) 531-2269

RESTAURANTS
Meat
Aladinos
Ingenieros Militares 255
Telephone: (55) 395-2959
Fax: (55) 395-9219

O Grill/Kosher House
37 Polanco, Mexico City
Telephone: (55) 280-1638
Fax: (55) 280-1638

Restaurant Pini
Ejercito Nacional 458d
Supervision: Maguen David

SYNAGOGUES
Agudas Achim
Montes de Oca 32, Condesa 6140
Telephone: (55) 553-6430

Bet Midrash Tecamachalco
Fuente de Marcela 23, Col. Tecamachalco
Telephone: (55) 251-8454

Beth Moshe
Tennyson No 134, Col. Polanco 11560
Telephone: (55) 280-6369 ;6375
Fax: (55) 281-3969
Email: monsinai@ort.org.mx

Beth Yehoshua
Fuente de San Sulpicio No. 16, Col. Tecamachalco 53950
Telephone: (55) 294-8617

Bircas Shumel
Plinio 311, Polanco
Telephone: (55) 280-2769

Jajam Elfasi
Fuente Del Pescador 168, Col. Tecamachalco
Shabbat services only.

Kolel Aram Zoba
Sofocles 346, Col. Polanco
Telephone: (55) 280-2669; 4886;

Kolel Maor Abraham
Lafontaine 344, Col. Polanco
Telephone: (55) 545-2482

Nidche Israel
Acapulco 70, Condesa
Telephone: (55) 211-0575

Or Damesek
Seneca 343
Telephone: (55) 280-6281

Ramat Shalom
Fuente del Pescador 35, Tecamachalco
Telephone: (55) 5251-3854
Fax: (55) 5251-4363
Email: www.ramat.org

Shaare Shalom
Av. de Los Bosques 53, Tecamachalco
Telephone: (55) 251-0973

Shuba Israel
Edgar Alan Poe 43, Col. Polanco
Telephone: (55) 5280-0136

Conservative
Bet El
Horacio 1722, Polanco los Morales
Telephone: (55) 281-2592
Fax: (55) 281-2467
Email: comunidad.betel@bigfoot.com

Beth Israel
Virreyes 114, Lomas
Telephone: (55) 520-8515
Fax: (55) 520-9559
Email: bethisrael@psi.net.mx
English-speaking.

Orthodox
Beth Itzjak de Polanco
Eujenio Sue 20, Polanco
Telephone: (55) 5280-9296
Fax: (55) 5280-0520
Email: bitzjak@prodigy.net.mx

Eliahu Fasja
Fuente de Templanza 13, Col. Tecamachalco
Telephone: (55) 294-9388

Midrash Latorah
Cerrada de Los Morales 8, Col. Polanco 11510
Telephone: (55) 280-0875
Fax: (55) 281-6801
Rabbi Asher Zrihen, formerly of London, will be happy to welcome and assist visitors.

Sephardi
Maguen David
Bernard Shaw 110, Polanco
Telephone: (55) 203-9964

Sephardi Synagogue
Monterey 359
Telephone: (55) 564-1197;1367

MONTERREY

COMMUNITY ORGANISATIONS
Centro Israelita de Monterrey
Canada 207, Nuevo León
Telephone: (81) 461-128
Includes a synagogue and mikva.

TIJUANA

CONTACT INFORMATION
JCC Chabad House
Centro Social Israelita de Baja California, Av. 16 Septiembre, Baja California 3000
Telephone: (664) 862-692; 862-693
Fax: (664) 341-532
Email: chabadtj@telnor.net
Synagogue and mikva on premises.

SYNAGOGUES
Tijuanua Hebrew Congregation
Amado Nervo 207, Baja California

MOLDOVA

Moldova used to be a Soviet Republic bordering Romania to the west and the Ukraine to the east. When the Jews first entered what is now Moldova, the area was known as Bessarabia, and was on an important trade route between Turkey and Poland. By the time of Russian rule in 1812, there was a permanent Jewish community. The Russians included the area in the 'Pale of Settlement', which held the majority of the Jews of their empire. By the end of the nineteenth century, there were over 200,000 Jews in the region. However, the twentieth century started with the infamous progrom in the capital Chisinev, where 49 Jews were killed and much damage was done to Jewish property. Emigration began to increase. The area fell under Romanian control between 1918 and 1940, but the community continued to lead a normal life until the Second World War, when many thousands of the pre-war community of over

250,000 were killed during the German occupation.

After the war, some survivors continued to live in Moldova, and Jews from other parts of the Soviet Union joined them. There is an umbrella society for Moldovan Jews, and there are synagogues and schools. The Lubavitch movement is active in building up religious life.

GMT +2 hours
Country calling code: **(+373)**
Total population: **4,335,000**
Jewish population: **15,000**
Emergency telephone:
Electricity voltage: **(Electricity voltage – 220)**

CHISINAU
Most of Moldova's Jews live in Chisinau (formerly Kishinev). This city was the scene for two notorious progroms in 1903 and 1905.

RELIGIOUS ORGANISATIONS
Yeshiva of Chisinau
Sciusev 5 277001
Telephone: (2) 274-362
Fax: (2) 274-331
Email: agudath@yeshiva.mldnet.com
In addition to Jewish studies, a mikva and kosher food supplies are on the premises.

SYNAGOGUES
Yakimovsky per. 8 277000
Telephone: (2) 221-215
A mikvah is on the premises and kosher food may be obtained.

TELENESHTY
SYNAGOGUES
4 28th June Street

TIRASPOL
CONTACT INFORMATION
Telephone: 336-495
Fax: 322-208
Details of the Jewish Community from Dr Vaisman.

MONACO

Some French Jews lived in Monaco before 1939, and the government issued them with false papers during the war, thus saving them from the Nazis. This tiny country has also attracted retired people from France, North Africa and the UK.

There is an official Jewish body, the Association Culturelle Israelite de Monaco, and there is a synagogue, a school and a kosher food shop. Half of the total Jewish population are Ashkenazi and the other half are Sephardi, and 60 per cent of the community is retired.

GMT +1 hour
Country calling code: **(+377)**
Total population: **32,000**
Jewish population: **800**
Emergency telephone: **(Police – 17) (Fire – 18)**
(Ambulance – 18)
Electricity voltage: **(Electricity voltage – 220)**

MONTE CARLO
COMMUNITY ORGANISATIONS
Association Culturelle Israelite de Monaco
15 Av. de la Costa
Telephone: 9330-1646

GROCERIES
Carrefour

SYNAGOGUES
15 Av. de la Costa, opp. Balmoral Hotel MC 98000
Telephone: 9330-1646
Services, Friday evening at 6.30pm and Saturday morning at 8.45am and Saturday afternoon at 5.30pm.

MOROCCO

There were Jews in Morocco before it became a Roman province (they first arrived after the destruction of the Temple in 587 BCE). Since the first century, the Jewish population settled in Morocco has increased steadily owing to several waves of immigration from Spain and Portugal following the expulsion of Jews by the Inquisition in 1492.

Under Moslem rule, the Jews experienced a general climate of tolerance, although they have suffered some persecution. During the Vichy period in the Second World War, Sultan Mohammed V protected the community. Almost 250,000 Jews have emigrated to Israel, Canada, France, Spain and Latin America, but they maintain strong links with the Kingdom.

Since ancient times, the Jewish community has succeeded in cohabiting harmoniously with the Berber and then with the Arab community. Today the present Jewish population is a living community, playing a significant role in Moroccan society although they have declined in number.

Country calling code: (+212)
Total population: 27,310,000
Jewish population: 6,000
Emergency telephone: (Police – 19) (Fire – 15) (Ambulance – 19)
Electricity voltage: (Electricity voltage – 110/170)

AGADIR

COMMUNITY ORGANISATIONS
Community Offices
Imm. Arsalane Av. Hassan II
Telephone: (8) 840091
Fax: (8) 822268

MIKVAOT
Av. Moulay Abdallah, cnr. rue de la Foire
Telephone: (8) 842339

SYNAGOGUES
Synagogue
Av. Moulay Abdallah, cnr. rue de la Foire
Telephone: (8) 842339

CASABLANCA
At the beginning of the 19th century around one quarter of the city's population was Jewish. The community thrived until restrictions were imposed by the Vichy government during the Second World War.

In 1948 the Jewish population amounted to 74,000. Since then it has declined and is now considered to be around 5000.

COMMUNITY ORGANISATIONS
Community Offices
Rue Abbou Abdallah al Mahassibi
Telephone: (2) 270976 & 222861
Fax: (2) 266953

MIKVAOT
32 rue Officier de Paix Thomas
Telephone: (2) 276688

RESTAURANTS
Americano
7 Place d'Aknoul

Aux Bon Delices
261 Blvd Ziraoui, opp. Lycee Lyautey

SYNAGOGUES
Benisty
13 rue Ferhat Achad

Bennaroche
24 rue Lusitania

Em Habanim
14 rue Lusitania

Hazan Synagogue
Rue Roger Farache

Ne'im Zemiroth
29 rue Jean-Jacques Rousseau

Temple Beth El
61 rue Jaber ben Hayane
Telephone: (2) 267-192

ESSAOUIRA (FORMERLY MOGADOR)
COMMUNITY ORGANISATIONS
Community Offices
2 rue Ziri Ben Atyah

SYNAGOGUES
2 rue Ziri Ben Atyah

FEZ
COMMUNITY ORGANISATIONS
Community Offices
rue Dominique Bouchery

CONTACT INFORMATION
Mrs Danielle Mamane, La Boutique, Hotel Palais Jamai, Fez
Telephone: (5) 5562 2353
Email: boutique.palaisjamai@iam.net.ma
Mrs Mamane will be pleased to assist all Jewish visitors.

MIKVAOT
Talmud Torah
rue Dominique Bouchery

RESTAURANTS
Meat
Centre Maimonide
24 rue Zerktouni, (adjacent to Hotel Splendide)
Telephone: (5) 620-593
Fax: (5) 659-412
Supervision: Local Rabbanut

SYNAGOGUES
Sadoun Synagogue
blvd Mohammed V.

Synagogue
rue de Beyrouth

Talmud Torah
rue Dominique Bouchery

KENITRA
COMMUNITY ORGANISATIONS
Community Offices
58 rue Sallah Eddine

MIKVAOT
58 rue Sallah Eddine

SYNAGOGUES
Synagogue
rue de Lyon

MARRAKECH
COMMUNITY ORGANISATIONS
Community Offices
PO Box 515
Telephone: (4) 448754

MIKVAOT
Blvd Zerktouni (Gueliz)
Telephone: (4) 448-754
Fax: (4) 438-676
Contact: Mme Kadoch

RESTAURANTS
Le Sepharade
31 Lotissement Hassania, Gueliz
Telephone: (4) 43 98 09

Le Viennois Hotel Pulman Mansour Eddahbi
Avenue de France, Marrakech
Telephone: (4) 339100

SYNAGOGUES
Bittoun
Medina, Rue Arset Laamach, Touareg
In course of renovation.

Rabbi Pinhas Ha Cohen
Medina Rue Arset, Laamach
Telephone: (4) 389-798

Salat Laazama
Rue Talmud Torah, Mellah, Hay Essalam
Telephone: (4) 403-798

MEKNES
MIKVAOT
5 rue de Ghana
Telephone: (5) 21968 or 22549
Tourists should telephone twenty-four hours in advance.

SYNAGOGUES
5 rue de Ghana
Telephone: (5) 21968 or 22549

OUJDA
COMMUNITY ORGANISATIONS
Community Offices
Texaco Maroc, 36 blvd Hassan Loukili

RABAT
COMMUNITY ORGANISATIONS
1 rue Boussouni

MIKVAOT
3 rue Moulay Ismail

RESTAURANTS
Cercle de l'Alliance
3 rue Mellila
Telephone: (7) 72 76 79

The Menora
Villa 5, rue Er Riyad
Telephone: (7) 26 01 03

SYNAGOGUES
3 rue Moulay Ismail

SAFI
SYNAGOGUES
Mursiand Synagogue
Rue de R'bat

Synagogue Beth El
Rue de R'bat

TANGIER
COMMUNITY ORGANISATIONS
Community Centre
1 rue de la Liberte
Telephone: (9) 931-633
Fax: (9) 937-609

MIKVAOT
Shaar Raphael
27 blvd Pasteur
Telephone: (9) 231304

SYNAGOGUES
27 blvd Pasteur
Telephone: (9) 231304

TOURIST SITES
Rue des Synagogues, off rue Siaghines.
There are a number of synagogues in this street which is in the old part of the town.

TETUAN
COMMUNITY ORGANISATIONS
Community Offices
16 rue Moulay Abbas

SYNAGOGUES
Benoualid Synagogue
The old Mellah

MOZAMBIQUE

The small community in Mozambique originally consisted of South African Jews who were forced out of South Africa by President Kruger for supporting the British at the beginning of the twentieth century. The synagogue was opened in 1926, and there is a cemetery in Alto Maha. The biggest Jewish community is in Maputo.

GMT +2 hours
Country calling code: (+258)
Total population: 16,917,000
Jewish population: Under 100
Emergency telephone: (Police – 119) (Fire – 198)
(Ambulance – 117)
Electricity voltage: (Electricity voltage – 220)

MAPUTO
COMMUNITY ORGANISATIONS
Jewish Community of Mozambique
Av. Tomas Nduda 235, PO Box 235
Telephone: (1) 494413
Email: xero_servicos@mail.garp.co.mz

MYANMAR

The first Jews came to Myanmar in the early eighteenth century from Iraq and other Middle Eastern countries. A synagogue was built in 1896. In the first years of the twentieth century Rangoon and Bassein both had Jewish mayors. The Jewish population swelled to 2,000 before 1939, but most of these fled to Britain and India before the Japanese invasion in the Second World War. Not many returned after the war (only a few hundred), and the community began to decline through intermarriage and conversion. The handful of remaining Jews are elderly and services are held only on the High Holy Days when a minyan is made up with help from the Israeli embassy.

There is also a tribe of Jews in the north of the country (the Karens), who have their own prayer houses and who believe that they are descended from the tribe of Menashe.

GMT +6 1/2 hours
Country calling code: (+95)
Total population: 46,402,000
Jewish population: Under 100
Emergency telephone: (Police – 199) (Fire – 191)
(Ambulance – 192)
In Yangon [Rangoon] only
Electricity voltage: (Electricity voltage – 220/230)

YANGON (FORMERLY RANGOON)
EMBASSY
Embassy of Israel
No. 15, Kha Baung Street, Hlaing Township
Telephone: 515115
Fax: 515116
Email: global56@yangon.mfa.gov.il

SYNAGOGUES
Musmeah Yeshua
85 26th Street
Telephone: 75062

NAMIBIA

Namibian Jewry began at the time when the country was a German colony, before the First World War. The cemetery at Swakopmund dates from that settlement. Keetmanschoop also had a congregation, but this no longer exists. The Windhoek synagogue is still in use, and was founded in 1924. Services are held on Shabbat and festivals.

South Africa provides some help for the community, such as a cantor on festivals, and the Cape Board of Jewish Education assists with Hebrew education. From approximately 100 Jewish families in the 1920s and 1930s, the number has dwindled.

GMT +2 hours
Country calling code: (+264)
Total population: 1,613,000
Jewish population: Under 100
Emergency telephone: (Police – 1011) (Fire – 2032270) (Ambulance – 2032276)
Electricity voltage: (Electricity voltage – 220/240)

WINDHOEK
SYNAGOGUES
Cnr. Tal & Post Streets, PO Box 563
Telephone: (61) 264-81-127-0800
Fax: (61) 264-61-291-6328
Email: groupgm@pupkewitz

NEPAL

Nepal has no Jewish history. It is however well visited by Israeli and other young Jewish tourists. Each year a large Seder is organised by the Lubavitch movement. In 2000 approximately 1,000 attended at the Radisson Hotel.

GMT +5.45 hours
Country calling code: (+977)
Total population: 22,591,000
Jewish population: Under 100
Emergency telephone:

KATHMANDU
EMBASSY
Embassy of Israel
Bishramalaya House, Lazimpat Street, G.P.O. Box 371
Telephone: (1) 411-811
Fax: (1) 413-920
Email: kathmandu@israel.org

NETHERLANDS

Although some historians believe that the first Jews in Holland lived there during Roman times, documentary evidence goes back only to the twelfth century. The contemporary settlement occurred when Portuguese Marranos found refuge from the Inquisition in Holland. Religious freedom was advocated in the early seventeenth century and Jews contributed much to the Netherlands' 'golden age' of prosperity and power.

By the time of Napoleon, the community had grown to 10,000 (the largest in Western Europe), mainly by incoming Jewish traders from eastern Europe. The Jews were emancipated in 1796, but the community began to decline slowly during the nineteenth century. Of the 140,000 Jews (including 30,000 German Jewish refugees) in Holland in 1939, the Germans transported 100,000 to various death camps in Poland, but the local Dutch population tended to behave sympathetically towards their Jewish neighbours, hiding many. Anne Frank and her family are the most famous of the hidden Jews from Holland. Amsterdam witnessed a strike in February 1941, called as a protest against the Jewish deportations.

Today, there are three Jewish councils in the Netherlands, representing the Ashkenazi, Reform and Orthodox communities. There are many synagogues in Amsterdam, as well as synagogues in other towns. There are kosher restaurants in Amsterdam, which also has many historical sites Anne Frank House, the Portuguese Synagogue, still lit by candlelight, and the Resistance Museum.

GMT +1 hour
Country calling code: (+31)
Total population: 15,604,000
Jewish population: 28,000
Emergency telephone: (Police – 112) (Fire – 112) (Ambulance – 112)
Electricity voltage: (Electricity voltage – 220)

AMERSFOORT

SYNAGOGUES

PO Box 1039 3800 BA
Telephone: 33-475-6722
Email: nigamersfoort@hetnet.nl

AMSTERDAM

The first Jews were said to have come to the city in 1598 following the Union of Utrecht when the northern provinces proclaimed their independence from Catholic Spain and abolished religious discrimination. It soon became the centre of the Converso Diaspora. The Jewish Historical Museum and the Anne Frank house are essential visits. The Rijksmuseum contains a number of paintings of Jewish interest including 'The Jewish Bride' by Rembrandt.

BAKERIES

Thee Boom

Bolestein 45-47
Telephone: (20) 642-7003
Supervision: Amsterdam Jewish Community
Hours: Sunday - Friday 9.00 am - 5.00 pm, closed on Tuesday. Trams: 12, 25.

Maasstraat 16
Telephone: (20) 662-4827
Supervision: Amsterdam Jewish Community

BOOKSELLERS

Joachimsthal's Boekhandel

Van Leijenberghlaan 116 1082 DB
Telephone: (20) 442-0762
Fax: (20) 404-1843
Email: joachims@xs4all.nl

Samech Books

Gunterstein 69
Telephone: (20) 642-1424
Fax: (20) 642-1424
Email: samech@dds.nl.

CHOCOLATE SHOPS

Chocolate shop Bonbon Jeannette

Hall Central Station Amsterdam, Stationsplein 15 1012 AB
Telephone: (20) 421-5194
Fax: (20) 421-5194
Their bitter and dairy chocolates and bonbons are kosher and are sanctioned by the Chief Rabbinate for the Netherlands. Open daily, 8 am to 9 pm.

DELICATESSEN

Mouwes Koshere Delicatessan

Kastelenstraat 261 1082
Telephone: (20) 661-0180

HOTELS

Golden Tulip Amsterdam Centre

Stadhouderskade 7 1054 ES
Telephone: (20) 685-1351
Fax: (20) 685-1611
Email: info@gtacentre.goldentulip.nl

Hotel Doria

Damstraat 3 1012 JL
Telephone: (20) 31-20-638-8826
Fax: (20) 31-20-638-8726
Email: doria@euronet.nl
Web site: www.intris.nl/hoteldoria
Kosher breakfast. Reception open 24 hours.

Hotel la Richelle

Holbeinstr 41
Telephone: (20) 671-7971
Fax: (20) 671-0541
Kosher breakfast on request.

JEWISH LIBRARY

Ets Haim Library - Livraria Montezinos

Mr. Visserplein 3 1011RD
Telephone: (20) 428-2596
Fax: (20) 428-2597
Email: biblio@etshaim.org
Web site: www.etshaim.org
Open for research only Monday-Thursday 10.00-16.00, Friday 10.00-12.30.

LIBRARIES
Bibliotheca Rosenthaliana
Singel 425 1012 WP
Telephone: (20) 525-2366
Fax: (20) 525-2311
Email: ros@uba.uva.nl
The Amsterdam University Library contains an extraordinary collection of Judaic and Hebrew writings given to the city in 1880 by the heirs of Lesser Rosenthal (1794-1868). The German occupation in the Second World War had severe repercussions for the Bibliotheca Rosenthaliana. The books were sent to Germany, where they were found by the Americans, and returned to Amsterdam in 1946. The collection now contains over 100,000 volumes, some dating back to the fifteenth century.

MEDIA
Newspaper
Nieuw Israelietisch Weekblad
Rapenburgerstr. 109 1011 VL
Telephone: (20) 627-6275
Fax: (20) 624-2519
Email: niw@xs4all.nl
Web site: www.xs4all.nl/~niw

MIKVAOT
Heinzestr. 3
Telephone: (20) 662-0178/671938
Mr. Visserplein 3
Telephone: (20) 625-6222

MUSEUMS
Anne Frank House
Prinsengracht 267
Telephone: (20) 0031-20-556-7105
Fax: (20) 0031-20-620-7999
Web site: www.annefrank.nl
The original hiding place of Anne Frank, where she wrote her diary. Open daily from 9am to 7pm (April 1st to September 1st daily from 9am to 9pm. January 1st and December 25th 12 noon to 5pm). Last entry thirty minutes before closing time.

Dutch Resistance Museum
Plantage Kerklaan 61 1018 CX
Telephone: (20) 020-620-2535
Fax: (20) 020-620-2960
Email: info@verzetsmuseum.org
Web site: www.verzetsmuseum.org
Open all year, except January 1st, April 30th and December 25th. Hours: 10am to 5pm, Tuesday to Friday, 12 noon to 5pm, Saturday to Monday. Permanent Exhibition: From 10 May 1940 to 5 May 1945, the Netherlands were occupied by Nazi Germany. Almost every Dutch person was affected by the consequences of the occupation. The Plancius Building, in which the museum is located, was built in 1876 as the social club for a Jewish choir.

Jewish Historical Museum
Jonas Daniël Meÿerplein 2-4 1011 RH
Telephone: (20) 626-9945
Fax: (20) 624-1721
Email: info@jhm.nl
Web site: www.jhm.nl
Housed in a complex of four former synagogues. Sandwich shop serving kosher food. Open daily from 11am to 5pm. Group visits by arrangement. Next to the permanent collection on the culture and the history of the Jews in the Netherlands, there are changing exhibitions and a program of events. Until the end of 2003: 'Where Mokum is home', an exhibition especially for children of the ages of 8-12 years (Awarded with the prestigious Museum Price 2002 of the Prince Bernhard Cultural Fund).

RELIGIOUS ORGANISATIONS
Ashkenazi Community Offices/Community Center
van der Boechorststr. 26, PO Box 7967 1008 AD
Telephone: (20) 646-0046
Fax: (20) 646-4357
Email: info@nihs.nl
Web site: www.nik.nl

RESTAURANTS

Nasj Viel Restaurant
Jewish Youth Center, De Lairessestraat 13, (near Concertgebouw) 1071
Telephone: (20) 676-7622
Fax: (20) 673-5215
Email: info@nasjviel.nl
Supervision: Amsterdam Rabbinate
Open: Sunday - Thursday, 6.00pm - 10.00pm (kitchen closes at 9.00pm). Groups can be accommodated - reserve in advance.

Sandwichshop Sal. Meijer
Scheldestraat 45 1078 GG
Telephone: (20) 673-1313
Fax: (20) 642-9020
Supervision: Amsterdam Jewish Community

Dairy

Museum Café
Jewish Historical Museum, Jonas Daniel Meijerplein 2-4
Telephone: (20) 626-9945
Fax: (20) 624-1721
Supervision: Amsterdam Jewish Community
Hours 11am to 5pm daily.

Meat

Carmel
Amstelveenseweg 224 1075 XT
Telephone: (20) 675-7636
Fax: (20) 773-5960
Supervision: Amsterdam Jewish Community
Hours: 12 pm to 11:30 pm, Sunday to Thursday. Caters for Shabbat meals for groups if ordered in advance. Transport: trams 6, 16, bus 15, 63, 170, 171, 172.

King Solomon Restaurant
Waterlooplein 239 1011 PG
Telephone: (20) 625-5860

Shabbes - Tisch
Plantage Westermanlaan 9 1018 DK
Telephone: (20) 623-4684
Supervision: Rabbinate of The Netherlands
Five minutes from Portuguese Synagogue. Friday night and Shabbath only. Reservations in advance.

Vegetarian

Bolhoed
Prinsengacht 60-62
Telephone: (20) 626-1803
Hours: 12 pm to 10 pm daily. Serves organic vegetarian and vegan food.

Restaurant Betty's
Rijnstraat 75 1079 GX
Telephone: (20) 644-5896

SYNAGOGUES

Liberal

Liberaal Joodse Gemeente
Jacob Soetendorpstr. 8 1079 RM
Telephone: (20) 642-3562
Fax: (20) 442-0337
Email: ljgadam@ljg.nl
Web site: www.ljg.nl
Also houses the Judith Druk Library and The Centre for Jewish Studies.

Orthodox

Gerard Doustraat Synagogue
Gerard Doustr. 238
Telephone: (20) 675-0932
Fax: (20) 867-1626
Email: gd_sjoel@joods.nl
Web site: www.joods.nl/gd_sjoel
Services: Saturday and Festival mornings.

Kehilas Ja'Akow (E. Europe)
Gerrit van der Veenstraat 26 1077 ED
Telephone: (20) 676-3602

Portuguese Jews' Congregation
Mr. Visserplein 3 1011 RD
Telephone: (20) 624-5351
Fax: (20) 625-4680
Email: pig-amsterdam@euronet.nl
This synagogue has been completely restored and is open from Sunday - Friday from 10 am to 4 pm. In August 2000 Holland's unique Sephardi Judaism collection was returned from safe keeping at The Hebrew University at Jerusalem.

Sephardi

Portuguese Synagogue & Community Centre
Texelstr. 82
Telephone: (20) 624-5351

TOURIST SITES

Portuguese Jewish Cemetery
Kerkstraat 7, 1191 JB, Ouderkerk aan de Amstel
Telephone: (20) 496-3498
Fax: (20) 496-5496
Email: bethaim@wxs.nl
Established 1614. One of the oldest Sephardic cemeteries still in use in Europe. Menasseh ben Israel is buried here, as are the parents of the philosopher Spinoza. Ten kilometres south-east of Amsterdam.

TOURS

Easy Rider Excursions
Majella 1, 1186 CE Amstelveen
Telephone: (20) 489-7045
Email: maxmeron@hotmail.com
Web site: www.easyriderexcursions.nl
Walk through the jewish history of Amsterdam. Licensed tour guides. By reservation only: 06-11292616, from June 1st till September 30th.

ARNHEM

SYNAGOGUES
Pastoorstr. 17a
Telephone: (26) 442-5154

Liberal
Liberaal Joodse Gemeente Arnhem
Veluws Hof 24, Ermelo 3852 JJ
Telephone: (26) 557-860
Email: elisjewa@hetnet.nl

BUSSUM

SYNAGOGUES
Orthodox
Kromme Englaan 1a
Telephone: (35) 691-4882
Fax: (35) 538-0236

DELFT

SYNAGOGUES
Beth Studentiem
Hillel House, Jewish Students Centre, Technical
University, Koornmarkt 9
Telephone: (15) 212-0300

EINDHOVEN

SYNAGOGUES
H. Casimirstr. 23
Telephone: (40) 751-1253

ENSCHEDE

SYNAGOGUES
Prinsestr. 16
Telephone: (53) 432-3479
Fax: (53) 430-9725
Email: jmhartog@vromen.nl

Liberal
Liberal Congregation Inquiries
Haaksbergen
Telephone: (53) 435-1330

GRONINGEN

SYNAGOGUES
Postbus 550 9700 AN
Telephone: (50) 312-3151
Email: NIG_Groningen@hotmail.com

HAARLEM

SYNAGOGUES
Kenaupark 7
Telephone: (23) 332-6899; 324-2051

HILVERSUM

CENTRAL ORGANISATIONS
Nederlandse Vegetariersbond
Larenseweg 26 1221 CM
Telephone: (35) 683-4796
Fax: (35) 683-6152
Email: info@vegetariers.nl
Web site: www.vegetariers.nl
Provides information on vegetarian hotels, restaurants
and guest houses.

SYNAGOGUES
Orthodox
Synagogue
Laanstr. 30
Telephone: (35) 621-2044
Fax: (35) 624-3654
Email: ipor@wxs.nl
The Inter-Provincial Chief Rabbinate is also based at this
address. Tel: 035-623-9238.

LEIDEN

ORGANISATIONS
Jewish Students Centre
Levendaal 8
Telephone: (71) 513-0382

SYNAGOGUES
Levendaal 14-16 2311 JL
Telephone: (71) 512-5793
Fax: (71) 512-5793

MAASTRICHT

SYNAGOGUES
Capucijnengang 2
The present synagogue was built in 1841. It is believed
however that there had been one in the town in the 14th
century

ROTTERDAM

SYNAGOGUES
Liberal
**Liberaal Joodse Gemeente Rotterdam
(Liberal Jewish Community of Rotterdam)**
Mozartlaan 99 3007
Telephone: (10) 461-2606
Fax: (10) 218-0322
Email: norbird@hetnet.nl
Mailing address: Postbox 91119, 3007 MA. Inquiries to
Secretary: 180 423474

Orthodox
Joodse Gemeente Rotterdam
A B N Davidsplein 2
Telephone: (10) 466-9765
Fax: (10) 467-5713
Email: nig.rotterdam@zonnet.nl
Mikva on premises.

THE HAGUE

DELICATESSEN
Jacobs
Haverkamp 220
Telephone: (70) 347-4980
Fax: (70) 347-4980

EMBASSY
Embassy of Israel
Buitenhof 47 2513 AH
Telephone: (70) 376-0500
Fax: (70) 376-0555
Email: ambassade@israel.nl

RESTAURANTS
Vegetarian
Restaurant De Wankele Tafel
Mauritskade 79 2514 HH
Telephone: (70) 364-3267

SYNAGOGUES
Liberal
Liberal Synagogue
Prinsessegracht 26
Telephone: (70) 365-6892
Fax: (70) 360-3883
Email: ljg-denhaag@hetnet.nl
Web site: www.ljgdenhaag.nl

Orthodox
Beis Jisroel
Doorniksestraat 152 2587 AZ
Telephone: (70) 358-6363
Fax: (70) 347-9002

Synagogue
Corn. Houtmanstraat 11, Bezuidenhout 2593 RD
Telephone: (70) 347-0222
Fax: (70) 347-9002
Email: raabinaat-haag@zonnet.nl
Mikva on premises, appointments should be made twenty-four hours in advance by telephoning 350-7621.

TOURIST SITES
Spinoza House
Paviljoensgracht
Spinoza House is of special interest, as is the eighteenth-century Portuguese synagogue in the Prinsessegracht, which is now used by the Liberal congregation.

UTRECHT

RESTAURANTS
Eetkafee De Baas
Lijnmarkt 8 3511 KM
Telephone: (30) 231-5185

SYNAGOGUES
Liberal
Liberal Synagogue
Telephone: (30) 644-2619
Email: batja@hetnet.nl
Inquiries to 030-603-9343

Orthodox
Springweg 164 3511 VZ
Telephone: (30) 231-4742
Fax: (30) 272-2091
Email: nigutrecht@hotmail.com

ZWOLLE

SYNAGOGUES
Samuel Hirschstr. 8, Postbox 1468 8001
Telephone: (38) 211412

Overseas Territories

CURAÇAO

EMBASSY
Consul General of Israel
Blauwduifweg 5, Willemstad
Telephone: 736-5068
Fax: 737-0707
Email: midalya@ibm.net

KASHRUT INFORMATION
There is no kosher restaurant in Curacao. However many kosher items may be purchased at the "food store" of the Congregation Shaarei Tsedek.

MUSEUMS
Jewish Cultural Historical Museum
Hanchi di Snoa 29, PO Box 322
Telephone: 461-1633
Fax: 465-4141
Opening hours: Monday to Friday 9.00 to 11.45am and 2.30 to 4.45pm. If there is a cruise ship in port, then also on Sundays from 9am to noon. Closed on Shabbats and Holy Days. On permanent display are a great many ritual, ceremonial and cultural objects, many of which date back to the seventeenth and eighteenth centuries and are still in use by the adjacent congregation Mikve Israel-Emanuel (founded 1651, oldest in the hemisphere).

SYNAGOGUES
Ashkenazi
Congregation Shaarei Tsedek
Leliweg 1a, PO Box 498
Telephone: 737-5738
Fax: 736-9546

Sephardi, Reconstructionist
United Congregation Mikve'Israel Emanuel
Hanchi di Snoa 29, PO Box 322
Telephone: 461-1067
Fax: 465-4141
Email: info@snoa.com
Sabbath services are Friday at 6.30pm (second Friday in the month is a family service), Saturday at 10am. Holy-day services at same times.

NEW ZEALAND

New Zealand Jewry is almost as old as the European presence in the country. The year 1829 marks the beginning of Jewish settlement, and Jews played a prominent role in the development of the country in the nineteenth century, especially in trading with Australia and Britain. Auckland Jewish community was founded in 1841, followed by Wellington in 1843. There was also a Jewish Prime Minister, Sir Julius Vogel, in the nineteenth century.

British Jews emigrated to New Zealand in the twentieth century, but New Zealand restricted immigration from Nazi Europe.

Today the community has six synagogues, four on the North Island and two on the South Island. Auckland and Wellington have Jewish day schools, and the 'Kosher Kiwi Guide' is published in Auckland. There has been recent Jewish immigration from South Africa.

GMT +12 hours
Country calling code: **(+64)**
Total population: **3,811,000**
Jewish population: **5,000**
Emergency telephone: **(Police – 111) (Fire – 111)**
(Ambulance – 111)
Electricity voltage: **(Electricity voltage – 230)**

AUCKLAND
COMMUNITY ORGANISATIONS
Auckland Jewish Council
80 Webb St, Wellington
Telephone: (9) 384-4229
Fax: (9) 384-4229
Has a small shop selling kosher food.

SYNAGOGUES
Orthodox
Auckland Hebrew Congregation
108 Greys Avenue
Telephone: (9) 373-2908
Fax: (9) 303-2147
Email: office@ahc.org.nz
New Zealands largest selection of kosher goods. Open Wednesday to Friday 8.30 am to 3.30pm. Sundays 9.00am to 11.00am.Mailing address: PO Box 68224 Newton Auckland

Progressive
Beth Shalom Progressive Synagogue
180 Manukau Road, Epsom 1003
Telephone: (9) 524-4139
Fax: (9) 524-7075
Email: bshalom@ihug.co.nz
Web site: www.bethshalom.org.nz

CHRISTCHURCH
COMMUNITY ORGANISATIONS
Christchurch Jewish Council
Telephone: (3) 358-8769

SYNAGOGUES
406 Durham Street
Telephone: (3) 365-7412
Fax: (3) 355-7982
Email: coxst@chch.planet.org.nz

WELLINGTON
COMMUNITY ORGANISATIONS
Wellington Jewish Community Centre
80 Webb Street
Telephone: (4) 384-5081
Fax: (4) 384-5081
Email: bethel@ihug.co.nz
There are no kosher restaurants in Wellington. Visitors who want kosher meals & kosher food should contact the office of the Community Centre or the Kosher Co-op, on 384-3136.

Wellington Regional Jewish Council
54 Central Terrace 5
Telephone: (4) 475-7622
Email: zwartz@actrix.gen.nz

DELICATESSEN
Dixon Street Delicatessen
Telephone: (4) 384-2436
Fax: (4) 384-8692
Not fully kosher but provides kosher challahs and various American & Israeli kosher foods.

EMBASSY
Embassy of Israel
Level 13, 111 The Terrace, Equinox House, P O Box 2171
Telephone: (4) 472-2368
Fax: (4) 499-0632
Email: israel-ask@israel.org.nz
Web site: www.webnz.co.nz/israel

GROCERIES
Kosher Co-op
80 Webb Street
Telephone: (4) 384-3136
Fax: (4) 384-5081
Email: clemclan@ihug.co.nz
Web site: www.go.to/koshernz
Open on Wednesday, Friday and Sunday for kosher
meats, cheese and imported products. Goods can be sent
anywhere in New Zealand.

MEDIA
Newspapers
New Zealand Jewish Chronicle
PO Box 27-156
Telephone: (4) 934-6077
Fax: (4) 934-6079
Email: mike@rifkov.co.nz
Monthly newspaper of local, Israeli and Jewish News.

MIKVAOT
Wellington Jewish Community Centre
80 Webb Street
Telephone: (4) 384-5081
Fax: (4) 384-5081
Email: bethel@ihug.co.nz

SYNAGOGUES
Orthodox
Beth-El Synagogue
80 Webb Street
Telephone: (4) 384-5081
Fax: (4) 384-5081
Email: bethel@ihug.co.nz

Progressive
Temple Sinai
147 Ghuznee Street
Telephone: (4) 385-0720
Fax: (4) 385-0572
Email: temple@actrix.co.nz
Web site: www.sinai.org.nz

NORWAY

The only way Jews could enter Norway before the nineteenth century was with a 'Letter of Protection', as Danish control limited the amount of Jewish entry. The situation changed in 1851, when a Norwegian liberal poet, Henrik Wergeland, argued for the admission of Jews into the country, and the parliament eventually agreed. There were only some 650 Jews in the country after emancipation in 1891, mainly in Oslo

and Trondheim. By 1920, the community numbered 1,457 and by the time of the Nazi invasion there were 1,800. Despite attempts by the Norwegian resistance to smuggle Jews to Sweden, 767 Jews were transported to Auschwitz, although 930 were able to reach Sweden. The Jewish survivors were joined after the war by Displaced Persons, especially invited by the Norwegian government.

The current situation forbids shechita, but there are no other restrictions on Jewish life. There is a synagogue in Oslo, and a kosher food shop. There is also a Jewish magazine. An old-age home was built in 1988. Trondheim, in the north of the country, has the northernmost synagogue in the world.

GMT +1 hour
Country calling code: (+47)
Total population: 4,445,000
Jewish population: 1,500
Emergency telephone: (Police – 112) (Fire – 110)
(Ambulance – 113)
Electricity voltage: (Electricity voltage – 220)

OSLO
Oslo is the major centre of Norwegian Jewry, with 900 Jews living in the capital. The Resistance Museum is of interest as is the Wergerland Monument in the Var Frisler Cemetery. A monument consisting of 8 empty chairs in remembrance of the Norwegian Jews who were killed during the War is located near Akershus fortification.

COMMUNITY CENTRE
Bergstien 13 131
Telephone: 2269-6570
Fax: 2246-6604
Email: kontor@dmt.oslo.no
Web site: www.dmt.oslo.no
Also has a kosher shop. Opening hours: Tuesday and Thursday 4.00pm to 6.00pm, Wednesday 2.00pm to 5.00pm, Friday 12 noon to 2.00pm (winter)/ 12 noon to 3.00pm (summer). Phone 2260-9166.

EMBASSY
Embassy of Israel
Parkveien 35, Oslo 258
Telephone: 2101-9500
Fax: 2101-9530
Email: israel@online.no

RESTAURANTS
Kosher Food Centre
Corner Bergstien/Waldemar Thranes gate 171
Telephone: 2260-9166
Supervision: Rabbi Michael Melchior
There are no kosher hotels or restaurants in Oslo but
there is the Kosher Food Centre. Open 4 pm to 6 pm
Tuesday and Thursday, and 12.00 noon to 2 pm on Friday.
Closed Shabbat.

SYNAGOGUES
Orthodox
Mosaiske Trossamfund (The Jewish Community)
Bergstien 13 172
Telephone: 2269-6570
Fax: 2246-6604
Email: kontor@dmt.oslo.no
Web site: www.dmt.oslo.no
Postal address: postboks 2722 St. Hanshaugen, 0131
Oslo, Norway

TOURIST SITES
Ostre Gravlund Cemetary
There is a Jewish war memorial here.

TRONDHEIM
SYNAGOGUES
Synagogue
Ark. Christiesgt. 1
Telephone: 7352-6568 or 4752-2030
Fax: 7353-1108
Email: palkom@online.no
The world's northernmost synagogue. The synagogue
also has a museum. Postal address Postboks 2722 St.
Hanshaugen, 0131 Oslo, Norway.

PANAMA

Some Jews, most of them pretending to be
Christians, came to Panama during colonial
times. Panama was an important crossroads
for trade and, as a result, many Jews passed
through the country on their journeys in
the region.

In 1849, immigrant Sephardic Jews in
Panama founded the Hebrew Benevolent
Society, the first Jewish congregation in the
Isthmus. They came from the pious congre-
gation of the Netherlands Antilles
(Curacao) to settle in Panama.

Jews from Saint-Thomas (Virgin Islands)
and Curacao founded in 1876 the Kol
Shearith Israel Synagogue in Panama City,

and in 1890 the Kahal Hakadosh Yangacob
in Colon.

By the end of the First World War, a number
of Middle Eastern Jews had settled in the
country and founded the Israelite
Benevolent Society Shevet Ahim. During
the years of the Second World War, immigrants from Europe arrived at Panama,
establishing Beth-El, the only Ashkenazi
community in the country. The majority of
Jewish community is Sephardi (around 80
per cent).

There have been two Jewish presidents in
Panama, the only country – apart from
Israel of course – where this has happened.

GMT -5 hours
Country calling code: (+507)
Total population: 2,719,000
Jewish population: 7,000
Emergency telephone: (Police – 104) (Fire – 103)
Electricity voltage: (Electricity voltage – 120)

PANAMA CITY
BAKERIES
Pita Pan
Plaza Bal Harbour, Paitilla
Telephone: 264-2786

BUTCHERS
Shalom Kosher
Plaza Bal Harbour, Paitilla
Telephone: 264-4411

Super Kosher
Calle San Sebastian, Paitilla
Telephone: 263-5254
Fax: 263-2067
Email: mzakay@skosher.com
Supervision: Shevet Ahim Rabinate
Mailing Address POB 8242 Panama 7. Also Kosher
supermarket, bakery and restaurant. Open from 8.30am
to 8.30 pm Sunday to Thursday. Friday until 4.30pm.

CHOCOLATE SHOPS
Candies Bazaar
Via Argentina, 155 L-2
Telephone: 269-4857

La Bonbonniere
Calle Juan XXIII, Paitilla
Telephone: 264-5704

COMMUNITY ORGANISATIONS
Consejo Central Comunitario Hebreo de Panama
P O Box 3309 4
Telephone: 263-8411
Fax: 264-7936

Jewish Centre: Centro Cultural Hebreo De beneficiencia
Calle 50 Final, PO Box 7166, 5 5
Telephone: 226-0455
Fax: 226-0869
(K) Restaurant open daily for lunch and supper. Closed Saturdays.

EMBASSY
Embassy of Israel
Edificio Grobman, Calle Manuel Maria Icaza, 5th Floor
Telephone: 264-8257

MIKVAOT
Beneficiencia Israelita Beth El
Calle 58E,, Urb. Obarrio
Telephone: 223-3383

Sociedad Israelita Shevet Ahim
Calle 44-27
Telephone: 225-5990
Fax: 227-1268

RESTAURANTS
Dairy
Pita Pan
Plaza Bal Harbour, Paitilla
Telephone: 264-2786

Meat
Shalom Kosher
Plaza Bal Harbour, Paitilla
Telephone: 264-4411

Pizzeria
Pizzeria Italiana
Centro Cultural Hebreo de Beneficiencia, Calle 50 Final
Telephone: 226-0455
Fax: 226-0869

SYNAGOGUES
Ashkenazi
Beneficiencia Israelita Beth El
Calle 58E, Urb. Obarrio
Telephone: 264-0058
Fax: 264-0058
Mikva on premises.

Orthodox Sephardi
Ahavat Sion
Calle Juan XXIII, Paitilla
Telephone: 265-1891
Daily Services. Mikva for women on premises.

Sociedad Israelita Shevet Ahim
Calle 44-27
Telephone: 225-5990
Fax: 227-1268
Daily services.

Reform
Kol Shearith Israel
Av. Cuba 34-16 5
Telephone: 225-4100

PARAGUAY

Jewish settlement in this land-locked country came late for this area of South America. The few who came over from Western Europe at the end of the nineteenth century rapidly assimilated into the general population. The first synagogue was founded early in the twentieth century by Sephardis from Palestine, Turkey and Greece. Ashkenazis arrived in the 1920s and 1930s from eastern Europe and some 15,000 came to the country to escape Nazism, intending to move on into Argentina. Some of these settled in Paraguay.

Paraguay, in more recent times, has accepted Jews from Argentina who were fleeing from the military regime.

Today there are three synagogues, a Jewish school and a Jewish museum in Asuncion. There is a high rate of intermarriage, but children of mixed marriages may receive a Jewish education.

GMT -5 hours
Country calling code: (**+507**)
Total population: **5,085,000**
Jewish population: **900**
Emergency telephone: (**Police – 00**) (**Fire – 00**) (**Ambulance – 00**)
Electricity voltage: (**Electricity voltage – 220**)

ASUNCION
COMMUNITY ORGANISATIONS
Consejo Representativo Israelita de Paraguay
General Diaz, 657, PO Box 756
Telephone: (21) 441-744
Fax: (21) 448-289

EMBASSY
Embassy of Israel
Calle Yegros No. 437 C/25 de Mayo, Edificio San
Rafael, Piso 8, PO Box 1212
Telephone: (21) 495-097; 496-043; 496-044
Fax: (21) 496-355

SYNAGOGUES
General Diaz, 657

PERU

The first Jews in Peru arrived with the first
Europeans, as many Conversos were leaders in the Spanish army which invaded the
country in 1532. After the Inquisition was
set up in 1570, the Jews were persecuted,
and many were burned alive. From 1870,
groups of Jews came over from Europe, but
tended to disappear into the general population. In 1880, a group of North African
Jews settled in Iquitos and worked in the
rubber industry. More Jewish immigration
occurred after the First World War, and later
Nazi refugees entered the country. By the
end of the Second World War the Jewish
population had reached 6,000, but this subsequently declined.

Almost all of the present Jewish population
are Ashkenazi. Two Jewish newspapers are
produced and most Jewish children go to
the Colegio Leon Pinelo school, which is
well known for its high standards. There is a
cemetery at Iquitos built by the nineteenth-
century community. The community is
shrinking owing to intermarriage and
assimilation.

GMT -5 hours
Country calling code: (+51)
Total population: 25,015,000
Jewish population: 3,000
Emergency telephone: (Police – 105) (Fire – 116)
(Ambulance – 470 5000)
Electricity voltage: (Electricity voltage – 220)

LIMA
COMMUNITY ORGANISATIONS
Asociacion Judia de Beneficencia y Culto de 1870
Libertad 375, Miraflores 18
Telephone: (1) 445-1089
Fax: (1) 445-1089
Email: AJBC1870@terra.com.pe

EMBASSY
Embassy of Israel
Natalio Sanchez 125 6to Piso, Santa Beatriz 1
Telephone: (1) 433-4431
Fax: (1) 433-8925

GROCERIES
Minimarket Kasher
Av. Gral. Juan A. Pezet 1472, San Isidro, 27
Telephone: (1) 264-2187
Fax: (1) 264-2187
Email: minimarket@terms.com.pe
Supervision: Rabbinate of the Union Israelita del Peru
Hours of opening: Monday-Thursday 9.00 am-6.00 pm,
Friday 9.00 am-3.00 pm.

HOTELS
Hotel Libertador
Los Eucaliptos 550, San Isidro, 27
Telephone: (1) 421-6680
Fax: (1) 442-3011
Web site: libertador.com.pe
A short walk away from the Union Israelita Synagogue

KASHRUT INFORMATION
Chief Rabbi Abraham Benhamu
Telephone: (1) 442-4505
Fax: (1) 442-8147
Email: absolben@terra.com.pe
Rabbi Benhamu is the Chief Rabbi of Peru.

KOSHER FOOD
Salon Majestic
Av. Bolivar 965, Pueblo Libre, 21
Telephone: (1) 463-0031
Fax: (1) 461-8912
Supervision: Chief Rabbi Abraham Benhamu
Catering for special groups and parties by prior
arrangement only.

MEDIA
Newspapers
Menora
Jose Quinones 290, Miraflores 18
Telephone: (1) 441-3461
Fax: (1) 422-5796
Email: jta_bnaibrith@terra.com.pe
Daily.

Shofar
Jose Bielovucic 1350, Lince 14
Telephone: (1) 440-0853
Fax: (1) 440-0853
Bimonthly.

MIKVAOT
Beit Jabad Peru
Av. Salaverry 3095, San Isidro, 27
Telephone: (1) 51-1-264-6060
Fax: (1) 51-1-264-5499
Email: chabadperu@unired.net.pe /
chabadperu@telefonica.net.pe
Mikveh, daily minyan, kosher meals.

Union Israelita
Ave. Gral. Juan A. Pezet 1472, San Isidro, 27
Telephone: (1) 264-2187
Sociedad Israelita Sefardi; Beit Jabad.

MUSEUMS
Inquisition and Congress Museum
Junin 548 Lima 1
Telephone: (1) 3117801 / 3117777 anexo 2910
Fax: (1) 3117801
Web site: www.congreso.gob.pe/museo.htm
The museum is opened from Monday to Sunday, from 9.00am to 5.00pm. The services are free and the tour is given in: spanish, english, french, italian, german and portuguese.

Museum of the Inquisition
Junin 548, Lima 1
Telephone: (1) 427-0365
Dungeon and torture chamber of the headquarters of the Inquisition for all Spanish South America from 1570 to 1820.

SYNAGOGUES
Conservative
Asociacion Judia de Beneficiencia y Culto de 1870
Jose Galvez 282, Miraflores 18
Telephone: (1) 445-1089 or445-5148
Fax: (1) 445-1089
Email: fambrons@junin.itete.com.pe

Orthodox
Beit Jabad
Av. Salaverry 3095, San Isidro, 27
Telephone: (1) 264-6060
Fax: (1) 264-5499
Email: chabadperu@unired.net.pe
Web site: www.lp.edu.pe/jabad
Synagogues (services daily), mikva, kosher food.

Sociedad de Beneficencia Israelita Sefardi
Enrique Villar 581, Santa Beatriz, 1
Telephone: (1) 471-7230
Fax: (1) 422-8147
Email: absolben@terra.com.pe

Union Israelita del Peru
Av. Dos de Mayo 1815, San Isidro 27 27
Telephone: (1) 421-3688
Fax: (1) 421-3684
Web site: orbita.starmedia.com/~uiperu
Services are held at the Centro Sharon.

TOURIST SITES
Pilatos House
Ancash 390, Lima 1
Telephone: (1) 427-5814
Seventeenth-century private mansion, now used by the Constitutional Court. On the 2nd floor was the synagogue of the Converso Jews. Located in front of the San Francisco Monastery.

PHILIPPINES REPUBLIC

Conversos who came with the Spanish in the sixteenth century were the first Jewish presence in the region. In the late nineteenth century, western European Jews came to trade in the area, and after the Americans occupied the country in 1898, more Jews arrived from a variety of places, including the USA and the Middle East. The first synagogue was built in 1924. The Philippines accepted refugees from Nazism, but the Japanese occupied the islands during the war and the Jewish population was interned. After the war many of the community emigrated. However, a new synagogue opened in 1983, and services are also held in the US Air Force bases around the country.

GMT +8 hours
Total population: **73,527,000**
Jewish population: **100**
Emergency telephone:
Electricity voltage: **(Electricity voltage – 220)**

MANILA
EMBASSY
Embassy of Israel
Trafalgar Plaza 23rd Floor, 105 H.V. dela Costa Street, Salcedo Village, Makati City 1200
Telephone: (2) 892-5329/30/31/34
Fax: (2) 894-1027
Email: israelembphl@netasia.net
Postal address: POB 1697 MCPO, Makati Metro, Manila 1299.

MIKVAOT
Jewish Association of the Philippines (Beth Yaacov Synagogue)
110 H.V. de la Costa corner Tordesillas West, Salcedo Village, Makati City, Metro Manila 1227
Telephone: (2) 815-0265
Fax: (2) 840-2566
Email: jap.manila@usa.net
By arrangement.

SYNAGOGUES

Orthodox, Sephardi
110 H.V. de la Costa corner Tordesillas West,
Salcedo Village, Makati City, Metro Manila 1227
Telephone: (2) 815-0265
Fax: (2) 840-2566
Email: jap.manila@usa.net
Services; Fri at 6.30pm, Sat at 9.30am.

POLAND

After just five years of German occupation in the Second World War, the thousand-year-old Jewish settlement in Poland, one of the largest Jewish communities in the world, had been almost totally eradicated. Jews came to Poland, in order to escape anti-semitism in Germany, in the early Middle Ages. They were initially welcomed by the rulers, and the Jews became greatly involved in the economy of the country.

Before the Second World War most Jews lived in the east and south of the country, under Russian and Austrian domination, respectively, until 1918. After 1918, Poland became an independent country once more, with over 3,000,000 Jews (300,000 in Warsaw.) The community continued to flourish before 1939, with Yiddish being the main language of the Jews. The community was destroyed in stages during the war, as Poland became the centre for the Nazi's destruction of European Jewry. After the war, the borders shifted again, and the 100,000 or so survivors mostly tried to emigrate. The few who remained endured several progroms even after the events of the Holocaust.

Today the community is comparatively small, and most of the members are elderly, but there is a functioning synagogue in Warsaw and many Jewish historical sites are scattered throughout the country. The Polish Tourist Board publishes information about the Jewish heritage in Poland.

GMT +1 hour
Country calling code: (+48)
Total population: 38,650,000
Jewish population: 5,000
Emergency telephone: (**Police – 997**) (**Fire – 998**) (**Ambulance – 999**)
Electricity voltage: (**Electricity voltage – 220**)

BIELSKO-BIALA

ORGANISATIONS
Elzbieta Wajs
ul. Mickiewicza 26 43-300
Telephone: (2) 22438

CRACOW

BOOKSELLERS
Jarden
2 Szeroka Street, Miodowa 41
Telephone: (12) 217166

COMMUNITY ORGANISATIONS
The Jewish Religion Congregation
2 Skawinska Street
Telephone: (12) 429-5735
Mondays to Thursdays 9.00am to 2.00pm, Friday 9.00am to 12.

CULTURAL FESTIVAL
Jewish Culture Festival
Telephone: (12) 429-2573
Email: office@jewishfestival.twelfth.pl
Web site: www.jewishfestival.pl
The twelth annual Jewish Culture Festival will be held between 28 June and 6 July 2003 in the restored Jewish quarter of Kasimierz.

HOTELS
Kosher
Hotel Eden
Ul. Ciemna 15, Cracow 31057
Telephone: (12) 430-6565
Fax: (12) 430-6767
Email: eden@hoteleden.pl
Web site: www.hoteleden.pl

MUSEUMS
Museum of the History and Culture of the Cracow Jews
The Old Synagogue, 24 Szeroka Street
Telephone: (12) 422-0962
Fax: (12) 431-0545
Email: alteszul@poczta.onet.pl

ORGANISATIONS
Judaica Foundation
ul. Rabina Meiselsa 17
Telephone: (12) 423-5595
Fax: (12) 423-5034
Email: uwrussek@cyf-kr.edu.pl

RESTAURANTS
Meat
Na Kazimierzu
ul Szeroka 39 31-053
Telephone: (12) 229-644
Fax: (12) 219-909
Billed as the 'only kosher restaurant in Cracow and the south of Poland'. Hours: 12 pm to 12 am everyday. Traditional Shabbat courses are available on Shabbat.

SYNAGOGUES
Isaac Synagogue
18 Kupa Street
Telephone: (12) 430-55-77
Fax: (12) 602-144-262
Email: synagogaizaaka@eranet.pl
Contact Dominik Dybek.

Remuh
ul. Szeroka 40
Built in 1557 the synagogue is named after Rabbi Moses Isserles the son of its founder, who is buried in the adjacent cemetery.
For information; contact 603 860 373 (Mobile)

TOURIST SITES
Temple Synagogue
24 Miodowa Street
Built in 1862 it was used by the Germans during the war as a stable during the War and is currently being restored.

GLIWICE
CONTACT INFORMATION
ul. Dolnych Walow 9 44100
Telephone: (32) 314797

KATOWICE
CONTACT INFORMATION
ul. Mlynska 13 40098
Telephone: (32) 537742

LEGNICA
CONTACT INFORMATION
ul. Chojnowska 37 59220
Telephone: (76) 22730

LODZ
COMMUNITY ORGANISATIONS
Jewish Congregation
Zachodnia 78
Telephone: (42) 335156

RELIGIOUS ORGANISATIONS
Jewish Chabad
Telephone: (42) 331221, 336825

LUBLIN
Once a major Jewish town in eastern Europe, Lublin today has fewer than a hundred Jews. Pre-war Lublin was a centre for Torah study, and a large yeshivah was built only a few years before the Second World War, and is now used as a dental college. Majdanek Concentration Camp lies within the city's boundary, clearly visible from a major road leading south east. There is a particularly moving memorial in the camp, consisting of the ashes from the camp's crematoria.

CONTACT INFORMATION
ul. Lubartowska 10 20080
Telephone: (81) 22353

OSWIECIM
MUSEUMS
Auschwitz - Birkenau State Museum
al .Wiezniow Oswiecimie 20 32-620
Telephone: 48.33.844.8102
Fax: 48.33.843.1934
Email: muzeum@auschwitz.org.pl
Web site: www.auschwitz.org.pl
Auschwitz Jewish Center and Chevra Lomdei Mishnayot Synagogue
Pl. Skarbka 5 32-600
Telephone: 33-844-7002
Fax: 33-844-7003
Email: info@ajcf.pl
Web site: www.ajcf.org
Hours of opening: April-September: 8.30am - 8.00pm; October-March: 8.30am - 6.00pm; The Center is closed on Saturday and Jewish holidays.

RZESZOW
SYNAGOGUES
Synagogue
ul Bonicza, edge of Pl. Ofiara Getta

SZCZECIN
CONTACT INFORMATION
ul. Niemcewicza 2 71553
Telephone: (91) 221674

WARSAW
Before the war, Warsaw had approximately 300,000 Jews. Now there are only a couple of thousand, mostly elderly. There are many sites which can be visited, such as surving fragments of the Ghetto walls and iA memorial Route to the struggle and Martyrdom of the Jews 1940-1943î known as îMemory Laneî The old Jewish cemetery, untouched by the Nazis, is very imposing, and is still in use. The Warsaw Ghetto fighters are included in the inscription to Tomb of the Unknown Soldier in the centre of the city. In 2002 the Nozyk synagogue celebrated its centenary.

EMBASSY

Embassy of Israel
ul. Krzywickiego 24 02-078
Telephone: (22) 0048-22-825-0028
Fax: (22) 0048-22-825-1607
Web site: http//warsaw.mfa.gov.il

MIKVAOT

Nozyk Synagogue
6 Twarda Street
Telephone: (22) 652-2805
Fax: (22) 652-2805
Email: varshe@jewish.org.pl
Contact: Sharona Kanofsky tel: 652 21 50.

MONUMENT

Monument to the Ghetto Heroes
Zamenhofa
Erected in 1948 this monument symbolises the heroic
Ghetto defiance of the 1943 uprising.

ORGANISATIONS

The Jewish Historical Institute
3/5 Tlomackie Street 90
Telephone: (22) 827-9221
Fax: (22) 827-8372
Email: zihinb@ikp.atm.com.pl
This establishment has a remarkable collection of
Judaica. It includes a library of documents on the
manuscripts stolen by the Germans from all over Europe.

RESTAURANTS

Menora
Plac Grzybowski 2
Telephone: (22) 203754

Nove Miasto Ecological Restaurant
Rynek Nowego Miasta 13/15
Telephone: (22) 831-4379
Fax: (22) 831-4379
Web site: www.novemiasto.waw.pl

Panorama
Al Witsoa 31
Telephone: (22) 642-0666

Salad Bar
ul. Tamka 37
Telephone: (22) 635-8463

SYNAGOGUES

Nozyk Synagogue, Jewish Community of Warsaw, Union of Jewish Communities in Poland.
6 Twarda Street 00-950
Telephone: (22) 6204324
Fax: (22) 6201037
Email: varshe@jewish.org.pl
The synagogue was renovated in 1977-83 and is well
worth a visit. It is the only pre-War synagogue still
standing in Warsaw. Visitors welcomed. Friday night
dinner available. Kosher store in the synagogue.

THEATRE

Jewish National Theatre
Plac Grzybowski 12/16
Performances are given in Yiddish.

TOURS

Shalom Travel Service
Twarda Street 6 00-105
Telephone: (22) 652-2802
Fax: (22) 652-2803
Email: shalom@jewish.org.pl

WROCKLAW

MUSEUMS

Historical Museum
Slezna Street 37
Telephone: (71) 678236

PORTUGAL

Portuguese Jewry had a parallel history to
Spanish Jewry until the twelfth century,
when the country emerged from Spain's
shadow, and Jews worked with the
Portuguese kings in developing the country.
However, they were heavily taxed and had to
live in special areas, although they were free
to practise their religion as they pleased. As a
result, the community flourished.

Persecution began during the period of the
Black Death, and the Church was a key
instigator of the riots which broke out
against the Jews. After the Inquisition in
neighbouring Spain, many Jews fled to
Portugal, but were expelled in 1496. Many
Jews converted in order to remain in the
country and help with the economy. These
became the Portuguese 'Conversos' and
some of their descendants are converting
back to Judaism today.

Over the last century and a half, Jews have
begun to re-enter the country, and many
others used it as an escape route to America
during the last war. Most of the community
are Sephardi, and there is a Sephardi synagogue in Lisbon. There is also a central
Jewish organisation which is a unifying
force for Jews in the country.

GMT +0 hours
Country calling code: (**+351**)
Total population: **9,921,000**
Jewish population: **800**
Emergency telephone: (Police – 115) (Fire – 115)
(Ambulance – 115)
Electricity voltage: (**Electricity voltage – 220**)

ALGARVE
COMMUNITY ORGANISATIONS
Jewish Community of Algarve
Rua Judice Biker 11-5°., Portimão 8500-701
Telephone: (282) 416-710
Fax: (282) 416-515

MUSEUMS
Faro Jewish Cemetery and Museum
Telephone: (282) 416-710
Fax: (282) 416-515
Only remaining vestige of the first post-Inquisition
Jewish presence in Algarve. Open weekday mornings
from 9:30 am to 12:30 pm. Situated opposite entrance to
Faro Hospital. Enquiries to Ralf Pinto, Jewish Community
of Algarve.

BELMONTE
COMMUNITY ORGANISATIONS
Jewish Community of Belmonte
Apt. 18, Bairo de Santa Maina, 6250 Belmonte
Telephone: (275) 912465
Fax: (275) 912465

LISBON
Jews settled in Lisbon in the 12th century. Many
Jews were prominent in court circles. In 1496
when the Jews were expelled Lisbon was chosen
as a point of embarkation.

In the Alfama district, London's oldest, is the
Rua de Judiara and at 8 Beco dos Barretas is the
site of what is believed to be an ancient
synagogue.

The first official synagogue dates from 1813. The
Shaar-7 kuah synagogue opened in 1904, was
constructed inside a garden because legislation
at that time did not permit non-Catholic places
of worship to be directly on a public highway. It
was classified as a "Building of Public Interest"
in 1997.

COMMUNITY ORGANISATIONS
Communal Offices
Rua do Monte Olivete 16-r/c 1200-280
Telephone: (21) 393-1130
Fax: (21) 393-1139
Email: secretaria@cilisboa.org
Web site: www.cilisboa.org

Jewish Club & Centre
Rua Rosa Araujo 10
Telephone: (21) 572041

EMBASSY
Embassy of Israel
Rua Antonio Enes 16-4 1020-025
Telephone: (21) 355-3640
Fax: (21) 355-3658
Email: israemb@mail.telepac.pt

JEWISH TOURS
Jewish Heritage Tours
Avenida 5 de Outubro, 321 1649-015
Telephone: (21) 7919-954
Fax: (21) 7919-959
Email: fit.lisboa@space.pt
Web site: www.jewisheritage.pt
Tours to explore Jewish ancestral roots in Portugal and to
meet the descendants of the Conversos, the 'secret' Jews.

KOSHER FOOD
Mrs R. Assor
Rua Rodrigo da Fonseca 38.1'D
Telephone: (21) 386-0396
Fax: (21) 386-6336
Email: iassor@mail.telepac.pt
Kosher meals and delicatessen are obtainable if prior
notice is given. For kosher meats, contact the communal
offices.

SYNAGOGUES
Ashkenazi
1 Avenida Elias Garcia 100

OPORTO
SYNAGOGUES
Rua Guerra Junqueiro 340

TOMAR
TOURIST SITES
There is an interesting Sephardi museum in the old
synagogue.

Overseas Region
PONTA DELGADA
SYNAGOGUES
The only synagogue in the Azores. It was built in 1836
and has been out of use since the 1950s. It is expected to
reopen during the early part of 2003.

PUERTO RICO

The Jewish community in Puerto Rico is just over 100 years old, with the first Jews arriving from Cuba in 1898 after the beginning of American rule. During the Second World War, many Jewish American servicemen went to the island, along with refugees from Nazism. The Jewish Community Centre dates from the early war years. After the war the community grew with an influx of Cuban and American Jews.

San Juan, the capital, has the largest Jewish population, and there are two synagogues. There is also a Hebrew school, held in the Community Centre. The first Chief Justice of Puerto Rico was Jewish.

GMT -4 hours
Country calling code: **(+1 787)**
Total population: **3,771,000**
Jewish population: **2,500**
Emergency telephone: **(Police – 343 2020) (Fire – 343 2330)**
Electricity voltage: **(Electricity voltage – 120)**

SAN JUAN-SANTURCE
SYNAGOGUES
Shaare Zedeck
903 Ponce de Leon Av., Santurce 00907
Telephone: (787) 724-4157
Fax: (787) 722-4157
Services: Monday 7.00am, Thursday 7.00am, Kabalat Shabat Friday 6.30pm, Shabat 9.00am, Sunday 9.00am

Reform
Temple Beth Shalom
San Jorge Av. & Loiza St., Santurce 907

ROMANIA

Romanian Jewry began at the time the Romans gave the country its name and language. In the fifteenth century, community life had begun to be organised, and settlement had spread to the town of Iasi and some Moldavian towns. Jews were welcomed from Poland and other east European countries, despite the opposition of the Church. Over the years, the community grew in size with further immigration, but emigration became the dominant factor

after 1878, when the Treaty of Berlin, which demanded equal rights for Jews, was not implemented in Romania. Following Romania's acquisition of the large area of Transylvania from Hungary after 1918, the Jewish population increased once more. The Jews were finally emancipated, but harsh discriminatory decrees were passed in 1937, and Romania's alliance with Nazi Germany during the war led to 385,000 of the 800,000 Romanian Jews being killed in the Holocaust.

It is ironic that Romanian Jewry was able to function relatively normally under the harsh Ceausescu regime. He was the only Warsaw Pact leader not to sever relations with Israel in 1967, and he allowed Jewish practices to continue, even permitting the then Chief Rabbi, Dr Moses Rosen, to have a seat in the parliament. This freedom also tolerated emigration to Israel, which was seen by Ceausescu as being advantageous to Romania. Post-1989, the community still has its central body, the Federation of Jewish Communities, and there are kosher cafeterias in several cities. The community is ageing, but many synagogues are still functioning, and there are also Jewish newspapers and a Yiddish theatre. The Choral Synagogue in Bucharest is of particular interest to visitors.

GMT +2 hours
Country calling code: **(+40)**
Total population: **22,520,000**
Jewish population: **12,000**
Emergency telephone: **(Police – 995) (Fire – 981) (Ambulance – 961)**
Electricity voltage: **(Electricity voltage – 220)**

ARAD
COMMUNITY ORGANISATIONS
Community Offices
10 Tribunal Dobra Street
Telephone: (257) 281310

RESTAURANTS
Ritual
22, 7 Episcopei Street
Telephone: (257) 280731

SYNAGOGUES
Muzeul Judetean
Piata George Enescu 1
Telephone: (257) 280114

Neologa
10 Tribunal Dobra Street

Orthodox
12 Cozia Street

BACAU
COMMUNITY ORGANISATIONS
Community Offices
11 Alexandru cel Bun Street
Telephone: (234) 134714

RESTAURANTS
11 Alexandru cel Bun Street

SYNAGOGUES
Avram A. Rosen Synagogue
31 V. Alecsandri Street

Cerealistilor
29 Stefan cel Mare Street

BOTOSANI
COMMUNITY ORGANISATIONS
Community Offices
220 Calea Nationala
Telephone: (231) 0315-14659

MIKVAOT
67 7 Aprilie Street

RESTAURANTS
69 7 Aprilie Street
Telephone: (231) 0315-15917

SYNAGOGUES
Great
1a Marchian Street

Mare
18 Muzicantilor Street

Yiddish
10 Gh. Dimitrov Street

BRASOV
COMMUNITY ORGANISATIONS
Community Offices
27 Poarta Schei Street
Telephone: (268) 143532

RESTAURANTS
27 Poarta Schei Street
Telephone: (268) 144440

SYNAGOGUES
27 Poarta Schei Street

BUCHAREST
COMMUNITY ORGANISATIONS
Federation of Jewish Communities of Romania
Str. Sf. Vineri 9-11, Sector 3
Telephone: (21) 313-2538
Fax: (21) 312-0869
Email: asivan@pcnet.ro
Kosher supervision on 11 restaurants in the main Jewish communities of Romania.

EMBASSY
Embassy of Israel
1 Dimitrie Cantemir Bd.
Telephone: (21) 613-2634/5/6

MIKVAOT
5 Negustori Street

MUSEUMS
Museum of the Jewish Community in Romania
3 Mamoulari Street
Telephone: (21) 615-0837
Hours: Wednesday and Sunday, 9 am to 1 pm.

RELIGIOUS ORGANISATIONS
Chief Rabbi of Romania
Strada Sf. Vineri 9
Telephone: (21) 613-2538
Fax: (21) 312-0869

RESTAURANTS
Jewish Community
18 Popa Soare Street
Telephone: (21) 322-4067
Fax: (21) 322-4067
Email: fcerdas@com.pcnet.ro
This restaurant is operated by the Jewish Community.

SYNAGOGUES
Choral Temple
Strada Sf. Vineri 9, Sector 3
Telephone: (21) 313-1782
Fax: (21) 312-0869
Email: ccmailb@dial.kappa.ro
Credinta
48 Vasile Toneanu Street

Sephardi
Great Synagogue
9-11 Vasile Adamache Street
Telephone: (21) 615-0846

THEATRE
Jewish State Theatre
15 Iuliu Barash Str., Sector 3 74212
Telephone: (21) 323-4530
Fax: (21) 323-2746
Email: tes@dnt.ro
Web site: www.dnt.ro/users/tes

CLUJ NAPOCA

COMMUNITY ORGANISATIONS
Community Offices
25 Tipografiei Street
Telephone: (264) 11667

MIKVAOT
16 David Fransisc Street

RESTAURANTS
5-7 Paris Street
Telephone: (264) 11026

SYNAGOGUES
Beth Hamidrash Ohel Moshe
16 David Fransisc Street

Sas Hevra
13 Croitorilor Street

Templul Deportatilor
21 Horea Street

CONSTANTA

COMMUNITY ORGANISATIONS
Jewish Community Office and Cultural Club
3 Sarmisagetuza Street
Telephone: (241) 611598

SYNAGOGUES
Great Temple Synagogue
2 C. A. Rosetti Street

Small
3 Sarmisagetuza Street

DOROHOI

COMMUNITY ORGANISATIONS
Community Office
95 Spiru Haret Street
Telephone: (31) 611797

SYNAGOGUES
Great Synagogue
4 Piata Unirii Street

GALATI

COMMUNITY ORGANISATIONS
Community Office
9 Dornei Street
Telephone: (236) 413662

RESTAURANTS
9 Dornei Street
Telephone: (236) 413662

SYNAGOGUES
Meseriasilor
11 Dornei Street

IASI (JASSY)

COMMUNITY ORGANISATIONS
Community Office
15 Elena Doamna Street
Telephone: (232) 114414

MIKVAOT
15 Elena Doamna Street

RESTAURANTS
15 Elena Doamna Street
Telephone: (232) 1117883

SYNAGOGUES
Schor
5 Sf. Constantin Street

ORADEA

COMMUNITY ORGANISATIONS
Community Office
4 Mihai Viteazu Street
Telephone: (259) 134843

MIKVAOT
5 Mihai Viteazu Street

RESTAURANTS
5 Mihai Viteazu Street
Telephone: (259) 131383

SYNAGOGUES
Great
4 Mihai Viteazu Street

PIATRA NEAMT

COMMUNITY ORGANISATIONS
Community Office
7 Petru Rares Street
Telephone: (33) 623815

SYNAGOGUES
Leipziger
12 Meteorului Street

Old Baal Shem Tov
7 Meteorului Street
Old historical monument.

RADAUTI

COMMUNITY ORGANISATIONS
Community Office
11 Aleea Primaverii, Block 14, Apt.1
Telephone: (30) 461333

SYNAGOGUES
Great
2, 1 Mai Street

Vijnitzer
49 Libertatii Street

SATU MARE

Satu Mare is the Romanian name for the town of Szatmar, where the famous Hassidic sect originated. It is in the north west of Romania, very near the border with Hungary. Before World War One, the town itself used to be in Hungary.

COMMUNITY ORGANISATIONS
Community Office
4 Decebal Street
Telephone: (61) 743783

SYNAGOGUES
Great
4 Decebal Street

SF. GHEORGHE

TRAVEL AGENTS
International Tourism and Trade
Jozef Bem Str. 2, Sf. Gheorghe 520023, PO Box 1/152
Telephone: 267-316-375
Fax: 267-351-551
Email: it&t@honoris.ro
Web site: www.loveromania.com

SIGHET

COMMUNITY ORGANISATIONS
Community Office
8 Basarabia Street
Telephone: (62) 511652

SYNAGOGUES
Great
8 Basarabia Street

SUCEAVA

COMMUNITY ORGANISATIONS
Community Office
8 Armeneasca Street
Telephone: (30) 213084

TIMISOARA

COMMUNITY ORGANISATIONS
5 Gh. Lazar Street
Telephone: (56) 132813

MIKVAOT
55 Resita Street

RESTAURANTS
10 Marasesti Street
Telephone: (56) 136924

SYNAGOGUES
Cetate
6 Marasesti Street

Fabric
2 Splaiul Coloniei
Iosefin
55 Resita Street

TIRGU MURES

COMMUNITY ORGANISATIONS
Community Office
10 Brailei Street
Telephone: (65) 115001

SYNAGOGUES
21 Aurel Filimon Street

TUSHNAD

HOTELS
Kosher
Olt Hotel
c/o Interom Tours
Telephone: 972-3924-6425
Fax: 972-3579-1720

VATRA DORNEI

COMMUNITY ORGANISATIONS
Community Office
54 M Eminescu Street
Telephone: (30) 371957

SYNAGOGUES
Vijnitzer
14 Luceafarul Street

RUSSIAN FEDERATION

In early Russian history, Jews were not allowed to settle, and the few who did were later expelled by various Czars. After 1772, however, Russia acquired a large area of Poland, in which lived a significant number of Jews. There were still restrictions against the Jews, but eventually they were allowed to settle in the 'Pale of Settlement', an area in the west of the Russian Empire. Between 1881 and 1914, 2,000,000 Jews emigrated from the Empire, escaping from anti-semitism.

Jews were only allowed into Russia itself in the mid-nineteenth century, and by 1890 there were 35,000 Jews in Moscow. Most were expelled the following year. The community grew after the Second World War, drawing Jewish immigration from Belarus and Ukraine to cities such as Moscow and

Leningrad. Birobidzhan was a failed experiment to give the Jews their own 'Autonomous District', and those who moved there (in the far east, near China) soon moved away. Under communism, both religious practices and emigration were restricted to Israel, but since 1991 there has been a revival in Jewish learning. There are synagogues functioning in many cities, and there are now 100 Jewish schools. The major threat is still from antisemitic right-wing groups, who are unfortunately increasing their activity.

GMT + 2 to +12 hours
Country calling code: (+7)
Total population: **146,100,000**
Jewish population: **300,000**
Emergency telephone: (**Police – 02**) (**Fire – 01**)
(**Ambulance – 03**)
Electricity voltage: (**Electricity voltage – 220**)

ASTRAKHAN
SYNAGOGUES
30 Babushkin Street

BIROBIDJAN
Birobidjan, the size of Belgium was created in 1934 as a Jewish homeland in the wilds of Siberia. It was not a success and was effectively terminated in the 1940s. There has, however, now been a resurgence of interest in what was known as the Jewish Autonomous District.

SYNAGOGUES
9 Chapaev Street, Khabarovsk Krai

BRYANSK
SYNAGOGUES
Narodov Vostoka Street
82 Lermontov Street

Lubavitch
Synagogue of Bryansk
27a Uritskovo Street 241000
Telephone: (832) 445-515

DERBENT
SYNAGOGUES
94 Tagi-Zade Street

Lubavitch
Jewish Community of Derbent
23 Kandelaky Street 368600
Telephone: (8724) 021-731

EKATERINBURG
SYNAGOGUES
18/2 Kirov Street
14 Kuibyshev Street

IRKUTSK
SYNAGOGUES
17 Karl Liebknecht Street

KAZAN
The capital of Tatarstan, an autonomous Russian republic, has 10,000 Jews an Ort school and its own Jewish newspaper.

SYNAGOGUES
Lubavitch
Synagogue of Kazan
15 Profsouznaya Street 420111
Telephone: (8432) 329-743

KOSTRAMA
SYNAGOGUES
Lubavitch
Synagogue of Kostrama
16a Sennoi Peroulok 156026
Telephone: (942) 514-388

KRASNOYARSK
SYNAGOGUES
Lubavitch
Synagogue of Krasnoyarsk
65 Surikova Street 660049
Telephone: (3912) 223-615
Fax: (3912) 440-137
Email: jckras@hotmail.com

KURSK
SYNAGOGUES
3 Bolshevitskaya Street

MAKHACHKALA
SYNAGOGUES
111 Yermoshkin Street

MOSCOW
Around 200,000 Jews now live in Moscow, and since the collapse of the USSR in 1991, the community has experienced a revival. The Choral Synagogue on Arkhipova Street, which was built in 1891 and was used during the Soviet regime, is again the focus of Jewish religious life. The Lubavitch movement has its own centre, and there has been an upsurge of interest in Jewish education.

CONTACT INFORMATION
Rabbi Pinchas Goldschmidt
Chief Rabbi of Moscow
Telephone: (95) 923-4788; 924-2424

EMBASSY
Embassy of Israel
Bolshaya Ordinka 56
Telephone: (95) 230-6777
Fax: (95) 238-1346

KOSHER FOOD
Spassoglinishevsky per., 10

LIBRARIES
Central Library
A Jewish literature reading hall opened in 2002. The hall
holds the State Library's Jewish literature collection.

RESTAURANTS
Kosher Food
The restaurant on Nikitskaya
Nikitskaya str., 47
Telephone: (95) 291-4045

Meat
King David Club
Bolshoi Spasoglinishchevsky per. (Arkhipova St) 6,
door code 77
Telephone: (95) 925-4601
Fax: (95) 924-4243
Email: ail@ail.msk.ru
Supervision: Rabbi Pinchas Goldschmidt, Chief Rabbi of
Moscow
This kosher food centre serves as a glatt kosher
restaurant and a mini hotel. Catering services are
available as are lunchboxes.

Na Monmartre
Vetoshny per., 9
Telephone: (95) 745-5230
Fax: (95) 745-5239
Supervision: Rabbi Berl Lazar
On the 5th floor of a modern shopping centre. (the
French Gallery Mall) near Redsquare.

SYNAGOGUES
Lubavitch
Chabad Lubavitch
4 Novousushevsky Peroulok 103055
Telephone: (95) 218-0001
Fax: (95) 219-9707
Email: lazar@glasnet.ru

Chabad Lubavitch Synagogue
6 Balshaya Bronya Street 103104
Telephone: (95) 202-4530
Fax: (95) 291-6483
Known as the Polyakov Synagogue after the railway and
banking family.

Darkei Shalom Synagogue
1 Novovladikinsky Peroulok 103055
Telephone: (95) 903-0782
Fax: (95) 903-2218

Orthodox
Moscow Choral Synagogue
Bolshoi Spasoglinishchevsky per. (Arkhipova St) 10
Telephone: (95) 924-2424

NALCHIK
SYNAGOGUES
73 Rabochaya Street, cnr. Osetinskaya

NIZHNY NOVGOROD
SYNAGOGUES
Lubavitch
Nizhny Novgorod Synagogue
5a Gruzinskaya Street 603000
Telephone: (8312) 336-345
Fax: (8312) 303-759

NOVOSIBIRSK
SYNAGOGUES
Synagogue
23 Luchezarnaya Street

Lubavitch
Synagogue of Novosibirsk
14 Kominististscheskaya
Telephone: (3832) 210-698

PENZA
SYNAGOGUES
15 Krasnaya Street

PERM
SYNAGOGUES
Pushkin Street
Kuibyshev Street

ROSTOV-NA-DONU
SYNAGOGUES
Lubavitch
Synagogue of Rostov-na-Dou
18 Gazetny Peroulok 344007
Telephone: (8632) 624-759
Fax: (8632) 624-119

SACHKHERE
SYNAGOGUES
145 Sovetskaya Street
105 Tsereteli Street

SAMARA
SYNAGOGUES
Synagogue
3 Chapaev Street

Lubavitch
Jewish Community Center of Samara Synagogue
84B Chapaevskaya St 443099
Telephone: (8462) 334-064
Fax: (8462) 320-242
Email: samara@fjc.ru
The community center has a mikva, and a kosher lemihadrin kitchen.

SARATOV
SYNAGOGUES
Posadskov Street

Synagogue
2 Kirpichnaya Street

Lubavitch
Synagogue of Saratov
208 Posadskovo Street 410005
Telephone: (8452) 249-592

ST PETERSBURG
With 100,000 Jews, St Petersburg is witnessing a similar Jewish revival to Moscow. There are opportunities to pray, learn and eat kosher ñ this was not the case (in general) before 1991 in the USSR. Americans and Israelis are the main motivators behind the revival, but St Petersburg Jewry is also eager to learn about religion, now that there is the freedom to do so.

MIKVAOT
2 Lermontovsky Prospekt
Telephone: (812) 114-4428
Fax: (812) 113-6209
Email: synagog@peterlink.ru

RESTAURANTS
Meat
Shalom
8 Koli Tomchaka Street
Telephone: (812) 327-5475

SYNAGOGUES
The Grand Choral Synagogue of St. Petersburg
2 Lermontovsky Prospekt 190121
Telephone: (812) 113-6209
Fax: (812) 113-6209
Email: synagog@peterlink.ru
This is the second street past the Mariinsky Opera & Ballet Theatre.

TSHELYABINSK
SYNAGOGUES
Lubavitch
Synagogue of Tshelyabinsk
PO Box 16187 454091
Telephone: (3512) 333-618
Fax: (3512) 332-468
Email: chabadural@mail.ru

TULA
SYNAGOGUES
15 Veresaevskaya Street

VLADIKAVKAZ
SYNAGOGUES
Revolutsiya Street

VOLGOGRAD
SYNAGOGUES
Chabad of Volgograd
Novorosiyskaya 43 400087
Telephone: (8442) 378-308
Email: volgograd@fjc.ru

Zekher Avoteinu

- General and Jewish sightseeing in Russia and Scandinavia
- Participation in cultural and social life of local communities
- Shabbat hospitality

www.zekhera.hypermart.net   e-mail: zekhera@hotmail.com

tel. in St. Petersburg +7-812-945-0874
tel./fax in New York +1-718-236-6037

YEKATRINBURG

SYNAGOGUES

Lubavitch

Yekatrinburg Synagogue
118/93 Shekmana Street 620144
Telephone: (3432) 236-440
Fax: (3432) 293-054

SINGAPORE

As Singapore developed into an important south-east Asian trading centre in the mid-nineteenth century, some Jewish traders from India and Iraq set up a community there in 1841. A synagogue was built in 1878, and another in 1904. By the time of the Japanese occupation in the Second World War, the community had grown to 5,000, and included some eastern European Jews. The Japanese imprisoned the community and took their property. After the war, emigration to Australia and the USA reduced numbers, but in recent years Israelis who work in the country and other Jews have moved in. Ninety per cent of the community are Sephardi.

David Marshall, who had been a POW in Japan, returned to Singapore and in 1955 became Chief Minister.

One of the two synagogues is used regularly, and there is a mikvahh and a newsletter. The Sir Manasseh Meyer Community Centre is the hub of Jewish life. The Jewish community today is small and mainly composed of professionals.

Country calling code: (+65)
Total population: **3,737,000**
Jewish population: **300**
Emergency telephone: (**Police – 999) (Fire – 999)**
(Ambulance – 999)
Electricity voltage: (**Electricity voltage – 220/240)**

COMMUNITY ORGANISATIONS

Jewish Welfare Board
Robinson Road, PO Box 474

CONTACT INFORMATION

Rabbi Abergel
Telephone: 737-9112
Email: mordehai@singnet.com.sg
Contact for more detailed information on the community and availability of kosher products.

EMBASSY

Embassy of Israel
58 Dalvey Road S-1025
Telephone: 235-0966
Fax: 733-7008

SYNAGOGUES

Orthodox

Chesed-El
2 Oxley Rise S-0923
Telephone: 732-8832
Services, Monday only, Shacharit and Mincha/Maariv.

Maghain Aboth Synagogue
24/26 Waterloo Street 187950
Telephone: 337-2189
Fax: 336-2127
Email: jewishwb@singnet.com.sg
Daily and Shabbat services are held, except for Monday when services are held at Chesed-El Synagogue, 2 Oxley Rise, at 7:30 am. Because Singapore has equatorial times, Mincha/Maariv commences at 6:45 pm throughout the year. Shacharit: weekdays, 7:30 am, Friday night Shabbat meal served after evening service. Shabbat 09.00 am. Every Shabbat lunch is served for the community. Breakfast is currently served every morning after services. Mikvah is available for use. For details please contact 737 9112 Rabbi Mordechai Abergel. There are kosher meat, cheeses, wine and other grocery items on sale at the synagogue.

SLOVAKIA

Slovakia has passed through the control of various countries over the centuries, finally gaining independence after the peaceful splitting of Czechoslovakia in 1992. Before 1918 the region was part of Hungary and many in southern Slovakia, near the Hungarian border, still speak Hungarian.

In 1939, the Jewish population in the Slovak area of Czechoslovakia numbered 150,000 but the Hungarians occupied the south of the country, and assisted the Germans in deporting Jews to Auschwitz and other camps. Many survivors emigrated after the war, but some remained, and are now rediscovering their Jewish heritage. Since independence, B'nai B'rith and Maccabi have been established, but anti-semitism has re-emerged. There are kosher restaurants in Bratislava and Kosice, and Jewish education is available once more.

GMT +1 hour
Country calling code: (+421)
Total population: **5,383,000**
Jewish population: **5,000**
Emergency telephone: (**Police – 158**) (**Fire – 150**)
(**Ambulance – 155**)
Electricity voltage: (**Electricity voltage – 220**)

BRATISLAVA

Known in German as Pressburg, Bratislava was a key centre of Judaism when Slovakia was under Hungarian rule before the First World War. Bratislava was especially famous for the number of Jewish scholars living there, including the Chatam Sofer. The preserved underground tomb of the Chatam Sofer and other rabbis is now a place of pilgramage.

BED AND BREAKFAST
Chez David
Zamocka 13, . 81101
Telephone: (2) 544-13 824; 544-16 943
Fax: (2) 544-12 642
Email: recepcia@chezdavid.sk
Web site: www.chezdavid.sk
Kashrut supervision of Rabbi Baruch Myers.

COMMUNITY ORGANISATIONS
Central Union of Jewish Religious Communities in the Slovak Republic
Kozia ul. 21 81447
Telephone: (2) 5441-2167; 5441-8357
Fax: (2) 5441-1106
Email: uzzno@netax.sk

MIKVAOT
Zamocka 13 81101
Telephone: (2) 544-17829
Fax: (2) 544-17814
Email: chabad@mail.eurotel.sk

MUSEUMS
The Museum of Jewish Culture
Zidovska Street 81101
Telephone: (2) 59349142/3/4
Fax: (2) 59349145
Contact: Prof. PhDr. Pavol Mest'an Dr. Sc.

Underground Mausoleum
Contains the graves of eighteen famous rabbis, including the Chatam Sofer. The key is available from the community offices.

RESTAURANTS
Meat
Chez David
Zamocka 13 81101
Telephone: (2) 544-13824, 544-16943
Fax: (2) 544-12642
Email: recepcia@chezdavid.sk
Web site: www.chezdavid.sk

SYNAGOGUES
Heydukova 11-13
Services held Monday, Thursday and Saturday.

GALANTA
MIKVAOT
Partizanska 907

SYNAGOGUES
Partizanska 907
Daily services held.

KOSICE
RESTAURANTS
Meat
Community Centre
Zvonarska Ul 5, Kaschau 4001
Telephone: (55) 622-1047

SYNAGOGUES
Puskinova Ul 3, Kaschau
Beth Hamidrash
Zvonarska Ul 5, Kaschau
Daily services held.

PIESTANY
CEMETERIES
Old Cemetery
Janosikova Ul 606

SYNAGOGUES
Hviezdoslavova 59
Shabbat and festival services held.

TRNAVA
MONUMENT
Monument to Deportees
Halenarska Ul 32
In the courtyard of the former synagogue.

SYNAGOGUES
Synagogue
Kapitulska Ul 7

SLOVENIA

Maribor was the centre for medieval Jewish life in what is now Slovenia. Expulsion followed after the Austrian occupation in the late Middle Ages, but in 1867 the Jews in the Austrian empire were emancipated and some returned to Solvenia. The community was never large. During the Second World War the members of the small Jewish community either escaped to Italy, fought with the Yugoslav partisans, or were deported.

There is a Jewish Community of Slovenia, connected to the Croatian community. There is one synagogue in Maribor, that is classed as an historic monument and dates from the Middle Ages. There are also some sites from medieval times such as the cemeteries in Ljubljana (the capital) and Murska Sobota.

GMT +1 hour
Country calling code: (+386)
Total population: 1,987,000
Jewish population: Under 100
Emergency telephone: (Police – 93) (Fire – 92) (Ambulance – 94)
Electricity voltage: (Electricity voltage – 220)

LJUBLJANA
COMMUNITY ORGANISATIONS
Jewish Community of Slovenia
Trzaska 2 1000
Telephone: (61) 2521-836
Fax: (61) 2521-836
Email: jss@siol.net
Web site: www.jewishcommunity.si

SOUTH AFRICA

Although some believe that Jews were present in the country at around the time of the first European settlement in the area in the seventeenth century, the community only really began in the nineteenth century, when religious freedom was granted. In 1836 the explorer Nathaniel Isaacs published 'Travels and Adventures on Eastern Africa', an important contemporary account of Zulu life and customs.

The year 1841 saw the first Hebrew Congregation in Cape Town, and the discovery of diamonds in the Transvaal later in the century prompted a wave of Jewish immigration.

The main immigration of Jews into South Africa occurred at the end of the nineteenth century, when many thousands left Eastern Europe, the majority from Lithuania (40,000 had arrived by 1910). Although the country did not officially accept refugees from the Nazis, about 8,000 Jews managed to enter the country after their escape from Europe.

Today the community is affluent and has good relations with the government. There is a South African Board of Deputies, and many international Jewish associations are present in the country. There are kosher hotels and restaurants, and Jewish museums. Kosher wine is produced at the Zaandwijk Winery.

GMT +2 hours
Country calling code: (+27)
Total population: 43,336,000
Jewish population: 80,000
Emergency telephone: (Police – 1011) (Fire – 1022) (Ambulance – 10222)
Electricity voltage: (Electricity voltage – 220/250)

Eastern Cape
EAST LONDON
SYNAGOGUES
Reform
Synagogue
Belgravia Crescent

PORT ELIZABETH

MUSEUMS
Jewish Pioneers' Memorial Museum
Raleigh Streetr cnr Edward Street
Telephone: (41) 373-5197
Fax: (41) 374-3612
Open between 10 am and noon every Sunday. The
museum has a ramp for disabled for access via
wheelchairs. It is also a National Monument. For further
information visitors may phone Dr Sam Abrahams (041)
583-3671.

SYNAGOGUES
Orthodox
Port Elizabeth Hebrew Congregation
Abraham Levy Centre, Barris Walk, Glendinningvale
6001
Telephone: (41) 373-1332
Fax: (41) 374-3612
Email: peheb@xsinet.co.za

Progressive
Temple Israel
Upper Dickens Street
Telephone: (41) 373-6642

Free State

BLOEMFONTEIN

RELIGIOUS ORGANISATIONS
United Hebrew Institutions
Community Centre, 1 Dickie Clark Street, PO Box
1152
Telephone: (51) 436-2207
Fax: (51) 436-6447
Mornings.

SYNAGOGUES
1 Dickie Clark Street, Dan Pienaar, PO Box 1152
9300
Telephone: (51) 436-2207
Fax: (51) 436-6447
Mikvah also available. Contact telephone number above.

Gauteng

BRAKPAN

RELIGIOUS ORGANISATIONS
Brakpan Synagogue
cnr. Victoria Avenue and Cavendish
Telephone: (53) 832-5652
For further information phone Mr Waner, Tel: (011) 740-
0903.

JOHANNESBURG

The largest city in South Africa has the largest
Jewish community in the country. About 70% of
the country's Jews live there (a community of
some 55,000) and the headquarters of many of
South African Jewry's Institutions are housed
there. There are more than fifty synagogues in
the city.

BAKERIES
Brooklyn Bagel
Shop 7, Lyndhurst Discount Centre, cnr
Modderfontein & Pretoria Rds, Lyndhurst
Telephone: (11) 882-2474
Fax: (11) 882-8565
Supervision: Johannesburg Beth Din

Friends Bakery
53 Ridge Road, Glenhazel
Telephone: (11) 440-5094
Fax: (11) 440-5096
Supervision: Johannesburg Beth Din

Shirley's
114 William Road, Norwood
Telephone: (11) 728-0974
Fax: (11) 728-2807
Supervision: Johannesburg Beth Din

Shula's
173 Oxford Road, Rosebank
Telephone: (11) 880-6989
Fax: (11) 880-6605
Supervision: Johannesburg Beth Din

BED AND BREAKFAST
Kosher Bed and Breakfast
124 Third Avenue, Fairmount
Telephone: (11) 485-5006
Fax: (11) 485-5518
Supervision: Johannesburg Beth Din

BOOKSELLERS
Chabad House Books
Fairmount Shopping Centre, George Street,
Fairmount
Telephone: (11) 485-1957

Kollel Bookshop
Pick 'N' Pay Shopping Centre, 54 Sixth Ave.,
Gardens
Telephone: (11) 728-1822
Fax: (11) 728-1813

BUTCHERS
Bolbrand Poultry Shoppe
74-76 George Avenue, Sandringham 2192
Telephone: (11) 640-4080
Supervision: Johannesburg Beth Din

Gallo Manor Kosher Butchery
Morning Glen Shopping Centre, cnr. Braides &
Kelvin Sts, Gallo Manor
Telephone: (11) 802-3539
Fax: (11) 802-6546
Supervision: Johannesburg Beth Din

Gardens Kosher
cnr. Grant & 6th Avenue, Norwood 2052
Telephone: (11) 483-3357
Fax: (11) 728-1562
Supervision: Johannesburg Beth Din

Maxi Discount Kosher Butcher
74 George Avenue, Sandringham 2192
Telephone: (11) 485-1485; 485-1486
Fax: (11) 485-2991
Supervision: Johannesburg Beth Din

Nussbaums
434 Louis Botha Avenue, cnr. Main St., Rouxville
Telephone: (11) 485-2303
Fax: (11) 640-4663
Supervision: Johannesburg Beth Din

Rishon Balfour
Checker Balfour Park, cnr. Louis Botha & Athol Sts,
Highlands North
Telephone: (11) 786-9626
Fax: (11) 885-1996
Supervision: Johannesburg Beth Din

Saveways Spar
Fairmount Shopping Centre, cnr. Sandler and
Livingstone St, Fairmount
Telephone: (11) 640-6592
Fax: (11) 640-3057
Supervision: Johannesburg Beth Din

Trevors
Bramley Gardens Shopping Centre
Telephone: (11) 885-3663
Fax: (11) 887-9502
Supervision: Johannesburg Beth Din

DELICATESSEN
Feigel's Kosher Delicatessan
Shop 3, Queens Place, Kingswood Road, Glenhazel
2192
Telephone: (11) 887-1364
Supervision: Johannesburg Beth Din
Bramley Gardens Shopping Centre, Shop 1, 280
Corlett Drive
Telephone: (11) 887-9505/6
Fax: (11) 887-9507
Supervision: Johannesburg Beth Din
Hours: Friday, 7:30 am to 4:30 pm; Sunday, 8 am to 1 pm;
Monday to Thursday, 10 am to 5 pm.

Kosher King
74 George Avenue, Sandringham
Telephone: (11) 640-6234
Supervision: Johannesburg Beth Din
Hours: Monday to Thursday, 8:30 am to 5 pm; Friday, 8
am to 3 pm; Sunday, 9 am to 1 pm.

Pick 'N Pay
Cnr. Grant Avenue & 6th Street, Norwood
Telephone: (11) 483-3357
Fax: (11) 728-1562
Supervision: Johannesburg Beth Din

Pie Works and Deli
Shop 35 Greenhill Road, Emmarentia 2195
Telephone: (11) 011-486-1502
Fax: (11) 011-486-0580
Email: feigfam@mweb.co.za
Supervision: Johannesburg Beth Din
Hours: Weekdays, 8.00am to 5.30pm; Friday to 4.00pm;
Sunday 9.00am to 2.00pm.

Saveways Spar Supermarket
Fairmount Shopping Centre, cnr. Livingston St &
Sandler Avenue, Fairmount 2192
Telephone: (11) 640-3056
Fax: (11) 640-3057
Supervision: Johannesburg Beth Din
Hours: Monday to Thursday, 8 am to 6 pm; Sunday and
public holidays, 8 am to 1 pm.

Shoshana's Bakery
Stan Tech House, cnr. Cross Road and Queens
Square, Glenhazel
Telephone: (11) 885-1039
Supervision: Johannesburg Beth Din

The Pie Works
74 George Avenue, Sea Point, Sandringham 2192
Telephone: (11) 485-2447
Supervision: Johannesburg Beth Din
Hours: weekdays, 8 am to 5 pm; Friday, to 4 pm; Sunday,
to 2 pm.

LIBRARIES
Kollel Library
5 Water Lane, Orchards 2198
Telephone: (11) 728-1308
Fax: (11) 728-8597

MEDIA
Newspapers
The S.A. Jewish Report
Suite 175, Postnet X10039, Randburg 2125
Telephone: (11) 886-0162
Fax: (11) 886-4202
Email: carro@global.co.za

Periodicals

Jewish Affairs
2 Elray Street, Raedene
Telephone: (11) 645-2500
Fax: (11) 645-2559
Email: sajbod@iafrica.com
Quarterly journal of the South African Jewish Board of Deputies.

Jewish Heritage
PO Box 3 7179, Birnham Park 2015
Telephone: (11) 880-1830

Jewish Tradition
PO Box 46559, Orange Grove 2119
Telephone: (11) 485-4865
Fax: (11) 640-7528
Email: isaacrez@yebo.co.za
Publication of the Union of Orthodox Synagogues of South Africa.

South African Jewish Observer
PO Box 29189, Sandringham 2131
Telephone: (11) 440-2206
Fax: (11) 786-8155
Email: mizrachi@netactive.co.za
A publication of the Mizrachi Organisation of South Africa.

MIKVAOT

Adase Yashurun Mikvah
34 Fortesque Road, Yeoville
Telephone: (11) 648-6300
By appointment only. Phone Mrs Levy. (011) 648-6751

Glenhazel Mikvah (Be'er Rachel)
65 Nicholson Avenue, Glenkay
Telephone: (11) 485-1555
Email: nisaacson@africakoshersafaris.com

Sandton Mikvah
211 Rivonia Road, Morningside
Telephone: (11) 883-4210

RELIGIOUS ORGANISATIONS

The Southern African Union for Progressive Judaism
357 Louis Botha Avenue, Highlands North
Telephone: (11) 640-6614

Union of Orthodox Synagogues of South Africa
58 Oaklands Road, Orchards 2192
Telephone: (11) 485-4865
Fax: (11) 640-7528
Email: jhb@uos.co.za
The office of the chief Rabbi as well as the Beth Din are located at the same address and phone number.

RESTAURANTS

Dairy

Brazilian Coffee Shop
Shop 174, Balfour Park Shopping Centre, cnr. Athol Road, Highlands North
Telephone: (11) 440-8822
Fax: (11) 466-1876
Supervision: Johannesburg Beth Din

Shula's
173 Oxford Road, Rosebank 2196
Telephone: (11) 880-6969
Fax: (11) 880-6605
Supervision: Johannesburg Beth Din
Pareve and milk restaurant. Hours: Sunday to Thursday, 7 am to 11 pm; Friday, to 4 pm; Motzei Shabbat to 1 am.

Meat

D.J's Take Away
Balfour Park Shopping Centre, Shop No. 232, Balfour Park 2090
Telephone: (11) 440-1792
Supervision: Johannesburg Beth Din

Marc Chagall's
Upper Level, Balfour Park Shopping Centre, cnr. Athol Road, Highlands North
Telephone: (11) 786-0593
Fax: (11) 786-0594
Supervision: Johannesburg Beth Din

On The Square
Shop No. 7, Shell Court, cnr. Craddock Avenue & Baker Street, Rosebank 2196
Telephone: (11) 880-4153; 447-4891
Supervision: Johannesburg Beth Din
Hours: Sunday to Thursday, 10 am to 3 pm; 6 pm to 10 pm; Motzei Shabbat, 1 hour after Shabbat to 12 am.

The Junction Grill
4 Dunnottar Street, Sydenham
Telephone: (11) 485-2585
Fax: (11) 485-3707
Supervision: Johannesburg Beth Din

SYNAGOGUES

There are more than fifty synagogues in Johannesburg. Please contact the appropriate Religious Organisation for details (Page 191).

TOURS

Africa Kosher Safaris
P O Box 51380, Raedene 2124
Telephone: (11) 485-3465
Email: yisaacson@africakoshersafaris.com

African Safari Experience
26 Kings Road, Bedfordview
Telephone: (11) 832-5652
Email: ase@cgs.co.za
Web site: www.asesouthafrica.co.za

Celafrica Tours
PO Box 357, Highlands North, 2037
Telephone: (11) 11-887-5262
Fax: (11) 11-885-3097
Email: celeste@celafrica.com
Web site: www.celafrica.com
The company specialises in kosher tours to southern
Africa, for people needing kosher food and Shabbat
arrangements.

KRUGERSDORP
SYNAGOGUES
Krugersdorp Synagogue
1 Cilliers Street, Monument
Telephone: (11) 954-1367
Fax: (11) 953-4905

PRETORIA
EMBASSY
Embassy of Israel
Embassy of Israel
3rd Floor, Dashing Centre, 339 Hilda Street, Hatfield
Telephone: (12) 342-2693

KASHRUT INFORMATION
Pretoria Council of BOD
Telephone: (12) 344-2372
Fax: (12) 344-2059

KOSHER FOOD
Pick 'N Pay
Brooklyn Square Mall, Middle Street, Muckleneuk
Telephone: (12) 346-8680
Kosher prepacked food under the Johannesburg Beth Din
Spar
Groenkloof Plaza, George Stonar Drive, Groenkloof
Telephone: (12) 346-5555
Kosher prepacked food under the Johannesburg Beth Din

MUSEUMS
Sammy Marks Museum
PO Box 4197, Old Brokhorstspruit 1
Telephone: (12) 802-1150
Fax: (12) 802-1292
Email: smarks@nfi.co.za
Web site: www.afsef.com/sammymarks
Hours of opening: Tuesdays - Sundays, 10.00-16.00

RESTAURANTS
JAFFA Old Age Home
42 Mackie Street, Baileys Muckleneuk 181
Telephone: (12) 346-2006
Fax: (12) 346-2008
Email: jaffa@smartnet.co.za
Web site: www.jaffa.org.za
Hotel as well. Prior booking necessary. Kosher catering,
resident mashgiach. Kosher meals, both meat and dairy,
available on request.

SYNAGOGUES
Orthodox
Adath Israel Centre
246 Schroder Stresst, Groenkloof
Telephone: (12) 460-7991
Fax: (12) 480-5911
Email: phc@netactive.co.za
Progressive
Temple Menorah
315 Bronkhorst Street, New Muckleneuk, PO Box
1497
Telephone: (12) 467-296

SPRINGS
SYNAGOGUES
Springs Synagogue
40 Charterland Avenue, Selcourt
Telephone: (11) 818-2572

KwaZulu-Natal
DURBAN
BED AND BREAKFAST
Beit Ya'akov
75 Windmill Road, PO Box 47314, Greyville 4023
Telephone: (31) 202-7275
Fax: (31) 202-7302
Email: koby@global.co.za
Run by family who are shomer mitzvot.

BUTCHERS
Pick 'N Pay
Musgrave Centre, Berea 4001
Telephone: (31) 201-4208
Bakery as well.

COMMUNITY ORGANISATIONS
Council of KwaZulu-Natal Jewry
44 Old Fort Road, Durban 4001
Telephone: (31) 337-2581
Fax: (31) 337-9600
Email: cknj@djc.co.za
Mailing address: PO Box 10797, Marine Parade, 4056
Durban Jewish Club
44 Old Fort Road, Durban 4001
Telephone: (31) 337-2581
Fax: (31) 337-9600
Email: cknj@djc.co.za
Mailing address: PO Box 10797, Marine Parade 4056.

RESTAURANTS
Café Shalom
Durban Hebrew Congregation, cnr. Essenwood &
Silverton Roads
Telephone: (31) 202-1205

Dairy
Great Synagogue cnr. Silverton & Essenwood
Roads, PO Box 50044, Musgrave Road 4062
Telephone: (31) 202-1205
Fax: (31) 209-2925
Email: studycentre1@freemail.absa.co.za

SYNAGOGUES

Orthodox
**Durban United Hebrew Congregation The
Great Synagogue**
Cnr. Essenwood & Silverton Roads, PO Box 50044,
Musgrave Road 4062
Telephone: (31) 201-5177
Fax: (31) 202-8925
Email: shul@duhc.org.za

The Vryheid Memorial Shul
Cnr. Old Fort & Playfair Rds
Telephone: (31) 201-5177
Fax: (31) 202-8925
Email: shul@duhc.org.za

Progressive
Durban Progressive Jewish Congregation
369 Ridge Road
Telephone: (31) 208-6105
Fax: (31) 209-2429

UMHLANGA

CONTACT INFORMATION
Chabad of Umhlanga
POBox 474 4320
Telephone: (31) 561-2487
Fax: (31) 561-5845
Web site: www.chabadonline.com/kwazulu-natal
Open all hours. Regular minyanim especially Shabbat
and Yomim Tovim. Ladies' mikvah twenty minutes away.
Kosher hospitality. For kosher tours in Southern Africa
contact Shlomo on the above numbers.

Northern Cape
KIMBERLEY
SYNAGOGUES
Orthodox
Griqualand West Hebrew Congregation
20 Synagogue Street 8301
Telephone: (53) 832-5652
Fax: (53) 832-3632
Email: ahorwitz@lantic.net

Western Cape
CAPE TOWN
Cape Town has approximately 17,000 Jews. A
visit to the Campus comprimising the Gardens
Synagogue (160 years old), the new South
African Jewish Museum, the Albow Centre –
housing the Holocaust Museum and the Gitlin
Library – and the Cafe Riteva, is a must for
Jewish visitors.

BAKERIES
Checkers
Gallaria Centre, Regent Road, Sea Point
Telephone: (21) 439-6159
Supervision: Cape Beth Din

BOOKSELLERS
Chabad Centre
20 S. Johns Road, Sea Point 8001
Telephone: (21) 021-434-3740
Email: reception@chabad.co.za
Supervision: Rabbi Mendel Popack

BUTCHERS
Claremont Kosher Butchers and Deli
150 Main Road, Corner Oliver, Sea Point, Claremont
7800
Telephone: (21) 439-6909
Fax: (21) 439-6920
Email: adlercaz@hixnet.co.za
Supervision: Cape Beth Din
Can deliver to your door.

Pick 'N Pay
Constantia Village
Telephone: (21) 794-5960
Supervision: Cape Beth Din
Main Road, Claremont
Telephone: (21) 683-2724
Supervision: Cape Beth Din
Prepacked with Beth Din hechser sign only.
Adelphi Centre, Main Road, Sea Point
Telephone: (21) 434-8987
Supervision: Cape Beth Din

COMMUNITY ORGANISATIONS
Astra Centre
20 Breda Street, Gardens 8001
Telephone: (21) 021-465-4200
Fax: (21) 021-465-4231
Email: jsec@iafrica.com
Web site: www.jsec.org.za

Cape Town Jewish Community Centre
87 Hatfield Street, Gardens 8001
Telephone: (21) 464-6700
Fax: (21) 461-5805
Email: sajbd2@ctjc.co.za

DELICATESSEN
Goldies Nosh Bar
64 Regent Road, Sea Point 8001
Telephone: (21) 434-1116
Fax: (21) 438-3851
Supervision: Cape Beth Din
Sit-down deli and take-away. Meat and pareve. Hours:
Sunday to Thursday, 7 am to 8 pm; Friday, to 5 pm.

GROCERIES
Pick 'N Pay
Centre Point Milnerton
Telephone: (21) 552-2057
Supervision: Cape Beth Din
Prepacked with Beth Din hechser only.

Spar
Regent Road, Sea Point
Telephone: (21) 439-0913
Supervision: Cape Beth Din
Prepacked with Beth Din hechser only.

HOTELS
Kosher
The Belmont Shareblock
3 Holmfirth Road, Sea Point 8005
Telephone: (21) 439-1155
Fax: (21) 434-9451
Supervision: Cape Beth Din
Breakfast and lunch only.

LIBRARIES
Jacob Gitlin Library
Albow Centre, 88 Hatfield Street 8001
Telephone: (21) 462-5088
Fax: (21) 465-8671
Email: gitlib@netactive.co.za

MIKVAOT
Arthur's Road Synagogue, Sea Point
Telephone: (21) 434-3148; 439-8787

Chabad Centre
20 S. Johns Road, Sea Point 8001
Telephone: (21) 021-434-3740
Email: reception@chabad.co.za
Supervision: Rabbi Mendel Popack

MUSEUMS
Cape Town Holocaust Centre
88 Hatfield Street, Gardens 8001
Telephone: (21) 27-21-462-5553
Fax: (21) 27-21-462-5554
Email: ctholocaust@mweb.co.za
Web site: www.museums.org.za/ctholocaust
Sunday to Thursday: 10.00 am - 5.00 pm. Friday: 10.00
am - 1.00 pm.

South African Jewish Museum
88 Hatfield Street, Gardens 8001
Telephone: (21) 27-21-465-1546
Fax: (21) 27-21-465-0284
Email: info@sajewishmuseum.co.za
Web site: www.sajewishmuseum.co.za
Open Sunday - Thursday 10.00am - 5.00pm; Fridays
10.00am - 2.00pm. Museum shop and café.

RESTAURANTS
Dairy
Café Riteve
88 Hatfield Street, Gardens
Telephone: (21) 465-1594
Fax: (21) 465-5980
Supervision: Cape Beth Din

Meat
Avron's Place Restaurant & Grill
19/33 Regent Road, Sea Point 8005
Telephone: (21) 021-439-7610
Fax: (21) 439-7599
Email: avronsplace@netactive.co.za
Supervision: Cape Beth Din
Delivery within 5km radius.

Goldies Bakery & Deli
66 Regent Road, Sea Point
Telephone: (21) 439-0628
Supervision: Cape Beth Din

Kaplan Student Canteen
University of Cape Town
Telephone: (21) 650-2688
Fax: (21) 650-3064
Supervision: Cape Beth Din
Lunches, take-away and orders. Meat and pareve. Open
Monday to Friday. Closed December/January for varsity
holidays and during summer vacation.

Sylvlah's Restaurant
11 Regent Road, Sea Point
Telephone: (21) 433-2303

SYNAGOGUES
Chabad Centre
20 S. Johns Road, Sea Point 8001
Telephone: (21) 021-434-3740
Email: reception@chabad.co.za
Supervision: Rabbi Mendel Popack

Orthodox
Arthur's Road
31 Arthur's Road, Sea Point
Telephone: (21) 434-8680
Fax: (21) 434-8880

Camps Bay
Chilworth Road, Camps Bay
Telephone: (21) 438-8082
Fax: (21) 438-8082
Email: cbhc@netactive.co.za

Cape Town Hebrew Congregation
84 Hatfield Street, Gardens
Telephone: (21) 465-1405
Fax: (21) 461-7659
Email: cthc@isoft.co.za
Web site: www.gardensshul.org

Claremont Hebrew Congregation
Grove Avenue (at Morris Rd), P.O. Box 23035,
Claremont 7735
Telephone: (21) 671-9006
Fax: (21) 683-3011
Email: clarshul@iafrica.com

Constantia Hebrew Congregation
Old Kendal Road, Constantia 7806
Telephone: (21) 713-1818
Fax: (21) 715-3110
Email: mkornblum@herzlia.com
Web site: www.shul.org.za

Green & Sea Point Hebrew Congregation
10 Marais Road, Sea Point
Telephone: (21) 439-7543
Fax: (21) 434-3760
Email: gspheb@mweb.co.za

Milnerton
29 Fitzpatrick Road, Cambridge Estate 7441
Telephone: (21) 551-0442
Fax: (21) 552-4285

Sephardi Hebrew Congregation
Weizmann Hall, 65 Regent Road, Sea Point
Telephone: (21) 439-1962
Fax: (21) 439-9620
Email: sephardicape@xsinet.co.za

Synagogue
Camp Road, Muizenberg
Telephone: (21) 785-5611
Fax: (21) 785-5611

Wynberg Hebrew Congregation
1 Mortimer Road, Wynberg 7806
Telephone: (21) 797-5029
Fax: (21) 797-5029

Reform
Temple Israel
Upper Portswood Road, Green Point
Telephone: (21) 434-9721
Fax: (21) 434-2400
Email: templect@iafrica.com

OUDTSHOORN
SYNAGOGUES
United Hebrew Institutions
291 Buitenkant Street
Telephone: (44) 272-3068
Fax: (44) 272-3068
There is a Jewish section in the C.P. Nel Museum.

PAARL
SYNAGOGUES
Synagogue
Herzlia School
Telephone: (21) 872-4087
For further information phone Mr. Kaufman (083) 325-6603.

SPAIN

Spain has an ancient connection with the Jews, and the term 'Sephardi' originates from the Hebrew word for Spain. Beginning in Roman times, the Jews have suffered the usual cycle of acceptance and persecution, with a 'golden age' under the Islamic Moorish occupation, which began in 711. Great Jewish figures arose from the Spanish community, such as Ibn Ezra and the Ramban. However, the situation changed when the Christians gained the upper hand, and blood libels began. In 1492, almost 100 years after a particularly violent period of persecution, the Jews were expelled from Spain. Many thousands were baptised but practised Judaism in secret (the Conversos), and many were caught and burnt at the stake.

Jewish life began again in the nineteenth century. The Inquisition ended in 1834 and by 1868 Spain had promulgated religious tolerance. Synagogues could be built after 1909, and Spain accepted many thousands of Jewish refugees before and during the Second World War. Angel Sanz-Briz alone helped to save thousands of Hungarian Jews by issuing 'letters of protection' and entry visas.

There has been a recent immigration from North Africa, and the community today has a central body and synagogues in several towns (including Torremolinos and Malaga). Rambam's synagogue in Cordoba can be visited, and there are several other old synagogues throughout the country.

GMT +1 hour
Country calling code: (+34)
Total population: 39,270,000
Jewish population: **14,000**
Emergency telephone: (**Police** – 092 or 091) (**Fire** – 080) (**Ambulance** – 092)
Electricity voltage: (**Electricity voltage** – 220)

ALICANTE
COMMUNITY ORGANISATIONS
Communidad Israelita
Apdo. 189, Playa de San Juan 3540
Telephone: (96) 515-1572
SYNAGOGUES
Vila Carlota, 15 Urb Montivoli, Villajoyosa

BARCELONA
The ancient community of the city lived in the area of the Calle (from the Hebrew Kahall) and the cemetery was in Montjuic (Mountain of the Jews). Most of the original tombstones are now in the Provincial Archaeological Museum.

BUTCHERS
Carniceria|
Porvenir 24
Telephone: (93) 200-3375
Supervision: Barcelona Rabanut

COMMUNITY ORGANISATIONS
Communidad Israelita de Barcelona
Porvenir 24 8071
Telephone: (93) 200 6148
Fax: (93) 200 6148

Community Centre
Porvenir 24 8071
Telephone: (93) 200-6148 or 8513
Kosher meals are available on request

KOSHER FOOD
Kosher Food Service
Telephone: (93) 34-93-4399934
Email: kosherservice@chabadbarcelona.org
Supervision: Rabbi Libersohn

MIKVAOT
Porvenir 24 8071
Telephone: (93) 200-6148, 8513

RESTAURANTS
Vegetarian
Comme Bio
Via Laietana 28 8003
Telephone: (93) 319-8986
Gran Via 603 8007
Telephone: (93) 301-0376

Self Naturista
Carrer de Santa Anna 11-17 08002
Telephone: (93) 93318-2684
Fax: (93) 93412-5413

SYNAGOGUES
Orthodox
Communidad Israelita de Barcelona
Porvenir 24 8021
Telephone: (93) 200-8513
The first synagogue to be built in Spain since the Inquisition.

Progressive
Comunitat Jueva ATID de Catalunya
Castanyer 27, Bajos, Izquierda 8022
Telephone: (93) 417-3704
Fax: (93) 417-3704
Email: atid@arquired.es
Web site: www.atid.freeservers.com

TOURS
Urban Cultours Project
Telephone: (93) 417-1191
Fax: (93) 417-1191
Web site: www.urbancultours.com
Walk of the Call (Jewish Quarter) by a Jewish American architect. Visits to other places of Jewish interest in Catalonia can also be arranged.

TRAVEL AGENCIES
Jewish Travel Agency
Viajes Moravia, Consejo de Ciento 380
Telephone: (93) 246-0300

BENIDORM
KASHRUT INFORMATION
Telephone: (96) 522-9360

BURGOS
During the 13th century Burgos was the largest Jewish community in North Castile. The Juderia was in the area of the Calle Fernan Gonzalez.

There are no other specific locations of interest to travellers.

CORDOBA
This is an ancient synagogue (declared as a monument). Near by, a statue of Maimonides has been erected in the Plazuela de Maimonides. The entrance to the ancient Juderia is near the Almodovar Gate.

TOURIST SITES
Calle de los Judios 20
This is an ancient synagogue built in 1315 and one of only three pre-expulsion ones remaining. It was declared a national monument in 1985, Nearby, a statue of Maimonides has been erected in the Plaza de Tiberiades.(named to perpetuate the connection between his birthplace and where he is buried).

EL ESCORIAL
LIBRARIES
San Lorenzo Monastery
The library of the San Lorenzo Monastery contains a magnificent collection of medieval Hebrew Bibles and illuminated manuscripts. On the walls of the Patio of Kings, in the Palace of Philip II, are sculpted effigies of six Kings of Judah.

ESTELLA
The Jewish community here was one of the most important in the kingdom of Navarre. The Santa Maria de Jus Castillo Church was once a synagogue.

There are no other specific locations of interest to travellers.

GIRONA
ORGANISATIONS
Patronat Municipal Call De Girona
8, Carrer de la Forca 17004
Telephone: 21 67 61
Fax: 21 46 18
Email: callgirona@ajgirona.org
Web site: www.ajgirona.org/call
Built where there was once a 15th century synagogue. It comprises the Museum of the History of the Jews and Nahmanides Institute for Jewish Studies. Open May to October: Monday - Saturday 10am to 8pm, Sunday and Bank Holidays 10am to 3pm; November - April: Monday to Saturday 10am to 6pm, Sundays and Bank Holidays 10am to 3pm

GRANADA
Originally the Jewish community was one of the most important in Spain.

It is believed that the "lion fountain", in the courtyard of the Alhambra, was a gift from the Jews of the city and is based upon a fountain in King Solomon's palace.

There are no other specific locations of interest to travellers.

HERVAS
This village in the Gredos Mountains, 150 miles west of Madrid, has a well-preserved Juderia, which has been declared a national monument. Its main street has been renamed Calle de la Amistad Judeo Cristiana.

There are no other specific locations of interest to travellers.

MADRID
About 3,500 Jews live in Madrid. A new synagogue was completed in 1968, and there is a community centre providing kosher food. The Prado has a number of paintings of Jewish interest.

BUTCHERS
Elias Shoshanna
35 calle Viriato
Telephone: (91) 446-7847
Supervision: Harav ben Dahan, rabbi of the community

COMMUNITY ORGANISATIONS
Community Centre
Calle Balmes 3
Telephone: (91) 591-3131
Fax: (91) 594-1517
Email: cjmsecretaria@terra.es

EMBASSY
Embassy of Israel
Calle Velasquez 150, 7th Floor 28002
Telephone: (91) 411-1357

GIFT SHOP
Sefarad Handicrafts
Gran Via 54
Telephone: (91) 548-2577, 547-6142
Fax: (91) 548-2577
Email: sefaradgalleries@bravored.com
Jewish religious articles.

MIKVAOT
Calle Balmes 3
Telephone: (91) 591-3131

MUSEUMS
Museo Arquelogico
Calle de Serrano 13
Permanent exhibition of casts of Hebrew inscriptions from medieval buildings.

RESTAURANTS
La Escudilla
Santisima Trinidad 16
Telephone: (91) 34-91-4457380

Meat
Community Centre
Calles Balmes 3
Telephone: (91) 591-3131
Fax: (91) 594-1517
Email: cjmsecretaria@terra.es
For groups only.

Vegetarian
El Estragon
Pel de la Paja 10, Austrias 28005
Telephone: (91) 365-8982

SYNAGOGUES
Conservative
Congregacion Bet El
5 Calle Boixy Morer
Telephone: (91) 277-013
Email: sinagoga@bet-el.org
Web site: www.bet-el.org

Orthodox
Calle Balmes 3
Telephone: (91) 591-3131
Fax: (91) 594-1517
Email: cjmsecretaria@terra.es
The capital's first synagogue since the expulsion of Jews in 1492 was opened in December 1968. The building also houses the Community Centre, as well as mikvah, library, classrooms, an assembly hall and the office of the community. Nearest underground station: Metro Iglesias.

TOURS
Alex Benarroch
Telephone: (91) 607-716-642
Email: koteltravel@hotmail.com
Web site:
www.puertademadrid.com/rentacellphone
Jewish heritage tours in Spain and Morocco. Discover Sefarad and Moroccan roots of most well known rabbis. Tours, hotels, kosher food delivered to your hotel, cell phone rental and all travel arrangements. Please contact Alex Benarroch, Cell (34) 607-716-642.

MALAGA
BUTCHERS
Carmiceria Kosher
Calle Somera 14 29001
Telephone: (95) 260-4201

MIKVAOT
Calle Somera 12 29001

SYNAGOGUES
Alameda Principal, 47,20.B 29001
Telephone: (95) 260-4094

TOURIST SITES
There is a statue of the eleventh-century Hebrew poet, Shlomo Ibn-Gabirol, a native of Malaga, in the gardens outside the Alcazaba Castle, in the heart of the city.

MARBELLA
COMMUNITY ORGANISATIONS
Community Centre
Paseo Maritima

GROCERIES
Hipercor
El Corte Ingles, Section No 16, Puerto Banus

Mrs Jacqueline Ohayon
Telephone: (95) 282-6649
Kosher poultry and wine.

MEDIA

Periodicals
Edificio Marbella 2000
Paseo Maritima
Focus
PO Box 145 29600
Community journal

SYNAGOGUES

Orthodox
Beth El
Urbanizacion El Real, KM 184,, Jazmines Str. 21
Telephone: (95) 277-9387
Email: cimarbella@yahoo.es
About two miles from the town centre to the east.
Services: Friday eve. (winter) 7.00pm, (summer)
8.30pm; Shabbat morning & all festivals 10am. Mikveh,
Catering for all occasions. Kosher food available on
request, rooms and apartments for rent.

SALAMANCA

RESTAURANTS
Vegetarian
El Trigal
Calle Libreros 20

SARAGOSSA

This city was once a very important Jewish
centre. A mikvahh has been discovered in the
basement of a modern building at 126-132 Calle
del Coso.

**There are no other specific locations of
interest to travellers.**

SEGOVIA

The Alcazar contains the 16-century 'Tower of
the Jews'. Calle de la Juderia Vieja and Calle de
la Juderia Nueva are the sites of the medieval
Jewish quarters, where the former synagogue
now houses the Corpus Christi Convent.

**There are no other specific locations of
interest to travellers.**

SEVILLE

The first mention of a Jewish community in
Seville was in the 4th century. In 1391 riots
broke out and many synagogues were converted
into churches. The most important of these and
well worth visiting is the Church of Santa Maria
la Blanca.

The Archives of the Indies holds an extensive
collection of documents relating to both north
and south America and include the account
books of Luis de Santagel, a Converso, who
financed Columbus and assisted Jews to leave
the country in 1492. It is being currently restored
and will reopen in 2003.

MUSEUMS

Casa de la Memoria
Calle Ximenez de Enciso, 28 41004
Telephone: 560-670
Email: memorias@teleline.es
A small museum which contains items from local pre-
expulsion Jewish homes.

SYNAGOGUES

Comunidad Israelita de Sevilla
Calle Bustos Tavera 8 41003
Telephone: (95) 427-5517

TARRAGONA

Tarragona Cathedral, Calle de Escribanias
Viejas. This has in its cloister a seventh-century
stone inscribed in Latin and Hebrew. Some very
old coins are preserved in the Provincial
Archaeological Museum. The gate to the
medieval Juderia still stands at the entrance to
Calle de Talavera.

**There are no other specific locations of
interest to travellers.**

TOLEDO

Though it now has no established community,
Toledo is the historical centre of Spanish
Judaism. Well worth a visit are two ancient
former synagogues. One is the El Transito (in
Calle de Samuel Levi), founded by Samuel Levi,
the treasurer of King Pedro I, in the 14th century.
It has been turned by the Spanish Government
into a museum of Sephardi culture. The other,
now the Church of Santa Maria la Blanca, is the
oldest Jewish monument in Toledo, having been
built in the 13th century. It stands in a quiet
garden in what was once the heart of the
Juderia, not far from the edge of the Tagus River.
Also of interest is the house of Samuel Levi, in
which El Greco, the famous painter, lived. The
house is now a museum of his works.

Plaza de la Juderia, half-way between El Transito
and Santa Maria la Blanca, was part of the city's
two ancient Jewish quarters, where many
houses and streets are still much as they were
500 years ago.

JUDAICA

Casa de Jacob
Calle del Angel 15 45002
Telephone: (925) 216-454
Fax: (925) 216-454
Email: libreria-judaica@casadejacob.com
Web site: www.casadejacob.com
We also stock some canned kosher food and wines

TORREMOLINOS

BAKERIES
Panaderia
c/Casablanca, 27 (Local 9B) 29620
Telephone: (95) 374-975
Email: www.perso.wanadoo.es/k
Close to the synagogue

HOTELS
N.CH Hotel
5, Plaza Gamba Alegre 29620
Telephone: (95) 0034.952.373.780
Fax: (95) 0034.952.382.724
Email: nch@n-chhotel.com
Web site: www.n-chhotel.com

RESTAURANTS
Meat
Little Jerusalem
Calle San-Miguel 52, 2nd Floor 29620
Telephone: (95) 205-3155

SYNAGOGUES
Beth Minzi
Calle Skal 13 29620
Telephone: (95) 383952
Fax: (95) 237-0444
Calle Skal La Roca is a small street at the seaward end of
the San Miguel pedestrian precinct, almost opposite the
Police Station. Sephardi and Ashkenazi services are held
on Sabbath morning at 9.30am and Friday evening
services are held at 6.30pm in winter and 8.30pm in
summer.

Rabbi Shaul Khalili
Av. Palma de Mallorca , Castillo S. Luis 29620
Telephone: (95) 952-377-414
Fax: (95) 952-054-114

TUDELA
The remains of the Juderia are near the
cathedral. There is a memorial stone to the great
Jewish traveller, Benjamin of Tudela author of
Book of Travels (1172/3).
**There are no other specific locations of
interest to travellers.**

VALENCIA
RESTAURANTS
Vegetarian
Buffet Chino Veg
Conde Altea 46
Telephone: (96) 334-7061
La Lluna
San Ramon 23
Telephone: (96) 392-214

SYNAGOGUES
Calle Asturias 7-4'
Telephone: (96) 334-3416
Services: Friday evening & festivals.

Conservative
La Javura
calle Uruguay 59, pta 13 46007
Telephone: (96) 380-2129
Email: atoscano@arrakis.es
Web site: www.uscj.org/world/valencia
Tours of medieval Jewish quarter. The synagogue is a
room in a private home.

Orthodox Sephardi
Comunidad Israelita de Valencia
Calle Ingeniero Joaquin Benlloch, 29, 1st Floor,
Apart #2 46006
Telephone: (96) 0034-963346848
Fax: (96) 0034-9633527981
Email: civ@ctv.es
Opening hours: Every Friday, 8.30pm, Jewish Holydays:
Morning 9.00am, Evening 8.30pm. Kosher food under
supervition of Madrid Cheaf Rabbi Mr. Moshe Bendahan.

VITORIA

The monument on the Campo de Judimendi commemorates the ancient Jewish cemetery which, following the edict of expulsion in 1492, the town council undertook to take care of, and never to build over it.

There are no other specific locations of interest to travellers.

Overseas Regions

CEUTA

KASHRUT INFORMATION
Calle Sargento Coriat 8

SYNAGOGUES
Calle Sargento Coriat 8

LAS PALMAS

SYNAGOGUES
Ap. Correos 2142 35080
Telephone: (928) 823-1976

MAJORCA

Majorca's Jewish population today numbers about 300, although fewer than 100 are registered with the community. Founded in 1971, it was the first Jewish community in Spain to be officially recognised since 1435. The Jewish cemetery is at Santa Eugenia, some 12 miles from Palma.

Palma Cathedral containes some interesting Jewish relics, including a candelabrum with 365 lights, which was originally in a synagogue. In the ëTesoroí room are two unique silver maces, over 6 feet long, converted from Torah ërimonimí brought from Sicily in 1493. The Santa Clara Church stands on the site of another pre-Inquisition synagogue. The Montezion Church was, in the 14th century, the Great Synagogue. In Calle San Miguel is the Church of San Miguel, which also stands on the site of a former synagogue. It is not far from the Calle de la Plateria, once a part of the Palma Ghetto.

COMMUNITY ORGANISATIONS
Communidad Israelita de Mallorca
Apartado Correos 389
Telephone: (971) 283799

SYNAGOGUES
Orthodox
Communidad Israelita de Mallorca (Jewish Community of Mallorca)
Palma de Mallorca 7014
Telephone: (971) 283-799
Email: r_ajkatz@hotmail.com
Web site:
www.fortunecity.com/victorian/coldwater/252
This synagogue was dedicated to the community in June 1987. Services are held on Fridays and Holy-days. A communal seder is also held. The community invites all congregants and guests to kiddush following the services.

MELILLA

KASHRUT INFORMATION
Calle General Mola 19
Telephone: 267-4057

SYNAGOGUES
Isaac Benarroch
Calle Marina 7

Jacob Almonznino
Calle Luis de Sotomayor 4

Salama
Calle Alfonso XII 6

Solinquinos
Calle O'Donnell

Yamin Benarroch
Calle Lopez Moreno 8

TENERIFE

COMMUNITY ORGANISATIONS
Comunidad Israelita de Tenerife
Telephone: (922) 247296, 247246

KASHRUT INFORMATION
General Mola 4, Santa Cruz, Holdings 38006
Telephone: (922) 274157
Welcomes all Jewish visitors.

SYNAGOGUES
Ap. De Correos 939, Villalba Hervas 38001
Telephone: (922) 224-6013

SRI LANKA

Islamic and Samaritan legend relates that Adam came to the island after his expulsion from Eden and that Noah's Ark came to rest there. Solid evidence for Jewish settlement was recorded about 1,000 years ago by Muslim travellers. There was a small Jewish community when the Dutch took the island as a colony. This attracted Jews from southern India to the island because of the possibilities of trade.

There was a plan put forward when the island came under British rule for mass Jewish immigration. The Chief Justice, Sir Alexander Johnston appeared to consider the idea a serious one, but the British government did not act on it. A coffee estate was founded in 1841 near Kandy by Jews from Europe.

There is no communual organisation on the island. The Sri Lankans appear to be supportive of Israel, despite the government's official pro-Arab stance. Diplomatic relations with Israel were resumed in May 2000.

GMT +5 1/2 hours
Country calling code: (+94)
Total population: 18,552,000
Jewish population: **Under 100**
Emergency telephone: **(Police – 43 3333) (Fire – 42 2222) (Ambulance – 42 2222)**
Electricity voltage: **(Electricity voltage – 230/240)**

COLOMBO
KASHRUT INFORMATION
82 Rosmead Place 7
Telephone: (1) 695-642
Fax: (1) 74715-306

SURINAME

Suriname's Jewish community is very old. The first Jews settled here in the seventeenth century, escaping from persecution in Brazil. Later Jews came from Britain, after the country had passed into British hands. Suriname welcomed more Jewish refugees from the Caribbean and the country became a Dutch colony in 1668, bringing Sephardi Jews from Amsterdam.

Eventually, half the white population in the country was Jewish, and there was a 'Jodensavanne' (Jewish savannah), where the Jews owned large sugar plantations. They called the plantations by Hebrew names and built a synagogue in 1685. The community began to decline in the nineteenth century. Recently, many have emigrated to Israel.

Today, there are two synagogues in Paramaribo, the capital. The Ashkenazi synagogue, like the one in CuraÁao, has a sandy floor, which is symbolic of the 40 years in the desert and was also said to have muffled the footsteps of the Conversos as they carried out their Judaism in secret.

GMT -3 hours
Country calling code: **(+597)**
Total population: **437,000**
Jewish population: **200**
Emergency telephone:
Electricity voltage: **(Electricity voltage – 110/220)**

PARAMARIBO
KASHRUT INFORMATION
Commewijnestr. 21
Telephone: 400236
Fax: 471154

ORGANISATIONS
Suriname Jewish Community
Keizerstraat 82-84
Telephone: 400236/473896
Fax: 402380/471154

SYNAGOGUES
Ashkenazi
Neveh Shalom
Keizerstr. 82

TOURIST SITES
Sights to see include Joden Savanah (Jewish Savanah), one of the oldest Jewish settlements in the Americas.

Sedek Ve Shalom
Herenstr. 20
The entire contents of this eighteenth century synagogue are currently on 'long term loan' to the Israel Museum in Jerusalem. The building is now being used as an Internet café.

SWEDEN

Sweden was under the influence of the Lutheran church until the late eighteenth century and was opposed to Jewish settlement. Aaron Isaac from Mecklenburg in Germany, a seal engraver, was the first Jew admitted into the country, in 1774. The emancipation of Jews in Sweden was a slow process; Jews had limited rights, as they were designated a 'foreign colony'. After a gradual lifting of restrictions in the nineteenth century, Jews were fully emancipated in 1870, although the right to hold ministerial office was closed to them until 1951.

The emancipation heralded the growth of the community, and many eastern European Jews found refuge in Sweden at the beginning of the twentieth century. The initial refusal to accept Jews fleeing the Nazis changed to sympathy as evidence for the Holocaust mounted, and in 1942 many Jews and other refugees were allowed into the country, followed, in 1943, by almost all of Danish Jewry. Sweden also accepted Hungarian, Czechoslovakian and Polish Jews after the war.

There is an Official Council of Jewish Communities in Sweden, and many international Jewish groups are represented. There are three synagogues in Stockholm, including the imposing Great Synagogue built in 1870. There are synagogues in other large towns. Although shechita is forbidden, kosher food is imported, and there are some kosher shops.

GMT +1 hour
Country calling code: (+46)
Total population: 8,847,000
Jewish population: 16,000
Emergency telephone: (Police – 112) (Fire – 112) (Ambulance – 112)
Electricity voltage: (Electricity voltage – 220)

BORAS

COMMUNITY ORGANISATIONS
Jewish Community of Boras & Synagogue
Varbergsvagen 21, Box 46 50305
Telephone: (33) 124892
Email: s. rytz@vertextrading.se

GOTHENBURG

COMMUNITY ORGANISATIONS
The Jewish Community of Gothenburg
Ostra Larmgatan 12 S-411 07
Telephone: (31) 31-177245
Fax: (31) 31-7119360
Email: kansli@judiskaforsamlingen.se

GROCERIES
Dr. Allards
gata 4
Telephone: (31) 741-1545

MEDIA
Radio
Thursdays at 9pm on 94.4 MHz.

SYNAGOGUES
Conservative
The Jewish Community of Gothenburg
Ostra Larmgatan 12 S-411 07
Telephone: (31) 31-177245
Fax: (31) 31-711-9360
Email: kansli@judiskaforsamlingen.se

Orthodox
Beilh Tefilah
Storgatan 5
Telephone: (31) 711-7872
Web site: www.welcome.to/minyan

MALMO

COMMUNITY ORGANISATIONS
Jewish Community Centre
Kamrergatan 11, Box 4198 20313
Telephone: (40) 611 6460; 8860; 976043 (Rabbi)
Fax: (40) 234-469
Email: rabeli@alfa.telenordia.se

MIKVAOT
Kamrergatan 11
Telephone: (40) 118860

SYNAGOGUES
Orthodox
Foreningsgatan
The Moorish style building celebrates its centenary during 2003.

STOCKHOLM
Stockholm has a number of Jewish facilities. In addition the Raoul Wallenberg Park is worth a visit.

COMMUNITY ORGANISATIONS
Jewish Community Centre
Judaica House, Nybrogatan 19, PO Box 5053 102 42
Telephone: (8) 5878-5867
Fax: (8) 5878-5870
Email: info@jf-stockholm.org
Web site: www.jf-stockholm.org

Jewish Community of Stockholm
Wahrendorffsgatan 3, PO Box 7427 103 91
Telephone: (8) 5878-5800
Fax: (8) 5878-5858
Email: info@jf-stockholm.org
Web site: www.jf-stockholm.org
Open Monday to Thursday 9am-5pm Friday 9am-4pm (closed for lunch noon-1pm).

EMBASSY
Embassy of Israel
Torstenssongatan 4, PO Box 14006 104 40
Telephone: (8) 663-1465
Fax: (8) 662-5301
Email: israel.embassy.swipnet.se

GIFT SHOP
Menorah: Community Centre Shop
Judaica House, Nybrogatan 19, PO Box 5053 102 42
Telephone: (8) 663-6580

GROCERIES
Kosherian Blecher & Co
Nybrogatan 19, PO Box 5053 102 42
Telephone: (8) 663-6580
Fax: (8) 663-6580
Kosher groceries. Also offers cooked meals such as burgers, sausages, meat sandwiches etc. Delivery to groups, hotels etc.

KASHRUT INFORMATION
Rabbi Meir Horden
Jewish Community House, Wahrendorffsgatan 3B, P.O.B. 7472 S-103 91
Telephone: (8) 08-587-858-00
Fax: (8) 08-587-858-58
Email: meir.horden@jf-stockholm.org
Web site: www.jf-stockholm.org/centret/judendom/kosher
Rabbi Meir Horden supervises kashrut in Stockholm. Look at www.jf-stockholm.org/kosher for the latest updated information.

LIBRARIES
The Jewish Library
Wahrendorffsgatan 3, PO Box 7427 103 91
Telephone: (8) 587-858 34
Fax: (8) 587-858 51
Email: judiska.biblioteket@jf-stockholm.org
The Raoul Wallenberg Room is also on the premises, it is named after the Swedish diplomat who saved scores of thousands of Hungarian Jews from the Nazis, was arrested by the Russians in Budapest in 1945 and disappeared.

MEDIA
Periodicals
Judisk Kronika
, PO Box 5053 102 42
Telephone: (8) 660-3872
Fax: (8) 660-3892
Email: judisk.kronika@swipnet.se

Menorah
, PO Box 5053 102 42
Telephone: (8) 667-6770
Fax: (8) 663-7676
Email: kh-uia@swipnet.se
Web site: www.menorah-sweden.com

MIKVAOT
Community Centre
Judaica House, Nybrogatan 19 102 42
Telephone: (8) 5878-5867
Fax: (8) 5878-5870
Email: info@jf-stockholm.org
Web site: www.jf-stockholm.org
The Mikva is located in the Judaica House. To get in touch please contact the Jewish Community Centre (5878-5867).

MONUMENT
The Holocaust Monument
Wahrendorffsgatan 3
The monument was opened in 1998 by King Carl Gustaf of Sweden, and records the over 8,500 holocaust victims who are relatives of Jews residing in Sweden.

MUSEUMS
Jewish Museum
Halsingegatan 2
Telephone: (8) 08-310143
Fax: (8) 8-318404
Email: info@judiska-museet.a.se
Web site: www.judiska-museet.a.se
The only one of its kind in the Nordic countries. Arranges exhibitions about the history of Swedish Jewry and is open every day, except Saturday, between noon and 4 pm.

RESTAURANTS
Community Centre
Nybrogatan 19 102 42
Telephone: (8) 663-6580
Email: info@jf-stockholm.org
Kosher lunches under Rabbi Meir Horden's supervision at the Community Centre are available during the summer. Dinners can also be arranged at the Community Centre for groups. Contact Mr Ike Tankus. Tel: 647-4475.

Lao Wai
Luntmakargatan 74
Telephone: (8) 673-7800
Supervision: Rabbi Meir Horden

Mino's Café
Tegnergatan 36
Telephone: (8) 30 77 42
Jewish North African Cuisine. All meat is said to be kosher but there is no kosher licence.

SYNAGOGUES
Masorti
Great Synagogue
Wahrendorffsgatan 3, PO Box 7427 103 91
Telephone: (8) 5878-5800
Fax: (8) 5878-5850
Email: kansli@jf-stockholm.org
Web site: www.jf-stockholm.org
The interior originally comes from a synagogue in Hamburg which survived Kristallnacht in Germany. Services: Monday and Thursday mornings, Friday evenings & Saturday morning. Open to tourists Monday - Friday from 10am till 2pm.

Orthodox
Adat Jeshurun
Riddargatan 5, PO Box 5053 102 42
Telephone: (8) 679-2900
Fax: (8) 663-6580
Daily services: Weekdays 7.45 am, Shabat 9 am, Sunday 8.30 am.

Adat Jisroel
St. Paulsgatan 13
Telephone: (8) 679-2900
Situated in an 18th century building it was renovated some 20 years ago. Daily Services: weekdays 7.30am, Shabbat 9.00am, Sunday 8.15am

UPPSALA
ORGANISATIONS
Jewish Students Club
Dalgatan 15
Telephone: (8) 125453

SWITZERLAND

Swiss Jewry originated in medieval times and their history followed the standard course of medieval European Jewry: working as money-lenders and pedlars, attacked by the local population, who accused them of causing the Black Death, then resettling a few years afterwards, only to be subsequently expelled.

By the late eighteenth century, when the Helvetic Confederation was formed, there were three small communities. Freedom of movement was allowed, and full emancipation was granted in 1866. Theodor Herzl held the first World Zionist Conference in Basle in 1897.

Although Switzerland accepted some refugees from Nazism, many were refused, and most of the new refugee Jewish population emigrated soon after the war. The community today has a central body, and is made up of various factions, from ultra-Orthodox to Reform. The major towns have synagogues, and kosher meat is imported. There are several hotels with kosher facilities. Over half of the community live in the German-speaking area, the French-speaking area has the second largest number, and a small population is found in the southern, Italian-speaking area.

Switzerland has elected its first Jewish (and first female) president, Ruth Dreifuss.

In 2001 it was reported that evidence had been found of an early Jewish presence in the country, being a ring bearing images of a menorah and a ram's horn and dating from 200CE.

GMT +1 hour
Country calling code: (+41)
Total population: 7,085,000
Jewish population: 18,000
Emergency telephone: (Police – 117) (Fire – 118) (Ambulance – 144)
Electricity voltage: (Electricity voltage – 220)

AROSA

HOTELS

Levin's Hotel Metropol
Telephone: (81) 377-4444
Fax: (81) 377-2100
Mikva on premises. Own kosher bakery.

BADEN

KOSHER FOOD

Atrium Hotel Blume
Kurplatz 4 5400
Telephone: (56) 222-5569
Fax: (56) 222-4298
Email: info@blume-baden.ch
Web site: www.blume-baden.ch
Prepacked kosher meals on request

SYNAGOGUES

Israelitische Kultusgemeinde Baden
Parkstrasse 17 5400
Telephone: (56) 221-5128
Fax: (56) 222-9447
Email: ikgb@dplanet.ch
Friday nights: Winter 18.30; Summer 19.30. Shabbat and Festivals: mornings 8.45am.

BASLE

The Jewish community dates back to the beginning of the 12th century. Thislasted for some two hundred years until the Jews had to flee from persecution.

They returned in the 16th century and Basle became a centre for jewish printing.

Basle is of course famous for the first Zionist Conference of 1897. A plaque on the wall of the Concert Hall commemorates this event.

BAKERIES

Bakery Schmutz
Austrasse 53
Telephone: (61) 272-4765

BOOKSELLERS

Victor Goldschmidt
Mostackerstrasse 17 4051
Telephone: (61) 261-6191
Fax: (61) 261-6123
Email: vgb.@econophone.ch

BUTCHERS

Juedische Genossenschafts-Metzgerei
Friedrichstrasse 26 4055
Telephone: (61) 301-3493
Fax: (61) 301-6882
Supervision: Both Basel Rabbinates
Also sells groceries and wine. Open 7.30am-12.00 noon, 3pm-6.00. Closed Friday afternoon.

HOTELS

Hotel Euler
Centralbahnplatz 14 4002
Telephone: (61) 275-8000
Fax: (61) 275-8050
Offers kosher meals on request. Has a synagogue and Mikvah on the premises.

MIKVAOT

Eulerstr. 10 4051
Telephone: (61) 301-6831
Thannerstrasse 60
Telephone: (61) 301-2220

MUSEUMS

Jewish Museum of Switzerland
Kornhausgasse 8 CH-4051
Telephone: (61) 0041-61-261-9514
Email: museum-judaistik@unibas.ch
Hours: Monday and Wednesday, 2 pm to 5 pm; Sunday, 11 am to 5 pm. Free entrance.

RESTAURANTS

Holbein Cafe
Leimenstrasse 67 4051
Telephone: (61) 270-6868
Fax: (61) 270-6810
Email: info@holbeinhof.ch
Supervision: Basle Rabbinate
Serves both meat and dairy.

Restaurant Topas
Leimenstrasse 24 4051
Telephone: (61) 206-9500
Fax: (61) 206-9501
Email: info@restaurant-topas.ch
Web site: www.restaurant-topas.ch
Supervision: Under the supervision of local rabbinical authority.
Hours: 11:30 am to 2 pm Sunday to Friday. 6:30 pm to 9 pm Sunday to Thursday. Friday night, Shabbat lunch and holidays by reservation before 2 pm of preceding day.

Vegetarian Kosher

Falafel- & Pitahaus
Oberwilerstrasse 46 4102
Telephone: (61) 423-7575
Fax: (61) 423-7575
Email: info@falafel-und-pitahaus.ch
Web site: www.falafel-und-pitahaus.ch

SYNAGOGUES

Israelitische Religionsgesellschaft
Ahornstrasse 14
Telephone: (61) 301-4898
Rabbi, Tel: 41-61-302-1434.

Orthodox
Israelitische Gemeinde Basel
Leimenstrasse 24 4003
Telephone: (61) 279-9850
Fax: (61) 279-9851
Email: igb@igb.ch

BERN
EMBASSY
Embassy of Israel
Alpenstrasse 32 3006
Telephone: (31) 356-3500
Fax: (31) 356-3556
Email: info@emb.israel.ch

SYNAGOGUES
Conservative Traditional
Synagogue & Community Center
Kapellenstrasse 2
Telephone: (31) 381-4992
Fax: (31) 382-3861
Email: info@jgb.ch
Web site: www.jgb.ch
Rabbiner Dr Michael Leipziger, Tel: 41-31 381-7303.

BIEL/BIENNE
SYNAGOGUES
Synagogue
Ruschlistrasse 3
Telephone: (32) 377-3619
Fax: (32) 377-3619

BREMGARTEN / AARGAU
CONTACT INFORMATION
Israelitische Cultusgemeinde
Werner Meyer-Moses, Ringstrasse. 37 CH-5620
Telephone: (56) 633-6626
Fax: (56) 633-6626

ENDINGEN
CONTACT INFORMATION
J. Bloch
Buckstr. 2 5304
Telephone: (56) 242-1546
Visits to the old synagogue and cemetery can be arranged.

ENGELBERG
HOTELS
Hotel Marguerite
6390 Engelberg
Telephone: (41) 637-2522
Fax: (41) 637-2926
Supervision: Agudas Achim, Zurich
Mikva on premises.

FRIBOURG
SYNAGOGUES
9 avenue de Rome
Telephone: (26) 322-1670

GENEVA
Originally Jews were not allowed to settle in Geneva itself but only the surrounding district. They had come in 1182 from France. In 1490 however they were expelled.

After Geneva's annexation by France, at the end of the 18th century, Jews allowed back in. They were not allowed civic rights however until 1841.

BAKERIES
Pouly
Rue des Eaux Vives 72
Ask for kosher bread.

BUTCHERS
Boucherie Kosher
Biton 21, rue de Montchoisi
Telephone: (22) 736-3168

EMBASSY
Permanent Mission of Israel to the United Nations
9 Chemin Bonvent, Cointrin 1216

MEDIA
Periodicals
Israelitsches Wochenblatt/Revue Juive
Avenue du Mail 5 1205
Telephone: (22) 800-1026
Fax: (22) 800-1028

MIKVAOT
Telephone: (22) 346-9732
Fax: (22) 736-9632

RESTAURANTS
Meat
Le Jardin Rose
10, rue St-Leger
Telephone: (22) 317-8910
Fax: (22) 317-8990
Only open for lunch but arrangements can be made so that lunches and dinners can be delivered to any hotel downtown.

R.Liebermann
Av. Jules Crosnier 4 1206
Telephone: (22) 346-0892
Fax: (22) 346-0830
Supervision: Machsike Hadas

SYNAGOGUES
Orthodox
Beth Habad
12 rue du Lac
Telephone: (22) 736-3682

The Geneva Synagogue (Ashkenazi)
Place de la Synagogue

Sephardi
Hekhal Haness
54 ter route de Malagnou
Telephone: (22) 736-9632

TOURIST SITES
Cathedrale St-Pierre
Place du Bourg-Four $ 1204
Telephone: (22) 311-7575
Fax: (22) 310-0225
There is an interesting stained glass window depicting
Moses in the Chapelle des Macchabees.

KREUZLINGEN
CONTACT INFORMATION
Louis Hornung
Schulstr. 7
Telephone: (71) 671-1630

LA-CHAUX-DE-FONDS
SYNAGOGUES
Rue de Parc 63 2300
Telephone: (39) 231-794
Jews first came to the town from Alsace in 1777. The
synagogue was built in 1896. It has been recently
refurbished.

LAUSANNE
COMMUNITY ORGANISATIONS
Communauté Israélite de Lausanne
3 avenue Georgette 1001
Telephone: (21) 021-341-7240
Fax: (21) 021-341-7241
Email: secretariat.cil@vtx.ch

GROCERIES
Kolbo Shalom
7 avenue Juste-Olivier
Telephone: (21) 312-1265

MIKVAOT
1 avenue Juste-Olivier
Telephone: (21) 617-5818

RESTAURANTS
Community Centre
3 avenue Georgette 1003
Telephone: (21) 341-7242
Serves lunch only, from 12 pm to 2 pm.

SYNAGOGUES
Orthodox
1 avenue Juste-Olivier
Telephone: (21) 320-9911
Cnr J. Olivier and av. Florimont.

LENGNAU
CONTACT INFORMATION
Telephone: (56) 241-1203
For visits to the old synagogue and cemetery.

LUCERNE
BUTCHERS
Judische Metzgerei
Bruchstrasse 26
Telephone: (41) 240-2560

MIKVAOT
Bruchstrasse 51
Telephone: (41) 320-4750

SYNAGOGUES
Bruchstrasse 51
Telephone: (41) 240-6400

LUGANO
GROCERIES
Koschere Lebensmittel erhaltlich bei
Frutor SA via Bagutti 4
Telephone: (91) 922-8522

HOTELS
Hotel Dan
Via Fontana 1 6902
Telephone: (91) 985-7030
Fax: (91) 985-7031
Email: danlugano@yahoo.com
Web site: pibt.de/l/dan.htm
Kashrut under the supervision of the rabbinate Lugano's
Jewish Community.

MIKVAOT
Via Maderno 11
Telephone: (91) 923-8952

SYNAGOGUES
Via Maderno 11
Telephone: (91) 923-5698

NEUKIRCH-EGNACH
CENTRAL ORGANISATIONS
Vegetarian society
**Schweizerische Vereinigung fur
Vegetarismus (SVV)**
Bahnhofstr 52 9315
Telephone: 071-477-3377
Fax: 071-477-3378
Email: svv@vegetarismus.ch
Web site: www.vegetarismus.ch
Can supply information on those who wish to eat
vegetarian in Switzerland.

ST GALLEN

SYNAGOGUES
Frongartenstrasse 18
Telephone: (71) 223-5923

ST MORITZ

HOTELS
Bermann's Hotel Edelweiss
Telephone: (81) 836-5555
Fax: (81) 833-5556

VEVEY

RESTAURANTS
Les Bergers du Leman
Telephone: 923-5355
Fax: 922-5923

WINTERTHUR

SYNAGOGUES
Rosenstrasse 5
Telephone: (52) 232-8136

YVERDON

CONTACT INFORMATION
Dr Maurice Ellkan
1400 Cheseaux-Noreaz
Telephone: (24) 425-1851

ZUG

RESTAURANTS
Restaurant Glashof
Baarerstr. 41 6301
Telephone: (42) 221-248
Prepared kosher meals are available.

ZURICH

Jews first arrived in Zurich in 1273. Over the following two centuries Jews were repeatedly expelled and allowed to return. There are five stained glass Chagall windows in the Fraumunster Church (located at Munsterhof Square) of which four are on themes from the Hebrew Bible.

BAKERIES
Ruben Bollag
Waffenplatzstrasse 5, (near Bahnhof Enge) 8002
Telephone: (1) 202-3045
Brauerstrasse 110 8004
Telephone: (1) 242-8700
Fax: (1) 291-4684

BOOKSELLERS
Morascha
Seestrasse 11 8002
Telephone: (1) 201.11.20
Fax: (1) 201.31.20
Email: morascha@bluemail.ch
Web site: www.morascha.com

BUTCHERS
Zukom
8 Aemtlerstrasse
Telephone: (1) 451-8384
Fax: (1) 451-8386
Supervision: Judische Gemeinde Aguda Achim and Israelitsche Religionsgellschaft.

GROCERIES
Jelmoli Department Store
Bahnhofstrasse
Has a kosher section.

Pick and Pay
Lavaterstrasse
Has a kosher section.

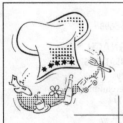

MEDIA

Periodicals

Jewish City Guide of Switzerland
Spectrum Press International, Im Tannegg 1,
Friesenbergstrasse 221 8055
Telephone: (1) 462-6411; 462-6412
Fax: (1) 462-6462
Email: info@jewishguide.ch
Web site: www.jewishguide.ch
Published quarterly in English and German, a guide to
Jewish communities throughout Switzerland.

Tachles Irevve Juive
Rudigerstr 10, Postfach 8027
Telephone: (1) 206-4200
Fax: (1) 206-4210
Email: redaktion@tachles.ch
Web site: www.tachles.ch
Weekly magazine.

MIKVAOT
Freigutstrasse 37
Telephone: (1) 201-7306
Appointment by phone between 9am & 11am.

RESTAURANTS
Restaurant Schalom
G. van Dijk, Lavaterstrasse 33-37 8002
Telephone: (1) 283-2233
Fax: (1) 283-2234
Email: catering.schalom@bleuwin.ch
Supervision: Rabbi Rothschild.

Dairy
Fein & Schein
Schontalstrasse 14, Corner/Ecke Hallwylstrasse
Telephone: (1) 241-3040
Fax: (1) 241-2112
Supervision: Rabbi Daniel Levy

Rimon Take Away
Zelgstr. 1 8003
Telephone: (1) 960-2323

Meat
Club Savjon
G. van Dijk-Neufeld., Lavaterstr. 33
Telephone: (1) 201-1476
Fax: (1) 201-1496
Email: catering.schalom@bluewin.ch
Supervision: Rabbi Rothschild

SYNAGOGUES
Freigutstrasse 37
Telephone: (1) 201-4998

Israel Religionsgesellschaft
Freigutstrasse 37 8002
Telephone: (1) 201-6746

Israelitische Cultusgemeinde Zurich
Lavaterstrasse 33 8002
Telephone: (1) 283-2222
Fax: (1) 283-2223
Email: info@icz.org

Judische Gemeinde Agudas Achim
Erikastrasse 8 8003
Telephone: (1) 463-8033
Fax: (1) 463-8045

Orthodox
Minjan Machsikei Hadass
Anwandstrasse 60
Telephone: (1) 241-3759
Fax: (1) 241-2668
Rabbi Schmerler: 01-242-9046

Minjan Wollishofen
Etzelstrasse 6 8038
Telephone: (1) 286-5010
Fax: (1) 286-5018
Email: minjan.wollishofen@schweiz.ch
Contact: Dr. Sigmund Pugatsch

TAIWAN

The US Army brought the first Jews to
Taiwan in the 1950s, when an American
base, now closed, was set up in the country.
In the 1970s, some Jewish businessmen
began to work on the island, serving two- or
three-year contracts with their companies.
Most are Americans, although there are
some Israelis and other nationalities.
Services are held on Shabbat in a hotel, and
there is a Jewish community centre.

GMT +8 hours
Country calling code: (+886)
Total population: 21,854,000
Jewish population: **Under 100**
Emergency telephone: (Police – 110) (Fire – 119)
(Ambulance – 119)
Electricity voltage: (Electricity voltage – 110)

TAIPEI
COMMUNITY ORGANISATIONS
Taiwan Jewish Community Centre
37 Lane 315, Shihpai road, Shihlin
Telephone: (2) 396-0159
Fax: (2) 396-4022
Email: thetjc@yahoo.com
Services are held on most Friday evenings at 7.30pm.
Visitors should check in advance. All Holy Days and major
festivals are celebrated.

SYNAGOGUES
Orthodox
Ritz Landis Hotel
41 Min Chuan East Road
Telephone: (2) 2597-1234
Fax: (2) 2596-9223
Email: ritz@theritz-taipei.com
Shabbat and festival services are held here, also, when minyan is available, Weekday Services.

TAJIKISTAN

One of the former Soviet Republics, Tajikistan has a small Jewish population but, after the fall of the Soviet Union, many Jews emigrated to Israel. The community is a mix of 40 per cent Bokharans and 60 per cent Soviet Jews from other parts of the former USSR who migrated to Tajikistan during the Second World War. The Bokharan Jews are believed to be descendants of Persian Jewish exiles. Dushanbe, the capital, and Shakhrisabz are provided with synagogues, and Dushanbe also has a library.

GMT +5 hours
Country calling code: (+7)
Total population: 5,513,000
Jewish population: 1,500
Emergency telephone:
Electricity voltage: (Electricity voltage – 220)

DUSHANBE
SYNAGOGUES
Ashkenazi
Synagogue
Proletarsky Street

Bokharan
Nazyina Khikmeta Street 26

SHAKHRISABZ
SYNAGOGUES
23 Bainal Minal Street

THAILAND

Although the first confirmed presence of Jews in Thailand was in 1890, Thai Jewry really began with Jews escaping Russia and eastern Europe in the 1920s and 1930s although most of them emigrated after 1945.

The present community arrived in the post-war period of the 1950s and 1960s. They came from Syria and Lebanon, and also from Europe and America. Some Israelis also came, and jewellery is an important source of trade with Israel. Another relatively large influx came in 1979 as Jews left Iran after the fall of the Shah.

Bangkok has Ashkenazi, Sephardi and Lubavitch synagogues. The community centre is based in the Ashkenazi synagogue. The Lubavitch synagogue offers several communual activities, including Seders at Passover, which have a large attendance.

GMT +7 hours
Country calling code: (+66)
Total population: 60.206,000
Jewish population: 250
Emergency telephone:
Electricity voltage: (Electricity voltage – 220)

BANGKOK
COMMUNITY ORGANISATIONS
Jewish Community of Thailand
Beth Elisheva Building, 121 Soi Sai, Nam Thip 2, Sukhumvit Soi 22
Telephone: (2) 663-0244
Fax: (2) 663-0245
Email: ykantor@ksc15.th.com
Web site: www.jewishthailand.com
Friday night and Shabbat services with Kiddush & Shabbat meal. Holidays services. Call to confirm.

EMBASSY
Embassy of Israel
'Ocean Tower II' 25th floor, 75 Sukhumvit Soi 19, Asoke Road 10110
Telephone: (2) 204-9200
Fax: (2) 204-9255
Email: consul.bkk@israelfm.org

KASHRUT INFORMATION
Telephone: (2) 318-1577
Telephone: (2) 234-0606
Telephone: (2) 237-1697

MIKVAOT
Jewish Community of Thailand
Beth Elisheva Building, 121 Soi Sai, Nam Thip 2, Sukhumvit Soi 22
Telephone: (2) 663-0244
Fax: (2) 663-0245
Email: ykantor@ksc15.th.com
Web site: www.jewishthailand.com

RESTAURANTS
Ohr Menachem - Chabad House
96 Ram Buttri Rd., Kaosarn Road, Banglampoo
Telephone: (2) 282-6388
Fax: (2) 629-1153
Supervision: Rabbi Y. Kantor
Open 12 noon to 9 pm daily. Bakery and store. Tel 629-2944/5.

SYNAGOGUES
Orthodox
Beth Elisheva
121 Soi Sai, Nam Thip 2, Sukhumvit Soi 22
Telephone: (2) 663-0244
Fax: (2) 663-0245
Email: ykantor@ksc15.th.com
Close to: Imperial Queens Park, Jade Pavilion, Rembrandt, and Sheraton Grande Hotels. Friday night service at candle lighting time followed by Shabbat meal. Shabbat services 10.00am with Kiddush & Shabbat meal. Call to confirm.

Even Chen
The Bossotel Inn 2nd floor, 55/12-14 Soi Charoenkrung, 42/1 New Road (Silom Road area)
Telephone: (2) 630-6120
Fax: (2) 237-3225
Email: ykantor@ksc15.th.com
Daily morning service. Regular Friday evening and Shabbat morning, afternoon and evening services. Light kosher meal after Shabbat service, by advance reservation.

Ohr Menachem - Chabad House
96 Ram Buttri Rd., Kaosarn Road, Banglampoo
Telephone: (2) 282-6388
Fax: (2) 629-1153
Email: chabadbangkok@yahoo.com
Daily services, Friday evenings at sundown with Shabbat meal, attracts young Jewish travellers.

TUNISIA

There is written proof of ancient Jewish settlement in Carthage in the year 200CE, when the region was under Roman control. The community was successful and was left in peace. Under the Byzantine Empire, conditions for the Jews did worsen, but after the Islamic conquest, the 'golden age' of Tunisian Jewry occurred. There was prosperity and many centres of learning were established. This did not continue into the Middle Ages, as successive Arab and Spanish invasions led to discrimination. Emancipation came from the French, but the community suffered under the Nazi-influenced Vichy government. After the war, many emigrated to Israel or to France and the community is currently shrinking.

There are several synagogues in the country, together with kindergartens and schools. Tunisia is not as extreme in its attitude towards Israel as some Arab states, and there has been communication between the two countries at a high level. An Israeli Interest Bureau in Tunis acts as an unofficial embassy. The Bardo Museum in Tunis has an exhibition of Jewish ritual objects.

GMT +1 hour
Country calling code: (+216)
Total population: 9,215,000
Jewish population: 1,500
Emergency telephone:
Electricity voltage: (Electricity voltage – 220)

JERBA
There are Jews in two villages on this small island off al Ghariba the Tunisian coast. There is also a magnificent synagogue, al Ghariba, many hundreds of years old. In the Hara al-Saghira which is in the centre of the island.

Each year a traditional Lag B'Omei celebration is held. Following the terrorist attack in 2001 attendance dropped from 7000 to 800. Jewish silversmiths are prominent in Hournt souk on rue Bizerte.

The community in Jerba is possibly the oldest continuous one outside Israel. There are two small Jewish towns; Hara Saghira and Hara Kebira. Most of the Jews live in Hara Kebira, where there is the Al Ghriba "extraordinary" synagogue which has a multicoloured interior and is a site of pilgrimage.

There are no other specific locations of interest to travellers.

TUNIS

COMMUNITY ORGANISATIONS
Community Offices
15 rue de Cap Vert
Telephone: (1) 282469, 287153

KASHRUT INFORMATION
26 rue de Palestine
Telephone: (1) 282406; 283540

SYNAGOGUES
Beth Yacob
3 rue Eve, Nohelle
Telephone: (1) 348964

Grande
43 Av. de la Liberte

Lubavitch Yeshiva
73 rue de Palestine
Telephone: (1) 791429

TURKEY

There have been Jews in Turkey since at least the fourth century BCE, making Turkey one of the earliest Jewish communities. The fifteenth and sixteenth centuries were periods of major prosperity for the Jews of Turkey.

After the Expulsion of the Jews from Spain in 1492, at a time when Jews were not tolerated in most of the Christian countries of Western Europe, what was then the Ottoman (Turkish) Empire was their principal land of refuge. The Sultan was reported to have said of the Spanish King: 'By expelling the Jews, he has impoverished his country and enriched mine'.

During the Second World War Turkey was neutral and accepted those Jews able to enter it.

GMT +2 hours
Country calling code: (+90)
Total population: **63,745,000**
Jewish population: **20,000**
Emergency telephone: (**Police – 155**) (**Fire – 110**)
(**Ambulance – 11**)
Electricity voltage: (**Electricity voltage – 220**)

ANKARA

EMBASSY
Embassy of Israel
Mahatma Gandhi Sok 85, Gaziosmanpasa
Telephone: (312) 446-3605
Fax: (312) 446-8071

BALAT

A coastal town about 20 miles west of Istanbul which has a 500-year- old synagogue. Now closed ,the keys are with the mosque next door.

There are no other specific locations of interest to travellers.

ISTANBUL

In the 12th century Benjamin Tudela said of the city "There is no city like her except Baghdad". At that time it was one of the most important Jewish centres in the world.

Since 1949 the Jewish community has had autonomy in its own affairs.

COMMUNITY ORGANISATIONS
Buyuk Hendek
Sokak No 61, Galata
Telephone: (212) 293-7566
Secretary General: Lina Filiba

EMBASSY
Consul General of Israel
Valikonag Caddesi No 73
Telephone: (212) 255-1040
Fax: (212) 225-1048
Email: isrcon@comnet.com.tr

MUSEUMS
Zulfari Museum
Telephone: (212) 274-2607
Fax: (212) 274-2607
The museum contains material relating to the Jewish members of the Ottoman Parliament, physicians at the Imperial Court, diplomats, academicians, police officers and civil servants. Contact Mr H Ojalvo (212-275-3944) for further information.

RELIGIOUS ORGANISATIONS
Chief Rabbinate
Yemenici Sokak 23, Beyoglu, Tunel 80050
Telephone: (212) 293-8794/5
Fax: (212) 244-1980

RESTAURANTS
Levi Restaurant
Tustempasamah Kalcin Sok, Cavustasa Han (2nd floor)
Telephone: (212) 512-1196

Meat
Carne Restaurant
Muallim Naci Cad. 17, Ortakoy
Telephone: (212) 260-8424

SYNAGOGUES
Askenazi Synagogue
Yuksekkaldinm Sok No 37, Galata
Telephone: (212) 252-2157
Fax: (212) 244-2975
Email: eskenazivakli@superonline.com

Beth Israel
Efe Sok No 4, Sisli
Telephone: (212) 240-6599
Every day.

Caddesbostan Synagogue
Tasmektep Sok, Goztepe
Telephone: (212) 356-5922
Every day.

Etz Ahayim Synagogue
Muallim Naci Cad No 40 & 41, Ortakoy
Telephone: (212) 260-1896
Every day.

Hemdat Israel Synagogue
Izettin Sok No 65, Kadikoy
Telephone: (212) 336-5293
Every day.

Hesed Leavraam Synagogue
Pancur Sok No 15, Buyukada
Telephone: (212) 382-5788
June-September including High Holy days.

Italian Synagogue
Sair Ziya Pasa Yokusu No 27, Karakoy, Galata
Telephone: (212) 293-7784

Neve Shalom Buyuk Hendek Sok
No 61, Galata
Telephone: (212) 293-7566
Saturdays only.

IZMIR

BUTCHERS
Kosher Meat
Telephone: (232) 148-395
Tuesday and Thursday. Enquire at the synagogue.

COMMUNITY ORGANISATIONS
Jewish Community Council
Azizler Sokak 920/44, Guzelyurt
Telephone: (232) 421-12-90
Fax: (232) 463-52-25
Email: isakalaluf@superonline.com.tr

SYNAGOGUES
Beth Israel
265 Mithatpasa Street, Karatas, Kanamursil District

Shaar Ashamayan
1390 Sokak 4/2, Bikur Holim

UKRAINE

The Ukraine has had a long and compli-
cated history, with areas of the present
country being under the rule of a number
of other countries, from Austria to Romania.
The history of the Jews who live in the
modern-day, independent Ukraine is both
long and tragic. From settlement in Kiev in
the tenth century, before the concept of a
Ukrainian national identity had been
formed, the Jewish community grew and
was joined by many Jews from central
Europe. The Chmielnicki massacre of 1648,
in which up to 100,000 were killed, was the
worst event to befall the Jews before the
Holocaust, and much destruction occurred
in the west of the country.

Throughout the nineteenth century, the
Ukraine was mainly under Russian domination. After 1918, the Ukraine attempted to
become independent, and many Jews were
killed in the fighting. The Ukraine absorbed
some of south-eastern Poland in 1939 and,
after the German invasion of the Soviet
Union, the Jewish community suffered ter-
rible losses in the Holocaust.

The community today remains fairly large,
and is slowly emerging from the atheist
Soviet times. Most Jews live in towns, and
Kiev (the capital) is a major centre. There
are now Jewish schools, and kosher food
can be obtained. In a similar way to Belarus,
there are many interesting places to visit
graves of famous Hassidic masters and the
monument to the Babi Yar massacre (near
Kiev) are frequent destinations. There have
been memorials erected (mainly after the
fall of Communism) all over the country to
events which happened during the
Holocaust.

GMT +2 hours
Country calling code: **(+380)**
Total population: **58,800,000**
Jewish population: **180,000**
Emergency telephone: **(Police – 02) (Fire – 01)**
(Ambulance – 03)
Electricity voltage: **(Electricity voltage – 220)**

BERDICHEV

MIKVAOT
4 Dzherzhinskaya Street
Telephone: (4143) 23938 / 20222

SYNAGOGUES
4 Dzherzhinskaya Street
Telephone: (4143) 23938 / 20222
Kosher kitchen on premises.

BEREGOVO

SYNAGOGUES
17 Sverdlov Street

BERSHAD

SYNAGOGUES
25 Narodnaya Street

CHERNIGOV

SYNAGOGUES
34 Kommunisticheskaya Street

CHERNOVTSY

SYNAGOGUES
24 Lukyana Kobylitsa Street
Telephone: 54878

CHMELNITSY

SYNAGOGUES
58 Komminnestnaya Street

DNEPROPETROVSK

SYNAGOGUES
Synagogue of Dnepropetrovsk
7 Kotsubinskovo St. 320030
Telephone: (56) 342-120
Fax: (56) 342-137
Email: dnepr@jewcom.dp.ua
Web site: www.jew.dp.ua

DONETSK

SYNAGOGUES
Synagogue of Donetsk
Oktiabrskaya str.36 83086
Telephone: (62) 062-345-0052
Fax: (62) 062-335-7725
Email: office@jewish-com.dn.ua

IVANO-FRANKIVSK

SYNAGOGUES
Synagogue of Ivano-Frankivsk
Strachenyh 7 284000
Telephone: (34) 22- 23029
Fax: (34) 325-367
Rabbi Rolesnik (22-34894) is prepared to assist those
doing historical or genealogical research in the Western
Ukraine (Galicia).

KHARKOV

SYNAGOGUES
48 Kryatkovskaya Street
Web site: www.kharkovejewish.com
Orthodox Union Project Reunite
Surnskaya 45
Telephone: (572) 408-378
Fax: (572) 439-209

Synagogue of Kharkov
12 Pushkinskaya Street 310057
Telephone: (572) 126-526
Fax: (572) 452-140
Email: chabad@kharkov.com

KHERSON

SYNAGOGUES
Synagogue of Kherson
27 Gorkovo Street 325025
Telephone: (552) 223-334
Fax: (552) 325-367

KIEV

Kiev's central position as a crossroad of Western
Europe and central Asia attracted Jewish settlers
as early as the eighth century. The unfortunate
usual cycle of persecution and resettlement then
began.

In 1911 Kiev was the location of a modern blood
libel case "the Beilis affair".

CENTRAL ORGANISATIONS
Vaad
6 Kurskaya Street
Telephone: (44) 276-1214

EMBASSY
Embassy of Israel
Lesi Ukrainki 34, GPE-S 252195

SYNAGOGUES
Orthodox
Podil Synagogue
29 Shcekovytska Street
Telephone: (44) 416-2442
The Central Synagogue
13 Shota Rustavely
Telephone: (44) 225-0246
Originally built in 1897 the synagogues was, under
Soviet rule, converted into a puppet theatre. Today, it is
both a puppet theatre and a synagogue.

Reform
Reform Congregation
7 Nemanskaya Street
Telephone: (44) 296-3961
Fax: (44) 295-9604

TOURIST SITES
Babi Yar Monument
Melnikova Street
The monument in the form of a menorah was erected in 1991, fifty years after the two days on which 33,371 Jews were murdered by the Nazis.

Sholom Aleichem Statue
Near Basseynye Street
Shalom Aleichem (Shalom Rabinovitz) was born in 1859 in Pereyaslav, near Kiev.

KOROSTEN
SYNAGOGUES
8 Shchoksa Street

KREMENCHUG
SYNAGOGUES
50 Sverdlov Street

LVIV
Situated on the edge of shifting imperial boundaries, this city has been under Austrian, Polish and Soviet control. It has had as many names as its number of rulers among them LwÛw in Polish and Lemberg in German. Now called Lviv in Ukrainian, there are 6,000 Jews in the city, once a major Jewish centre in Galicia. A couple of synagogues are still functioning, and a number of monuments have been erected commemorating the Holocaust. Many Jews on ëheritage toursí use the town as a base to explore the region, and guides (generally Yiddish-speaking) are available.

SYNAGOGUES
Beis A'aron V'Yisroel
4 Brativ Michnovskich Street 79018
Telephone: (322) 333-535
Email: bald@link.lviv.ua
Restaurant orders must be placed in advance. Tourist information.

NIKOLAYEV
SYNAGOGUES
Synagogue of Nikolayev
13 Karl Libknechta Street 327001
Telephone: (512) 358-310
Fax: (512) 353-072

ODESSA
SYNAGOGUES
Chabad
21 Osipovo St. 270011
Telephone: (482) 218-890
Fax: (482) 496-301

Main Synagogue
25 Evreyskaya Street
Telephone: (482) 243-694
Fax: (482) 347-850

SIMFEROPOL
JEWISH CENTRE
Mironova 24, Crimea 95001
Telephone: (52) 510-773
Email: chabadcrimea@cris.crimea.ua

SYNAGOGUES
Orthodox
Krasna Znamyonaya 78
Telephone: (52) 510-773
Fax: (52) 510-773
Also has a mikvah. Information on kosher matters is available from the main office.

SLAVUTA
SYNAGOGUES
Kuzovskaya Street 2
Telephone: (447) 925-452
The first edition of Tanya was printed here by the Shapira family whose tombs are in the cemetery.

UMAN
Each year followers of the Breslau Chassidic sect visit the grave of Rabbi Lachman of Breslau, its founder for Rosh Hashana. In 2000 there were a reported 13,000 visitors.

There are no other specific locations of interest to travellers.

ZAPAROZHE
SYNAGOGUES
Synagogue of Zaparozhe
22 Turgeneva Street. 330063
Telephone: (612) 642-961

ZHITOMIR
SYNAGOGUES
Synagogue
59 Lubarskaya Street
Telephone: (412) 373-468
Reb Ze'ev Wolf, disciple of Dov Baer, is buried in the Smolanka cemetery.

Synagogue of Zhitomire
7 Malaya. Berdishevskaya St. 262001
Telephone: (412) 226-608
Fax: (412) 373-428

UNITED KINGDOM

There were probably individual Jews in England in Roman and (though less likely) in Anglo-Saxon times, but the historical records of any organised settlement start after the Normal Conquest of 1066. Jewish immigrants arrived early in the reign of William the Conqueror and important settlements came to be established in London (at a site still known as Old Jewry), Lincoln and many other centres. In 1190 massacres of Jews occured in many cities, most notably in York. This medieval settlement was ended by Edward I's expulsion of the Jews in 1290, after which date, with rare and temporary exceptions, only converts to Christianity or secret adherents of Judaism could live in the country.

After the expulsion of the Jews from Spain in 1492, a secret Converso community became established in London, but the present Anglo-Jewish community dates in practice from the period of the Commonwealth. In 1650 Menasseh ben Israel, of Amsterdam, began to champion the cause of Jewish re-admission to England, and in 1655 he led a mission to London for this purpose. A conference was convened at Whitehall and a petition was presented to Oliver Cromwell. Though no formal decision was then recorded, in 1656 the Spanish and Portuguese Congregation in London was organised. It was followed towards the end of the seventeenth century by the establishment of an Ashkenazi community, which increased rapidly inside London as well as throwing out offshoots before long to a number of provincial centres and seaports. The London community, however, has always comprised the largest section of Anglo-Jewry.

Although Jews in Britain had achieved a virtual economic and social emancipation by the early nineteenth century, they had not yet gained 'political emancipation'. Minor Jewish disabilities were progressively removed and Jews were admitted to municipal rights and began to win distinction in the professions.

During the 19th century British Jews diversified from those callings which had hitherto been regarded as characteristic of the Jews.

There has always been a steady stream of immigration into Britain from Jewish communities in Europe, originally from the Iberian Peninsula and northern Italy, later from western and central Europe. The community was radically transformed by the large influx of refugees which occured between 1881 and 1914, the result of the intensified persecution of Jews in the Russian Empire. The Jewish population rose from about 25,000 in the middle of the nineteenth century to nearly 350,000 by 1914. It also became far more dispersed geographically.

From 1933 a new emigration of Jews commenced, this time from Nazi persecution, and again many settled in this country. Since the end of the Second World War and notably since 1956, smaller numbers of refugees have come from Iran, Arab countries and eastern Europe.

Counties are currently being restructured into Counties and Unitary Authorities. The new designations are not yet in common use and for this year the 'old' County names and areas have been retained.

GMT
Country calling code: (**+44**)
Emergency telephone: (**Police – 999**) (**Fire – 999**) (**Ambulance – 999**)
Electricity voltage: (**Electricity voltage – 240**)

Avon

BRISTOL

Bristol was one of the principal Jewish centres of medieval England. Even after the Expulsion from England in 1290 there were occasional Jewish residents or visitors. A community of Conversos lived here during the Tudor period. The next Jewish settlement in Bristol was around 1754 and its original synagogue opened in 1786. The present building dates from 1871 and incorporates fittings from the earlier building.

DELICATESSEN
British Hebrew Congregation
Telephone: (0117) 970-6938
Open alternate Sundays at 10 am.

ORGANISATIONS
Hillel House
45 Oakfield Road, Clifton BS8 2BA
Telephone: (0117) 946-6589

RESTAURANTS
Vegetarian
Cherries
122 St Michaels Hill, BS2 8BU
Telephone: (0117) 929-3675

Millwards Vegetarian Restaurant
40 Alfred Place, Kingsdown BS2 8HD
Telephone: (0117) 924-5026

SYNAGOGUES
Bristol Hebrew Congregation
9 Park Row BS1 5LP
Telephone: (0117) 927-3334
Email: simon770@aol.com
Services: Friday night at 183 Bishop Road BS7. Summer 7.45 pm, Winter 7 pm. Saturday at synagogue 9.45 am

Progressive
Bristol & West Progressive Jewish Congregation
43 Bannerman Road, Easton BS5 0RR
Telephone: (0117) 954-1937
Email: webmaster@bwpjc.org
Web site: www.bwpjc.org
Secretary: 973-8744

Bedfordshire
LUTON
SYNAGOGUES
PO Box 215 LU1 1HW
Telephone: (01582) 25032
Friday night and Sabbath morning. services. Office open 9.30am to 12.30pm on Sundays.

Berkshire
MAIDENHEAD
SYNAGOGUES
Reform
Synagogue
Grenfell Lodge, Ray Park Road SL6 8QX
Telephone: (01628) 673012
Fax: (01628) 625536
Email: mheadsyn@aol.com
Services: Friday 8.30pm; Saturday 10.30am

READING
SYNAGOGUES
Orthodox
Goldsmid Road RG1 7YB
Telephone: (0118) 9571018
Email: secretary@rhc.org.uk
Web site: www.rhc.org.uk

Progressive
Thames Valley Progressive Jewish Community
6 Church Street
Telephone: (0118) 781971

Buckinghamshire
MILTON KEYNES
BUTCHERS
Gilbert's Kosher Foods
Kestrel House, Mount Avenue MK1 1LJ
Telephone: (01908) 646-787
Fax: (01908) 646-788
Supervision: London Board of Shechita

Cambridgeshire
CAMBRIDGE
COMMUNITY ORGANISATIONS
Cambridge University Jewish Society
33 Thompson's Lane CB5 8AQ
Telephone: (01223) 354783
Email: soc-cujs@lists.cam.ac.uk
Web site: www.cam.ac.uk/societies/cujs

Chabad Centre
19 Regent Terrace CB2 1AA
Telephone: (01223) 565388
Email: cambridge@lubavitchuk.com
Supervision: Rabbi Reuven and Rochel Leigh

The Cambridge University CUlanu Centre
33 Bridge Street CB2 1UW
Telephone: (01223) 366-338
Fax: (01223) 366-338
Email: dansilverstein@hotmail.com
The CUlanu Centre organises, with the Cambridge University Jewish Society a programme of education events, debates and socials. There are regular Friday night meals.

GROCERIES
Telephone: (01223) 352145
There is a kosher canteen during term time serving lunch most weekdays and Friday night and Shabbat meals.

KOSHER FOOD
Derby Stores
Derby Street
Telephone: (01223) 354391
Stocks a range of kosher food and wine; fresh bread products each Thursday lunchtime. Can purchase goods to order.

SYNAGOGUES
Orthodox
Cambridge Synagogue
Syn/Student Centre, 3 Thompsons Lane CB5 8AQ
Telephone: (01223) 354783 or 368346 answer phone
Email: ctjcorguk@aol.com
Web site: www.ctjc.org.uk
Daily morning and evening service during term time. Friday evening and Saturday morning during vacations, other services by arrangement.

Reform
Beth Shalom Reform Synagogue
Telephone: (01223) 365614

Cornwall
TRURO
SYNAGOGUES
Reform
Kehillat kernow
Telephone: (01209) 719672
Contact: Owl Cottage, 11 Mill Road, Penponds TR14 0QH

Cumbria
GRASMERE
HOTELS
Vegetarian
Lancrigg Vegetarian Country House Hotel
Easedale LA22 9QN
Telephone: (01539) 435317

Devon
EXETER
In pre-Expulsion times, Exeter was an important Jewish centre. Jews were first mentioned in 1181, After the resettlement a community was again established in 1728.

SYNAGOGUES
Hebrew Congregation
Synagogue Place, Mary Arches Street EX4 3BA
Telephone: (01392) 251529
Fax: (01392) 772338
Email: fjg@exetersynagogue.org.uk
Web site: www.exetersynagogue.org.uk
The synagogue was built in 1763, and the cemetery in Magdalen Road dates from 1757. The synagogue, a Grade II* listed building, has just had a major refurbishment.

PLYMOUTH
The congregation was founded in 1752 and a synagogue erected ten years later. This is now the oldest Ashkenazi synagogue building in England still used for its original purpose. It is a scheduled historical monument. In 1815 Plymouth was one of the most important provincial centres of Anglo-Jewry.

LIBRARIES
Holcenberg Collection
Plymouth Central Library, Drake Circus PL4 8AL
Telephone: (01752) 305907/8
Fax: (01752) 305905
Email: ref@plymouth.gov.uk
Web site: www.plymouthlibraries.info
A Jewish collection of fiction and non-fiction books, mainly lending copies.

RESTAURANTS
Vegetarian
Plymouth Arts Centre Vegetarian Restaurant
38 Looe Street PL4 0EB
Telephone: (01752) 202-616
Fax: (01752) 206-118
Email: arts@plymouthac.org.uk
Hours: lunch, Monday to Saturday, 12 noon to 2 pm; dinner, Tuesday to Saturday, 5 pm to 8.30 pm. Light refreshments served from 10 am.

SYNAGOGUES
Orthodox
Plymouth Hebrew Congregation
Catherine Street PL1 2AD
Telephone: (01752) 301955
Email: info@plymouthsynagogue.co.uk
Services: Fri., 6pm; Sat., 9:30am. The congregation offers free use of minister's modern flat as holiday accommodation in return for conducting Orthodox Friday evening and Saturday morning services.

TORQUAY

SYNAGOGUES
Old Town Hall, Abbey Road TQ1 1BB
Telephone: (01803) 607197
Covering also Brixham and Paignton. Services first
Sabbath of every month and festivals, 10.30am.

Dorset

BOURNEMOUTH
The Bournemouth Hebrew Congregation was
established in 1905, when the Jewish population
numbered fewer than 20 families. Today, the
town's permanent Jewish residents number
3,500 out of a total population of some 15,000.
During the holiday season, however, there are
many more Jews in Bournemouth, for it is an
extremely popular resort, with kosher hotels,
guest houses and other holiday accommodation.

COMMUNITY ORGANISATIONS
Bournemouth Jewish Representative Council
Telephone: (01202) 762101

DELICATESSEN
Louise's Butchers & Deli
164 Old Christchurch Road BH1 1NU
Telephone: (01202) 295-979
Fax: (01202) 295-979

HOTELS
Kosher
New Ambassador Hotel
Meyrick Road, East Cliff BH1 3DP
Telephone: (01202) 555-453
Fax: (01202) 311-077
Email: sales@newamb.co.uk
Web site: www.newamb.com
Supervision: London Beth Din
112 rooms, all with bathroom en suite.

Normandie Hotel
Manor Road, East Cliff BH1 3HL
Telephone: (01202) Reservation phone no: 01202-
291770
Fax: (01202) 291-178
Email: normandiehotel@aol.co.uk
Web site: www.thenormandiehotel.co.uk
Supervision: Kedassia
71 rooms.

MIKVAOT
Bournemouth Hebrew Congregation
Synagogue Chambers, Wootton Gardens BH1 1PW
Telephone: (01202) 557-443

SYNAGOGUES
Orthodox
Synagogue Chambers, Wootton Gardens BH1 1PW
Telephone: (01202) 557-433
Fax: (01202) 557-578
Email: bhc.1@virgin.net

Reform
Bournemouth Reform Synagogue
53 Christchurch Road BH1 3PN
Telephone: (01202) 01202-557736
Email: synagogue@btinternet.com

Essex

CHIGWELL
SYNAGOGUES
Orthodox
Limes Avenue, Limes Farm Estate IG7 5NT
Telephone: (0208) 8500-2451
Email: chshul@btinternet.com

COLCHESTER
SYNAGOGUES
Independent
Colchester and District Jewish Community Synagogue
Fennings Chase, Priory Street CO1 2QG
Telephone: (01206) 545-992
Email: tanenb@essex.ac.uk
Services every Friday at 8pm, on the High Holydays and most festivals.

HARLOW
SYNAGOGUES
Reform
Harlow Jewish Community
Harberts Road CM20 4DT
Telephone: (01279) 432503

LOUGHTON
SYNAGOGUES
Orthodox
Loughton Synagogue
Borders Lane IG10 1TE
Telephone: (020) 8508-0303
Email: loughtonsynagogue@lineone.net
Friday evening. 7.00pm; Saturday morning 9.00am

REDBRIDGE
BAKERIES
Golan Bakery
388 Cranbrook Road, Ilford
Telephone: (020) 8554-8202
Supervision: London Beth Din

BUTCHERS
N. Goldberg
12 Claybury Broadway, Redbridge IG
Telephone: (020) 8551-2828
Supervision: London Board for Shechita

DELICATESSEN
Deli on the Lane
13 Beehive Lane, Redbridge
Telephone: (020) 8554-5008
Supervision: Beth Din of the Federation of Synagogues

GROCERIES
Brownstein's
24a Woodford Avenue, Gants Hill
Telephone: (020) 8550-3900
Email: deli@brownsteins.co.uk
Web site: www.brownsteins.co.uk
Supervision: London Beth Din

MIKVAOT
Ilford Mikvah Federation of Synagogues
463 Cranbrook Road, Ilford IG
Telephone: (020) 8554-2551 (Evenings: 8554-8532).
Correspondence to 367 Cranbrook Road, Ilford.

SOUTHEND-ON-SEA
Jews began settling in the area in the late 19th century, mainly from the East End of London. The first temporary synagogue was built in 1906. The Jewish population is 4,500.

BOOKSELLERS
Dorothy Young
21 Colchester Road SS2 6HW
Telephone: (01702) 331218
Email: dorothy@dorothyyoung.co.uk
Web site: www.dorothyyoung.co.uk
Religious articles, Israeli giftware, etc., also stocked. Jewish software ordered. Call for appointment.

COMMUNITY ORGANISATIONS
Southend & District Representative Council
Telephone: (01702) 343192

SYNAGOGUES
Southend and Westcliff Hebrew Congregation
Finchley Road SSO 8AD
Telephone: (01702) 344900
Fax: (01702) 391131
Email: swhc@btclick.com
Web site: www.swhc.org.uk

Southend Reform Synagogue
851 London Road, Westcliff SSO
Telephone: (01702) 75809

WESTCLIFF ON SEA
HOTELS
The Riverside Hotel
4 Cobham Road SSO 8EA
Telephone: (01702) 346885

Gloucestershire
CHELTENHAM
The congregation was established in 1824 and the present synagogue opened in 1839. However, after two generations, the congregation declined and the synagogue was closed in 1903. At the outbreak of the Second World War, the synagogue was re-opened following the influx of Jewish newcomers to the town.

RESTAURANTS
Vegetarian
The Orange Tree
317 High Street GL50 3HW
Telephone: (01242) 234232
Fax: (01242) 234232
Email: shaipateluk@yahoo.co.uk
Strictly vegan & vegetarian cuisine. Fully licensed with selection of organic wines & beers.

SYNAGOGUES
Cheltenham Hebrew Congregation
St James Square GL50 5PU
Telephone: (01242) 578893
Fax: (01242) 578893
Services every Friday at 7.00pm and High Holydays as advised.

Hampshire
ALDERSHOT
CONTACT INFORMATION
Jewish Committee for H.M. Forces
25 Enford Street W1H 2DD
Telephone: (01252) 724-7778
Fax: (01252) 706-1710
Email: jmcouncil@btinternet.com
Web site: www.jmcouncil.org
Inquiries to Senior Jewish Chaplain.

PORTSMOUTH & SOUTHSEA
The Portsmouth community was founded in 1746. Its first synagogue was in Oyster Row, but the congregation moved to a building in White's Row which it continued to occupy for almost two centuries. A new building was erected in 1936. The cemetery is in a street which was once known as Jews' Lane.

SYNAGOGUES
Synagogue Chambers
The Thicket, Southsea PO5 2AA
Telephone: (023) 9282 1494

SOUTHAMPTON

LIBRARIES
Hartley Library
University of Southampton SO17 1BJ
Telephone: (023) 592721
Fax: (023) 593007
Email: archives@soton.ac.uk
Houses both the Parkes Library and the Anglo-Jewish Archives.

SYNAGOGUES
Moordaunt Road, The Inner Avenue SO2 0GP
Services Sat. morn 10am

Hertfordshire

BUSHEY

BUTCHERS
J.D Glass & Co
100 High Road, Bushey Heath, Bushey WD2 3JE
Telephone: (020) 8420-4443
Supervision: London Board for Shechita

SYNAGOGUES
Orthodox
Bushey and District
177 Sparrows Herne WD23 1AJ
Telephone: (020) 8950-7340
Fax: (020) 8421-8267
Email: administrator@busheyus.org

HEMEL HEMPSTEAD

SYNAGOGUES
Morton House
Midland Road HD1 1RP
Telephone: (01923) 232007

SAWBRIDGEWORTH

BANQUETING SUITE
Manor of Groves
High Wych CM21 0JU
Telephone: (01279) 600777
Fax: (01279) 600374
Email: info@manorofgroves.co.uk
Web site: www.manorofgroves.com

ST ALBANS

SYNAGOGUES
Masorti
St Albans Masorti Synagogue
PO Box 23 AL1 4PH
Telephone: (01727) 860642
Email: info@e-sams.org
Web site: www.e-sams.org

Orthodox
Oswald Road AL1 3AQ
Telephone: (01727) 825925

WATFORD

SYNAGOGUES
Orthodox
16 Nascot Road WD17 3RE
Telephone: (01923) 222755
Fax: (01923) 222755
Email: wadshul@btopenworld.com
Covers also Abbots Langley, Carpenters Park, Croxley Garden, Garston, Kings Langley and Rickmansworth.

WELWYN GARDEN CITY

SYNAGOGUES
Orthodox
Barn Close, Handside Lane AL8 6ST
Telephone: (01707) 890575
Email:
doraprag@aol.com/gunter.tuch@ntlworld.com

Humberside

GRIMSBY

SYNAGOGUES
Orthodox
Sir Moses Montefiore Synagogue
Heneage Road DN32 9DZ
Telephone: (01472) 351-404
Services every Friday 7:00pm and all major festivals.

HULL

In Hull, as in other English port towns, a Jewish community was formed earlier than in inland areas. The exact date is unknown, but it is thought to be the early 1700s. There were enough Jews in Hull to buy a former Roman Catholic chapel, damaged in the Gordon Riots of 1780, and turn it into a synagogue. Hull was then the principal port of entry from northern Europe, and most Jewish immigrants came through it. Both the Old Hebrew Synagogue in Osborne Street and the Central Synagogue in Cogan Street were destroyed in air raids during the Second World War.

MUSEUMS
Hull Synagogue Museum
Linneaus Street HU3 2PD
Telephone: (01482) 217153
Fax: (01482) 216565
Email: info@jcsc.info
Correspondence to: Old Synagogue, Linnaeus Street, HU3 2PD.

Perfect for any occasion

A splendid Georgian Manor House set within 160 acres of beautiful Hertfordshire countryside – perfect for any occasion. Sample the beauty of the glass conservatory Manor Suite overlooking the oriental gardens.

We can supply our magnificent facilities for your own Kosher caterers to host the perfect event. Stay with your guests in our newly refurbished bedrooms on our special stop-over rate.

Our experienced Duty Manager will be on hand during the event, to liaise with both host and caterers, leaving you to enjoy your day from beginning to end.

 MANOR *of* GROVES

Hotel, Golf & Country Club

For full details contact our Wedding Co-ordinator
on **01279 600777**

SYNAGOGUES
Orthodox
Hull Hebrew Congregation
30 Pryme Street, Anlaby HU10 6SH
Telephone: (01482) 653242

Reform
Reform Synagogue
Great Gutter Lane, West Willerby HU10 7JT
Telephone: (01482) 658312
Fax: (01482) 342836
Email: iansugarman@isa.karoo.co.uk

Kent
CANTERBURY
TOURIST SITES
The Old Synagogue
King Street CT
The Old Synagogue, an Egyptian-style building of 1847, stands in King Street and is now used by the Kings School for recitals.

MARGATE
SYNAGOGUES
Godwin Road, Cliftonville CT9 2HA
Telephone: (01843) 223219

RAMSGATE
SYNAGOGUES
Montefiore Endowment
Hereson Road

Montefiore Mausoleum & Synagogue
33 Luton Avenue, Broadstairs
Telephone: (01843) 862507

ROCHESTER
SYNAGOGUES
Magnus Memorial Synagogue
366 High Street ME1 1DJ
Telephone: (01634) 847665
Grade 2, listed building known as The Chatham Memorial Synagogue.

Lancashire
BLACKPOOL
DELICATESSEN
The Deli
6 Station Road, Lytham St Annes
Telephone: (01253) 735861

SYNAGOGUES
Orthodox
United Hebrew Congregation
Synagogue Chambers, Leamington Road FY1 4HD
Telephone: (01253) 28164

Reform
Reform Jewish Congregation
40 Raikes Parade FY1 4EX
Telephone: (01253) 623-687

LANCASTER
BED AND BREAKFAST
Lancaster University Jewish Society
Interfaith Chaplaincy Centre, University of Lancaster, Bailrigg Lane LA1 4YW
Telephone: (01524) 594075
Jewish rooms and kosher kitchen. Contact Rev Malcolm Wiseman.

ST ANNES ON SEA
SYNAGOGUES
Orthodox
Orchard Road FY8 1PJ
Telephone: 721831
Services 7.30am and 8pm

Leicestershire
LEICESTER
There has been a Jewish presence here since the Middle Ages, but the first record of a 'Jews' Synagogue' dates from 1861 in the Leicester Directory. In 2001 the Leicester City Council finally renounced a ban on Jews living in the city which was originally imposed in 1731.

LIBRARIES
Jewish Library and Bookshop
Community Hall, Highfield Street LE2 0NQ
Telephone: (0116) 212-8920

MIKVAOT
Synagogue Building, P.O.Box 6836 LE2 1WZ
Telephone: (0116) 270-6672
Fax: (0116) 270-8796
Email: stanley.lidiker@btopenworld.com
Mailing address: PO Box 6836, Leicester, LE2 1WZ

RESTAURANTS
Vegetarian
The Good Earth
19 Free Lane LE1 1JX
Telephone: (0116) 262-6260

SYNAGOGUES
Progressive Jewish Congregation
24 Avenue Road
Telephone: (0116) 271-5584
Fax: (0116) 271-7571
Email: jeffrey@kaufmans.co.uk

Orthodox
Synagogue
Highfield Street LE2 1WZ
Telephone: (0116) 254-0477
Mikvah on premises. Mailing address: PO Box 6836, Leicester, LE2 1WZ

Lincolnshire
LINCOLN
Lincoln was one of the centres of medieval Jewry. One of England's oldest stone houses in the city is known as Aaron the Jew's House. The site of Old synagogue is remembered now at Jews' Court. In the cathedral is a recent token of ecclesiastical apology for the 13th-century incident of the "blood libel", retold in Chaucer. Jews returned to the area in the 19th century. The current community is of very recent date.

COMMUNITY ORGANISATIONS
Lincolnshire Jewish Community
3 West End Road, Ulceby
Telephone: (01469) 588951

TOURIST SITES
Aaron the Jew's house
47 Steep Hill
Believed to be the home of Aaron of Lincoln (c1123-1186) the most prominent Anglo-Jewish financier of the time. A Grade I listed building.

Jews' Court
2 Steep Hill
Site of the pre-expulsion synagogue. A Grade I listed building.

London
LONDON
Jews came to London with the Normans following their conquest of the country in 1066. A Jewish area in London is first mentioned in 1128; it was known as 'the Jewish quarter' and was situated around Old Jewry, a street in the City of London close to the Bank of England. Nearby to the west is the church of St Lawrence of Jewry and about one mile to the east is Jewry Street. The community expanded and until 1177 had the only Jewish cemetery in the country. Although there is now no evidence of early Jewish life, the remains of a mikveh were found in October 2001 in Milk Street, close to Old

Jewry. It is one of the earliest pieces of physical evidence of Jews in Europe and is the only identifiable structure that has survived from the then Jewish community. It is intended that it be dismantled and moved to the Bevis Marks synagogue.

The community flourished as arrivals, including a number of scholars, came into the country. In 1194 it contributed a large sum towards the levy raised to ransom Richard I.

In due course, anti-Jewish feeling developed and Jews were expelled from the whole country in 1290. At that time the population was estimated to be around 500.

Until the resettlement the only Jews in London, apart from the converts to Christianity who lived in the Domus Conversorum, a home established for that purpose in New Street, now Chancery Lane, were rare occasional visitors. After the expulsion from Spain in 1492, however, services were held in the city in secret by groups of crypto-Jews.

In December 1656, with resettlement, the approximately 20 families then living in the country established a synagogue in Creechurch Lane (a plaque now commemorates this just under one mile east of the original settlement), and in the following year a cemetery was acquired.

Following the accession of William of Orange to the throne, the number of Spanish and Portuguese Jews arriving from Holland increased. Included among these were merchants and brokers. As a result, in 1697 'Jew Brokers' were allowed to trade on the Royal Exchange. In due course, Ashkenazi settlers arrived, establishing their own community in 1690.

During the 19th century both communities expanded. In 1835 David Salomons (1797-1873) was elected a sheriff of the city. In 1847 he became the first Jewish alderman and in 1855 the first Jewish lord mayor of the City of London. In 1851 he had been elected a member of parliament but was unable to take his seat as he refused to take the oath of allegiance 'on the true faith of a Christian'. After the oath was amended in 1858, he sat as a member from 1859 until his death. The first Jew to take his seat, however, was Lionel de Rothschild, some months earlier in 1858.

From the 1880s until controls on immigration were established by the 1905 Aliens Act, around 100,000, generally poor, Jews arrived from Russia, Poland and other eastern European countries both to avoid pogroms and as 'economic migrants'.

A Reform community was established in 1840. Jews College (now London School of Jewish

Studies) was established in 1855 and the Board of Guardins for the Relief of the Jewish Poor in 1859.

Jewish London is split into a number of areas. Central, the East End and the city, the traditional home of immigrants into England; North London, which contains Stamford Hill, the most Orthodox area; and the North-West where the majority of London Jews now live. The remaining parts of London, the South and the East, have communities but offer little interest to a visitor.

Central London
The Hebrew section of the British Library, situated in Euston, has a large collection of interest to all Jewish visitors to the city. There is a Holocaust Memorial Garden in Hyde Park in the centre of London.

The East End and the City
There is little remaining of Jewish life apart from the historical Jewish sites. Of particular interest is Bevis Marks Synagogue, which was built in 1701 and is almost a duplicate of the Spanish and Portuguese Great Synagogue in Amsterdam. It is the oldest synagogue in the country (some of the oak benches come from the original synagogue in Creechurch Lane). It is still almost exactly the same now as it was 300 years ago, even still being lit by candles. Also worth a visit is the Spitalfields Heritage Centre, devoted to the history of immigration into the country. It is on the site of Princelet Street synagogue, which itself was originally a Huguenot family house.

North London
Stamford Hill is the centre of London Jewish hassidic life. It is full of shteibels and small Jewish shops. also in Stamford Hill is the Jewish Military Museum. Nearby in Camden Town is the Ben Uri Art Gallery and the Jewish Museum dealing with Jews in Britain and throughout the world. The Jewish Museum further north in Finchley covers the social history of London Jewry itself. It is in the grounds of the Sternberg Centre for Judaism, which also includes Leo Baeck College.

North-West
Apart from two restaurants in the West End of London, this is the place to go if one wishes to eat kosher. The area around Golders Green and Edgware abounds in restaurants of varying cuisine and quality. There is also an abundance of many Jewish shops of many kinds.

South London
Visitors to London should endeavour to go to the Holocaust Exhibition at the Imperial War Museum in Lambeth. In addition to the exhibition itself, the Imperial War Museum has much of interest.

Currently, around three-quarters of the approximate 300,000 Jews living in Britain live in London.

BAKERIES

Carmelli Bakeries Ltd
126-128 Golders Green Road, Golders Green NW11
Telephone: (020) 8455-2074
Fax: (020) 8455-2789
Email: orders@carmelli.co.uk
Web site: www.carmelli.co.uk
Supervision: London Beth Din, Kedassia

Crème de la Crème
5 Temple Fortune Parade, Bridge Lane NW11 1QN
Telephone: (020) 8458-9090
Supervision: Kedassia

Daniel's Bagel Bakery
12-13 Hallswelle Parade, Finchley Road, Golders Green NW11 0DL
Telephone: (020) 8455-5826
Fax: (020) 8455-5826
Supervision: London Beth Din

David Bagel Bakery
38 Vivian Avenue, Hendon NW4 3XP
Telephone: (020) 8203-9995
Supervision: London Beth Din, Kedassia

Dinos Bakeries
11 Edgwarebury Lane, Edgware HA8 8LH
Telephone: (020) 8958-1554
Fax: (020) 8958-2554
Supervision: London Beth Din, Kedassia
106 Brent Street, Hendon NW4 2HH
Telephone: (020) 8203-6623
Supervision: London Beth Din, Kedassia

Hendon Bagel Bakery
55-57 Church Road, Hendon NW4
Telephone: (020) 8203-6919
Fax: (020) 8203-8843
Supervision: Kedassia

J.Grodzinski & Daughters
9 Northways Parade NW3 5EN
Telephone: (020) 7722-4944
Email: grodzinskibakers@aol.com
Supervision: Kedassia and London Beth Din

M & D Grodzinski
223 Golders Green Road, Golders Green NW119ES
Telephone: (020) 8458-3654
Fax: (020) 8905-5382
Supervision: London Beth Din & Kedassia

Parkway Patisserie Ltd.
30a North End Road, Golders Green NW11
Telephone: (020) 8455-5026
Supervision: London Beth Din, Kedassia
204 Preston Road, Wembley HA9
Telephone: (020) 8904-7736
Supervision: London Beth Din, Kedassia

Parkway Patisseries Ltd.
326-328 Regents Park Road, Finchley N3
Telephone: (020) 8346-0344
Supervision: London Beth Din, Kedassia

The Cake Company
2 Sentinel Square, Hendon NW4 2EL
Telephone: (020) 8202-2327
Fax: (020) 202-8058
Email: cakes@thecakecompany.co.uk
Web site: www.thecakecompany.co.uk
Supervision: London Beth Din, Kedassia

Woodberry Down Bakery
47 Brent Street, Hendon NW4
Telephone: (020) 8202-9962
Supervision: London Beth Din, Kedassia

BED AND BREAKFAST
Harold Godfrey Hillel House
25 Louisa Street, Stepney E1 4NF
Telephone: (020) 7790-9557
Summer accommodation in London. Twenty-three rooms, self-catering separate meat and milk kitchens. Very close to Stepney Green tube station with easy access to all London attractions. Please contact the warden at the above address for more information or to book a room.

Orthodox
Kacenberg's Guest House
1 Alba Gardens, Near Alba Court, Golders Green NW11 9NS
Telephone: (020) 8455-3780
Fax: (020) 8381-4250
Shabbat meals available. "Strictly Orthodox".

BOOKSELLERS
Boreham Wood Judaica
11 Croxdale Road, Boreham Wood WD6 4QD
Telephone: (020) 8381-5559

Carmel Gifts
62 Edgware Way, Middx
Telephone: (020) 8958-7632
Fax: (020) 8958-6226
Email: info@carmelgifts.co.uk
Web site: www.carmelgifts.co.uk

ירושלים של זהב

Jerusalem The Golden
World of Judaica

THOUSANDS OF BOOKS and ספרים

Judaica and religious requisites for the home and the Synagogue
Large selection of 925 Sterling Silver Craftsmanship of high elegance
including for V.I.P. and Royalty.

Special coin sets for PIDYON HABEN sanctified by Israel's Chief Rabbinate.
Generous discounts on Books for Synagogues, Schools and Youth Organisations.

וראה כטוב ירושלים

146a-148 Golders Green Road, London NW11 8HE
Tel: 020 8455 4960 Fax: 020 8203 7808
Opening Times: Sunday to Thursday 9.30am-10.00pm
Fridays 9.30am-2.00pm Winter
Motzaei Shabbat 1 hour after Shabbat terminates until 10pm

Hebrew Book and Gift Centre
24 Amhurst Parade, Amhurst Park N16 5AA
Telephone: (020) 8802-0609
Fax: (020) 8802-0609
Web site: www.hebrewbooks.co.uk

J. Aisenthal
11 Ashbourne Parade, Finchley Road, Temple
Fortune NW11 0AD
Telephone: (020) 8455-0501
Email: infor@aisenthal.co .uk
Web site: www.aisenthal.co.uk

Jerusalem the Golden
146a Golders Green Road, Golders Green NW11
8HE
Telephone: (020) 8455-4960
Fax: (020) 8203-7808

Menorah Book and Gift Centre
16 Russell Parade, Golders Green Road NW11 9NN
Telephone: (020) 8458-8289
Fax: (020) 8731-8403

Steimatzky Hasifria
46 Golders Green Road NW11 8LL
Telephone: (020) 8458-9774
Fax: (020) 8458-3449
Email: hasifria@hotmail.com
Web site: www.hasifria.com

Torah Treasures
4 Sentinel Square, Brent Street, Hendon NW4 2EL
Telephone: (020) 8202-3134
Fax: (020) 8202-3161
Email: torahtreasures@btinternet.com
Seforim, Judaica and gifts.

BUTCHERS

A. Perlmutter & Son
1-2 Onslow Parade, Hampden Square, Southgate
N14 5JN
Telephone: (020) 8361-5441/2
Fax: (020) 8361-5442
Supervision: London Board of Shechita

Frohwein's
1095 Finchley Road, Temple Fortune NW11
Telephone: (020) 8455-9848
Supervision: Kedassia
Deli and cooked food available for weekends and
Shabbat.

Golders Green Kosher
132 Golders Green Road, Golders Green NW11 8HB
Telephone: (020) 8381-4450
Fax: (020) 8731-6450

Greenspans
9-11 Lyttelton Road N2 0DW
Telephone: (020) 8455-9921
Fax: (020) 8455-3484
Supervision: London Board of Shechita

Jack Schlagman
112 Regents Park Road, Finchley N3
Telephone: (020) 8346-3598
Supervision: London Board of Shechita

La Boucherie
4 Cat Hill, East Barnet EN4 8JB
Telephone: (020) 8449-9215
Fax: (020) 8441-1848
Supervision: London Board of Shechita

Louis Mann
23 Edgwarebury Lane, Edgware HA8
Telephone: (020) 8958-3789
Supervision: London Board of Shechita

M. Lipowicz
9 Royal Parade, Ealing W5
Telephone: (020) 8997-1722
Fax: (020) 8997-0048
Supervision: London Board of Shechita

Mehadrin Meats
25 Belfast Road, Stamford Hill N16
Telephone: (020) 8806-0000
Fax: (020) 8880-0500
Supervision: Kedassia
19 Russell Parade, Golders Green NW11 9NN
Telephone: (020) 8455-9992
Fax: (020) 8455-3777/8599 0984
Supervision: Kedassia

Menachem's
15 Russell Parade, Golders Green Road, Golders Green NW11
Telephone: (020) 8201-8629
Fax: (020) 8201-8629
Supervision: London Board of Shechita

R. Wolff
84 Edgware Way, Edgware HA8 8JS
Telephone: (020) 8958-8454
Supervision: London Board of Shechita

COMMUNITY ORGANISATIONS
Board of Deputies of British Jews
6 Bloomsbury Square WC1A 2LP
Telephone: (020) 7534-5400
Fax: (020) 7534-0010
Email: info @bod.org.uk
Web site: www.bod.org.uk

The Sephardi Centre
2 Ashworth Road W9 1JY
Telephone: (020) 7266-3682
Fax: (020) 7289 5957
Email: sephardicentre@spsyn.org.uk

CONTACT INFORMATION
Jewish Community Information (JCI)
6 Bloomsbury Square WC1A 2LP
Telephone: (020) 7543-5421
Fax: (020) 7543-0100
Email: jci@bod.org.uk
The basic information service for all aspects of the Jewish Community in Britain. Available Monday to Friday throughout the year, 10.00am to 4.30pm (1.30pm on Fridays) excluding Public and Jewish Holidays.

The International Jewish Vegetarianism Society
Bet Teva, 855 Finchley Road NW11 8LX
Telephone: (020) 8455-0692
Fax: (020) 8455-1465
Email: ijvs@yahoo.com
The International Jewish Vegetarian Society was formed 35 years ago to promote vegetarianism from a Jewish perspective.

DELICATESSEN

Kosher King
293 Hale Lane, Edgware HA8 7AX
Telephone: (020) 8281-1656
Supervision: London Beth Din

Munch Box
41 Greville Street EC1
Telephone: (020) 7242-5487
Supervision: London Beth Din

EMBASSY

Consul General of Israel
15a Old Court Place, Kensington W8 4QB
Telephone: (020) 7957-9500
Fax: (020) 957-9577
Web site: www.israel-embassy.org.uk/london
Nearest tube station: High Street Kensington. Consular office hours: Monday to Thursday, 10 am to 1 pm; Friday, 10 am to 12 pm. Postal address: Consulate Section, Embassy of Israel, 2 Palace Green, London W8 4QB.

Embassy of Israel
2 Palace Green, Kensington W8 4QB
Telephone: (020) 7957-9500
Fax: (020) 7957-9555
Email: info-assist@london.mfa.gov.il
Web site: http://london.mfa.gov.il

FISHMONGERS

Leveyuson
47a Brent Street, Hendon NW4
Telephone: (020) 8202-7834
Supervision: London Beth Din

Sam Stoller
28 Temple Fortune Parade, Finchley Road, Golders Green NW11 0QS
Telephone: (020) 8455-1957; 8458-1429
Fax: (020) 8445-1957
Supervision: Sephardi Kashrut Authority

GROCERIES

B Kosher
91 Bell Lane, Hendon NW4
Telephone: (020) 8202-1711
Opposite Vincent Court.

Carmel Fruit Shop
40 Vivian Avenue, Hendon NW4
Telephone: (020) 8202-9587
Fresh fruit and vegetables as well as a good supply of kosher products, cakes and biscuits.

Kosher King
235 Golders Green Road, Golders Green NW11 9ES
Telephone: (020) 8455-1429
Fax: (020) 8201-8924
Email: koshking@aol.com
Supervision: London Beth Din

Kosher Paradise
10 Ashbourne Parade, Finchley Road, Temple Fortune NW11 0AD
Telephone: (020) 8455-2454
Fax: (020) 8731-6919

Maxine's
20 Russell Parade, Golders Green Road, Golders Green NW11
Telephone: (020) 8458-3102
Fax: (020) 8455-3632
Kedassia Deli. Deliveries.

Pelter Stores
82 Edgware Way, Edgware HA8
Telephone: (020) 8958-6910
Supervision: Beth Din of the Federation of Synagogues

Steve's Kosher Delicatessen
5 Canons Corner, Stanmore, Middx HA8 8AE
Telephone: (020) 8958-9446
Fax: (020) 8905-4700
Email: stephen@mrbutler.net
Web site: www.mrbutler.net
Supervision: London Beth Din
Freshly cooked deli food and take-away. Made on premises

Yarden
123 Golders Green Road, Golders Green NW11
Telephone: (020) 8458-0979
Free delivery on orders over £25. Hours: Sunday,
Wednesday, Thursday, 8 am to 10 pm; Monday, Tuesday,
8 am to 9 pm; Friday, 8 am.

GUEST HOUSE
Sharon Guest House
7 Woodlands Close, Golders Green
Telephone: (020) 8458-8531
Email: jlazenga@aol.com
Although not officially supervised it is said to be Shomer
Shabbat Dati.

HOTELS
Central Hotel
35 Hoop Lane, Golders Green NW11 8BS
Telephone: (020) 8458-5636
Fax: (020) 8455-4792
Private bathrooms and parking.

Croft Court Hotel
44 Ravenscroft Avenue, Golders Green NW11 8AY
Telephone: (020) 8458-3331
Fax: (020) 8455-9175

King Solomon Palace Hotel
155-159 Golders Green Road NW11 9BX
Telephone: (020) 8201-9000
Fax: (020) 8201-9853
Kosher
Kadimah Hotel
146 Clapton Common, Stamford Hill E5 9AG
Telephone: (020) 8800-5960
Fax: (020) 8800-6237
Supervision: Kedassia

KASHRUT INFORMATION
Federation of Synagogues Kashrus Board - KF
65 Watford Way, London NW4 3AQ
Telephone: (020) 8202-2263
Fax: (020) 8203-0610
Email: info@kfkosher.org
Web site: www.kfkosher.org

Joint Kashrus Committee-Kedassia (Union of Orthodox Hebrew Congregations)
140 Stamford Hill, Stamford Hill N16 6QT
Telephone: (020) 8800 6833
Fax: (020) 8809-7092

London Beth Din
735 High Road, Finchley N12 0US
Telephone: (020) 8343-6255 (Kashrut hotline: 8343-6333)
Fax: (020) 8343-6254
Email: info@kosher.org.uk
Web site: www.kosher.org.uk
Publishes 'The Really Jewish Food Guide', which contains a list of all the establishments it certifies, as well as guidance for the shopper in buying general consumer products.

National Council of Shechita Boards
Elscot House, Arcadia Avenue, Finchley N3 2JU
Telephone: (020) 8349-9160
Fax: (020) 8346-2209
Email: shechita@tiscali.co.uk

Sephardi Kashrut Authority
2 Ashworth Road, Maida Vale W9 1JY
Telephone: (020) 7289-2573
Fax: (020) 7289-7663
Email: dvsteinhof@onetel.net.uk

KOSHER FOOD
Kosher Corner
42, St. George's Rd, Wimbledon SW19 4ED
Telephone: (020) 8944-1581
Email: Lubwdon@aol.com

LIBRARIES
British Library, Asia, Pacific and Africa Collections - Hebrew Section
96 Euston Road NW1 2DB
Telephone: (020) 7412-7646
Fax: (020) 7412-7641/7870
Email: ilana.tahan@bl.uk
Web site: www.bl.uk/collections/hebrew.html
The Hebrew section contains over 70,000 printed books, 3,000 manuscripts and some 10,000 Genizah fragments. Oriental reading room open to holders of readers' passes: Monday 10.00am-5.00pm; Tuesday-Saturday 9.30am-5.00pm. Hebrew manuscripts on permanent display. The Golden Haggadah is included in the electronic "Turning the Pages" programme.

Institute of Contemporary History and Wiener Library
4 Devonshire Street W1W 5BH
Telephone: (020) 7636-7247
Fax: (020) 7436-6428
Email: info@wienerlibrary.co.uk
Web site: www.wienerlibrary.co.uk
The world's oldest institution dedicated to the documentation of Nazi Germay and the Holocaust. The collection includes 60,000 books and pamphlets, periodicals, documents, videos and photographs as well as extensive press cuttings from 1933 onwards. Other subjects include 20th-century Jewish history, anti-semitism, refugees, minorities, fascism, citizenship, etc.

The Jewish Studies Library
University College London Library, Gower Street WC1E 6BT
Telephone: (020) 7679-2598
Fax: (020) 7679-7373
Email: library@ucl.ac.uk
In addition to materials purchased for the College's Department of Hebrew Studies, it incorporates the Mocatta Library, Altmann Library, William Margulies Yiddish Library and the Library of the Jewish Historical Society of England. Applications to use or view the collections should be made in advance in writing to the Librarian.

MEDIA
Directory
Jewish Year Book
Vallentine Mitchell, Crown House, 47 Chase Side, Southgate N14 5BP
Telephone: (020) 8920-2100
Fax: (020) 8447-8548
Email: jyb@vmbooks.com
Annual directory of all information relating to the British Jewish Community.

Internet
Brijnet
11 The Lindens, Prospect Hill, Waltham Forest E17 3EJ
Telephone: (020) 8520-3531
Email: info@brijnet.org
Web site: www.brijnet.org

Listings
The Diary
32 Bell Lane NW4 2AD
Telephone: (020) 8922-5437
Fax: (020) 8922-8709

Newspapers
Essex Jewish News
Crown House, 47 Chase Side, Southgate N14 5BP
Telephone: (020) 8920-2100
Fax: (020) 8447-8548
Quarterly publication serving East London and Essex.

Hamodia
149 Kyverdale Road N16 6PS
Telephone: (020) 8806 7577
Fax: (020) 8806 1222
Email: Post@Hamodia.demon.co.uk

Jewish Chronicle
25 Furnival Street EC4A 1JT
Telephone: (020) 7415-1500
Fax: (020) 7405-9040
Email: editorial@thejc.com
Web site: www.thejc.com
Established 1841. Weekly publication.

London Jewish News
Unit 611 Highate Studios, 53-79 Highate road,
Kentish Town NW5 1TL
Telephone: (020) 7692-6929
Fax: (020) 7692-6689
Email: info@totallyjewish.com
Web site: www.totallyjewish.com

MIKVAOT
Adath Yisroel Synagogue Mikvah
40a Queen Elizabeth's Walk, Stamford Hill N16 0HH
Telephone: (020) 8802-2554

Craven Walk Mikvah
72 Lingwood Road, Stamford Hill N16
Telephone: (020) 8800-8555
Evening telephone number: 020-8809-6279.

Edgware & District Communal Mikvah
Edgware United Synagogue Grounds, 22 Warwick
Avenue Drive, Edgware HA8
Telephone: (020) 8958-3233
Fax: (020) 8958-4004
Email: estrin@clara.co.uk

North West London Communal Mikvah
10a Shirehall Lane, Hendon NW4
Telephone: (020) 8202-1427 (Evenings: 8202-
8517/5706).

Satmar Mikvah
62 Filey Avenue, Stamford Hill N16
Telephone: (020) 8806-3961

South London Mikvah
42 St Georges Road, Wimbledon SW19 4ED
Telephone: (020) 8944-7149
Fax: (020) 8944-7563
Email: lubwdon@aol.com

Stamford Hill and District Mikvah
Margaret Road, Stamford Hill N16
Telephone: (020) 8806-3880
Other telephone numbers: 020-8809-4064 or 020-8800-
5119.

The New Central London Mikveh
21 Andover Place NW6 5ED
Telephone: (020) 7372-7237
By appointment only.

The Sternberg Centre for Judaism
80 East End Road, Finchley N3 2SY
Telephone: (020) 8349-2568
Fax: (020) 8349-5699
Email: sylvia.morris@reformjudaism.org.uk
Web site: www.refsyn.org.uk
Hours: 9.30 - 5.30 Monday to Thursday, Friday 9.30 - 3.30
/4.

Union of Orthodox Hebrew Congregations
140 Stamford Hill, Stamford Hill N16 6QT
Telephone: (020) 8802-6226
Fax: (020) 8809-7097

MUSEUMS
Ben Uri Art Society & Gallery
126 Albert Street NW1 7NE
Telephone: (020) 7482-1234
Fax: (020) 7482-1414
Email: benuri@ort.org
The aim of the Society, which is a registered charity
founded 1915, is to promote Jewish art as part of the
Jewish cultural heritage. The Gallery provides a showcase
for exhibitions of contemporary art as well as for the
Society's own collection of over 800 works by Jewish
artists, including David Bomberg, Mark Gertler, Jacob
Epstein, Reuven Rubin and Leon Kossof. Open Monday-
Thursday 10-4, Sunday afternoons during exhibitions
2pm-5pm. Closed Jewish Holy-days and Bank Holidays.

Jewish Military Museum and Memorial Room
AJEX House, East Bank, Stamford Hill N16 5RT
Telephone: (020) 8800-2844
Fax: (020) 8800-1117
Email: ajexuk@talk21.com
Web site: www.ajex.org.uk
Memorabilia, artefacts, medals, letters, documents,
pictures and uniforms all illustrating British Jewry's
contribution to the Armed Forces of the Crown from the
Crimea to the present day. By appointment, Sunday to
Thursday, 11 am to 4 pm.

Museum of Immigration
19 Princelet Street E1

A museum devoted to the history of immigration into Great Britain. Included in the site is Princelet street Synagogue, a 1870 synagogue built onto a Grade II* listed Georgian town house.

The Holocaust Exhibition
Imperial War Museum, Lambeth Road SE1 6HZ
Telephone: (020) 7416-5320
Fax: (020) 7416-5374
Email: rbjones@iwm.org.uk
Web site: www.iwm.org.uk

The Exhibition covers two floors and uses original artefacts, film, documents and photographs to tell the story of the Nazis' genocidal programme. It brings to the UK for the first time rare and important historical material, some lent by former concentration and extermination camp inmates. Special talks can be arranged for groups visiting the exhibition. Opening hours: 10am to 6pm daily.

The Jewish Museum
Raymond Burton House, 129-131 Albert Street, Camden Town NW1 7NB
Telephone: (020) 7284-1997
Fax: (020) 7267-9008
Email: admin@jmus.org.uk
Web site: www.jewishmuseum.org.uk

The Museum's attractive premises include a History Gallery, Ceremonial Art Gallery and a Temporary Exhibitions gallery offering a varied programme of changing exhibitions. The Museum has been awarded Designated status by the Museums and Galleries Commission in recognition of its outstanding collections of Jewish ceremonial Art, which are amongst the finest in the world. Open Monday to Thursday 10am - 4pm, and Sunday 10am to 5pm. Closed Jewish festivals and Public Holidays. Group visits by prior arrangement. Admission charge.

The Sternberg Centre, 80 East End Road, Finchley N3 2SY
Telephone: (020) 8349-1143
Fax: (020) 8343-2162
Email: enquiries@jewishmuseum.org.uk
Web site: www.jewishmuseum.org.uk

Permanent exhibitions trace history of London Jewry with reconstructions of a tailoring and a furniture workshop. Holocaust education is also a major feature of the Museum's work and the Museum's displays include a moving exhibition on London-born Holocaust survivor, Leon Greenman. Open Monday to Thursday: 10.30am - 5.00pm, and Sunday 10.30am to 4.30pm. Closed Jewish festivals and Public Holidays and 25 December to 5 January.

RELIGIOUS ORGANISATIONS
Assembly of Masorti Synagogues
1097 Finchley Road, Golders Green NW11 0PU
Telephone: (020) 8201-8772
Fax: (020) 8201-8917
Email: office@masorti.org.uk
Web site: www.masorti.org.uk

Reform Synagogues
The Sternberg Centre for Judaism, 80 East End Road, Finchley N3 2SY
Telephone: (020) 8349-5640
Fax: (020) 8343-5699
Email: admin@reformjudaism.org.uk
Web site: www.reformjudaism.org.uk

Spanish & Portuguese Jews' Congregation
2 Ashworth Road, Maida Vale W9 1JY
Telephone: (020) 7289-2573
Fax: (020) 7289-2709
Email: howardmiller@spsyn.org.uk

Union of Liberal and Progressive Synagogues
The Montagu Centre, 21 Maple Street W1T 4BE
Telephone: (020) 7580-1663
Fax: (020) 7436-4184
Email: montagu@ulps.org
Web site: www.ulps.org

Union of Orthodox Hebrew Congregations
140 Stamford Hill, Stamford Hill N16 6QT
Telephone: (020) 8802-6226
Fax: (020) 8809-7902

United Synagogue
Adler House, 735 High Road, Finchley N12 0US
Telephone: (020) 8343-8989
Fax: (020) 8343-6262
Web site: www.unitedsynagogue.org.uk

RESTAURANTS
Bevis Marks The Restaurant
Bevis Marks EC3
Telephone: (020) 7283-2220
Fax: (020) 7283-2221
Email: enquiries@BevisMarksTheRestaurant.com

Dairy
Art 2 Heart
109a Golders Green Road, London NW11
Telephone: (020) 8201-9991
Supervision: London Beth Din

Bon Baggeute
122 Golders Green Road NW11 8HB
Telephone: (020) 8209-0232
Supervision: London Beth Din

Café Dan
14 Halleswelle Parade, Finchley Road NW11 8HB
Telephone: (020) 8455-3731
Supervision: London Beth Din

Café on the Green
122 Golders Green Road, Golders Green NW11 8HB
Telephone: (020) 8209-0232
Supervision: London Beth Din
Chalav Yisrael. Open Motzei Shabbat in winter.

Cassit
225 Golders Green Road, Golders Green NW11 9PN
Telephone: (020) 8455-8195
Fax: (020) 8458-4837
Supervision: Beth Din of the Federation of Synagogues

Isola Bella Café
63 Brent Street, Hendon NW4 2EA
Telephone: (020) 8203-2000
Supervision: Beth Din of the Federation of Synagogues,
Sephardi Kashrut Authority

Milk n' Honey
124 Golders Green Road, Golders Green NW11 8HB
Telephone: (020) 8455-0664
Supervision: Kedassia
Vegetarian/dairy restaurant/coffee shop/air-conditioned.
Menus in English and Hebrew. Also take-away available.

Orli Cafe
96 Brent Street, Hendon NW4 2HH
Telephone: (020) 8203-7555
Supervision: Kedassia
108 Regents Park Road, Finchley N3 3JG
Telephone: (020) 8371-9222
Supervision: Kedassia
295 Hale Lane, Edgware HA8 7AX
Telephone: (020) 8958-1555

Taboon
17 Russell Parade, Golders Green Road NW11 9NN
Telephone: (020) 8455-7451
Supervision: Sephardi Kashrut Authority, Kedassia

Tasti Pizza
252 Golders Green Road, Golders Green NW11
Telephone: (020) 8209-0023
Supervision: London Beth Din, Kedassia

Tasty Pizza
23 Amhurst Parade, Amhurst Park, Stamford Hill
N16 5AA
Telephone: (020) 8802-0018
Supervision: London Beth Din, Kedassia

Meat
Amor
8 Russell Parade, Golders Green NW11
Telephone: (020) 8458-4221
Supervision: Kedassia

Aviv
87 High Street, Edgware
Telephone: (020) 8952-2484
Fax: (020) 8952-0200
Email: info@avivrestaurant.com
Web site: www.avivrestaurant.com
Supervision: Beth Din of the Federation of Synagogues

Blooms Restaurant
130 Golders Green Road, Golders Green NW11 8HB
Telephone: (020) 8455-1338
Fax: (020) 8455-1338
Web site: www.blooms-restaurant.co.uk
Supervision: London Beth Din
Free delivery service, air-conditioned. Open until 1.00am
Sunday to Thursday; Friday lunchtime and Saturday
nights 1 hour after Shabbos until 4.00am.

Dizengoff
118 Golders Green Road, Golders Green NW11 8HB
Telephone: (020) 8458-7003
Fax: (020) 8381-4902
Email: shurkin@btopenworld.com
Supervision: Sephardi Kashrut Authority
Hours: Sunday to Thursday, 11 am to midnight; Friday, to
4 pm; Saturday night, winter only.

Folman's Restaurant
134 Brent Street NW4
Telephone: (020) 8202-5592
Supervision: London Beth Din

Kaifeng
51 Church Road, Hendon NW4 4DU
Telephone: (020) 8203-7888
Fax: (020) 8203-8263
Web site: www.kaifeng.co.uk
Supervision: London Beth Din
Chinese restaurant with take-away and delivery service.
Free delivery with minimum order of £25. Hours: Sunday
to Thursday, 12:30 pm to 2:30 pm, 6 pm to 11 pm; Open
Saturday evening, September to April.

Kinneret
313 Hale Lane HA8 7AX
Telephone: (020) 8958-4955
Supervision: Beth Din of the Federation of Synagogues

La Fiesta
239 Golders Green Road NW11 9PN
Telephone: (020) 8458-0444
Fax: (020) 8455-2003
Supervision: London Beth Din

Lemonade
87 Brent St. NW4
Telephone: (020) 8201-5222
Supervision: Sephardi Kashrut Authority

Marcus's
5 Hallswelle Parade, Finchley Road, Golders Green
NW11 0DL
Telephone: (020) 8458-4670
Web site: www.marcuss.co.uk
Supervision: London Beth Din

Reubens
79 Baker Street W1M 1AJ
Telephone: (020) 7486-0035
Fax: (020) 7486-7079
Supervision: Sephardi Kashrut Authority
Open daily except for Shabbat; open Friday until two
hours before sundown.

Sami's Restaurant
157 Brent Street, Hendon NW4 4DJ
Telephone: (020) 8203-8088
Fax: (020) 8203-1040
Supervision: Beth Din of the Federation of Synagogues
Glatt kosher Middle Eastern cuisine.

Six13 Restaurant
19 Wigmore Street W1H 9LA
Telephone: (020) 7629-6133
Fax: (020) 7629-6135
Email: inquiries@six13.com
Web site: www.six13.com
Supervision: London Beth Din
Opening times: Mon-Thurs Lunch 12.00-2.30pm, Dinner
5.00-10.30pm. Weekends for exclusive hire

Solly's
148a Golders Green Road, Golders Green NW11
Telephone: (020) 8455-0004
Supervision: London Beth Din

Solly's Exclusive
146-150 Golders Green Road, Golders Green NW11
Telephone: (020) 8455-2121
Supervision: London Beth Din

Tavlin
1-4 Belmont Parade, Finchley Road NW11 6XP
Telephone: (020) 8458-1999
Fax: (020) 8458-2999
Supervision: Kedassia

The White House Restaurant
10 Bell Lane, Hendon NW4
Telephone: (020) 8203-2427
Supervision: Beth Din of the Federation of Synagogues,
Sephardi Kashrut Authority

Uncle Shloime's
204 Stamford Hill, Stamford Hill N16
Telephone: (020) 8802-9355
Supervision: Kedassia

Snack Bar

Sue Harris Student Centre
B'nai B'rith-Hillel Foundation, 1-2 Endsleigh Street
WC1H 0DS
Telephone: (020) 7388-0801
Fax: (020) 7916-3973
Email: info@hillel.co.uk
Web site: www.hillel.co.uk
Supervision: London Beth Din
Hours: Monday to Thursday. Please phone for details of
summer months opening. Re-opens for students and all
other visitors mid-September.

SELF-CATERING
Yamor
, Golders Green **?more details of address**
Telephone: (020) 07968-387499
Fax: (020) 020-8455-4231
Web site: www.yamor.com

TRAVEL AGENTS
Goodmos Tours
Dunstan House, 14a St Cross Street EC1N 8XA
Telephone: (020) 7430-2230
Fax: (020) 7405-5049

LestAir Services
80 Highfield Ave, Golders Green NW11 9TT
Telephone: (020) 8455-9654
Fax: (020) 455-9654
Email: family.schleimer@ukgateway.net
Promoting Jewish Heritage Tours to the Czech Republic,
Poland, Hungary, Byelorus, Latvia and Lithuania and can
be contacted for detailed information and guidance.

Longwood Travel
3 Bourne Court, Southend Road, Woodford Green
IG8 8HD
Telephone: (020) 8551-4466
Fax: (020) 8551-5588

Peltours
11-19 Ballards Lane, Finchley N3 1UX
Telephone: (020) 8346-9144
Fax: (020) 8343-0579
Email: sales@peltours.com
Web site: www.peltours.com

Peltours AMG Travel
70 Edgware Way, Edgware HA8 8JS
Telephone: (020) 8958-3188
Fax: (020) 8958-8898

Sabra Travel Ltd.
9 Edgwarebury Lane, Edgware HA8 8LH

Telephone: (020) 8958-3244-7
Travelink Group Ltd.
50 Vivian Avenue NW4 3XH
Telephone: (020) 8931-8000
Fax: (020) 8931-8877
Email: info@travelinkuk.com
Web site: www.travelinkuk.com

West End Travel
Barratt House, 341 Oxford Street W1R 2LE
Telephone: (020) 7629-6299
Fax: (020) 7499-0865
Email: admin@westendtravel.co.uk

Manchester (Greater)
CHEADLE
BUTCHERS
Hymark Kosher Meat Ltd
39 Wilmslow Road, Cheadle, Cheshire SK
Telephone: (0161) 428-3400
Supervision: Manchester Beth Din
Meat department only.

DELICATESSEN
Hyman's Delicatessen
41 Wilmstow Road, Cheadle M
Telephone: (0161) 491-1100
Fax: (0161) 491-1100
Supervision: Manchester Beth Din

SYNAGOGUES
Orthodox
Yeshurun Hebrew Congregation
Coniston Road, Gatley-Cheadle, Cheshire SK8 4AP
Telephone: (0161) 428-8242
Fax: (0161) 491-5265
Email: yeshurun@btinternet.com
Web site: www.yeshurun.co.uk

HALE BARNS
BUTCHERS
Hymark of Hale
The Square, Hale Barns, Cheshire
Telephone: (0161) 980-2836
Supervision: Manchester Beth Din

MIKVAOT
Naomi Greenberg South Manchester Mikvah
Hale Synagogue, Shay Lane, Hale Barns
Telephone: (0161) 904-8296
Use is by appointment only.

RESTAURANTS
Aviv Restaurant
18 The Square, Hale Barns
Telephone: (0161) 980-0009
Supervision: Manchester Beth Din

SYNAGOGUES
Orthodox
Hale and District Hebrew Congregation
Shay Lane, Hale Barns, Cheshire WA15 8PA
Telephone: (0161) 980-8846
Fax: (0161) 980-1802

MANCHESTER
The Manchester Jewish community is the second largest in the United Kingdom, numbering about 35,000. There was no organised community until 1780. The present Great Synagogue claims to be the direct descendant of this earliest community. The leaders of Manchester Jewry in those early days came from the neighbouring relatively important Jewish community of Liverpool. In 1871 a small Sephardi group from North Africa and the Levant drew together and formed a congregation, which extended to fill two handsome synagogues. One has now been turned into a Jewish museum.

BAKERIES
State Fayre Bakeries
Unit 1, Empire Street M3
Telephone: (0161) 832-2911
Supervision: Manchester Beth Din

BUTCHERS
J.A. Hyman (Titanic) Ltd
123/9 Waterloo Road M8
Telephone: (0161) 792-1888
Supervision: Manchester Beth Din
Suppliers of meat and poultry, cooked meats and delicatessen products.

Lloyd Grosberg (J. Kreger)
102 Barlow Moor Road M20
Telephone: (0161) 445-4983
Supervision: Manchester Beth Din

GROCERIES
State Fayre
77 Middleton Road M8
Telephone: (0161) 740-3435
Supervision: Manchester Beth Din

KASHRUT INFORMATION
Manchester Beth Din
435 Cheetham Hill Road M8 0PF
Telephone: (0161) 740-9711
Fax: (0161) 721-4249
Contact them to ensure that an establishment is still certified.

LIBRARIES
Central Library
St Peter's Square M2 5PD
Telephone: (0161) 234-1983; 1984
Fax: (0161) 234-1927
Email: socsci@libraries.manchester.gov.uk
Large collection of Jewish books for reference and loan, including books in Hebrew. Contact the Social Sciences Library.

MUSEUMS
Manchester Jewish Museum
190 Cheetham Hill Road M8 8LW
Telephone: (0161) 834-9879; 832-7353
Fax: (0161) 834-9801
Email: info@manchesterjewishmuseum.com
Web site: www.manchesterjewishmuseum.com
Exhibitions, Heritage trails, Demonstrations and Talks.
Details of events available on request. Educational visits
for schools and adult groups must be booked in advance.
Open Monday-Thursday, 10.30am to 4pm Sundays
10.30am to 5pm. Admission charge. Contact Don
Rainger.

RESTAURANTS
Antonio's Restaurant
JCLC, Corner Bury Old Road & Park Road
Telephone: (0161) 795-8911
Fax: (0161) 795-8911
Supervision: Manchester Beth Din
Open Monday-Thursday 5.00pm-11.00pm ; Sunday
1.00pm to 11.00pm. In winter 1 1/2 hours after Shabbat
until 2.00 am.

SYNAGOGUES
Orthodox
Cheetham Hebrew Congregation
Jewish Cultural Centre, Bury Old Road M7 4QY
Telephone: (0161) 740-7788

Heaton Park Hebrew Congregation
Ashdown, Middleton Road M8 6JX
Telephone: (0161) 740-4766

United Synagogue
Meade Hill Road M8 4LR
Telephone: (0161) 740-9586

Reform
Cheshire Reform Congregation Menorah Synagogue
Altrincham Road M22 4RZ
Telephone: (0161) 428-7746
Fax: (0161) 428-0937
Email: office@menorah.org

Manchester Reform Synagogue
Jackson's Row M2 5NH
Telephone: (0161) 834-0415
Fax: (0161) 834-0415

TRAVEL AGENTS
ITS: Israel Travel Service
427/430 Royal Exchange, Old Bank Street M2 7EP
Telephone: (0161) 839-1111
Fax: (0161) 839-0000
Email: all@itstravel.co.uk
Web site: www.itstravel.co.uk
Freephone 0800 0181 839

Peltours Ltd
27-29 Church Street M4 1QA
Telephone: (0161) 834-3721
Fax: (0161) 832-9343

PRESTWICH
BAKERIES
Swiss Cottage Patisserie
118 Rectory Lane, Prestwich M25
Telephone: (0161) 798-0897
Fax: (0161) 798-8212
Supervision: Manchester Beth Din

BOOKSELLERS
B. Horwitz
20 King Edwards Buildings, Bury Old Road,
Prestwich M7 4QJ
Telephone: (0161) 740-5897
Open 9.30am-5.30pm Monday to Friday; 10.00am-
1.00pm Sunday; 9.00am-2.00pm Fridays during winter.

B. Horwitz Judaica World
2 Kings Road, Prestwich M25 0LE
Telephone: (0161) 773-4956
Fax: (0161) 773-4956
Email: horbroom@aol.com

BUTCHERS
Kosher Foods
49 Bury New Road, Prestwich M25
Telephone: (0161) 773-1308
Supervision: Manchester Beth Din
Sells groceries as well.

Kosher Supreme
61 Bury Old Road, Prestwich M25
Telephone: (0161) 773-2020
Supervision: Manchester Beth Din

Vidal's Kosher Meats
75 Windsor Road, Prestwich M25
Telephone: (0161) 740-3365
Supervision: Manchester Beth Din

DELICATESSEN
Deli King
Kings Road, Prestwich M25 8LQ
Telephone: (0161) 798-7370
Fax: (0161) 798-5654
Supervision: Manchester Beth Din
Hours: Sunday to Friday, 8:30 am to 6 pm.

Haber's
8 Kings Road, Prestwich M25 0LE
Telephone: (0161) 773-2046
Fax: (0161) 773-9101
Supervision: Manchester Beth Din

MEDIA

Newspaper
Jewish Telegraph
Telegraph House, 11 Park Hill, Bury Old Road,
Prestwich M25 0HH
Telephone: (0161) 740-9321
Fax: (0161) 740-9325
Email: manchester@jewishtelegraph.com
Web site: www.jewishtelegraph.com

MIKVAOT
Manchester & District Mikva (Machzikei Hadass)
Sedgley Park Road, Prestwich M25
Telephone: (0161) 773-1537; 795-2223

RESTAURANTS
Asher's
5 Kings Road, Prestwich
Telephone: (0161) 773-1414
Supervision: Manchester Beth Din

Meat
J.S. Kosher Restaurant
7 Kings Road, Prestwich M25 0LE
Telephone: (0161) 798-7776
Supervision: Manchester Beth Din
Glatt kosher.

SYNAGOGUES

Orthodox
Higher Prestwich
445 Bury Old Road, Prestwich M25 1QP
Telephone: (0161) 773-4800

Holy Law South Broughton Congregation
Bury Old Road, Prestwich M25 0EX
Telephone: (0161) 792-6349/721-4705
Fax: (0161) 720-6623
Email: office@holylaw.org.uk

Prestwich Hebrew Congregation
Bury New Road M25 9WN
Telephone: (0161) 773-1978
Fax: (0161) 773-7015

Sedgley Park (Shomrei Hadass)
Park View Road, Prestwich M25 5FA
Telephone: (0161) 773-4828/740-1969
Email: laurencemiller@hotmail.com

SALE

SYNAGOGUES
Orthodox
Sale & District Hebrew Congregation
14 Hesketh Road, Sale M33 5AA
Telephone: (0161) 973-2172

SALFORD

BAKERIES
Brackman's
45 Leicester Road, Salford M7
Telephone: (0161) 792-1652
Supervision: Manchester Beth Din

BOOKSELLERS
Hasefer Book Store
18 Merrybower Road, Salford M7
Telephone: (0161) 740-3013
Fax: (0161) 721-4649

J. Goldberg
11 Parkside Avenue, Salford M7 0HB
Telephone: (0161) 740-0732

Jewish Book Centre
25 Ashbourne Grove, Salford M7 4DB
Telephone: (0161) 792-1253
Fax: (0161) 661-5505
Hours: Sunday to Thursday, 9 am to 9 pm; Friday, 9.00am-1.00pm.

BUTCHERS
Halberstadt Ltd
55 Leicester Road, Salford M7 4AS
Telephone: (0161) 792-1109
Supervision: Manchester Beth Din
Open full day Tuesday, Wednesday, and Thursday. Open half day Sunday, Monday and Friday. Only Glatt Beth Yosef Meat-Mehadrin Poultry. Electric doors/disabled ramp.

GROCERIES
Halperns Kosher Food Store
57-59 Leicester Road, Salford M7 4DA
Telephone: (0161) 792-1752 Office 792-2992
Fax: (0161) 708-8881
Email: halperns.kosherfood@virgin.net
Supervision: Manchester Beth Din

HOTELS
Fulda's Hotel
144 Old Bury Road, Salford M7 4QY
Telephone: (0161) 740-4551
Fax: (0161) 795-5920
Web site: www.here.at/fuldas.com
Supervision: Manchester Beth Din
Four-star hotel open all year. Glatt kosher. Within easy access of motorways, and uniquely placed in the heart of the Manchester Jewish community in Broughton Park. Within easy walking distance of numerous synagogues and shopping facilities.

MIKVAOT
Manchester Communal Mikvah
Broome Holme, Tetlow Lane, Salford M7 0BU
Telephone: (0161) 792-3970
During opening hours only. For appointments for Friday
night and YomTov evenings: 740-4071; 740-5199. For
tevilat kelim, 795-2272.

RESTAURANTS
Dairy
Brackman's Bakery & Coffee Shop
45 Leicester Road
Telephone: (0161) 792-1652
Supervision: Manchester Beth Din

SYNAGOGUES
Orthodox
Adass Yeshurun
Cheltenham Crescent, Salford M7 0FE
Telephone: (0161) 792-1233

Adath Yisroel Nusach Ari
Upper Park Road, Salford M7 0HL
Telephone: (0161) 740-3905

**Central & North Manchester (incorporating
Hightown Central and Beth Jacob)**
Leicester Road, Salford M7 4GP
Telephone: (0161) 740-4830

Congregation of Spanish and Portuguese
18 Moor Lane, Kersal, Salford M7 4WX
Telephone: (0161) 792-7406
Fax: (0161) 792-7406
Email: ahodari@antonyhodari.co.uk
Web site: www.18moorlane.freeserve.co.uk

Higher Crumpsall & Higher Broughton
Bury Old Road, Salford M7 4PX
Telephone: (0161) 740-1210

Kahal Chassidim Lubavitch
62 Singleton Road, Salford M7 4LU
Telephone: (0161) 740-1629

Machzikei Hadass
17 Northumberland Street, Salford M7 0FE
Telephone: (0161) 792-1313

Manchester Great & New Synagogue
Stenecourt, Holden Road, Salford M7 4LN
Telephone: (0161) 792-8399
Fax: (0161) 792-1991

North Salford
2 Vine Street, Salford M7 0NX
Telephone: (0161) 792-3278

Ohel Torah
132 Leicester Road, Salford M7 0EA
Telephone: (0161) 740-2568
Fax: (0161) 745-8876

TRAVEL AGENTS
Goodmos Tours (Man) Ltd.
23 Leicester Road, Salford M7 0AS
Telephone: (0161) 792-7333
Fax: (0161) 792-7336
Email: goodmos836@aol.com

WHITEFIELD
BUTCHERS
Park Lane Kosher Meats
142 Park Lane, Whitefield M45 7PX
Telephone: (0161) 766-5091
Supervision: Manchester Beth Din
Hours: Sunday 8.30am - 1.00pm; Monday & Friday
8.00am - 1.00pm; Tuesday, Wednesday & Thursday
8.00am - 6.00pm.

DELICATESSEN
Cottage Deli
83 Park Lane, Whitefield M
Telephone: (0161) 766-6216
Supervision: Manchester Beth Din

MIKVAOT
Whitefield Mikvah
Park Lane, Whitefield M45 7PB
Telephone: (0161) 796-1054
Fax: (0161) 767-9453
Ansaphone. Evenings only: 773-7830. Use is by
appointment only.

SYNAGOGUES
Orthodox
Hillock Hebrew Congregation
Beverley Close, Ribble Drive, Whitefield M25 6NJ
Telephone: (0161) 959-5663
Mailing address is 13 Mersey Close, Whitefield,
Manchester, M45 8LB

Whitefield Hebrew Congregation
Park Lane, Whitefield M45 7PB
Telephone: (0161) 766-3732
Fax: (0161) 767-9453
Email: mail@whitefieldshul.co.uk

Reform
**Sha'arei Shalom North Manchester Reform
Synagogue**
Elms Street, Whitefield M45 8GQ
Telephone: (0161) 796-6736
Fax: (0161) 796-6736

Merseyside
LIVERPOOL
There is evidence of an organised community before 1750, believed to have been composed of Sephardi Jews and to have had some connection with the West Indies and with Dublin, although some authorities believe they were mainly German Jews. The largely Ashkenazi community, who arrived later, were to some degree intending emigrants for the USA and the West Indies who changed their minds and stayed in Liverpool. By 1807 the community had a building in Seel Street, the parent of today's synagogue in Princes Road, one of the handsomest in the country.

BOOKSELLERS
Liverpool Jewish Book & Gift Centre
Harold House, Dunbabin Road L15 6XL
Telephone: (0151) 475-5671
Fax: (0151) 475-2212
Full range of Jewish books, artefacts and gifts. Sundays 11.00am to 1.00pm.

COMMUNITY ORGANISATIONS
Merseyside Jewish Representative Council
433 Smithdown Road L15 3JL
Telephone: (0151) 733-2292
Fax: (0151) 734-0212
Email: mjrcshifrin@hotmail.com
Web site: www.merseyside-jewish-community.org.uk

KASHRUT INFORMATION
Liverpool Kashrut Commission (inc. Liverpool Shechita Board)
c/o Shifrin House, 433 Smithdown Road L15 3JL
Telephone: (0151) 733-2292
Fax: (0151) 734-0212

MEDIA
Newspaper
Jewish Telegraph
Harold House, Dunbabin Road L15 6XL
Telephone: (0151) 475-6666
Fax: (0151) 475-2222
Email: liverpool@jewishtelegraph.com
Web site: www.jewishtelegraph.com

MIKVAOT
Childwall Hebrew Congregation
Dunbabin Road L15 6XL
Telephone: (0151) 722-2079
Fax: (0151) 722-2079

RESTAURANTS
JLGB Centre
Telephone: (0151) 475-5825; 475-5671
Open Sun, Tues., Thurs. 6.30-11.00pm. Licensed bar. Out-of-town visitors welcome. Also take-away service.

Kosher
The Liverpool Jewish Youth and Community Centre Harold House
Dunbabin Road L15 6XL
Telephone: (0151) 475-5671/5825
Fax: (0151) 475-2212
Email: info@liverpooljewish.com
Web site: www.liverpooljewish.com
Supervision: Liverpool Kashrut Commission
Also does take-away.

Vegetarian
Munchies Eating House
Myrtle Parade
Telephone: (0151) 709-7896

SYNAGOGUES
Orthodox
Allerton Hebrew Congregation
cnr. Mather & Booker Avenues, Allerton L18 9TB
Telephone: (0151) 427-6848

Childwall Hebrew Congregation
Dunbabin Road L15 6XL
Telephone: (0151) 722-2079
Fax: (0151) 722-2079

Greenbank Drive Hebrew Congregation
Greenbank Drive L17 1AN
Telephone: (0151) 733-1417
Fax: (0151) 733-3862

Liverpool Old Hebrew Congregation
Synagogue Chambers, Princes Road L8 1TG
Telephone: (0151) 709-3431
Fax: (0151) 709-3431
Email: lohc1@aol.com
Grade II Listed Building. Guided talks available during the week daily. Pre-booking essential. Other times by special arrangement.

Progressive
Liverpool Progressive Synagogue
28 Church Road North L15 6TF
Telephone: (0151) 733-5871

SOUTHPORT
COMMUNITY ORGANISATIONS
Southport Jewish Representative Council
Telephone: (01704) 540704
Fax: (01704) 540704

SYNAGOGUES
Orthodox
Southport Hebrew Congregation
Arnside Road PR9 0QX
Telephone: (01704) 532964
Fax: (01704) 514002
Mikvah on premises.

Reform
New (Reform) Synagogue
Portland Street PR8 1LR
Telephone: (01704) 535950
Email: snewsyn@aol.com

Middlesex
STAINES
SYNAGOGUES
Orthodox
Staines & District Synagogue
Westbrook Road, South Street TW18 4PR
Telephone: (01784) 254604
Fax: (01784) 254604
Email: staines.synagogue@btinternet.com
Includes Slough and Windsor.

Norfolk
NORWICH
Norwich is the site of the first recorded "blood libel" in Europe when in 1144, William of Norwich was found murdered. At that time Jews were connected with the woollen and worsted trades for which the city was at that time famous. Resettlement took place in the early 18th century and the present community was established in 1813.

SYNAGOGUES
3a Earlham Road NR2 3RA
Telephone: (01603) 503434

Progressive Jewish Community of East Anglia
c/o Frimette Carr NR
Telephone: (01603) 714162

Northamptonshire
NORTHAMPTON
SYNAGOGUES
Overstone Road BB1 3JW
Telephone: (01604) 33345
Services on Friday night.

Nottinghamshire
NEWARK
HOLOCAUST MEMORIAL CENTRE
Beth Shalom
Laxton, Newark, Notts NG22 0PA
Telephone: (01623) 836627
Fax: (01623) 836647
Beth Shalom Holocaust Memorial Centre was conceived as a place where some of the implications of the Holocaust can be faced. It is an education centre where Jews and non-Jews work together to forge a united front against the perils of anti-Semitism and racism in society today.

NOTTINGHAM
Jews settled in Nottingham as early as medieval times, and centres of learning and worship are known to have existed in that period. The earliest known record of an established community dates from 1822 when a grant of land for burial purposes was made by the Corporation.

The synagogue in Shakespeare Street (originally a Methodist Church) is a Grade II listed building.

RESTAURANTS
Vegetarian
Maxine's Salad Table
56 Upper Parliament Street NG1 2AG
Telephone: (0115) 947-3622

SYNAGOGUES
Orthodox
Shakespeare Street NG1 4FQ
Telephone: (0115) 947-2004

Progressive
Nottingham Progressive Jewish Congregation
Lloyd Street, Sherwood NG5 4BP
Telephone: (0115) 962-4761
Email: npjc@ulps.org
Web site: www.npjc.org.uk

Oxfordshire
OXFORD
There was an important medieval community, and the present one dates back to 1842. The Oxford Synagogue and Jewish Centre, opened in 1974, serves both the city and the university. It is available for all forms of Jewish worship.

COMMUNITY ORGANISATIONS
L'Chaim Society
Albion House, Little Gate OX
Telephone: (01865) 794-462

SYNAGOGUES
The Synagogue and Jewish Centre
21 Richmond Road OX1 2JL
Telephone: (01865) 553042
Email: information@oxford-synagogue.org.uk
Regular Orthodox, Masorti and Progressive Services.
Wide range of communal activities. A kosher meals
service operates during term-time. Phone or email for
information.

Staffordshire
STOKE ON TRENT
SYNAGOGUES
Birch Terrace, Hanley ST1 3JN
Telephone: (01782) 616417

Surrey
GUILDFORD
SYNAGOGUES
Orthodox
Guildford & District Synagogue
York Road GU1 4DR
Telephone: (01483) 576470
Email: gould.harry@net.ntl.com
Web site:
www.geocities.com/guildfordjewishcommunity

Correspondence: Mrs B. Gould, Lynwood, Hillier Road,
Guildford, Surrey, GU1 2JG.

TOURIST SITES
Enquiries about the important discovery in 2000 of a
medieval synagogue in the town may be addressed to
the Guildford Museum.

Sussex (East)
BRIGHTON AND HOVE
The first known Jewish resident of Brighton
lived here in 1767. The earliest synagogue was
founded in Jew Street in 1789. Henry Solomon,
vice-president of the congregation, was the first
Chief Constable of the town. His brother-in-law,
Levi Emanuel Cohen, founded the *Brighton
Guardian*, and was twice elected president of the
Newspaper Society of Great Britain. The town's
Jewish population today is about 8,000.

COMMUNITY ORGANISATIONS
Lubavitch Chabad House
15 The Upper Drive BN3 6GR
Telephone: (01273) 321-919
Fax: (01273) 821-518

KOSHER SERVICES WORLDWIDE

Presents its services to the Jewish traveler, holiday maker & host

★★★★★

Kosher functions catered anywhere in the world

★★★

Kosher fresh cooked food anywhere in the world
If you have the venue we will provide the food
(not pre-packed but freshly cooked)

★★★

Kosher Cruises throughout the world
cruises@lotustours.info

★★★

Kosher Villa at Sosua in the Dominican Republic,
Fully staffed. With fresh cooked kosher food
Donaldr@afpimaging.com

★★★

Kosher catering in the United Kingdom
(Under Supervision Brighton & Hove Kashrut Committee)

★★★

Kosher hotel for Pesach in Brighton, England
(Under Supervision Brighton & Hove Kashrut Committee)

★★★

Kosher catering throughout Israel
(Rabbinate Netanya Supervision)

Kosher Services Worldwide

Koshercaterer@yahoo.co.uk   kosherisrael@013.net.il

Israel +97298626442   England +1273 772406

DELICATESSEN
Cantor's of Hove
20 Richardson Road, Hove BN3 5BB
Telephone: (01273) 723-669

MEDIA
Newspaper
Sussex Jewish News
PO Box 2178 BN3 3SZ
Telephone: (01273) 330-550
Fax: (01273) 736-342
Email: doris@sjnews.fsnet.co.uk
Web site: www.jewishsussex.com

MIKVAOT
Prince Regent Swimming Pool Complex, Church
Street BN1 1YA
Telephone: (01273) 321-919

ORGANISATIONS
Hillel House
18 Harrington Road BN1 6RE
Telephone: (01273) 503-450
Closed during summer vacation. Friday evening meals
available.

RELIGIOUS ORGANISATIONS
Brighton and Hove Joint Kashrus Committee
c/o B.H.H.C., 31 New Church Road, Hove BN3 4AD
Telephone: (01273) 888855
Fax: (01273) 888810

RESTAURANTS
Vegetarian
Food for Friends
17-18 Prince Albert Street, The Lanes
Telephone: (01273) 202-310
Fax: (01273) 774-171
Email: simon@foodies.freeserve.co.uk
Web site: www.foodforfriends.com

Vegetarian
Wai Kika Moo Kau Limited
42 Meeting House Lane
Telephone: (01273) 323-824

SYNAGOGUES
Orthodox
Brighton & Hove Hebrew Congregation
Middle Street Synagogue, 66 Middle Street BN1
1AL
Telephone: (01273) 888855
Fax: (01273) 888810
The synagogue, which was built in 1874 when Brighton
was very fashionable, has an elaborate Victorian interior.
It is a Grade II listed building.

Hove Hebrew Congregation
79 Holland Road, Hove BN3 1JN
Telephone: (01273) 732035
West Hove Synagogue
31 New Church Road, Hove BN3 4AD
Telephone: (01273) 888855
Fax: (01273) 888810
Email: bhhc@breathemail.net

Progressive
Progressive Synagogue
6 Landsdowne Road BN3 1FF
Telephone: (01273) 737223
9.30am to 1pm

Reform
New (Reform)
Palmeira Avenue BN3 3GE
Telephone: (01273) 735343
Fax: (01273) 734537
Email: office@bhns.org
Web site: www.bhns.org

EASTBOURNE
SYNAGOGUES
Orthodox
22 Susans Road BN21 3TJ
Telephone: (01323) 640441

HASTINGS
CONTACT INFORMATION
Alfred Ross
PO Box 74, Bexhill on Sea
Telephone: (01424) 848344

Tyne & Wear
GATESHEAD
A community with many schools, yeshivot and
other training institutions.

BAKERIES
Stenhouse
215 Coatsworth Road NE8 1SR
Telephone: (0191) 477-2001

BOOKSELLERS
J. Lehmann
28-30 Grasmere Street NE8 1TS
Telephone: (0191) 477-3523
Fax: (0191) 430-0555
Email: info@lehmanns.co.uk
Also has wholesale and mail order, Unit E, Rolling Mill
Road, NE32 3DP. Tel: 0191 430-0333

BUTCHERS
K.L. Kosher Butcher
83 Rodsley Avenue NE8
Telephone: (0191) 477-3109
Kosher.

MIKVAOT
180 Bewick Road NE8 1UF
Telephone: (0191) 477-3552

SYNAGOGUES
138 Whitehall Road NE8 1TP
Telephone: (0191) 477-3012
180 Bewick Road NE8 1UF
Telephone: (0191) 477-0111

NEWCASTLE UPON TYNE
The community was established before 1831, when a cemetery was acquired. Jews have lived in Newcastle since 1775. There are about 1,200 Jews in the city today.

GROCERIES
Zelda's Delicatessen
Unit 7, Kenton Park Shopping Centre, Gosforth NE3 4RU
Telephone: (0191) 213-0013
Fax: (0191) 213-0013
Email: zeldasdeli@aol.com
Supervision: Newcastle Kashrus Committee, Rabbi Yehuda Black

KASHRUT INFORMATION
Kashrus Committee
Lionel Jacobson House, Graham Park Road, Gosforth NE3 4BH
Telephone: (0191) 284-0959
Fax: (0191) 284-0959

MEDIA
Newspapers
The North-East Jewish Recorder
24 Adeline Gardens NE3 4JQ
Telephone: (0191) 285-1253
Fax: (0191) 242-1316
Email: clivando@hotmail.com
Web site: www.northeastjewish.org.uk

MIKVAOT
Graham Park Road NE3 4BH
Telephone: (0191) 284-0959

RELIGIOUS ORGANISATIONS
Representative Council of North-East Jewry
Telephone: (0191) 215-6253
Fax: (0191) 215-6080

RESTAURANTS
Vegetarian
The Supernatural
2 Princess Square NE1 8ER
Telephone: (0191) 261-2730

SYNAGOGUES
Orthodox
United Hebrew Congregation
Graham Park Road NE3 4BH
Telephone: (0191) 284-0959
Mikva on premises.

Reform
Newcastle Reform Synagogue
The Croft, off Kenton Road NE3 4RF
Telephone: (0191) 284-8621

SUNDERLAND
MIKVAOT
11 The Oaks East, Ryhope Road SR2 8EX
Telephone: (191) 565-0224

SYNAGOGUES
Orthodox
Sunderland Hebrew Congregation
Ryhope Road SR2 7EQ
Telephone: (191) 565-8093
This building has been given Grade II listed status.

West Midlands
BIRMINGHAM
This Jewish community is one of the oldest in the Provinces, dating from at least 1730. Birmingham was a centre from which Jewish pedlars covered the surrounding country week by week, returning home for Shabbat.

The first synagogue of which there is any record was in The Froggery in 1780. There was a Jewish cemetery in the same neighbourhood in 1730. The synagogue of 1780 was extended in 1791, 1809 and 1827. A new and larger synagogue, popularly known as 'Singers Hill', opened in 1856. Today's Jewish population stands at about 2,300.

BOOKSELLERS
Lubavitch Bookshop
95 Willows Road B12 9QF
Telephone: (0121) 440-6673
Fax: (0121) 446-4199

DELICATESSEN
Gee's Butchers Ltd
75 Pershore Road B5 7NX
Telephone: (0121) 440-2160
Kosher butcher, baker and deli.

INFORMATION AND RESOURCE CENTRE
Israel Information Centre for the Midlands
Singers Hill, Ellis Street B1 1HL
Telephone: (0121) 643-2688
Fax: (0121) 643-2688
Email: rjacobs@iicmids.u-net.com
Hours of opening: 10am-4pm Monday, Tuesdays,
Thursdays or by appointment.

KASHRUT INFORMATION
Shechita Board
Singers Hill, Ellis Street B1 1HL
Telephone: (0121) 643-0884

MIKVAOT
Birmingham Central Synagogue
133 Pershore Road B5 7PA
Telephone: (0121) 440-4044
Fax: (0121) 440-5405

SYNAGOGUES
Liberal
Progressive Synagogue
4 Sheepcote Street B16 8AA
Telephone: (0121) 643-5640
Fax: (0121) 633-8372
Email: bps@uips.org
Web site: www.bps-pro-syn.co.uk

Orthodox
Bimingham Hebrew Congregation
Singer's Hill, Ellis Street B1 1HL
Telephone: (0121) 643-0884
Fax: (0121) 643-5950

Central Synagogue
133 Pershore Road, Edgbaston B5 7PA
Telephone: (0121) 440-4044
Fax: (0121) 440-5405

COVENTRY
SYNAGOGUES
Orthodox
Coventry Hebrew Congregation
Barras Lane CV1 3BW
Telephone: (024) 7622-0168
The Jewish presence in Coventry dates back to 1775, if
not earlier.

Reform
Coventry Jewish Reform Community
Telephone: (024) 7667-2027

SOLIHULL
SYNAGOGUES
Orthodox
Solihull & District Hebrew Congregation
3 Monastery Drive B91 1DW
Telephone: (0121) 707-5199
Fax: (0121) 706-8736
Email: shul@solihullshul.org
Web site: www.solihullshul.org
Services: Friday evening 6.30pm winter, 8.00 pm
summer; Saturday 9.45am, Sunday 9am

Yorkshire (North)
HARROGATE
SYNAGOGUES
Orthodox
Harrogate Hebrew Congregation
St Mary's Walk
Telephone: (01423) 871713
Fax: (01423) 879143
Email: philip.morris@ukgateway.net
Services: Saturday 9.30 am. First Friday evening in month
- Winter 6 pm. / Summer 7 pm.

YORK
TOURS
Yorkwalk
3 Fairway, Clifton, York YO30 5QA
Telephone: (01904) 622303
Fax: (01904) 656244
Email: admin@yorkwalk.fsnet.co.uk
Web site: www.yorkwalk.co.uk
Introduced new walk called 'The Jewish Heritage Walk',
recalling the Jewish contribution to York's history. The
walk finishes at Clifford's Tower, the site of a dreadful
massacre in 1190.

Yorkshire (South)
SHEFFIELD
SYNAGOGUES
Orthodox
Sheffield Jewish Congregation and Centre
Kingfield Synagogue, Brincliffe Crescent S11 8UX
Telephone: (0114) 255-2296
There is a mikveh in the building. There is also a kosher
restaurant and butcher on Thursdays only.

Reform
Sheffield & District Reform Jewish Congregation
PO Box 675 S11 8TE
Telephone: (0114) 209259
Fax: (0114) 236-2982
Web site: www.shef-ref.co.uk
Service alternate Friday evenings and Saturday mornings, and high Holy Days

Yorkshire (West)

BRADFORD
The Jewish community, although only about 140 years old, has exercised much influence on the city's staple industry: wool. Jews of German descent developed the export trade of wool yarns and fabrics.

SYNAGOGUES
Orthodox
Bradford Hebrew Congregation
Springhurst Road, Shipley BD18 3DN
Telephone: (01274) 581189
Fax: (01274) 374101
Services 10am monthly on Shabbat Mevorachim, High Holy Days & certain festivals.

Reform
Bradford Synagogue
Bowland Street, Manningham Lane BD1 3BW
Telephone: (01274) 01274-728925
Service Sat 11am; Festivals, 6pm & 11am. A Grade II listed building, built in 1873 in the Moorish style.

LEEDS
The Leeds Jewish community is the second largest in the provinces, and numbers about 12,000. The community dates only from the 1820s, although a few Jews are known to have lived there in the previous half-century. The first synagogue was built in 1860.

The population which peaked at around 20,000 in the 1920s, and was possibly the city which had largest population of Jews in the country, is now less than 8,000.

BAKERIES
Chalutz Bakery
378 Harrogate Road LS17 6PY
Telephone: (0113) 269-1350
Supervision: Leeds Beth Din
Hours: Monday to Thursday, 8 am to 6 pm; Friday, to one hour before Shabbat; Saturday, from one hour after Shabbat to 2 pm Sunday.

BUTCHERS
Fisher's Deli
391 Harrogate Road LS17 6DJ
Telephone: (0113) 268-6944
Supervision: Leeds Beth Din
Butcher and deli.

Gourmet Foods
Sandhill Parade, 584 Harrogate Road LS17 8DP
Telephone: (0113) 268-2726
Supervision: Leeds Beth Din
Butcher and deli.

COMMUNITY ORGANISATIONS
Leeds Jewish Representative Council
c/o Shadwell Lane Synagogue LS17
Telephone: (0113) 269-7520
Fax: (0113) 237-0851
Publishes Year Book.

DELICATESSEN
The Kosherie
410 Harrogate Road LS17 6PY
Telephone: (0113) 268-2943
Fax: (0113) 269-6979
Supervision: Leeds Beth Din

HOTELS
Beegee's Guest House
18 Moor Allerton Drive, off Street Lane, Moortown LS17 6RZ
Telephone: (0113) 293-5469
Fax: (0113) 275-3300
Near all synagogues.

LIBRARIES
Jewish Library
Porton Collection; Leeds Central Library, Municipal Buildings LS1 3AB
Telephone: (0113) 247-8282
Fax: (0113) 247-8426
Web site: www.leeds.gov.uk

MEDIA
Newspaper
Jewish Telegraph
1 Shaftesbury Avenue LS8 1DR
Telephone: (0113) 295-6000
Fax: (0113) 295-6006
Email: leeds@jewishtelegraph.com
Web site: www.jewishtelegraph.com

MIKVAOT
Makor Jewish and Israel Centre
411 Harrogate Road LS17 7BY
Telephone: (0113) 268-0899

RELIGIOUS ORGANISATIONS
Beth Din
Etz Chaim Synagogue LS17 6BY
Telephone: (0113) 269-6902
Fax: (0113) 237-0893
Information about kosher food and accommodation may
be obtained here.

RESTAURANTS
Hansa's Gujarati Restaurant
72 North Street LS2 7PN
Telephone: (0113) 244-4408
Web site: www.hansasrestaurant.co.uk
Indian Vegetarian restaurant.

SYNAGOGUES
Orthodox
Beth Hamidrash Hagadol
399 Street Lane LS17 6HQ
Telephone: (0113) 269-2181
Fax: (0113) 237-0113
Email: office@bhhs.freeserve.co.uk

Chassidishe
c/o Donisthorpe Hall, Shadwell Lane LS17 6AW

Etz Chaim
411 Harrogate Road LS17 7BY
Telephone: (0113) 266-2214

Queenshill Synagogue
26 Queenshill Avenue LS17 6AX
Telephone: (0113) 2687364
Email: sabrah2936.aol.com
Mailing address: 49 Queenshill Drive, Moortown, LS17
5BG.

**Shadwell Lane Synagogue (United Hebrew
Congregation)**
151 Shadwell Lane LS17 8DW
Telephone: (0113) 269-6141
Fax: (0113) 269-6141
Email: minyan@uhcleeds.fsnet.co.uk
Web site: www.uhcleeds.com

Shomrei Hadass
368 Harrogate Road LS17 6QB
Telephone: (0113) 268-1461

Reform
Sinai
Roman Avenue, off Street Lane LS8 2AN
Telephone: (0113) 266-5256
Fax: (0113) 266-1539
Email: synagogue@sinaileeds.freeserve.co.uk

ISLE OF MAN

DOUGLAS
SYNAGOGUES
Hebrew Congregation
Telephone: (01624) 24214
There are more than 70 Jews on the island.

Channel Islands

ALDERNEY

LONGY
MEMORIAL
Corblets Road
There is a memorial to the victims of the Nazis during
their occupation of the Channel Islands during the
Second World War. It bears plaques in English, French,
Hebrew and Russian.

JERSEY

ST BRELADE
CONTACT INFORMATION
16 La Rocquaise, La Route des Genets, St Brelade
JE3 8HY
Telephone: (01534) 742-819
Fax: (01534) 747-554
Honorary secretary of the Jersey Jewish Congregation.

SYNAGOGUES
Jersey Jewish Congregation
La Petite Route des Mielles, St Brelade JE3 8FY
Telephone: (01534) 865-333
Fax: (01534) 861-431
Shabbat morning service, 10:30 am; Holy days, 7 pm and
10 am.

NORTHERN IRELAND

BELFAST
There were Jews living in Belfast in the year
1652, but the present community was founded
in 1869.

ORGANISATIONS
Vegetarian & Vegans Northern Ireland
66 Ravenhill Gardens BT6 8GQ
Telephone: (028) 9028-1640

RESTAURANTS
Jewish Community Centre
49 Somerton Road BT15 3LH
Telephone: (028) 9077-7974
Open Sunday 6.30 pm to 9.30 pm. Phone ahead as the centre closing during the summer. Both Meat and Dairy.

SYNAGOGUES
Orthodox
49 Somerton Road BT15 3LH
Telephone: (028) 9077-7974
Services: Saturday, Sunday, Monday, & Thursday; am. Friday pm.

SCOTLAND

Fife
DUNDEE
SYNAGOGUES
St Mary Place DD1 5RB
Telephone: (01382) 223557

DUNOON
SYNAGOGUES
Argyll & Bute Jewish Community
Telephone: (01369) 705118

ST ANDREWS
CONTACT INFORMATION
Jewish Student's Society
c/o Sec., Students' Union, University of St Andrews KY16 9UY

Grampian
ABERDEEN
RESTAURANTS
Vegetarian
Lemon Tree Café
5 West North Street AB24 5AT
Telephone: (01224) 621610
Fax: (01224) 630888
Email: bar@lemontree.org
12 noon to 4.00pm Tuesday - Sunday.

SYNAGOGUES
74 Dee Street AB11 6DS
Telephone: (01224) 582135

Lothian
EDINBURGH
The Town Council and Burgess Roll minutes of 1691 and 1717 record applications by Jews for permission to live and trade in Edinburgh.

KASHRUT INFORMATION
Rabbi D Sedley
Telephone: (0131) 667-9360

RESTAURANTS
Vegetarian
Black Bo's
Blackfriars Street EH
Telephone: (0131) 557-6136

Henderson's
94 Hanover Street EH2 1DR
Telephone: (0131) 225-2131
Fax: (0131) 220-3542
Email: mail@hendersonsofedinburgh.co.uk
Web site: www.hendersonsofedinburgh.co.uk
Hours 8.00am - 10.30pm, closed on Sundays. Adjoining Bistro is also vegetarian, (Open on Sunday).

Kalpna Restaurant
2/3 St Patrick Sq. EH8 9EZ
Telephone: (0131) 667-9890
Fax: (0131) 443-8782
Email: kalpnarestaurant@yahoo
Web site: www.kalpna.co.uk
Hours: Lunch 1100am to 2.00pm. Dinner 5.30pm to 11.00pm.

SYNAGOGUES
Orthodox
4 Salisbury Road EH16 5AB
Telephone: (0131) 667-3144
Fax: (0131) 01324-613-750
Email: ray.taylor@lineone.net

Strathclyde
GLASGOW
The Glasgow Jewish community dates back to 1823. The oldest synagogue building is the Garnethill Synagogue, now also the home of the Scottish Jewish Archives, which opened in 1879. The community grew rapidly from 1891 with many Jews settling in the Gorbals. In recent years the community has gradually spread southwards and is now mainly situated in the Giffnock and Newton Mearns areas.

BOOKSELLERS
J & E Levingstone
47/55 Sinclair Drive G42 9PT
Telephone: (0141) 649-2962
Fax: (0141) 649-2962
Religious requisites also stocked.

Well of Wisdom
Giffnock Synagogue G46
Telephone: (0141) 577-8260
Fax: (0141) 620-0823

COMMUNITY ORGANISATIONS
Jewish Community Centre
222 Fenwick Road G46 6UE
Telephone: (0141) 577-8200
Fax: (0141) 577-8202
Email: glasgow@j-scot.org
Web site: www.j-scot.org/glasgow

DELICATESSEN
Hello Deli
200 Fenwick Road G46
Telephone: (0141) 638-8267
Fax: (0141) 621-2290

Marlenes Kosher Deli
2 Burnfield Road G46 7QB
Telephone: (0141) 638-4383

Michael Morrison and Son
52 Sinclair Drive G42 9PY
Telephone: (0141) 632-0998
Fax: (0141) 632-6091
Email: kosher@talk21.com
Not under official supervision. Stockist of many glatt kosher items. Will deliver to hotels.

HOTELS
Giffnock Guest House
10 Forres Avenue G46 6LJ
Telephone: (0141) 638-5554 (mobile: 07801 666-864)
Fax: (0141) -571-9301
Email: stay@giffnockguesthouse.co.uk
Web site: www.giffnockguesthouse.co.uk
Not kosher. 5 minute walk to Synagogue.

Guest House
26 St Clair Avenue G46 7QE
Telephone: (0141) 638-3924
Kosher, but not supervised. 2 twin bedded rooms

KOSHER FOOD
Mindelicious
Unit 2, Block 8, Thornliebank Industrial Estate G77 5PZ
Telephone: (0141) 620-0787
Fax: (0141) 638-4411
Email: chef@mindelicious
Web site: www.mindelicious.com
Delivers to hotels.

MEDIA
Newspaper
Jewish Telegraph
May Terrace, Giffnock G46 6DL
Telephone: (0141) 621-4422
Fax: (0141) 621-4333
Email: glasgow@jewishtelegraph.com
Web site: www.jewishtelegraph.com

MIKVAOT
Giffnock & Newlands Synagogue
Maryville Avenue G46 7NE
Telephone: (0141) 577-8269
Fax: (0141) 577-8252

SYNAGOGUES
Orthodox
Garnethill
129 Hill Street G3 6UB
Telephone: (0141) 332-4151
Shabbat services 10am. Yomtov services 9.45 am.

Giffnock & Newlands Hebrew Congregation
Maryville Avenue G46 7NE
Telephone: (0141) 577-8250
Fax: (0141) 577-8252
Email: rabbimrubin@talk21.com

Langside
125 Niddrie Road G42 8QA
Telephone: (0141) 423-4062

Netherlee & Clarkston
Clarkston Road at Randolph Drive G44
Telephone: (0141) 637-8206/639-7194
Fax: (0141) 616-0743

Newton Mearns
14 Larchfield Court G77 5BH
Telephone: (0141) 639-4000
Fax: (0141) 639-4000
Email: nmhc@btconnect.com

Reform
Glasgow New Synagogue
147 Ayr Road, Newton Mearns G77 6RE
Telephone: (0141) 639-4083
Fax: (0141) 639-4083
Email: shul@gns.org.uk
Web site: www.gns.org.uk

WALES

Glamorgan (South)
CARDIFF
MIKVAOT
Wales Empire Pool Building, Wood Street CF1 1PP
Telephone: (029) 2038-2296

RESTAURANTS
Vegetarian
Munchies Wholefood Co-op
60 Crwys Road, Cathays CF2 4NN
Telephone: (029) 2039-9677

SELF-CATERING
Hillel House CF2 5NR
Telephone: (029) 2022-8845
Self-catering for students.

SYNAGOGUES
Orthodox
Cardiff United Synagogue
Cyncoed Gardens, Cyncoed CF23 5SL
Telephone: (029) 2047-3728
Fax: (029) 2047-3728
Email: C.U.S@btopenworld.co.uk
Web site: www.cardiffunited.org.uk

Reform
Cardiff New Synagogue
Moira Terrace CF24 0EJ
Telephone: (029) 2049-1689
Email: info@cardiffnewsyn.org
Web site: www.cardiffnewsyn.org

Glamorgan (West)
SWANSEA
RESTAURANTS
Vegetarian
Chris's Kitchen
The Market SA1 3PE
Telephone: (01792) 643455
8.30am to 5.30pm Mon.-Sat

SYNAGOGUES
Ffynone
17 Ffynone Drive SA1 6DB
Telephone: (01792) 473333

Gwent
NEWPORT
SYNAGOGUES
Newport Mon Hebrew Congregation
Risca Road NP9 5HH
Telephone: (01633) 262308
Fax: (01633) 266362
Communication: 45 St Marks Crescent, Newport, S.
Wales, NP20 5HE.

Gwynedd
LLANDUDNO
HOTELS
Vegetarian
Plas Madoc Vegetarian Guesthouse
60 Church Walks LL30 2HL
Telephone: (01492) 876514
Email: plasmadoc@vegetarianguesthouse.com
Web site: www.vegetarianguesthouse.com
Synagogue 100 yards away.

SYNAGOGUES
28 Church Walks LL30 2HL
Telephone: (01492) 572549
No resident minister, but visiting ministers during
summer months. Friday night services held throughout
year, 6.15pm (winter) and 8pm (summer).

UNITED STATES OF AMERICA

The first Jews came to what is now the United States of America in 1654. The ship had come from the West Indies and included 23 Jews from Brazil, attempting to escape the arrival of the Inquisition following Portugal's recapture of Brazil from the Dutch earlier that year. It is believed that they thought they were travelling to Amsterdam in the Netherlands, rather than to New Amsterdam (as New York was then called). Within ten years, however, the commuity was moribund. The surrender of New Amsterdam to the British in 1664 brought substantial changes to the Jewish settlement as some restrictions to both civil and religious rights were lifted. In a few colonies they were even granted the right to vote.

Following the English takeover communities were established along the eastern coast, and by 1700 there were between 200 and 300 Jews in the country. At the time of the Revolution there were between 1,500 and 2,000 Jews and they served both in the Militia (which was compulsory) and as officers and soldiers. In the decades immediately before the Civil War, the Jewish population rose from 15,000 to 150,000 as a result of emigration, mainly from German areas. During that war Jews served on both sides with their respective communities.

Immigration was at its peak between 1880 and 1925 (when free emigration ended) and during this period the Jewish population grew from 280,000 to 4,500,000. Unfortunately, during the 1930s, only a small number of the Jewish refugees trying to escape from Germany were able to enter the USA. America's numerical position in world Jewry has declined, with its population being in 1948 as much as ten times the population of Israel, to its current approaching parity. The largest concentration by far has always been in New York.

Each of the main religious groups has its own association of synagogues and rabbis and, unlike many other countries, there is no central religious organisation. There is therefore no central supervision of kashrut. Instead there are many hashgachot issued by both individual local communal organisations and rabbis, as well as by companies who issue such certificates on a commercial basis. Travellers may always check with a local rabbi to ascertain the appropriate supervisory body in a relevant location.

Travellers should also be aware that, following a decision in the Brooklyn (New York) District Court in July 2000, discussions are under way in several other jurisdictions to prepare for the eventuality that New York's kosher laws may be rendered unconstitutional on appeal.

Country calling code: **(+1)**
Total population: **274,520,000**
Jewish population: **5,700,000**
Emergency telephone: **(Police – 911) (Fire – 911) (Ambulance – 911)**
Electricity voltage: **(Electricity voltage – 110/220)**

Alabama

BIRMINGHAM

COMMUNITY ORGANISATIONS
Birmingham Jewish Federation
3966 Montclair Road 35213
Telephone: (205) 803-0416
Fax: (205) 803-1526

CONTACT INFORMATION
Rabbi Avraham Shmidman
3225 Montevallo Road 35223
Telephone: (205) 879-1664
Fax: (205) 879-5774
Email: kicongreg@aol.com

DELICATESSEN
Browdy's
2607 Cahaba Road 35223
Telephone: (205) 879-6411

MIKVAOT
Knesseth Israel
3225 Montevallo Rd 35213
Telephone: (205) 879-1464
Supervision: (O)

SYNAGOGUES
Conservative
Beth-El
2179 Highland Avenue 35205
Telephone: (205) 933-2740
Fax: (205) 933-2747

Orthodox
Knesseth Israel
3225 Montevallo Road 35223
Telephone: (205) 879-1464
Fax: (205) 879-5774
Email: knessethisrael@aol.com

Reform
Emanu-El
2100 Highland Avenue 35205
Telephone: (205) 933-8037

HUNTSVILLE
SYNAGOGUES
Conservative
Etz Chayim
7705 Bailey Cove Road 35802
Telephone: (256) 882-2918
Fax: (256) 881-6160

MOBILE
SYNAGOGUES
Reform
Spring Hill Avenue Temple
1769 Spring Hill Avenue 36607
Telephone: (334) 478-0415

MONTGOMERY
COMMUNITY ORGANISATIONS
Jewish Federation
PO Box 20058 36120
Telephone: (334) 277-5820
Fax: (334) 277-8383

SYNAGOGUES
Conservative
Agudath Israel
3525 Cloverdale Road 36111
Telephone: (334) 281-7394

Orthodox
Etz Ahayem (Sephardi)
725 Augusta Road 36111
Telephone: (334) 281-9819

Reform
Beth Or
2246 Narrow Lane 36106

Alaska
ANCHORAGE
GROCERIES
Carr's Market
Diamond Boulevard and Seward Hwy
Telephone: (907) 341-1020

SYNAGOGUES
Orthodox
Congregation Shomrei Ohr
1210 E. 26th 99508
Telephone: (907) 279-1200
Fax: (907) 279-7890
Email: lubavitchofak@gci.net

Reform
Beth Sholom
7525 E. Northern Lights Blvd 99504
Telephone: (907) 338-1836
Fax: (907) 337-4013
Email: sholom@alaska.net

JUNEAU
SYNAGOGUES
Reform
Juneau Jewish Community
Telephone: (907) 463-4333

Arizona
PHOENIX
COMMUNITY ORGANISATIONS
Jewish Federation of Greater Phoenix
32 W. Coolidge, Suite 200 85013
Telephone: (602) 274-1800

Orthodox Rabbinical Council of Greater Phoenix
515 E. Bethany Home Road 85012
Telephone: (602) 277-8858
Fax: (602) 274-0713
Email: Bethjoseph515@hotmail.com
Supervision: Rabbi David Rebibo

KASHRUT INFORMATION
Rabbi David Rebibo
Phoenix Vaad Hakashruth, 515 E. Bethany Home
Rd. 85012
Telephone: (602) 602-277-8858
Fax: (602) 602-274-0713
Email: bethjoseph515@hotmail.com

MEDIA
Newspapers
Jewish News of Greater Phoenix
1625 E. Northern Ave., Suite 106 85020
Telephone: (602) 870-9470
Fax: (602) 870-0426
Email: editor@jewishaz.com
Web site: www.jewishaz.com

Shalom Arizona
32 W. Coolidge, Suite 200 85013
Telephone: (602) 274-1800

RESTAURANTS
King Solomon's Pizza
4810 N. 7th Street
Telephone: (602) 870-8655

Meat
Segal's Kosher Foods
4818 N. 7th Street
Telephone: (602) 285-1515
Fax: (602) 277-5760
Email: segalkosh@aol.com
Supervision: Vaad Hakashrut of Phoenix

SYNAGOGUES
Conservative
Beth El Congregation
1118 W. Glendale 85021
Telephone: (602) 944-3359
Fax: (602) 944-3565
Web site: www.bethelphoenix.com

Temple Beth Sholom
3400 N Dobson Road, Chandler 85224
Telephone: (602) 897-3636
Fax: (602) 897-3633
Email: office@templebethsholomaz.org
Web site: www.templebethsholomaz.org

Orthodox
Congregation Beth Joseph
515 E. Bethany Home Road 85012
Telephone: (602) 602-277-8858
Fax: (602) 602-274-0713
Email: bethjoseph515@hotmail.com
Supervision: Rabbi David Rebibo

Congregation Shaarei Tzedek
7608 N. 18th Avenue 85021
Telephone: (602) 944-1133

Young Israel of Phoenix
745 E Maryland Avenue, Ste.120 85014
Telephone: (602) 265-8888
Fax: (602) 265-8867
Email: cnsil5@home.com

Reform
Temple Beth Ami
4545 N. 36th Street, No. 211 85018
Telephone: (602) 956-0805

Temple Chai
4545 East Marilyn Rd 85032
Telephone: (602) 971-1234

SCOTTSDALE
MUSEUMS
Sylvia Plotkin Judaica Museum
10460 N. 56th St, Scottsdale 85253
Telephone: (480) 951-0323
Fax: (480) 951-7150
Email: museum@templebethisrael.org
Web site: www.spjm.org

SYNAGOGUES
Conservative
Beth Emeth of Scottsdale
5406 E. Virginia Avenue 85254
Telephone: (480) 947-4604

Har Zion
5929 E. Lincoln Drive 85253
Telephone: (480) 991-0720

Orthodox
Chabad of Scottsdale
10215 North Scottsdale Road 85253
Telephone: (480) 998-1410
Web site: www.chabadofscottsdale.org

Reform
Temple Kol Ami
15030 N. 64th Street 85254
Telephone: (480) 951-9660
Fax: (480) 951-5231
Email: templekolami@aol.com

Temple Solel
6805 E. MacDonald Drive 85253
Telephone: (480) 991-7414
Fax: (480) 451-0829
Email: mleano@templesolel.org
Web site: www.templesolel.org

SIERRA VISTA
SYNAGOGUES
Reform
Temple Kol Hamidbar
PO Box 908 Sierra Vista 85636
Telephone: (520) 458-8637 (Ans. phone only)
Email: tkh85636@hotmail.com
Web site: www.uahcweb.org/congs/az/tkh/

SUN CITY
SYNAGOGUES
Reform
Beth Shalom of Sun City
12202 101st Avenue 85351
Telephone: 977-3240
Fax: 977-3214
Email: tbsaz@goodnet.com

SUN CITY WEST
SYNAGOGUES
Conservative
**Beth Emeth Congregation of the Sun Cities &
West Valley of Phoenix**
13702 West Meeker Blvd., 85375
Telephone: (602) 623-584-7210
Fax: (602) 623-975-2976
Email: info@bethemethaz.org
Web site: www.bethemethaz.org

TEMPE
COMMUNITY ORGANISATIONS
Tri-City Jewish Community Center
1965 E. Hermosa Drive 85282
Telephone: (602) 897-0588

SYNAGOGUES
Orthodox
Chabad-Lubavitch Center
23 W. 9th Street 85281
Telephone: (602) 966-5163

Reform
Temple Emanuel
5801 Rural Road 85283
Telephone: (602) 838-1414

TUCSON
BAKERIES
Nadine's Pastry Shoppe
4553 Broadway Blvd.
Telephone: (520) 326-0735

BUTCHERS
Feig's Kosher Market & Deli
5071 E. 5th Street 85711
Telephone: (520) 325-2255
Fax: (520) 325-2978
Supervision: Rabbi R. Eisen.

COMMUNITY ORGANISATIONS
Jewish Federation of Southern Arizona
3822 E. River Rd. 85718
Telephone: (520) 577-9393
Fax: (520) 577-0734
Email: stumellan@jon.cjfny.org

SYNAGOGUES
Conservative
Congregation Bet Shalom
3881 E. River Road 85718
Telephone: (520) 577-1171
Fax: (520) 577-8903
Email: cbs3881@juno.com
Supervision: Rabbi Leo M Abrami

Orthodox
Congregation Chofetz Chayim
5150 E. 5th Street 85711
Telephone: (520) 747-7780
Fax: (520) 745-6325
Email: ewbecker@flash.net
Young Israel of Tucson
2443 E 4th Street 85710
Telephone: (520) 326-8362

Arkansas

EL DORADO
SYNAGOGUES
Reform
Beth Israel
1130 E. Main Street

HELENA
SYNAGOGUES
Reform
Temple Beth-El
406 Perry Street 72342
Telephone: (501) 338-6654

HOT SPRINGS
SYNAGOGUES
Reform
House of Israel
300 Quapaw Avenue 71901
Telephone: (501) 623-5821
Fax: (501) 622-3500
Email: houseofi@direclynx.net

LITTLE ROCK
COMMUNITY ORGANISATIONS
Jewish Federation of Arkansas
425 N. University Ave., Little Rock 72205
Telephone: (501) 663-3571
Fax: (501) 663-7286
Email: jfalr@aristotle.net

SYNAGOGUES
Orthodox
Agudath Achim
7901 W. 5th St. 72205
Telephone: (501) 225-1683

Reform
B'nai Israel
3700 Rodney Parham Rd. 72212
Telephone: (501) 225-9700
Fax: (501) 225-6058
Email: elevy@snider.net

California
As the general population of California continues to increase, the Jewish community is growing as well. Places of worship abound, from Eureka in the north to San Diego in the south, but the major part of the community lives in the Los Angeles metropolitan area.

ALAMEDA
SYNAGOGUES
Reform
Temple Israel
3183 McCartney Road 94502
Telephone: (510) 522-9355
Fax: (510) 522-9356
Email: tialameda@prodigy.net

BAKERSFIELD
SYNAGOGUES
Conservative
B'nai Jacob
600 17th Street 93301
Telephone: (661) 325-8017

Reform
Temple Beth El
2906 Loma Linda Drive 93305
Telephone: (661) 322-7607
Fax: (661) 322-7807
Email: kernjew@aol.com
Web site: www.templebethel_ca.homestead.com

BERKELEY
MIKVAOT
Mikvah Taharas Israel
2520 Warring St. 94704-3111
Telephone: (510) 510-848-7221
Fax: (510) 510-217-3596
Email: vaad@flash.net

MUSEUMS
Judah L. Magnes Museum
2911 Russell St. 94705
Telephone: (510) 549-6950
Fax: (510) 849-3673
Email: info@magnesmuseum.org
Web site: www.judahmagnesmuseum.org

RESTAURANTS
Dairy
Noah's Bagels
1883 Solano Avenue
Telephone: (510) 525-4447
Supervision: The Vaad Kakashrus of Northern California

SYNAGOGUES
Conservative
Netivot Shalom
1841 Berkeley Way 94708
Telephone: (510) 549-9447
Fax: (510) 549-9448
Email: administrator@netivotshom.org
Web site: www.netivotshalom.org

Egalitarian
Berkeley Hillel Foundation
2736 Bancroft Way 94704
Telephone: (510) 845-7793
Fax: (510) 845-7753

Jewish Renewal
Aquarian Minyan
c/o Goldfarb, 2020 Essex 94703
Kehilla
PO Box 3063 94703

Orthodox
Chabad House
2643 College Avenue 94704
Telephone: (510) 540-5824
Congregation Beth Israel
1630 Bancroft Way 94703
Telephone: (510) 510-843-5246
Fax: (510) 510-843-5058
Email: office@beth-israel.berkeley.ca.us
Web site: www.beth-israel.berkeley.ca.us

Reform
Congregation Beth El
2301 Vine Street 94708
Telephone: (510) 848-3988
Fax: (510) 848-9434
Email: frontoffice@bethelberkeley.org
Web site: www.bethelberkeley.org

BONITA

SYNAGOGUES

Orthodox

Beth Eliyahu Torah Center
5012 Central Avenue, Bonita 91902
Telephone: (619) 472-2144
Fax: (619) 472 0718

BURLINGAME

SYNAGOGUES

Reform

Peninsula Temple Sholom
1655 Sebastian Drive 94010
Telephone: (415) 697-2266
Fax: (415) 697-2544

CARMEL

SYNAGOGUES

Reform

Congregation Beth Israel
5716 Carmel Valley Road 93923
Telephone: (831) 624-2015
Fax: (831) 624-4786
Email: shalomcbi@aol.com

CASTRO VALLEY

SYNAGOGUES

Reform

Shir Ami
4529 Malabar Avenue 94546
Telephone: (415) 537-1787

CHULA VISTA

SYNAGOGUES

Conservative

Temple Beth Sholom
208 Madrona Street, Chula Vista 91910
Telephone: (619) 420-6040
Email: bethsholomcv@aol.com
Web site: www.ascj.org/pacsw/chulavista/1ntel.

COSTA MESA

COMMUNITY ORGANISATIONS

Jewish Federation of Orange County
250 E. Baker Street, Suite #A 92626
Telephone: (714) 755-5555 ext 241
Fax: (714) 755-0307
Email: info@jfoc.org
Web site: www.jewishorangecounty.org

GIFT SHOP

The Golden Dreidle
1835 Newport Blvd. #A111 92627
Telephone: (714) 645-3878
Fax: (714) 646-5081

DALY CITY

SYNAGOGUES

Conservative

B'nai Israel
1575 Annie Street 94015
Telephone: (415) 756-5430

DAVIS

SYNAGOGUES

Reform

Davis Jewish Fellowship
1821 Oak Avenue 95616
Telephone: (916) 758-0842

ENCINITAS

SYNAGOGUES

Reform

Temple Solel
552 S.Camino Real, Encinitas 92024
Telephone: (760) 436-0654
Fax: (760) 436-2748
Email: info@templesolel.net

EUREKA

SYNAGOGUES

Reform

Beth El
Hodgson & T Streets, PO Box 442 95502
Telephone: (707) 444-2846

FRESNO

COMMUNITY ORGANISATIONS

Jewish Federations Office
1340 W. Herndon, Suite 103 93711

SYNAGOGUES

Conservative

Beth Jacob
406 W. Shields Avenue 93705
Telephone: (209) 222-0664

Reform

Temple Beth Israel
6622 N. Maroa Avenue 93704
Telephone: (209) 432-3600

LA JOLLA

SYNAGOGUES

Conservative

Congregation Beth El
8660 Gilman Drive, La Jolla 92037
Telephone: (619) 452-1734
Fax: (619) 452 5578
Email: congregationbethel.com

Orthodox
Congregation Adat Yeshurun
8950 Villa La Jolla Drive, Suite 1224, La Jolla 92037
Telephone: (619) 535-1196
Fax: (619) 535-0037
Email: adatyeshurun.org
8625 La Jolla Scenic Dr., N. 92037
Telephone: (619) 535-1196
Fax: (619) 535-0037
Email: info@adatyeshurun.org
Web site: www.adatyeshurun.org

LA MESA
MEDIA
Newspapers
San Diego Jewish Times
4731 Palm Avenue, La Mesa 91941
Telephone: (619) 463-5515
Fax: (619) 463-1309
Email: jewishtimes@earthlink.net

LAGUNA HILLS
DELICATESSEN
The Kosher Bite
23595 Moulton Parkway 92653
Telephone: (949) 770-1818
Fax: (949) 770-5321
Email: kosherbite.com
Supervision: Rabinical Council of Orange County

LAKEWOOD
SYNAGOGUES
Conservative
Temple Beth Zion Sinai
6440 Del Amo Blvd. 90713
Telephone: (310) 429-0715
Fax: (310) 429-0715
Email: tbzs@jps.net

OAKLAND
COMMUNITY ORGANISATIONS
Berkeley/Richmond JCC
1414 Walnut St.,, Berkeley 94709
Telephone: (510) 848-0237
Fax: (510) 848-0170
Email: info@brjcc.org
Web site: www.brjcc.org
Jewish Community Federation of the Greater East Bay
300 Grand Ave 94610
Web site: www.jfed.org

DELICATESSEN
Holy Land Restaurant
677 Rand Avenue 94610
Telephone: (510) 272-0535

MIKVAOT
Beth Jacob Synagogue
3778 Park Blvd 94610
Telephone: (510) 482-1147
Fax: (510) 482-2374
Email: bjc-office@eb.jfed.org

SYNAGOGUES
Conservative
Beth Abraham
327 MacArthur Blvd. 94610
Telephone: (510) 832-0936
Beth Sholom
642 Dolores, San Leandro 94577

Independent
B'nai Israel of Rossmoor
c/o Fred Rau, 2601 Ptarmigan #3, Walnut Creek 94595
Beth Chaim
PO Box 23632, Pleasant Hill 94523

Orthodox
Beth Jacob Synagogue
3778 Park Blvd 94610
Telephone: (510) 482-1147
Fax: (510) 482-2374
Email: bjc-office@eb.jfed.org

Reform
Beth Emek
PO Box 722, Livermore 94550
Beth Hillel
801 Park Central, Richmond 94803
Temple Beth Torah
42000 Paseo Padre Pkwy, Fremont 94538
Telephone: (510) 656-7141
Web site: www.bethtorah-fremont.org
Temple Isaiah
3800 Mt. Diablo Blvd., Lafayette 94549
Temple Sinai
2808 Summit 94609
Telephone: (510) 451-3263
Fax: (510) 465-0603
Email: templeoffice@oaklandsinai.org

PALM SPRINGS
SYNAGOGUES
Conservative
Temple Isaiah
332 W. Alejo Road 92262
Telephone: (760) 325-2281
Fax: (760) 325-3235

Orthodox
Chabad of Palm Springs
425 Avenue, Ortega
Telephone: (760) 325-0774

Desert Synagogue
1068 N. Palm Canyon Drive 92262
Telephone: (760) 327-4848
Fax: (760) 322-5238
Email: theshul@earthlink.net
Web site: www.desertshul.org

PALO ALTO
COMMUNITY ORGANISATIONS
Albert L. Schultz Community Center
655 Arastradero Road 94306
Telephone: (650) 493-9400

GROCERIES
Garden Fresh
1245 W. El Camino Road, Mount View 94040
Telephone: (650) 961-7795

SYNAGOGUES
Orthodox
Chabad of Greater South Bay
3070 Louis Road 94303
Telephone: (650) 424-9800
Fax: (650) 493-3425
Email: chabad@jewish.org

Palo Alto Orthodox Minyan
260 Sheridan Avenue 94306
Telephone: (650) 948-7498

POWAY
SYNAGOGUES
Orthodox
Chabad of Poway
16934 Chabad Way 92064
Telephone: (858) 451-0455
Fax: (858) 673-0299

Reform
Temple Adat Shalom
15905 Pomerado Road, Poway 92064
Telephone: (858) 451-1200
Fax: (858) 451 2409

RAMONA
SYNAGOGUES
Reform
Etz Chaim
PO Box 1138, Ramona 92065
Telephone: (760) 789-7393

SACRAMENTO
COMMUNITY ORGANISATIONS
Jewish Federation of Sacramento
2351 Wyda Way 95825
Telephone: (916) 486-0906
Fax: (916) 486-0816
Email: jfed@juno.com
Web site: www.jewishsac.org

MIKVAOT
1024 Morse Ave 95864
Telephone: (916) 481-1158

RESTAURANTS
Meat
Bob's Butcher Block
6436 Fair Oaks Blvd., Carmichael Oaks Shopping Ctr
Telephone: (916) 482-6884

SYNAGOGUES
Conservative
Mosaic Law
2300 Sierra Blvd. 95825
Telephone: (916) 488-1122
Fax: (916) 488-1165
Web site: www.mosaiclaw.org

Orthodox
KenessethIsrael Torah Center
1024 Morse Avenue 95864
Telephone: (916) 481-1159
Fax: (916) 481-2096
Email: itc1159@earthlink.net
Web site: www.kitsacramento.org

Reform
B'nai Israel
3600 Riverside Blvd. 95818
Telephone: (916) 446-4861

Beth Shalom
4746 El Camino Avenue 09608
Telephone: (916) 485-4478
Fax: (916) 485-0776
Email: office@cbshalom.org
Web site: www.cbshalom.org

SAN BERNARDINO
SYNAGOGUES
Reform
Emanu El
3512 N. E Street 92405
Telephone: (909) 886-4818
Fax: (909) 883-5892
Email: cee@emanuelsb.org

SAN CARLOS

CONTACT INFORMATION
Jewish Travel Network
PO Box 283 94070
Telephone: (650) 368-0880
Fax: (650) 599-9066
Email: info@jewishtravelnetwork.com
Web site: www.jewishtravelnetwork.com/

SAN DIEGO

BAKERIES
Sheila's Café & Bakery
4577 Clairemont Drive 92117
Telephone: (619) 270-0251
Fax: (619) 274-5797
Email: SheilasSanDiego@hotmail.com
Web site: www.sheilascafe.com

COMMUNITY ORGANISATIONS
United Jewish Federation of San Diego County
4950 Murphy Canyon 92123-4325
Telephone: (619) 571-3444
Fax: (619) 571-0701
Email: outreach@ujfsd.org
Web site: www.jewishinsandiego.org

MEDIA
Newspapers
San Diego Jewish Press Heritage
PO Box 19363
Telephone: (619) 265-0808
Fax: (619) 265-0850
Email: sdheritage@cox.net

RESTAURANTS
Dairy
Aarons Glatt Kosher Market
4488 Convoy Street 92111
Telephone: (619) 636-7979
Fax: (619) 636-7980
Web site: www.kosherfooddelivery.com

Sababa, Kosher Restaurant
7520 El Cajon Blvd.
Telephone: (619) 337-1880
Fax: (619) 523-9963

Shmoozers Vegetarian & Pizzeria
6366 El Cajon Blvd 92115
Telephone: (619) 583-1636
Fax: (619) 583 1635
Email: shmoozers1@aol.com
Supervision: Vaad HaRabbanim of San Diego

Dairy Market
Lang's Premium Kosher
6165 El Cajon Blvd 92115
Telephone: (619) 287-7306; 800-60-LANGS
Fax: (619) 582-1545
Web site: www.kosherbread.com
Supervision: Vaad of San Diego

Meat
Sheila's Café & Bakery
4577 Clairemont Dr. 92117
Telephone: (619) 270-0251
Fax: (619) 274-5797
Email: SheilasSanDiego@hotmail.com
Web site: www.sheilascafe.com

SYNAGOGUES
Conservative
Congregation Beth Am
5050 Black Mtn. Road 92130
Telephone: (619) 481-8454
Fax: (619) 481-6068
Email: betham@betham.com

Ner Tamid
16770 West Bernardo Drive, Suite A 92127
Telephone: (619) 592-9141
Fax: (619) 592-4889
Email: nertamid@altavista.com

Tifereth Israel Synagogue
6660 Cowles Mountain Blvd 92119
Telephone: (619) 697-6001
Fax: (619) 697 1102
Email: tiferethisrael.com

Orthodox
Beth Jacob Synagogue
4855 College Avenue 92115
Telephone: (619) 287-9890
Fax: (619) 287-0578

Chabad
6115 Montezuma Road 92115
Telephone: (619) 619-265-0519
Fax: (619) 619-265-0346
Email: ChabadHouseSD@aol.com

Chabad of La Jolla
3813 Governor Drive, Suite N 92122
Telephone: (619) 455-1670
Fax: (619) 451 1443

Ohr Shalom
1260 Morena Blvd, Suite 100 92100
Telephone: (619) 275-9299
Fax: (619) 275-2078

Young Israel of San Diego
7291 Navajo Road, Suite 102 92119
Telephone: (619) 589-1447

Reconstructionist
Congregation Dor Hadash
4858 Ronson Court, Suite A 92111
Telephone: (619) 268-3674
Fax: (619) 794 4087

Reform
Congregation Beth Israel of San Diego
9001 Towne Centre Drive 92122
Telephone: (619) 535-1111
Fax: (619) 535-1130
Email: bmiller@cbisd.org
Web site: www.cbisd.org

Temple Emanu-El
6299 Capri Drive 92120
Telephone: (619) 286-2555
Fax: (619) 286 3176

SAN FRANCISCO
BAKERIES
Noahs Bagels
3519 California Street, Willow Glen
Telephone: (415) 387-3874

COMMUNITY ORGANISATIONS
Jewish Com. Fed. of San Francisco, the Peninsula, Marin & Sonoma Counties
121 Steuart St. 94105
Telephone: (415) 777-4545
Fax: (415) 495-6635
Email: jewishNfo@sfjcf.org
Web site: www.jewishfed.org

EMBASSY
Consul General of Israel
Suite 2100, 456 Montgomery Street 94104

GROCERIES
Jacob's Kosher Meats
2435 Noriega Street 94122
Telephone: (415) 564-7482

Kosher Meats Israel & Cohen Kosher Meats
5621 Geary Blvd 94121
Telephone: (415) 752-3064

Kosher Nutrition Kitchen
Montefiore Senior Center, 3200 California Av.,
Supervision: Orthodox Rabbinical Council

Tel Aviv Strictly Kosher Meats
2495 Irving Street 94122
Telephone: (415) 661-7588
Fax: (415) 661-8258
Supervision: Orthodox Rabbinical Council

LIBRARIES
Holocaust Library & Research Center
601 14th Avenue 94118
Telephone: (415) 751-6040

MIKVAOT
Mikva
3355 Sacramento Street 94118
Telephone: (415) 921-4070

MUSEUMS
The Magnes Museum
121 Steuart St 94105
Telephone: (415) 591-8800
Fax: (415) 591-8815
Email: info@magnesmuseum.org
Web site: www.magnesmuseum.org

RESTAURANTS
Meat
Sabra
419 Grant Avenue, Chinatown
Telephone: (415) 982-3656
Fax: (415) 982-3650
Supervision: Vaad Hakashrus of Northern California

This Is It
430 Geary Street 94210
Telephone: (415) 749-0201

SYNAGOGUES
Conservative
B'nai Emunah
3595 Taraval Street 94116
Telephone: (415) 664-7373
Fax: (415) 664-4209
Email: emuna@jps.net
Web site: www.bnaiemunahsf.org

Beth Israel-Judea
625 Brotherhood Way 94132
Telephone: (415) 586-8833

Beth Sholom
1301 Clement Street 94118
Telephone: (415) 221-8736
Fax: (415) 221-3944
Email: enichol@bethsholomsf.org
Web site: www.bethsholomsf.org

Ner Tamid
1250 Quintara Street 94116
Telephone: (415) 661-3383

Orthodox
Adath Israel
1851 Noriega Street 94122
Telephone: (415) 564-5565

Anshey Sfard
1500 Clement Street 94118
Telephone: (415) 752-4979

Chevra Tehilim
751 25th Avenue 94121
Telephone: (415) 752-2866

Keneseth Israel
873 Sutter Street 94109
Telephone: (415) 771-3420

Torat Emeth
768 27th Avenue 94121
Telephone: (415) 386-1830

Young Israel of San Francisco
1806 A Noriega Street 94122
Telephone: (415) 387-1774

Reform
Emanu-El
Arguello Blvd. & Lake Street 94118
Telephone: (415) 751-2535
Fax: (415) 751-2511
Email: mail@emanuelsf.org

Sha'ar Zahav
290 Dolores Street 94103
Telephone: (415) 861-6932
Fax: (415) 841-6081
Email: office@shaarzahav.org

Sherith Israel
2266 California Street 94115
Telephone: (415) 346-1720
Fax: (415) 673-9439
Email: ed@sherithisrael.org

Sephardi
Magain David
351 4th Avenue 94118
Telephone: (415) 752-9095

TOURIST INFORMATION
Jewish Community Information & Referral
121 Steuart St 94105
Telephone: (415) 415-777-4545
Fax: (415) 415-495-4897
Email: Info@jewishNfo.org
Web site: www.jewishNfo.org

SAN JOSE
BOOKSELLERS
Alef Bet Judaica
14103-0 Winchester Blvd, Los Gatos 95032
Telephone: (408) 370-1818
Fax: (408) 725-8269
Email: nurit@best.com

COMMUNITY ORGANISATIONS
Jewish Federation of Greater San Jose
14855 Oka Road, Los Gatos 95030
Telephone: (408) 358-3033
Fax: (408) 356-0733

MIKVAOT
Mikvah Society of San Jose
1670 Phantom Avenue 95152
Telephone: (408) 408-371-9548 for appointments;
408-264-3138 for info
Email: davidbergman@msn.com

RESTAURANTS
Meat
Willow Glen Kosher Market
1185 Lincoln Avenue 95125
Telephone: (408) 297-6604
Email: kosher@visto.com
Supervision: Va'ad Hakashrus of San Jose

SYNAGOGUES
Conservative
Congregation Beth David
19700 Prospect Road, Saratoga 95070
Telephone: (408) 257-3333
Fax: (408) 257-3338
Email: admin@beth-david.org
Web site: www.beth-david.org

Congregation Emeth
PO Box 1430, Gilroy 95021
Telephone: (408) 847-4111

Congregation Sinai
1532 Willowbrae Avenue 95125-4450
Telephone: (408) 264-8542
Fax: (408) 264-4316
Email: sinai_sj@juno.com

Orthodox
Ahavas Torah
1537-A Meridian Avenue 95125
Telephone: (408) 266-2342
Fax: (408) 264-3139
Email: ahavastorahsj@aol.com
Web site: www.ahava.org

Almaden Valley Torah Center
1422 Helmond Lane 95118
Telephone: (408) 408-445-1770

Am Echad Community
1504 Meridian Avenue 95125
Telephone: (408) 267-2591
Email: info@amechad.org
Web site: www.amechad.org

Reform
Congregation Shir Hadash
16555 Shannon Road, Los Gatos 95032
Telephone: (408) 358-1751
Fax: (408) 358-1753
Web site: www.shirhadash.org

Temple Beth Sholom
2270 Canoas Garden Avenue 95125
Telephone: (408) 978-5566
Temple Emanu-El
1010 University Avenue 95126
Telephone: (408) 292-0939

SAN RAFAEL
SYNAGOGUES
Reform
Rodef Sholom
170 N. San Pedro Rd 94903
Telephone: (415) 479-3441

SANTA BARBARA
SYNAGOGUES
Orthodox
Chabad of Santa Barbara
6047 Stow Canyon Road, Goleta 93117
Telephone: (805) 683-1544
Fax: (805) 683-1545
Email: rabbi@sbchabad.org
Young Israel of Santa Barbara
1826 C Cliff Drive 93109
Telephone: (805) 966-4565

Reform
Congregation B'nai B'rith
1000 San Antonio Creek Road 93111
Telephone: (805) 964-7869
Fax: (805) 683-6473
Email: cbbrav@aol.com

SANTA MONICA
SYNAGOGUES
Orthodox
Chabad House
1428 17th Street 90404
Young Israel of Santa Monica
21 Hampton Avenue
Telephone: (310) 399-8514

Reform
Beth Shir Sholom
1827 California Avenue 90403
Telephone: (310) 310-453-3361
Fax: (310) 310-453-6827
Web site: www.bethshirsholom.com

SANTA ROSA
SYNAGOGUES
Conservative
Beth Ami
4676 Mayette Avenue 95405
Telephone: (707) 545-4334

Reform
Congregation Shomrei Torah
1717 Yulupa Avenue 95405
Telephone: (707) 578-5519
Fax: (707) 578-3967
Email: shomrei@pacbell.net

STOCKTON
Stockton is one of the oldest communities west of the Mississippi River, founded in the days of the California Gold Rush. Temple Israel was founded as Congregation Ryhim Ahoovim in 1850 and erected its first building in 1855.

SYNAGOGUES
Reform
Temple Israel
5105 N. El Dorado St. 95207
Telephone: (209) 477-9306

SUNNYVALE
SYNAGOGUES
Bar Yohai Sefardic Minyan
1030 Astoria Drive 94087
Email: jpbraun@aol.com
Web site: www.baryohai.org

THOUSAND OAKS
SYNAGOGUES
Conservative
Temple Etz Chaim
1080 E. Janss Rd 91360
Telephone: (805) 497-6891
Fax: (805) 497-0086

TIBURON
SYNAGOGUES
Conservative
Congregation Kol Shafar
215 Blackfield Dr 94920
Telephone: (415) 388-1818

VALLEJO
SYNAGOGUES
Unaffiliated
Congregation B'nai Israel
1256 Nebraska St. 94590
Telephone: (707) 642-6526

VENTURA
COMMUNITY ORGANISATIONS
Jewish Community Centre
259 Callens Road
Telephone: (805) 658-7441

SYNAGOGUES
Reform
Temple Beth Torah
7620 Foothill Road 93004
Telephone: (805) 647-4181

WALNUT CREEK
COMMUNITY ORGANISATIONS
Contra Costa JCC
2071 Tice Valley Blvd. 94595
Telephone: (925) 938-7800
Fax: (925) 937-0765

SYNAGOGUES
Conservative
Congregation B'nai Shalom
74 Eckley Lane 94596
Telephone: (925) 934-9446
Fax: (925) 934-9450
Email: office@bshalom.org
Web site: www.bshalom.org
Contra Costa Jewish Community Center
2071 Tice Valley Blvd 94595

Orthodox
Chabad of Contra Costa
1671 Newell Ave. 94595
Telephone: (925) 925-937-4101
Email: info@chabadcoco.com
Web site: www.chabadcoco.com

Reform
Congregation B'nai Tikvah
25 Hillcroft Way 94595
Telephone: (925) 933-5397

WHITTIER
SYNAGOGUES
Conservative
Beth Shalom Synagogues Center
14564 E. Hawes Street 90604
Telephone: (310) 914-8744

LOS ANGELES (GREATER)

ANAHEIM
RESTAURANTS
Disneyland
SYNAGOGUES
Conservative
Temple Beth Emet
1770 W. Cerritos Avenue 92804
Telephone: (714) 772-4720
Fax: (714) 772-4710
Email: tbe-anaheim@tea-house.com

ARCADIA
SYNAGOGUES
Conservative
Congregation Shaarei Torah
550 S. 2nd Avenue 91006
Telephone: (818) 445-0810

BEVERLY HILLS
SYNAGOGUES
Orthodox
Beth Jacob
9030 Olympic Boulevard 90211
Telephone: (310) 278-1911
Fax: (310) 278-9186

Young Israel of Beverly Hills
8701 Pico Blvd, (Between Robertson & La
Cienega) 90035
Telephone: (310) 275-3020
Fax: (310) 275-3031
Email: rabbispan@yahoo.com

Young Israel of North Beverly Hills
9350 Civic Center Drive, North Beverly Hills 90210
Telephone: (310) 203-0170

Orthodox Sephardi
Magen David
322 N. Foothill 90210

BURBANK
SYNAGOGUES
Conservative
Temple Emanu-El
1302 N. Glenoaks Avenue, Burbank 91504
Telephone: (818) 845-1734

DOWNEY
SYNAGOGUES
Reform
Temple Ner Tamid
10629 Lakewood Boulevard 90241
Telephone: (310) 861-9276

ENCINO
SYNAGOGUES
Conservative
Valley Beth Shalom
15739 Ventura Blvd, Encino 91316
Telephone: (818) 788-6000

Orthodox
Chabad House
4915 Hayvenhurst, Encino 91346

Reform
Shir Chadash
17000 Ventura Blvd, Encino

GARDENA
SYNAGOGUES
Conservative
Southwest Temple Beth Torah
14725 S. Gramercy Place 90249
Telephone: (310) 327-8734

GRANADA HILLS
COMMUNITY ORGANISATIONS
North Valley Center
16601 Rinaldi Street, Granada Hills 91344

HOLLYWOOD
KASHRUT INFORMATION
Kosher Information Bureau
15365 Magnolia Blvd, Sherman Oaks 91403
Telephone: (818) 762-3197 & 262-5351
Fax: (818) 766-8537
Email: eeidlitz@kosherquest.org
Web site: www.kosherquest.org

LONG BEACH
BAKERIES
Fairfax Kosher Market & Bakery
11196-98 Los Alamitos Blvd 90720
Telephone: (562) 828-4492

COMMUNITY ORGANISATIONS
**Jewish Federation of Greater Long Beach &
W. Orange County**
3801 E. Willow St. 90815
Telephone: (562) 426-7601

MEDIA
Newspapers
Jewish Community Chronicle
3801 E. Willow St. 90815-1791

MIKVAOT
3847 Atlantic Avenue 90807

SYNAGOGUES
Orthodox
Congregation Lubavitch
3981 Atlantic Avenue 90807
Telephone: (562) 596-1681

Young Israel of Long Beach
PO Box 7041 90807-0041
Telephone: (562) 527-3163

Reform
Temple Beth David
6100 Hefley Street, Westminster 92683
Telephone: (562) 892-6623
Fax: (562) 897-5306
Email: tbdavid@aolcom
Web site: www.templebethdavid.org
Temple Israel
338 E. 3rd Street 90812

LOS ANGELES
Los Angeles is America's, and the world's, second largest Jewish metropolis, with a Jewish population of around 600,000. Fairfax Avenue and Beverly Blvd together form the crossroads of traditional Jewish life, while a growing Orthodox enclave centers around Pico and Robertson Blvds.

Important note: Area telephone codes have recently been split to 310 and 213 for central Los Angeles. We have endeavoured in all cases to correct our information, but cannot guarantee the accuracy of those who did not send in updates.

BAKERIES
Noah's New York Bagels
1737 Santa Rita Road #400, Pleasanton 94566
Telephone: (213) 485-1921
Email: noah@noahs.com
Supervision: California Rabbinical Council

Schwartz Bakery
441 N. Fairfax Ave. 90036
Telephone: (213) 653-1683
Fax: (213) 653-6142
Supervision: RCC
8616 W. Pico Blvd
Telephone: (213) 854-0592
Fax: (213) 653-6142
Supervision: RCC

COMMUNITY ORGANISATIONS
Board of Rabbis of Southern California
6505 Wilshire Blvd, Suite 430 90048
Telephone: (213) 761-8600
Fax: (213) 761-8603

Jewish Federation of Greater Los Angeles
6505 Wilshire Blvd 90048
Telephone: (213) 761-8000
Fax: (213) 761-8123
Web site: www.jewishla.org

Los Angeles West Side Community Center
5870 W. Olympic Blvd 90036
Telephone: (213) 938-2531
Fax: (213) 954-9175
Email: westsidejcc@jcc-gla.org

DELICATESSEN
Pico Kosher Deli
8826 W. Pico Blvd 90035
Telephone: (213) 273-9381
Fax: (213) 273-8476
Supervision: RCC

EMBASSY
Consul General of Israel
Suite 1700, 6380 Wilshire Blvd 90048
Telephone: (213) 852-5523
Fax: (213) 852-5555
Email: israinfo@primenet.com
Web site: www.israelemb.org/la

GROCERIES
PS Kosher Food Services
9760 W. Pico Blvd 90035
Telephone: (213) 553-8804
Fax: (213) 275-3031
Email: psfood@juno.com
Web site: www.pskosherfood.com

HOSPITAL
Cedars Sinai Hospital
8700 Beverly Blvd
Telephone: (213) 855-4797
Supervision: RCC

KASHRUT INFORMATION
Rabbi Bukspan
6407 Orange Street 90048
Telephone: (213) 653-5083

MEDIA
Newspapers
Heritage Southwest Jewish Press
20201 Sherman Way, Ste, 204, Winnetka 91306
Jewish Journal
Weekly publication, coming out on Fridays.

MIKVAOT
Los Angeles Mikva
9548 W. Pico Blvd., 90035
Telephone: (213) 550-4511

MUSEUMS
Museum of Tolerance
9786 West Pico Boulevard 90035
Telephone: (213) 800-900-9036
Fax: (213) 310-553-4521
Web site: www.museumoftolerance.com
Museum of Tolerance (Beit Hashoah)
9786 West Pico Blvd 90035
Telephone: (213) 553-8403
Fax: (213) 553-4521
Email: information@wiesenthal.net
Web site: www,wiesenthal.com/library

ORGANISATIONS
Jewish Social Action Organisation
Simon Wiesenthal Center, 1399 South Roxbury Dr.
90035
Telephone: (213) 553-9036
Fax: (213) 553-4521
Email: information@wiesenthal.net
Web site: www.wiesenthal.com

RESTAURANTS
Dairy
Fish Grill
7226 Beverly Blvd
Telephone: (213) 937-7162

Fish Place Restaurant
9340 W. Pico Blvd
Telephone: (213) 858-8737
Supervision: Kehila Kosher

Milk & Honey
8837 W. Pico Blvd
Telephone: (213) 858-8850

Nagila Pizza Restaurant
9411 W. Pico Blvd.
Telephone: (213) 788-0111

Pizza Delight
435 N. Fairfax Avenue
Telephone: (213) 655-7800

Pizza World
368 S. Fairfax Ave
Telephone: (213) 653-2896

Meat
Chick 'N Chow
9301 W. Pico Blvd
Telephone: (213) 274-5595

Cohen Restaurant
316 E. Pico Blvd 90015
Telephone: (213) 742-8888
Fax: (213) 742-0066
Supervision: RCC

Encino Grill & Wok
16340 Ventura Blvd.
Telephone: (213) 905-8622

Glatt Hut
9303 W. Pico Blvd
Telephone: (213) 246-1900

Jeff's Gourmet Sausage Factory
8930 W. Pico Blvd.
Telephone: (213) 310-858-8590
Fax: (213) 310-858-8138
Email: links@jeffsgourmet.com
Web site: www.jeffsgourmet.com

Kabob & Chinese Food
11330 santa Monica
Telephone: (213) 914-3040

La Gondola Ristorante Italiano
6405 Wilshire Blvd.
Telephone: (213) 852-1915

Magic Carpet
8566 W. Pico Blvd 90035
Telephone: (213) 310-652-8507
Fax: (213) 310-652-3568
Supervision: Kehillah of Los Angeles

Mr. Pickles Deli
13354 Washington Blvd.
Telephone: (213) 822-7777

Nathan's Famous
9216 W. Pico Blvd.
Telephone: (213) 273-0303

Simon's La Glatt
446 N. Fairfax Avenue
Telephone: (213) 658-7730

Pizzerias
Pizza Delight
435 N. Fairfax Avenue 90036
Telephone: (213) 655-7800
Fax: (213) 655-1142
Supervision: Kehillah of Los Angeles

Shalom Pizza
8715 W. Pico Blvd
Telephone: (213) 271-2255
Email: shalompizza@la.com
Supervision: RCC

SYNAGOGUES
Conservative
Adat Shalom
3030 Westwood Blvd 90034
Telephone: (213) 475-4985

Sinai Temple
10400 Wilshire Blvd 90024
Telephone: (213) 474-1518
Fax: (213) 474-6801

Temple Beth Am
1039 S. La Cienega Blvd 90035
Telephone: (213) 652-7353
Fax: (213) 652-2384
Email: betham@tbala.org
Web site: www.tbala.org

Orthodox
Chabad House
741 Gayley Avenue, West Los Angeles 90025

Etz Jacob Congregation
7659 Beverly Blvd 90036
Telephone: (213) 938-2619
Fax: (213) 930-2373
Email: office@etzjacob.org

Ohel David
7967 Beverly Blvd

Young Israel of Century City
9317 West Pico Blvd, Century City 90035
Telephone: (213) 273-6954
Fax: (213) 273-7103
Email: shuloffice@yicc.org
Web site: www.yicc.org

Young Israel of Hancock Park
225 South La Brea
Telephone: (213) 931-4030
Fax: (213) 935-3819

Young Israel of Los Angeles
660 N. Spaulding Avenue 90036
Telephone: (213) 655-0300
Fax: (213) 655-0322

Orthodox Sephardi
Kahal Joseph
10505 Santa Monica Blvd 90025
Telephone: (213) 474-0559

Temple Tifereth Israel
10500 Wilshire Blvd 90024
Telephone: (213) 475-7311
Fax: (213) 470-9238

Reconstructionist
Kehillat Israel
16019 Sunset Blvd, Pacific Palisades 90272
Telephone: (213) 459-2328
Fax: (213) 573-2098
Email: kihome@aol.com

Reform
Leo Baeck Temple
1300 N. Sepulveda Blvd 90049
Telephone: (213) 476-2861

Stephen S. Wise Temple
15500 Stephen S. Wise Drive, Bel Air 90024
Telephone: (213) 476-8561
Fax: (213) 476-3587

Temple Akiba
5249 S. Sepulveda Blvd, Culver City 90230
Telephone: (213) 398-5783
Fax: (213) 398-1637
Web site: www.temakiba

Temple Isaiah
10345 W. Pico Blvd 90064

University Synagogue
11960 Sunset Blvd 90049
Telephone: (213) 472-1255
Fax: (213) 476-3237

Wilshire Blvd Temple
3663 Wilshire Blvd 90010
Telephone: (213) 388-2401
Fax: (213) 388-2595

NORTH HOLLYWOOD
KASHRUT INFORMATION
The Kashrus Information Bureau
12753 Chandler Blvd, N. Hollywood 91607
Telephone: (818) 762-3197 & 262-5351
Fax: (818) 766-8537
Email: eeidlitz@kosherquest.org
Web site: www.kosherquest.org

MIKVAOT
Teichman Mikvah Society
12800 Chandler Blvd, N. Hollywood 91607
Telephone: (818) 506-0996

RESTAURANTS
Meat
Flora Falafel
12450 Burbank Blvd, N. Hollywood
Telephone: (818) 766-6567
Supervision: RCC

Golan
13075 Victory Blvd.
Telephone: (818) 763-5375

SYNAGOGUES
Orthodox
Adat Ari El Synagogue
5540 Laurel Canyon Blvd, N. Hollywood 91607
Telephone: (818) 766-9426

Shaarey Zedek
12800 Chandler Blvd, N. Hollywood 91607
Telephone: (818) 763-0560
Fax: (818) 763-8215

NORTHRIDGE
SYNAGOGUES
Conservative
Temple Ramat Zion
17655 Devonshire Avenue, Northridge
Telephone: (818) 360-1881

Orthodox
Young Israel of Northridge
17511 Devonshire Street 91325
Telephone: (818) 818-368-2221
Fax: (818) 818-581-5754
Email: rabbi@yion.org
Web site: www.yion.org

Reform
Temple Ahavat Shalom
11261 Chimineas Avenue, Northridge

PASADENA
SYNAGOGUES
Conservative
Pasadena Jewish Temple and Center
1434 North Altadena Drive 91107
Telephone: (626) 798-1161

SAN FERNANDO VALLEY
BAKERIES
Continental Kosher Bakery
12419 Burbank Blvd
Telephone: (818) 762-5005

RESTAURANTS
Apropo Falafel
6800 Reseda Blvd
Telephone: (818) 881-6608

Hadar Restaurant and Catering
12514 Burbank Blvd 91607
Telephone: (818) 762-1155
Supervision: RCC

Meat
Sportsman Lodge
Sherman Oaks
Telephone: (818) 984-0202

Pizzerias
La Pizza
12515 Burbank Blvd
Telephone: (818) 760-8198

SYNAGOGUES
Conservative
Beth Meier Congregation
11725 Moorpark, Studio City 91604
Telephone: (818) 818-769-0515
Fax: (818) 818-769-7127
Email: congbethmeier@sbcglobal.net
Temple B'nai Hayim
4302 Van Nuys Blvd, Sherman Oaks
Telephone: (818) 788-4664

SHERMAN OAKS
RESTAURANTS
Dairy
Fish Grill
13628 Ventura Blvd
Telephone: (818) 788-9896

TARZANA
BAKERIES
Unique Pastry Bakery and Café
18385 Ventura Blvd. 91356
Telephone: (818) 818-757-3100
Fax: (818) 818-757-3144

BOOKSELLERS
Steimatzky
19566 Ventura Blvd, Tarzana 91356
Telephone: (818) 708-2347
Fax: (818) 708-2319
Email: stmla@earthlink.net

SYNAGOGUES
Reform
Temple Judea
5429 Lindley Avenue, Tarzana

TUSTIN
SYNAGOGUES
Conservative
Congregation B'nai Israel
655 S. "B" St 92680
Telephone: (714) 259-0655

VAN NUYS
COMMUNITY ORGANISATIONS
Valley Cities Center
13164 Burbank Blvd., Van Nuys 91401

VENICE
SYNAGOGUES
Orthodox
National Council of Young Israel West Coast Regional Office
1050 Indiana Avenue 90291
Telephone: (310) 396-3935
Fax: (310) 581-0904
Email: ncyi.west@youngisrael.org
Pacific Jewish Center
Shul on the Beach 505 Ocean Front Walk , Venice Beach 90291
Telephone: (310) 392-8749
Fax: (310) 392-4557
Email: office@pjcenter.com
Web site: www.pjcenter.com

WEST HILLS
COMMUNITY ORGANISATIONS
West Valley Center
22622 Vanowen Street, West Hills 91307

SYNAGOGUES
Conservative
Shomrei Torah Synagogue
7353 Valley Circle, West Hills 91304
Telephone: (818) 818-346-0811
Fax: (818) 818-346-3956
Email: shomrei@sbcglobal.net
Web site: www.shomreitorahsynagogue.org

Colorado

BOULDER
COMMUNITY ORGANISATIONS
Boulder JCC
3800 Kalmia Avenue 80301
Telephone: (303) 998-1900
Fax: (303) 998-1965
Email: linda@boulderjcc.org
Web site: www.bjcf.org

ORGANISATIONS
Lubavitch of Boulder County
4900 Sioux Drive 80303
Telephone: (303) 494-1638
Fax: (303) 938-8350
Email: lubavbldr@cs.com
Web site: www.lubavitchofboulder.org

SYNAGOGUES
Hillel Foundation
2795 Colorado Avenue, University of Colorado
Telephone: (303) 442-6571

Conservative
Congregation Bonai Shalom
1527 Cherryvale Rd, 80303
Telephone: (303) 442-6605
Fax: (303) 442-7545
Email: bonaishalom@aol.com
Web site: www.bonaishalom.org

Orthodox
Chabad
4900 Sioux Drive 80303
Telephone: (303) 494-1638
Email: lubofbldr@juno.com

Reform
Congregation Har Hashem
3950 Baseline Road 80303
Telephone: (303) 499-7077

Jewish Renewal Community of Boulder
5001 Pennsylvania 80303
Telephone: (303) 271-3541

COLORADO SPRINGS
SYNAGOGUES
Conservative & Reform
Temple Shalom
1523 E. Monument Street 80909
Telephone: (719) 634-5311
Fax: (719) 447-9385
Email: Tshalom@qwest.net
Web site: www.Templeshalom.com

DENVER
BAKERIES
The Bagel Store
942 South Monaco 80224
Telephone: (303) 388-2648
Supervision: Vaad Hakashrus of Denver

COMMUNITY ORGANISATIONS
Allied Jewish Federation of Colorado - Events Office
300 S. Dahlia Street 80246
Telephone: (303) 316-6491
Fax: (303) 322-8328
Email: mgardenswartz@ajfcolorado.org
Web site: www.jewishcolorado.org

Jewish Family & Children's Service
1355 S. Colorado Blvd 80222
Telephone: (303) 759-4890
Fax: (303) 759-5998
Email: jfs@jewishfamilyservice.org
Web site: www.jewishfamilyservice.org

GROCERIES
Auerbach's
4810 Newport St.
Telephone: (303) 289-4521

Cub Foods
1985 Sheridan Blvd, Edgewater
Telephone: (303) 232-8972

King Soopers
890 S.Monaco Parway
Telephone: (303) 333-1535
6470 East Hampden Avenue
Telephone: (303) 758-1210

Safeway
7150 Leetsdale Drive (& Quebec)
Telephone: (303) 377-6939
6460 E. Yale (& Monaco)
Telephone: (303) 691-8870

KASHRUT INFORMATION
Scoll K Vaad Hakashrus of Denver
1350 Vrain 80204
Telephone: (303) 595-9349
Fax: (303) 629-5159

MEDIA
Newspaper
Intermountain Jewish News
1275 Sherman Avenue, Suite 214 80203
Telephone: (303) 861-2234
Fax: (303) 832-6942
Email: email@ijn.com

MIKVAOT
Mikvah of Denver
1404 Quitman 80204
Telephone: (303) 893-5315
Fax: (303) 825-5810

RELIGIOUS ORGANISATIONS
Synagogue Council of Greater Denver
PO Box 102732 80250
Telephone: (303) 759-8484

RESTAURANTS
Meat
Jeff's Diner
731 Quebec Street 80220
Telephone: (303) 333-4637

Pizzeria
Pete's Kosher Pizza
5606 E. Cedar Avenue 80204
Telephone: (303) 355-5777

SYNAGOGUES
Conservative
Beth Shalom
2280 East Noble Place, Littleton 80121
Telephone: (303) 794-6643

Hebrew Educational Alliance (HEA)
3600 South Ivanhoe St. 80237
Telephone: (303) 758-9400
Fax: (303) 758-9500
Email: info@headenver.org

Rodef Shalom
450 S. Kearney 80224
Telephone: (303) 399-0035
Fax: (303) 399-7623
Email: mainoffice@rodef-shalom.org
Web site: www.rodef-shalom.org

Orthodox
Aish/Ahavas Yisroel; A Center for Jewish Learning
9550 E Belleview Ave, Greenwood Village 80111
Telephone: (303) 220-7200
Fax: (303) 290-9191
Email: ymeyer@aish.com

Bais Medrash Kehillas Yaakov
295 S. Locust Street 80222
Telephone: (303) 377-1200
Fax: (303) 355-6010
Email: tai@jewishpeople.com

Congregation Zera Abraham
1560 Winona Court 80204
Telephone: (303) 825-7517

Reform
Beth Shalom
2280 E. Noble Place 80121
Telephone: (303) 794-6643

Temple Micah
2600 Leyden Street 80207
Telephone: (303) 303-388-4239

Email: office@micahdenver.org
Web site: www.micahdenver.org
Temple Sinai
3509 South Glencoe Street 80237
Telephone: (303) 759-1827
Fax: (303) 759-2519
Email: mail@sinaidenver.org
Web site: www.sinaidenver.org

Traditional
B.M.H.-BJ Congregation
560 S. Monaco Pkwy. 80224
Telephone: (303) 388-4203
Fax: (303) 388-4210

EVERGREEN
SYNAGOGUES
Liberal
Congregation Beth Evergreen
2931 Evergreen Parkway 80439
Telephone: (303) 670-4294
Fax: (303) 836-6470
Email: shalom@bethevergreen.org
Web site: www.bethevergreen.org

PUEBLO
SYNAGOGUES
Conservative
United Hebrew Congregation
106 W. 15th Street 81003
Telephone: (719) 544-9897, 583-8303

Reform
Temple Emanuel
1325 Grand Avenue 81003
Telephone: (719) 544-6448
Email: pavisilva@earthlink.net

Connecticut

BRIDGEPORT
COMMUNITY ORGANISATIONS
Jewish Center for Community Services of Eastern Fairfield County
4200 Park Avenue 06604
Telephone: (203) 372-6567
Fax: (203) 374-0770
Email: info@jccs.org

MEDIA
Radio
WVOF Radio
c/o Fairfield University, Fairfield 06430
Telephone: (203) 254-4111

MIKVAOT
Mikveh Israel
1326 Stratfield Road, Fairfield 06432

RELIGIOUS ORGANISATIONS
Va'ad of Fairfield County
1571 Stratfield Road, Fairfield 06432
Telephone: (203) 372-6529
Fax: (203) 373-0467
Email: rbaun64732@aol.com

RESTAURANTS
Cafe Shalom
c/o Abel, Community Center
Telephone: (203) 372-6567

SYNAGOGUES
Conservative
B'nai Torah
5700 Main St., Trumbull 06611

Rodeph Sholom
2385 Park Avenue 06604
Telephone: (203) 334-0159
Fax: (203) 334-1411
Email: cong.rodeph.sholom@suet.net
Web site: www.rodephsholom.com

Orthodox
Agudas Achim
85 Arlington Street 06606

Bikur Cholim
Park & Capitol Avenues 06604
Telephone: (203) 336-2272
Email: jbm@ou.org
Web site: www.ou.org

Reconstructionist
Congregation Shirei Shalom
PO Box 372, Monroe 06468

Reform
Temple B'nai Israel
2710 Park Avenue 06604
Telephone: (203) 336-1858
Fax: (203) 367-7889
Email: welcome@congregationbnaiisrael.org

DANBURY
COMMUNITY ORGANISATIONS
Jewish Federation
105 Newtown Road 06810
Telephone: (203) 203-792-6353
Fax: (203) 203-748-5099
Email: info@thejf.org
Web site: www.thejf.org

SYNAGOGUES
Conservative
Congregation B'nai Israel
193 Clapboard Ridge Road 06811
Telephone: (203) 792-6161
Fax: (203) 792-8315
Email: cbi193clab@juno.com

Orthodox
Chabad
9 Golden Heights Road 06811
Telephone: (203) 790-4700
Email: lgurkov@juno.com

Reform
United Jewish Center
141 Deer Hill Avenue 06810
Telephone: (203) 748-3355

FAIRFIELD
BAKERIES
Carvel Ice Cream Bakery
1838 Black Rock Turnpike
Telephone: (203) 384-2253
Supervision: Vaad Hakashrus of Fairfield County

SYNAGOGUES
Conservative
Congregation Beth El
1200 Fairfield Woods Rd, Fairfield 06825
Telephone: (203) 374-5544
Fax: (203) 374-4962
Email: congbethel@aol.com
Web site: www.uscj.org/ctvalley/fairfield

Orthodox
Congregation Ahavath Achim
1571 Stratfield Road, Fairfield 06825
Telephone: (203) 372-6529
Fax: (203) 373-0647
Web site: www.ahavathachim.org

HARTFORD
COMMUNITY ORGANISATIONS
Jewish Federation of Hartford
333 Bloomfield Avenue 06117
Telephone: (860) 232-4483

KASHRUT INFORMATION
Kashrut Commission
162 Brewster Road 06117
Telephone: (860) 563-4017

MEDIA
Guide
All Things Jewish
333 Bloomfield Avenue 06117
Telephone: (860) 232-4483

MIKVAOT
Mikva
61 Main Street 06119

SYNAGOGUES
Conservative
Beth El
2626 Albany Avenue, West Hartford 06117

Beth Tefilah
465 Oak St, East Hartford 06118

Congregation B'nai Sholom
26 Church St, Newington 06111-4401
Telephone: (860) 667-0826
Fax: (860) 667-0827
Email: president@cbsnewington.com
Web site: www.cbsnewington.org

Emanuel Synagogue
160 Mohegan Dr, West Hartford 06117
Telephone: (860) 236-1275
Fax: (860) 231-8890
Email: emansyn@emanuelsynagogue.org

Orthodox
Agudas Achim
1244 N. Main St, West Hartford 06117

Beth David Synagogue
20 Dover Road, West Hartford 06119
Telephone: (860) 236-1241
Fax: (860) 232-8272
Email: rabbi@bethdavidwh.org

Teferes Israel
27 Brown St, Bloomfield 06002

United Synagogue of Greater Hartford
840 N. Main St, West Hartford 06117

Reform
Temple Sinai
41 W. Hartford Road, Newington 06011

MANCHESTER
SYNAGOGUES
Conservative
Temple Beth Sholom
400 Middle Turnpike E 06040
Telephone: (603) 643-9563
Fax: (603) 643-9565
Email: riplavin@prodigy.net
Web site: www.uscj.org/ctvalley/manchestertbs

MERIDEN
SYNAGOGUES
Conservative
B'nai Abraham
127 E. Main St 06450
Telephone: (203) 235-2581

MIDDLETOWN
SYNAGOGUES
Conservative
Adath Israel
48 Church St 06457
Telephone: (860) 346-4709

NEW BRITAIN
SYNAGOGUES
Conservative
B'nai Israel
265 W. Main St 06051
Telephone: (860) 224-0479

Orthodox
Tephereth Israel
76 Winter Street 06051

NEW HAVEN
COMMUNITY ORGANISATIONS
Jewish Federation of Greater New Haven
360 Amity Road, Woodbridge Ct. 06525
Telephone: (203) 387-2424

CONTACT INFORMATION
Young Israel House at Yale University
c/o Joseph Slifka Center, 80 Wall Street 06510
Telephone: (203) 432-1134
Fax: (203) 776-4212
Email: Rabbiisaacs@cs.com
Web site: www.yale.edu/hillel/orgs/yihy.html

DELICATESSEN
The Westville
1460 Whalley Avenue 06515
Telephone: (203) 397-0839
Fax: (203) 387-4129
Email: pweinb@aol.com

Zackey's
1304 Whalley Avenue 06515
Telephone: (203) 387-2454

GROCERIES
Westville Kosher Meat Market
95 Amity Road 06525
Telephone: (203) 389-1723

LIBRARIES
Center Cafe & Jewish Library
360 Amity Road 06525
Telephone: (203) 387-2424

MIKVAOT
86 Hubinger Street 06511
Telephone: (203) 387-2184

RESTAURANTS
Dairy
Claire's Gourmet Vegetarian Restaurant & Caterer
1000 Chapel Street 06510
Telephone: (203) 562-3888
Supervision: Young Israel of New Haven

SYNAGOGUES
Conservative
Beth-El Keser Israel
85 Harrison Street 06515
Telephone: (203) 389-2108

Orthodox
Beth Hamedrosh Westville
74 West Prospect Street 06515
Telephone: (203) 389-9513

Congregation Bikur Cholim Sheveth Achim
112 Marvel Road 06515
Telephone: (203) 387-4699

Yeshiva of New Haven
765 Elm Street, New Haven 06511
Telephone: (203) 777-2200
Fax: (203) 777-7198
Email: info@yeshivanewhaven.org
Web site: www.yeshivanewhaven.org

NEW LONDON
COMMUNITY ORGANISATIONS
Jewish Federation of Eastern Connecticut
28 Channing Street 06320
Telephone: (203) 442-8062

NORWICH
SYNAGOGUES
Orthodox
Brothers of Joseph
Broad & Washington Avs. 06360
Telephone: (203) 887-3777

STAMFORD
COMMUNITY ORGANISATIONS
United Jewish Federation of Greater Stamford, New Canaan and Darien
1035 Newfield Avenue, Suite 200 06905-2591
Telephone: (203) 321-1373
Fax: (203) 322-3277
Email: office@ujf.org
Web site: www.ujf.org

DELICATESSEN
Delicate-Essen at the JCC
1035 Newfield Avenue 06902
Telephone: (203) 322-0944
Fax: (203) 322-5160
Supervision: Vaad Hakashrus of Fairfield County

GROCERIES
Delicate-Essen
111 High Ridge Road 06905
Telephone: (203) 316-5570
Fax: (203) 316-5573
Email: bhert2b111@aol.com
Supervision: Vaad Hakashrus of Fairfield County

SYNAGOGUES
Orthodox
Young Israel of Stamford
69 Oak Lawn Avenue 06905
Telephone: (203) 348-3955

WATERBURY
COMMUNITY ORGANISATIONS
Jewish Communities of Western CT, Inc.
73 Main Street, South Woodbury 06798
Telephone: (203) 263-5121
Fax: (203) 263-5143
Email: jfedwtby@aol.com

WEST HARTFORD
BOOKSELLERS
The Judaica Store
31 Crossroads Plaza 06117
Telephone: (860) 236-9956
Fax: (860) 236-9956

SYNAGOGUES
Orthodox
Young Israel of West Hartford
2240 Albany Avenue 06117
Telephone: (860) 233-3084
Fax: (860) 232-6417
Email: westhartfordrav@aol.com
Web site: www.youngisraelwh.org

Reform
Congregation Beth Israel
701 Farmington Avenue 06119
Telephone: (860) 233-8215
Fax: (860) 523-0223
Email: bethisrael@cbict.org
Web site: www.cbict.org

WESTPORT
SYNAGOGUES
Orthodox
215 Post Road West 06880
Telephone: (203) 226-6901

WOODBRIDGE

LIBRARIES
Department of Jewish Education Library
360 Amity Road 06525
Telephone: (203) 387-2424 ext. 330
Fax: (203) 387-1818
Email: library@jewishnewhaven.org

Delaware

DOVER
SYNAGOGUES
Conservative
Congregation Beth Sholom of Dover
PO Box 223 19903
Telephone: (302) 734-5578

NEWARK
SYNAGOGUES
Reconstructionist
Temple Beth El
101 Possum Park Rd 19711
Telephone: (302) 366-8330

WILMINGTON
COMMUNITY ORGANISATIONS
Jewish Community Center
101 Garden of Eden Road 19803
Telephone: (302) 478-5660
Fax: (302) 478-6068
Email: jccinfo@jccdelaware.org

SYNAGOGUES
Conservative
Beth Shalom
18th St. and Baynard Blvd 19802

Orthodox
Adas Kodesh Shel Emeth
Washington Blvd & Torah Drive 19802
Telephone: (302) 762-2705
Fax: (302) 762-3236
Web site: www.akse.org

Reform
Beth Emeth
300 W. Lea Blvd. 19802
Telephone: (302) 764-2393
Fax: (302) 764-2395

District of Columbia

WASHINGTON
CONTACT INFORMATION
Eruv in Georgetown
Telephone: (202) 338-ERUV

DELICATESSEN
Hunan Deli
H Street
Telephone: (202) 833-1018
Posins Bakery & Deli
5756 Georgia Avenue
Telephone: (202) 726-4424

EMBASSY
Embassy of Israel
3514 International Drive 20008
Telephone: (202) 364-5500
Fax: (202) 364-5423

KASHRUT INFORMATION
Rabbinical Council of Greater Washington
7826 Eastern Avenue 20012
Telephone: (202) 291-6052
Fax: (202) 291-5377
Email: capitalkdc@ad.org
Web site: www.capitolk.org

MEDIA
Newspaper
The Jewish Week
1910 "K" Street 20006

MUSEUMS
B'nai B'rith Klutznick National Jewish Museum
1640 Rhode Island Av. 20036
Telephone: (202) 857-6583
Fax: (202) 857-1099
Email: eberman@bnaibrith.org
Web site: www.BBInet.org

Lillian & Albert Small Museum
701 3rd Street N. W. 20001
Telephone: (202) 789-0900
Fax: (202) 789-0485
Email: info@jhsgw.org

National Museum of American Jewish Military History
1811 R. Street N.W. 20009
Telephone: (202) 265-6280
Fax: (202) 462-3192
Email: mnmajmh@nmajmh.org
Web site: www.nmajmh.org

Smithsonian Institute
The Natural History Building, 10th & Constitution Avs N.W. 20001

The National Portrait Gallery
F Street between 7th & 8th Sts.

United States Holocaust Memorial Museum
100 Raoul Wallenberg Place S.W. 20024-2150
Telephone: (202) 488-0400
Fax: (202) 488-2606
Email: group_visit@ushmm.org
Web site: www.ushmm.org

ORGANISATIONS
Jewish Historical Society of Greater Washington
701 3rd Street N. W. 20001
Telephone: (202) 202-789-0900
Fax: (202) 202-789-0485
Email: info@jhsgw.org

RESTAURANTS
Jewish Community Centre
16th Street at Q
Supervision: Va'ad Hakashrut of Washington

TOURIST SITE
John F. Kennedy Center
2700 "F" Street

Florida

BOCA RATON
COMMUNITY ORGANISATIONS
Jewish Federation of South Palm Beach County
9901 Donna Klein Blvd 33428-1788
Telephone: (561) 852-3100

JUDAICA
Holyland Judaica
Del Mar Shopping Village, 7080 Beracasa Way
Telephone: (561) 367-8277

MIKVAOT
Boca Raton Synagogue
7900 Montoya Circle 33433
Telephone: (561) 394-5854

RESTAURANTS
Dairy
Campus Café
Cultural Arts Building, 9801 Donna Klein Blvd 33428-1788
Telephone: (561) 852-3200 ext. 4103
Fax: (561) 852-3282
Supervision: Jewish Federation of South Palm Beach County

Eilat Café
6853 SW 18th Street, Wharfside Shopping Center 33428-1788
Telephone: (561) 368-6880

Jon's Place
22191 Powerline Road, (southwest corner Palmetto & Powerline)
Telephone: (561) 338-0008

My Favorite Café
3369 Sheridan Street
Telephone: (561) 965-0111

Meat
Café Haifa
2901 N. Federal Highway 33431
Telephone: (561) 955-8500

City Grill
Delmar Shopping Village, 7158 N. Beracasa Way 33434
Telephone: (561) 417-8936

Jerusalem
8255 International Drive
Telephone: (561) 248-9494
Email: www.jerusalemglatt.com
Supervision: Rabbi Konig

Jerusalem Grill
19635 US Highway 411, Boca Plaza Greens 33428
Telephone: (561) 470-1120

Sagi's Falafel Armon
22767 State Road 7 33428
Telephone: (561) 477-0633

SYNAGOGUES
Conservative
Beth Ami Congregation
1401 N.W. 4th Avenue 33432
Telephone: (561) 347-0031
Fax: (561) 393-5326
Email: bethamicong@aol.com

Orthodox
Boca Raton Synagogue
7900 Montoya Circle 33433
Telephone: (561) 394-5732
Fax: (561) 394-0180
Email: www.brsweb.org

Young Israel of Boca Raton
7200 Palmetto Circle Blvd 33433
Telephone: (561) 391-3235
Fax: (561) 391-5509
Email: yiboca@bellsouth.net

Reform
Congregation B'nai Israel
2200 Yamato Road 33431
Telephone: (561) 241-8118
Fax: (561) 241-8118

CLEARWATER

COMMUNITY ORGANISATIONS

Jewish Federation of Pinellas County
13191 Starkey Road, Suite 8, Largo 33773-1438
Telephone: (727) 530-3223
Fax: (727) 531-0221
Email: jewishfed@tbi.net
Web site: www.jfedpinellas.org

SYNAGOGUES

Conservative
Beth Shalom
1325 S. Belcher Road 33764
Telephone: (727) 531-1418
Fax: (727) 531-0798

Reform
B'nai Israel
1685 S. Belcher Road 34624
Telephone: (727) 531-5829

Temple Ahavat Shalom
1575 Curlew Road, Palm Harbor 34683
Telephone: (727) 785-8811
Fax: (727) 785-8822
Email: rabgar@tampabay.rr.com

DAYTONA BEACH

COMMUNITY ORGANISATIONS

Jewish Federation of Volusia & Flagler Counties
470 Andalusin Ave, Ormond Beach 32174
Telephone: (904) 672-0294
Fax: (904) 673-1316

SYNAGOGUES

Conservative
Temple Israel
1400 S. Peninsula Drive 32118
Telephone: (904) 252-3097

Reform
Temple Beth El
579 N. Nova Road, Ormond Beach 32174
Telephone: (904) 677-2484

DEERFIELD BEACH

SYNAGOGUES

Orthodox
Young Israel of Deerfield Beach
1880 W. Hillsboro Blvd 33442
Telephone: (954) 421-1367
Fax: (954) 426-9127

DELRAY BEACH

GROCERIES

Meat Market
Oriole Kosher Market, 7345 West Atlantic Ave., 33446

SYNAGOGUES

Conservative
Temple Anshei Shalom of West Delray
Oriole Jewish Center, 7099 W. Atlantic Avenue 33446
Telephone: (561) 495-1300

Temple Emeth
5780 W. Atlantic Avenue 33446
Telephone: (561) 498-3536

Orthodox
Anshei Emuna
16189 Carter Road 33445
Telephone: (561) 499-9229

Reform
Temple Sinai of Palm Beach County
2475 W. Atlantic Avenue 33445
Telephone: (561) 561-276-6161
Fax: (561) 561-276-3485
Email: sinai2475@att.net
Web site: www.TempleSinaiPBC.org

FORT LAUDERDALE

DELICATESSEN

East Side Kosher Restaurant & Deli
6846 W. Atlantic Blvd, Margate 33063

KOSHER FOOD

Meat
Galt Kosher Market
3515 Galt Ocean Drive 33308
Telephone: (954) 563-2026

RESTAURANTS

Amore' Ristorante
8067 West Oakland Park Blvd, Sunrise
Telephone: (954) 749-6888
Supervision: Glatt kosher

SYNAGOGUES

Orthodox
Temple Ohel B'nai Raphael
4351 West Oakland Park Boulevard 33313
Telephone: (954) 733-7684

Sephardi
B'nai Sephardim
3670 Stirling Rd, Ft Lauderdale

FORT MEYERS

SYNAGOGUES

Reform
Temple Beth El
16225 Winkler Road Ext 33908
Telephone: (941) 433-0018

FORT PIERCE

SYNAGOGUES

Reform
Temple Beth-El Israel
4600 Oleander Drive 34982
Telephone: (407) 461-7428

HALLANDALE

RESTAURANTS

Dairy
Fressers at Tierra Mar
1960 S. Ocean Dr.
Telephone: 889-0075

Meat
Kosher World
514 - 41st St.
Telephone: 532-2210

Pita Loca South Beach Israeli Restaurant
601 Collins Ave., #5
Telephone: 305-673-3388
Fax: 305-673-6051
Web site: www.pitaloca.8m.com

HOLLYWOOD & VICINITY

COMMUNITY ORGANISATIONS

Jewish Federation of South Broward
2719 Hollywood Blvd 33020
Telephone: (954) 921-8810

JUDAICA

Holyland Judaica
5650 Stirling Road, Hollywood
Telephone: (954) 964-4288

KOSHER FOOD

Ilana's Cookies
5650 Stirling Road, Hollywood
Telephone: (954) 963-6130

MIKVAOT

Mikveh/Young Israel of Hollywood - Ft. Lauderdale
3291 Stirling Road, Fort Lauderdale 33312
Telephone: (954) 963-3952
Fax: (954) 962-5566

RESTAURANTS

Dairy
Sara's
3944 N. 46th Avenue 33021
Telephone: (954) 986-1770
Fax: (954) 986-2602

Meat
Pita King
5650 Stirling Road 33021
Telephone: (954) 985-8028

Pizzerias
Jerusalem Pizza
5650 Stirling Road 33021
Telephone: (954) 964-6811
Fax: (954) 964-2911

SYNAGOGUES

Conservative
B'nai Aviv
1410 Indian Trace, Weston 33326

Century Pines Jewish Center
13400 S.W. 10 St., Pembroke Pines 33027
Telephone: (954) 431-3300

Hallandale Jewish Center
416 N.E. Eighth Ave., Hallandale 33009
Telephone: (954) 454-9100

Temple Beth Ahm Israel
9730 Stirling Rd 33024
Telephone: (954) 431-5100

Temple Judea of Carriage Hills
6734 Stirling Rd, Hollywood

Temple Sinai of Hollywood
1400 N. 46 Avenue, Hollywood 33021
Telephone: (954) 987-0026

Orthodox
Chabad of Southwest Broward
11251 Taft St., Pembroke Pines

Congregation Ahavat Shalom
315 Madison St., PO Box 220918 33022-0918
Telephone: (954) 954-922-4544
Fax: (954) 954-922-4523

Congregation Levi Yitzchok-Lubavitch
1295 E. Hallandale Beach Blvd, Hallandale 33009
Telephone: (954) 458-1877
Fax: (954) 458-1651
Email: chai@dialisdn.com

Young Israel of Hollywood/Ft Lauderdale
3291 Stirling Road, Ft Lauderdale 33312
Telephone: (954) 966-7877
Fax: (954) 962-5566
Email: yih@bellsouth.net

Young Israel of Pembroke Pines
13400 S.W. 10 St., Pembroke Pines

Reform
Temple Beth El
1351 S. 14 Av, Hollywood 33020
Telephone: (954) 920-8225

Temple Beth Emet
4807 South Flamingo Road, Cooper City,
Pembroke Pines
Telephone: (954) 680-1882
Email: bethemet@aol.com

Temple Solel
5100 Sheridan St., Hollywood 33021
Telephone: (954) 989-0205

JACKSONVILLE
COMMUNITY ORGANISATIONS
Jacksonville Jewish Federation
8505 San Jose Blvd 32217
Telephone: (904) 448-5000

MIKVAOT
Etz Chaim
10167 San Jose Blvd 32257
Telephone: (904) 262-3565

ORGANISATIONS
Kosher Nutrition Center
5846 Mt Carmel Terrace. 32216
Telephone: (904) 737-9075

SYNAGOGUES
Orthodox
Eitz Chaim Synagogue
10167 San Jose Boulevard 32217
Telephone: (904) 262-3565

KENDALL
SYNAGOGUES
Orthodox
Young Israel of Kendall
7880 SW 112th Street 33156
Telephone: (305) 305-232-6833
Fax: (305) 305-232-6418
Email: yikendall@aol.com

KEY WEST
SYNAGOGUES
Conservative
B'nai Zion
750 United Street 33040-3251
Telephone: (305) 294-3437

LAKELAND
SYNAGOGUES
Conservative
Temple Emanuel
600 Lake Hollingsworth Drive 33803
Telephone: (813) 682-8616

MELBOURNE
GROCERIES
Brevard Kosher Zone
416N Harbor City Blvd., 1/4 mile south of Eau
Gallie
Telephone: (321) 752-8000
Fax: (321) 752-8000
Email: bkz1@mindspring.com

MIAMI/MIAMI BEACH
BOOKSELLERS
Jerusalem Judaica
459 41st Street 33140
Telephone: (305) 535-8888

EMBASSY
Consul General of Israel
Suite 1800, 100N Biscayne Blvd 33132

GROCERIES
Kosher World-Fine Food Market
514 W. 41st Street 33140
Telephone: (305) 532-2210
Fax: (305) 532-8816

HOTELS
Saxony Hotel
3201 Collins Avenue, Miami Beach 33140
Telephone: (305) 538-6811
Fax: (305) 672-3721
Supervision: National Kashruth

MEDIA
Directory
Jewish Life in Dade County
4200 Biscayne Blvd 33137
Telephone: (305) 576-4000
Fax: (305) 573-8115
Web site: www.jewishmiami.org

Radio
Shalom South Florida (WAXY 790 AM)

MIKVAOT
B'nai Israel & Greater Miami Youth
Synagogue Mikveh
16260 S. W. 288th Street, Naranja 33033
Telephone: (305) 264-6488

Congregation and Mikvah Adas Dej
225 37th Street 33140
Telephone: (305) 305-674-8204

Daughters of Israel
2530 Pinetree Drive 33140
Telephone: (305) 305-672-3500

Mikveh Blima of North Dade, Inc.,
1054 N.E. Miami Gardens Drive 33179
Telephone: (305) 949-9650

Rabbi Meisel's Mikveh
Washington Av. & 2nd Street 33139
Telephone: (305) 673-4641

Shul of Bal Harbour Mikvah
9540 Collins Avenue, Surfside 33154
Telephone: (305) 868-1411
Email: info@theshul.org

MUSEUMS
Jewish Museum of Florida
301 Washington Avenue, Miami Beach 33139-6965
Telephone: (305) 672-5044
Fax: (305) 672-5933
Email: mzerivitz@aol.com
Web site: www.jewishmuseum.com

RELIGIOUS ORGANISATIONS
Young Israel Southern Regional Office
173575 NE 7th Avenue 33162
Telephone: (305) 770-3993
Fax: (305) 770-3993
Email: ncyi.south@youngisrael.org

RESTAURANTS
Pita Loca glatt Kosher
601 Collins Ave #5, (on 6th Street between Collins Ave & Ocean Dr. in South Beach) 33139
Telephone: 305-673-3388

Dairy
Bagel Time
3915 Alton Road 33140
Telephone: (305) 538-0300
Supervision: Star-K

Gitty's Hungarian Kitchen
6565 Collins Avenue, Sherry Frontenac Hotel 33141
Telephone: (305) 865-4893

Milky Way
530 41st Street
Telephone: (305) 534-4144

Meat
Embassy Peking Tower Suite
4101 Pine Tree Drive, Tower 41 33140
Telephone: (305) 538-7550
Fax: (305) 538-7570
Supervision: NK

Europa Grill
5445 Collins Avenue
Telephone: (305) 993-3924

Jerusalem Peking
4299 Collins Avenue, Miami Beach
Telephone: (305) 522-2263

Mexico Bravo
16850 Collins Avenue, Sunny Isles Beach
Telephone: (305) 945-1999
Fax: (305) 949-5560
Supervision: Star-K Supervision

Original Pita Hut
530-41st St.
Telephone: (305) 534-4144

Shalom Tokyo Steak House
5101 Collins Avenue, Miami Beach
Telephone: (305) 866-6039

Pizzerias
Shemtov's Pizza
514 41st Street 33140
Telephone: (305) 305-538-2123
Fax: (305) 305-534-4213
Supervision: Star-K

SYNAGOGUES
Orthodox
National Council of Young Israel Southern Regional Office
1035 NE 170th Terrace 33162
Telephone: (305) 770-3993
Email: ncyi.south@youngisrael.org
The Shul of Bal Harbor, Bay Harbor & Surfside
9540 Collins Avenue 33154
Telephone: (305) 868-1411
Email: info@theshul.org
Young Israel of Miami Beach
4221 Pine Tree Drive 33140
Telephone: (305) 538-9462

NORTH MIAMI / NORTH MIAMI BEACH
RESTAURANTS
Dairy
The Noshery
Saxony Hotel, 3201 Collins Ave., 33140
Telephone: (305) 538-6811
Yummy Miami
18090 Collins Ave.
Telephone: 466-1010

Meat
China Kikar Tel Aviv
5005 Collins Avenue 33140
Telephone: (305) 866-3316
Giuliani's Café
3439 NE 163rd Street, North Miami Beach
Telephone: (305) 940-8141
Kosher World
514 - 41st.
Telephone: (305) 532-2263
Mexico Bravo
16850 Collins Avenue, Sunny Isles Beach
Telephone: (305) 945-1999
Shalom Haifa
18533 W. Dixie Hwy, Aventura
Telephone: (305) 936-1800
Fax: (305) 936-1811
Subrific
1688 NE Street
Telephone: (305) 949-7811
Tani Guchi's Place
2224 N.E. 123rd St, North Miami
Telephone: (305) 892-6744
Fax: (305) 892-1035
Supervision: Glatt Kosher
Thai Treat
2176 123rd Street
Telephone: 892-1118

Wing Wan II
1640 N.E, 164 Street 33162
Telephone: (305) 945-3585
Pizzerias
Jerusalem Pizza
761 N.E. 167th Street 33162
Telephone: (305) 653-6662
Sarah's Kosher Pizza
2214 N.E. 123 Street 33181
Telephone: (305) 891-3312
1127 N. E. 163 Street 33162
Telephone: (305) 948-7777

SYNAGOGUES
Orthodox
Young Israel of Greater Miami
990 NE 171st Street, North Miami Beach 33162
Telephone: (305) 651-3591
Young Israel of Sky Lake
1850 NE 183rd Street, North Miami Beach 33179
Telephone: (305) 945-8712/8715
Young Israel of Sunny Isles
17395 North Bay Road, North Miami Beach 33160
Telephone: (305) 935-9095

ORLANDO
COMMUNITY ORGANISATIONS
Jewish Federation of Greater Orlando
851 N. Maitland Avenue, Maitland 32751
Telephone: (407) 407-645 5933
Fax: (407) 407-645 1172
Email: postmaster@orlandojewishfed.org

DELICATESSEN
Market Place Deli, Hyatt Orlando
6375 W. Irlo Bronson Highway
Telephone: (407) 396-1234

GROCERIES
Amira's Catering and Specialty
1351 E. Altamonte, Altamonte Springs
Telephone: (407) 767-7577

HOTELS
Quality Inn Kosher Hotel
4944 W. 192 Orlando-Kissimmee 34746
Telephone: (407) 787-3400
Fax: (407) 397-1116
Web site: www.kosherinflorida.com

MIKVAOT
Mikvah Yisrael
8 Lake Howell Road 32751
Telephone: (407) 644-2362

RESTAURANTS
The Lower East Side Restaurant
8548 Palm Parkway 32836
Telephone: (407) 465-0565
Fax: (407) 238-6427
Supervision: Florida Kosher Services

SYNAGOGUES
Conservative
Congregation Beth Shalom
13th & Center Streets, Leesburg 32748
Telephone: (407) 742-0238

Congregation Ohev Shalom
5015 Goddard Avenue 32804
Telephone: (407) 298-4650

Congregation Shalom Aleichem
PO Box 424211, Kissimmee 34742-4211

Congregation Shalom (Williamsburg)
11821 Soccer Lane, c/o Sydney Ansell 32821-7952

Southwest Orlando Jewish Congregation
11200 S. Apopka-Vineland Road 32836
Web site: www.sojc-orlando.org

Temple Israel
4917 Eli Street 32804
Telephone: (407) 647-3055

Orthodox
Cong. Ahavas Yisrael/Chabad
708 Lake Howell Road, Maitland 32751
Telephone: (407) 644-2500
Fax: (407) 644-7763
Email: rabbidubov@aol.com

Reform
Congregation of Liberal Judaism
928 Malone Drive 32810
Telephone: (407) 645-0444

PALM BEACH
SYNAGOGUES
Conservative
Temple Emanu-el
190 N. County Road 33480
Telephone: (561) 832-0804

Orthodox
Palm Beach Orthodox Synagogue
120 North County Road 33480
Telephone: (561) 561-838-9002
Fax: (561) 561-838-5356
Web site: www.pbos.org

PALM CITY
SYNAGOGUES
Conservative
Treasure Coast Jewish Center-Congregation Beth Abraham
3998 S.W. Leighton Farms Avenue 34990
Telephone: (407) 287-8833

PALM COAST
SYNAGOGUES
Conservative
Temple Beth Shalom
40 Wellington Drive, POB 350557 32135-0557
Telephone: (904) 445-3006

PEMBROKE PINES
SYNAGOGUES
Orthodox
Young Israel of Pembroke Pines
13400 SW 10th Street 33027
Telephone: (954) 433-8666

PENSACOLA
SYNAGOGUES
Conservative
B'nai Israel
1829 N. 9th Avenue, PO Box 9002 32513
Telephone: (805) 433-7311
Fax: (805) 435-9597

Reform
Beth El
800 N. Palafox Street 32501
Telephone: (805) 438-3321

ROCKLEDGE
COMMUNITY ORGANISATIONS
Jewish Federation of Brevard
108A Barton Avenue
Telephone: (321) 636-1824
Fax: (321) 636-0614
Email: jfbrevard@aol.com

SARASOTA
COMMUNITY ORGANISATIONS
Sarasota-Manatee Jewish Federation
580 S. McIntosh Road 34232-1959
Telephone: (941) 371-4546
Fax: (941) 378-2947
Email: smjf@jon.cjfny.org

SYNAGOGUES

Conservative

Temple Beth Shalom
1050 South Tuttle Avenue 34237
Telephone: (941) 955-8121

ST AUGUSTINE

SYNAGOGUES

Orthodox

The First Congregation Sons Of Israel
161 Cordova Street 43084

ST PETERSBURG

DELICATESSEN

JO-EL's Delicatessen & Marketplace
2619 23rd Ave N 33713
Telephone: (727) 321-3847
Fax: (727) 327-0682
Email: catercat@Tampabay.rr.com

GROCERIES

Jo-El's Specialty Foods
2619 23rd Avenue N. 33713
Telephone: (727) 321-3847
Fax: (727) 327-0682

SYNAGOGUES

Conservative

B'nai Israel
300 58th Street North 33710
Telephone: (727) 381-4900
Fax: (727) 344-1307
Email: rabbissec@cbistpete.org

Beth Shalom
1844 54th Street S. 33707
Telephone: (727) 321-3380

Reform

Beth-El
400 Pasadena Avenue S. 33707
Telephone: (727) 347-6136

TALLAHASSEE

SYNAGOGUES

Conservative

Congregation Shomrei Torah
4858 Kerry Forest Parkway 32308
Telephone: (850) 893-9674
Email: shomreitorah@aol.com

TAMARAC

SYNAGOGUES

Orthodox

Young Israel of Taramac
8565 W McNab Road 33321
Telephone: (954) 726-3586

TAMPA

COMMUNITY ORGANISATIONS

Tampa Jewish Federation
13009 Community Campus Drive 33625-4000
Telephone: (813) 813-264-9000
Fax: (813) 813-265-8450
Email: info@jewishtampa.com
Web site: www.jewishtampa.com

MIKVAOT

Bais Tefilah
14908 Pennington Road 33624
Telephone: (813) 963-2317

SYNAGOGUES

Conservative

Congregation Rodeph Sholom
2713 Bayshore Blvd. 33629
Telephone: (813) 837-1911
Fax: (813) 832-4168
Email: rsholom@tampabay.rr.com
Web site: www.rsholom.org

Kol Ami
3919 Moran Road 33618
Telephone: (813) 962-6338

Temple David
2001 Swann Avenue 33606
Telephone: (813) 254-1771

Orthodox

Hebrew Academy
14908 Penington Road 33624
Telephone: (813) 963-0706

Young Israel of Tampa
3721W Tacon Street 33629
Telephone: (813) 832-3018

Reform

Schaarai Zedek
3303 Swann Avenue 33609
Telephone: (813) 876-2377

Temple Shalom
4630 Pine Ridge Road 34119
Telephone: (813) 455-3030
Fax: (813) 455-4361
Web site: www.naplestemple.org

VERO BEACH

SYNAGOGUES

Reform

Temple Beth Shalom
365 43rd Avenue 32968
Telephone: (772) 569-4700
Fax: (772) 569-4701
Email: tbsoff@aol.com

WEST PALM BEACH

COMMUNITY ORGANISATIONS

Jewish Federation of Palm Beach County
4601 Community Drive 33417
Telephone: (561) 478-0700
Fax: (561) 478-9696

DELICATESSEN

Mr Glatt Mart
4869 Okeechobee Blvd 33417
Telephone: (561) 721-9000
Fax: (561) 689-2595
Email: rav613@hotmail.com
Supervision: Star K

Georgia

ATHENS

SYNAGOGUES

Reform
Congregation Children Of Israel
Dudley Drive 30606
Telephone: (404) 549-4192

ATLANTA

COMMUNITY ORGANISATIONS

Jewish Federation
1753 Peachtree Road, NE 30309
Telephone: (404) 873-1661
Fax: (404) 874-7043

EMBASSY

Consul General of Israel
Suite 440, 1100 Spring Street, NW 30309-2823

HOTELS

Bed & Breakfast Atlanta
1608 Briarcliff Road, Suite 5 30306
Telephone: (404) 875-0525
Fax: (404) 875-8198
Web site: www.bedandbreakfast.com

KASHRUT INFORMATION

Atlanta Kashrut Commission
1855 La Vista Road, N.E. 30329
Telephone: (404) 634-4063
Fax: (404) 634-4254
Email: akc613@usa.com

RESTAURANTS

Dairy
Broadway Café
2166 Briarcliff Road 30329
Telephone: (404) 329-0888
Fax: (404) 329-9888
Supervision: Atlanta Kashrut Commission

Wall Street Pizza
2470 Briarcliff Road, 30329
Telephone: (404) 633-2111
Supervision: Atlanta Kashrut Commission

Glatt Kosher Chinese
Chai Peking
2205 La Vista Road, N.E. (inside Kroger) 30329
Telephone: (404) 327-7810
Fax: (404) 327-7811
Web site: www.chaipeking.com
Supervision: Atlanta Kashruth Commission

Meat
Quality Kosher
2153 Briarcliff Road 30329
Telephone: (404) 636-1114
Fax: (404) 636-8675
Supervision: Atlanta Kashrut Commission

SYNAGOGUES

Conservative
Ahavath Achim
600 Peachtree Battle Avenue
Telephone: (404) 355-5222

Orthodox
Anshi S'Fard
1324 North Highland Avenue, N.E. 30306
Telephone: (404) 874-4513
Email: greggbrenner@aol.com

Congregation Beth Jacob
1855 La Vista Road NE 30329
Telephone: (404) 633-0551
Fax: (404) 320-7912
Email: cbj@mindspring.com
Web site: www.toll-free.com/bethjacob

Young Israel of Toco Hills
2074 La Vista Road, Toco Hills 30329
Telephone: (404) 315-1417
Fax: (404) 315-1417
Email: info@yith.org
Web site: www.yith.org

Reform
Temple Sinai
5645 Dupree Drive, N.W. 30327
Telephone: (404) 252-3073

The Temple
1589 Peachtree Road
Telephone: (404) 873-1731

Sephardi
Ner Hamizrach
1858 La Vista Road, N.E. 30329
Telephone: (404) 315-9020

AUGUSTA

BAKERIES
Sunshine Bakery
1209 Broad Street 30902

DELICATESSEN
Parti-Pal
Daniel Village 30904

Strauss
965 Broad Street 30902

SYNAGOGUES
Orthodox
Adas Yeshuron
935 Johns Road, Walton Way 30904
Telephone: (404) 733-9491

COLUMBUS

SYNAGOGUES
Conservative
Shearith Israel
2550 Wynnton Road 31906
Telephone: (614) 323-1443

Reform
Temple Israel
1617 Wildwood Avenue 31906
Telephone: (614) 323-1617

DECATUR

RESTAURANTS
Meat
Twelve Oaks Barbecue
1451 Scot Blvd.
Telephone: (404) 377-0120

TOURS OF JEWISH INTEREST
Kosher Expeditions
2932 Westbury Drive, Suite 100
Telephone: (404) 441-2545
Fax: (404) 234-5170
Email: dl@kosherexpeditions.com
Web site: www.kosherexpeditions.com

MACON

SYNAGOGUES
Conservative
Sha'arey Israel
611 First Street 31201
Telephone: (478) 745-4571
Fax: (478) 745-5892
Web site: www.csimacon.org

Reform
Beth Israel
892 Cherry Street 31201
Telephone: (478) 745-6727

SAVANNAH

COMMUNITY ORGANISATIONS
Savannah Jewish Federation
5111 Abercorn Street 31405
Telephone: (912) 355-8111
Fax: (912) 355-8116
Email: sharon@savj.org

CONTACT INFORMATION
Rabbi Avigdor Slatus
5444 Abercorn Street 31405
Telephone: (912) 354-2359
Fax: (912) 354-5272

GUEST APARTMENTS
Buckingham South
5450 Abercorn Street 31405
Telephone: (912) 355-5550
Fax: (912) 353-9393
Email: information@buckinghamsouth.com
Supervision: Rabbi Avigdor Slatus

SYNAGOGUES
Conservative
Agudath Achim
9 Lee Blvd. 31405
Telephone: (912) 352-4737

Orthodox
B'nai B'rith Jacob
5444 Abercorn Street 31405
Telephone: (912) 354-7721
Fax: (912) 354-9923

Reform
Mickve Israel
Bull & Gordon Sts. 31401
Telephone: (912) 233-1547

Hawaii

HAWAII

KONA

SYNAGOGUES
Reform
Kona Beth Shalom Kailua-Kona
Telephone: (808) 322-4192 or 322-6004

MAUI

KIHEI

SYNAGOGUES
Reform
Congregation Gan Eden
PO Box 555, Kihei Road 96753
Telephone: (808) 879-9221
Fax: (808) 874-8570

OAHU

HONOLULU

GROCERIES

Down To Earth
King's Street, Near University Av.,

Foodland Supermarket Beretania
1460 S. Beretania St.

SYNAGOGUES

Conservative
Congregation Sof Ma'arav
2500 Pali Highway 96817
Telephone: (808) 595-3678

Reform
Temple Emanu-El
2550 Pali Highway 96817
Telephone: (808) 595-7521

WAIKIKI

SYNAGOGUES

Orthodox
Chabad
Hawaiian Monarch Hotel, Nieu St
Telephone: (808) 735-8161

Illinois

CHAMPAIGN-URBANA

COMMUNITY ORGANISATIONS

Champaign-Urbana Jewish Federation
503 E. John St 61820
Telephone: (217) 217-367-9872
Fax: (217) 217-344-1540
Email: cujf@shalomcu.org
Web site: www.shalomcu.org

SYNAGOGUES

Reform
Sinai Temple
3104 Windsor Road 61821
Telephone: (217) 352-8140

CHICAGO

BOOKSELLERS

Chicago Hebrew Book Store
2942 W. Devon 60659
Telephone: (312) 973-6636
Fax: (312) 973-6465

Rosenblum's World of Judaica, Inc.
2906 W. Devon Ave 60659
Telephone: (312) 262-1700
Fax: (312) 262-1930
Email: avi@alljudaica.com
Web site: www.alljudaica.com

The Bariff Shop at the Spertus Museum
618 S. Michigan Avenue 60605
Telephone: (312) 322-1740
Fax: (312) 922-6406
Email: bariff_shop@spertus.edu
Web site: www.bariff.org

DELICATESSEN

Romanian Kosher Sausage
7200 N. Clark 60625
Telephone: (312) 761-4141
Supervision: Orthodox Union

EMBASSY

Consul General of Israel
Suite 1308, 111 East Wacker Drive 60601

MIKVAOT

Bnei Ruven
6350, N. Whipple 60659
Telephone: (312) 743-4282

MUSEUMS

Spertus Museum
Spertus Institute of Jewish Studies, 618 S.
Michigan Avenue 60605
Telephone: (312) 322-1747
Fax: (312) 922-3934
Email: musm@spertus.edu
Web site: www.spertus.edu

RESTAURANTS

Dairy
Jerusalem Kosher Restaurant
3014 W. Devon 60659
Telephone: (312) 262-0515
Supervision: OK

Meat
Great Chicago Food & Beverage Co.
3149 W. Devon 60659
Telephone: (312) 465-9030
Fax: (312) 465-9011
Email: gcfbken@aoi.com
Supervision: Chicago Rabbinical Council

Mi Tsu Yun Kosher Chinese Rest.
3010 W. Devon 60659
Telephone: (312) 262-4630
Fax: (312) 262-4835
Supervision: Chicago Rabbinical Council

Shallots
2324 N. Clark St. 60614
Telephone: (312) 755-5205
Web site: www.shallots-chicago.com

SYNAGOGUES

Conservative

Anshe Emet Synagogue
3760 N. Pine Grove 60613
Telephone: (312) 281-1423
Fax: (312) 281-2813
Web site: ansheemet.org

Orthodox

K.I.N.S of West Rogers Park
2800 W. North Shore Avenue 60645
Telephone: (312) 761-4000
Fax: (312) 761-4959
Email: congkins@cs.com

Lake Shore Drive Synagogue
70 E. Elm Street 60611
Telephone: (312) 337-6811

Loop Synagogue
16 S Clark Street 60603

Young Israel of Chicago
4931 North Kimball Street 60625
Telephone: (312) 338-6380

Young Israel of West Rogers Park
2706 West Touhy Avenue 60645
Telephone: (312) 743-9400

HIGHLAND PARK

DELICATESSEN

Best's Kosher Outlet Store
1630 Deerfield Rd. 60035
Telephone: (847) 831-9435
Fax: (847) 831-9440

Now we're cooking grill
710 Central 60035
Telephone: (847) 432-7310
Fax: (847) 432-8352
Supervision: Chicago Kashrut Association Inc

SYNAGOGUES

Conservative

North Surburban Synagogue Beth El
1175 Sheriden Road 60035
Telephone: (847) 432-8900

NORTHBROOK

SYNAGOGUES

Orthodox

Young Israel of Northbrook
3545 Walters Road 60062
Telephone: (847) 480-9462
Fax: (847) 205-1967

PEORIA

SYNAGOGUES

Orthodox

Agudas Achim
5614 N. University 61614
Telephone: (309) 692-4848
Fax: (309) 692-7255

Reform

Anshai Emeth
5614 North University Street 61614
Telephone: (309) 691-3323
Email: rariel@aol.com

ROCK ISLAND

COMMUNITY ORGANISATIONS

Jewish Federation of the Quad Cities
209 18th Street 61201
Telephone: (309) 793-1300
Fax: (309) 793-1345

ROCKFORD

COMMUNITY ORGANISATIONS

Jewish Federation of Greater Rockford
1500 Parkview Avenue 61107
Telephone: (815) 399-5497
Fax: (815) 399-9835
Email: rockfordfederation@juno.com

SYNAGOGUES

Conservative

Ohave Sholom
3730 Guildford Road 61107
Telephone: (815) 226-4900

Reform

Temple Beth El
1203 Comanche Drive 61107
Telephone: (815) 398-5020

SKOKIE

BAKERIES

Chaim's Kosher bakery
4964 Dempster Street 60077
Telephone: (847) 675-1005
Fax: (847) 675-0028
Web site: www.chaimskosher.com

JUDAICA

Hamakor Gallery Ltd.
4150 Dempster 60076
Telephone: (847) 677-4150
Fax: (847) 677-4160
Email: gallery@jewishsource.com
Web site: www.jewishsource.com

MEDIA
Newspaper
Chicago Jewish Star
PO Box 268 60076
Telephone: (847) 674-7827
Fax: (847) 674-0014
Email: chicago-jewish-star@mcimail.com

RESTAURANTS
Dairy
Bagel Country
9306 Skokie Blvd, Skokie, IL 60077
Telephone: (847) 673-3030
Fax: (847) 673-4040
Email: bcskokie@aol.com
Supervision: Chicago Rabbinical Council

Da'Nali's
4032 W. Oakton 60076
Telephone: (847) 677-2782
Supervision: Chicago Rabbinical Council

Meat
Bugsy's Charhouse
3355 W. Dempster 60076
Telephone: (847) 679-4030
Fax: (847) 835-3354
Email: gcfbken@aol.com
Supervision: Chicago Rabbinical Council

Hy Life
4120 W. Dempster, Skokie 60076
Telephone: (847) 674-2021
Supervision: Chicago Rabbinical Council

Ken's Diner
3353 W. Dempster 60076
Telephone: (847) 679-4030
Fax: (847) 835-3354; 3835- Deli
Email: gcfbken@aoi.com
Supervision: Chicago Rabbinical Council

Vegetarian
Mysore Woodlands
2548 Devon Avenue 60659
Telephone: (847) 338-8160
Fax: (847) 338-8162
Supervision: CKA

SYNAGOGUES
Orthodox
Young Israel of Skokie
3740 W. Dempster 60076
Telephone: (847) 329-0990

SPRINGFIELD
SYNAGOGUES
Conservative
Temple Israel
1140 West Governor Street 62704
Telephone: (413) 546-2841
Fax: (413) 726-9857
Email: templeisrael@springnet1.com

Indiana

BLOOMINGTON
SYNAGOGUES
Orthodox
Chabad House
516 E. 17th Street 47408
Telephone: (812) 332-6784

Reform
Congregation Beth Shalom
3750 E. Third 47401
Telephone: (812) 334-2440

EAST CHICAGO
SYNAGOGUES
Orthodox
B'nai Israel
3517 Hemlock Street 46312

EVANSVILLE
SYNAGOGUES
Conservative
Temple Adath B'nai Israel
3600 E. Washington Avenue 47715
Telephone: (812) 477-1577
Fax: (812) 477-1577
Email: tabi@evansville.net

Reform
Tempe
Washington Avenue Temple, 100 Washington
Avenue 47714

FORT WAYNE
SYNAGOGUES
Conservative
B'nai Jacob
7227 Bittersweet Moors Drive 46814
Telephone: (219) 672-8459
Fax: (219) 672-8928

Reform
Congregation Achduth Vesholom
5200 Old Mill Road 46807
Telephone: (219) 260-744-4245
Fax: (219) 260-744-4246
Email: office@TempleCAV.org

GARY
SYNAGOGUES
Reform
Temple Israel
601 N. Montgomery Street 46403
Telephone: (219) 938-5232

HAMMOND
SYNAGOGUES
Conservative
Beth Israel
7105 Hohman Avenue 46324
Telephone: (219) 931-1312

Reform
Temple Beth-El
6947 Hohman Avenue 46324
Telephone: (219) 932-3754

HIGHLAND
COMMUNITY ORGANISATIONS
Jewish Federation of North West Indiana
2939 Jewett Street, Highland 48322-3005
Telephone: (219) 661-0840
Fax: (219) 661-4204
Email: info@holocaustcenter.org
Web site: www.holocaustcenter.org

INDIANAPOLIS
COMMUNITY ORGANISATIONS
Jewish Federation of Greater Indianapolis
6705 Hoover Road 70002-4826
Telephone: (317) 888-2209

SYNAGOGUES
Conservative
Congregation Shaarey Tefilla
5879 Central Avenue 46220-2509
Telephone: (317) 253-4591
Fax: (317) 253-8529
Email: execdir@shaareytefilla.org
Web site: www.shaareytefilla.org

Conservative/Reconstructionist
Beth-El Zedeck
600 W. 70th Street 46260
Telephone: (317) 317-253-3441
Fax: (317) 317-259-6849
Email: bez613@bez613.org
Web site: www.bez613.org

Orthodox
B'nai Torah
6510 Hoover Road 46260
Telephone: (317) 253-5253
Fax: (317) 253-5459
Email: scrandall@iquest.net

Etz Chaim Sephardic Congregation
826 West 64 Street 46260
Telephone: (317) 251-6220

Reform
Indianapolis Hebrew Congregation
6501 N. Meridian Street 46260
Telephone: (317) 255-6647

LAFAYETTE
SYNAGOGUES
Orthodox
Sons of Abraham
661 N. 7th Street 47906
Telephone: (317) 742-2113
Email: retrovir@bragg.bio.purdue.edu

MICHIGAN CITY
SYNAGOGUES
Reform
Sinai Temple
2800 S. Franklin Street 46360
Telephone: (219) 874-4477

MUNCIE
SYNAGOGUES
Reform
Temple Beth El
525 W. Jackson Street, cnr. Council Street 47305
Telephone: (317) 288-4662

SOUTH BEND
COMMUNITY ORGANISATIONS
Jewish Federation of St. Joseph Valley
3202 Shalom Way 46615
Telephone: (574) 574-233-1164
Fax: (574) 574-288-4103
Email: mgardner@jfedsjv.org
Web site: www.jfedsjv.org

CONTACT INFORMATION
Rabbi Y. Gettinger
Hebrew Orthodox Congregation, 3207 S. High
Street 71301

KASHRUT INFORMATION
Hebrew Orthodox Congregation
3207 S. High Street 02108
Telephone: (574) 367-9100
Fax: (574) 367-9310
Email: thejewishadvocate@thejewishadvocate.com
Web site: www.thejewishadvocate.com

SYNAGOGUES
Conservative
Sinai
1102 E. Laselle Street 46617
Telephone: (574) 234-8584
Fax: (574) 234-6856
Email: sinai@michiana.org
Web site: www.uscj.org/midwest/southbend

Orthodox
Hebrew Orthodox Congregation
3207 S. High Street 46614
Telephone: (574) 291-4239
Fax: (574) 291-9490

Reform
Beth-El
305 W. Madison Street 46601
Telephone: (574) 234-4402

TERRE HAUTE
DELICATESSEN
Kosher Meat & Sandwiches
410 W. Western Avenue 71301
Telephone: (812) 445-9367
Fax: (812) 445-9369

VALPARAISO
SYNAGOGUES
Conservative
Temple Israel
PO Box 2051 46383

WEST LAFAYETTE
SYNAGOGUES
Reform
620 Cumberland Street 47906
Telephone: (765) 463-3455
Fax: (765) 463-4650
Email: temple@iquest.net

WHITING
SYNAGOGUES
Orthodox
B'nai Judah
116th Street & Davis Avenue 46394
Telephone: (219) 659-0797

Iowa

CEDAR RAPIDS
SYNAGOGUES
Reform
Temple Judah
3221 Lindsay Lane S.E. 52403
Telephone: (319) 362-1261

DAVENPORT
SYNAGOGUES
Reform
Temple Emanuel
12th Street & Mississippi Avenue 52803

DES MOINES
COMMUNITY ORGANISATIONS
Jewish Federation of Greater Des Moines
910 Polk Blvd 71104
Telephone: (515) 221-4129

DELICATESSEN
The Nosh
800 First Street 70898
Telephone: (515) 291-5895

SYNAGOGUES
Conservative
Tifereth Israel
924 Polk Blvd 50312
Telephone: (515) 255-1137

Orthodox
Beth El Jacob
954 Cummins Parkway 50312
Telephone: (515) 274-1551
Fax: (515) 274-1552
Email: rav613@hotmail.com
Web site: www.cyberconnect.com/bej

Reform
Temple B'nai Jeshurun
5101 Grand Avenue 50312
Telephone: (515) 274-4679
Fax: (515) 274-2072
Email: arptbj@aol.com
Web site:
www.shamash.org/reform/uahc/congs/ia/ia001

DUBUQUE
SYNAGOGUES
Reform
Beth El
475 W. Locust Street 52001
Telephone: (563) 583-3483

FORT DODGE
SYNAGOGUES
Conservative
501 N. 12th Street 50501
Telephone: (515) 572-8925

IOWA CITY
SYNAGOGUES
Conservative & Reform
Agudas Achim Congregation
602 E. Washington Street 52240
Telephone: (319) 319-337-3813
Fax: (319) 337-6764
Email: agudasachim@aol.com
Web site: www.uscj.org/central/iowacity

POSTVILLE
SYNAGOGUES
Orthodox
440 South Lawlor Street
Telephone: (319) 863-3013

SIOUX CITY
SYNAGOGUES
Conservative
Congregation Beth Shalom
815 38th Street 51104
Telephone: (712) 255-1990
Fax: (712) 258-0619
Email: drosen4005@aol.com

Orthodox
United Orthodox
Nebraska & 14th Street 51105
Telephone: (712) 255-4455

Kansas
LAWRENCE
SYNAGOGUES
Lawrence Jewish Community Center
917 Highland Drive 66046
Telephone: (913) 784-841-7636
Email: ljcc@sunflower.com
Web site: www.ljcc.info

Kansas
OVERLAND PARK
BUTCHERS
Jacobsons Strictly Kosher Foods
5200 West 95th Street 70115
Telephone: (913) 897-8246

SYNAGOGUES
Orthodox
Congregation Beth Israel Abraham & Voliner
9900 Antioch 66212
Telephone: (913) 341-2444
Fax: (913) 341-2467

Kehilath Israel Synagogue
10501 Conser 66212
Telephone: (913) 642-1880
Fax: (913) 642-7332

Reform
Congregation Beth Torah
6100 W 127th Street 66209
Telephone: (913) 498-2212
Fax: (913) 498-1071

PRAIRIE VILLAGE
SYNAGOGUES
Conservative
Ohev Sholom
5311 W. 75th Street 66208
Telephone: (913) 642-6460
Fax: (913) 642-6461
Email: rabbidanny@aol.com

TOPEKA
COMMUNITY ORGANISATIONS
Topeka Lawrence Jewish Federation
4200 Munson Street 70002
Telephone: (785) 828-2125
Fax: (785) 828-2827

SYNAGOGUES
Reform
Beth Sholom
4200 SW Munson Avenue 66604-1818
Telephone: (785) 272-6040

WICHITA
GROCERIES
Dillon's
21st Street & Rock Road 70002
Telephone: (316) 828-2125
Fax: (316) 828-2827
Email: jewishnews@jewishnola.com
13th Street & Woodlawn Street 70002
Telephone: (316) 888-2010
Fax: (316) 888-2014
Web site: www.koshercajun.com
Foodbarn Woodlawn & Central Sts 68154
Telephone: (316) 334-8200

The Bread Lady
20205 Rock Road, #80 67208

SYNAGOGUES
Orthodox
Hebrew Congregation
1850 N. Woodlawn 67208
Telephone: (316) 685-1139

Reform
Congregation Emanu-El
7011 E. Central Street 67206
Telephone: (316) 685-5148

Kentucky

LEXINGTON
COMMUNITY ORGANISATIONS
Central Kentucky Jewish Federation
340 Romany Road 67208

SYNAGOGUES
Conservative
Lexington Havurah
685 Shasta Circle 40503
Telephone: (859) 223-1299

Ohavay Zion
2048 Edgewater Ct. 40502
Telephone: (859) 266-8050
Fax: (859) 268-3357
Email: ozslex@gte.net
Web site: www.ozs.org

Reform
Adath Israel
124 N. Ashland Avenue 40502
Telephone: (859) 269-2979
Fax: (859) 269-7347

LOUISVILLE
COMMUNITY ORGANISATIONS
Jewish Community Federation
3630 Dutchman's Lane 67208

SYNAGOGUES
Conservative
Adath Jeshurun
2401 Woodbourne Avenue 40205
Telephone: (502) 458-5359
Fax: (502) 451-5634
Email: webmaster@adathjeshurun.com
Web site: www.adathjeshurun.com

Knesseth Israel
2531 Taylorsville Road 40205
Telephone: (502) 459-2780

Orthodox
Anshei Sfard
3700 Dutchman's Lane 40205
Telephone: (502) 451-3122

Reform
Temple Shalom
4615 Lowe Road 40220
Telephone: (502) 458-4739
Fax: (502) 451-9750
Email: rsmiles@pipeline.com

The Temple
5101 Brownsboro Road 40241
Telephone: (502) 423-1818
Fax: (502) 423-1835
Email: gronkin@thetempleaibs.org
Web site: www.uahcweb.org/ky/thetemple

PADUCAH
SYNAGOGUES
Reform
Temple Israel
330 Joe Clifton Drive, PO Box 1141 42001
Telephone: 442-4104

Louisiana

ALEXANDRIA
CONTACT INFORMATION
Jewish Welfare Federation
Telephone: (318) 445-4785

GROCERIES
Dr & Mrs B Kaplan
100 Park Place 66211
Telephone: (318) 327-8100
Fax: (318) 327-8110
Email: www.jewishkc.org

LIBRARIES
Meyer Kaplan Memorial Library (Judiaca)
c/o B'nai Israel, 1908 Vance Street 66604

SYNAGOGUES
Conservative
B'nai Israel
1907 Vance Street 71301
Telephone: (318) 445-9367

Reform
Gemiluth Chassodim
2021 Turner Street 71301
Telephone: (318) 445-3655

BATON ROUGE
COMMUNITY ORGANISATIONS
Jewish Federation of Greater Baton Rouge
PO Box 80827 66207
Telephone: (504) 648-3880

SYNAGOGUES
Reform
B'nai Israel
3354 Kleinert Avenue 70806
Telephone: (504) 343-0111

Beth Shalom
9111 Jefferson Highway 70809
Telephone: (504) 924-6773

LAFAYETTE
SYNAGOGUES
Reform
Temple Sholom
603 Lee Avenue, PO Box 53711 70505
Telephone: (317) 234-3760

NEW ORLEANS
COMMUNITY ORGANISATIONS
Jewish Federation of Greater New Orleans
3500 N. Causeway Blvd., #1240, Metairie 66204

DELICATESSEN
Kosher Cajun Deli & Grocery
3519 Severn St, Metairie 63146
Telephone: (504) 569-2770

GROCERIES
Casablanca
3030 Seven Avenue, Metrairie 63146
Telephone: (504) 569-2770
Fax: (504) 569-2774
Touro Infirmary
1401 Foucher Street 63146

GUEST HOUSE
2405 St. Charles Avenue
Telephone: (504) 581-5858
Fax: (504) 891-5626
Email: paulag@sunshinebrokers.com

MEDIA
Newspaper
The Jewish News
Goldring-Woldenberg Jewish Community Campus,
Harry & Jeanette Weinberg Building, 3747 West
Esplanade Avenue, Metaire 70002
Telephone: (504) 780-5614
Fax: (504) 780-5601
Email: jfedstl@jfedstl.org
Web site: www.neworleansjewishnews.com

MIKVAOT
Beth Israel
7000 Canal Blvd 64114

RESTAURANTS
Meat
Casablanca
3030 Severn Avenue, Metairie
Telephone: (504) 888-2209
Fax: (504) 888-5605
Web site: www.kosherneworleans.com
Supervision: Lubavitch Shechita & Chabad.
Creole Kosher Kitchen
115 Chartres Street
Telephone: (504) 529-4120
Supervision: Beth Israel Congregation

SYNAGOGUES
Orthodox
Anshe Sfard
2230 Carondelet Street 70130
Telephone: (504) 522-4714
Chabad House
7037 Freret Street
Telephone: (504) 866-5164

SHREVEPORT
SYNAGOGUES
Conservative
Agudath Achim
9401 Village Green Drive 71115
Telephone: (318) 797-6401
Fax: (318) 797-6402

Reform
B'nai Zion
245 Southfield Road 71105
Telephone: (318) 861-2122

Maine

AUBURN
COMMUNITY ORGANISATIONS
Lewiston-Auburn Jewish Federation
74 Bradman Street 04210
Telephone: (207) 786-4201
Fax: (207) 786-4202
Email: temple6359@aol.com

SYNAGOGUES
Conservative
Congregation Beth Abraham
Main Street & Laurel Avenue 04210
Telephone: (207) 783-1302
Temple Shalom
74 Bradman Street 04210
Telephone: (207) 786-4201
Fax: (207) 786-4202
Email: temple6359@aol.com

AUGUSTA
SYNAGOGUES
Reform
Temple Beth El
PO Box 871, Woodlawn Street 04330
Telephone: (404) 622-7450

BANGOR
RESTAURANTS
Bagel Central
33 Central Street 04401
Telephone: (207) 947-1654
Supervision: Beth Abraham Rabbi Fred Neble

SYNAGOGUES
Conservative
Congregation Beth Israel
144 York Street 04401
Telephone: (207) 945-3433
Fax: (207) 945-3840

Orthodox
Beth Abraham
145 York Street 04401
Telephone: (207) 942-8093
Email: rabbi@jewishbangor.com
Web site: www.jewishbangor.com

OLD ORCHARD BEACH
KASHRUT INFORMATION
Eber Weinstein
187 E. Grand Avenue 04064
Telephone: (207) 934-7522

PORTLAND
BUTCHERS
Penny Wise Super Market
182 Ocean Avenue 55812
Telephone: (503) 724-8857

COMMUNITY ORGANISATIONS
Jewish Fed.-Com. Council of Southern Maine
57 Ashmont Street 55907
Telephone: (503) 288-7500
Fax: (503) 286-9329
Email: rabbigreene@charter.net

MIKVAOT
Shaarey Tphiloh
76 Noyes Street 55416
Telephone: (503) 381-3410
Fax: (503) 381-3401
Email: jschachtman@jccminneapolis.org

SYNAGOGUES
Conservative
Temple Beth El
400 Deering Avenue 04103
Telephone: (503) 774-2649
Fax: (503) 774-7518
Email: office@templebethel-maine.org

Orthodox
Shaarey Tphiloh
76 Noyes Street 04103
Telephone: (503) 773-0693

ROCKLAND
SYNAGOGUES
Conservative
Adas Yoshuron
Willow Street
Telephone: (207) 594-4523

Maryland
Bethesda, Bowie, Chevy Chase, Gaithersburg, Greenbelt, Hyattsville, Kensington, Laurel, Lexington Park, Olney, Potomac, Rockville, Silver Spring & Wheaton and Temple Hills are all part of Greater Washington, DC.

ANNAPOLIS
SYNAGOGUES
Conservative
Congregation Kol Ami
1909 Hidden Meadow Lane 21401
Telephone: (410) 266-6006
Email: kolami2@toadmail.toad.net

Reform
Temple Beth Shalom
1461 Baltimore-Anaapolis Blvd., 21012

BALTIMORE
BAKERIES
Alder's Bakery
1860D Reisterstown Road
Telephone: (410) 653-1119

Dunkin Donuts
1508 Reisterstown Road 21208
Telephone: (410) 653-8182
Supervision: Rabbi Salfer
7000 Reisterstown Road 21215
Telephone: (410) 764-6846
Supervision: Rabbi Salfer

Goldman's Kosher Bakery
6848 Reistertown Road, Fallstaff Shopping Center 48108
Telephone: (410) 677-0100
Fax: (410) 677-0109
Email: info@jewishannarbor.org

Pariser's Kosher Bakery
6711 Reisterstown Road 48104
Telephone: (410) 995-3276
Fax: (410) 996-2479
Email: chabad@jewmich.com

Schmell & Azman Kosher Bakery
1351 Lamberton Drive 48075
Telephone: (410) 559-5005/06
Fax: (410) 559-5202

Schmell-Azman
7006 Reisterstown Road 21215
Telephone: (410) 484-7373
Supervision: Star K

BUTCHERS
Shlomo Meat & Fish Market
4135 Amos Ave., (Menlo Industrial Park) 21215
Telephone: (410) 358-9633

Wasserman & Lemberger
7006-D Reisterstown Road 20208
Telephone: (410) 486-4191

COMMUNITY ORGANISATIONS
Associated Jewish Community Federation of Baltimore
101 W. Mount Royal Avenue 55416
Telephone: (410) 926-3829
Fax: (410) 920-2184
Email: office@kenessethisrael.org

Jewish Information and Referral Service
5750 Park Heights Avenue 48075
Telephone: (410) 410-466-4636
Fax: (410) 410-664-0551
Email: cordetroit@hotmail.com
Web site: www.jirs.info

DELICATESSEN
Knish Shop
508 Reisterstown Road 21208
Telephone: (410) 484-5850

Liebes Kosher Deli Carry Out
607 Reistertown Road 48303

GROCERIES
Seven Mile Market
4000 Seven Mile Lane 21208
Telephone: (410) 653-2000; 2002
Email: SevenMileMarket@covad.net
Supervision: Star-K

Shlomo Meat & Fish
506 Reisterstown Road 48237

Wasserman & Lemberger
7006-D Reisterstown Road 48237
Telephone: (410) 443-2425

KASHRUT INFORMATION
Star-K Kosher Certification
122 Slade Avenue, Suite 300 48075
Telephone: (410) 443-2425

MIKVAOT
Mikva of Baltimore Inc.,
3207 Clarks Lane 50312
Telephone: (410) 277-6321

MUSEUMS
The Jewish Museum of Maryland
15 Lloyd Street 55116

RESTAURANTS
Café Shalom
2401 West Belvedere Avenue 21215
Telephone: (410) 601-5000 ext 3971
Fax: (410) 601-6312
Supervision: Star-K

Goldberg's Bagels
708 Reisterstown Road
Telephone: (410) 415-7001
Supervision: Star-K

Krispy Kremes
10021 Reisterstown Road (nr Painters Mill Rd).
Telephone: (410) 356-2655
Supervision: Star-KD

Mama Leah's Pizza
1852 Reisterstown Road
Telephone: (410) 653-7600
Supervision: Star-K

Dairy
Caramel's Pizza & Ice Cream
700 Reisterstown Road
Telephone: (410) 486-2365
Supervision: Star-K

Milk and Honey Bistro
Commercecentre, 1777 Reisterstown Road
Telephone: (410) 484-3544
Supervision: Star-K

Meat
David Chu's China Bistro
7105 Reisterstown Road 21215
Telephone: (410) 602-5008
Supervision: Star-K

Kosher Bite
6309 Reisterstown Road 48502
Telephone: (410) 767-5922
Fax: (410) 767-9024
Email: fjf@tm.net

Royal Restaurant
7006 Reistertown Road 48322
Telephone: (410) 661-1000
Fax: (410) 661-3680

Szechuan Dynasty
1860C Reisterstown Road
Telephone: (410) 602-1817

The Brasserie
Pomona Square Shopping Center, 1700
Reisterstown Rd 50265

Pizzeria
Tov Pizza
6313 Reisterstown Road
Telephone: (410) 358-5238

TOURS OF JEWISH INTEREST
Holocaust Memorial
Gay & Lombard Sts 51105
Telephone: (410) 258-0618

CUMBERLAND
SYNAGOGUES
Conservative
Beth Jacob
1 Columbia Street 21502
Telephone: (301) 777-3717

Reform
B'Er Chayim
107 Union Street 21502
Telephone: (301) 722-5688
Web site: www.berchayim.org

HAGERSTOWN
SYNAGOGUES
Reform
B'nai Abraham
53 E. Baltimore Street 21740
Telephone: (301) 733-5039

HYATTSVILLE
SYNAGOGUES
Conservative
Beth Torah Congregation
6700 Adelphi Road 20782
Telephone: (301) 927-5525
Email: bethtorah@starpower.net
Web site: www.bethtorah.ws

LAUREL
SYNAGOGUES
Reconstructionist
Oseh Shalom
8604 Briarwood Drive 20708
Telephone: (301) 498-5151

LEXINGTON PARK
SYNAGOGUES
Conservative
Beth Israel Congregation
PO Box 1683, 21780 Bunker Hill Drive 20653
Telephone: (301) 862-2021
Email: bethisraelsyna@geocities.com
Web site: www.geocities.com/bethisraelsyna

POCOMOKE
SYNAGOGUES
Conservative
Temple Israel
3rd Street 21851

SALISBURY
SYNAGOGUES
Conservative
Beth Israel
600 Camden Ave 21801
Telephone: (410) 410-742-2564
Fax: (410) 410-742-2697
Email: bethisrael1231@cs.com
Web site: www.bethisraelsailisbury.org

TEMPLE HILLS
SYNAGOGUES
Conservative
Shaare Tikva
5405 Old Temple Hills Road 20748
Telephone: (301) 894-4303

GREATER WASHINGTON

BETHESDA
COMMUNITY ORGANISATIONS
United Jewish Appeal Federation of Greater Washington
7900 Wisconsin Avenue 48034

BOWIE
SYNAGOGUES
Conservative
Nevey Shalom
12218 Torah Lane 20715
Telephone: (301) 262-9020
Fax: (301) 262-9015
Email: neveyshalom@maxinter.net

Reform
Temple Solel
2901 Mitchelville Road 20716
Telephone: (301) 249-2424

CHEVY CHASE
SYNAGOGUES
Conservative
Ohr Kodesh
8402 Freyman Drive 20815
Telephone: (301) 589-3880
Fax: (301) 495-4801
Email: okcjmm@erols.com

Reform
Temple Shalom
8401 Grubb Road 20815
Telephone: (301) 587-2273

GAITHERSBURG
SYNAGOGUES
Conservative
Kehilat Shalom
9915 Apple Ridge Road 20886
Telephone: (301) 869-7699
Fax: (301) 977-7870
Email: mail@kehilatshalom.org
Web site: www.kehilatshalom.org

GREENBELT
SYNAGOGUES
Conservative
Mishkan Torah
Westway and Ridge Road 20770
Telephone: (301) 474-4223

KEMP MILL
SYNAGOGUES
Kemp Mill Synagogue
11910 Kemp Mill Road
Telephone: (301) 593-0966

KENSINGTON
SYNAGOGUES
Reform
Temple Emanuel
10101 Connecticut Avenue 20895
Telephone: (301) 942-2000
Fax: (301) 942-9488

OLNEY
SYNAGOGUES
Conservative
B'nai Shalom
18401 Burtfield Drive 20832
Telephone: (301) 774-0879

POTOMAC
RESTAURANTS
Meat
Hunan Gourmet
350 Fortune Terrace 46615
Telephone: (301) 233-1164
Fax: (301) 288-4103
Email: mgardner@jfedsjv.org
Web site: www.jfedsv.org

SYNAGOGUES
Conservative
Har Shalom
11510 Falls Road 20854
Telephone: (301) 299-7087
Email: shalom@harshalom.org
Web site: www.harshalom.org

Orthodox
Beth Sholom Congregation and Talmud Torah
11825 Seven Locks Road 20854
Telephone: (301) 279-7010
Fax: (301) 279-5815
Email: bethsholom.org
Young Israel Ezras Israel of Potomac
11618 Seven Locks Road 20854
Telephone: (301) 299-2827
Web site: www.yieip.org

ROCKVILLE
GROCERIES
Katz Supermarket
4860 Boiling Brook Parkway
Telephone: (301) 468-0400

RESTAURANTS
Dairy
Siena's
Nicholson Road
Telephone: (301) 770-7474

Meat
Royal Dragon
4840 Boiling Brook Parkway
Telephone: (301) 468-1922

Meat and Dairy
Kat'z Kafe
4860 Boiling Brook Parkway 46614
Telephone: (301) 291-4239
Fax: (301) 291-9490

SYNAGOGUES
Conservative
B'nai Israel
6301 Montrose Road 20852
Telephone: (301) 881-6550
Fax: (301) 881-6221
Tikvat Israel
2200 Baltimore Road 20851
Telephone: (301) 762-7338
Fax: (301) 424-4399

Orthodox
Magen David Sephardic Congregation
11215 Woodglen Drive, Rockville, MD 20852
Telephone: (301) 770-6818
Fax: (301) 881-0498

Reform
Temple Beth Ami
14330 Travilah Road 20850
Telephone: (301) 340-6818
Fax: (301) 738-0094
Email: cgs@bethami.org

SILVER SPRING
BAKERIES
Kosher Pastry Oven
2521 Ennalls Avenue
Telephone: (301) 946-0159

Schmell and Azman
Kemp Mill Shopping Center, Arcola Avenue
Telephone: (301) 593-4785

The Wooden Shoe Pastry Shop
11301 Georgia Avenue 20902
Telephone: (301) 942-9330

Virtuoso
11230a Lockwood Avenue 50901
Telephone: (301) 593-6034

BOOKSELLERS
Lisbon's Hebrew Books & Gifts
2305 University Blvd West, Wheaton 46260
Telephone: (301) 726-5450
Fax: (301) 205-0307
Email: hnadler@jewishinindy.org

The Jewish Bookstore
11252 Georgia Avenue 40502
Telephone: (301) 268-0672
Fax: (301) 268-0775
Email: ckjf@jewishlexington.org

GROCERIES
Shalom
2309 University Blvd 21215
Telephone: (301) 764-1448
Fax: (301) 578-0018

Shaul & Hershel Meat Market
Telephone: (301) 949-8477

MIKVAOT
Mikva
8901 Georgia Avenue 46322
Telephone: (301) 972-2251
Fax: (301) 972-4779

RESTAURANTS
Dairy
Ben Yehuda Pizza
Kemp Mill Shopping Center, off Arcola Avenue

The Nut House
11419 Georgia Avenue 40205
Telephone: (301) 451-8840
Fax: (301) 458-0702
Email: jfed@iglou.com

Meat
Max's
2309 University Blvd
Telephone: (301) 949-6297

SYNAGOGUES
Conservative
Har Tzeon-Agudath Achim
1840 University Blvd. W 20902

Shaare Tefila Congregation
11120 Lockwood Drive 20901
Telephone: (301) 593-3410
Fax: (301) 593-3860
Email: mgreen@shaaretefila.org
Web site: www.shaaretefila.org

Orthodox
Silver Spring Jewish Center
1401 Arcola Avenue 46614
Telephone: (301) 291-4239
Fax: (301) 291-9490

South-East Hebrew Congregation
10900 Lockwood Drive 20902

Woodside Synagogue Ahavas Torah
9001 Georgia Avenue 20910
Telephone: (301) 301587-8252
Email: information@wsat.org
Web site: www.wsat.org

Young Israel of White Oak
PO Box 10613, White Oak 20914
Telephone: (301) 369-1531

Young Israel Shomrai Emunah of Greater Washington
1132 Arcola Avenue 20902
Telephone: (301) 593-4465
Fax: (301) 593-2330
Email: yise@erols.com

Massachusetts
ACTON
SYNAGOGUES
Independent
Beth Elohim
10 Hennessy Drive 07120
Telephone: (978) 263-8610

AMHERST
SYNAGOGUES
Independent
Jewish Community
742 Main Street 21215
Telephone: (413) 358-6349
Supervision: Star-K

ANDOVER

SYNAGOGUES

Reform
Temple Emanuel
7 Haggett's Pond Road 01810
Telephone: (978) 978-470-1356
Fax: (978) 978-470-1783
Email: info@templeemanuel.net
Web site: www.templeemanuel.net

ATHOL

SYNAGOGUES

Conservative
Temple Israel
107 Walnut Street 01331
Telephone: (978) 249-9481

ATTLEBORO

SYNAGOGUES

Reconstructionist
Agudas Achim Congregation
901 N. Main Street 02703
Telephone: (508) 222-2243
Email: agudasachim@netzero.net
Web site: www.shamash.org/jrf/agudasma

AYER

SYNAGOGUES

Independent
Congregation Anshey Sholom
Cambridge Street 01432
Telephone: (508) 772-0896

BELMONT

SYNAGOGUES

Reform
Beth El Temple Center
2 Concord Avenue 02478
Telephone: (617) 484-6668
Fax: (617) 484-6020
Web site: www.uahc.org/ma/betc

BEVERLY

SYNAGOGUES

Conservative
B'nai Abraham
200 E. Lothrop Street 01915
Telephone: (978) 927-3211
Fax: (978) 922-5281
Email: TBA200East@cs.com

BOSTON

EMBASSY

Consul General of Israel
1020 Statler Office Blvd 02116

KASHRUT INFORMATION

Synagogue Council of Massachusetts
1320 Centre Street, Newton Centre 21215
Telephone: (617) 358-9625
Fax: (617) 358-5859
Email: mcohn@comcast.net

The Kashruth Commission
177 Tremont Street 02111
Telephone: (617) 764-1700

MEDIA

Guide
Jewish Guide to Boston and New England
15 School Street 02108
Telephone: (617) 617-367-9100
Fax: (617) 617-367-9310
Email: thejewishadvocate@thejewishadvocate.com

Newspapers
Boston Jewish Times
15 School Street 02108
Telephone: (617) 484-3544
Supervision: Star-K

The Jewish Advocate
15 School Street 02108
Telephone: (617) 617-367-9100
Fax: (617) 617-367-9310
Email: thejewishadvocate@thejewishadvocate.com
Web site: www.thejewishadvocate.com
Supervision: Star-K

RELIGIOUS ORGANISATIONS

Rabbinical Council of New England
177 Tremont Street 02111
Telephone: (617) 301-593-4785

RESTAURANTS

Dairy
50 Milk Street 21208
Telephone: (617) 486-4191

SYNAGOGUES

Orthodox
Chabad House
491 Commonwealth Avenue 02215
Telephone: (617) 424-1190
Fax: (617) 266-5997
Email: chabad@peoplepc.com

The Boston Synagogue (at Charles River Park)
55 Martha Road 02114
Telephone: (617) 523-0453
Fax: (617) 723-2863

Zvhil-Mezbuz Beis Medrash
15 School Street 02108
Telephone: (617) 227-8200
Fax: (617) 227-8420
Web site: www.rebbe.org

Reform
Temple Israel
Longwood Ave & Plymouth Street 02215
Telephone: (617) 566-3960
Fax: (617) 731-3711
Web site: www.tisrael.org

BRAINTREE
SYNAGOGUES
Conservative
Temple Bnai Shalom
41 Storrs Avenue 02184
Telephone: (781) 843-3687

BRIGHTON
MIKVAOT
Daughters of Israel
101 Washington Street, Brighton 02135
Telephone: (617) 466-4636
Fax: (617) 664-0551
Email: jirs@jfs.org
Web site: www.jirs.info

SYNAGOGUES
Conservative
Temple B'nai Moshe
1845 Commonwealth Avenue, Brighton 02135
Telephone: (617) 254-3620
Fax: (617) 254-3620
Email: templebnaimoshe.org

Orthodox
Chai Odom
77 Englewood Av 02135
Telephone: (617) 734-5359
Web site: www.chaiodom.org

Congregation Kadimah-Toras Moshe
113 Washington Street, Brighton 02135
Telephone: (617) 254-1333

Lubavitch Shul of Brighton
239 Chestnut Hill Avenue, Brighton 02135
Telephone: (617) 782-8340

Talner Congregation Beth David
64 Corey Road 02135
Telephone: (617) 232-2349

BROCKTON
SYNAGOGUES
Conservative
Temple
479 Torres Street 02401
Telephone: (508) 583-5810

Orthodox
Agudas Achim
144 Belmont Avenue 02301
Telephone: (508) 583-0717

BROOKLINE
BAKERIES
Catering by Andrew
402 Harvard Street 02446
Telephone: (617) 731-6585
Fax: (617) 232-3788
Email: cbandrew@aol.com
Supervision: Vaad Harabonim of Massachusetts

Kupel's
421 Harvard Street
Telephone: (617) 566-9528

GROCERIES
Beacon Kosher
1706 Beacon Street
Telephone: (617) 734-5300

JUDAICA
Israel Book Shop, Inc.
410 Harvard Street
Telephone: (617) 323-7723

RESTAURANTS
Dairy
Café Eilat
420 Harvard Street 02446
Telephone: (617) 277-7770

Meat
Rami's
324 Harvard Street 02446
Telephone: (617) 738-3577

Rubin's Kosher Deli and Restaurant
500 Harvard Street, Brookline 02146
Telephone: (617) 731-8787

Ruth's Kitchen
401 Harvard Street 02446
Telephone: (617) 484-4110
Fax: (617) 653-9294
Email: star-k@star-k.org
Web site: www.star-k.org

Shalom Hunan
92 Harvard Street 02445-46
Telephone: (617) 731-9778
Fax: (617) 731-9760

Taam China
423 Harvard Street
Telephone: (617) 264-7274

SYNAGOGUES

Conservative
Kehillath Israel
384 Harvard St 2146
Telephone: (617) 277-9155

Orthodox
Beth Pinchas (Bostoner Rebbe)
1710 Beacon Street 02146
Telephone: (617) 734-5100
Fax: (617) 739-0163
Email: rofeh@world.std.com

Congregation Lubavitch
100 Woodcliff Road 02467
Telephone: (617) 469-5000
Fax: (617) 469-0089
Email: lubavitch@jvnv.com

Young Israel of Brookline
62 Green Street 02446
Telephone: (617) 734-0276
Fax: (617) 734-7195
Email: office@yibrookline.org
Web site: www.yibrookline.org

Reform
Ohabei Shalom
1187 Beacon St 2446
Telephone: (617) 277-6610
Email: dberman@ohabei.org
Web site: www.ohabei.org

Temple Sinai
50 Sewall Av, Coolidge Corner 02146
Telephone: (617) 277-5888

Sephardi
Sephardic Congregation
1566 Beacon St 02146
Telephone: (617) 566-8171

BURLINGTON

SYNAGOGUES
Reform
Temple Shalom Emeth
14-16 Lexington Street 01803
Telephone: (718) 272-2351

CAMBRIDGE

KASHRUT INFORMATION
Harvard Hillel
Harvard University, 52 Mt. Auburn St 21202
Telephone: (617) 732-6400
Fax: (617) 732-6451
Email: info@jewishmuseummd.org
Web site: www.jewishmuseummd.org

RESTAURANTS
52 Mt Auburn Street 02138
Telephone: (617) 495-4695
Fax: (617) 864-1637
Email: linda@hillel.harvard.edu
Web site: www.hillel.harvard.edu

Meat
M.I.T. Hillel
40 Massachusetts Avenue 02139
Telephone: (617) 253-2982
Fax: (617) 253-3260
Email: hillel@mit.edu
Supervision: Vaad Harabonim of Massachusetts

SYNAGOGUES
Conservative
Temple Beth Shalom of Cambridge
8 Tremont Street 02139
Telephone: (617) 864-6388
Fax: (617) 864-0507
Email: office@tremontstreetshul.org

Orthodox
Chabad
38 Banks Street 02138
Telephone: (617) 547-6124
Email: rebharvard@aol.com

Harvard Hillel
52 Mt Auburn Street 01238
Telephone: (617) 495-4695
Fax: (617) 864-1637
Email: linda@hillel.harvard.edu
Web site: www.hillel.harvard.edu

CANTON

SYNAGOGUES
Conservative
Beth Abraham
1301 Washington Street 02021
Telephone: (781) 828-5250

Reform
Temple Beth David of the South Shore
1060 Randolph Street 02021
Telephone: (781) 828-2275
Fax: (781) 821-3997
Email: info@templebethdavid.com
Web site: www.templebethdavid.com

CAPE COD
SYNAGOGUES
Orthodox
Beth Israel
cnr. of Onset Avenue & Locust Street, PO Box 24,
Onset 02558
Telephone: (508) 295-9185
Email: capeshul@att.net
Web site: www.home.att.net/capeshul

CHELMSFORD
SYNAGOGUES
Reform
Congregation Shalom
Richardson Road 01824
Telephone: (978) 251-8090

CLINTON
SYNAGOGUES
Independent
Shaarei Zedeck
Water Street 01510
Telephone: (978) 365-3320

EAST FALMOUTH
SYNAGOGUES
Reform
Falmouth Jewish Congregation
7 Hatchville Road 02536
Telephone: (508) 540-0602
Fax: (508) 540-8094
Web site: www.falmouthjewish.org

EASTON
SYNAGOGUES
Traditional
Temple Chayai Shalom
238 Depot Street 02334
Telephone: (508) 238-6385

EVERETT
SYNAGOGUES
Traditional
Tifereth Israel
34 Malden Street 02149
Telephone: (617) 387-0200

FALL RIVER
COMMUNITY ORGANISATIONS
Fall River Jewish Community Council
Room 327, 56 N. Main St 21201
Telephone: (508) 727-4828

SYNAGOGUES
Conservative
Beth El
385 High Street 02720
Telephone: (508) 674-9761

Orthodox
Adas Israel
1647 Robeson Street 02720
Telephone: (508) 674-9761
Fax: (508) 678-3195

FRAMINGHAM
RESTAURANTS
Meat
Rami's of Framington
341 Cochituate Rd 01701
Telephone: (508) 370-3577

SYNAGOGUES
Conservative
Temple Beth Sholom
50 Pamela Road 01701
Telephone: (508) 877-2540
Fax: (508) 877-8278
Web site: www.beth-sholom.org

Orthodox
Chabad House
74 Joseph Road 01701
Telephone: (508) 877-5313
Fax: (508) 877 5313

Reform
Beth Am
300 Pleasant Street 01701
Telephone: (508) 872-8300
Fax: (508) 872-9773
Email: tempbetham@aol.com

Temple Beth Am
300 Pleasant Street 01701
Telephone: (508) 508-872-8300
Fax: (508) 508-872-9773
Email: shalom@templebetham.org
Web site: www.templebetham.org

GLOUCESTER
SYNAGOGUES

Conservative
Ahavat Achim
86 Middle Street 01930
Telephone: (978) 281-0739
Fax: (978) 281-0739

GREENFIELD
SYNAGOGUES

Conservative
Temple Israel
27 Pierce Street 01301
Telephone: (413) 773-5884

HAVERHILL
SYNAGOGUES

Orthodox
Anshe Sholom
427 Main Street 01830
Telephone: (508) 372-2276

Reform
Temple Emanu-El
514 Main Street 01830
Telephone: (508) 373-3861

HINGHAM
SYNAGOGUES

Reform
Congregation Sha'aray Shalom
1112 Main Street 02043
Telephone: (781) 749-8103
Fax: (781) 740-1480
Email: cssadm@aol.com

HOLBROOK
SYNAGOGUES

Conservative
Temple Beth Shalom
95 Plymouth Street 02343
Telephone: (617) 767-4922

HOLLISTON
SYNAGOGUES

Conservative
Temple Beth Torah
2162 Washington Street 01746
Telephone: (508) 429-6268
Fax: (508) 429-7729
Email: tbt@bethtorah.org

HOLYOKE
SYNAGOGUES

Conservative
Sons of Zion
378 Maple Street 01040
Telephone: (413) 534-3369

Orthodox
Rodphey Sholom
1800 Northampton Street 01040
Telephone: (413) 534-5262

HULL
SYNAGOGUES

Conservative
Temple Beth Sholom
600 Nantasket Avenue 02045
Telephone: (617) 925-0091
Fax: (617) 925-9053

Temple Israel of Nantasket
9 Hadassah Way 02045
Telephone: (617) 925-0289

HYANNIS
SYNAGOGUES

Reform
Cape Cod Synagogue
145 Winter Street 02601
Telephone: (508) 775-2988

HYDE PARK
SYNAGOGUES

Conservative
Temple Adas Hadrath Israel
28 Arlington Street 02136
Telephone: (617) 364-2661

LAWRENCE
COMMUNITY ORGANISATIONS
Jewish Com. Council of Greater Lawrence
580 Haverhill Street 20910
Telephone: (913) 565-3737

SYNAGOGUES

Orthodox
Anshai Sholum
411 Hampshire Street 01843
Telephone: (913) 683-4544

LEOMINSTER
SYNAGOGUES
Conservative
Congregation Agudat Achim
268 Washington Street 01453
Telephone: (508) 534-6121

LEXINGTON
SYNAGOGUES
Conservative
Temple Emunah
9 Piper Road 02421
Telephone: (859) 861-0300
Fax: (859) 861-7141
Email: rholmes@emunahlex.org
Web site: www.templeemunah.org

Orthodox
Chabad Center
9 Burlington Street 02173
Telephone: (859) 863-8656

Reform
Temple Isaiah
55 Lincoln Street 02173
Telephone: (859) 862-7160

LONGMEADOW
MIKVAOT
Mikveh Association
1104 Converse, Long. MA 2558
Telephone: (413) 295-9820

SYNAGOGUES
Conservative
B'nai Jacob
2 Eunice Dr 01106
Telephone: (413) 567-3163

Orthodox
Beth Israel
1280 Williams St 01106
Telephone: (413) 567-3210
Lubavitcher Yeshiva Synagogue
1148 Converse St 01106
Telephone: (413) 567-8665

LOWELL
MIKVAOT
Mikvah
48 Academy Drive
Telephone: (978) 933-1800
Fax: (978) 933-7466
Email: slisbon@idsonline.com

SYNAGOGUES
Conservative
Temple Beth El
105 Princeton Blvd. 01851
Telephone: (978) 453-7744

Orthodox
Montefiore Synagogue
460 Westford Street 20902
Telephone: (978) 649-4425
Fax: (978) 649-1274

Reform
Temple Emanuel of Merrimack Valley
101 W. Forest Street 01851
Telephone: (978) 454-1372
Email: info@temv.org
Web site: www.temv.org

LYNN
SYNAGOGUES
Orthodox
Ahabat Sholom
151 Ocean Street 01902
Telephone: (617) 593-9255
Fax: (617) 593-9255
Email: ahabat@juno.com
Web site: www.ahabatsholom.org
Anshai Sfard
150 South Common Street 01905
Telephone: (617) 599-7131

MALDEN
SYNAGOGUES
Conservative
Ezrath Israel
245 Bryant Street 02148
Telephone: (781) 322-7205

Orthodox
Congregation Beth Israel
10 Dexter Street 02148
Telephone: (781) 322-5686
Fax: (781) 322-6678
Email: congbi@aol.com
Young Israel of Malden
45 Holyoke Street 02148
Telephone: (781) 961-9817

Reform
Tifereth Israel
539 Salem Street 02148
Telephone: (781) 322-2794

Traditional
Agudas Achim
160 Harvard Street 02148
Telephone: (781) 322-9380

MARBLEHEAD
SYNAGOGUES
Conservative/Masorti
Temple Sinai
1 Community Road 01945
Telephone: (617) 631-2763
Fax: (617) 631-2244
Email: Tmpsinai@gis.net

Orthodox
Orthodox Congregation of the North Shore
4 Community Road 01945
Telephone: (617) 598-1810

Reform
Temple Emanu-El
393 Atlantic Avenue 01945
Telephone: (617) 631-9300

MARLBORO
SYNAGOGUES
Conservative
Temple Emanuel
150 Berlin Road 01752
Telephone: (508) 485-7565

MEDFORD
SYNAGOGUES
Conservative
Temple Shalom
475 Winthrop Street 02155
Telephone: (781) 396-3262

MELROSE
SYNAGOGUES
Reform
Temple Beth Shalom
21 E. Foster Street 02176
Telephone: (617) 665-4520

MILFORD
SYNAGOGUES
Conservative
55 Pine Street 01757
Telephone: (508) 473-1590
Web site: www.templebethshalom.com

MILLIS
SYNAGOGUES
Conservative
Ael Chunon
334 Village Street 02054
Telephone: (508) 376-5984
Fax: (508) 533-3802
Email: TNULB@mediaone.net

MILTON
SYNAGOGUES
Conservative
Temple Shalom
180 Blue Hill Avenue 02186
Telephone: (617) 698-3394
Fax: (617) 696-9265
Email: templeshalom@yahoo.com
Web site: www.uscj.org/neweng/milton

Orthodox
B'nai Jacob
100 Blue Hill Parkway 02187
Telephone: (617) 698-0698
Supervision: Rabbi Nathan Korff

NATICK
SYNAGOGUES
Conservative
Temple Israel
145 Hartford Street 01760
Telephone: (508) 650-3521
Fax: (508) 655-3440
Web site: www.tiofnatick.org

NEEDHAM
SYNAGOGUES
Conservative
Temple Aliyah
1664 Central Avenue 02492
Telephone: (781) 781-444-8522
Fax: (781) 781-449-7066
Web site: www.templealiyah.com

Reform
Temple Beth Shalom
670 Highland Avenue 02494
Telephone: (781) 781-444-0077
Fax: (781) 781-449-3274
Email: tbshalom@ix.netcom.com
Web site: www.templebethshalom.info

NEW BEDFORD

COMMUNITY ORGANISATIONS
Jewish Federation of Greater New Bedford
467 Hawthorn Street, N. Dartmouth 20902
Telephone: (508) 942-5900

SYNAGOGUES
Conservative
Tifereth Israel
145 Brownell Avenue 02740
Telephone: (508) 997-3171
Fax: (508) 997-3173

Orthodox
Ahavath Achim
385 County Street 02740
Telephone: (508) 994-1760
Fax: (508) 994-8186
Email: rabbibarry@aol.com
Web site: www.members.aol.com/rabbibarry

NEWBURYPORT

SYNAGOGUES
Conservative
Congregation Ahavas Achim
Washington & Olive Streets 09150
Telephone: (508) 462-2461

NEWTON

COMMUNITY ORGANISATIONS
Jewish Community Center of Greater Boston
333 Nahanton Street 20902
Telephone: (617) 946-6500
Fax: (617) 946-1041

RESTAURANTS
Rosenfeld Bagels
1280 Centre Street, Newton Center 02459
Telephone: (617) 527-8080

SYNAGOGUES
Orthodox
Beth El Ateret Israel
561 Ward Street 02459
Telephone: (617) 244-7233

Congregation B'nai Jacob (Zvhil-Mezbuz Rebbe)
955 Beacon Street
Telephone: (617) 227-8200
Fax: (617) 227-8420
Web site: www.rebbe.org

Shaarei Tefilla
35 Morseland Avenue 02459
Telephone: (617) 527-7637

NORTH ADAMS

SYNAGOGUES
Conservative
Congregation Beth Israel
265 Church Street 01247
Telephone: (413) 663-5830
Fax: (413) 663-5830
Email: cbi@bcn.net

NORTHAMPTON

SYNAGOGUES
Conservative
B'nai Israel
253 Prospect Road 01060
Telephone: (413) 584-3593

NORWOOD

SYNAGOGUES
Conservative
Temple Shaare Tefilah
556 Nichols Street 02062
Telephone: (781) 762-8670
Fax: (781) 762-8670
Web site: www.uscj.org/neweng/norwood

ONSET

HOTELS
Bridge View Hotel
12 S. Water Street 20814
Telephone: (508) 652-6480

PEABODY

SYNAGOGUES
Conservative
Temple Ner Tamid
368 Lowell Street 001960
Telephone: (508) 532-1293
Fax: (508) 532-0101
Email: audrey368@aol.com
Web site: www.templenertamid.org

Independent
Congregation Tifereth Israel
Pierpont Street 01960
Telephone: (508) 531-8135

Reform
Beth Shalom
489 Lowell Street 01960
Telephone: (508) 535-2100
Fax: (508) 536-3115

Traditional
Congregation Sons of Israel
Park & Spring Streets 01960
Telephone: (508) 531-7576

PITTSFIELD
COMMUNITY ORGANISATIONS
Jewish Federation of the Berkshires
235 East Street 20782
Telephone: (413) 927-5525

PLYMOUTH
SYNAGOGUES
Reform
Congregation Beth Jacob
Synagogue on Pleasant Street, Community Center
on Court Street, PO Box 3284 02361
Telephone: (508) 746-1575
Email: cbethjacob@juno.com

QUINCY
SYNAGOGUES
Conservative
Adas Shalom
435 Adams Street 02169
Telephone: (617) 471-1818
Email: adasshalom@aol.com

Temple Beth El
1001 Hancock Street 02169
Telephone: (617) 479-4309

Orthodox
Beth Israel
33 Grafton Street, PO Box 690388 02269-0388
Telephone: (617) 472-6796

RANDOLPH
BOOKSELLERS
Davidson's Hebrew Book Store
1106 Main Street 4130

SYNAGOGUES
Orthodox
**Young Israel - Kehillath Jacob of Mattapan &
Randolph**
374 N. Main Street, PO Box 880 02368
Telephone: (781) 986-6461
Email: Youngisrael@Juno.com

REVERE
DELICATESSEN
Myer's Kosher Kitchen
168 Shirley Avenue 4103
Telephone: (617) 773-7254

SYNAGOGUES
Independent
Temple B'nai Israel
1 Wave Avenue 02151
Telephone: (617) 284-8388

Orthodox
Ahavas Achim Anshei Sfard
89 Walnut Way 02151
Telephone: (617) 289-1026

Tifereth Israel
43 Nahant Avenue 02151
Telephone: (617) 284-9255

SALEM
COMMUNITY ORGANISATIONS
Jewish Federation of the North Shore
21 Front Street 20902
Telephone: (508) 942-2237
Fax: (508) 933-5464

SYNAGOGUES
Conservative
Temple Shalom
287 Lafayette Street 01970
Telephone: (508) 741-4880
Fax: (508) 741-4882
Web site: www.templeshalomsalem.org

SHARON
HOTELS
Sharon Woods Inn
80 Brook Road 02067
Telephone: (781) 784-9401
Fax: (781) 784-5162
Email: kctova@yahoo.com

MIKVAOT
Chevrat Nashim
9 Dunbar Street 4103
Telephone: (781) 773-0693

RELIGIOUS ORGANISATIONS
Eruv Society
Telephone: (781) 997-7471

SYNAGOGUES
Conservative
Adath Sharon
18 Harding Street 02067
Telephone: (781) 784-2517

Temple Israel
125 Pond Street 02067
Telephone: (781) 784-3986
Fax: (781) 784-0719

Orthodox
Chabad Center
101 Worcester Road 02067
Telephone: (781) 784-8167

Young Israel of Sharon
100 Ames Street 02067
Telephone: (781) 784-6112
Fax: (781) 784-7758
Web site: www.yisharon.org

Reform
Temple Sinai
25 Canton Street 02067
Telephone: (781) 784-6081
Fax: (781) 784-2616
Email: office@temple-sinai.com

SOMERVILLE
SYNAGOGUES
Independent
B'nai B'rith of Somerville
201 Central Street 02144
Telephone: (617) 625-0333
Email: tbb@templebnaibrith.org
Web site: www.templebnaibrith.org

SPRINGFIELD
COMMUNITY ORGANISATIONS
Jewish Community Center
1160 Dickinson Street 02607
Email: blev@springfieldjcc.org
Web site: www.springfieldjcc.org

GROCERIES
Waldbaum's Food Mart
355 Belmont Avenue 2368
Telephone: (413) 961-4929

RESTAURANTS
Vi's Coffee Shoppe
Jewish Community Center, 1160 Dickinson Street
01108
Telephone: (413) 739-4715
Fax: (413) 739-4747
Email: agoldsmith@springfieldjcc.org

SYNAGOGUES
Orthodox
Congregation Kodimoh
124 Sumner Avenue, Springfield 01108
Telephone: (413) 781-0171
Fax: (413) 737-8002
Email: kodimoh@TheSpa.com

Kesser Israel
19 Oakland Street 01108
Telephone: (413) 732-8492

Reform
Temple Sinai
1100 Dickinson Street 01108
Telephone: (413) 736-3619

STOUGHTON
BAKERIES
Ruth's Bake Shop
987 Central Street 02072
Telephone: (781) 344-8993
Supervision: Vaad Harabonim of Massachusetts

SYNAGOGUES
Conservative
Adhavath Torah Congregation
1179 Central Street 02072
Telephone: (781) 344-8733
Fax: (781) 344-4315

SUDBURY
SYNAGOGUES
Independent
Congregation B'nai Torah
Woodside Road 01776
Telephone: (978) 443-2082

Reform
Congregation Beth El
105 Hudson Road 01776
Telephone: (978) 443-9622
Fax: (978) 443-9629
Email: secretary@bethelsudbury.org
Web site: www.bethelsudbury.org

SWAMPSCOTT
SYNAGOGUES
Conservative
Beth El
55 Atlantic Avenue 01907
Telephone: (617) 599-8005
Fax: (617) 599-1860

Temple Israel
837 Humphrey Street 01907
Telephone: (617) 595-6635
Fax: (617) 595-0033
Web site: www.templeisraelswampscott.org

VINEYARD HAVEN
SYNAGOGUES
Reform
Martha's Vineyard Hebrew Center
Center Street 02568
Telephone: (508) 693-0745

WAKEFIELD
SYNAGOGUES
Conservative
Temple Emmanuel
120 Chestnut Street 01880
Telephone: (781) 245-1886
Web site: www.geocities.com/temple_emanuel

WALTHAM

SYNAGOGUES

American Jewish Historical Society (Brandeis University campus)
2 Thornton Road 02154
Telephone: (617) 891-8110
Fax: (617) 899-9208

Conservative
Beth Israel
25 Harvard Street 02154
Telephone: (617) 894-5146

WAYLAND

SYNAGOGUES

Reform
Templr Shir Tikva
141 Boston Post Road 01778
Telephone: (508) 358-5312

WELLESLEY HILLS

SYNAGOGUES

Reform
Beth Elohim
10 Bethel Road 02181
Telephone: (617) 235-8419

WEST ROXBURY

SYNAGOGUES

Reconstructionist
Hillel B'nai Torah
120 Corey St, W. Roxbury 02132
Telephone: (617) 617-323-0486
Fax: (617) 617-327-8338
Email: office@templehbt.org
Web site: www.templehbt.org
Supervision: www.templehbt.org

WESTBORO

SYNAGOGUES

Reform
B'nai Shalom
117 E. Main Street, PO Box 1019 01581-6019
Telephone: (508) 366-7191

WESTWOOD

SYNAGOGUES

Reform
Beth David
40 Pond Street 02090
Telephone: (617) 769-5270

WINCHESTER

SYNAGOGUES

Reform
Temple Shir Tikvah
PO Box 373 01890
Telephone: (617) 792-1188

WINTHROP

SYNAGOGUES

Conservative
Tifereth Israel
93 Veterans Road 02152
Telephone: (617) 846-1390

Orthodox
Tifereth Abraham
283 Shirley Street 02152
Telephone: (617) 846-5063

WORCESTER

COMMUNITY ORGANISATIONS

Jewish Community Centre of Worcester
633 Salisbury Street
Telephone: (508) 508-756-7109

Jewish Federation
633 Salisbury Street 2159
Telephone: (508) 558-6522

CONTACT INFORMATION

Agudath Israel of America Hachnosas Orchim Committee
69 S. Flagg Street 01602
Telephone: (508) 754-3681

Rabbi Hershel Fogelman
22 Newton Avenue 2138
Telephone: (508) 495-4696
Fax: (508) 864-1637
Email: linda@hillel.harvard.edu

MIKVAOT

Mikva
Huntley Street 2151

SYNAGOGUES

Conservative
Beth Israel
15 Jamesbury Drive
Telephone: (508) 508-756-6204
Web site: www.bethisraelworc.org

Orthodox
Young Israel of Worcester
889 Pleasant Street 01602
Telephone: (508) 754-3681

Reform
Temple Emanuel
280 May Street
Telephone: (508) 508-755-1257
Web site: www.temple-emanuel.org

Temple Sinai
661 Salisbury Street
Telephone: (508) 508-755-2519

Michigan
ANN ARBOR
COMMUNITY ORGANISATIONS
Jewish Federation of Washtenaw County
2939 Birch Hollow Drive 2135
Telephone: (734) 782-9433

MIKVAOT
Chabad House
715 Hill 2111
Telephone: (734) 330-9600

SYNAGOGUES
Orthodox
Ann Arbor Orthodox Minyan
1429 Hill Street 48104
Telephone: (734) 994-5822

BENTON HARBOR
SYNAGOGUES
Conservative
Temple B'nai Shalom
2050 Broadway 49022
Telephone: (212) 925-8021

DETROIT
COMMUNITY ORGANISATIONS
Jewish Federation of Metr. Detroit
Telegraph Road, Bloomfield Hills 2111
Telephone: (313) 426-2139
Fax: (313) 426-6268
Email: kvh613@aol.com

GROCERIES
One Stop Kosher
Greenfield Road, north of Ten Mile Road
Telephone: (313) 569-5000

KASHRUT INFORMATION
Council of Orthodox Rabbis of Greater Detroit
16947 W. Ten Mile Road, Southfield 1602
Telephone: (313) 755-1257

MEDIA
Newspaper
Jewish News
Franklin Road, Southfield 1970
Telephone: (313) 745-4222
Fax: (313) 741-7507
Email: mail@jfns.org

MIKVAOT
Mikvah Israel
15116 W. Ten Mile Road, Oak Park 48237
Telephone: (313) 967-5402
Fax: (313) 967-5403

ORGANISATIONS
Machon L'Torah (The Jewish Network of Michigan)
W. 10 Mile Road 1851
Telephone: (313) 459-9400

RELIGIOUS ORGANISATIONS
Council of Orthodox Rabbis of Detroit (Vaad Harabonim)
16947 W. Ten Mile Road, Southfield 2108
Telephone: (313) 367-9100
Fax: (313) 367-9310
Email: thejewishadvocate@thejewishadvocate.com

Jewish Community Center of Metr. Detroit
6600 W. Maple Road, W. Bloomfield 2111
Telephone: (313) 426-2139
Fax: (313) 426-6268

RESTAURANTS
Dairy
Jerusalem Pizza
26025 Greenfield, Southfield 48034
Telephone: (313) 552-0088
Fax: (313) 552-0087

Meat
Unique Kosher
25270 Greenfield, Southfield
Telephone: (313) 967-1161

EAST LANSING
SYNAGOGUES
Conservative & Reform
Shaarey Zedek
1924 Coolidge Road 48823

FLINT
COMMUNITY ORGANISATIONS
Flint Jewish Federation
619 Wallenberg Street 1201
Telephone: (810) 442-4360

SYNAGOGUES
Conservative
Congregation Beth Israel
5240 Calkins Road 48532
Telephone: (810) 732-6310
Fax: (810) 732-6314
Email: cbiflint@tir.com
Web site: www.uscj.org/michigan/flint/

Orthodox
Chabad House
5385 Calkins 48532
Telephone: (810) 230-0770

Reform
Temple Beth El
501 S. Ballenger Highway 48532
Telephone: (810) 232-3138

GRAND RAPIDS
SYNAGOGUES
Conservative
Congregation Ahavas Israel
2727 Michigan Street N.E. 49506
Telephone: (616) 949-2840
Fax: (616) 949-6929
Email: office@ahavasisrael.org
Web site: www.ahavasisraelgr.org

Orthodox
Chabad House of Western Michigan
2615 Michigan Street N.E. 49506
Telephone: (616) 957-0770

Reform
Temple Emanuel
1715 E. Fulton Street 49503
Telephone: (616) 459-5976

JACKSON
SYNAGOGUES
Reform
Temple Beth Israel
801 W. Michigan Avenue 49202
Telephone: (517) 784-3862

KALAMAZOO
SYNAGOGUES
Conservative
Congregation of Moses
2501 Stadium Drive 49008
Telephone: (616) 342-5463

LANSING
SYNAGOGUES
Reconstructionist
Kehillat Israel
2014 Forest Road 48910-3711
Telephone: (517) 517-882-0049
Fax: (517) 517-882-9270
Email: kilori@msu.edu
Web site: www.kehillatisrael.net
Supervision: Rabbi Michael Zimmerman

SAGINAW
SYNAGOGUES
Conservative
Temple B'nai Israel
1424 S. Washington Avenue 48601
Telephone: (517) 753-5230

Reform
Congregation Beth El
100 S. Washington Avenue 48607
Telephone: (517) 754-5171

SOUTH HAVEN
SYNAGOGUES
Orthodox
First Hebrew Congregation
249 Broadway 49090
Telephone: (616) 637-1603

SOUTHFIELD
SYNAGOGUES
Orthodox
Young Israel of Southfield
27705 Lahser Road 48034
Telephone: (248) 358-0154
Fax: (248) 358-0154
Email: rabg@aol.com

WEST BLOOMFIELD
MUSEUMS
Holocaust Memorial Center
6602 W. Maple Road 2067
Telephone: (248) 784-7444

SYNAGOGUES
Orthodox
Young Israel of West Bloomfield
6111 West Maple Road, Suite 408 48322
Telephone: (248) 661-4182

Minnesota
DULUTH
COMMUNITY ORGANISATIONS
Jewish Federation & Com. Council
1602 E. 2nd Street 1108
Telephone: (218) 737-4313

SYNAGOGUES
Conservative & Reform
Temple Israel
1602 E. 2nd Street 55812
Telephone: (218) 724-8857

Orthodox
Adas Israel
302 E. Third Street 55802
Telephone: (218) 722-6459

MINNEAPOLIS
COMMUNITY ORGANISATIONS
Sabes Jewish Community Center
4330 Cedar Lake Rd S., 1108
Telephone: (612) 739-4715
Fax: (612) 739-4747

GROCERIES
Fishman's Kosher Market
4100 Minnetonka Blvd, St Louis Park 55416
Telephone: (612) 926-5611

MIKVAOT
Knesseth Israel
4330 W. 28th Street, St Louis Park 1108
Telephone: (612) 732-3866

RESTAURANTS
Dairy
Calypso Coffee Co.
3238 W. Lake St. 55416
Telephone: (612) 929-6245

SYNAGOGUES
Orthodox
Congregation Bais Yisroel
4221 Sunset Blvd 55416
Telephone: (612) 924-0654
Fax: (612) 926-2936
Email: BaisLine@mninter.net
Web site: www.baisyisroel.org

Kenesseth Israel
4330 W. 28th Street, St Louis Park 55416
Telephone: (612) 920-2183
Fax: (612) 920-2184
Email: rabbi@kennessethisrael.org
Web site: www.kennessethisrael.org

ROCHESTER
HOME HOSPITALITY
Lubavitch Bais Chaya Moussia Hospitality Center
730 2nd Street S.W. 1106
Telephone: (716) 567-1607

SYNAGOGUES
Reform
B'nai Israel Synagogue
621 SW 2nd Street 55902
Telephone: (716) 288-5825
Email: bnaisrael@aol.com

ST PAUL
GROCERIES
L'chaim
655 Snelling Avenue 1002
Telephone: (612) 256-0160
Fax: (612) 256-1588
Email: JCA.info@verizon.net
Web site: www.j-c-a.org

RESTAURANTS
Dairy
Old City Cafe
1571 Grand Avenue
Telephone: (612) 291-6240

Mississippi
GREENVILLE
SYNAGOGUES
Reform
Hebrew Union Congregation
504 Main Street 38701
Telephone: (662) 332-4153

GREENWOOD
SYNAGOGUES
Orthodox
Ahavath Rayim
Market & George Streets, PO Box 1235 38935-1235
Telephone: (662) 453-7537

JACKSON
SYNAGOGUES
Reform
Congregation Beth Israel
5315 Old Canton Road 39211
Telephone: (517) 956-6215
Email: bic5315@mindspring.com

NATCHEZ
SYNAGOGUES
Reform
B'nai Israel
Washington & S. Commerce Streets, PO Box 2081
39120

TUPELO
SYNAGOGUES
Conservative
Marshall & Hamlin Streets 38801
Telephone: (601) 842-9169

Missouri
JEFFERSON CITY
SYNAGOGUES
Reform
Temple Beth El
238 East High Street 65101
Telephone: (573) 635-8727

KANSAS CITY
RESTAURANTS
Sensations
1148 W. 103 Street
Telephone: (816) 424-0191

SYNAGOGUES
Conservative
Congregation Beth Shalom
9400 Wornall road 64114
Telephone: (816) 361-2990
Fax: (816) 361-4495

Reform
Temple B'nai Jehudah
712 E. 69th Street 64131
Telephone: (816) 363-1050
Fax: (816) 363-8610

The New Reform Temple
7100 Main 64114
Telephone: (816) 523-7809
Fax: (816) 523-2454
Email: nrt7100@aol.com

ST JOSEPH
SYNAGOGUES
Conservative
Temple B'Nai Sholem
615 S. 10th Street 64501
Telephone: (816) 279-2378
Fax: (816) 361-4495

ST LOUIS
BAKERIES
Schnuck's Nancy Ann Bakery
Olive & Mason
Telephone: (314) 569-0727
Fax: (314) 569-1723

BUTCHERS
Diamant's Kosher Meat Market
618 North & South Road
Telephone: (314) 712-9624

S. Kohn's
10405 Old Olive St. Road
Telephone: (314) 569-0727

Sol's Kosher Meat Mart
8627 Olive Street
Telephone: (314) 721-9624

COMMUNITY ORGANISATIONS
Jewish Federation of St Louis
12 Millstone Campus Drive
Telephone: (314) 542-FOOD
Fax: (314) 451-5FAX
Supervision: Orthodox Rabbinic Council of Greater
Boston

GROCERIES
Simon Kohn's Kosher Meat & Deli
10405 Old Olive Street
Telephone: (314) 752-5791

LIBRARIES
The Brodsky Jewish Community Library
12 Millstone Campus Drive
Telephone: (314) 734-9810

MIKVAOT
Mikva
4 Millstone Campus
Telephone: (314) 784-6112

MUSEUMS
Holocaust Museum and Learning Center
12 Millstone Campus Drive
Telephone: (314) 432-0020
Fax: (314) 432-1277
Email: dreich@jfedstl.org
Web site: www.hmlc.org

RELIGIOUS ORGANISATIONS
**The Vaad Hoeir (United Orthodox Jewish
Community of St Louis)**
4 Millstone Campus
Telephone: (314) 970-2008

RESTAURANTS
Meat
Diamant's
618 North & South Rd.
Telephone: (314) 291-6050

Simon Kohn's
10405 Old Olive Street
Telephone: (314) 434-7323

The Empire Steak Building
8600 Olive Blvd., just off McKnight
Telephone: (314) 993-9977
Fax: (314) 993-6647
Web site: www.chef2-go.com

SYNAGOGUES
Orthodox
Young Israel of St Louis
8101 Delmar Blvd 63130
Telephone: (314) 727-1880
Fax: (314) 727-2177
Email: yi-stl@juno.com

Montana
BILLINGS
SYNAGOGUES
Reform
Congregation Beth Aaron
1148 N. Broadway 59101
Telephone: (406) 248-6412

GREAT FALLS
SYNAGOGUES
Reform
Aitz Chaim
PO Box 6192 59406-6192
Telephone: (406) 468-2073
Email: aaron@weissman.com

MISSOULA
SYNAGOGUES
Har Shalom
PO Box 7581 59807
Telephone: (406) 523-5671

Nebraska
LINCOLN
SYNAGOGUES
Conservative
Congregation Tifereth Israel
3219 Sheridan Blvd. 68502
Telephone: (402) 423-8569
Fax: (402) 423-0178

Reform
South Street Temple B'nai Jeshurun
20th & South Streets 68502
Telephone: (402) 435-8004

OMAHA
COMMUNITY ORGANISATIONS
Jewish Federation of Omaha
333 S. 132nd Street
Telephone: (402) 993-9977

MIKVAOT
Com. Mikva
323 S. 132nd Street
Telephone: (402) 334-8200
Fax: (402) 334-1330
Email: pmonsk@top.net
Web site: www.jewishomaha.org

SYNAGOGUES
Conservative
Beth El Synagogue
14506 California Street 68154
Telephone: (402) 402-492-8550
Fax: (402) 402-492-8520
Email: exec@bethel-omaha.org
Web site: www.bethel-omaha.org

Orthodox
Beth Israel
1502 N. 52nd Street 68104
Telephone: (402) 556-6288

Beth Israel Synagogue
1502 North 52nd Street 68104
Telephone: (402) 556-6288
Email: bethisrael@novia.net

Reform
Temple Israel
7023 Cass Street 68132
Telephone: (402) 556-6536

Nevada
LAS VEGAS
DELICATESSEN
Casba Glatt Kosher
2845 Las Vegas Blvd
Telephone: (702) 791-3344

Rafi's Place
6135 West Sahara 89102
Telephone: (702) 253-0033

Sara's Place
4972 S. Maryland

KASHRUT INFORMATION
Community Relations
Telephone: (702) 732-0556

MIKVAOT
1260 S. Arville
Telephone: (702) 259-0770 ext 8

RESTAURANTS
Meat
Haifa Restaurant
855 E. Twain
Telephone: (702) 791-1956
Fax: (702) 791-2966

Las Vegas Kosher Deli
3317 L.V. Blvd S.
Telephone: (702) 892-9080

Shalom Hunan
4850 W Flamingo Road
Telephone: (702) 871-3262
Fax: (702) 871-3083
Email: yosstheboss@earthlink.net
Supervision: Chabad of Southern Nevada

SYNAGOGUES
Conservative
Temple Emanu-El
4925 South Torrey Pines Drive 89118
Telephone: (702) 254-3270

Orthodox
Chabad of Southern Nevada
1261 S. Arville
Telephone: (702) 259-0770
Fax: (702) 877-4700
Email: chabadlv@aol.com
Web site: www.chabadlv.org

Congregation Or-Bamidbar
2991 Emerson Ave.
Telephone: (702) 369-1175

Young Israel of Las Vegas
9590 West Sahara 89117
Telephone: (702) 360-8909
Fax: (702) 360-9627
Email: ywyne@aish.com
Web site: www.aish.combranches/las_vegas

Reform
Adat Ari El
3310 S. Jones Blvd.
Telephone: (702) 221-1230
Fax: (702) 221-1385
Email: info@adatariel.com

Congregation Ner Tamid
2761 Emerson Ave.
Telephone: (702) 733-6292
Fax: (702) 733-8553
Email: info@lvnertamid.org
Web site: www.lvnertamid.org

Temple Bet Emet
St. Andrew Lutheran Church, 8901 Del Webb
Blvd., Sun City
Telephone: (702) 243-5781

Temple Beth Am
9001 Hillpointe Road
Telephone: (702) 254-5110
Fax: (702) 254-0997

Traditional
Chabad of Summerlin
2620 Regatta Dr. #117
Telephone: (702) 259-0770
Fax: (702) 242-4318

RENO
SYNAGOGUES
Reform
Temple Sinai
3405 Gulling Road 89503
Telephone: (775) 747-5508
Fax: (775) 747-1911
Email: temple.sinai@juno.com

New Hampshire
BETHLEHEM
HOTELS
Arlington Hotel
Telephone: (603) 869-3353

MIKVAOT
Machzikei Hadas
Lewis Hill Road 03574
Telephone: (603) 869-3336

SYNAGOGUES
Conservative
Bethlehem Hebrew Congregation
Strawberry Hill 03574
Telephone: (603) 869-5465

Orthodox
Machzikei Hadas
Lewis Hill Road 03574
Telephone: (603) 869-3336

CONCORD
SYNAGOGUES
Reform
Temple Beth Jacob
67 Broadway 03301
Telephone: (603) 228-8581
Email: tbjconcord@aol.com

MANCHESTER
COMMUNITY ORGANISATIONS
Jewish Federation of Greater Manchester
698 Beech Street 03104
Telephone: (603) 627-7679
Fax: (603) 627-7963

MEDIA
Newspaper
The Reporter
698 Beech Street 03104
Telephone: (603) 627-7679
Fax: (603) 627-7963

SYNAGOGUES
Orthodox
Lubavitch
7 Camelot Drive 03104
Telephone: (603) 647-0204

Reform
Adath Yeshurun
152 Prospect Street 03104
Telephone: (603) 669-5650

PORTSMOUTH
SYNAGOGUES
Conservative
Temple Israel
200 State Street 03801
Telephone: (603) 436-5301

New Jersey
ABERDEEN
SYNAGOGUES
Orthodox
Bet Tefilah
479 Lloyd Road 07747
Telephone: (732) 583-6262

ATLANTIC CITY
RESTAURANTS
Meat
Jerusalem
6410 Ventnor Ave, Ventnor 08406
Telephone: (609) 822-2266
Supervision: Rabbi Abraham Spacirer

SYNAGOGUES
Conservative
Beth El
500 N. Jerome Ave, Margate 08402
Fax: (609) 823-1810
Beth Judah
700 N Swarthmore Avenue, Ventnor 08406
Telephone: (609) 822-7116
Fax: (609) 822-4654
Email: congbethjudah@aol.com
Chelsea Hebrew Congregation
4001 Atlantic Av 08401
Telephone: (609) 345-0825
Community Synagogue
Maryland & Pacific Avs 08401
Telephone: (609) 345-3282

Orthodox
Rodef Shalom
3833 Atlantic Av 08401
Telephone: (609) 345-4580

Reform
Beth Israel
2501 Shore Rd, Northfield 08225
Telephone: (609) 641-3600
Temple Emeth Synagogue
8501 Ventnor Av, Margate 08402
Telephone: (609) 822-4343

BAYONNE
COMMUNITY ORGANISATIONS
Jewish Community Centre
1050 Kennedy Blvd 07002
Telephone: (201) 436-6900

SYNAGOGUES
Conservative
Temple Emanuel
735 Kennedy Blvd 07002
Telephone: (201) 436-4499

Orthodox
Ohab Sholom
1016-1022 Ave. C 07002
Ohav Zedek
912 Ave. C 07002
Telephone: (201) 437-1488
Uptown Synagogue
49th St. & Ave. C 07002

Reform
Temple Beth Am
111 Ave. B 07002
Telephone: (201) 858-9052

BELMAR
SYNAGOGUES
Orthodox
Sons of Israel Congregation
PO Box 298 07719
Telephone: (973) 681-3200

BERGENFIELD
BUTCHERS
Glatt World
89 Newbridge Road
Telephone: (201) 439-9675
Fax: (201) 439-0342
Supervision: RCBC

DELICATESSEN
Foster Village Kosher Delicatessen & Catering
469 S. Washington Avenue 07621
Telephone: (201) 384-7100
Fax: (201) 384-0303
Supervision: Quality Kashrut Supervisory Service

SYNAGOGUES
Conservative
Congregation Beth Israel of Northern Valley
169 N. Washington Avenue 07621
Telephone: (201) 384-3911
Fax: (201) 384-3738
Email: cbitemple@juno.com
Web site: www.uscj.org/njersey/bergenfield

BRADLEY BEACH
SYNAGOGUES
Orthodox
Congregation Agudath Achim
301 McCabe Avenue 07720
Telephone: (973) 774-2495

BRIDGETON
SYNAGOGUES
Conservative
Congregation Beth Abraham
330 Fayette Street 08302

BURLINGTON
SYNAGOGUES
Conservative
B'nai Israel
212 High Street 08332
Telephone: (718) 386-0406

CHERRY HILL
BUTCHERS
Cherry Hill Kosher Market
907 W. Marlton Pike 08002
Telephone: (856) 428-6663
Fax: (856) 216-0752

DELICATESSEN
Leo's Deli
J.C.C. 1301 Springdale Road
Telephone: (856) 424-4444 Ext 158
Supervision: Tri-County Vaad

MIKVAOT
Sons of Israel
720 Cooper Landing Road 08002
Telephone: (856) 667-3515
Email: Tasha.flecha@verizon.net

RESTAURANTS
Meat
Maxim's Restaurant
404 Route 70
Telephone: (856) 428-5045

SYNAGOGUES
Conservative
Beth El
2901 W. Chapel Avenue 08002
Telephone: (856) 667-1300

Beth Shalom
1901 Kresson Road 08003
Telephone: (856) 751-6663

Congregation Beth Tikva
115 Evesboro-Medford Road, Marlton

Orthodox
Congregation Sons of Israel
720 Cooper Landing Road 08002
Telephone: (856) 667-9700
Fax: (856) 667-9765
Email: Tasha.flecha@verizon.net

Reform
Congregation M'kor Shalom
850 Evesham Road
Telephone: (856) 424-4220
Fax: (856) 424-2890

Temple Emmanuel
1101 Springdale Road

CINNAMINSON
SYNAGOGUES
Conservative
Temple Sinai
2101 New Albany Road 08077
Telephone: (609) 829-0658
Fax: (609) 829-0310
Email: tsoffice@snip.net
Web site: www.uscj.org/njersey/cinnaminson

CLARK
SYNAGOGUES
Conservative
Temple Beth O'r
111 Valley Road 07066
Telephone: (732) 381-8403
Fax: (732) 381-8403

CLIFTON
COMMUNITY ORGANISATIONS
Jewish Federation of Greater Clifton-Passaic
199 Scoles Avenue 07012
Telephone: (973) 777-7031
Fax: (973) 777-6701
Email: planned.giving@verizon.net

MEDIA
Newspaper
Jewish Community News
199 Scoles Avenue 07012

RESTAURANTS
Jerusalem II Pizza
224 Brook Avenue 07055
Telephone: (973) 778-0960

SYNAGOGUES
Conservative
Clifton Jewish Center
18 Delaware Street 007011
Telephone: (973) 772-3131

Reform
Beth Shalom
733 Passaic Avenue 07012
Telephone: (973) 773-0355

COLONIA
SYNAGOGUES
Conservative
Ohev Shalom
220 Temple Way 07067
Telephone: (908) 388-7222

CRANBURY
SYNAGOGUES
Conservative
Jewish Congregation of Concordia
c/o Club House 08512
Telephone: (609) 655-8136

CRANFORD
CONTACT INFORMATION
Rabbi Hoffberg
Telephone: (201) 276-9231

SYNAGOGUES
Conservative
Temple Beth El Mekor Chayim
338 Walnut Avenue 07016
Telephone: (201) 276-9231
Fax: (201) 276-6570
Web site: www.uscj.org/njersey/cranfotb

DEAL
RESTAURANTS
Pizzerias
Jerusalem II Pizza
106 Norwood Avenue 07723
Telephone: (732) 531-7936

SYNAGOGUES
Orthodox
128 Norwood Avenue 07723
Telephone: (732) 531-3200

Ohel Yaacob Congregation
6 Ocean Avenue, PO Box 225 07723
Telephone: (732) 531-0217/531-2405

EAST BRUNSWICK
BUTCHERS
East Brunswick Kosher Meats
1020 State Highway 18 08816
Telephone: (908) 257-0007

SYNAGOGUES
Conservative
E. Brunswick Jewish Center
511 Ryders Lane 08816
Telephone: (908) 257-7070

Reform
Temple B'nai Shalom
Fern & Old Stage Road, PO Box 957 08816
Telephone: (908) 732-251-4300

EDISON

COMMUNITY ORGANISATIONS
Jewish Community Center of Middlesex County
1775 Oak Tree Road 8820
Telephone: (732) 494-3232
Fax: (732) 548-2850

SYNAGOGUES
Conservative
Beth El
91 Jefferson Blvd 08817
Telephone: (732) 985-7272

ELIZABETH

RESTAURANTS
Dairy
Dunkin' Donuts
186 Elmora Avenue 07202

Meat
New Kosher Special
163 Elmora Avenue 07202
Telephone: (908) 353-1818

Pizzerias
Jerusalem Restaurant
150 Elmora Avenue 07202
Telephone: (908) 289-4810

SYNAGOGUES
Orthodox
Adath Israel
1391 North Avenue 07208
Telephone: (908) 355-4850
Fax: (908) 289-5245
Email: www.theJEC.org

Bais Yitzchak
153 Bellevue Street 07202
Telephone: (908) 354-4789

ELMWOOD PARK

COMMUNITY ORGANISATIONS
Elmwood Park Jewish Center
100 Gilbert Ave.,
Telephone: (201) 797-7320/797-9749

ENGLEWOOD

GROCERIES
Kosher By the Case & Less
255 Van Nostrand Avenue 07631
Telephone: (201) 568-2281
Fax: (201) 568-5681
Supervision: RCBC

MIKVAOT
Mikva
89 Huguenot Avenue
Telephone: (201) 567-1143

RESTAURANTS
Meat
Sol & Sol
34 E Palisade Avenue 07631
Telephone: (201) 541-6880
Fax: (201) 541-6883
Supervision: Kashrut Committee of Bergen County

SYNAGOGUES
Conservative
Temple Emanu-El
147 Tenafly Road 07631
Telephone: (201) 567-1300
Fax: (201) 569-7580

Orthodox
Ahavath Torah
240 Broad Avenue 07631
Telephone: (201) 568-1315
Fax: (201) 568-2991
Email: egorlyn@ahavathtorah.org
Web site: www.ahavathtorah.org

Shomrei Emunah
89 Huguenot Avenue 07631
Telephone: (201) 567-9420

FAIR LAWN

BAKERIES
New Royal Bakery
19-09 Fair Lawn Avenue 07410
Telephone: (201) 796-6565
Fax: (201) 796-8501
Supervision: RCBC

BUTCHERS
Food Showcase
24-28 Fair Lawn Avenue 07410
Telephone: (201) 475-0077
Fax: (201) 794-6728
Supervision: RCBC

RESTAURANTS
Dairy
J.C. Pizza of Fairlawn
14-20 Plaza Road 07410
Telephone: (201) 703-0801
Supervision: RCBC

SYNAGOGUES
Orthodox
Bris Arushon
22-04 Fairlawn Avenue 07410
Telephone: (201) 791-7200

FORT LEE
BUTCHERS
Blue Ribbon Self-Service Kosher Meat Market
1363 Inwood Terr. 07024
Telephone: (201) 224-3220
Fax: (201) 224-7281
Email: koshercomida@msn.com

DELICATESSEN
Al's Kosher Deli
209 Main Street 07024
Telephone: (201) 461-3044
Fax: (201) 461-7188
Supervision: Quality Kashrut Supervisory Service

SYNAGOGUES
Conservative
Jewish Community Center of Fort Lee
1449 Anderson Avenue 07024
Telephone: (201) 947-1735
Fax: (201) 947-1530
Email: aschafer@jcc.org

Orthodox
Young Israel of Fort Lee
1610 Parker Avenue 07024
Telephone: (201) 592-1518
Fax: (201) 592-8414

FREEHOLD
RESTAURANTS
Fred and Murry's
Pond Road Shopping Center, Route 9 07728
Telephone: (732) 462-3343
Web site: www.fredandmurrys.com

SYNAGOGUES
Orthodox
Agudath Achim/Freehold Jewish Center
Broad & Stokes Streets 07728
Telephone: (732) 462-0254
Fax: (732) 462-0217

HACKENSACK
COMMUNITY ORGANISATIONS
Jewish Federation of Community Services of Bergen County
170 State Street 07601

SYNAGOGUES
Conservative
Temple Beth El
280 Summit Avenue 07601
Telephone: (201) 342-2045

HADDONFIELD
BUTCHERS
Sarah's Kosher Kitchen
63 Ellis Road

HASBROUCK HEIGHTS
SYNAGOGUES
Reform
Temple Beth Elohim
Bourlevard & Charlton Aves
Telephone: (201) 393-7707

HIGHLAND PARK
GROCERIES
Berkley Bakery
405 Raritan Avenue 08904
Telephone: (847) 220-1919

Kosher Catch
239 Raritan Avenue
Telephone: (847) 572-9052

MIKVAOT
Park Mikva
112 S. 1st Avenue 08904
Telephone: (847) 249-2411

SYNAGOGUES
Conservative
Highland Park Conservative Temple & Center
201 S. 3rd Ave. 08904
Telephone: (847) 545-6482
Fax: (847) 246-3100

Orthodox
Congregation Ahavas Achim
Telephone: (847) 247-0532
Fax: (847) 247-6739
Email: aa613@juno.com

Congregation Etz Ahaim (Sephardi)
230 Denison St 08904
Telephone: (847) 247-3839
Fax: (847) 545-3191
Email: etzahaim@earthlink.net
Web site: www.home.earthlink.net/~etzahaim

Congregation Ohav Emeth
415 Raritan Avenue 08904
Telephone: (847) 247-3038
Fax: (847) 247-1438
Email: office@ohavemeth.org

HILLSIDE
SYNAGOGUES
Conservative
Shomrei Torah Ohel Yosef Yitzchok
910 Salem Avenue 07205
Telephone: (908) 289-0770

Orthodox
Congregation Sinai Torath Chaim
1531 Maple Avenue 7205
Telephone: (908) 923-9500

JAMESBURG
SYNAGOGUES
Rossmoor Jewish Congregation Meeting Room
Telephone: (609) 655-0439

JERSEY CITY
SYNAGOGUES
Orthodox
Congregation Mount Sinai
128 Sherman Avenue 07307
Telephone: (201) 659-4267
Fax: (201) 659-4267
Email: congmtsinai@netzero.net
Web site: www.mtsinai.net

LAKEWOOD
BAKERIES
Gelbsteins Bakery
415 Clifton Avenue 08701
Telephone: (310) 363-3636
Supervision: Orthodox supervision

Lakewood Heimishe Bakeshop
225-2nd St 08701
Telephone: (310) 905-9057
Supervision: Orthodox supervision

BOOKSELLERS
Torah Treasures
254-2nd St. 08701
Telephone: (310) 901-1911
Fax: (310) 905-6482

BUTCHERS
Shloimy's Kosher World
23 E. County Line Road 08701
Telephone: (310) 363-3066

COMMUNITY ORGANISATIONS
Ocean County Jewish Federation
301 Madison Avenue 08701
Telephone: (310) 363-0530
Fax: (310) 363-2097
Email: ocjf@optonline.net

KASHRUT INFORMATION
KCC - Cashrus Council of Lakewood
Telephone: (310) 901-1888

MIKVAOT
Congregation Mikvah Tahara
1101 Madison Avenue 08701
Telephone: (310) 370-1666

RESTAURANTS
Dairy
Bagel Nosh
380 Clifton Avenue 08701
Telephone: (310) 363-1115
Fax: (310) 363-5745

Meat
R. & S. Kosher Restaurant and Deli
416 Clifton Avenue 08701
Telephone: (310) 363-6688
Supervision: Kashrus supervision: Lakewood Satmar Dayan

Yum Mee Glatt
116 Clifton Avenue 08701
Telephone: (310) 886-9688

Pizzeria
Pizza Plus
241 4th St 08701
Telephone: (310) 367-0711
Supervision: Orthodox supervision

SYNAGOGUES
Conservative
Ahavat Shalom
Forest Avenue & 11th Street 08701
Telephone: (310) 363-5190
Fax: (310) 363-5225
Email: ahavat_shalom_nj@netzero.com
Web site: www.uscj.org/njersey/lakewood

Orthodox
Kol Shimshon
323 Squamkum Road 08701
Telephone: (310) 901-6680

Lakewood Yeshiva
617 Private Way (Sixth Street) 08701
Telephone: (310) 367-1060

Sons of Israel
Madison Avenue & 6th Street 08701
Telephone: (310) 364-2230

Reform
Beth Am
Madison Avenue & Carey Street 08701
Telephone: (310) 363-2800

LAWRENCEVILLE
SYNAGOGUES
Orthodox
Young Israel of Lawrenceville
2556 Princeton Pike 08648
Telephone: (609) 883-8833
Web site: www.yiol.com

LINDEN
SYNAGOGUES
Conservative
Mekor Chayim Suburban Jewish Center
Deerfield Road & Academy Terrace 07036
Telephone: (908) 925-2283

Orthodox
Congregation Anshe Chesed
100 Orchard Terrace at St George Ave. 07036
Telephone: (908) 486-8616

LIVINGSTON
RESTAURANTS
Dairy
Jerusalem Restaurant
99-101 West Mt Pleasant Avenue 07039
Telephone: (973) 533-1424
Fax: (973) 533-9275
Supervision: Vaad Hakashrus of the Council of Orthodox
Rabbis Metrowest

Meat
Moshavi
515 S. Livingston Avenue 07039
Telephone: (973) 740-8777
Supervision: Vaad Hakashrus of the Council of Orthodox
Rabbis Metrowest

SYNAGOGUES
Conservative
Temple Beth Shalom
193 E. Mt Pleasant Ave. 07039
Telephone: (973) 992-3600

Independent
Temple B'Nai Abraham
300 East Northfield Road 07039
Telephone: (973) 994-2290
Fax: (973) 992-1838
Email: lwold@tbanj.org
Web site: www.tbanj.org

Orthodox
Etz Chaim Synagogue
304 Mt Pleasant Avenue 07039
Telephone: (973) 597 1655

Synagogue of the Suburban Torah Center
85 W. Mount Pleasant Avenue 07039
Telephone: (973) 994-0122; 994-2620
Fax: (973) 535-3898
Email: execdirector@suburbantorah.org
Web site: www.suburbantorah.org

Reform
Temple Emanu-el of West Essex
264 W. Northfield Rd 07039
Telephone: (973) 992-5560

MAHWAH
SYNAGOGUES
Reform
Temple Beth Haverim
280 Remjo Valley Road
Telephone: (201) 512-1983

MAPLEWOOD
BOOKSELLERS
Skybook
1923 Springfield Avenue, Maplewood 07040
Telephone: (973) 763-4244/5
Fax: (973) 763-1412

METUCHEN
SYNAGOGUES
Conservative
Neve Shalom
250 Grove Avenue 08840
Telephone: (732) 548-2238
Fax: (732) 603-7976
Email: neveshal@webspan.net

MORRIS PLAINS
DELICATESSEN
Jonathan's Deli Restaurant
2900 Route 10 West 07950
Telephone: (973) 539-6010
Fax: (973) 539-6011

MORRISTOWN
KASHRUT INFORMATION
Rabbinical College of America
226 Sussex Avenue 07960
Telephone: (973) 267-9404
Fax: (973) 267-5208
Email: rca226@aol.com

MIKVAOT
**Mikvah Bais Chana, Sarah Esther Rosenhaus
Mikvah Institutue**
93 Lake Road 07960
Telephone: (973) 973-292-3932

SYNAGOGUES

Conservative
Morristown Jewish Center
177 Speedwell Avenue 07960
Telephone: (973) 538-9292

Orthodox
Congregation Ahavath Yisrael
9 Cutler Street 07960
Telephone: (973) 267-4184
Fax: (973) 898-1711
Email: sofernj@aol.com

Congregation Levi Yitzchok
226 Sussex Avenue 07960
Telephone: (973) 984-6326

NEW BRUNSWICK
SYNAGOGUES

Conservative
Congregation B'nai Tikvah
1001 Finnegans Lane 08902
Telephone: (732) 297-0696
Fax: (732) 297-2673
Email: administrator@bnaitikvah.org
Web site: www.bnaitikvah.org

Orthodox
Chabad House Friends of Lubavitch
8 Sicard St 08901
Telephone: (732) 828-9191

Congregation Poile Zedek
145 Neilson St. 08901
Telephone: (732) 545-6123
Email: admin@poilezedek.org
Web site: www.poilezedek.org

Reform
Anshe Emeth Memorial Temple
222 Livingston Av 08901
Telephone: (732) 545-6484
Fax: (732) 745-7448
Email: temple@aemt.net
Web site: www.aemt.net

OLD BRIDGE
SYNAGOGUES

Conservative
Ohav Shalom
3018 Bordertown Avenue 08859
Telephone: (201) 727-4334

PARAMUS
BUTCHERS
Harold's Self-Service Kosher Meat
67-A E. Ridgewood Avenue 07652
Telephone: (201) 262-0030

COMMUNITY ORGANISATIONS
Jewish Center of Paramus
304 Midland Ave.,
Telephone: (201) 262-7691

SYNAGOGUES
Conservative
Jewish Community Center of Paramus
E-304 Midland Ave., 07652
Telephone: (201) 262-7691
Fax: (201) 262-6516
Email: jccparam@mail.idt.net
Web site: www.uscj.org/njersey/paramus

PARSIPANNY
DELICATESSEN
Arlington Kosher Deli, Restaurant & Caterers
Arlington Shopping Center, 744 Route 46W 07054
Telephone: (973) 335-9400

PASSAIC
DELICATESSEN
B&Y Kosher Korner Inc.,
200 Main Avenue 07055
Telephone: (973) 777-1120

SUPERMARKET
Kosher Konnection
200 Main Avenue 07055
Telephone: (973) 777-1120
Fax: (973) 777-4991

SYNAGOGUES
Orthodox
Young Israel of Passaic-Clifton
200 Brook Avenue 07055
Telephone: (973) 778-7117

PATERSON
SYNAGOGUES
Conservative
Temple Emanuel
151 E. 33rd Street 07514
Telephone: (973) 684-5565

PERTH AMBOY
SYNAGOGUES
Conservative
Beth Mordechai
224 High Street 08861
Telephone: (732) 442-2431

Orthodox
Shaarey Teflioh
15 Market Street 08861
Telephone: (732) 826-2977

PLAINFIELD
SYNAGOGUES
Orthodox
United Orthodox Synagogue
526 W. 7th Street 07060
Telephone: (908) 755-0043

Reform
Temple Sholom
815 W. 7th Street 07063
Telephone: (908) 756-6447

PRINCETON
SYNAGOGUES
Conservative
The Jewish Center of Princeton
435 Nassau Street 08540
Telephone: (609) 609-921-0100
Fax: (609) 609-921-7531
Email: info@thejewishcenter.org
Web site: www.thejewishcenter.org

RAHWAY
SYNAGOGUES
Conservative
Temple Beth Torah
1389 Bryant Street 07065
Telephone: (609) 576-8432

RANDOLPH
SYNAGOGUES
Orthodox
Mount Freedom Jewish Center
1209 Sussex Turnpike 07970
Telephone: (781) 895-2100

RIDGEWOOD
SYNAGOGUES
Conservative
Temple Israel
475 Grove Street
Telephone: (201) 444-9320

RIVER EDGE
SYNAGOGUES
Reform
Temple Sholom
385 Howland Avenue 07661
Telephone: (201) 489-2463
Fax: (201) 489-0775
Web site: www.uahcweb.org/nj/tsholomre/

ROSELLE
MEDIA
Guide Book
Shalom Book
843 St Georges Avenue 07203
Telephone: (908) 298-8200
Fax: (908) 298-8220

RUMSON
SYNAGOGUES
Conservative
Congregation B'nai Israel
Hance & Ridge Roads 07760
Telephone: (908) 842-1800

SCOTCH PLAINS
COMMUNITY ORGANISATIONS
Jewish Federation of Central New Jersey
1391 Martine Avenue 07076
Telephone: (908) 889-5335
1391 Martine Avenue 07076
Telephone: (908) 908-351-5060

SYNAGOGUES
Conservative
Congregation Beth Israel
1920 Cliffwood Street 07076
Telephone: (908) 889-1830
Fax: (908) 889-5523

SHORT HILLS
SYNAGOGUES
Reform
B'Nai Jeshurun
1025 South Orange Ave. 07078
Telephone: (973) 379-1555
Fax: (973) 379-4345
Email: info@tbj.org

SOMERSET
SYNAGOGUES
Conservative
Temple Beth El
1945 Amwell Road 08873
Telephone: (201) 873-2325

SOUTH ORANGE
GROCERIES
Zayda's Super Value Meat Market & Deli
309 Irvington Avenue 07079
Telephone: (973) 762-1812

SYNAGOGUES

Conservative
Oheb Shalom Congregation
170 Scotland Rd 07079
Telephone: (973) 762-7067

Reform
Temple Sharey Tefilo-Israel
432 Scotland Rd 07079
Telephone: (973) 763-4116

SOUTH RIVER

COMMUNITY ORGANISATIONS
Jewish Federation of Greater Middlesex County
230 Old Bridge Turnpike, South River, Middlesex County 08882
Telephone: (732) 732-432-7711
Fax: (732) 732-432-0292
Email: middlesexfed@aol.com
Web site: www.jfgmc.org

SYNAGOGUES
Traditional
Congregation Anshe Emeth of South River
88 Main Street 08882
Telephone: (732) 257-4190
Fax: (732) 254-8819
Web site: www.members.home.net/ebweiss

SPOTSWOOD

SYNAGOGUES
Reform
Monroe Township Jewish Center
11 Cornell Avenue 08884
Telephone: (201) 251-1119

TEANECK

BAKERIES
Butterflake Bake Shop
448 Cedar Lane 07666
Telephone: (201) 836-3516
Fax: (201) 836-3056
Supervision: RCBC

Gruenebaum Bakeries
477B Cedar Lane 07666
Telephone: (201) 839-3128

Korn's Bakery
1378 Queen Anne Road 07666
Telephone: (201) 833-0114

Sammy's New York Bagels
1443 Queen Anne Road 07666
Telephone: (201) 837-0515
Fax: (201) 837-9733
Supervision: Kof-K

BOOKSELLERS
Zoldan's Judaica Center
406 Cedar Lane 07666
Telephone: (201) 907-0034

BUTCHERS
Glatt Express
1400 Queen Anne Road 07666
Telephone: (201) 837-8110
Fax: (201) 837-0084
Supervision: RCBC

DELICATESSEN
Chopstix
172 West Englewood Avenue 07666
Telephone: (201) 833-0200
Fax: (201) 833-8326
Supervision: RCBC

JUDAICA
Judaica House
478 Cedar Lane
Telephone: (201) 801-9001

MIKVAOT
Mikveh
1726 Windsor Road 07666
Telephone: (201) 837-8220

RESTAURANTS
Dairy
Jerusalem Pizza
496 Cedar Lane 07666
Telephone: (201) 836-2120
Fax: (201) 836-2261
Supervision: RCBC

Plaza Pizza & Restaurant
1431 Queen Anne Road 07666
Telephone: (201) 837-9500
Fax: (201) 836-2261
Supervision: RCBC

Shelly's
482 Cedar Lane 07666
Telephone: (201) 692-0001
Fax: (201) 692-1890
Email: shellys@noahsark.net
Supervision: RCBC

Meat
Hunan Teaneck
515 Cedar Lane 07666
Telephone: (201) 692-0099
Fax: (201) 692-1907
Supervision: RCBC

Noah's Ark
493 Cedar Lane 07666
Telephone: (201) 692-1200
Fax: (201) 692-1890
Email: info@noahsark.net
Supervision: RCBC

SYNAGOGUES
Conservative
Congregation Beth Sholom
354 Maitland Avenue 07666
Telephone: (201) 833-2620
Fax: (201) 833-2323
Email: bsteaneck@aol.com
Web site: www.uscj.org/njersey/teaneckcbs

Jewish Center of Teaneck
70 Sterling Place 07666
Telephone: (201) 833-0515
Fax: (201) 833-0511
Email: execdir@aol.com
Web site: www.jewishcenterofteaneck.org

Orthodox
Congregation Beth Aaron
950 Queen Anne Rd 07666
Telephone: (201) 836-6210
Fax: (201) 836-0005
Email: mail@bethaaron.org
Web site: www.bethaaron.org

Congregation Bnai Yeshurun
641 W. Englewood Avenue 07666
Telephone: (201) 201-836-8916
Fax: (201) 201-836-1888
Email: bnaiyeshurun@aol.com
Web site: www.bnaiyeshurun.org

Rinat Yisrael
389 W. Englewood Av 07666
Telephone: (201) 837-2795
Fax: (201) 837-7881
Email: office@rinat.org

Roemer Synagogue
Whittier School, W. Englewood Av., 07666

Reform
Congregation Beth Am
1148 Converse Street 01106
Telephone: (201) 413-567-8665
Fax: (201) 410-567-2233
Email: rabbink@comcast.net
Web site: www.lya.org

Temple Emeth
1666 Windsor Rd 07666
Telephone: (201) 833-1322
Fax: (201) 833-4831
Email: temple@emeth.org
Web site: www.emeth.org

TENAFLY
SYNAGOGUES
Reform
Temple Sinai of Bergen County
1 Engle Street 07670
Telephone: (201) 568-3035
Fax: (201) 568-6095
Email: temsinai@idt.net
Web site: www.uahc.org/congs.nj/nj009

TRENTON
COMMUNITY ORGANISATIONS
Jewish Federation of Mercer & Bucks Counties
999 Lower Ferry Road 08628
Telephone: (609) 883-5000

UNION
SYNAGOGUES
Conservative
Beth Shalom
2046 Vauxhall Road 07083
Telephone: (908) 686-6773

Temple Israel
2372 Morris Avenue 07083
Telephone: (908) 686-2120

VAUXHALL
RESTAURANTS
Meat
Mosaica
2933 Vauxhall Road
Telephone: 206-9911

VINELAND
COMMUNITY ORGANISATIONS
Jewish Federation of Cumberland County
1063 East Landis Avenue, Suite B 08360-3785
Telephone: (856) 696-4445
Fax: (856) 696-3428
Email: jfedcc@aol.com

SYNAGOGUES
Conservative
Beth Israel
1015 E. Park Avenue 08630
Telephone: (856) 691-0852

Orthodox
Ahavas Achim
618 Plum Street 08360
Telephone: (856) 691-2218

Sons of Jacob Congregation
321 Grape Street 08360
Telephone: (856) 692-4232
Fax: (856) 691-4985

WARREN
SYNAGOGUES
Reform
Mountain Jewish Community Center
104 Mount Horeb Road 07060
Telephone: (908) 356-8777

WASHINGTON TOWNSHIP
SYNAGOGUES
Reform
Temple Beth Or
56 Ridgewood Rd
Telephone: (201) 664-7422

WAYNE
COMMUNITY ORGANISATIONS
Jewish Federation of New Jersey
1 Pike Drive 07470
Telephone: (973) 595-0555

SYNAGOGUES
Conservative
Shomrei Torah
30 Hinchman Avenue 07470
Telephone: (973) 694-6274

Reform
Temple Beth Tikvah
950 Preakness Avenue 07470
Telephone: (973) 595-6565
Fax: (973) 595-8192

WEST CALDWELL
DELICATESSEN
David's Deco-Tessen
555 Passaic Avenue 07006
Telephone: 973-808-3354
Fax: 973-808-5806
Email: davidsdecotessen@aol.com
Supervision: Rabbi Herman Savitz (Conservative)

WEST NEW YORK
SYNAGOGUES
Orthodox
Congregation Shaare Zedek
5308 Palisade Avenue 07093
Telephone: (201) 867-6859

WEST ORANGE
GROCERIES
Gourmet Galaxy
659 Eagle Rock Avenue 07052
Telephone: (973) 736-0060
Supervision: Vaad Hakashrus of the Council of Orthodox Rabbis Metrowest

JUDAICA
Lubavitch Center of Essex County
456 Pleasant Valley Way 07052
Telephone: (973) 731-0770
Fax: (973) 731-6821

RESTAURANTS
Meat
Eden Wok
478 Pleasant Valley Way 07052
Telephone: (973) 243-0115
Fax: (973) 243-1332
Supervision: Vaad Hakashrus of the Council of Orthodox Rabbis Metrowest
Pleasantdale Kosher Meat
470 Pleasant Valley Way 07052
Telephone: (973) 731-3216

SYNAGOGUES
Conservative
B'Nai Shalom
300 Pleasant Valley Way 07052
Telephone: (973) 731-0160
Fax: (973) 731-1160
Email: bnai@aol.com

Orthodox
Congregation Ahawas Achim B'nai Jacob and David
700 Pleasant Valley Way 07052
Telephone: (973) 736-1407
Fax: (973) 736-8006
Email: shul.aabjdmail@verizon.com

WESTFIELD
SYNAGOGUES
Reform
Temple Emanu-El
756 E. Broad Street 07090
Telephone: (908) 908-232-6770
Fax: (908) 908-233-3959
Email: cshane@tewnj.org
Web site: www.westfieldnj.com/temple

WHIPPANY
COMMUNITY ORGANISATIONS
United Jewish Federation of Metrowest
901 Route 10 07981
Telephone: (973) 884-4800
Fax: (973) 884-7361

MEDIA
Newspaper
The New Jersey Jewish News
901 Route 10 07981
Telephone: (973) 887-8500
Fax: (973) 887-4152
Email: njjewnews@aol.com

WILLINGBORO
SYNAGOGUES
Reform
Adath Emanu-El
299 John F. Kennedy Way 08046
Telephone: (609) 871-1736

WOODBRIDGE
SYNAGOGUES
Conservative
Adath Israel
424 Amboy Avenue 07095
Telephone: (203) 634-9601
Fax: (203) 634-1593
Email: lina1330@bellatlantic.net

WYCKOFF
SYNAGOGUES
Reform
Temple Beth Rishon
585 Russell Ave
Telephone: (201) 891-4466
Fax: (201) 891-0508
Email: bethrish@bellatlantic.net

New Mexico

ALBUQUERQUE
COMMUNITY ORGANISATIONS
Jewish Federation of Greater Albuquerque
5520 Wyoming Blvd N.E. 87109
Telephone: (505) 821-3214
Fax: (505) 821-3351
Email: reception@jewishnewmexico.org
Web site: www.jewishnewmexico.org

KASHRUT INFORMATION
JFGA
Telephone: (505) 821-3214

MEDIA
Newspaper
The Link
5520 Wyoming Blvd 87109
Telephone: (505) 821-3214
Fax: (505) 821-3351

SYNAGOGUES
Conservative
Congregation B'nai Israel
4401 Indian School Road 87110
Telephone: (505) 505-266-0155
Fax: (505) 505-268-6136
Web site: www.bnaiisrael-nm.org

Orthodox
Chabad of New Mexico
4000 San Pedro 87110
Telephone: (505) 880-1181

LAS CRUCES
SYNAGOGUES
Reform
Temple Beth El
702 Parker Road, at Melendres 88004
Telephone: (505) 524-3380
Fax: (505) 521-3737
Email: rabbikane@cs.nmsu.edu
Web site: www.uahc.org/nm/nm002/

LOS ALAMOS
SYNAGOGUES
Conservative
Los Alamos Jewish Center
2400 Canyon Road 87544
Telephone: (505) 662-2440

RIO RANCHO
SYNAGOGUES
Reform
Rio Rancho Jewish Center
2009 Grande Blvd 87124
Telephone: (505) 892-8511

SANTA FE
SYNAGOGUES
Orthodox
Chabad Jewish Center
242 West S. Mateo (corner Galisteo)
Telephone: (505) 983-2000
Fax: (505) 983-2055
Email: ChabadSantaFe@aol.com
Web site: www.chabadsf.com

Pardes Yisroel
1307 Don Diego Avenue 87505
Telephone: (505) 986-1603
Email: shammes@pardes-yisroel.org
Web site: www.pardes-yisroel.org/py/

Reform
Congregation Beit Tikvah
PO Box 2112 87504
Telephone: (505) 820-2991
Fax: (505) 820-2991
Email: rap1818@aol.com
Web site: www.beittikva.org

Temple Beth Shalom
205 E. Barcelona Road 87505
Telephone: (505) 982-1376
Fax: (505) 983-7446
Email: tbs@santafe-newmexico.com
Web site: www.santafe-newmexico.com/~tbs

New York

New York City encompasses so much territory and so much activity that it can sometimes be easy to forget that there is also a whole state named New York. The Empire State stretches from New York City in the south to the Canadian border at Quebec and Ontario provinces in the north; from the New England border with Connecticut, Massachusetts and Vermont in the east to Pennsylvania and the Great Lakes of Erie and Ontario in the southwest and west.

Within this 50,000 square mile expanse lie metropolis, suburb, small town, large city, village, vast state parks and preserves, seashores, islands, high mountains and rolling foothills, and abundant natural wilderness.

To New York City residents, anything outside the five boroughs (Manhattan, Queens, Brooklyn, the Bronx, and Staten Island) is either upstate or Long Island. But within those areas are numerous large and thriving Jewish communities. The cities of Buffalo, Rochester, Binghamton, Syracuse, and Schenectady, the suburban counties of Westchester and Rockland, and the Long Island counties of Nassau and Suffolk count hundreds of thousands of Jews among their residents.

Jewish settlement began in New York in early September 1654 when twenty-three Sephardic and Ashkenazi Jews disembarked at the harbour of New Amsterdam from the French ship St Catherine. They had escaped the Spanish Inquisition in Recife, Brazil to settle in the Dutch colony. Though Governor Peter Stuyvesant forbade their admission to his jurisdiction, the travellers' protests to his bosses at the Dutch West India Company were accepted and the Jews were allowed to settle. Ten years later, in 1664, four British men-of-war appropriated New Amsterdam in the name of King Charles II of England, who, in turn, made a gift of it to his brother, James, Duke of York. Hence the name, New York.

Jewish immigration was sparse for the next 150 years, but it increased dramatically, especially in New York City between 1880 and 1924, as more than two million Jews made their way to 'der goldene medinah' (the golden door) from eastern and central Europe.

From that original group of twenty-three Jews in 1654, some made their way up the Hudson River as far as Albany (now the state capital). Two of them, Asser Levy and Jacob de Lucena, became Hudson River traders and also dealt in real estate in the Albany and Kingston areas. South of Albany, in nearby Newburgh, Jewish merchants established a trading post in 1777, but no Jewish community existed there until 1848.

New York's first Jewish community outside of New York City was the town of Sholom in the Catskill mountains in Ulster county. Founded by twelve families, it no longer exists. The oldest existing community is Congregation Beth El, founded in 1838 in Albany and later merged with Congregation Beth Emeth.

Westchester (just north of New York City) county's present Jewish population of close to 150,000 dates from 1860.

Rockland

Southeast of the Catskills, in Rockland county just north of New York City, are a number of communities with large Hasidic and Orthodox populations. New Square, a corruption of the name Skvir, was founded by the Skvirer Hasidim and is incorporated as a separate village within the town of Ramapo. With such an administrative and legal designation, New Square has its own zoning rules, its own village council, its own mayor, etc., and is run on strictly orthodox precepts. Monroe, Monsey and Spring Valley have very large Orthodox and Hasidic communities. Though observant Jews are predominant, these communities are also home to non-Jews and less-observant Jews. There are a number of villages in the area which have been incorporated with the express purpose of keeping Orthodox and Hasidim out, through regulations such as zoning to prevent synagogues from being built too close to residences and through the prohibition of having a synagogue in one's house.

ALBANY

GROCERIES

Price Chopper Market
1892 Central Avenue 12205
Telephone: (518) 456-2970
Supervision: Vaad Hakashruth
Full service kosher department.

JEWISH STUDENT CENTRE

Shabbos House
State University of New York, 316 Fuller Road
Telephone: (518) 438-4227
Email: shabbos@albany.net
Web site: www.shabboshouse.com
Is also a synagogue.

MIKVAOT

340 Whitehall Road
Telephone: (518) 437-1303

SYNAGOGUES

Conservative
Ohav Shalom
New Krumkill Rd 12208
Telephone: (518) 489-4706

Temple Israel
600 New Scotland Ave. 12208
Telephone: (518) 518-438-7858
Fax: (518) 518-482-5762
Email: timain@templeisraelalbany.org
Web site: www.templeisraelalbany.org

Orthodox
Beth Abraham-Jacob
380 Whitehall Rd 12208
Telephone: (518) 489-5819; 489-5179
Fax: (518) 489-5179
Email: mbomzer@aol.com

Chabad-Lubavitch Center of the Capital District
122 S. Main Av 12208
Telephone: (518) 482-5781
Fax: (518) 482-3684
Email: albanychabad@knick.net
Web site: www.chabadonline.com/albany

Shomray Torah
463 New Scotland Av 12208
Telephone: (518) 438-8981

Reform
B'nai Sholom
420 Whitehall Rd 12208
Telephone: (518) 482-5283

Beth Emeth
100 Academy Rd 12208
Telephone: (518) 436-9761
At this 160-year-old congregation, Rabbi Isaac Mayer Wise, founder of American Reform Judaism, served when he first arrived in the United States.

Daughters of Sarah Senior Community
180 Washington Avenue Extension 12203
Telephone: (518) 456-7831
Fax: (518) 456-1563
Email: info@daughtersofsarah.org
Web site: www.daughtersofsarah.org
Traditional service, Saturday 9:15 am. Reform service, Friday 3 pm. Traveller's advisory and kosher facility.

AMSTERDAM
SYNAGOGUES
Conservative
Congregation of Sons of Israel
355 Guy Park Avenue 12010
Telephone: (518) 842-8691

BEACON
SYNAGOGUES
Conservative
Hebrew Alliance
55 Fishkill Avenue 12508
Telephone: (845) 831-2012

BINGHAMTON
MIKVAOT
Beth David Synagogue
39 Riverside Drive 13905
Telephone: (607) 722-1793
Fax: (607) 722-7121
Email: bethdavidrabbi@aol.com

SYNAGOGUES
Community Center
500 Clubhouse Road 13903
Telephone: (607) 724-2417
Fax: (607) 824-2311
Email: JCC13850@AOL.com

Conservative
Temple Israel
Deerfield Place, Vestal 13850
Telephone: (607) 723-7461

Reform
Temple Concord
9 Riverside Drive 13905
Telephone: (607) 723-7355

BUFFALO
COMMUNITY ORGANISATIONS
Jewish Federation of Greater Buffalo
787 Delaware Avenue 14209
Telephone: (716) 886-7750
Fax: (716) 886-1367

DELICATESSEN
Tops Kosher Deli
Cnr of North Bailey and Maple Road
Telephone: (716) 615-0076

GROCERIES
Corner of North Bailey and Maple Road
Telephone: (716) 515-0075

MEDIA
Guide
Shalom Buffalo
787 Delaware Ave. 14209
Telephone: (716) 886-7750
Fax: (716) 886-1367

Newspaper
Buffalo Jewish Review
15 Mohawk Street 14203
Telephone: (716) 854-2192

MIKVAOT
Mikva
1248 Kenmore Avenue 14216
Telephone: (716) 632-1531

MUSEUMS

Benjamin & Dr. Edgar R. Cofeld Judaic Museum
805 Delaware Av. 14209
Telephone: (716) 836-6565
Fax: (716) 831-1126
Email: TBZ@TBZ.org
A collection of more than a thousand Judaic artifacts dating from the tenth century to the present. There are unique Ben Shahn stained glass windows in the building.

SYNAGOGUES

Conservative
Hillel of Buffalo
Campus Center for Jewish Life, 520 Lee Entrance, The Commons/Suite #204, Amherst, NY 14228
Telephone: (716) 639-8361
Fax: (716) 639-7817

Shaarey Zedek
621 Getzville Rd 14226
Telephone: (716) 838-3232

Temple Beth El of Greater Buffalo
2368 Eggert Road, Tonawanda 14150
Telephone: (716) 836-3762
Fax: (716) 836-3764
Email: templebethel@juno.com
Web site: http://bethelbuffalo.uscjhost.net

Orthodox
B'nai Shalom
1675 N. Forest Rd 14221
Telephone: (716) 689-8203

Beth Abraham
1073 Elmwood Av 14222
Telephone: (716) 874-4786

Chabad House
3292 Main St., & N. Forest Rd 14214 &14068
Telephone: (716) 688-1642

Saranac Synagogue
85 Saranac Avenue 14216
Telephone: (716) 876-1284
Fax: (716) 833-7178
Daily Minyan.

Young Israel of Greater Buffalo
105 Maple Rd, Williamsville 14221
Telephone: (716) 634-0212

Reconstructionist
Temple Sinai
50 Alberta Dr., Amherst 14226
Telephone: (716) 834-0708
Fax: (716) 838-2597
Email: templesinai@juno.com

Reform
Beth Am
4660 Sheridan Dr 14221
Telephone: (716) 633-8877
Fax: (716) 633-8952
Email: rabbif@aol.com

Congregation Havurah
6320 Main St. 14221
Telephone: (716) 874-3517

Temple Beth Zion
805 Delaware Avenue 14209
Telephone: (716) 886-7150
Fax: (716) 831-1126
Email: tbz@tbz.org
Web site: www.tbz.org

Traditional
Kehilat Shalom
700 Sweet Home Rd 14226
Telephone: (716) 885-6650

CATSKILLS

ELLENVILLE

MIKVAOT
Congregation Ezrath Israel
Rabbi Herman Eisner Square 12428
Telephone: (845) 647-4450/72
Fax: (845) 647-4472
Email: ezrathisrael@cs.com
Mikvah - call for hours.

FLEISCHMANNS

HOTELS
Kosher
Oppenheimer's Regis
PO Box 700, Fleischmanns 12430
Telephone: 254-5080
Fax: 254-4399
Email: kurtopp@aol.com
Supervision: Rabbinate of K'hal Adas Jeshurun, NYC
Open from Pesach to Succos. Off-season: Fax 1-732-367-5417.

LOCH SHELDRAKE

RESTAURANTS
Meat
Kikar Tel Aviv
Vacation Village
Telephone: (845) 434-0600

SYNAGOGUES
Orthodox
Young Israel of Vacation Village
PO Box 650 12759
Telephone: (845) 436-8359

MONTICELLO
HOTELS
Kutsher's Country Club
Kutshers Road 12701
Telephone: (845) 794-6000
Fax: (845) 794-0157
Email: kutshers@warwick.net
Daily services.

MIKVAOT
Mikva
16 North Street 12701
Telephone: (845) 794-6757
Summer: opens at sunset for two hours. Winter: by appointment only.

SYNAGOGUES
Orthodox
Landfield Avenue Synagogue
18 Landfield Avenue 12701
Telephone: (845) 794-8470
Fax: (845) 794-8478
Daily services.

Reform
Temple Sholom
Port Jervis & Dillon Roads 12701
Telephone: (845) 794-8731
Daily services.

SHARON SPRINGS
HOTELS
Yarkony's Adler Spa Hotel
PO Box 328 13459
Telephone: (845) 284-2285 or 1 800 448-4314
Fax: (845) 284-2215
Supervision: OU

WOODRIDGE
HOTELS
The Lake House Hotel
Telephone: (845) 434-7800
Glatt kosher. Chalav Yisrael products only. Open Pesach to Succot.

CLIFTON PARK
SYNAGOGUES
Conservative
Beth Shalom
Clifton Park, Center Road 12065
Telephone: (716) 371-0608

DELMAR
SYNAGOGUES
Orthodox
Chabad House of Delmar
109 Elsmere Avenue 12054
Telephone: (518) 439-8280
Fax: (518) 439-3226
Email: DelmarChabadSimon@juno.com

Reconstructionist
Reconstructionist Havurah of the Capital District
98 Meadowland Street 12054
Telephone: (518) 439-5870

ELMIRA
SYNAGOGUES
Orthodox
Shomray Hadath
Cobbles Park 14905
Telephone: (607) 732-7410

Reform
B'nai Israel
Water & Guinnip Streets 14905
Telephone: (607) 734-7735

GENEVA
SYNAGOGUES
Reform
Temple Beth El
755 South Main Street 14456
Telephone: (315) 789-9710
Email: rosenfield@hws.edu

GLENS FALLS
SYNAGOGUES
Conservative
Shaaray Tefila
68 Bay Street 12801
Telephone: (518) 792-4945
Fax: (518) 792-5966
Email: Shaarayt@localnet.com

Reform
Temple Beth El
3 Marion Avenue 12801
Telephone: (518) 792-4364

GLOVERSVILLE
SYNAGOGUES
Community Center
28 E. Fulton Street 12078

Conservative
Knesseth Israel
34 E. Fulton Street 12078
Telephone: (518) 725-0649

HUDSON
SYNAGOGUES
Conservative
Anshe Emeth
240 Jolsen Blvd. 12534
Telephone: (518) 828-9040

ITHACA
SYNAGOGUES
Conservative
Temple Beth El
402 N. Tioga Street 14850
Telephone: (607) 607-273-5775
Fax: (607) 607-273-5804
Email: rabbi@tbeithaca.org
Web site: www.tbeithaca.org

Orthodox
Young Israel of Cornell
106 West Avenue 14850
Telephone: (607) 272-5810

LAKE PLACID
SYNAGOGUES
Lake Placid Synagogue
30 Saranac Avenue, Post Office Box 521 12946
Telephone: (518) Answering machine: 518-523-3876
Email: learlan@adelphia.net
Web site: www.lakeplacidsynagogue.org

Traditional
30 Saranac Avenue, PO Box 521 12946-0521
Telephone: (518) 523-3876
Fax: (518) 891-2629

LONG ISLAND

Nassau County

BALDWIN
RESTAURANTS
Ben's Kosher Delicatessen
933 Atlantic Avenue
Telephone: (516) 868-2072
Fax: (516) 868-2062
Email: info@bensdeli.net
Web site: www.bensdeli.net
Supervision: Supervised

CEDARHURST
BAKERIES
Zomick's Bake Shop
444 Central Avenue, Cedarhurst
Telephone: (516) 569-5520
Supervision: Vaad HaKashrus of the Five Towns

BOOKSELLERS
Judaica Plus
530 Central Avenue, Cedarhurst
Telephone: (516) 295-4343

JUDAICA
530 Central Avenue
Telephone: (516) 295-4343

RESTAURANTS
Dairy
Ruthie's Kosher Dessert and Dairy Café
560A Central Avenue, Cedarhurst
Telephone: (516) 569-1818
Supervision: Vaad HaKashrus of the Five Towns

Meat
Burger Express
140 Washington Ave
Telephone: (516) 295-2040
Supervision: Supervised

K.D.'s El Passo BBQ
546 Central Avenue, Cedarhurst
Telephone: (516) 569-2920
Supervision: Supervised

K Roasters
72 Columbia Avenue, Cedarhurst
Telephone: (516) 791-5100
Supervision: Vaad HaKashrus of the Five Towns

King David Delicatessen
550 Central Avenue, Cedarhurst
Telephone: (516) 569-2920
Supervision: Vaad HaKashrus of the Five Towns
Glatt kosher, Shomer Shabbat. Ten minutes from JFK International Airport.

Wok Tov
594 Central Avenue, Cedarhurst
Telephone: (516) 295-3843
Fax: (516) 295-3865
Supervision: Vaad HaKashrus of the Five Towns

GREAT NECK
BUTCHERS
Great Neck Glatt
501 Middle Neck Road 11023
Telephone: (516) 773-6328
Fax: (516) 773-4694
Supervision: Vaad Harabonim of Queens

MEDIA

Newspapers
Long Island Jewish Week
98 Cutter Mill Road 11020
Telephone: (516) 773-3679

Long Island Jewish World
115 Middle Neck Road 11021
Telephone: (516) 829-4000

MIKVAOT
26 Old Mill Road 11023
Telephone: (516) 487-2726

RESTAURANTS
Meat
Bistro Grill
132 Middle Neck Road
Telephone: (516) 829-4428
Fax: (516) 829-3320

Chattanooga
37 Cuttermill Road
Telephone: (516) 487-4455

Colbeh
75 N. Station Plaza, Greatneck
Telephone: (516) 466-8181
Supervision: Kof-K

Danny's
624 Middle Neck Road
Telephone: (516) 487-6666

Hunan
507 Middle Neck Road, Greatneck
Telephone: (516) 482-7912
Supervision: Vaad Rab. of Queens

Kings Kosher Pizza
605 Middle Neck Road
Telephone: (516) 482-0400

Soprano's
113 Middle Neck Road
Telephone: (516) 482-0000
Fax: (516) 482-0560

GREENVALE
RESTAURANTS
Meat
Ben's Kosher Delicatessen
140 Wheatley Plaza
Telephone: (516) 621-3340
Fax: (516) 621-2178
Email: info@bensdeli.net
Web site: www.bensdeli.net
Supervision: Supervised

JERICHO
DELICATESSEN
437 No. Broadway
Telephone: (516) 939-2367
Fax: (516) 939-2294
Email: info@bensdeli.net
Web site: www.bensdeli.net
Supervision: Supervised

LAWRENCE
BAKERIES
Tasty Heimish Bakery
343 Central Avenue, Lawrence
Telephone: (508) 569-5551/5552

RESTAURANTS
Dairy
Dairy Review
143 Washington Avenue, Lawrence
Telephone: (508) 295-7417
Supervision: Vaad HaKashrus of the Five Towns

Primavera
357 Central Avenue, Lawrence
Telephone: (508) 374-5504
Fax: (508) 374-5589
Supervision: Supervised

Meat
Burger Express
140 Washington Avenue, Lawrence
Telephone: (508) 374-1714
Supervision: Vaad HaKashrus of the Five Towns

Cho-Sen Island
367 Central Avenue, Lawrence 11559
Telephone: (508) 374-1199
Fax: (508) 374-1459
Supervision: Vaad HaKashrus of the Five Towns

Traditions
302 Central Avenue
Telephone: (508) 295-3630

LONG BEACH
MIKVAOT
Sharf Manor, 274 W. Broadway 11561
Telephone: (310) 431-7758

SYNAGOGUES
Conservative
Beth Shalom of Long Beach and Lido
700 E. Park Ave 11561
Telephone: (310) 432-7464

Orthodox
Temple Beth El
570 W. Walnut Street 11561
Telephone: (310) 432-1678

SYOSSET

COMMUNITY ORGANISATIONS
Conference of Jewish Organisations of Nassau County
North Shore Atrium, 6900 Jericho Turnpike 11791
Telephone: (516) 364-4477
Fax: (516) 921-5092

WEST HEMPSTEAD

MIKVAOT
775 Hempstead Avenue 11552
Telephone: (516) 489-9358

RESTAURANTS
Meat
Wing Wan
248 Hempstead Avenue
Telephone: (616) 482-7912

WOODBURY

RESTAURANTS
Ben's Kosher Delicatessen
7971 Jericho Turnpike
Telephone: (516) 496-4236
Fax: (516) 496-4354
Email: info@bensdeli.net
Web site: www.bensdeli.net
Supervision: Supervised

WOODMERE

KASHRUT INFORMATION
Vaad HaKashrus of the Five Towns
859 Peninsula Blvd., Woodmere 11598
Telephone: (516) 569-4536
Fax: (516) 295 4212

RESTAURANTS
Soprano's
1034 Broadway 11598
Telephone: (516) 792-9800
Fax: (516) 792-0409

SYNAGOGUES
Orthodox
Young Israel of North Woodmere
634 Hungry Harbor Road, North Woodmere 11581
Telephone: (516) 791-5099
Email: info@yinw.org

Suffolk County

COMMACK

COMMUNITY ORGANISATIONS
Suffolk Council of Jewish Organizations
74 Hauppauge Road 11725
Telephone: (516) 631-462-5826
Email: suffolkCOJO@att.net
Web site: www.lijewishlinks.org
Publishes "Suffolk Jewish Directory".

RESTAURANTS
Meat
Pastrami 'N Friends
110a Commack Road 11725
Telephone: (516) 499-9537

SYNAGOGUES
Orthodox
Young Israel of Commack
40 Kings Park Road 11725
Telephone: (516) 543-1441

DIX HILLS

TOURIST INFORMATION
Jewish Genealogy Society of Long Island
37 Westcliff Drive 11746-5627
Telephone: (631) 549-9532
Email: jgsli@suffolk.lib.ny.us
Web site: www.jewishgen.org/jgsli
Offers assistance to Jewish travellers on their New York or US roots.

WESTHAMPTON BEACH

RESTAURANTS
Beach Bakery Café
112 Main Street 11978
Telephone: (631) 288-6552
Supervision: Rabbi Ariel Konstantyn

SYNAGOGUES
Orthodox
Hampton Synagogue
154 Sunset Avenue 11978
Telephone: (631) 288-0534

MONROE

SYNAGOGUES
Reform
Temple Beth-El
Monroe Temple of Liberal Judaism, 314 N. Main St. 10950
Telephone: (845) 845-783-2626
Email: monroetemplebeth-el.org

NEWBURGH

KASHRUT INFORMATION
Agudas Israel
290 North Street 12550
Telephone: (845) 562-5604
Fax: (845) 562-5622
Email: agudasisrael@aol.com

MUSEUMS
Gomez Mill House
Millhouse Road, Marlboro 12542
Telephone: (845) 236-3126
Fax: (845) 236-3365
Email: gomezmillhouse@juno.com
Web site: www.gomez.org
Oldest Jewish residence now maintained as a museum.

NEW YORK CITY

Nowhere in the United States is there a city richer in Jewish heritage than New York. From the city's beginnings as a Dutch trading post in the 17th century up to the present day, Jews have flocked to New York, made it their home, and left an indelible mark on the city's heritage, language, culture, physical structure, and day-to-day life. There are more Jews in the New York metropolitan area than in any other city in the world, and more than in any country except Israel. So, without a great deal of effort, just being in this largest urban Jewish community in history affords you the opportunity to be a tourist without concern about the ease of observing kashrut and Shabbat.

New York City is the largest Jewish community in the world outside Israel. The estimated Jewish population of New York City proper is just over one million. Another million or so live in the immediate suburbs, which include not only New York, but also New Jersey and Connecticut. Roughly one-third of American Jews live in and around New York City and virtually every national Jewish organization has its headquarters here.

New York City neighbourhoods with large Jewish populations are the upper west and upper east sides of Manhattan (modern Orthodox and secular Jewish), Borough Park, Williamsburg (Orthodox and Hasidic) and Brighton Beach (Russian) in Brooklyn, Forest Hills (Israelis and Russians), Kew Gardens, Kew Garden Hills (Orthodox) in Queens, Riverdale in the Bronx, and Staten Island.

In this largest urban Jewish community in history, the Jewish traveller is overwhelmed with choices of where to eat, where to find a minyan, what to see of Jewish interest and so on. And the variety of kosher restaurants makes choosing a pleasure: Chinese, Moroccan, Italian (both meat and dairy), traditional European, Indian, Japanese and seafood.

Though Jews from numerous countries of origin live together throughout New York's Jewish communities, many groups tend to congregate in their own neighbourhoods or sections of neighbourhoods.

Ever since the fateful year of 1654 Jews have been coming to New York City. Sometimes a few, sometimes more, and sometimes by the boatload, as was the case between 1880 and 1924 when some two million Jews entered the United States. And though one might argue cause and effect, New York City is still the commercial, intellectual and financial center of the country.

Synagogues

Hundreds if not thousands of synagogues, chavurot and shtiblech lie within the city, representing the myriad expressions of Judaism: Orthodox, Hasidic, Conservative, Reform and Reconstructionist.

Complete lists of synagogues in all five boroughs can be obtained from the various umbrella organizations listed in the beginning of the section on the USA.

The 1,300-seat, Moorish-style Central Synagogue (Reform) at 652 Lexington Avenue in Manhattan reopened its doors in October 2001, three years after a devastating fire. It is the city's oldest synagogue on an original site and is an official New York City landmark; the oldest Ashkenazi congregation, founded in 1825, is Bínai Jeshrun (Conservative) at 270 West 89th Street; Shearith Israel, the Spanish and Portuguese synagogue on Central Park West at 70th Street, is one of the oldest congregations in the United States and originated with those 23 refugees from the Spanish Inquisition in Brazil in 1654. The present building still has religious items from the earliest days of the congregation and its small chapel is representative of the American colonial period; Temple Emanu-El (Reform) at Fifth Avenue and 65th Street is not only the city's largest, but the world's largest synagogue. The congregation was founded in 1848 and the building, built in 1929, can seat over 2,000 people; the Fifth Avenue synagogue at 5 East 62nd Street was, until early 1967, presided over by the then Rabbi Dr Immanuel Jakobovits, who later became the Chief Rabbi of Great Britain and the Commonwealth; the Park East synagogue at 163 East 67th Street, on the very fashionable Upper East Side, was founded in 1890 and is a historic landmark. Kehilath Jeshurun (Orthodox), 125 East 85th Street, is a popular option if you are on the Upper East Side. On the Upper West Side, Lincoln Square Synagogue (Orthodox), 200 Amsterdam Avenue at 69th Street, and Ohab Zedek (Orthodox), 118 West 95th Street, are both very popular options.

Visitors may be interested in a late 9 am minyan on the Upper West Side at 303 W.91st East between West End Avenue and Riversdale Drive.

Libraries, Museums, and Institutes of Learning

New York's newest educational research center and one of the country's most important resources for Jewish scholarship opened in October 2000 and is located at 15 West 16th Street. The centre is a partnership of five major institutions of Jewish scholarship: American Jewish Historical Society, American Sephardi Federation, Leo Baeck Institute, Yeshiva University Museum and YIVO Institute for Jewish Research. The combined collections and the professional staff of these five institutions create an opportunity for an unparalleled comprehensive study of modern Jewish history.

The Jewish Museum (Fifth Avenue and 92nd Street, 212-423-3200) has been in existence since 1904. Under the auspices of the Conservative Jewish Theological Seminary, the museum has permanent and changing exhibits and programmes and an excellent collection of Jewish ritual and ceremonial objects.

The library at the Jewish Theological Seminary (3080 Broadway at 122nd Street, 212-678-8000) houses one of the greatest collections of Judaica and Hebraica in the world. Its holdings include a rare manuscript by Maimonides (the Rambam). Other libraries with large Judaica collections are at Yeshiva University (212-960-5400), the Judaica Collection at the New York Public Library (212-340-0849), New York University (212-998-1212), Columbia University (212-854-1754), the House of Living Judaism at Temple Emanu-El (212-744-1400) and the Leo Baeck Institute (212-744-6400). Inquire at each one individually as to availability of the collections.

One of New York's living museums is the Eldridge Street Synagogue (14 Eldridge Street, 212-219-0888). At over 100 years old, the Eldridge Street synagogue is a ghost of its former splendour. But, in its heyday at the turn of the century, it was among the busiest synagogues on the Lower East Side, and the first built for that purpose by New York's eastern European Jews. An official New York City landmark, and listed on the National Register of Historic Places, the synagogue is an ongoing restoration project. The synagogue functions as a museum and has a whole host of programmes.

In the same neighbourhood and sociologically related is the Lower East Side Tenement Museum (97 Orchard Street, 212-431-0233). Contrary to popular opinion, the word tenement does not mean slum housing, but a particular building design devised to house the masses of immigrants who came to New York in the latter part of the 19th century. Tenements are five- or six-storey walk-up buildings distinguished by narrow entry halls and a central air shaft. Each floor contained four apartments. Toilet facilities, located in the hallway, were shared by all the residents. Baths were taken at numerous local public bath houses. The museum, located in a restored tenement built in 1863, shows visitors what tenement life was like via a model apartment. In addition, actors in period dress present 90-minute shows in a small theatre. This is how the vast majority of Jews lived when they first came to New York City.

Ellis Island National Monument (212-269-5755) was once the point of entry for Jews and other immigrants. Some five million Jews came to the United States between 1850 and 1948 and most were processed through immigration at Castle Garden (the present ferry ticket office) or, after 1890, Ellis Island.

Neighbourhoods and areas of historical interest

Manhattan

The Lower East Side has physically changed very little in over a century. Cramped tenements and crowded, dirty streets have always characterised the area. But for the absence of vendors calling out 'I cash clothes' one can get a pretty good idea of what life looked like for Jews newly arrived in New York City from eastern European countries, although it is difficult to imagine the strangeness of a new language or being away from home for the first time.

Although the Lower East Side is not as Jewish as it once was and many Jewish shops have closed, it is appropriate that historical jaunts in New York begin in its tangle of streets and alleys. For the ancestors of some 80 per cent of American Jews, this was the first piece of America they saw. Now other immigrant groups call the Lower East Side home. Settlement houses such as the Henry Street Settlement and the Educational Alliance on East Broadway once served the Jewish immigrant population in their need to learn English and become Americanised. Still in existence, they provide services to current residents, Jewish and non-Jewish alike.

Many Jews still do business in the neighbourhood and the area is full of historic buildings, Jewish shops, foodstores and stores selling all manner of ritual items (kipot, taliltot, tefilin, siddurim, etc.). Look along Essex, Orchard, Grand, Rivington, Hester and Canal streets.

One of the best guidebooks for this area (as well as the rest of New York City) is the 'AIA [American Institute of Architects] Guide to New York City' by Elliot Willensky and Norval White. An organization called Big Onion Walking Tours gives Lower East Side tours and they are worth a telephone call (212-439-1090).

You may notice that a number of churches on the Lower East Side used to be synagogues. They were re-consecrated as churches when the Jewish community dwindled. But in many cases you still can tell which were synagogues. Look for things like Stars of David on building cornerstones, darkened mezuzah shaped areas on doorposts, and shadows of Stars of David on building facades. They are quite evident if you look.

Synagogues of note in the area are the Bialystoker synagogue (7 Wilet Street); Beth Midrash HaGadol (60 Norfolk Street); First Roumanian American Congregation (89 Rivington Street); and the Eldridge Street Synagogue (14 Eldridge Street).

The only kosher winery in Manhattan is Schapiro's kosher Winery (126 Rivington Street, 674-4404), founded in 1899. Call for tour information.

Along Second Avenue below 14th Street you can still see the remnants of the scores of Yiddish theatres that once lined the street. Note particularly the movie theatre on Second Avenue at 12th Street, currently the City Cinemas Village East. In the upper level auditorium you can get an idea of what the place looked like when stars like Molly Picon and Boris Tomeshevsky held forth on the stage.

Forty-seventh Street between Fifth Avenue and Avenue of the Americas is the diamond centre. Some 75 per cent of all the diamonds which enter the United States pass through here. As this is overwhelmingly a Jewish and Hasidic business, the street is bustling with diamond dealers concluding deals in the open market atmosphere that is pervasive. Most deals are made with a handshake. There are a number of kosher restaurants up and down the block and on the mezzanines of office buildings.

Historical Cemeteries

Manhattan

Shearith Israel Cemeteries

Vestiges of early Jewish settlement in New York can be gleaned from the remnants of the community's first cemeteries. The following three are owned by New York's oldest congregation, Shearith Israel, the Spanish Portuguese Synagogue.

First: Shearith Israel Graveyard: 55 St. James Place (between Oliver and James St), the first Jewish cemetery in New Amsterdam, was consecrated in 1656 and was located near the present Chatham Square. Its remains were moved to this location. It contains the remains of Sephardic Jews who emigrated from Brazil.

Second: Cemetery of the Spanish and Portuguese Synagogue (1805–1829): 72–76 West 11th Street, just east of Sixth Avenue on the south side of the street.

Third: Cemetery of the Spanish and Portuguese Synagogue (1829–1851): 98–110 West 21st Street, just west of Sixth Avenue on the south side of the street.

Brooklyn

Green-Wood Cemetery (Fifth Avenue and Fort Hamilton Parkway, Brooklyn) contains the graves of many prominent Jewish figures.

Queens

Fourth Cemetery of the Spanish and Portuguese Synagogue: Cypress Hills Street and Cypress Avenue, Queens. The beautiful chapel and gate were built in 1885.

Arts and Entertainment

As American entertainment is largely a secular Jewish enterprise, one need not look very far for Jewish references in plays and musicals. However, there are some dedicated Jewish theatrical companies and venues: the Jewish Repertory Company (212-831-2000); the American Jewish Theater (212-633-1588); the YM & YWHA (212-427-6000) has several outstanding lecture series, some with specific Jewish themes. For other events of Jewish interest consult one of the weekly listings magazines such as *Time Out New York* or *New York Magazine*, or the Sunday Arts & Leisure section of the *New York Times*. Jewish newspapers with events listings are *Jewish Week*, *Forward* and *Jewish Press*, all available at most newsstands.

Jewish Neighbourhoods of Interest outside Manhattan

Brooklyn

Williamsburg was for many years the centre of Hasidic life in New York City. But in the last decade many rebbes and their followers have moved to the suburbs, particularly Rockland county. However, a trip to Williamsburg is still worthwhile.

Boro Park is almost completely Orthodox and is a world apart from the rest of the city.

Crown Heights is populated by Hasidim of many sects, but particularly the Lubavitch, whose world headquarters is at 770 Eastern Parkway. The neighbourhood is not totally Jewish and there are often clashes (sometimes violent) between the Caribbean residents and Jewish residents.

New Jersey

Many towns in northern and central New Jersey are less than 40 minutes travel time by either car or public transport from Manhattan, and as such are part of metropolitan New York. They are:

Bayonne, Clifton, Elizabeth, Englewood, Fairlawn, Hackensack, Hoboken, Jersey City, Newark, Passaic, Teaneck, Union and West New York.

Restaurants

By law in New York State, the selling of non-kosher food as kosher is a punishable fraud. Administered by the kosher Law Enforcement Section of the New York State Department of Agriculture, heavy penalties are imposed on violators. An Orthodox rabbi oversees the operation. Businesses selling kosher food must display proper signage, indicating under whose hashgacha they operate, and establishments which sell both kosher and non-kosher food must display that as well, with a sign in block letters no smaller than four inches high.

In July 2000 a Federal Judge ruled that this law violated the First Amendment. In September 2002 there was a further stay of this ruling pending appeal.

'The Kosher Directory', issued by the Union of Orthodox Jewish Congregations, lists foods and services which bear the symbol. It is available for a charge by calling 212-563-4000. Other reliable kashruth insignias also exist.

Note that kosher packaged foods, including bread, meat, fish, cake, biscuits and virtually anything you can think of, are widely available in supermarkets throughout the New York metropolitan area. Many foodstores, especially on the Upper West Side of Manhattan and in Jewish neighbourhoods in Brooklyn and Queens, sell fresh kosher prepared meals as well.

BRONX

RESTAURANTS

Second Helping
3532 Johnson Avenue 10463
Telephone: (616) 548-1818
Supervision: Vaad Harabonim of Riverdale
Take-out food only; Glatt kosher.

Yeshiva University: Bronx Center
Eastchester Rd & Morris Park Avenue 10461
Telephone: (616) 430-2131

Dairy

Main Event
3708 Riverdale Avenue, Riverdale 10463
Telephone: (616) 601-6246
Fax: (616) 601-0008
Email: maineventc@aol.com
Supervision: Rabbi Jonathan Rosenblatt, Riverdale Jewish Center

Meat

Riverdelight
3534 Johnson Avenue, Riverdale 10463
Telephone: (616) 543-4270
Fax: (616) 543-7545
Supervision: Vaad Harabonim of Riverdale
Glatt kosher. Grill, deli and Middle-Eastern cuisine.
Take-out and catering.

BROOKLYN

HOTELS

Avenue Plaza Hotel
4624 13th Avenue 11219
Telephone: (616) 552-3200
Fax: (616) 552-3276
Email: info@theavenueplaza.com
Web site: www.theavenueplaza.com

Midwood Suites
1078 East 15 St. 11230
Telephone: (616) 253-9535
Fax: (616) 253-3269
Email: shalom@midwoodsuites.com

Scharf's Ateret of Midwood
1410 East 10th Street 11230
Telephone: (616) 998-5400
Fax: (616) 645-8600
Email: ateretavoth@aol.com
Daily Minyon. Under strict Hashgocha. Cholov Yisroel/Glatt Kosher

The Crown Palace Hotel
570-600 Crown Street
Telephone: (616) 604-1777
Glatt kosher.

LIBRARIES

Levi Yitzhak Library
305 Kingston Avenue 11213

MUSEUMS

The Chasidic Art Institute
375 Kingston Avenue

RESTAURANTS

Broadway's J-2 N.Y.C. Pizza
926 3rd Ave.
Telephone: (616) 768-7437

Dairy

Bella Luna
557 Kings Highway
Telephone: (616) 376-2999

Chapp-u-Ccino
4815 12th Avenue
Telephone: (616) 633-4377
Supervision: Rabbi Amrom Roth

Fontana Bella
2086 Coney Island Avenue
Telephone: (616) 627-3904
Supervision: Rabbi Gornish

Gio Caffe
448 Avenue P
Telephone: (616) 375-5437

Milk 'N Honey
5013 - 10 Ave.
Telephone: (616) 871-4319
Fax: (616) 871-4297
Supervision: Rabbi Friedlander

Sunflower Café
1223 Kings Highway, cor. E. 13th St.
Telephone: (616) 336-1340
Supervision: Rabbi Gornish

Tea For Two Café
547 Kings Highway
Telephone: (616) 998-0020
Supervision: Rabbi Gornish

Wendy's Plate
434 Avenue U
Telephone: (616) 376-3125
Fax: (616) 871-4297
Supervision: Rabbi Friedlander

Meat
1st Jerusalem Steak House
533 Kings Highway
Telephone: (616) 336-5115

47th St. Kosher Restaurant
274 - 47th Street , (off 3rd Ave.)
Telephone: (616) 492-2000
Fax: (616) 492-4199

A-Kosher Delight
4600 13th Ave.
Telephone: (616) 435-8500
Fax: (616) 435-1669

Bamboo Garden
904 Kings Highway
Telephone: (616) 375-8501
Supervision: Rabbi Yisroel P. Gornish

Cancun
448 Avenue P.
Telephone: (616) 375-4916
Supervision: Vaad Harabonim of Flatbush

Chap-A-Nosh Plus
1424 Elm Avenue 11230
Telephone: (616) 627-0072
Fax: (616) 645-6336
Supervision: Rabbi G. Reisman

China Glatt
4413 - 13th Ave
Telephone: (616) 438-2576

Dougies
4310 18th Ave, Bet. McDonald Ave. & E. 2nd St,
Off Ocean Parkway
Telephone: (616) 686-8080
Supervision: Udvar Kashruth of America

Essex on Coney
1359 Coney Island Ave
Telephone: (616) 253-1002
Supervision: Vaad Harabonim of Flatbush

Fuji Hana
512 Av. U
Telephone: (616) 336-3888
Supervision: Vaad Harabonim of Flatbush

Glatt-a-la-Carte
5502 18th Ave.
Telephone: (616) 621-3697
Supervision: R'Yechiel Babad

Jerusalem Steak House II
1316 Ave. M
Telephone: (616) 376-0680

Kaosan
1387 Coney Island Ave.
Telephone: (616) 252-6969

Kineret Steak House
521 Kings Highway, Bet. E. 2nd - E. 3rd Sts
Telephone: (616) 336-8888
Supervision: Kehilah Kashruth

McFleishig's
5508 16th Avenue
Telephone: (616) 435-2779
Supervision: Rabbi Babad, Tartikover

Olympic Pita
1419 Coney Island Avenue, Bet. J & K
Telephone: (616) 258-6222
Fax: (616) 258-3106
Supervision: Kehilah Kashrus

Shang-Chai
2189 Flatbush Ave.
Telephone: (616) 377-6100

Tokyo of Brooklyn
2954 Ave. U., off Nostrand Ave.
Telephone: (616) 891-6221
Supervision: Kehilah Kashrus

Yunkee
1424 Elm Ave, (cor. E. 15th/St & Ave. M)
Telephone: (616) 627-0072
Fax: (616) 645-6336
Supervision: Rabbi G. Reisman

SYNAGOGUES
Orthodox
Lubavitch Movement
770 Eastern Parkway 11213
Telephone: (616) 774-4000
Fax: (616) 774-2718
Email: info@lubavitch.com
Web site: www.lubavitch.com

MANHATTAN
There are of course a large number of
synagogues of all kinds in New York.
The major synagogues in Manhattan, and of
possible interest to visitors, are the following.

Conservative
Bínai Jeshrun
270 West 89th Street, NY, 10010
Telephone: (212) 787 7600

Park Avenue Synagogue
50 East 87th Street, NY 10128
Telephone: (212) 369 2600
Fax: (212) 410 7879

Visitors wishing to ascertain details of other synagogues
in Manhattan or of synagogues in outlying areas should
contact the appropriate central authority as detailed
below.

United Synagogue of America
155 Fifth Avenue, NY 10010
Telephone (212) 533 7800
World Council of Synagogues can be found at the same
location.

Orthodox
Agudat Israel World Organization
84 William Street, NY 10038
Telephone: (212) 797 9600
Fax: (212) 269 2843

Fifth Avenue Synagogue
5 East 62nd Street, NY, 10021
Telephone: (616) 838 2122

Kehilath Jeshurun
125 East 85th Street, NY, 10028
Telephone: (212) 427 1000

Lincoln Square
220 Amsterdam Avenue at 69th Street, NY, 10023
Telephone: (212) 874 6100

Lubavitch Movement
770 Eastern Parkway,
Brooklyn, NY 11213
Telephone: (718) 221 0500
Fax: (718) 221 0985

National Council of Young Israel National Office
3 West 16th Street, NY 10011
Telephone: (212) 929 1525
Fax: (212) 727 9526
Email: nyci

Ohab Zedeck
118 West 95th Street, NY, 10025
Telephone: (212) 749 5150

Park East
163 East 67th Street, NY, 10021
Telephone: (212) 737 6900
Fax: (212) 570 648

Union of Orthodox Jewish Congregations of America
333 Seventh Avenue, NY 10001
Telephone: (212) 563 4000
Fax: (212) 613 8333

Progressive
World Union for Progressive Judaism
838 Fifth Avenue, NY 10021
Telephone: (212) 650 4090
Fax: (212) 650 4090
Email: 5448032

Reform
Central Synagogue
652 Lexington Avenue, NY, 10022
Telephone: (212) 838 5122

Temple Emanuel-El
1 East 65th Street, NY, 10023
Telephone: (212) 744 1400

Union of America Hebrew Congregations
838 Fifth Avenue, NY 10021
Telephone: (212) 650 4085
Fax: (212) 650 4169

Sephardi
Shearith Israel
2 West 70th Street, NY, 10023

Union of Sephardi Congregations
8 West 70th Street, NY 10023
Telephone: (212) 873 0300

BAKERIES
H & H / The Excellent Bagel
2239 Broadway 10024
Telephone: (616) 595-8000
Supervision: Kof-K

BOOKSELLERS
J.Levine Judaica
5 West 30th Street
Telephone: (616) 695-6888
Web site: LevineJudaica.Com

EMBASSY
Consul General of Israel
800 Second Avenue 10017
Telephone: (616) 499-5400
Fax: (616) 499-5555

JUDAICA
Eichler's of Manhattan
62 West 45th St.
Telephone: 1-877-EICHLERS
Web site: www.EICHLERS.com

LIBRARIES
Butler Library of Colombia University
Broadway at 116th Street 10027
Has some 6,000 Hebrew books and pamphlets, plus 1,000 manuscripts and a Hebrew psalter printed at Cambridge University in 1685 and used by Samuel Johnson at the graduation of the first candidates for bachelor's degrees.

The Jewish Division of the New York Public Library
Fifth Avenue at 42nd Street 10018
Telephone: (616) 930-0601
Fax: (616) 642-0141
Has 125,000 volumes of Judaica and Hebraica, along with extensive microfilm and bound files of Jewish publications, one of the finest collections in existence.

MUSEUMS
Center for Jewish History
15 West 16th Street 10011
Telephone: (616) 294-8301
Fax: (616) 294-8302
Email: cjh@cjh.org
Web site: www.cjh.org
The Center has brought together the following five institutes to create the largest single repository for Jewish history in the Diaspora: American Jewish Historical Society, American Sephardi Federation, Leo Baeck Institute, Yeshiva University Museum and YIVO Institute for Jewish Research. It has over 500,000 volumes and over 100 million documents. A wide variety of exhibitions illustrate the diversity of Jewish art, history and culture. Tours are available and there is a kosher dairy cafe open Monday to Thursday 9.15 am to 4.30 pm and Sunday 11.00 am to 4.30 pm.

Jewish Theological Seminary of America
3080 Broadway at 122nd Street 10027
Telephone: (616) 678-8975
Email: shmintz@jtsa.edu
The Library of the Jewish Theological Seminary is one of the world's premier research libraries of Judaica and Hebraica. More than a thousand years of written history are to be found within the library's 375,000 rare books, 40,000 Genizah fragments and thousands of rare documents and prints. The remarkable treasures represent scholarship in the areas of Bible, liturgy, rabbinics, kabbala, philosophy and history. Throughout the year, exhibitions featuring selected pieces from the collection, showcase the library's treasures. Sundays, 10am to 5pm; Monday through Thursday, 9am to 6pm; Fridays, 9am to 2pm; closed Saturday.

Lower East Side Tenement Museum
90 Orchard Street 10002
Telephone: (616) 431-0233
Fax: (616) 431-0402
Web site: www.tenement.org
Housed in a 1863 structure, the Museum presents and interprets the variety of immigrant experience on Manhattan's Lower East side, "A gateway to America".

The House of Living Judaism
5th Avenue and 65th Street
Frequently shows paintings and ritual objects. Twelve marble pillars symbolise the Twelve Tribes.

The Jewish Museum
1109 Fifth Avenue 10128
Telephone: (616) 423-3200
This is one of the outstanding museums in the city and a 'must' not just for Jewish visitors but for all interested in art. The permanent display consists of one of the finest collection of Jewish ritual and ceremonial art in the world, along with notable paintings and sculptures.

The Museum of Jewish Heritage
18 First Place, Battery Park City 10004
Telephone: (616) 509-6130
Web site: www.mjhnyc.org

The Museum's core exhibition combines archival material with modern media as a living memorial to the Holocaust.

Theological Seminary of America
Fifth Avenue & 92nd Street 10028
An outstanding museum, with permanent displays of Jewish ritual and ceremonial art, along with notable paintings and sculptures.

ORGANISATIONS
UJA-Federation Resource Line
130 E. 59th Street 10022
Telephone: (616) 753-2288
Fax: (616) 888-7538
Email: resourceline@ujafedny.org
Web site: www.ujafedny.org

RESTAURANTS
Ben's Kosher Delicatessen
209 West 38th Street
Telephone: (616) 398-2367
Fax: (616) 398-3354
Email: info@bensdeli.net
Web site: www.bensdeli.net
Supervision: Supervised
Hours: 11am to 9.30 pm.

CENTER FOR JEWISH HISTORY

15 West 16 Street
(between 5th and 6th Avenue)

For more information
212-294-8301
or, see our website
www.cjh.org

Public Tours
every Tuesday and
Thursday, 2 p.m.

Millions of archival documents... half a million books... tens of thousands of photographs, artifacts, paintings, and works of art.

- Study these extraordinary collections

- View the many exhibitions

- Attend lectures, concerts, films, and literary evenings

- Visit our café and Center Shop.

Yeshiva University: Main Center
500 W. 185th Street 10033-3201
Telephone: (616) 960-5248
Fax: (616) 960-0070

Dairy
American Café
160 Broadway
Telephone: (616) 732-1426

Bagels & Co.
1428 York Ave., cnr. E. 76th St.
Telephone: (616) 717-0505
Supervision: New York Kosher

Broadway's Jerusalem 2
1375 Broadway, at 38th Street 10018
Telephone: (616) 398-1475
Fax: (616) 212-398-6797
Email: n.y.pies@.com
Supervision: OU
Chalav Yisrael, Prs Yisruel. Home of the N.Y. Flying
Pizza Pies. Visit the 'Jewish Wall of Fame', 7.00 am to
12.00 pm. Saturday nights to 2.00 am.

Café 18
8 East 18th Street, Bet. 5th and Broadway
Telephone: (616) 620-4182

Cafe Roma Pizzeria
175 W. 90th Street
Telephone: (616) 875-8972

Diamond Dairy Kosher Lunchonette
4 W. 47th Street 10036
Telephone: (616) 719-2694
On the gallery overlooking the diamond & jewelry
exchange. Hours: Monday to Thursday, 7:30 am to 5
pm; Friday, to 2 pm.

EEE's Bakery & Café
105 East 34th Street

Gusto va Mare
237 E. 53rd St.
Telephone: (616) 583-9300
Supervision: Organised Kashrut

JT Café
226 W. 72 St.
Telephone: (616) 724-2424

Mom's Bagels of NY
240 West 35th Street 10001
Telephone: (616) 494-0440
Fax: (616) 494-0402
Email: info@momsbagelsnyc.com
Supervision: Kof-K
Chulov Yisruel

My Most Favorite Desert
120 West 45th Street
Telephone: (616) 997-5130
Fax: (616) 997 5046
Supervision: OU
Chalav Yisrael.

Provi, Provi
228 W, 72nd St., Bet. B'way and West End Ave.
Telephone: (616) 875-9020
Supervision: Organised Kashrut

Va Bene
1589 Second Avenue 10028
Telephone: (616) 517-4448
Fax: (616) 517-2258
Supervision: OU
Chalav Yisrael Italian restaurant.

Vegetable Garden
48 East 41st St., (Bet. Mad & Park)
Telephone: (616) 883-7668

Kosher Vegetarian
Great American Health Bar
35 W. 57th Street
Telephone: (616) 355-5177
Web site: www.57thstreetkosher.com

Meat
A-Kosher Delight
1359 Broadway
Telephone: (616) 563-3366
Fax: (616) 268-9352

Abigael's Grill and Caterers
9 East 37th Street 10016
Telephone: (616) 725-0130
Fax: (616) 725-3577
Supervision: Kof-K
Glatt kosher.

Abigael's on Broadway
1407 Broadway, at 39th Street 10016
Telephone: (616) 575-1407
Fax: (616) 866-0666
Supervision: Kof-K
Glatt kosher. Lunch Monday-Friday 12pm-3pm. Dinner
Sun-Thursday 5pm-10pm.

Cafe Classico
35 West 57th Street
Telephone: (616) 355-5411
Email: www.57thstreetkosher.com
Glatt kosher.

Colbeh
43 West 39 St, (Mid Town)
Telephone: (616) 354-8181

Deli Kasbah
2553 Amsterdam Avenue
Telephone: (616) 568-4600

Domani Ristorante
1590 First Ave., Bet. 82nd-83rd St.
Telephone: (616) 717-7575/7557
Supervision: Organised Kashrut

Dougies
222 West 72nd
Telephone: (616) 724-2222
Fax: (616) 724-3421
Web site: www.Dougiesbbq.com

Eden Wok
127 W. 72 Street 10023
Telephone: (616) 787-8700
Fax: (616) 787-9801
Supervision: OU

Essex on Coney Downtown
17 Trinity Place
Telephone: (616) 809-3000

Estihana
221 W. 79 St.
Telephone: (616) 501-0393
Fax: (616) 501-0458
Web site: www.estihana.com
Japanese cuisine, glatt kosher

Glatt Dynasty
1049 Second Avenue, East 55th & East 56th Street
10022
Telephone: (616) 888-9119
Fax: (616) 888-9163
Supervision: Kof-K
Glatt kosher.

Haikara
1016 2nd Avenue 10022
Telephone: (616) 355-7000
Supervision: OU

Hapisgah Steakhouse
147-25 Union Turnpike, Kew Gardens Hills
Telephone: (616) 380-4449

Il Patrizio
206 East 63rd St., Bet. 2nd and 3rd Aves
Telephone: (616) 980-4007
Supervision: OU

Jasmine
11 East 30 Street, between Madison and 5th
Avenues
Telephone: (616) 251-8884
Supervision: Vaad l'Kashrut Badatz Sepharadic
Glatt kosher Persian and Middle Eastern cuisine. Open
Sunday to Friday, for lunch and dinner.

Jerusalem Pita
212 E. 45th Street
Telephone: (616) 922-0009
Fax: (616) 922-0018
Supervision: Glatt Kosher "Ner Tamid H", Rabbi Dov
Hazdan

Jewish Theological Seminary Dining Hall
3080 Broadway at 122nd Street 10027
Telephone: (616) 678-8822
Open September through to July (closed August) for
breakfast and lunch: 7.30am to 10.00am; 11.00am to
2.00pm. Strictly kosher, Shomer Shabbat.

Kasbah Restaurant
251 W. 85th Street
Telephone: (616) 496-1500
Fax: (616) 496-2273
Supervision: Circle K
Hours: Sunday to Thursday, 12 pm to 11 pm. American
and Mediterranean food.

Kosher Delight
1359 Broadway (37th Street)
Telephone: (616) 563-3366

Kosher Deluxe
10 W. 46th St, (Off 5th Avenue)
Telephone: (616) 869-6699

Le Marais
150 W. 46th Street 10036
Telephone: (616) 869-0900
Fax: (616) 869-1016
Supervision: Circle K
Glatt kosher. Hours: Sunday to Thursday, 12 pm to 12
am; Friday, to 3 pm; Saturday, October to May, one hour
after sundown to 1 am.

Le Marais 2
15 John St
Telephone: (616) 285-8585
Fax: (616) 791-3280
Supervision: Organised Kashrut

Levana
141 West 69th Street 10023
Telephone: (616) 877-8457
Fax: (616) 595-7522
Email: info@levana.com
Web site: www.levana.com
Supervision: Orthodox Union
Glatt kosher.

Mendy's
Rockfeller Center, 30 Rockfeller Plaza
Telephone: (616) 262-9600
Galleria, 115 east 57th Street

Mendy's West
208 West 70th Street 10023
Telephone: (616) 877-6787
Supervision: OU

Mr Broadway
1372 Broadway, (Bet. 37 & 38 St)
Telephone: (616) 921-2152

Penguin
258 W. 15th St., Bet. 7-8 Ave.
Telephone: (616) 255-3601
Supervision: Vaad Hakashrus

Pita Express
1470 2nd Avenue (77th Street)
Telephone: (616) 249-1300
Glatt kosher.

Prime Grill
60 East 49th St.
Telephone: (616) 692-9292
Fax: 883-8752

Second Avenue Delicatessen-Restaurant
156 2nd Avenue, cnr. 10th Street
Telephone: (616) 677-0606
Fax: (616) 477-5327
Email: 2ndavedeli@quicklink.com
Hours - Sunday-Thursday 7.30am-12.00am. Friday & Saturday 7.30am-3.00am.

Shallots
550 Madison Avenue, New York 10022
Telephone: (616) 833-7800
Email: shallotsny.com
In the Sony Plaza Atrium. Between 55th and 56th Sts

Tevere "84"
155 E. 84 St.

The Box Tree
250 East 49th Street
Telephone: (616) 758-8320

Tuscan Grill
228 West 72nd Street, (Bet. Bway & West End)
Telephone: (616) 875-9020

Village Crown Moroccan
96 Third Avenue 10003
Telephone: (616) 674-2061
Fax: (616) 388-9639
Email: info@villagecrown.com
Web site: www.villagecrown.com
Supervision: Kof-K: Glatt Kosher
11.30am to 11.00pm Sunday through Thursday,
11.30am to 2.00pm Friday. One hour after Shabbat until
12.00am Saturday (September thru June)

Wolf & Lamb Steakhouse
10 E. 48th St., Nr Rockerfeller Ctr., Between 5th & Madison 10017
Telephone: (616) 317-1950
Fax: (616) 317-0159
Supervision: Organised Kashrut

Organic
Caravan of Dreams
405 East 6th Street, Bet. 1st Ave. & Ave. A
Telephone: (616) 254-1613
Email: angel@caravanofdreams.net
Supervision: Orthodox Rabbinical Supervision

Vegetarian
Maharani Restaurant
156 W. 29 St, (Bet. 6 & 7 Ave.)
Telephone: (616) 868-0707/2211

Quintessence
566 Amsterdam Ave.
Telephone: (616) 501-9700 or (646)-654-1823

Saffron (Indian Vegetarian Cuisine)
81 Lexington Avenue 10016
Telephone: (616) 696-5130
Fax: (616) 696-5146

SYNAGOGUES
Orthodox
Union of Orthodox Jewish Congregations of America
11 Broadway 10004
Telephone: 212-563-4000
Fax: 212-564-9058
Email: info@ou.org
Web site: www.ou.org

THEATRE
Jewish Repertory Theatre
c/o Midtown YMHA, 344 E. 14th Street
Telephone: (616) 505-2667; 674-7200

QUEENS
BUTCHERS
Herskowitz Glatt Meat Market
164-08 69th Avenue, Hillcrest 11365
Telephone: (718) 591-0750
Fax: (718) 591-0750
Supervision: Vaad Harabonim of Queens

DELICATESSEN
Berso Foods
64-20 108th Street, Forest Hills 11375
Telephone: (718) 275-9793
Supervision: Vaad Harabonim of Queens
Take-out only.

Meal Mart
72-10 Main Street, Flushing 11367
Telephone: (718) 261-3300
Fax: (718) 261-3435
Supervision: Vaad Harabonim of Queens
Catering and take out.

RESTAURANTS
Ben's Best Deli Restaurant
96-40 Queens Blvd, Rego Park, Rego Park 11374
Telephone: (718) 897-1700
Fax: (718) 997-6503
Email: bensbest@worldnet.att.net

Dairy
Habustan Mediterranean Cuisine
188-202 Union Turnpike, Jamaica Estate

Kosher Corner Dairy
73-01 Main Street, Kew Gardens Hills
Telephone: (718) 263-1177

Zen Pavillion
251-15 Northern Blvd, Little Neck
Telephone: (718) 281-1500

Meat
Burger Nosh
69-48 Main Street, Kew Gardens Hills
Telephone: (718) 520-1933

Cho-Sen Garden
64-43 108th Street, Forest Hills 11375
Telephone: (718) 275-1300
Supervision: Vaad Harabonim of Queens
Chinese food.

Colbeh
68-34 Main Street, Flushing
Telephone: (718) 268-8181
Supervision: Kof-K

Da Mikelle II
102-39 Queens Blvd, Forest Hills
Telephone: (718) 997-6166

Dougie's
73-27 Main Street, Kew Gardens Hills
Telephone: (718) 793-4600
Fax: (718) 793-9003
Supervision: Vaad Harabonim of Queens

Glatt Kosher International Restaurant
JFK Airport, Terminal 4, 3rd floor, Forest Hills
Telephone: (718) 751-4787
Email: erwin7@nyc.rr.com
Supervision: Vaad Harabonim of Queens

Glatt Wok Express
190-11 Union Turnpike, Jamaica 11366
Telephone: (718) 740-1675
Supervision: Vaad Harabonim of Queens
Chinese food. Take-away service available.

Hapisgah Steakhouse
147-25 Union Turnpike, Kew Gardens Hills
Telephone: (718) 380-4449

La France
111-08 Queens Blvd
Telephone: (718) 520-6488

Pita House
98-102 Queens Blvd, Bet. 66-67th Ave., Flushing
Telephone: (718) 897-4829
Supervision: Rabbi David Katz

Vegetarian
Budda Bodai
42-96 Main Street, Flushing
Telephone: (718) 939-1188
Supervision: Rabbi Mayer Steinberg

STATEN ISLAND
KASHRUT INFORMATION
Directories
Organised Kashrus Laboratories
PO Box 218, Brooklyn
Telephone: (616) 851-6428
Including the Circle K trademark.

NIAGARA FALLS
COMMUNITY ORGANISATIONS
Jewish Federation of Niagara Falls
c/o of Beth Israel
Telephone: (716) 284-4575

SYNAGOGUES
Conservative
Beth Israel
College & Madison Avenues 14305
Telephone: (716) 285-9894

Reform
Beth El
720 Ashland Avenue 14301
Telephone: (716) 282-2717
Call for time of services.

POUGHKEEPSIE
COMMUNITY ORGANISATIONS
Jewish Community Center of Dutchess County
110 Grand Avenue 12603
Telephone: (845) 471-0430

SYNAGOGUES
Conservative
Temple Beth El
118 Grand Avenue 12603
Telephone: (845) 454-0570
Fax: (845) 454-7257
Web site: www.uscj.org/empire/poughktb

Orthodox
Shomre Israel
18 Park Avenue 12603
Telephone: (845) 454-2890

Reform
Vassar Temple
140 Hooker Avenue 12601
Telephone: (845) 454-2570

ROCHESTER
BAKERIES
Brighton Donuts
Monroe Avenue
Telephone: (716) 271-6940

COMMUNITY ORGANISATIONS
Jewish Community Federation
441 E. Avenue 14607
Telephone: (716) 461-0490

DELICATESSEN
Brownstein's Deli and Bakery
1862 Monroe Avenue 14618

Fox's Kosher Restaurant and Deli
3450 Winton Place 14623

MEDIA
Newspaper
Jewish Ledger
2525 Brighton-Henrietta Town Line R 14623

RESTAURANTS
Meat
Jewish Home of Rochester Cafeteria
2021 S. Winton Road 14618

SYNAGOGUES
Conservative
Temple Beth Hamedrash-Beth Israel
1369 East Avenue 14610
Telephone: (716) 244-2060

Orthodox
Congregation Beth Sholom
1161 Monroe Avenue 14620
Telephone: (716) 473-1625

Rockland County

HAVERSTRAW
SYNAGOGUES
Orthodox
Congregation Sons of Jacob
37 Clove Avenue 10927
Telephone: (845) 429-4644

MONSEY
BAKERIES
Bubba's Bagels
Wesley Hills Plaza, Wesley Hills 10952
Telephone: (845) 362-1019
Fax: (845) 362-0549
Supervision: Va'ad Harabonim of Greater Monsey

DELICATESSEN
Sammy's Bagels
421 Route 59 10952
Telephone: (845) 356-3030

RESTAURANTS
Dairy
Al di La
455 Route 306, Wesley Hills 10952
Telephone: (845) 354-2672
Supervision: Va'ad Harabonim of Greater Monsey
Italian/Dairy. Cholov Yisrael.

Chai Pizza
94 Route 59 10952
Telephone: (845) 356-2135

Jerusalem Pizza & Restaurant
190 Route 59 10952
Telephone: (845) 426-1500

Kol Tov Pizza
118 Rte 59
Telephone: (845) 356-5455

Meat
Glat Wok
106 Rte 59
Telephone: (845) 426-3600

Kyo Sushi and Steak
419 Rte 59
Telephone: (845) 371-5855

SYNAGOGUES
Orthodox
Young Israel of Monsey and Wesley Hills Inc
58 Parker Blvd 10952
Telephone: (845) 362-1838

NEW CITY
DELICATESSEN
Steve's Deli-Bake
179 South Main Street 10956
Telephone: (845) 634-8749

GROCERIES
M&S Kosher Meats
191a South Main Street 10956
Telephone: (845) 638-9494

SYNAGOGUES
Conservative
New City Jewish Center
47 Old Schoolhouse Road 10956
Telephone: (845) 634-3619
Fax: (845) 634-3481
Email: ncjc@j51.com
Web site: www.uscj.org/metny/newcity/index.html

Reform
Temple Beth Sholom
228 New Hempstead Road 10956
Telephone: (845) 638-0770
Fax: (845) 638-1696
Web site: www.templebethsholom.info

ORANGEBURG
SYNAGOGUES
Conservative
Orangetown Jewish Center
8 Independence Avenue 10962
Telephone: (845) 359-5920

SPRING VALLEY
DELICATESSEN
GPG Deli
Main Street 10977

HOME HOSPITALITY
Mendel & Margalit Zuber
32 Blauvelt Road, Monsey 10952
Telephone: (845) 425-6213
The Zuber's write 'Anyone wishing to spend a Shabbat or Yom Tov with us is more than welcome. We are Lubavitch Chasidim, glatt kosher.'

RESTAURANTS
Eli's Bagel Shop
58 N. Myrtle Avenue 10977
Telephone: (845) 425-6166
Hours: Sunday - Thursday 6.30am-5.00pm. Friday 6.30am-2.00pm. Open Motzei Shabbos from after Succos until Pesach. Catering and Platters for all occasions. Under the Hashgocha of Rabbi B. Gruber/Yoshen.

Mehadrin Restaurant
82 Route 59, Monsey 10952

Dairy
Sheli's Café and Pizza
126 Maple Avenue 10977
Telephone: (845) 426-0105
Fax: (845) 362-5004
Email: shely@ucs.net
Supervision: Rabbi Breslaver

SYNAGOGUES
Orthodox
Young Israel of Spring Valley
23 Union Road 10977
Telephone: (845) 356-3363

SUFFERN
SYNAGOGUES
Orthodox
Bais Torah
89 West Carlton Road 10901
Telephone: (845) 352-1343
Fax: (845) 352-0841
Email: yhaber@ou.org

SARATOGA SPRINGS
SYNAGOGUES
Conservative
Shaare Tefilah
84 Weibel Avenue 12866
Telephone: (518) 584-2370

Orthodox
Congregation Mikveh Israel
26 Lafayette Street 12866
Telephone: (518) 584-6338
Services in July & August. Kosher food available.

Orthodox Minyan
510 1/2 Broadway 12866
Telephone: (518) 437-1738

SCHENECTADY
SYNAGOGUES
Conservative
Agudat Achim
2117 Union Street 12309
Telephone: (518) 393-9211

Orthodox
Beth Israel
2195 Eastern Parkway 12309
Telephone: (518) 377-3700

Reform
Gates of Heaven
852 Ashmore Avenue 12309
Telephone: (518) 374-8173

SYRACUSE
SYNAGOGUES
Orthodox
Young Israel Shaarei Torah of Syracuse
4313 E. Genesee Street 13214
Telephone: (315) 446-6194
Fax: (315) 446-7936

TROY

MIKVAOT
Troy Chabad Center
2306 15th Street 12180
Telephone: (518) 274-5572

SYNAGOGUES
Conservative
Temple Beth El
411 Hoosick Street 12180
Telephone: (518) 272-6113

Reform
Congregation Berith Shalom
167 3rd Street 12180
Telephone: (518) 272-8872
Fax: (518) 272-8984

UTICA

COMMUNITY ORGANISATIONS
Jewish Community Federation of the
Mohawk Valley
2310 Oneida Street, Utica, NY 13501
Telephone: (315) 733-2343
Fax: (315) 733-2346
Email: jcci@borg.com
The Federation supports the Jewish Community Center.

SYNAGOGUES
Conservative
Temple Beth El
1607 Genesee Street 13501
Telephone: (315) 724-4751

Orthodox
Congregation Zvi Jacob
112 Memorial Parkway 13501
Telephone: (315) 724-8357

Reform
Temple Emanu-El
2710 Genesee Street 13502
Telephone: (315) 724-4177

VESTAL

COMMUNITY ORGANISATIONS
Jewish Federation of Broome County
500 Clubhouse Road 13850
Telephone: (607) 607-724-2332
Fax: (607) 607-724-2311
Email: earlejfbc@stny.rr.com

MEDIA
Newspaper
The Reporter
500 Clubhouse Road 13850
Telephone: (607) 607724-2360
Fax: (607) 607-724-2311
Email: treporter@aol.com

Westchester County

HARRISON
SYNAGOGUES
Orthodox
Young Israel of Harrison
207 Union Avenue 10528
Telephone: (914) 777-1236

MOUNT VERNON
SYNAGOGUES
Orthodox
Brothers of Israel
116 Crary Avenue 10550
Telephone: (914) 667-1302
Fax: (914) 667-0278

Fleetwood
11 East Broad Street 10552
Telephone: (914) 664-5581
Fax: (914) 699-6954
Email: rabbi@fleetwoodsynagogue.org
Web site: www.fleetwoodsynagogue.org

NEW ROCHELLE
RESTAURANTS
Eden Wok
1327 North Avenue 10804
Telephone: (914) 637-9363
Fax: (914) 637-9371
Supervision: Vaad of Westchester

SYNAGOGUES
Conservative
Bethel
Northfield Road

Orthodox
Cong. Anshe Sholom
50 North Avenue, New Rochelle, NY 10805
Telephone: (914) 632-9220
Fax: (914) 632-8182
Email: asnewroch@aol.com

Young Israel of New Rochelle
1228 North Avenue 10804
Telephone: (914) 777-1236
Contact Rabbi on 835-5581

Reform
Temple Israel
1000 Pine Brook Blvd. 10804

PEEKSKILL
SYNAGOGUES
Conservative
First Hebrew Congregation
1821 E. Main Street 10566
Telephone: (914) 739-0500
Fax: (914) 739-0684

PORT CHESTER
RESTAURANTS
Vegetarian
Green Symphony
427 Boston Post Road 10573
Telephone: (914) 937-6537

Vegetarian Kosher
427 Boston Post Road
Telephone: (914) 937-6537

SYNAGOGUES
Conservative
Kneses Tifereth Israel
575 King Street 10573
Telephone: (914) 939-1004
Fax: (914) 939-1086

SCARSDALE
SYNAGOGUES
Orthodox
Young Israel of Scarsdale
1313 Weaver Street 10583
Telephone: (914) 636-8686
Fax: (914) 636-1209
Email: yisecy@yahoo.com

Orthodox Sephardi
Magen David Sephardic Congregation
1225 Weaver Street, P O B 129H 10583
Telephone: (914) 633-3728
Fax: (914) 636-0608
Email: mitchser@aol.com

WHITE PLAINS
SYNAGOGUES
Conservative
Temple Israel Center
280 Old Mamaroneck Road, at Miles Avenue
10605
Telephone: (914) 948-2800
Fax: (914) 948-4755

Orthodox
Hebrew Institute of White Plains
20 Greenridge Avenue 10605
Telephone: (914) 914-948-3095
Fax: (914) 914-949-4676
Email: office@hiwp.org
Young Israel of White Plains
135 Old Mamaroneck Road, NY 10605
Telephone: (914) 683-YIWP
Email: yiwp.org
Web site: www.yiwp.org

Reconstructionist
Bet Am Shalom
295 Soundview Avenue 10606
Telephone: (914) 946-8851

Reform
Jewish Community Center
252 Soundview Avenue 10606
Telephone: (914) 949-4717

YONKERS
SYNAGOGUES
Conservative
Agudas Achim
21 Hudson Street 10701

Lincoln Park Center
323 Central Park Avenue 10704
Telephone: (914) 965-7119

Reform
Temple Emanu-El
306 Rumsey Road 10705
Telephone: (914) 963-0575

WEST POINT
SYNAGOGUES
**United States Military Academy Jewish
Chapel**
Building 750 10096
Telephone: (845) 938-2766
Fax: (845) 446-7706
With a local community of over 200 the Chapel was
designed by the firm responsible for the United Nations
building and the Lincoln Center.

North Carolina

ASHEVILLE

SYNAGOGUES

Conservative
Congregation Beth Israel
229 Murdock Avenue 28804
Telephone: (704) 252-8431
Fax: (704) 252-3882
Email: bethisrael@buncombe.main.nc.us

Reform
Beth Ha-Tephila
43 N. Liberty Street 28801
Telephone: (704) 253-4911
Email: tephila@worldnet.att.net

CHARLOTTE

COMMUNITY ORGANISATIONS
Jewish Federation
5007 Providence Road 28226
Telephone: (704) 366-5007

DELICATESSEN
The Kosher Mart & Delicatessen
Amity Gardens Shopping Center, 3840 E.
Independence Blvd 28205
Telephone: (704) 563-8288
Fax: (704) 532-9111
Email: koshermartusa@mindspring.com
Web site: www.koshermartusa.com

LIBRARIES
Speizman Jewish Library
5007 Providence Road 28226

MEDIA
Newspaper
Charlotte Jewish News
Telephone: (704) 366-5007

MIKVAOT
Chabad House
6619 Sardis Road 28270
Telephone: (704) 366-3984
Fax: (704) 362-1423

SYNAGOGUES
Conservative
Temple Israel
4901 Providence Road
Telephone: (704) 362-2796
Fax: (704) 362-1098
Email: templeisraelnc.org

Orthodox
Chabad House
6619 Sardis Road 28270
Telephone: (704) 366-3984
Fax: (704) 362-1423
Email: sardis@earthlink.net

Reform
Temple Beth El
5101 Providence Road 28207
Telephone: (704) 366-1948

DURHAM

COMMUNITY ORGANISATIONS
Durham-Chapel Hill Jewish Federation and Community Council
205 Mt. Bolus Road, Chapel Hill 27514
Telephone: (919) 967-6916

KASHRUT INFORMATION
Leon Dworsky
1100 Leon Street, Apt. 28 27705

SYNAGOGUES
Conservative
Beth El
1004 Watts Street 27701
Telephone: (919) 682-1238

Reform
Judea Reform Congregation
1955 Cornwallis Road 27705
Telephone: (919) 489-7062
Fax: (919) 489-0611
Email: infobox@judeareform.org

FAYETTEVILLE

SYNAGOGUES
Conservative
Beth Israel Congregation
2204 Morganton Road 28303
Telephone: (910) 484-6462

GREENSBORO

COMMUNITY ORGANISATIONS
Greensboro Jewish Federation
5509 C West Friendly Avenue 27410-4211
Telephone: (336) 852-5433
Fax: (336) 852-4346
Email: mfcgsonc@jon.cjfny.org

SYNAGOGUES
Conservative
Beth David
804 Winview Drive 27410
Telephone: (336) 294-0006
Fax: (336) 294-7011
Email: info@bethdavidsynagogue.org

HENDERSONVILLE

SYNAGOGUES

Conservative
Agudas Israel Congregation
328 N. King Street, PO Box 668 28793

RALEIGH

GROCERIES
Eshel Kosher Market
5540 Atlantic Springs Road
Telephone: (919) 872-7757

MIKVAOT
Congregation of Sha'arei Israel
7400 Falls of the Neuse Road 27615
Telephone: (919) 847-8986

SYNAGOGUES

Conservative
Beth Meyer
504 Newton Road 27615
Telephone: (919) 848-1420

Orthodox
Congregation of Sha'arei Israel - Lubavitch
7400 Falls of the Neuse Road 27615
Telephone: (919) 847-8986
Fax: (919) 847-3142

Reform
Temple Beth Or
5315 Creedmoor Road 27612
Telephone: (919) 781-4895
Fax: (919) 781-4697
Email: tempbethor@aol.com
Web site: www.templebethor-raleigh.org

WILMINGTON

SYNAGOGUES

Conservative
B'nai Israel
2601 Chestnut Street 28405
Telephone: (302) 762-1117

Reform
Temple Emanuel
201 Oakwood Drive 27103
Telephone: (302) 722-6640

Temple of Israel
1 South 4th Street 28401
Telephone: (302) 762-0000

North Dakota

BISMARK

SYNAGOGUES

Reform
Bismark Hebrew Congregation
703 North Fifth Street 58103
Telephone: (701) 258-3572

FARGO

SYNAGOGUES

Reform
Temple Beth El
809 11th Avenue S. 58103
Telephone: (701) 232-0441

Ohio

AKRON

COMMUNITY ORGANISATIONS
Jewish Community Board of Akron
750 White Pond Drive 44320
Telephone: (330) 869-2424
Fax: (330) 867-8498
Web site: www.jewishakron.org

MIKVAOT
Telephone: (330) 867-6798

SYNAGOGUES

Conservative
Beth El
464 S. Hawkins Avenue 44320
Telephone: (330) 864-2105

Orthodox
Anshe Sfard Synagogue
646 N.Revere Road 44333
Telephone: (330) 867-7292
Fax: (330) 867-7719

Reform
Temple Israel
133 Merriman Road 44303
Telephone: (330) 762-8617
Fax: (330) 762-8619
Email: rabbi@neo.rr.com

CANTON

COMMUNITY ORGANISATIONS
Jewish Community Federation
2631 Harvard Avenue 44709
Telephone: (781) 452-6444

SYNAGOGUES

Conservative
Shaaray Torah
423 30th Street N.W. 44709
Telephone: (781) 492-0310

Orthodox
Agudas Achim
2508 Market Street N. 44704
Telephone: (781) 456-8781

Reform
Temple Israel
333 25th Street N.W. 44709
Telephone: (781) 455-5197

CINCINNATI

BAKERIES
Just Desserts
6964 Plainfield Road 45236
Telephone: (513) 793-6627

COMMUNITY ORGANISATIONS
Jewish Community Center of Cincinnati
7420 Montgomery Road 45236
Telephone: (513) 513-761-7500
Fax: (513) 513-761-0084
Email: info@jcc-cinci.com
Web site: www.jcc-cinci.com

Jewish Federation
1811 Losantiville, Suite 320 45237
Telephone: (513) 351-3800

DELICATESSEN
Bilkers
7648 Reading Road 45237

LIBRARIES
The Hebrew Union College-Jewish Institute of Religion
3101 Clifton Avenue 45220
Telephone: (513) 221-1875
Fax: (513) 221-0519
Email: klau@cn.huc.edu

MEDIA

Newspaper
American Israelite
906 Main Street 45202

MIKVAOT
Kehelath B'nai Israel
1546 Beaverton Avenue 45237
Telephone: (513) 761-5260

RESTAURANTS

Dairy
Dunkin' Donuts
9385 Colerain Avenue 45231
Telephone: (513) 385-0930

Marx Hot Bagels
9701 Kenwood Road, Blue Ash 45242
Telephone: (513) 891-5542
Fax: (513) 891-1063

Meat
Pilder's Deli
4070 East Galbraith Road 45236
Telephone: (513) 792-9961
Fax: (513) 792-9605

SYNAGOGUES

Conservative
Northern Hills Synagogue - Congregation B'nai Avraham
715 Fleming Road 45231
Telephone: (513) 931-6038
Fax: (513) 931-6147
Email: berniceu@fuse.net
Web site: www.nhs-cba.org

Orthodox
Downtown Synagogue
Bartlett Building, 36 E. Fourth, 7th Floor 45202
Telephone: (513) 241-3576

Golf Manor Synagogue
6442 Stover Avenue 45237
Telephone: (513) 531-6654

Sephardic Beth Shalom
Manss Avenue, PO Box 37431 45222
Telephone: (513) 793-6936

Reform
Isaac M. Wise Temple
8329 Ridge Road 45236
Telephone: (513) 793-2556

CLEVELAND

BAKERIES
Breadsmith
9708 Kenwood Road, Blue Ash 45242
Telephone: (216) 791-8817

BUTCHERS
Tibor's Glatt Meat Market
2185 S. Green Road, S. Euclid 44121
Telephone: (216) 381-7615
Fax: (216) 381-5215

COMMUNITY ORGANISATIONS
Jewish Community Federation of Cleveland
1750 Euclid Avenue 44115
Telephone: (216) 566-9200
Fax: (216) 861-1230
Email: info@jcfcleve.org
Web site: www.jewishcleveland.org

DELICATESSEN
Unger's Kosher Market and Bakery
1831 S. Taylor Road, Cleveland Heights 44118
Telephone: (216) 321-7176
Fax: (216) 321-0777

MEDIA
Newspaper
Cleveland Jewish News
3645 Warrensville Center Road, Suite 230 44122

MIKVAOT
Cleveland Heights
Telephone: (216) 387-1040

Charlotte Goldberg Community Mkvah of the Park Synagogue
3300 Mayfield Road, Cleveland Heights 44118
Telephone: (216) 371-2244 ext 198
Fax: (216) 321-0639

K'hal Yereim Synagogue
1771 S. Taylor Road, Cleveland Heights 44118
Telephone: (216) 321-5855

MUSEUMS
Park Synagogue
3300 Mayfield Road 44118

RESTAURANTS
Dairy
Issi's Place
14100 Cedar Road, Waterstone Medical Bldg.,
University Heights 44121
Telephone: (216) 291-4251

Meat
Abba's Market and Grille
13937 Cedar Road, S. Euclid 44121
Telephone: (216) 321-5660
Fax: (216) 321-4135

Contempo Cuisine
13898 Cedar Road, University Heights 44118
Telephone: (216) 397-3520
Fax: (216) 397-3523

Empire Kosher Kitchen
2234 Warrensville Center Road, University Heights
Telephone: (216) 691-0006

Ruchama's Singapore
2172 Warrensville Center Road, University Heights
44118
Telephone: (216) 321-1100
Fax: (216) 321-1485

SYNAGOGUES
Orthodox
Congregation Shomre Shabbos
1801 S. Taylor Road, Cleveland Heights 44118
Telephone: (216) 371-0033

K'hai Yereim
1771 S. Taylor Road, Cleveland Heights 44118
Telephone: (216) 321-6855

Young Israel of Greater Cleveland
2463 South Green Road, Beachwood 44122
Telephone: (216) 1-216-382-5740
Fax: (216) 1-216-382-8722
Email: office@yigc.org
Web site: www.yigc.org

COLUMBUS
RESTAURANTS
Dairy
Sammy's New York Bagels
40 N. James Road 43213
Telephone: (614) 237-2444
Fax: (614) 235-4177
Supervision: Vaad Ho-ir of Columbus

SYNAGOGUES
Orthodox
Agudas Achim Synagogue
2767 E. Broad Street 43209
Telephone: (614) 237-2747

Orthodox
Congregation Ahavas Sholom
2568 E. Broad Street 43209
Telephone: (614) 252-4815
Fax: (614) 252-1316
Email: ahavas@beol.net
Web site: www.ahavas-sholom.org

DAYTON
BAKERIES
Rinaldo's Bakery
910 West Fairview Avenue 45406
Telephone: (937) 274-1311
Supervision: Rabbi Hillel Fox, Beth Jacob Congregation.

COMMUNITY ORGANISATIONS
Jewish Federation of Greater Dayton
4501 Denlinger Road 45426
Telephone: (937) 854-4150

HOME HOSPITALITY
Shomrei Emunah
1706 Salem Avenue 45406
Telephone: (937) 274-6941
Fax: (937) 274-7511
Email: shomrei@earthlink.net

MEDIA

Newspapers
Dayton Jewish Observer
4501 Denlinger Road 45426
Telephone: (937) 854-4150
Fax: (937) 854-2850
Email: dayjobs@aol.com

The Dayton Jewish Advocate
Telephone: (937) 854-4150 ext. 118

MIKVAOT
556 Kenwood Avenue 45406
Telephone: (937) 275-1436

SYNAGOGUES

Orthodox
Beth Jacob Congregation
7020 North Main Street 45415
Telephone: (937) 274-2149
Fax: (937) 274-9556
Email: bethjacob1@aol.com
Web site: www.bethjacobcong.org
Supervision: Rabbi Hillel Fox, Beth Jacob Congregation

Shomrei Emunah/Young Israel of Dayton
1706 Salem Avenue 45406
Telephone: (937) 274-6941
Fax: (937) 274-6941

LORAIN
SYNAGOGUES
Conservative
Agudath B'nai Israel
1715 Meister Road 44053
Telephone: (216) 282-3307

TOLEDO
SYNAGOGUES
Conservative
B'nai Israel
2727 Kenwood Blvd. 43606
Telephone: (419) 531-1677

Orthodox
Congregation Etz Chayim
3852 Woodley Road 43606
Telephone: (419) 473-2401

Reform
The Temple-Congregation Shomer Emunium
6453 Sylvania Avenue 43560
Telephone: (419) 883-3341

YOUNGSTOWN
COMMUNITY ORGANISATIONS
Youngstown Area Jewish Federation
505 Gypsy Lane 44501
Telephone: (330) 746-3251

MIKVAOT
Children of Israel
3970 1/2 Logan Way 44505
Telephone: (330) 759-2167

SYNAGOGUES
Conservative
Beth Israel Temple Center
2138 E. Market Street, Warren 44483-6104
Telephone: (330) 395-3877
Fax: (330) 394-5918
Email: bethisrael1@juno.com

Ohev Tzedek-Shaarei Torah
5245 Glenwood Avenue 44512
Telephone: (330) 758-2321
Fax: (330) 758-2322
Email: ot20@juno.com

Temple El Emeth
3970 Logan Way 44505
Telephone: (330) 759-1429

Reform
Rodef Sholom
Elm Street & Woodbine Avenue 44505
Telephone: (330) 744-5001

Oklahoma

OKLAHOMA CITY
BAKERIES
Ingrid's Kitchen
2309 N.W. 36th Street 73112

KASHRUT INFORMATION
Chabad House
6401 Lenox Avenue, Oklahoma City 73116
Telephone: (405) 810-1770
Fax: (405) 810-1772

SYNAGOGUES
Conservative
Emanuel Synagogue
900 N.W. 47th Street 73106
Telephone: (405) 528-2113

Reform
Temple B'nai Israel
4901 N. Pennsylvania Avenue 73112
Telephone: (405) 848-0965

TULSA

COMMUNITY ORGANISATIONS
Jewish Federation
2021 E. 71st Street 74136
Telephone: (918) 495-1100
Fax: (918) 495-1220
Email: federation@jewishtulsa.org

KASHRUT INFORMATION
Chabad House
6622 S. Utica Avenue 74136
Telephone: (918) 492-4499; 493-7006
Fax: (918) 492-4499

MEDIA
Newspaper
Tulsa Jewish Review
2021 E. 71st Street 74136
Telephone: (918) 495-1100

MIKVAOT
Congregation B'nai Emunah
1719 S. Owasso 74120
Telephone: (918) 583-7121
Fax: (918) 747-9696
Email: thenicepeople@tulsagogue.com
Web site: www.tulsagogue.com

Mikva Shoshana - Chabad
6622 So. Utica Avenue 74136
Telephone: (918) 493-7006

MUSEUMS
The Sherwin Miller Museum of Jewish Art
2021 East 71st Street 74136
Telephone: (918) 918-492-1818
Fax: (918) 918-492-1888
Email: info@jewishmuseum.net
Web site: www.jewishmuseum.net

RESTAURANTS
Congregation B'nai Emunah
1719 S. Owasso 74120
Telephone: (918) 583-7121
Fax: (918) 747-9696
Email: thesynagogue@bnaiemunah.com

SYNAGOGUES
Conservative
1719 S. Owasso 74120
Telephone: (918) 583-7121
Fax: (918) 747-9696
Email: thesynagogue@bnaiemunah.com

Orthodox
Chabad House
6622 S Utica Avenue 74136
Telephone: (918) 492-4499; 493-7006
Fax: (918) 492-4499

Reform
Temple Israel
2004 E. 22nd Place 74114
Telephone: (918) 747-1309
Fax: (918) 747-3564
Email: templeis@ionet.net

Oregon

ASHLAND
SYNAGOGUES
Reform
Temple Emek Shalom-Rogue Valley Jewish Community
1081 East Main St
Telephone: (541) 488-2909
Fax: (541) 488-2814
Email: TEShalom@emekshalom.org
Web site: www.emekshalom.org

EUGENE
SYNAGOGUES
Conservative
Temple Beth Israel
42 W. 25th Avenue 97405
Telephone: (541) 485-7218

PORTLAND
COMMUNITY ORGANISATIONS
Jewish Federation of Portland
6680 S.W. Capitol Highway 97219
Telephone: (503) 245-6219
Fax: (503) 245-6603
Email: federation@jewishportland.org
Web site: www.jewishportland.org

GROCERIES
Albertson's
5415 SW Beaverton Hillsdale Highway 97221
Telephone: (503) 246-1713

MIKVAOT
Ritualarium
1425 S.W. Harrison Street 97219
Telephone: (503) 224-3409

MUSEUMS
Oregon Jewish Museum
310 NW Davis Street 97209
Telephone: (503) 226-3600
Fax: (503) 226-1800
Email: museum@ojm.org
Web site: www.ojm.org

RESTAURANTS
Mittleman Jewish Community Center (Kosher restaurant)
6651 S. W. Capitol Highway 97219
Telephone: (503) 244-0111

SYNAGOGUES
Conservative
Congregation Neveh Shalom
2900 SW Peaceful Lane 97239
Telephone: (503) 246-8831
Fax: (503) 246-7553
Email: frothstein@nevehshalom.org
Web site: www.nevehshalom.org

Orthodox
Ahavath Achim
3225 S.W. Barbur Blvd 97201
Telephone: (503) 775-5895

Kesser Israel
136 S.W. Meade Street 97201
Telephone: (503) 222-1239

Shaare Torah
920 N.W. 25th Avenue 97210
Telephone: (503) 226-6131
Fax: (503) 226-0241
Email: info@shaarietorah.org
Web site: www.shaarietorah.org

Reform
Temple Beth Israel
1972 NW Flanders 97209
Telephone: (503) 222-1069

SALEM
SYNAGOGUES
Reconstructionist
Beth Shalom
1795 Broadway NE 97303
Telephone: (508) 362-5004
Temple Beth Shalom
1795 Broadway, NE 97303
Telephone: (508) 362-5004

Pennsylvania
ALLENTOWN
COMMUNITY ORGANISATIONS
Jewish Federation
702 22nd Street 18104
Telephone: (610) 821-5500

MIKVAOT
1834 Whitehall Street 18104
Telephone: (610) 776-7948

RESTAURANTS
Meat
Glatt Kosher Community Center
702 N. 22nd Street 18104
Telephone: (610) 435-3571

SYNAGOGUES
Conservative
Temple Beth El
1702 Hamilton Street 18104
Telephone: (610) 435-3521

Orthodox
Congregation Agudas Achim
625 North Second Street 18102
Telephone: (610) 432-4414

Congregation Sons of Israel
2715 Tilghman Street 18104
Telephone: (610) 433-6089
Fax: (610) 433-6080
Email: rabbi@att.net
Web site: www.sonsofisrael.net

Reform
Congregation Keneseth Israel
2227 Chew Street 18104
Telephone: (610) 435-9074
Email: congki@enter.net

BENSALEM
MIKVAOT
Bucks County Mikveh
2454 Bristol Road 19020
Telephone: (215) 891-5565

SYNAGOGUES
kehillas B'nai Shalom
2446 Bristol Road 19020
Telephone: (215) 215-750-0604
Fax: (215) bjoc613
Supervision: Rabbi Moshe Travitsky - Orthodox

BETHLEHEM
SYNAGOGUES
Conservative
Congregation Brith Sholom
Macada & Jacksonville Roads 18017
Telephone: (603) 866-8009

Orthodox
Agudath Achim
1555 Linwood Street 18017
Telephone: (603) 866-8891

EASTON
SYNAGOGUES
Conservative
B'nai Abraham
16th & Bushkill Streets 18042
Telephone: (508) 258-5343

Reform
Temple Covenant of Peace
1451 Northampton Street 18042
Telephone: (508) 253-2031
Fax: (508) 253-7973
Email: tcp@ fast.net

ELKINS PARK
TOURIST SITE
Beth Sholom
8231 Old York Park 19027
Telephone: 887-1342

ERIE
COMMUNITY ORGANISATIONS
Jewish Community Council
Suite 405, Professional Building, 161 Peach St.,
16501
Telephone: (814) 455-4474
Fax: (814) 455-4475

SYNAGOGUES
Conservative
Brith Sholom Jewish Center
3207 State Street 16508
Telephone: (814) 454-2431
Fax: (814) 452-0790

Reform
Temple Anshe Hesed
930 Liberty Street 16502
Telephone: (814) 454-2426
Fax: (814) 454-2427
Email: anshhsd@velocity.net

HARRISBURG
COMMUNITY ORGANISATIONS
**United Jewish Community of Greater
Harrisburg**
100 Vaughn Street 17110
Telephone: (717) 236-9555

GROCERIES
Bakeries Giant Food Store and Weis Market
Linglestown Road

Quality Kosher
7th Division Street 17110

KOSHER FOOD
Norman Gras Catering
3000 Green Street 17110-1234
Telephone: (717) 234-2196
Fax: (717) 234-3943
Email: normangras@aol.com

SYNAGOGUES
Conservative
Beth El
2637 N. Front Street 17110
Telephone: (717) 232-0556
Fax: (717) 232-6240

Chisuk Emuna
5th & Division Streets 17110
Telephone: (717) 232-4851
Fax: (717) 232-7950
Email: muroff@juno.com

Orthodox
Kesher Israel
2945 N. Front Street 17110
Telephone: (717) 238-0763

Reform
Ohev Sholom
2345 N. Front Street 17110
Telephone: (717) 233-6459
Fax: (717) 236-7844

HAZELTON
SYNAGOGUES
Conservative
Agudas Israel
77 N. Pine Street 18201
Telephone: (717) 455-2851

Reform
Beth Israel
98 N. Church Street 18201
Telephone: (717) 455-3971

HERSHEY
SNACK BAR
Meat
Central PA's Kosher Mart
Hershey Park
Telephone: (717) 392-1503

JOHNSTOWN
COMMUNITY ORGANISATIONS
United Jewish Federation of Johnstown
700 Indiana Street 15905
Telephone: (814) 536-0647

SYNAGOGUES

Conservative

Beth Sholom Congregation
700 Indiana Street 15905
Telephone: (814) 536-0647

LANCASTER

COMMUNITY ORGANISATIONS

Jewish Federation
2120 Oregon Pike 17601
Telephone: (717) 597-7354

SYNAGOGUES

Conservative

Beth El
1836 Rohrerstown Road 17601
Telephone: (717) 581-7891
Fax: (717) 581-7870
Email: templebethel@dejazzd.com

Orthodox

Degel Israel
1120 Columbia Avenue 17603
Telephone: (717) 397-0183
Fax: (717) 509-6188
Email: ourkehilla@mail.com

Reform

Temple Shaarei Shomayim
N. Duke & James Streets 17602
Telephone: (717) 397-5575

MCKEESPORT

SYNAGOGUES

Conservative

Tree of Life-Sfard
Cypress Avenue 15131
Telephone: (412) 673-0938

Orthodox

Gemilas Chesed
1400 Summit Street, White Oak 15131
Telephone: (412) 678-9859

Reform

B'nai Israel
536 Shaw Avenue 15132
Telephone: (412) 678-6181
Fax: (412) 678-6908
Email: tbi536@juno.com or tbi536@aol.com

PHILADELPHIA

BAKERIES

Arthur's Bakery
Academy Plaza, Red Lion and Academy Roads
19114
Telephone: (215) 637-9146
Supervision: Rabbinical Assembly

Best Cake Bakery
7594 Haverford Avenue 19151
Telephone: (215) 878-1127
Email: rugalach@aol.com
Supervision: Orthodox Vaad of Philadelphia

Buy the Dozen
219 Haverford Avenue, Narberth 19072
Telephone: (215) 610-667-9440
Supervision: Orthodox Vaad of Philadelphia

Dante's Bakery
Richboro Centre, Bustleton and Second Street
Pikes, Richboro 18954
Telephone: (215) 357-9599
Supervision: Rabbinical Assembly

Hesh's Eclair Bake Shoppe
7721 Castor Avenue 19152
Telephone: (215) 742-8575
Supervision: Vaad Hakashruth

Hutchinson's Classic Bakery
13023 Bustleton Pike 19116
Telephone: (215) 676-8612
Supervision: Rabbinical Assembly

Kaplan's New Model Bakery
901 North 3rd Street 19123
Telephone: (215) 627-5288
Supervision: Rabbi Solomon Isaacson

Lipkin and Sons Bakery
8013 Castor Avenue 19152
Telephone: (215) 342-3005
Supervision: Rabbi Abraham Novitsky

Michael's
6635 Castor Avenue 19149
Telephone: (215) 745-1423
Supervision: Rabbi Dov Brisman

Moish's Addison Bakery
10865 Bustleton Avenue 19116
Telephone: (215) 469-8054
Supervision: Rabbinical Assembly

Rilling's Bakery
2990 Southampton Road 19154
Telephone: (215) 698-6171
Supervision: Rabbinical Assembly

Viking Bakery
39 Cricket Avenue, Ardmore 19003
Telephone: (215) 642-9227
Supervision: Rabbi Joshua Toledano

Weiss Bakery
6635 Castor Avenue 19149
Telephone: (215) 722-4506
Supervision: Rabbi Dov Brisman

Zach's Bakery
6419 Rising Sun Avenue 19111
Telephone: (215) 722-1688
Supervision: Rabbinical Assembly

BOOKSELLERS
Gratz College
Old York Road and Melrose Avenue,
Melrose Park 19027
Telephone: (215) 635-7300
Fax: (215) 635-7320
Email: gratzinfo@aol.com

Jerusalem Israeli Gift Shop
7818 Castor Avenue 19152
Telephone: (215) 342-1452

Rosenberg Hebrew Book Store
409 Old York Road, Jenkintown 19046
Telephone: (215) 884-1728; 800-301-8608
Fax: (215) 884-6648
6408 Castor Avenue 19149

BUTCHERS
Aries Kosher Meats
6530 Castor Avenue 19149
Telephone: (215) 533-3222
Supervision: Vaad Hakashruth

Best Value Kosher Meat Center
8564 Bustleton Avenue 19152
Telephone: (215) 342-1902
Fax: (215) 342-5775
Supervision: Rabbi Dov Brisman

Bustleton Kosher Meat Market
6834 Bustlton Avenue 19149
Telephone: (215) 332-0100
Supervision: Rabbi Shalom Novoseller

Glendale Meats
7730 Bustleton Avenue 19152
Telephone: (215) 725-4100
Supervision: Vaad Hakashruth

Main Line Kosher Meats
75621 Haverford Avenue 19151
Telephone: (215) 877-3222
Supervision: Vaad Hakashruth

Simons Kosher Meats and Poultry
6926 Bustleton Avenue 19149
Telephone: (215) 624-5695
Supervision: Vaad Hakashruth

Wallace's Krewstown Kosher Meat Market
8919 Krewstown Road 19115
Telephone: (215) 464-7800
Supervision: Vaad Hakashruth

CONTACT INFORMATION
Jewish Information and Referral Service
2100 Arch Street, 7th Floor 19103
Telephone: (215) 832-0821
Fax: (215) 832-0833
Email: lyouman@philafederation.org

EMBASSY
Consul General of Israel
230 South 15th Street 19102
Telephone: (215) 546-5556
Fax: (215) 545-3986
Email: info.ph@israelfm.org
Web site: www.israelemb.org/pa

GROCERIES
Best Value Kosher Meat Center
8564 Bustleton Avenue 19152
Telephone: (215) 342-1902
Supervision: Rabbi Dov Brisman

Milk and Honey
7618 Castor Avenue 19152
Telephone: (215) 342-3224
Supervision: Vaad Hakashruth

HISTORIC SITE
Congregation Beth T'fillah of Overbrook Park
7630 Woodbine Avenue 19151
Telephone: (215) 477-2415
Fax: (215) 477-2417

Mikveh Israel Cemetery
8th and Spruce Streets 19107
Telephone: (215) 922-5446

The Frank Synagogue
Albert Einstein Medical Center, Old York and Tabor
Roads 19141
Telephone: (215) 456-7890

JUDAICA
Bala Judaica and Jewelry Center
222 Bala Avenue, Bala Cynwyd 19004
Telephone: (215) 610-664-1303
Fax: (215) 610-664-4319
Email: jewishwedding@erols.com

KASHRUT INFORMATION
Board of Rabbis of Greater Philadelphia
2100 Arch Street - 3rd Floor 19103
Telephone: (215) 832-0675
Fax: (215) 832-0689
Email: info@brdavphila.com

Ko Kosher Service
5871 Drexel Road 19131
Telephone: (215) 696-0408
Fax: (215) 696-9249
Email: ko_kosher_service@msm.com
Web site: www.ko-kosher-service.org

Orthodox Vaad of Philadelphia
7505 Brookhaven Road 19151
Telephone: (215) 658-1967
Fax: (215) 473-6220

Rabbinical Assembly
United Synagogue of Conservative, Judaism, 1510 Chestnut Street 19102
Telephone: (215) 563-8814

Rabbinical Council of Greater Philadelphia
44 North 4th Street, Philadelphia 19106
Telephone: (215) 215-922-5446
Fax: (215) 215-922-1550
Supervision: (O)

Vaad Hakashruth and Beth Din of Philadelphia
1147 Gilham Street, Philadelphia 19111
Telephone: (215) 725-5181
Fax: (215) 725-5182
Supervision: (O)

LIBRARIES

Annenberg Research Institute
420 Walnut Street 19106
Telephone: (215) 238-1290

Philadelphia Jewish Archives Center
Balch Institute for Ethnic Studies, 18 South 7th Street 19106
Telephone: (215) 925-8090

Reconstructionist Rabbinical College Library
Church Road and Greenwood Avenue, Wyncote 19095
Telephone: (215) 576-0800

Talmudical Yeshivah Library
6063 Dexel Road 19131
Telephone: (215) 477-1000
Fax: (215) 477-5065

Temple University
Paley Library, 13th Street and Berks Mall 19122
Telephone: (215) 787-8231

The Free Library of Philadelphia
Central Library, Logan Square 19103
Telephone: (215) 686-5392
Fax: (215) 563-3628
Web site: www.library.phila.gov

Tuttleman Library
Gratz College, Mandell Education Campus, 7605 Old York Road, Melrose Park 19027
Telephone: (215) 635-7300 ext. 169
Fax: (215) 635-7320
Email: libraryinfo@gratz.edu

University of Pennsylvania
Van Pelt Library, 3420 Walnut Street 19104
Telephone: (215) 898-7556

MEDIA

Newspapers

Jewish Exponent
Jewish Publishing Group, 2100 Arch Street, Philadelphia 19103
Telephone: (215) 832-0700
Fax: (215) 832-0786
Email: dalpher@jewishexponent.com

Jewish Post
P.O.Box 442, Yardley 19067
Telephone: (215) 321-3443

Jewish Times
Jewish Publishing Group, 103A Tomlinson Road, Huntingdon Valley 19006
Telephone: (215) 938-1177

Mir
P.O. Box 6162, Philadelphia 19115
Telephone: (215) 934-5512

Periodicals

Inside Magazine
Jewish Publishing Group, 2100 Arch Street 19103
Telephone: (215) 893-5797
Fax: (215) 546-3957
Email: rleiter@jewishexponent.com

Jewish Quarterly Review
420 Walnut Street 19106
Telephone: (215) 238-1290
Email: jqroffice@sas.upenn.edu

Shofar Magazine
P.O. Box 51591 19115
Telephone: (215) 676-8304

Radio

Meridian
Telephone: (215) 962-8000

Radio & TV

Barry Reisman Show
Telephone: (215) 365-5600

Bucks County Jewish Life
Telephone: (215) 949-1490

Comcast Cablevision of Philadelphia
4400 Wayne Avenue 19140
Telephone: (215) 673-6600

Pulse
WSSJ, Camden
Telephone: (215) 365-5600

MEMORIAL

Monument to the Six Million Jewish Martyrs
16th Street and the Benjamin, Franklin Parkway 19103

MIKVAOT
Mikveh Association of Philadelphia (Ardmore)
Torah Academy, Wynnewood and Argyle Roads, Ardmore 19003
Telephone: (215) 642-8679

Mikveh association of Philadelphia (Northern)
7525 Loretto Avenue, Philadelphia 19111
Telephone: (215) 745-3334

MUSEUMS
Balch Institute for Ethnic Studies
18 South 7th Street 19106
Telephone: (215) 925-8090

Borowsky Gallery
Jewish Community Centers of Greater, Philadelphia, 401 South Broad Street 19147
Telephone: (215) 545-4400
Email: www.gershmany.org

Fred Wolf Jr Gallery
Jewish Community Centers of Greater, Philadelphia, 10100 Jamison Avenue 19116
Telephone: (215) 698-7300

Holocaust Awareness Museum
Gratz College, Mandell Education Campus, 7601 Old York Road, Melrose Park 19027
Telephone: (215) 635-6480

National Museum of American Jewish History
55 North 5th Street, Independence Mall East 19106-2197
Telephone: (215) 923-3811
Fax: (215) 923-0763
Email: nmajh@nmajh.org
Web site: www.nmajh.org

Philadelphia Congregation Rodeph Shalom
615 North Broad Street 19123
Telephone: (215) 627-6747

Rosenbach Museum & Library
2010 Delancey Place 19103
Telephone: (215) 732-1600
Fax: (215) 545-7529
Email: info@rosenbach.org

Temple Judea Museum of Keneseth Israel
8339 Old York Road, Elkins Park, PA 19027
Telephone: (215) 887-2027; 887-8700
Fax: (215) 887-1070
Email: tjmuseum@aol.com

RESTAURANTS
Dairy
Cherry Street Chinese vegetarian
1010 Cherry Street 19107
Telephone: (215) 923-3663
Supervision: Rabbinical Assembly

Pizzerias
Holyland Pizza
8010 Castor Avenue
Telephone: (215) 725-7444

Shalom Pizza
7598a Haverford Avenue
Telephone: (215) 878-1500
Email: shalom2u@rcn.com

SYNAGOGUES
Center City Eruv Corporation
44 North 4th Street 19106
Telephone: (215) 215-922-5446
Fax: (215) 215-922-1550
Email: info@mikvehisrael.org
Web site: www.mikvehisrael.org

Conservative
Congregation Beth El
21 Penn Valley Road, Fallsington, Levittown 19054
Telephone: (215) 945-9500

Ohev Shalom
2 Chester Road, Wallingford 19086
Telephone: (215) 874-1465
Web site: www.uscj.org/delvlly/wallingford

Tiferet Bet Israel
1920 Skippack Pike, Blue Bell 19422
Telephone: (215) 275-8797

Orthodox
Young Israel of Elkins Park
7715 Montgomery Avenue, Elkins Park 19027
Telephone: (215) 635-3152
Email: host@yiep.org
Web site: www.yiep.org

Young Israel of Oxford Circle
6427 Large Street 19149
Telephone: (215) 215-743-2848

Young Israel of the Main Line
273 Montgomery Ave, Bala-Gynwyd 19004
Telephone: (215) 610-667-3255
Email: audveag@evols.com

Orthodox Sephardi
Congregation Mikveh Israel
44 North Fourth Street 19106
Telephone: (215) 216-922-5446
Fax: (215) 216-922-1550
Email: info@mikvehisrael.org
Web site: www.mikvehisrael.org

Reform
Congregation Rodeph
615 North Broad Street
Telephone: (215) 627-6747

Temple Shalom
Edgley Road, off Mill Creek Pkwy., Levittown 19057
Telephone: (215) 945-4154

THEATRE
Theatre Ariel/Habima Ariel
PO Box 0334, Merion Station 19066
Telephone: (215) 567-0670

TOURS OF JEWISH INTEREST
American Jewish Committee Historic Tour
117 South Seventeenth Street, Suite 1010
Telephone: (215) 665-2300
Fax: (215) 665-8737

PITTSBURGH
BAKERIES
Pastries Unlimited
2119 Murray Avenue 15217
Telephone: (412) 521-6323

BOOKSELLERS
Pinskers Judaica Center
2028 Murray Avenue 15217
Telephone: (412) 421-3033;1- 800-JUDAISM (1-800-583-2476)
Fax: (412) 421-6103
Email: info@judaism.com
Web site: www.judaism.com

COMMUNITY ORGANISATIONS
United Jewish Federation of Greater Pittsburgh
234 McKee Place 15213
Telephone: (412) 681-8000
Fax: (412) 681-3980
Email: enaveh@ujf.net
Web site: www.ujf.net

GROCERIES
Brauner's Emporium
2023 Murray Avenue 15217

MEDIA
Newspaper
Pittsburgh Jewish Chronicle
5600 Baum Blvd 15206
Telephone: (412) 687-1000
Fax: (412) 687-5119
Email: news@pittchron.com
Web site: www.pittchron.com

MIKVAOT
2326 Shady Avenue 15217
Telephone: (412) 422-8010

MUSEUMS
Holocaust Center of the United Jewish Federation of Greater Pittsburgh
5738 Darlington Road 15217
Telephone: (412) 421-1500
Fax: (412) 422-1996
Email: lhurwitz@ujf.net
Web site: www.ujfhc.net

RESTAURANTS
Meat
Greenberg's Kosher Poultry
2223 Murray Avenue 15217

Platters Restaurant
2020 Murray Avenue 15217
Telephone: (412) 422-3370

Prime Kosher
1916 Murray Avenue 15217
Telephone: (412) 421-1015

SYNAGOGUES
Conservative
Ahavath Achim
500 Chestnut St., Carnegie 15106
Telephone: (412) 279-1566

Beth El of South Hills
1900 Cochran Rd 15220
Telephone: (412) 561-1168

Beth Shalom
Beacon & Shady Avs 15217
Telephone: (412) 421-2288
Fax: (412) 421-5923
Web site: www.bethshalom-pgh-org

New Light
1700 Beechwood Blvd. 15217
Telephone: (412) 421-1017

Parkway Jewish Center
300 Princeton Dr. 15235
Telephone: (412) 412-823-4338
Fax: (412) 412-823-4338
Web site: http://members.aol.com/pghpjc

Tree of Life
Wilkins & Shady Avs 15217
Telephone: (412) 521-6788
Fax: (412) 521-7846
Email: tolpon@aol.com

Orthodox
B'nai Emunoh Congregation
4315 Murray Av. 15217
Telephone: (412) 521-1477
Fax: (412) 521-1762
Email: drmaimon@netzero.net

B'nai Zion
6404 Forbes Av. 15217
Telephone: (412) 521-1440

Beth Hamedrash Hagodol - Beth Jacob Congregation
1230 Colwell St. 15219
Telephone: (412) 471-4443
Fax: (412) 281-1965

Bohnei Yisroel
6401 Forbes Av. 15217
Telephone: (412) 521-6047

Kether Torah
5706 Bartlett St. 15217
Telephone: (412) 521-9992

Poale Zedeck
6318 Phillips Avenue 15217
Telephone: (412) 421-9786
Fax: (412) 421-3383
Email: mil313@aol.com
Web site: www.pzonline.com

Shaare Tefillah
5741 Bartlett St. 15217
Telephone: (412) 521-9911

Shaare Torah
2319 Murray Av. 15217
Telephone: (412) 421-8855

Torath Chaim
728 N. Negley Av. 15206
Telephone: (412) 362-7736; 362-0036
Email: joeberger1@juno.com

Young Israel of Greater Pittsburgh
5831 Bartlett Street 15217-1636
Telephone: (412) 421-7224

Reconstructionist
Dor Hadash
6401 Forbes Av. 15217

Reform
Rodef Shalom
4905 5th Av. 15213
Telephone: (412) 621-6566
Fax: (412) 621-5475
Email: herzog@rodefshalom.org

Temple David
4415 Northern Pike, Monroeville 15146

Temple Emanuel of South Hills
1250 Bower Hill Rd. 15243
Telephone: (412) 279-2600
Fax: (412) 279-7628

Temple Sinai
5505 Forbes Av. 15217
Telephone: (412) 421-9715

POTTSTOWN
SYNAGOGUES
Conservative
Congregation Mercy & Truth
575 N. Keim Street 19464
Telephone: (610) 326-1717

READING
COMMUNITY ORGANISATIONS
Jewish Federation
1700 City Line St 19604
Telephone: (610) 921-2766
Fax: (610) 921-2766
Email: sramati@epix.net

SYNAGOGUES
Conservative
Kesher Zion
Eckert & Perkiomen Streets 19602
Telephone: (610) 374-1763

Orthodox
Shomrei Habrith
2320 Hampden Blvd. 19604
Telephone: (610) 610-921-0881
Fax: (610) 610-685-3866
Email: lipsker@aol.com
Web site: www.l-chaim.org
Supervision: Rabbi Yosef Lipsker

Reform
Reform Congregation Oheb Sholom
555 Warwick Drive, Wyomissing 19610
Telephone: (610) 375-6034
Fax: (610) 375-6036
Email: office@ohebsholom.org
Web site: www.ohebsholom.org

SCRANTON
BUTCHERS
Blatt's Butcher Block
420 Prescott Avenue 18510
Telephone: (570) 342-3886
Fax: (570) 342-9711
Supervision: Rabbi Fine and Rabbi Herman of Scranton Rabbinate

COMMUNITY ORGANISATIONS
Jewish Federation of Northeastern Pennsylvania
601 Jefferson Avenue 18510
Telephone: (570) 961-2300
Fax: (570) 346-6147
Email: jfednepa@epix.net

MUSEUMS
Houdini Museum Tour and Magic Show
1433 N. Main 18508
Telephone: (570) 342-5555
Email: magicusa@microserve.net
Web site: www.houdini.org

SYNAGOGUES
Conservative
Temple Israel
Gibson Street & Monroe Avenue 18510
Telephone: (570) 342-0350
Fax: (570) 342-7250
Email: tiscran@epix.net

Orthodox
Beth Shalom
Clay Avenue at Vine Street 18510
Telephone: (570) 346-0502
Fax: (570) 346-8800
Email: bethshalom2@aol.com

Congregation Machzikeh Hadas
600 Monroe Avenue 18510
Telephone: (570) 570-342-6271

Ohev Zedek
1432 Mulberry Street 18510
Telephone: (570) 343-2717

Reform
Temple Hesed
Lake Scranton 18505
Telephone: (570) 344-7201

SHARON
SYNAGOGUES
Reform
Temple Beth Israel
840 Highland Road 16146
Telephone: (781) 346-4754
Fax: (781) 981-4424

WILKES-BARRE
COMMUNITY ORGANISATIONS
Jewish Federation of Greater Wilkes-Barre & Community Center
60 S. River Street
Telephone: (570) 822-4146
Fax: (570) 824-5966

SYNAGOGUES
Conservative
Temple Israel
236 S. River Street 18702
Telephone: (570) 824-8927

Orthodox
Ohav Zedek
242 S. Franklin Street 18701
Telephone: (570) 825-6619
Fax: (570) 825-6634
Email: info@ohavzedek.org

Reform
B'nai B'rith
408 Wyoming Street, Kingston 18704

WILLIAMSPORT
SYNAGOGUES
Conservative
Ohev Sholom
Cherry & Belmont Streets 17701
Telephone: (717) 322-4209

Reform
Beth Ha-Sholom
425 Center Street 17701
Telephone: (717) 323-7751

Rhode Island

BARRINGTON
SYNAGOGUES
Reform
Temple Habonim
165 New Meadow Road 02806
Telephone: (401) 245-6536

CRANSTON
SYNAGOGUES
Conservative
Temple Torat Yisrael
330 Park Avenue 02905
Telephone: 785-1800

Reform
Temple Sinai
30 Hagan Avenue 02920
Telephone: 942-8350

MIDDLETOWN
SYNAGOGUES
Conservative
Temple Shalom
223 Valley Road 02842
Telephone: (860) 846-9002
Fax: (860) 682-2417

NARRAGANSETT

SYNAGOGUES

Conservative
Congregation Beth David
Kingstown Road 02882
Telephone: (401) 846-9002

NEWPORT

HOTELS
Admiral Weaver Inn
28 Weaver Avenue 02840
Telephone: (401) 849-0051
Fax: (401) 847-5902
Email: olgat@gis.net
Web site: www.kosherbedandbreakfast.com

TOURS OF JEWISH INTEREST
Touro Synagogue
85 Touro Street 02840
Telephone: (401) 847-4794
Fax: (401) 847-8121

PROVIDENCE

COMMUNITY ORGANISATIONS
Jewish Federation of Rhode Island
130 Sessions Street 02906
Telephone: (401) 421-4111

Rhode Island Jewish Historical Association
Telephone: (401) 863-2805

KASHRUT INFORMATION
Brown University-RISD Hillel
80 Brown Street 02906
Telephone: (401) 863-2805
Fax: (401) 863-1591
Email: spf@brown.edu

Vaad Hakashrut
Telephone: (401) 621-9393
Fax: (401) 331-9393
Email: bethshalom1@juno.com

MEDIA
Periodical
L'Chaim
130 Sessions Street 02906
Telephone: (401) 421-4111

MIKVAOT
401 Elmgrove Avenue 02906
Telephone: (401) 751-0025

MUSEUMS
Rhode Island Holocaust Memorial Museum
401 Elmgrove Avenue 02906
Telephone: (401) 861-8800

SYNAGOGUES
Conservative
Temple Emanu-El
99 Taft Avenue 02906
Telephone: (401) 331-1616

Orthodox
Beth Sholom
275 Camp Avenue 02906
Telephone: (401) 621-9393
Fax: (401) 331-9393
Email: bethsholom1@hotmail.com

Congregation Sons of Jacob
24 Douglas Avenue 02908
Telephone: (401) 274-5260

Mishkon Tfiloh
203 Summit Avenue 02906
Telephone: (401) 521-1616

Shaare Zedek
688 Broad Street 02907
Telephone: (401) 751-4936

Reform
Beth El
70 Orchard Avenue 02906
Telephone: (401) 331-6070

WARWICK

SYNAGOGUES
Conservative
Temple Am David
40 Gardiner Street 02888
Telephone: (401) 463-7944

WESTERLY

SYNAGOGUES
Orthodox
Congregation Shaare Zedek
Union Street 02891
Telephone: (401) 596-4621

WOONSOCKET

SYNAGOGUES
Conservative
Congregation B'nai Israel
224 Prospect Street 02895
Telephone: (401) 762-3651
Fax: (401) 767-5243
Email: cbi_synagogue@juno.com
Web site: www.shalom-cbi.org

South Carolina

CHARLESTON

BAKERIES

Ashley Bakery
1662 Savannah Highway 29407
Telephone: (843) 763-4125

Cookie Bouquet
280 W. Coleman Road
Telephone: (843) 881-0110

COMMUNITY ORGANISATIONS

Jewish Federation and Community Center
1645 Raoul Wallenberg Blvd, PO Box 31298 29416
Telephone: (843) 571-6565
Fax: (843) 556-6206

DELICATESSEN

Nathan's Deli
1836 Ashley River Road 29407
Telephone: (843) 556-3354

SYNAGOGUES

Orthodox

Brith Sholom Beth Israel
182 Rutledge Avenue
Telephone: (843) 577-6599
Fax: (843) 577-6699
Email: sholomsc@aol.com
Web site: www.bs-bi.com

Reform

Beth Elohim
90 Hasell Street 29401
Telephone: (843) 843-723-1090
Fax: (843) 843-723-0537
Email: office@kkbe.org
Web site: www.kkbe.org

COLUMBIA

COMMUNITY ORGANISATIONS

Columbia Jewish Federation
4540 Trenholm Road, Cola 29206
Telephone: (803) 787-2023

DELICATESSEN

Groucho's
Five Points 29205

SYNAGOGUES

Conservative

Beth Shalom
5827 North Trenholm Road 29206
Telephone: (803) 782-2500
Fax: (803) 782-5420
Email: bethshalom@bellsouth.net
Web site:
www.midnet.sc.edu/beth_shalom/index.htm

Reform

Tree of Life
6719 Trenholm Road 29206
Telephone: (803) 787-2182
Fax: (803) 787-0309

GEORGETOWN

CEMETERIES

Old Cemetery

MYRTLE BEACH

RESTAURANTS

Jerusalem Kosher
1007 Withers Dr.
Telephone: (803) 946-6650

Jerusalem Kosher Restaurant
1007 Withers Drive
Telephone: (803) 946-6650

SYNAGOGUES

Conservative

Temple Emanuel
406 65th Ave N. 29577
Telephone: (803) 449-5552

Orthodox

Beth El
401 Highway 17 N., 56th Avenue 29577
Telephone: (803) 449-3140

Chabad Lubavitch
2803 N. Oak Street
Telephone: (803) 448-0035
Fax: (803) 626-6403

South Dakota

ABERDEEN

SYNAGOGUES

Conservative

Congregation B'nai Isaac
202 North Kline Street 57401
Telephone: (732) 225-7360
Email: beapre@iw.net

RAPID CITY

SYNAGOGUES

Reform

Synagogue of the Hills
417 N. 40th Street 57702
Telephone: (605) 348-0805
Email: bhshul@rapidnet.com

Tennessee

CHATTANOOGA

COMMUNITY ORGANISATIONS

Jewish Community Federation
5326 Lynnland Terrace 47311
Telephone: (423) 894-1317
Fax: (423) 894-1319

SYNAGOGUES

Conservative

B'nai Zion
114 McBrien Road 37411
Telephone: (423) 894-8900

Orthodox

Beth Sholom
20 Pisgah Avenue 37411
Telephone: (423) 894-0801

Reform

Mizpah Congregation
923 McCallie Avenue 37403
Telephone: (423) 423-237-9771
Fax: (423) 423-267-9773
Email: mizpah@mizpahcongregation.org

Siskin Museum of Religious Artifacts
1 Siskin Plaza 37403
Telephone: (423) 267-9771
Fax: (423) 634-1717

MEMPHIS

COMMUNITY ORGANISATIONS

Jewish Federation and Community Center
6560 Poplar Avenue 38138
Telephone: (901) 767-7100

DELICATESSEN

Kroger Kosher Deli
540 S. Mendenhall
Telephone: (901) 683-8846

Schnuck's Kosher Deli
799 Truse Parkway
Telephone: (901) 682-2989

KASHRUT INFORMATION

Vaad Hakehilloth of Memphis
Memphis Orthodox Jewish Community Council,
PO Box 41133 38104
Telephone: (901) 767-2263
Fax: (901) 761-3788

MIKVAOT

Anshei Sphard
120 E. Yates Rd.
Telephone: (901) 682-6302

Baron Hirsch Congregation
400 South Yates Road 38120
Telephone: (901) 901-683-7485
Fax: (901) 901-683-7499
Email: general@baronhirsch.org
Web site: www.baronhirsch.org

SYNAGOGUES

Orthodox

Anshei Sephard-Beth El Emeth
120 E.Yates Road N. 38117
Telephone: (901) 682-1611

Baron Hirsch Cong.
369 Winter Oak
Telephone: (901) 683-7485

Kesser Torah
531 S. Yates
Telephone: (901) 761-6060

Reform

Temple Israel
1376 E. Massey Road
Telephone: (901) 761-3130

NASHVILLE

COMMUNITY ORGANISATIONS

Jewish Federation of Nashville and Middle Tennessee
801 Percy Warner Blvd. 37205
Telephone: (615) 356-3242
Fax: (615) 352-0056

MIKVAOT

Sherith Israel
3600 West End Avenue 37205
Telephone: (615) 292-6614
Fax: (615) 463-8260
Email: SylvL@AOL.com

RESTAURANTS

Vegetarian

Grins
Schulman Centre, Corner of 25th Av. S. and
Vanderbilt Place
Supervision: Sherith Israel

SYNAGOGUES

Conservative

West End Synagogue
3814 West End Avenue 37205
Telephone: (615) 269-4592
Fax: (615) 269-4695
Email: office@westendsyn.org or
exec@westendsyn.org

Reform
The Temple
5015 Harding Road 37205
Telephone: (615) 352-7620
Fax: (615) 352-9365

OAK RIDGE
SYNAGOGUES

Conservative
Jewish Congregation of Oak Ridge
101 W. Madison Lane 37830
Telephone: (423) 482-3581

Texas
AMARILLO
SYNAGOGUES

Reform
Temple B'nai Israel
4316 Albert Street 79106
Telephone: (806) 352-7191

ARLINGTON
MEDIA

Newspaper
Texas Jewish Post
3120 South Freeway , Ft. Worth 76110
Telephone: (817) 927-2831
Fax: (817) 429-0840
Email: news@texasjewishpost.com

SYNAGOGUES

Reform
Congregation Beth Shalom
1210 Thannisch Drive 76011
Telephone: (817) 860-5448
Email: bethshalom.org

AUSTIN
COMMUNITY ORGANISATIONS
Jewish Federation and Community Center of Austin
7300 Hart Lane 78731
Telephone: (512) 331-1144
Fax: (512) 331-7059

SYNAGOGUES

Conservative
Agudas Achim
4300 Bull Creek Road 78731
Telephone: (512) 459-3287

Congregation Beth El
8902 Mesa Drive 78759
Telephone: (512) 346-1776
Fax: (512) 233-004
Email: difriedman@aol.com

Reform
Temple Beth Israel
3901 Shoal Creek Blvd. 78756
Telephone: (512) 454-6806

BAYTOWN
SYNAGOGUES

Unaffiliated
K'nesseth Israel
100 W. Sterling, PO Box 702 77522
Telephone: (281) 424-8765

BEAUMONT
SYNAGOGUES

Reform
Temple Emanuel
1120 Broadway 7740
Telephone: (409) 832-6131

CORPUS CHRISTI
SYNAGOGUES

Conservative
B'nai Israel
3434 Fort Worth Street 78411
Telephone: (361) 855-7308
Fax: (361) 855-7309
Email: CGDK@aol.com

Reform
Temple Beth El
4402 Saratoga Street 78413
Telephone: (361) 857-8181

DALLAS
COMMUNITY ORGANISATIONS
Jewish Federation of Greater Dallas
7800 Northaven Road 75230
Telephone: (214) 369-3313
Fax: (214) 369-8943
Email: contact@jfgd.org
Web site: www.jewishdallas.org

HOTELS
The Westin Galleria, Dallas
13340 Dallas Parkway
Telephone: (214) 934-9494
Fax: (214) 851-2869
Email: galas@westin.com

MIKVAOT
Mikvah Association
5640 McShan 75230
Telephone: (214) 776-0037

RELIGIOUS ORGANISATIONS
Dallas Area Torah Association (Kollel)
5840 Forest Lane 75230
Telephone: (214) 987-3282
Fax: (214) 987-1764
Email: data@datanet.org
Web site: www.datanet.org

SITE
Zaide Reuven's Esrog Farm
Telephone: (214) 931-5596
Fax: (214) 931-5476
Email: zrsesrog@aol.com
Web site: www.members.aol.com/arsesrog

SYNAGOGUES
Orthodox
Chabad of Dallas
7008 Forest Lane 75230
Telephone: (214) 361-8600
Fax: (214) 361-8680
Email: shull@airmail.net
Web site: www.chabadcenters.com/dallas

Ohr HaTorah
12800 Preston Road
Telephone: (214) 404-8980

Shaare Tefilla
6131 Churchill Way, off Preston Road 75230
Telephone: (214) 661-0127
Fax: (214) 661-0150
Email: shaaretefilla@juno.com

Reform
Temple Emanu-El
8500 Hillcrest Road 75230
Telephone: (214) 706-0000
Fax: (214) 706-0025
Web site: www.tedallas.org

Sephardi
Magen David Congregation
7314 Campbell Road, Dallas, Texas 75248
Telephone: (214) 386-7166

EL PASO
COMMUNITY ORGANISATIONS
Chabad House
6515 Westwind 79912
Telephone: (915) 584-8218
Web site: www.chabadelpaso.com

MUSEUMS
El Paso Holocaust Museum and Study Center
401 Wallenberg Drive 79912
Telephone: (915) 833-5656
Fax: (915) 833-9523
Email: epholo@flash.net
Web site: www.flash.net/~epholo.com

SYNAGOGUES
Conservative
B'nai Zion
805 Cherry Hill Lane 79912
Telephone: (915) 833-2222

Reform
Sinai
4408 N. Stanton Street 79902
Telephone: (915) 532-5959

HOUSTON
BAKERIES
Kroger's
S. Post Oak 77096
Telephone: (713) 721-7691
Supervision: Houston Kashruth Association

New York Bagel Shop
9724 Hillcroft 77096
Telephone: (713) 723-5879
Supervision: Houston Kashruth Association

Randall's Bakery
Supervision: Houston Kashruth Association

Three Brothers Bakery
4036 S. Braeswood 77025
Telephone: (713) 666-2551
Supervision: Houston Kashruth Association

BUTCHERS
Kroger's
S. Post Oak 77096
Telephone: (713) 721-7691
Supervision: Houston Kashruth Association

COMMUNITY ORGANISATIONS
Jewish Federation of Greater Houston
5603 S. Braeswood Blvd. 77096
Telephone: (713) 729-7000
Fax: (713) 721-6232
Web site: www.houstonjewish.org

EMBASSY
Consul General of Israel
Suite 1500, 24 Greenway Plaza 77046

GROCERIES
Albertson's
S. Braeswood
Telephone: (713) 271-1180
Supervision: Houston Kashruth Association

KASHRUT INFORMATION
Houston Kashrut Association
9001 Greenwillow 77096
Telephone: (713) 723-3850
Fax: (713) 723-3852

TORCH - Torah & Outreach Resource Center of Houston
7000 Westview, Suite 121 77055
Telephone: (713) 721-6400
Fax: (713) 721-6900
Email: ypolatsek@torchweb.com
Web site: www.torchweb.com

MIKVAOT
Chabad Lubavitch Center
10900 Fondren Road 77096
Telephone: (713) 777-2000

United Orthodox Synagogues
4221 S. Braeswood Blvd., 77096
Telephone: (713) 723-3850

RESTAURANTS
Dairy
Saba's Mediterranean
9704 Fondren
Telephone: (713) 270-7222
Supervision: Houston Kashruth Association

Meat
Nosher's at the Jewish Community Centre
5601 S. Braeswood 77096
Telephone: (713) 729-3200
Supervision: Houston Kashruth Association

Vegetarian
Madras Pavilion
3910 Kirby Drive 77098
Telephone: (713) 521-2617
Supervision: Houston Kashruth Association

Wonderful Vegetarian Restaurant
7549 Westheimer 77063
Telephone: (713) 977-3137
Supervision: Houston Kashruth Association

SYNAGOGUES
Conservative
B'rith Shalom
4610 Bellaire Blvd. 77401
Telephone: (713) 667-9201

Beth Am
1431 Brittmore Rd. 77043
Telephone: (713) 461-7725
Fax: (713) 461-7773
Email: ebbe@earthlink.net
Web site: www.bethamtx.org

Beth Yeshurun
4525 Beechnut St. 77096
Telephone: (713) 666-1881
Fax: (713) 666-7767
Email: arthur@bethyeshurun.org
Web site: www.bethyeshurun.org

Congregation Shaar Hashalom
16020 El Camino Real 77062
Telephone: (713) 488-5861
Fax: (713) 488-3561
Email: stuartfederow@hotmail.com
Web site: www.shaarshalom.org

Orthodox
Chabad Lubavitch of Houston
10900 Fondren Road 77096
Telephone: (713) 777-2000

Congregation Beth Rambam
11333 Braesridge Blvd. 77071
Telephone: (713) 723-3030
Fax: (713) 726-8737
Email: gez@flash.net
Web site: www.flash.net/~bentzion/br.htm

United Orthodox Synogogues
9001 Greenwillow 77096
Telephone: (713) 723-3850
Web site: www.uosh.org

Young Israel of Houston
7823 Ludinton Road 77071
Telephone: (713) 729-0719
Web site: www.youngisraelofhouston.org

Reform
Beth Israel
5600 N. Braeswood Blvd. 77096
Telephone: (713) 771-6221
Fax: (713) 771-5705
Web site: www.Beth-Israel.org

Congregation Emanu El
1500 Sunset Blvd. 77005
Telephone: (713) 529-5771
Fax: (713) 529-0703
Email: emanuelhouston.org
Web site: www.emanuel.org

Congregation for Reform Judaism
801 Bering Dr. 77057
Telephone: (713) 782-4162
Fax: (713) 782-4167

Jewish Community North
5400 Fellowship Lane 77379
Telephone: (713) 376-0016
Fax: (713) 251-1033
Email: jcn@wt.net

Temple Sinai
783 Country Place Dr. 77079
Telephone: (713) 496-5950
Fax: (713) 496-1537

LUBBOCK
GROCERIES
Albertson's
Telephone: (806) 794-6761

Lowe's Supermarket
82nd & Slide Rd

SYNAGOGUES
Reform
Congregation Shaareth Israel
6928 3rd Street 79424
Telephone: (806) 794-7517

SAN ANTONIO
COMMUNITY ORGANISATIONS
Jewish Federation
8434 Ahern Drive 78216
Telephone: (210) 341-8234

DELICATESSEN
Delicious Food
7460 Callaghan Road 78229
Telephone: (210) 366-1844

MUSEUMS
Holocaust Memorial
12500 N W Military Highway 78231
Telephone: (210) 302-6807
Fax: (210) 408-2332
Email: cohenm@jfstx.org

SYNAGOGUES
Conservative
Agudas Achim
1201 Donaldson Avenue 78228
Telephone: (210) 734-4216

Orthodox
Rodfei Sholom
3003 Sholom Drive 78230
Telephone: (210) 493 3558
Fax: (210) 492 0629
Email: rodfei@world-net.net
Web site: www.ou.org

Reform
Beth El
211 Belknap Place 78212

WACO
SYNAGOGUES
Conservative
Agudath Jacob
4925 Hillcrest Drive 76710
Telephone: (254) 772-1451
Fax: (254) 772-2471
Email: Agudath@stonemedia.com
Web site: www.agudath-jacob.org

Reform
Rodef Sholom
1717 N. New Road 76707
Telephone: (254) 754-3703
Fax: (254) 754-5538

Utah

SALT LAKE CITY
COMMUNITY ORGANISATIONS
United Jewish Federation of Utah
2416 East, 1700 South 84108
Telephone: (801) 581-0102
Fax: (801) 581-1334

DELICATESSEN
Kosher on the Go
1575 S. 1100 East
Telephone: (801) 463-1786

SYNAGOGUES
Orthodox
Chabad Lubavitch of Utah
1433 South 1100 East 84105
Telephone: (801) 467-7777
Fax: (801) 486-7526
Email: chabadutah@aol.com
Web site: www.chabadutah.com

Reconstructionist
Chavurah B'yachad
Jubilee Center, 309 East 100 South 84111
Telephone: (801) 596-8996
Email: byachad@aol.com

Reform
Congregation Kol Ami
2425 E. Heritage Way 84109
Telephone: (801) 484-1501
Fax: (801) 484-1162
Email: clyon@conkolami.org
Web site: www.conkolami.org

Vermont

BURLINGTON
SYNAGOGUES
Conservative
Ohavi Zedek
188 N. Prospect Street 05401
Telephone: (718) 802-864-0218
Fax: (718) 802-864-0219
Email: office@ohavizedek.com
Web site: www.ohavizedek.com

Orthodox
Ahavath Gerim
cnr. Archibald & Hyde Streets 05401
Telephone: (718) 862-3001

Reform
Temple Sinai
500 Swift Street 05401
Telephone: (718) 862-5125

MONTPELIER
SYNAGOGUES
Congregation Beth Jacob
10 Harrison Avenue 05602
Telephone: (802) 229-9429

Virginia
ALEXANDRIA
SYNAGOGUES
Conservative
Agudas Achim
2908 Valley Drive 22302
Telephone: (318) 998-6460

Reform
Beth El Hebrew Congregation
3830 Seminary Road 22304
Telephone: (318) 370-9400
Fax: (318) 370-7730
Email: bethelhc@erols.com

ARLINGTON
SYNAGOGUES
Conservative
Congregation Etz Hayim
2920 Arlington Blvd. 22204
Telephone: (817) 703-979-4466
Fax: (817) 703-979-4468
Email: office@etzhayim.net
Web site: www.arfax.org

CHARLOTTESVILLE
SYNAGOGUES
The Hillel Jewish Center
The University of Virginia, 1824 University Circle
22903
Telephone: (804) 295-4963

Reform
Congregation Beth Israel
301 E. Jefferson Street 22902
Telephone: (804) 295-6382
Fax: (804) 296-6491
Email: office@cbicville.org
Web site: www.cbicville.org

DANVILLE
SYNAGOGUES
Reform
Temple Beth Sholom
Sutherlin Avenue
Telephone: (804) 792-3489

FAIRFAX
SYNAGOGUES
Conservative
Congregation Olam Tikvah
3800 Glenbrook Road 22031
Telephone: (703) 425-1880
Fax: (703) 425-0835

FALLS CHURCH
SYNAGOGUES
Reform
Temple Rodef Shalom
2100 Westmoreland Street 22043
Telephone: (703) 532-2217
Email: trsfcva@erols.com

HAMPTON
SYNAGOGUES
Conservative
Rodef Sholom
318 Whealton Road, Hampton 23666
Telephone: (757) 826-5894
Email: rabbirst@erols.com

Traditional
B'nai Israel
3116 Kecoughtan Road, Hampton 23661
Telephone: (757) 772-0100

NEWPORT NEWS
BAKERIES
Brenner's Warwick Bakery
240 31st Street, Newport News 23607
Supervision: Va'ad Hakashrut

COMMUNITY ORGANISATIONS
United Jewish Community of the Virginia Peninsula
2700 Spring Road, Newport News 23606
Telephone: (757) 930-1422

MIKVAOT
Adath Jeshurun
12646 Nettles Drive, Newport News 23606
Telephone: (757) 930-0820
Email: adathjeshurun@juno.com

SYNAGOGUES
Reform
Temple Sinai
11620 Warwick Blvd., Newport News 23601
Telephone: (757) 596-8352

NORFOLK
COMMUNITY ORGANISATIONS
United Jewish Federation of Tidewater
5029 Corporate Woods Drive, Suite 225, Virginia Beach 23462
Telephone: (757) 671-1600
Fax: (757) 671-7613

GROCERIES
The Kosher Place
738 W. 22nd Street
Telephone: (757) 623-1770
Fax: (757) 623-2237
Web site: www.kosherplacecafe.com
Supervision: Vaad Hakashrus of Tidewater

HOTELS
Sheraton Norfolk Waterside Hotel
777 Waterside Drive 23510
Telephone: (757) 622-6664
Supervision: Va'ad

KASHRUT INFORMATION
Vaad Hakashrus of Tidewater
PO Box 11082 23517
Telephone: (757) 627-7358
Fax: (757) 627-8544
Email: mostsky@hotmail.com
Web site: www.vaadoftidewater.com

MIKVAOT
B'nai Israel Congregation
420 Spotswood Avenue 23517
Telephone: (757) 627-7358
Fax: (757) 627-8544
Email: office@bnaiisrael.org
Web site: www.bnaiisrael.org

SYNAGOGUES
Conservative
Beth El
422 Shirley Av. 23517
Telephone: (757) 625-7821
Fax: (757) 627-4905
Email: office@bethelnorfolk.com

Temple Israel
7255 Granby St. 23505
Telephone: (757) 489-4550

Orthodox
B'nai Israel
402 Spotswood Avenue 23517
Telephone: (757) 627-7358

Reform
Ohef Sholom
Stockley Gdns at Raleigh Av. 23507
Telephone: (757) 625-4295

The Commodore Levy Chapel
Frazier Hall, Building C-7 (inside Gate 2), Norfolk US Navy Station
Telephone: (757) 444-7361
Fax: (757) 444-7362
Email: chaplain@nsn.cmar.navy.mil

RICHMOND
COMMUNITY ORGANISATIONS
Jewish Community Federation
5403 Monument Avenue 23226
Telephone: (804) 288-0045
Fax: (804) 282-7507
Email: www.jewishrichmond.org

HOTELS
The Farbreng-Inn Kosher Retreat Center
1800 SEE Virginia 23233
Telephone: (804) 740-2000/800-733-8474
Fax: (804) 750-1341
Email: info@chabadofva.org

MIKVAOT
Young Israel
4811 Patterson Avenue 23226
Telephone: (804) 353-3831
Fax: (804) 288-4381
Email: adere@juno.com

MUSEUMS
Beth Ahabah Museum & Archive
1117 W. Franklin Street 23220
Telephone: (804) 353 -0268

SYNAGOGUES
Conservative
Or Atid
501 Parham Road 23229
Telephone: (804) 740-4747

Orthodox
Keneseth Beth Israel
6300 Patterson Avenue 23226
Telephone: (804) 288-7953
Fax: (804) 673-9558
Email: kbi6300@erols.com

Young Israel of Richmond
4811 Patterson Avenue 23226
Telephone: (804) 353-5831
Email: yosefb@juno.com

Reform
Or Ami
9400 N. Huguenot Road 23235
Telephone: (804) 272-0017

VIRGINIA BEACH
MEDIA
Newspapers
Southeastern Virginia Jewish News
5029 Corporate Woods Drive, Suite 225 23462
Telephone: (757) 671-1600
Fax: (757) 671-7613
Email: news@ujft.org
Web site: www.jewishva.org

Periodical
**Southeastern Virginia Jewish News &
RENEWAL Magazine**
5041 Corporate Woods Drive #150 23462-4381
Telephone: (757) 757-671-1600
Fax: (757) 757-671-7613
Email: news@ujft.org
Web site: www.jewishva.org

SYNAGOGUES
Conservative
Kempsville Conservative
952 Indian Lakes Blvd. 23464
Telephone: (757) 495-8510
Web site: www.uscj.org/seabd/virginiabeach/

Temple Emanuel
25th Street 23451
Telephone: (757) 428-2591

Orthodox
Chabad Lubavitch
533 Gleneagle Drive 23462
Telephone: (757) 499-0507

Reform
Beth Chaverim
3820 Stoneshore Road 23452-7965
Telephone: (757) 463-3226
Fax: (757) 463-1134
Email: bethchaverim@ddaccess.com

Washington
ABERDEEN
SYNAGOGUES
Conservative
Temple Beth Israel
1219 Spur Street 98520
Telephone: (732) 533-3784

MERCER ISLAND
COMMUNITY ORGANISATIONS
**Stroum Jewish Community Center of Greater
Seattle**
Mercer Island Facility, 3801 E. Mercer Way 98040
Telephone: (206) 232-7115
Fax: (206) 232-7119
Email: info@sjcc.org
Web site: www.sjcc.org

OLYMPIA
SYNAGOGUES
Progressive
Temple Beth Hatfiloh
802 South Jefferson, SE 98057
Telephone: (206) 754-8519

SEATTLE
BAKERIES
Bagel Deli
340 15th Ave. E.
Telephone: (206) 322-2471

COMMUNITY ORGANISATIONS
Jewish Federation of Greater Seattle
2031 3rd Avenue 98121
Telephone: (206) 443-5400

**Stroum Jewish Community Center of Greater
Seattle**
Northend Facility, 8606 35th Avenue NE 98115
Telephone: (206) 526-8073
Fax: (206) 526-9958
Email: NeReception@sjcc.org
Web site: www.sjcc.org

Washington Association of Jewish Communities
2031 3rd Avenue 98121

JEWISH STUDENT CENTRE
Hillel, Foundation for Jewish Campus Life at the University of Washington
4745 17th Av. N.E. 98105
Telephone: (206) 527-1997
Fax: (206) 527-1999
Email: mail@hilleluw.org
Web site: www.hilleluw.org

KASHRUT INFORMATION
Va'ad HaRabanim of Greater Seattle
5305 S. 52nd Ave S, Suite 102 98118-2502
Telephone: (206) 760-0805
Fax: (206) 725-0347
Email: vaad@w-link.net
Web site: www.seattlevaad.org

MEDIA
Periodicals
The Jewish Transcript
2031 3rd Avenue 98121
Telephone: (206) 441-4553
Fax: (206) 441-2736
Email: jewishtran@aol.com

MUSEUMS
Community Center
3801 E. Mercer Way, Mercer Island 98040
Telephone: (206) 232-7115

RESTAURANTS
Dairy
Leah's Deli
65 St. between 21st and 22nd
Telephone: (206) 524-3870

Panini Grill
2118 NE 65 St.
Telephone: (206) 522-2730

Vegetarian
Bamboo Garden
364 Roy Street, near Seattle Center 98109
Telephone: (206) 282-6616
Fax: (206) 284-2775
Email: bamboogarden@aol.com
Web site: www.bamboogarden.net
Supervision: Va'ad HaRabanim of Greater Seattle

Teapot Vegetarian House
125 E. 15th Ave
Telephone: (206) 325-1010

SPOKANE
COMMUNITY ORGANISATIONS
Jewish Community Council
North 221 Wall, Suite 500, Spokane 99201
Telephone: (509) 838-4261

SYNAGOGUES
Conservative
Temple Beth Shalom
1322, 30th Street 99203
Telephone: (509) 747-3304

West Virginia
CHARLESTON
SYNAGOGUES
Reform
Temple B'nai Israel
2312 Kanawha Boulevard 25311
Telephone: (843) 342-5852

Traditional
Congregation B'nai Jacob
1599 Virginia Street East 25311
Telephone: (843) 304-346-4722
Fax: (843) 304-344-4167
Email: wvrabbi@chater.net
Web site: www.bnaijacob.com

HUNTINGTON
SYNAGOGUES
Conservative & Reform
B'nai Sholom
949 10th Avenue 25701
Telephone: (304) 522-2980

Wisconsin
MADISON
COMMUNITY ORGANISATIONS
Madison Jewish Community Council
6434 Enterprise Lane 53179
Telephone: (608) 278-1808
Fax: (608) 278-7814
Email: mjcc@mjcc.net
Web site: www.jewishmadison.org

SYNAGOGUES
Conservative
Beth Israel Center
1406 Mound Street 53711
Telephone: (608) 256-7763
Fax: (608) 256-9434
Email: office@bethisraelcenter.org
Web site: www.bethisraelcenter.org

Orthodox
Chabad House
1722 Regent Street 53705
Telephone: (608) 231-3450
Fax: (608) 231-3790

Reform
Beth El
2702 Arbor Drive 53711
Telephone: (608) 238-3123

MILWAUKEE
COMMUNITY ORGANISATIONS
Coalition for Jewish Learning
6401 North Santa Monica Boulevard 53217
Telephone: (414) 962-8860
Fax: (414) 962-8852

MEDIA
Directory
Milkwaukee Jewish Federation
1360 N. Prospect Avenue 53202
Telephone: (414) 271-2992

Newspapers
Wisconsin Jewish Chronicle
1360 N. Prospect Avenue 53202
Telephone: (414) 390-5888
Fax: (414) 271-0487
Email: milwaukeej@aol.com

RESTAURANTS
Meat
Kosher Meat Klub
4731 West Burleigh 53210
Telephone: (414) 449-5980
Fax: (414) 449-5985

SYNAGOGUES
Orthodox
Agudas Achim Chabad
2233 West Mequon Road, Mequon 53092
Telephone: (414) 242-2235
Fax: (414) 242-2268
Email: chabadmequon@aol.com
Web site: www.chabadmequon.org

Beth Jehudah
3100 North 52nd Street 53216
Telephone: (414) 442-5730
Fax: (414) 442-6171
Email: bethjehudah@juno.com
Web site: www.bethjehudah.org

Congregation Anshai Leibowitz
2415 West Mequon Road 53092
Telephone: (414) 512-1195
Fax: (414) 512-1695

SHEBOYGAN
SYNAGOGUES
Traditional
Temple Beth El
1007 North Avenue 53083
Telephone: (920) 452-5828
Email: bethelsheboygan@juno.com

Wyoming

CASPER
SYNAGOGUES
Reform
4105 S. Poplar, PO Box 3534 82602
Telephone: (307) 237-2330

CHEYENNE
SYNAGOGUES
Conservative
Mount Sinai
2610 Pioneer Avenue 82001
Telephone: (307) 634-3052

LARAMIE
SYNAGOGUES
Reform
Laramie JCC
PO Box 202 82073
Telephone: (307) 760-9275
Email: www.uahc.org/wy/wy001

URUGUAY

After the Conversos in the sixteenth century, there was no known Jewish community in Uruguay until the late nineteenth century, when the country served as a stopover on the way to Argentina. The Jewish population rose in the twentieth century, with immigration from the Middle East and eastern Europe. A synagogue was opened by 1917. Despite restrictive immigration laws imposed against European Jews fleeing Nazism, 2,500 Jews managed to enter the country between 1939 and 1940. Further Jewish immigration followed, from Hungary and the Middle East, in the post-war period.

There are many Jewish organisations functioning in Urugauy, including Zionist and women's organisations. Kosher restaurants exist in Jewish institutions, and there are a number of synagogues.

GMT -3 hours
Country calling code: **(+598)**
Total population: **3,221,000**
Jewish population: **25,000**
Emergency telephone: **(Police – 999) (Fire – 999) (Ambulance – 999)**
Electricity voltage: **(Electricity voltage – 220)**

MONTEVIDEO
With approximately 10,000 families in the capital of Uruguay, Montevideo contains almost all of the country's Jewish community. There is a Museum of the Holocaust in Montevideo, and near the Teatro Solis opera house stands a Golda Meir monument. An Albert Einstein monument can be found in Rodo Park.

COMMUNITY ORGANISATIONS
Centro Lubavitch
Av. Brasil 2704, CP 11300
Telephone: (2) 709-3444; 708-5169
Fax: (2) 711-3696
Email: shemtov@chasque.apc.org

Comite Central Israelita Del Uruguay
Rio Negro 1308, P. 5 11100
Telephone: (2) 903-0464
Fax: (2) 900-6562
Email: cciu@adinet.com.uy

EMBASSY
Embassy of Israel
Bulevar Artigas 1585-89
Telephone: (2) 400-4164
Fax: (2) 409-5821
Email: emisuyur@adlnet.com.uy

GROCERIES
Yavne
Cavia 2800
Telephone: (2) 908-7869
Fax: (2) 707-0866

MEDIA
Newspaper
Semanario Hebreo
Soriano 875/201
Telephone: (2) 925-311
Spanish-language weekly. Editor also directs daily Yiddish radio programme.

MIKVAOT
Adat Yiereim
Durazno 1183
Telephone: (2) 711-1686
Fax: (2) 711-7736

MUSEUMS
Centro Recordatorio del Holocausto
Canelones 1084, P.3 11100
Telephone: (2) 902-5750
Fax: (2) 902-5740
Email: centroshoa@conectate.com.uy
First Museum of the Shoah in South America

RESTAURANTS
Kasherissimo
Camacua 623
Telephone: (2) 915-0128
Fax: (2) 208-1536
Supervision: Chief Rabbi Yosef Bitton
The restaurant is situated in the Hebraica Macabi building.

Dairy
Best Western Armon Suites
2885 21st September Rd

SYNAGOGUES
Comunidad Israelita Hungara
Durazno 972
Telephone: (2) 900-8456
Fax: (2) 900-8456

Social Isralite Adat Yeshurun
Alarcon 1396

Ashkenazi
Comunidad Israelita de Uruguay
Canelones 1084, Piso 1
Telephone: (2) 902-5750
Fax: (2) 902-5740
Email: kehila@adinet.com.uy

Conservative
Nueva Congregacion Israelita
Wilson Ferreira Aldunate 1168
Telephone: (2) 902-6620
Fax: (2) 902-0589
Email: nci@adinet.com.uy

Orthodox
Vaad Ha'ir
Canelones 828
Telephone: (2) 900-6106
Fax: (2) 711-7736
Email: marebis@com.uy

Sephardi
Comunidad Israelita Sefardi
Buenos Aires 234, 21 de Setiembre 3111
Telephone: (2) 710-179

Templo Sefardi
de Pocitos L. Franzini 888

TOURIST SITES
Memorial to Golda Meir
Reconquista y Ciudadela
Email: cciu@adinet.com.uy

UZBEKISTAN

The ancient Jewish community in this central Asian republic is believed to have originated from Persian exiles in the fifth century. The Jews were subject to harsh treatment under the various rulers of the region, but still managed to become important traders in this area, which straddled the route between Europe and China and the Far East. In the late Middle Ages Jewish weavers and dyers were asked to help in the local cloth industry, and Bukhara became a key Jewish city after it became the capital of the country in the 1500s. Once the area had been incorporated into the Russian Empire in 1868, many Jews from the west of the Empire moved into Uzbekistan. A further influx occurred when Uzbekistan was used to shelter Jews during the Nazi invasion of the Soviet Union – many subsequently set up home there.

The original Bukharan Jews are generally more religious than the Ashkenazim who entered the area in the nineteenth and twentieth centuries. There are Jewish schools in the area, and although there is no central Jewish organisation, there are many Jewish bodies operating on separate levels for the Ashkenazim and the Bukharans.

GMT +5 hours
Country calling code: **(+7)**
Total population: **21.206,000**
Jewish population: **15,000**
Emergency telephone: **(Police – 03) (Fire – 03) (Ambulance – 03)**
Electricity voltage: **(Electricity voltage – 220)**

ANDIZHAN
SYNAGOGUES
7 Sovetskaya Street

BUKHARA
SYNAGOGUES
20 Tsentralnaya Street

KATTA-KURGAN
SYNAGOGUES
1 Karl Marx Alley

KERMINE
SYNAGOGUES
36 Narimanov Street

KOKAND
SYNAGOGUES
Dekabristov Street, Fergan Oblast

MARGELAN
SYNAGOGUES
Turtkilskaya Street, Fergan Oblast

NAVOY
SYNAGOGUES
36 Narimanov Street

SAMARKAND
3,000 Jews live in Samarkand. Many are Bukharan, and live in the special mahala, the quarter designated to Jews.

SYNAGOGUES
18 Esayva Street

TASHKENT

EMBASSY
Embassy of Israel
16A Shakhrisabz Street, 5th floor
Telephone: (71) 152911
Fax: (71) 1521378
Email: isremb@online.ru

SYNAGOGUES
Gorbunova Street 62
Telephone: (71) 1525978
Fax: (71) 1525978
Email: jewish@bcc.com.uz
Web site: www.jewish.uz
9 Chkalov Street

Ashkenazi
77 Chempianov Street

Sephardi
3 Sagban Street
Telephone: (71) 40-0768

VENEZUELA

Settlement in Venezuela began in the early nineteenth century from the Caribbean. The Jews were granted freedom early (between 1819 and 1821), which encouraged more settlement. The community at that time was not religious. At the beginning of the twentieth century, some Middle Eastern Jewish immigrants organised a central committee for the first time. The powerful influence of the Catholic Church meant few Jews were accepted as immigrants in the pre-war rush to escape Nazi Europe.

After the war, however, the community began to expand, with arrivals from Hungary and the Middle East. The successful oil industry and the excellent Jewish education system attracted immigrants from other South American countries.

Today most Jews live in Caracas, the capital. Fifteen synagogues serve the country. The Lubavitch movement is present and maintains a yeshivah. Caracas has a Jewish bookshop and a weekly Jewish newspaper. Venezuela has an expanding Jewish community, in contrast to many of its South American neighbours. The oldest Jewish cemetery in South America, in Coro, with tombstones dating from 1832, is still in use today.

GMT -4 hours
Country calling code: (+58)
Total population: 22,777,000
Jewish population: 22,000
Emergency telephone: (Ambulance – 545 4545) (Dr. – 02 483 7021)
Electricity voltage: (Electricity voltage – 220)

CARACAS

The first real Jewish settlement in the city dates from 1880 only although there is mention of them being in the territory in the early 18th century. The present community is basically Sephardi.

BAKERIES
Le Notre
Avenida Andres Bello
Telephone: (2) 782-4448

Pasteleria Kasher
Avenida Los Proceres
Telephone: (2) 515-086

BOOKSELLERS
Libreria Cultural Maimonides
Av Altamira Edif. Carlitos PB, (near Av. Galapen), San Bernardino
Telephone: (2) 551-6356
Fax: (2) 552-9127
Email: judaico@tecel.net.ve

CONTACT INFORMATION
Chabad-Lubavitch Centre
Apartado 5454 1010A
Telephone: (2) 523-887

DELICATESSEN
La Belle Delicatesses
Av. Bogotá, Edif Santa María, Local 2, Los Caobos
Telephone: (2) 781-7204
Fax: (2) 781-7182
Kosher delicatessen and mini-market, restaurant and take-away.

EMBASSY
Embassy of Israel
Avenida Francisco de Miranda, Centro Empresarial Miranda, 4 Piso Oficina 4-D, Apartado Postal Los Ruices 70081
Telephone: (2) 239-4511; 239-4921
Fax: (2) 239-4320

GROCERIES
Mini Market
Avenida Los Caobas
Telephone: (2) 781-7204
Take-away.

MEDIA
Newspaper
Nuevo Mundo Israelita
Av Marques del Toro 9, Los Caobos

MIKVAOT
Shomrei Shabbat Association Synagogue
Av Anauco, San Bernardino
Telephone: (2) 517-197

Union Israelita de Caracas Synagogue & Community Centre
Av Marques del Toro 9, San Bernardino
Telephone: (2) 552-8222
Fax: (2) 552-7628
Email: rabino@brener@eldish.net

SYNAGOGUES
Ashkenazi
Great Synagogue of Caracas
Av Francisco Javier Ustariz, San Bernardino
Telephone: (2) 511-869

Shomrei Shabbat Assoc. Synagogue
Av Anauco, San Bernardino
Telephone: (2) 517-197

Union Israelita de Caracas Synagogue & Community Centre
Av Marques del Toro 9, San Bernardino
Telephone: (2) 552-8222
Fax: (2) 552-7628
Email: rabino@brener@eldish.net
If notified in advance, they can arrange kosher lunches. There is also a meat snack bar open in the evening.

Sephardi
Bet El
Av Cajigal, San Bernardino
Telephone: (2) 522-008

Keter Tora
Av Lopez Mendez, San Bernardino

Shaare Shalom
Av Bogota, Quinta Julieta, Los Caobos

Tiferet Yisrael
Av Mariperez, Los Caobos
Telephone: (2) 781-1942

MARACAIBO
COMMUNITY ORGANISATIONS
Associación Israelita de Maracaibo
Calle 74 No 13-26
Telephone: (61) 70333

PORLAMAR
SYNAGOGUES
Or Meir
Calle Carnevali, Margarita Island
Telephone: (95) 634-433
Mikva on premises.

VIRGIN ISLANDS (USA)

Jews first began to settle on the island in 1655, taking advantage of liberal Danish rule. They were mainly traders in sugar cane, rum and molasses, and by 1796 a synagogue had been founded. The Jewish population of 400 in 1850 made up half of the islands' white community. There have been three Jewish governors; one being Gabriel Milan, the first governor who was appointed by King Christian of Denmark.

The community began to shrink after the Panama Canal was opened in 1914, and by 1942 only 50 Jews remained. Since 1945, the community has expanded again, with families arriving from the US mainland.

GMT -4 hours
Country calling code: **(+1 340)**
Total population: **115,000**
Jewish population: **300**
Emergency telephone:

ST THOMAS
SYNAGOGUES
Hebrew Congregation of St. Thomas
PO Box 266 00804-0266
Telephone: (340) 774-4312
Fax: (340) 774-3249
Email: hebrewcong@islands.vi
Web site: www.onepaper.com/synagogue
This synagogue built in 1833, was restored in 2000. Services are held on Fridays at 6.30pm and Saturday at 10.30am. Open to visitors: Monday to Friday 9am to 4pm.

YUGOSLAVIA

(Yugoslavia at present comprises Serbia and Montenegro.) The history of Serbian Jewry is both long and comparatively happy, with initial settlement occurring in Roman times. Afte the onset of Turkish domination in 1389, the community continued to thrive and also prospered under Austrian rule in the eighteenth century. The nineteenth century saw some measures being taken against the Jews after Serbia became independent, but these were quickly redressed in 1889, following the Treaty of Berlin.

After 1918, Serbia was united with Croatia, Slovenia and the other south Slavic states into one country, known as Yugoslavia. The community suffered heavily under Nazi domination. The Jews were active among the Yugoslav partisans and, after liberation, many who had hidden or fought with the partisans began to return to their homes. Before the break-up of Yugoslavia, the Jews were allowed contact with other communities, including Israel. Since the civil war, some Jews have remained in the country, and there is a synagogue and a Talmud Torah school in Belgrade.

GMT +1 hour
Country calling code: (+381)
Total population: **10,597,000**
Jewish population: **2,500**
Emergency telephone: (**Police – 92**) (**Fire – 93**) (**Ambulance – 94**)
Electricity voltage: (**Electricity voltage – 220**)

BELGRADE

Some 2,000 Jews now live in the capital of Serbia, compared with hardly any during the latter stages of World War Two. There is an Ashkenazi synagogue which follows Sephardi tradition (or nusach), and there is a community centre, although kosher food is not available.

COMMUNITY ORGANISATIONS
Federation of Jewish Communities
7 Kralja Petra Street 71a/111, PO Box 841 11001
Telephone: (11) 624-359/621-837
Fax: (11) 626-674
Email: savezjev@infosky.net

MUSEUMS
Jewish Historical Museum
Kralja Petra Street 71a/1 11001
Telephone: (11) 622-634
Fax: (11) 626-674
Email: muzej@eunet.yu
Web site: www.jim-bg.org
Open daily from 10.00 to 12.00.

SYNAGOGUES
Birjuzova Street 19
Services are held Friday evenings and Jewish holidays.

TOURIST SITES
Jewish Cemetery
There are monuments here to fallen fighters and martyrs of Fascism, fallen Jewish soldiers in the Serbian army in the First World War. In 1990 a new monument to Jews killed in Serbia was erected by the Danube, in the pre-War Jewish quarter Dorcol.

NOVI SAD

COMMUNITY ORGANISATIONS
Community Offices
Jevrejska 11
Telephone: (21) 613-882

TOURIST SITES
Jewish Cemetery
There is a monument to the Jews who fell in the War and the victims of Fascism. The synagogue here is no longer open but it's reported to be extremely beautiful, and is currently being converted to a concert hall.

SUBOTICA

COMMUNITY ORGANISATIONS
Community Offices
Dimitrija Tucovica Street 13
Telephone: 28483

TOURIST SITES
The Subotica Synagogue built in 1901 and considered one of the finest Art Nouveau buildings in Europe is currently being restored.

ZAMBIA

The Jewish community began in the early twentieth century, with cattle ranching being the main attraction for Jewish immigrants. The community grew, and the copper industry was developed largely by Jewish entrepreneurs. With refugees from Nazism and a post-war economic boom, the Jewish community in the mid-1950s totalled 1,200. The community declined after independence in 1964.

Today, the Council for Zambian Jewry (founded in 1978) fulfils the role of the community's central body.

GMT +2 hours
Country calling code: **(+260)**
Total population: **9,715,000**
Jewish population: **Under 100**
Emergency telephone: **(Police – 999) (Fire – 999) (Ambulance – 999)**
Electricity voltage: **(Electricity voltage – 220)**

LUSAKA
COMMUNITY ORGANISATIONS
Council for Zambian Jewry
P O Box 30089 10101
Telephone: (1) 229-556
Fax: (1) 223-798
Email: galaun@zamnet.zm

SYNAGOGUES
Lusaka Hebrew Congregation
Chachacha Road, POB 30020
Telephone: (1) 229-190
Fax: (1) 221-428
Email: galaun@zamnet.zm

ZIMBABWE

Jews were among the earliest pioneers in Zimbabwe (formerly Rhodesia). The first white child born there (April 1894) was Jewish. The first synagogue in Zimbabwe (formerly Rhodesia) was set up in 1894, in a tent in Bulawayo. In 1897 a Jew was elected as the first mayor of Bulawayo. The first Jews came from Europe (especially Lithuania), and they became involved in trade and managing hotels. They were joined in the 1920s and 1930s by Sephardis from Rhodes. Some senior politicians in the country were Jewish, including one prime minister.

The 1970s saw the turbulent transition to Zimbabwe and many Jews emigrated to escape the unrest. The community is now mainly Ashkenazi, with an important Sephardi component. Harare has both an Ashkenazi and a Sephardi synagogue; Bulawayo has a Ashkenazi synagogue. There are community centres in both the towns, and schools, although the latter have many local, non-Jewish pupils.

GMT +2 hours
Country calling code: **(+263)**
Total population: **12,294,000**
Jewish population: **900**
Emergency telephone: **(Police – 999) (Fire – 999) (Ambulance – 999)**
Electricity voltage: **(Electricity voltage – 220/240)**

BULAWAYO
SYNAGOGUES
Bulawayo Hebrew Congregation
Jason Moyo Street, PO Box 337
Telephone: (9) 237-335

HARARE
COMMUNITY ORGANISATIONS
Zimbabwe Jewish Board of Deputies
PO Box 1954
Telephone: (4) 702-507
Fax: (4) 702-506
Email: cazo@zol.co.zw
Hours of opening 8.30 am. to 12 noon

SYNAGOGUES
Harare Hebrew Congregation
Milton Park Jewish Centre, Lezard Avenue, PO Box 342
Telephone: (4) 727-576

Sephardi Congregation
54 Josiah Chinamano Avenue, PO Box 1051
Telephone: (4) 722-899

International Access Dialling Codes

In order to phone from one country to another one must use the appropriate International Access Dialling Code.

Most International Access Dialling Codes are 00. The following however are the exceptions.

Australia	0011
Bahamas	11
Belarus	810
Canada	011
Colombia	9
Finland	varies
Hong Kong	1
Israel	varies
Japan	varies
Lithuania	810
Mexico	98
Russia	810
Singapore	1
South Africa	09
South Korea	varies
Taiwan	2
Thailand	1
Ukraine	810
United States of America	011
Uzbekistan	810
Yugoslavia	99

The procedure is as follows:

FIRST dial the International Access Code for the country you are calling from (as shown above).

SECOND dial the country calling code (as shown on the appropriate page of this guide) for the country you are dialling to.

THIRD dial the area code for the location you are dialling to (some countries do not require an area code).

FOURTH dial the local phone number.

Kosher Fish in Europe

CYPRUS

Antzouva (Anchovy)
Bacceliaos (Cod)
Barbouni (Pike)
Cephalos (Perch)
Glossa (Sole)
Lavraki (Bass)
Sardella (Pilchard)
Scoumbri (Mackerel)
Tonos (Tuna)
Tsipoura (Bream)

CZECH REPUBLIC

Ancovicka (Anchovy)
Belicka (Roach)
Kambala (Brill)
Kapr (Carp)
Lin (Tench)
Losos (Salmon)
Makrela (Mackerel)
Okoun (Perch)
Parmice (Mullet)
Platejs (Dab)
Platyz (Plaice)
Plotice (Sole)
Prazama (Bream)
Pstruh (Trout)
Sardinka (Sardine)
Sled (Herring)
Sprota (Sprat)
Stika (Pike)
Treska (Haddock)
Tunak (Tuna)

DENMARK

Aborre (Perch)
Ansjos (Anchovy)
Bars (Bass)
Brasen (Bream)
Brisling (Sprat)
Gedde (Pike)
Helleyflynder
 (Halibut)
Hvilling (Whiting)

Ising (Dab)
Karpe (Carp)
Knurhane (Gunard)
Kuller (Haddock)
Kulmule (Hake)
Laks (Salmon)
Lange (Ling)
Lubbe (Pollack)
Makrel (Mackerel)
Multe (Mullet)
Orred (Trout)
Rodspaette (Plaice)
Sardin (Sardine)
Sild (Herring)
Skalle (Roach)
Skrubbe (Flounder)
Slethvarre (Brill)
Suder (Tench)
Torsk (Cod)
Tun fisk (Tuna)
Tunge (Sole)

FRANCE

Aiglefin (Haddock)
Anchois (Anchovy)
Bar Commun (Bass)
Barbue (Brill)
Breme (Bream)
Brochet (Pike)
Cabillaud (Cod)
Carpe (Carp)
Carrelet (Plaice)
Daurade (Bream)
Epirlan (Smelt)
Flet (Flounder)
Fletan (Halibut)
Gardon (Roach)
Grondin (Gunard)
Hareng (Herring)
Lieu Jaune (Pollack)
Limande (Dab)
Lingue (Ling)
Maquereau
 (Mackerel)

Merlan (Whiting)
Merlu (Hake)
Mulet (Mullet)
Perche (Perch)
Pilchard (Pilchard)
Plie (Plaice)
Sardine (Sardine)
Saumon (Salmon)
Sole (Sole)
Sprat (Sprat)
Tanche (Tench)
Thon (Tuna)
Truite (Trout)

GERMANY

Barsch (Perch)
Brasse (Bream)
Flunder (Flounder)
Forelle (Trout)
Glattbutt (Brill)
Hecht (Pike)
Heilbutt (Halibut)
Hering (Herring)
Kabeljau (Cod)
Knurrhahn (Gunard)
Lachs (Salmon)
Leng (Ling)
Makrele (Mackerel)
Meerasche (Mullet)
Pilchard (Pilchard)
Plotze (Roach)
Pollack (Pollack)
Sardelle (Anchovy)
Sardine (Sardine)
Scharbe (Dab)
Schellfisch (Haddock)
Schlei (Tench)
Scholle (Plaice)
Seebarsch (Bass)
Seehecht (Hake)
Seezunge (Sole)
Sprotte (Sprat)
Thun (Tuna)
Weissfisch (Carp)

Wittling (Whiting)

GREECE

Antjuga (Anchovy)
Bakaliaros (Cod)
Chematida
 (Flounder)
Chromatida (Dab)
Gados (Haddock)
Giavros (Anchovy)
Glinia (Tench)
Glossa (Sole)
Glossaki (Plaice)
Hippoglossa (Halibut)
Kaponi (Gunard)
Kephalos (Mullet)
Kyprinos (Carp)
Lavraki (Bass)
Lestia (Bream)
Papalina (Sprat)
Pentiki (Ling)
Perca chani (Perch)
Pestropha (Trout)
Pissi (Brill)
Regha (Herring)
Romvos (Brill)
Sardella (Pilchard)
Sardine (Sardine)
Scoumbri (Mackerel)
Solomos (Salmon)
Tonnos (Tuna)
Tourna (Pike)
Tsironi (Roach)

ITALY

Acciuga (Anchovy)
Aringa (Herring)
Asinello (Haddock)
Brama (Bream)
Carpa (Carp)
Cefalo (Mullet)
Halibut (Halibut)
Limanda (Dab)
Luccio (Pike)

Maccerello (Mackerel)
Merlano (Whiting)
Merluzzo Bianco (Cod)
Merluzzo Giallo
  (Pollack)
Molva (Ling)
Nasello (Hake)
Passera (Plaice)
Passera Pianuzza
  (Flounder)
Pesce (Perch)
Pesce Capone
  (Gunard)
Rombo Liscio (Brill)
Salmone (Salmon)
Sardina (Sardine)
Sogliola (Sole)
Spigola (Bass)
Spratto (Sprat)
Tinca (Tench)
Tonno (Tuna)
Triotto (Roach)
Trota (Trout)

NETHERLANDS
Aaldoe (Mullet)
Ansjovis (Anchovy)
Baars (Perch)
Blankvoorn (Roach)
Bot (Flounder)
Brasem (Bream)
Forel (Trout)
Griet (Brill)
Harder (Mullet)
Haring (Herring)
Heek (Hake)
Helibot (Halibut)
Kabeljauw (Cod)
Karper (Carp)
Leng (Ling)
Makree (Mackerel)
Pelser (Sardine)
Poon (Gunard)
Salm (Salmon)
Sardien (Sardine)
Schar (Dab)

Schelvis (Haddock)
Schol (Plaice)
Snoek (Pike)
Sprot (Sprat)
Tong (Sole)
Tonijn (Tuna)
Wijting (Whiting)
Witte koolvis
  (Pollack)
Zeebaars (Bass)
Zeelt (Tench)

PORTUGAL
Alabote (Halibut)
Anchova (Anchovy)
Arenque (Herring)
Arinca (Haddock)
Atum (Tuna)
Bacalhau (Cod)
Badejo (Pollack)
Biqueirao (Anchovy)
Carpa (Carp)
Donzela (Ling)
Espadilha (Sprat)
Linguado (Sole)
Lucio (Pike)
Perca (Perch)
Pescada (Hake)
Petruca (Flounder)
Robalo (Bass)
Rodovalho (Brill)
Ruivaca (Roach)
Ruivo (Gunard)
Salmao (Salmon)
Sarda (Mackerel)
Sardinha (Sardine)
Sargo (Bream)
Solha (Plaice)
Solhao (Dab)
Tainha (Mullet)
Tenca (Tench)
Truta (Trout)

SPAIN
Abadejo (Pollack)
Anchoa (Anchovy)

Arenque (Herring)
Atun (Tuna)
Bacalao (Cod)
Bermejuela (Roach)
Boqueron (Anchovy)
Caballa (Mackerel)
Carpa (Carp)
Eglefino (Haddock)
Espadin (Sprat)
Halibut (Halibut)
Lenguado (Sole)
Limanda (Dab)
Lisa (Mullet)
Lubina (Bass)
Lucio (Pike)
Maruca (Ling)
Merlan (Whiting)
Merluza (Hake)
Perca (Perch)
Platija (Flounder)
Remol (Brill)
Rubios (Gunard)
Salmon (Salmon)
Sardina (Sardine)
Solla (Plaice)
Tenca (Tench)
Trucha (Trout)

TURKEY
Alabalik (Trout)
Bakalyaro (Whiting)
Berlam (Hake)
Caca (Sprat)
Civisiz kalkan (Brill)
Derepissi (Flounder)
Dil baligi (Sole)
Gelincik (Ling)
Hamsi (Anchovy)
Kadife baligi   (Tench)
Kefal (Mullet)
Kirlangic (Gunard)
Kizilgoz (Roach)
Levrek (Bass)
Morina (Cod)
Palatika (Sprat)
Pisi baligi (Dab)

Ringa (Herring)
Sardalya (Sardine)
Sardayalo (Pilchard)
Sazan (Carp)
Som baligi (Salmon)
Tahta baligi (Bream)
Tatlisu levregi (Perch)
Ton baligi (Tuna)
Turna baligi (Pike)
Uskumru (Mackerel)

UNITED KINGDOM
Anchovy
Barbel
Bass
Bloater
Bonito
Bream
Brill
Brisling
Buckling
Carp
Coalfish
Cod
Coley
Dab
Dace
Flounder
Fluke
Grayling
Gurnard
Haddock
Hake
Halibut
Herring
Hoki
John Dory
Keta Salmon
Kipper
Ling
Mackerel
Megrim
Mock Halibut
Mullet Grey
Mullet Red
Norway Haddock

Parrot Fish	Redfish	Smelt	Tilapia
Perch	Roach	Snapper	Trout
Pike	Saithe	Snoek	Tuna (Tunny)
Pilchard	Salmon	Sole Dover	Whitebait
Plaice	Sardine	Sole Lemon	Whiting
Pole	Shad	Sprat	Witch
Pollack	Sild	Tench	

Kosher Fish outside Europe

AUSTRALIA

Anchovy
Baramundi
Barracouta
Barracuda
Blue Eye
Blue Grenadier
Bream
Butterfly-fish
Cod
Coral Perch
Duckfish
Flathead
Flounder
Garfish
Groper
Gurnard
Haddock
Hake
Harpuka
Herring
Jewfish
John Dory
Lemon Sole
Mackerel
Morwong
Mullet
Murray Cod
Murray Perch
Orange Roughy
Perch

Pike
Pilchard
Red Emperor
Redfin
Salmon
Sardine
Sea Perch
Shad
Sild
Snapper
Tailor
Tasmanian Trumpeter
Terakiji
Trevally
Trout
Tuna:
   Albacore, Bluefin
    North bluefin
    South bluefin
    Skipjack (striped)
    Yellowfin
Whiting
Yellowtail

CANADA

Albacore
Anchovy
Bass
Boston Bluefish
Carp
Cisco

Cod
Flounder
Goldeye
Haddock
Hake
Halibut
Herring
Mackerel
Orange Roughy
Perch
Pickerel
Pike
Pollock
Pompano
Salmon
Sardine
Silverside
Smelt
Snapper
Sole
Sunfish
Tarpon
Trout
Tuna

CARIBBEAN

Bonito
Grouper
Kingsish
Mullet
Muttonfish

Pompano
Roballo
Smelt
Snapper Red/Yellow
Spanish Mackerel
Trout
Tuna

HONG KONG

Anchovy
Bigeyes
Carp
Crevalles
Croakers
Giant Perch
Grey Mullet
Grouper
Japanese Sea Perch
Leopard Coral Trout
Pampano
Pilchard
Red Sea Bream
Round Herring
Sardine
Scad
Whitefish

NEW ZEALAND

Hoki
John Dory
Kingfish

Mackerel
Mullet
Orange Roughy
Perch
Piper
Salmon
Smooth Black
Snapper
Sole
Southern Whiting
Terakihi
Trevally
Trout

SOUTH AFRICA

Albacore Tuna
Anchovies
Butterfish
Carp
Euthynnus Tuna
Haddock
Hake
Herring
Kabeljou
Kingklip
Maas Banker
Mackerel
Pilchards
Red Roman

Salmon
Sardines
Seventy Four
Skipjack Tuna
Snoek
Sole
Steembras
Stock Fish
Stump Nose
Tongol Tuna
Trout
Yellowfin Tuna

UNITED STATES OF AMERICA

Albacore
Alewife
Amberjack
Anchovies
Angelfish
Barb
Barracouta
Barracuda
Bass
Bigeyes
Black Cod
Blackfish
Blueback
Bluefish

Bluegill
Bonito
Bream
Brill
Capelin
Carp
Cero
Char
Chub
Cisco
Coalfish
Cod
Crevalle
Dab
Flounders
Fluke
Gag
Grayling
Grouper
Haddock
Hake
Halibut
Herrings
John Dory
Kingfish
Mackerel
Mahi Mahi
Merluccio
Mullet

Parrot Fish
Perch
Pike
Pilchard
Plaice
Pollock
Pomfrets
Red Snapper
Roach
Saithe
Salmon
Sardine
Shad
Sierra
Skipjack
Smelts
Snapper
Sole
Sprat
Tench
Tilapia
Trout
Tuna
Wahoo
Whitefish
Whiting
Yellowtail

Jewish Calendar

2004 (5764-5765)

Fast of Esther	Thursday	March 4th
Purim	Sunday	March 7th
First Day Pesach	Tuesday	April 6th
Second Day Pesach	Wednesday	April 7th
Seventh Day Pesach	Monday	April 12th
Eighth Day Pesach (Yizkor)	Tuesday	April 13th
Holocaust Memorial Day	Sunday	April 18th
Israel Independence Day	Monday	April 26th
Lag B'Omer	Sunday	May 9th
First Day Shavout	Wednesday	May 26th
Second Day Shavout (Yizkor)	Thursday	May 27th
Fast of Tammuz	Tuesday	July 6th
Fast of Av	Tuesday	July 27th
First Day Rosh Hashanah	Thursday	September 16th
Second Day Rosh Hashanah	Friday	September 17th
Fast of Gedaliah	Sunday	September 19th
Yom Kippur (Yizkor)	Saturday	September 25th
First Day Succot	Thursday	September 30th
Second Day Succot	Friday	October 1st
Shemini Atseret (Yizkor)	Thursday	October 7th
Simchat Torah	Friday	October 8th
First Day Chanukah	Wednesday	December 8th

2005 (5765-5766)

Fast of Esther	Thursday	March 24th
Purim	Friday	March 25th
First Day Pesach	Sunday	April 24th
Second Day Pesach	Monday	April 25th
Seventh Day Pesach	Saturday	April 30th
Eighth Day Pesach (Yizkor)	Sunday	May 1st
Israel Independence Day	Thursday	May 12th
Lag B'Omer	Friday	May 27th
Holocaust Memorial Day	Thursday	June 5th
First Day Shavout	Monday	June 13th
Second Day Shavout (Yizkor)	Tuesday	June 14th
Fast of Tammuz	Sunday	July 24th
Fast of Av	Sunday	August 14th
First Day Rosh Hashanah	Tuesday	October 4th
Second Day Rosh Hashanah	Wednesday	October 5th
Fast of Gedaliah	Thursday	October 6th
Yom Kippur (Yizkor)	Thursday	October 13th
First Day Succot	Tuesday	October 18th
Second Day Succot	Wednesday	October 19th
Shemini Atseret (Yizkor)	Tuesday	October 25th
Simchat Torah	Wednesday	October 26th
First Day Chanucah	Monday	December 26th

Index

Bern	198	Bremgarten / Aargau	198	Casale Monferrato	132
Bershad	206	Brest (Belarus)	20	Casper	375
Besancon	62	Brest (France)	66	Castro Valley	254
Bethesda	293	Bridgeport	268	Cavaillon	84
Bethlehem (NH)	312	Bridgeton	314	Cayman Islands	46
Bethlehem (PA)	355	Bridgetown	19	Cedar Rapids	287
Beverly	296	Brighton	297	Cedarhurst	330
Beverly Hills	261	Brighton and Hove	239	Celle	94
Beziers	83	Brisbane	9	Ceuta	192
Biel/Bienne	198	Bristol	208	Chalkis	103
Bielsko-Biala	166	Brno	54	Chalons-sur-Marne	63
Billings	311	Brockton	297	Chalon-sur-Saone	63
Binghamton	327	Bronx	336	Chambery	63
Birkirkara	147	Brookline	297	Champaign-Urbana	283
Birmingham (AL)	249	Brooklyn	336	Champigny	77
Birmingham (UK)	242	Brussels	23	Charleroi	24
Birobidjan	174	Bryansk	174	Charleston (SC)	365
Bischeim-Schiltigheim	66	Bucharest	171	Charleston (WV)	374
Bishkek	143	Budapest	106	Charlotte	349
Bismark	350	Buenos Aires	2	Charlottesville	371
Bitche	62	Buffalo	327	Chateauroux	67
Blackpool	216	Bukhara	377	Chatham	39
Blida	1	Bulawayo	381	Chattanooga	366
Bloemfontein	180	Bulgaria	33	Cheadle	233
Bloomington	285	Burbank	261	Chelles	77
Bobigny	76	Burgos	187	Chelmsford	299
Bobruisk	20	Burlingame	254	Cheltenham	213
Boca Raton	273	Burlington (MA)	298	Chernigov	206
Bogota	49	Burlington (NJ)	314	Chernovtsy	206
Bolivia	25	Burlington (VT)	370	Cherry Hill	314
Bologna	132	Bushey	214	Chevy Chase	293
Bondy	76	Bussum	158	Cheyenne	375
Bonita	254			Chicago	283
Bonn	94	**C**		Chigwell	212
Boras	194			Chile	46
Bordeaux	89	Caen	66	Chimkent	142
Borisov	20	Caesarea	116	China	47
Boskovice	54	Cairo	59	Chisinau	150
Bosnia-Hercegovina	26	Calgary	34	Chmelnitsy	206
Boston	296	Cali	50	Choisy-le-Roi	77
Botosani	171	Caluire- et- Cuire	83	Christchurch	160
Boulay	62	Cambridge (MA)	298	Chula Vista	254
Boulder	266	Cambridge (UK)	209	Cincinnati	351
Boulogne sur Seine	76	Campinas	30	Cinnaminson	315
Boulogne-sur-Mer	63	Campos	28	Clark	315
Bournemouth	211	Canada	34	Clearwater	274
Bouzonville	63	Canberra	6	Clermont-Ferrand	84
Bowie	293	Cannes	83	Cleveland	351
Bradford	244	Canterbury	216	Clichy-sur-Seine	77
Bradley Beach	314	Canton (MA)	298	Clifton	315
Braintree	297	Canton (OH)	350	Clifton Park	329
Brakpan	180	Cape Cod	299	Clinton	299
Brasilia	27	Cape Town	184	Cluj Napoca	172
Brasov	171	Caracas	378	Coblenz (Koblenz)	95
Bratislava	178	Cardiff	248	Cochabamba	25
Braunschweig	94	Carmel	254	Cochin	108
Brazil	26	Carpentras	84	Colchester	212
Bremen	94	Casablanca	151	Colmar	63

Cologne	95	Delmar	329	Ellenville	328
Colombia	49	Delray Beach	274	Elmira	329
Colombo	193	Denmark	56	Elmwood Park	316
Colonia	315	Denver	267	Emmendingen	95
Colorado Springs	267	Derbent	174	Encinitas	254
Columbia	365	Des Moines	287	Encino	261
Columbus (GA)	282	Detroit	307	Endingen	198
Columbus (OH)	352	Dieuze	63	Engelberg	198
Commack	332	Dijon	63	Enghien	77
Compiegne	63	Dix Hills	332	Englewood	316
Concord	313	Dnepropetrovsk	206	Enschede	158
Concordia	5	Dominican Republic	57	Epernay	63
Constanta	172	Donetsk	206	Epinal	63
Copenhagen	56	Dorohoi	172	Erechim	29
Coquitlam	35	Dortmund	95	Erfurt	95
Cordoba (Argentina)	6	Douglas	245	Erie	356
Cordoba (Spain)	187	Dover	272	Ernakulam	108
Corfu	103	Downey	261	Esch-Sur-Alzette	145
Cork	110	Dresden	95	Essaouira (formerly Mogador)	
Corpus Christi	367	Druskininkai	144		151
Corsica	90	Dublin	111	Essen	95
Costa Mesa	254	Dubrovnik	51	Essingen	96
Costa Rica	50	Dubuque	287	Estella	188
Coventry	243	Duluth	309	Estonia	60
Cracow	166	Dundee	246	Ethiopia	60
Cranbury	315	Dunkirk	63	Eugene	354
Cranford	315	Dunoon	246	Eureka	254
Cranston	363	Durban	183	Evansville	285
Créteil	77	Durham	349	Everett	299
Croatia	51	Dushanbe	202	Evergreen	268
Cuba	52	Dusseldorf	95	Evian	84
Cuernavaca	147			Exeter	210
Cumberland	293	**E**		Eze-Village	84
Cuneo	132				
Curaçao	159	East Brunswick	315	**F**	
Curitiba	28	East Chicago	285		
Cyprus	53	East Falmouth	299	Fair Lawn	316
Czech Republic	53	East Lansing	307	Fairfax	371
		East London	179	Fairfield	269
D		Eastbourne	241	Fall River	299
		Easton (MA)	299	Falls Church	371
Dallas	367	Easton (PA)	356	Fargo	350
Daly City	254	Ecuador	58	Faulquemont-Crehange	63
Dan	116	Edinburgh	246	Fayetteville	349
Danbury	269	Edison	316	Ferrara	132
Danville	371	Edmonton	34	Fez	151
Daugavpils	143	Egypt	58	Fiji	60
Davenport	287	Eilat	116	Finland	61
Davis	254	Eindhoven	158	Fleischmanns	328
Dayton	352	Eisenstadt	15	Flint	307
Daytona Beach	274	Ekaterinburg	174	Florence	133
Dead Sea	116	El Dorado	252	Fontainebleau	77
Deal	315	El Escorial	188	Fontenay aux Roses	77
Deauville	67	El Paso	368	Fontenay sous Bois	78
Decatur	282	El Salvador	59	Forbach	63
Deerfield Beach	274	Elbeuf	67	Fort Dodge	287
Degania Alef	116	Elizabeth	316	Fort Lauderdale	274
Delft	158	Elkins park	356	Fort Lee	317

Fort Meyers	275	Greenbelt	294	Helsinki	61
Fort Pierce	275	Greenfield	300	Hemel Hempstead	214
Fort Wayne	285	Greensboro	349	Hendersonville	350
Framingham	299	Greenvale	331	Herford	97
France	62	Greenville	309	Hershey	356
Frankfurt	96	Greenwood	309	Hervas	188
Fredericton	37	Grenoble	84	Herzlia	120
Freehold	317	Grimsby	214	Highland	286
Freeport	19	Grodno	20	Highland Park (IL)	284
Freiburg	96	Groningen	158	Highland Park (NJ)	317
Frejus	84	Grosbliederstroff	63	Hildesheim	97
Fresno	254	Guadalajara	147	Hillside	318
Fribourg	198	Guadeloupe	90	Hilversum	158
Friedberg	96	Guaruja	30	Hingham	300
Furth	96	Guatemala	104	Hinterglemm	16
		Guatemala City	104	Hiroshima	141
G		Guildford	239	Hobart	10
		Gush Etzion	118	Hof	97
Gaithersburg	294			Holbrook	300
Galanta	178	**H**		Holesov	54
Galati	172			Holliston	300
Galilee	117	Haarlem	158	Hollywood (CA)	262
Gardena	262	Hackensack	317	Hollywood & Vicinity (FL)	275
Garges-les-Gonesse	78	Haddonfield	317	Holyoke	300
Gary	286	Hadera	118	Honduras	105
Gateshead	241	Hagen	97	Hong Kong	48
Gelsenkirchen	97	Hagerstown	293	Honolulu	283
Geneva (NY)	329	Hagondange	63	Hornbaek	57
Geneva (Switzerland)	198	Haguenau	63	Hot Springs	252
Genoa	133	Haifa	118	Houston	368
Georgetown	365	Haiti	104	Hudson	330
Georgia	91	Hale Barns	233	Hull (MA)	300
Germany	91	Halifax	38	Hull (UK)	214
Ghent	24	Hallandale	275	Hungary	105
Gibraltar	101	Halle	97	Huntington	374
Girona	188	Hamburg	97	Huntsville	250
Glace Bay	38	Hamilton (Bermuda)	25	Hyannis	300
Glasgow	246	Hamilton (Canada)	39	Hyattsville	293
Glens Falls	329	Hammond	286	Hyde Park	300
Gliwice	167	Hampton	371	Hyeres	84
Gloucester	300	Hanita	120		
Gloversville	330	Hanover	97	**I**	
Golan Heights	118	Haon	120		
Gold Coast	9	Harare	381	Iasi (Jassy)	172
Gomel	20	Harlow	212	Ichenhausen	97
Gori	91	Harrisburg	356	India	107
Gorizia	133	Harrison	347	Indianapolis	286
Gothenburg	194	Harrogate	243	Ingenheim	97
Granada	188	Hartford	269	Ingwiller	63
Granada Hills	262	Hasbrouck Heights	317	Innsbruck	16
Grand Cayman	46	Hastings	241	Insming	63
Grand Rapids	308	Havana	52	Ioannina	103
Grasmere	210	Haverhill	300	Iowa City	288
Graz	15	Haverstraw	345	Iquique	46
Great Falls	311	Hazelton	356	Iran	110
Great Neck	330	Hazorea	120	Irish Republic	110
Greater Rio de Janeiro	28	Heidelberg	97	Irkutsk	174
Greece	102	Helena	252	Isfahan	110

Isle of Man	245	Kiev	206	Latvia	143
Israel	112	Kihei	282	Launceston	10
Issy-Les-Moulineaux	78	Kimberley	184	Laurel	293
Istanbul	204	Kingston (Canada)	39	Lausanne	199
Italy	131	Kingston (Jamaica)	141	Lawrence (KS)	288
Ithaca	330	Kippenheim	97	Lawrence (MA)	300
Ivano-Frankivsk	206	Kitchener	39	Lawrence (NY)	331
Izieu	84	Klaipeda	144	Lawrenceville	319
Izmir	205	Knokke	24	Le Blanc Mesnil	78
		Kobe	141	Le Chesnay	78
J		Kobersdorf	16	Le Havre	67
		Kokand	377	Le Kremlin-Bicetre	78
Jackson (MI)	308	Kolkata	108	Le Mans	67
Jackson (MS)	309	Kona	282	Le Perreux Nogent	78
Jacksonville	276	Konstanz	98	Le Raincy	78
Jaffa	120	Korazim	125	Le Vesinet	78
Jamaica	140	Korosten	207	Leeds	244
Jamesburg	318	Kosice	178	Leghorn	134
Japan	141	Kostrama	174	Legnica	167
Jefferson City	310	Krasnoyarsk	174	Leicester	216
Jerba	203	Krefeld	98	Leiden	158
Jericho	331	Kremenchug	207	Lengnau	199
Jersey	245	Kreuzlingen	199	Leominster	301
Jersey City	318	Krugersdorp	183	Les Lilas	78
Jerusalem	120	Kuba	19	Levallois Perret	79
Johannesburg	180	Kursk	174	Lexington (KY)	289
Johnstown	356	Kutaisi	91	Lexington (MA)	301
Juneau	250	Kyrgyzstan	143	Lexington Park	293
				Liberec	54
K		**L**		Libourne	89
				Liège	24
Kaifeng	49	La Ciotat	85	Liepaja	143
Kaiserslautern	97	La Courneuve	78	Lille	63
Kalamazoo	308	La Garenne-Colombes	78	Lima	164
Kansas City	310	La Jolla	254	Limoges	89
Karlovy Vary	54	La Mesa	255	Lincoln (NE)	311
Karlsruhe	97	La Paz	25	Lincoln (UK)	217
Kathmandu	154	La Rochelle	89	Linden	319
Katowice	167	La Serena	46	Linz	16
Katta-Kurgan	377	La Seyne-sur-Mer	85	Lisbon	169
Kaunas	144	La Varenne St-Hilaire	78	Lithuania	144
Kazakhstan	142	La-Chaux-de-Fonds	199	Little Rock	252
Kazan	174	Lafayette (IN)	286	Liverpool	237
Kelowna	35	Lafayette (LA)	290	Livingston	319
Kemp Mill	294	Laguna Hills	255	Ljubljana	179
Kendall	276	Lake Placid	330	Llandudno	248
Kenitra	152	Lakeland	276	Loch Sheldrake	328
Kensington	294	Lakewood (CA)	255	Lod	125
Kenya	142	Lakewood (NJ)	318	Lodz	167
Kermine	377	Lancaster (PA)	357	Lohamei Hagetaot	126
Key West	276	Lancaster (UK)	216	London (Canada)	39
Kfar Giladi	125	Landau	98	London (UK)	217
Khamasa	108	Lansing	308	Long Beach (CA)	262
Kharkov	206	Laramie	375	Long Beach (NY)	331
Kherson	206	Larissa	103	Longmeadow	301
Kibbutz Harduf	125	Las Cruces	325	Longy	245
Kibbutz Yotvata	125	Las Palmas	192	Lorain	353
Kiel	97	Las Vegas	311	Lorient	67

Los Alamos	325	Marlboro	302	Montevideo	376
Los Angeles	262	Marrakech	152	Montgomery	250
Loughton	212	Marseilles	86	Monticello	329
Louisville	289	Martinique	90	Montpelier	371
Lowell	301	Massy	79	Montpellier	87
Lubbock	370	McKeesport	357	Montreal	44
Lubeck	98	Meaux	79	Montreuil	79
Lublin	167	Medellin	50	Montrouge	79
Lucerne	199	Medford	302	Morocco	151
Lugano	199	Meknes	152	Morris Plains	319
Luneville	64	Melbourne (Australia)	11	Morristown	319
Lusaka	381	Melbourne (FL)	276	Moscow	174
Luton	209	Melilla	192	Moshav Shoresh	126
Luxembourg	145	Melrose	302	Mount Vernon	347
Luxembourg City	145	Melun	79	Mozambique	153
Lviv	207	Memphis	366	Mulheim	98
Lynn	301	Menton	87	Mulhouse	64
Lyons	85	Merano	134	Mumbai	108
		Mercer Island	373	Muncie	286

M

		Meriden	270	Munich	98
		Merlebach	64	Myanmar	153
Maagan	126	Metuchen	319	Myrtle Beach	365
Maastricht	158	Metz	64		
Maayan Harod	126	Meudon-La-Foret	79		

N

Macedonia	146	Mexico	147		
Macon (France)	86	Mexico City	147	Nagasaki	141
Macon (GA)	282	Miami/Miami Beach	276	Nahariya	126
Madison	374	Michelstadt	98	Nairobi	142
Madrid	188	Michigan City	286	Nalchik	175
Magdeburg	98	Middletown (CT)	270	Namibia	154
Mahanayim	126	Middletown (RI)	363	Nancy	64
Mahwah	319	Mikulov	54	Nantes	67
Maidenhead	209	Milan	134	Naples	135
Mainz	98	Milford	302	Narragansett	364
Maisons Alfort	79	Millis	302	Nashville	366
Majorca	192	Milton	302	Nassau	19
Makhachkala	174	Milton Keynes	209	Natchez	310
Malaga	189	Milwaukee	375	Natick	302
Malaysia	146	Minden	98	Navoy	377
Malden	301	Minneapolis	309	Nazareth	126
Malmo	194	Minsk	20	Needham	302
Malta	146	Mississauga	40	Negev	126
Manaus	27	Missoula	311	Nepal	154
Manchester (CT)	233	Mobile	250	Netanya	126
Manchester (NH)	313	Modena	135	Netherlands	154
Manchester (UK)	270	Moghilev	21	Neuilly	79
Manhattan	338	Mogi Das Cruzes	30	Neukirch-Egnach	199
Manila	165	Moldova	149	Neustadt	99
Mantua	134	Monaco	150	New Bedford	303
Maplewood	319	Monchengladbach	98	New Britain	270
Maputo	153	Moncton	37	New Brunswick	320
Maracaibo	379	Monroe	332	New City	345
Marbella	189	Mons	25	New Delhi	109
Marblehead	302	Monsey	345	New Haven	270
Marburg an der Lahn	98	Montauban	89	New London	271
Margate	216	Montbeliard	64	New Orleans	290
Margelan	377	Monte Carlo	150	New Rochelle	347
Marignane	86	Monterrey	149	New Zealand	160

Newark (DE)	272	Orangeburg	346	Petach Tikva	127
Newark (UK)	238	Orlando	278	Peterborough	40
Newburgh	333	Orleans	67	Petropolis	29
Newburyport	303	Orsha	21	Phalsbourg	64
Newcastle	7	Oshawa	40	Philadelphia	357
Newcastle upon Tyne	242	Osijek	51	Philippines Republic	165
Newport (RI)	364	Oslo	161	Phoenix	250
Newport (UK)	248	Osnabruck	99	Piatra Neamt	172
Newport News	371	Ostend	25	Piestany	178
Newton	303	Oswiecim	167	Pilsen	54
Niagara Falls (Canada)	40	Ottawa	40	Pisa	135
Niagara Falls (NY)	344	Oudtshoorn	186	Pittsburgh	361
Nice	87	Oujda	152	Pittsfield	304
Nicosia	53	Overland Park	288	Plainfield	321
Nikolayev	207	Owen Sound	40	Plovdiv	33
Nimes	88	Oxford	238	Plymouth (MA)	304
Niteroi	29			Plymouth (UK)	210
Nizhny Novgorod	175	**P**		Pocomoke	293
Noisy Le Sec	80			Poitiers	89
Norfolk	372	Paarl	186	Poland	166
North Adams	303	Paderborn	99	Polna	54
North Bay	40	Padua	135	Ponta Delgada	169
North Hollywood	265	Paducah	289	Porlamar	379
North Miami / North Miami		Palm Beach	279	Port au Prince	104
Beach	278	Palm City	279	Port Chester	348
Northampton (MA)	303	Palm Coast	279	Port Elizabeth	180
Northampton (UK)	238	Palm Springs	255	Portland (ME)	291
Northbrook	284	Palo Alto	256	Portland (OR)	354
Northern Ireland	245	Panama	162	Porto Alegre	29
Northridge	265	Panama City	162	Portsmouth (NH)	313
Norway	161	Panevezys	144	Portsmouth & Southsea (UK)	
Norwich (CT)	271	Pantin	80		213
Norwich (UK)	238	Paraguay	163	Portugal	168
Norwood	303	Paramaribo	193	Postville	288
Nottingham	238	Paramus	320	Poti	91
Novi Sad	380	Paravur	109	Potomac	294
Novosibirsk	175	Paris	67	Pottstown	362
		Parma	135	Poughkeepsie	344
O		Parsipanny	320	Poway	256
		Pasadena	265	Prague	54
Oak Ridge	367	Passaic	320	Prairie Village	288
Oakland	255	Passo Fundo	29	Prestwich	234
Oakville	40	Paterson	320	Pretoria	183
Obernai	64	Pau	89	Princeton	321
Odenbach	99	Peabody	303	Providence	364
Odessa	207	Peekskill	348	Pueblo	268
Offenbach	99	Pelotas	29	Puerto Rico	170
Oklahoma City	353	Pembroke Pines	279	Pune	109
Old Bridge	320	Pensacola	279		
Old Orchard Beach	291	Penza	175	**Q**	
Olney	294	Peoria	284		
Olomouc	54	Périgveux	89	Qatzrin	128
Olympia	373	Perm	175	Quebec City	45
Omaha	311	Perpignan	88	Queens	343
Onni	91	Perth	14	Quincy	304
Onset	303	Perth Amboy	320	Quito	58
Oporto	169	Peru	164		
Oradea	172	Perugia	135		

R

Ra'anana	128
Rabat	152
Radauti	172
Rahway	321
Raleigh	350
Ramat Gan	128
Ramat Hanegev	128
Ramat Yohanan	128
Ramona	256
Ramsgate	216
Rancagua	46
Randolph (MA)	304
Randolph (NJ)	321
Rapid City	365
Reading (PA)	362
Reading (UK)	209
Rechitsa	21
Recife	28
Redbridge	212
Regensburg	99
Regina	45
Rehovot	128
Reims	64
Rennes	67
Reno	312
Réunion	90
Revere	304
Rezhitsa	143
Rhodes	103
Riccione	135
Richmond (Canada)	35
Richmond (VA)	372
Richmond Hill	41
Ridgewood	321
Riga	143
Rijeka	52
Rio Rancho	325
Ris-Orangis	80
River Edge	321
Roanne	88
Rochester (MN)	309
Rochester (NY)	345
Rochester (UK)	216
Rock Island	284
Rockford	284
Rockland	291
Rockledge	279
Rockville	294
Roissy-En-Brie	80
Romania	170
Rome	136
Rosario	6
Roselle	321
Rosh Hanikra	128
Rosh Pina	128
Rosny-Sous-Bois	80

Rostov-na-Donu	175
Rotterdam	158
Rouen	67
Rousse	33
Rumson	321
Russian Federation	173
Rzeszow	167

S

Saarbrucken	99
Sachkhere	175
Sacramento	256
Safed	128
Safi	152
Saginaw	308
Saint Germain	80
Saint John	38
Saint-Avold	64
Saint-Die	64
Saint-Etienne	88
Saint-Fons	88
Saint-Laurent-du-Var	88
Saint-Leu-La-Foret	80
Saint-Louis	64
Saint-Ouen-L'Aumône	80
Saint-Quentin	65
Salamanca	190
Sale	235
Salem (MA)	304
Salem (OR)	355
Salford	235
Salisbury	293
Salt Lake City	370
Salvador	27
Salzburg	16
Samara	176
Samarkand	377
San Antonio	370
San Bernardino	256
San Carlos	257
San Diego	257
San Fernando Valley	265
San Francisco	258
San Jose (CA)	259
San Jose (Costa Rica)	50
San Juan-Santurce	170
San Pedro Sula	105
San Rafael	260
San Salvador	59
Santa Barbara	260
Santa Cruz	26
Santa Fe	325
Santa Monica	260
Santa Rosa	260
Santiago	46
Santo Andre	30
Santo Domingo	58

Santos	30
Sao Caetano do Sul	30
Sao Jose dos Campos	30
Sao Paulo	30
Saragossa	190
Sarajevo	26
Sarasota	279
Saratoga Springs	346
Saratov	176
Sarcelles	80
Sardinia	138
Sarrebourg	65
Sarreguemines	65
Sartrouville	81
Saskatoon	45
Satu Mare	173
Savannah	282
Savigny sur Orge	81
Sawbridgeworth	214
Scarsdale	348
Schenectady	346
Schwerin	99
Scotch Plains	321
Scotland	246
Scottsdale	251
Scranton	362
Seattle	373
Sedan-Charleville	65
Segovia	190
Selestat	65
Senigallia	138
Sens	65
Seville	190
Sevran	81
Sf. Gheorghe	173
Shakhrisabz	202
Shanghai	49
Sharon (MA)	304
Sharon (PA)	363
Sharon Springs	329
Sheboygan	375
Sheffield	243
Sherman Oaks	266
Shiauliai	145
Short Hills	321
Shreveport	290
Sicily	138
Siena	138
Sierra Vista	251
Sighet	173
Silver Spring	295
Simferopol	207
Singapore	177
Sioux City	288
Skokie	284
Skopje	146
Slavuta	207
Slovakia	177

Slovenia	179	Sudbury (MA)	305	Thunder Bay	41
Sofia	33	Suffern	346	Tiberias	130
Solihull	243	Sukhumi	91	Tiburon	260
Somerset	321	Sun City	252	Tijuana	149
Somerville	305	Sun City West	252	Timisoara	173
Sopron	107	Sunderland	242	Tirana	1
Sorocaba	32	Sunnyvale	260	Tiraspol	150
Sosua	58	Surami	91	Tirgu Mures	173
South Africa	179	Suriname	193	Tokyo	141
South Bend	286	Suva	61	Toledo (OH)	353
South Haven	308	Swampscott	305	Toledo (Spain)	190
South Orange	321	Swansea	248	Tomar	169
South River	322	Sweden	194	Topeka	288
Southampton	214	Switzerland	196	Toronto	41
Southend-on-Sea	213	Sydney (Australia)	7	Torquay	211
Southfield	308	Sydney (Canada)	38	Torremolinos	191
Southport	237	Syosset	332	Toul	66
Spain	186	Syracuse	346	Toulon	88
Speyer	99	Szczecin	167	Toulouse	90
Spezia	138			Tours	67
Split	52	**T**		Trappes	81
Spokane	374			Trenton	323
Spotswood	322	Tahiti	90	Trier	100
Spring Valley	346	Taipei	201	Trieste	138
Springfield (IL)	285	Taiwan	201	Trikkala	103
Springfield (MA)	305	Tajikistan	202	Trnava	178
Springs	183	Tallahassee	280	Trondheim	162
Sri Lanka	193	Tallinn	60	Troy	347
St Albans	214	Tamarac	280	Troyes	66
St Andrews	246	Tampa	280	Truro	210
St Annes On Sea	216	Tangier	152	Tshelyabinsk	176
St Augustine	280	Tarragona	190	Tshkinvali	91
St Brelade	245	Tarzana	266	Tskhakaya	91
St Catharine's	41	Tashkent	378	Tucson	252
St Gallen	200	Ta-Xbiex	147	Tucuman	6
St Joseph	310	Tbilisi	91	Tudela	191
St Louis	310	Teaneck	322	Tula	176
St Moritz	200	Tegucigalpa	105	Tulsa	354
St Paul	309	Tehran	110	Tunis	204
St Petersburg (FL)	280	Tel Aviv	129	Tunisia	203
St Petersburg (Russia)	176	Teleneshty	150	Tupelo	310
St Thomas	379	Tempe	252	Turin	138
St. John's	38	Temple Hills	293	Turkey	204
Staines	238	Temuco	47	Turku	61
Stains	81	Tenafly	323	Tushnad	173
Stamford	271	Tenerife	192	Tustin	266
Staten Island	344	Teplice	55		
Ste. Agathe des Monts	45	Terezin	55	**U**	
Stockholm	194	Terre Haute	287		
Stockton	260	Tetuan	153	Ukraine	205
Stoke On Trent	239	Thailand	202	Uman	207
Stoughton	305	Thane	109	Umhlanga	184
Strasbourg	65	The Hague	159	Union	323
Straubing	100	Thessaloniki	103	United Kingdom	208
Stuttgart	100	Thiais	81	United States of America	249
Subotica	380	Thionville	66	Uppsala	196
Suceava	173	Thornhill	41	Urbino	139
Sudbury (Canada)	41	Thousand Oaks	260	Uruguay	376

Utica	347	Volgograd	176	Wiesbaden	100
Utrecht	159	Volos	104	Wilkes-Barre	363
Uzbekistan	377			Williamsport	363

W

				Willingboro	325
				Wilmington (DE)	272
V		Waco	370	Wilmington (OH)	350
Valdivia	47	Waikiki	283	Winchester	306
Valence	89	Wakefield	305	Windhoek	154
Valencia	191	Wales	248	Windsor	43
Valenciennes	66	Walnut Creek	261	Winnipeg	37
Vallejo	260	Waltham	306	Winterthur	200
Valparaiso (Chile)	47	Warren	324	Winthrop	306
Valparaiso (IN)	287	Warsaw	167	Woodbridge (CT)	272
Van Nuys	266	Warwick	364	Woodbridge (NJ)	325
Vancouver	35	Washington	272	Woodbury	332
Vani	91	Washington Township	324	Woodmere	332
Vatra Dornei	173	Wasselonne	66	Woodridge	329
Vauxhall	323	Waterbury	271	Woonsocket	364
Veitshochheim	100	Waterloo	25	Worcester	306
Venezuela	378	Watford	214	Worms	100
Venice (CA)	266	Wayland	306	Wrocklaw	168
Venice (Italy)	139	Wayne	324	Wuppertal	100
Venissieux	89	Wellesley Hills	306	Wurzburg	100
Ventura	260	Wellington	160	Wyckoff	325
Vercelli	140	Welwyn Garden City	214		
Verdun	66	West Bloomfield	308	**Y**	
Vero Beach	280	West Caldwell	324		
Verona	140	West Hartford	271	Yangon (formerly Rangoon)	153
Versailles	81	West Hempstead	332	Yarmouth	38
Vestal	347	West Hills	266	Yekatrinburg	177
Vevey	200	West Lafayette	287	Yerres	82
Viareggio	140	West New York	324	Yonkers	348
Vichy	89	West Orange	324	York	243
Victoria	36	West Palm Beach	281	Youngstown	353
Vienna	16	West Point	348	Yugoslavia	380
Villejuif	81	West Roxbury	306	Yverdon	200
Villeneuve-la-Garenne	81	Westboro	306		
Villiers Sur Marne	82	Westcliff on Sea	213	**Z**	
Villiers-le-Bel-Gonesse	82	Westerly	364		
Vilnius	145	Westfield	324	Zagreb	52
Vincennes	82	Westhampton Beach	332	Zambia	381
Vineland	323	Westport	271	Zaparozhe	207
Vineyard Haven	305	Westwood	306	Zhitomir	207
Virgin Islands (USA)	379	Whippany	324	Zichron Ya'achov	131
Virginia Beach	373	White Plains	348	Zimbabwe	381
Vitoria	192	Whitefield	236	Zug	200
Vitry-sur-Seine	82	Whiting	287	Zurich	200
Vittel	66	Whittier	261	Zwolle	159
Vladikavkaz	176	Wichita	288		

Index to Advertisers

Please complete and return Jewish Travel Guide form to us by 1 September 2004

Please reserve the following advertising space in

Jewish Travel Guide 2005:

☐ Full Page   £475   181 x 115 mm

☐ Half Page   £245   91 x 115 mm

☐ Quarter Page   £145   45 x 115 mm

(UK advertisers please note that the above rates are subject to VAT)

Special positions by arrangement

☐ **Please insert the attached copy (If setting is required a 10% setting charge will be made.)**

☐ **Copy will be forwarded from our Advertising Agents (*see below*)**

Contact Name: _____

Advertisers Name: _____

Address for invoicing: _____

_____

Tel:_____ Fax: _____

Signed: _____ Title:_____

VAT No:_____

Date:_____

Agency Name (if applicable): _____

Address: _____

_____

Tel:_____ Fax: _____

All advertisements set by the publisher will only be included if they have been signed and approved by the advertiser.

To the Advertising Department
Jewish Travel Guide
Vallentine Mitchell & Co. Ltd.
Crown House, 47 Chase Side, Southgate, London N14 5BP
Tel. No.: + 44(0)208 447 8798 Fax: + 44(0)208 447 8548.
E-mail: jtg@vmbooks.com

Update for *Jewish Travel Guide* 2005

PUBLISHER'S REQUEST

Readers are asked kindly to draw attention to any omissions or errors. If errors are discovered, it would be appreciated if you could give appropriate up-to-date information, referring to the appropriate page, and send this form to the Editor at the address given below.

Alternatively, you can email us.

With reference to the following entry:

Page:

Country:

Entry should read:

Signed:_____ Date: _____

Name (BLOCK CAPITALS) _____

Address: _____

_____

Telephone: _____

SEND TO:

The Editor
Jewish Travel Guide
Vallentine Mitchell & Co. Ltd.
Crown House, 47 Chase Side,
Southgate, London N14 5BP
Tel. No.: + 44(0)208 447 8798 Fax: + 44(0)208 447 8548.
E-mail: jtg@vmbooks.com